The International Library of Essays on Capital Punishment, Volume I

The International Library of Essays on Capital Punishment

Series Editor: Peter Hodgkinson

Titles in the Series

The International Library of Essays on Capital Punishment, Volume I
Justice and Legal Issues
Peter Hodgkinson

The International Library of Essays on Capital Punishment, Volume II
Abolition and Alternatives to Capital Punishment
Peter Hodgkinson

The International Library of Essays on Capital Punishment, Volume III
Policy and Governance
Peter Hodgkinson

The International Library of Essays on Capital Punishment, Volume I

Justice and Legal Issues

Edited by

Peter Hodgkinson

Westminster University Law School, UK

Routledge
Taylor & Francis Group
LONDON AND NEW YORK

First published 2013 by Ashgate Publishing

2 Park Square, Milton Park, Abingdon, Oxfordshire OX14 4RN
711 Third Avenue, New York, NY 10017

Routledge is an imprint of the Taylor & Francis Group, an informa business

First issued in paperback 2018

British Library Cataloguing in Publication Data
A catalogue record for this book is available from the British Library.

The Library of Congress has cataloged the printed edition as follows: 2013943929

ISBN 13: 978-1-4094-6135-7 (hbk)
ISBN 13: 978-1-138-37990-9 (pbk)

In fond memory of
Hugo Adam Bedau
(1926–2012)
Mentor, Inspiration, and Friend
An uncompromising foe of capital punishment in any guise

Contents

Acknowledgements *ix*
Series Preface *xi*
Introduction *xiii*

PART I LEGAL ISSUES

1 Yvonne McDermott (2010), '*Yong Vui Kong v. Public Prosecutor* and the Mandatory Death Penalty for Drug Offences in Singapore: A Dead End for Constitutional Challenge?', *International Journal on Human Rights and Drug Policy*, **1**, pp. 35–52. 3
2 Sandra Babcock (2012), 'The Limits of International Law: Efforts to Enforce Rulings of the International Court of Justice in U.S. Death Penalty Cases', *Syracuse Law Review*, **62**, pp. 183–97. 21
3 Douglas L. Mendes (2009), 'The Mandatory Death Penalty – An International and Comparative Perspective', in *Judges, Prosecutors and Counsel – A Penalty without Legitimacy: The Mandatory Death Penalty in Trinidad and Tobago*, London: The Death Penalty Project, pp. 1–17. 37
4 Lilian Chenwi (2006), 'Fair Trial Rights and their Relation to the Death Penalty in Africa', *International and Comparative Law Quarterly*, **55**, pp. 609–33. 55
5 Jon Yorke (2009), 'The Right to Life and Abolition of the Death Penalty in the Council of Europe', *European Law Review*, **34**, pp. 205–29. 81
6 Leah Ambler (2007), 'The People Decide: The Effect of the Introduction of the Quasi-Jury System (*Saiban-In Seido*) on the Death Penalty in Japan', *Northwestern Journal of International Human Rights*, **6**, pp. 1–23. 107
7 Caycie D. Bradford (2010–11), 'Waiting to Die, Dying to Live: An Account of the Death Row Phenomenon from a Legal Viewpoint', *Interdisciplinary Journal of Human Rights Law*, **5**, pp. 77–96. 131
8 William A. Schabas (2008), 'The United Nations and Abolition of the Death Penalty', in Jon Yorke (ed.) *Against the Death Penalty*, Farnham: Ashgate, pp. 9–41. 151
9 Andy Boon and Peter Hodgkinson (1966), 'Life and Death in the Lawyer's Office: The Internship in Capital Punishment Studies', *Law Teacher*, **30**, pp. 253–69. 185
10 Esther Gumboh (2011), 'The Penalty of Life Imprisonment under International Criminal Law', *African Human Rights Law Journal*, **11**, pp. 75–92. 203
11 Joyce G. Reed and Glenn E. Rohrer (2000), 'Death Penalty Mitigation: A Challenge for Social Work Education', *Journal of Teaching in Social Work*, **20**, pp. 187–99. 221
12 Kerry Ann Akers (2013), 'The Global Capital Punishment Litigation Landscape', in Peter Hodgkinson (ed.) *The International Library of Essays on Capital Punishment: Volume I*, Farnham: Ashgate, pp. 235–48. 235

PART II INNOCENCE

13 Morris B. Hoffman (2007), 'The Myth of Factual Innocence', *Chicago-Kent Law Review*, **82**, pp. 663–90. 251

14 Michael L. Radelet (2008), 'The Role of the Innocence Argument in Contemporary Death Penalty Debates', *Texas Tech Law Review*, **41**, pp. 199–220. 279

PART III RACE AND RELIGIOUS DISCRIMINATION

15 Greg Wallance (1978), 'South Africa: Racism and the Death Penalty', *Race & Class*, **19**, pp. 404–16. 303

16 Hugo Adam Bedau (2008–2009), 'Racism, Wrongful Convictions, and the Death Penalty', *Tennessee Law Review*, **76**, pp. 615–24. 317

PART IV GENDER AND SEXUALITY ISSUES

17 Barrie Sander (2010), 'A Nation at War with Itself: The Potential Impact of Uganda's Anti-Homosexuality Bill, *Centre for Capital Punishment Studies Internship Report*, pp. 58–76. 329

18 Steven F. Shatz and Naomi R. Shatz (2012), 'Chivalry is not Dead: Murder, Gender, and the Death Penalty', *Berkeley Journal of Gender Law and Justice*, **64**, pp. 64–112. 349

19 Aminu Adamu Bello (2013) 'Zina (Adultery) under Islamic Law in Nigeria: The Gender Issues in Amina Lawal's Case', *The International Library of Essays on Capital Punishment*: *Volume I*, Farnham: Ashgate, pp. 399–417. 399

PART V JUVENILES

20 Jeffrey Fagan (2007) 'End Natural Life Sentences for Juveniles', *Criminology and Public Policy*, **6**, pp. 735–46. 421

21 Kathleen M. Heide and Jessica McCurdy (2010), 'Juvenile Parricide Offenders Sentenced to Death, *Victims and Offenders*, **5**, pp. 76–99. 433

PART VI VICTIM ISSUES

22 Walter C. Long (2011), 'Trauma Therapy for Death Row Families', *Journal of Trauma & Dissociation*, **12**, pp. 482–94. 459

23 Nancy Berns (2009), 'Contesting the Victim Card: Closure Discourse and Emotion in Death Penalty Rhetoric', *Sociological Quarterly*, **50**, pp. 383–406. 473

24 Peter Hodgkinson, Seema Kandelia and Rupa Reddy (2009), 'Capital Punishment: Creating More Victims?', in Nancy Loucks, Sally Smith Holt and Joanna R. Adler (eds), *Why We Kill: Understanding Violence Across Cultures and Disciplines*, London: Willan Press, pp. 63–82. 497

Name Index 517

Acknowledgements

Ashgate would like to thank the researchers and contributing authors who provided copies, along with the following for their permission to reprint copyright material.

American Society of Criminology for the essay: Jeffrey Fagan (2007) 'End Natural Life Sentences for Juveniles', *Criminology and Public Policy*, **6**, pp. 735–46. Copyright © 2007 by the American Society of Criminology.

Berkeley Law, University of California for the essay: Steven F. Shatz and Naomi R. Shatz (2012), 'Chivalry is not Dead: Murder, Gender, and the Death Penalty', *Berkeley Journal of Gender Law and Justice*, **64**, pp. 64–112. Copyright © 2012 by Regents of the University of California.

Cambridge University Press for the essay: Lilian Chenwi (2006), 'Fair Trial Rights and their Relation to the Death Penalty in Africa', *International and Comparative Law Quarterly*, **55**, pp. 609–33. Copyright © 2006 British Institute of International and Comparative Law, published by Cambridge University Press, reproduced with permission.

Chicago-Kent Law Review for the essay: Morris B. Hoffman (2007), 'The Myth of Factual Innocence', *Chicago-Kent Law Review*, **82**, pp. 663–90.

The Council for American Students in International Negotiations (CASIN) for the essay: Caycie D. Bradford (2010–11), 'Waiting to Die, Dying to Live: An Account of the Death Row Phenomenon from a Legal Viewpoint', *Interdisciplinary Journal of Human Rights Law*, **5**, pp. 77–96. Copyright © 2011 by the Council for American Students in International Negotiations.

Institute of Race Relations for the essay: Greg Wallance (1978), 'South Africa: Racism and the Death Penalty', *Race & Class*, **19**, pp. 404–16. Copyright © 1978 Institute of Race Relations.

JUTA Law for the essay: Esther Gumboh (2011), 'The Penalty of Life Imprisonment under International Criminal Law', *African Human Rights Law Journal*, **11**, pp. 75–92.

Yvonne McDermott for the essay: Yvonne McDermott (2010), '*Yong Vui Kong v. Public Prosecutor* and the Mandatory Death Penalty for Drug Offences in Singapore: A Dead End for Constitutional Challenge?', *International Journal on Human Rights and Drug Policy*, **1**, pp. 35–52. Copyright © 2011 International Centre on Human Rights and Drugs Policy.

Douglas L. Mendes for the essay: Douglas L. Mendes (2009), 'The Mandatory Death Penalty – An International and Comparative Perspective', in *Judges, Prosecutors and Counsel – A Penalty without Legitimacy: The Mandatory Death Penalty in Trinidad and Tobago*, London: The Death Penalty Project, pp. 1–17. Copyright © 2009 Douglas L. Mendes.

Northwestern University School of Law for the essay: Leah Ambler (2007), 'The People Decide: The Effect of the Introduction of the Quasi-Jury System (*Saiban-In Seido*) on the Death Penalty in Japan', *Northwestern Journal of International Human Rights*, **6**, pp. 1–23. Copyright © 2007 Northwestern University School of Law.

Syracuse Law Review for the essay: Sandra Babcock (2012), 'The Limits of International Law: Efforts to Enforce Rulings of the International Court of Justice in U.S. Death Penalty Cases', *Syracuse Law Review*, **62**, pp. 183–97.

Taylor & Francis Group for the essays: Andy Boon and Peter Hodgkinson (1966), 'Life and Death in the Lawyer's Office: The Internship in Capital Punishment Studies', *Law Teacher*, **30**, pp. 253–69. Copyright © 1966 The Association of Law Teachers reprinted by permission of Taylor and Francis Ltd, http://www.tandfonline.com, on behalf of The Association of Law Teachers; Joyce G. Reed and Glenn E. Rohrer (2000), 'Death Penalty Mitigation: A Challenge for Social Work Education', *Journal of Teaching in Social Work*, **20**, pp. 187–99. Copyright © 2000 by the Haworth Press, Inc.; Kathleen M. Heide and Jessica McCurdy (2010), 'Juvenile Parricide Offenders Sentenced to Death, *Victims and Offenders*, **5**, pp. 76–99. Copyright © 2010 Taylor & Francis Group, LLC; Walter C. Long (2011), 'Trauma Therapy for Death Row Families', *Journal of Trauma & Dissociation*, **12**, pp. 482–94. Copyright © 2011 Taylor & Francis Group, LLC.

Tennessee Law Review Association for the essay: Hugo Adam Bedau (2008–2009), 'Racism, Wrongful Convictions, and the Death Penalty', *Tennessee Law Review*, **76**, pp. 615–24.

Texas Tech Law Review for the essay: Michael L. Radelet (2008), 'The Role of the Innocence Argument in Contemporary Death Penalty Debates', *Texas Tech Law Review*, **41**, pp. 199–220.

Thomson Reuters for the essay: Jon Yorke (2009), 'The Right to Life and Abolition of the Death Penalty in the Council of Europe', *European Law Review*, **34**, pp. 205–29. Copyright © 2009 Thomson Reuters (Legal) Limited and Contributors.

John Wiley & Sons for the essay: Nancy Berns (2009), 'Contesting the Victim Card: Closure Discourse and Emotion in Death Penalty Rhetoric', *Sociological Quarterly*, **50**, pp. 383–406. Copyright © 2009 Midwest Sociological Society.

Every effort has been made to trace all the copyright holders, but if any have been inadvertently overlooked the publishers will be pleased to make the necessary arrangement at the first opportunity.

Publisher's Note

The material in this volume has been reproduced using the facsimile method. This means we can retain the original pagination to facilitate easy and correct citation of the original essays. It also explains the variety of typefaces, page layouts and numbering.

Series Preface

The American experience has long been the staple diet of capital punishment research and activism and continues in the 21st century to shape the debate even when it is not relevant to the analysis globally. Difficult though it has been to unearth country and topic specific research especially that authored by local scholars, I have, wherever possible, drawn on non-US sources to inform my selection.

My approach and contribution to this debate is holistic and, in some respects, critical of the *status quo* and challenging of the received wisdom of the capital punishment discourse. It is my contention that abolition of capital punishment requires far more than the repeal of executions, important though this is. The claims of abolitionists are greatly exaggerated and any achievements are diminished, and occasionally neutralised, if not accompanied by root and branch reform of the fundamental flaws that characterize its implementation; it is these principles that inform my approach to this collection.

Questions need to be asked about what some would consider to be a profligate use of scarce resources expended by the abolitionist industry especially when the actions they stage, such as national and international conferences, are of questionable value. These are resources I believe could be more effectively spent developing and supporting the infrastructure changes essential to the transition to lasting abolition marked by fundamental improvements to the socio-legal and socio-political landscape. June 2013 will mark the staging of the Fifth World Congress in Madrid, Spain by the ECPM in association with the World Coalition at huge expense. These two groups are representative of the multi-nationals of the abolitionist movement and cater to a global audience of activists who, in essence, support abolition with nary a supporter of capital punishment in sight.

I believe it to be crucial in the interest of good governance and evaluating effectiveness to assess value for money especially when one considers the astronomical sums of money expended on a variety of initiatives. What benefits flow from these activities that can be demonstrated to have contributed to the building of sustainable capacity sufficient to justify the costs? It is difficult to judge how such events progress abolition or estimate their lasting effects. Who are the target audiences for such occasions and what proportion attend as believers and leave as abolitionists? I suspect very few.

Having spent the past two to three years researching the content and purpose of this collection, and its bespoke sister collection *Capital Punishment: New Perspectives*, I have been driven reluctantly to the conclusion that the bulk of abolition activities are directed at abolitionists rather than at the abolition of capital punishment.

I have no clear recollection of my earlier views about the death penalty even though I grew up through the last two executions in Britain [1964] and its abolition in 1965, neither of which engaged me. The experience that possibly triggered my decision to give serious thought to the issue of capital punishment, and subsequently its abolition, was the probation exchange visit I made to Texas in 1980 during which I visited several prisons, including the 'Walls' unit in Huntsville that houses the execution chamber. I recall thinking at the time that those sentenced to death in Texas were indistinguishable from those convicted of murder with whom I worked in the UK who, when deemed appropriate, were released under supervision to the community where, overwhelmingly, they led productive lives. On a comparative note I was also struck by the fact that in Dallas alone in the first nine months of that year there had been 800 homicides [pop. approximately one million] compared to some 500/600 in the whole of the UK [approximately 55 million] – not a very effective deterrent I thought.

It was not until 1992 when I founded two initiatives – Death Watch [an abolitionist group] and the Centre for Capital Punishment Studies [CCPS] – that my stance on the death penalty began to mature. This lead to my decision to allow the abolitionist initiative to wither on the vine. I was no longer persuaded that the rhetoric of the abolitionist industry was helpful, accurate or effective. To talk simplistically in terms of abolition ignores such crucial issues as people's fear of crime, the needs of victims and the raft of legal and criminal justice issues that need addressing in the transition from removing the death penalty and implementing its alternative. I chose instead to invest my energies developing the CCPS into an applied research and humane advocacy project, one which authoritatively informs the debate regarding the implementation of capital punishment. Since the early 1990s many of the problems associated with the implementation of the death penalty across the world have been partly addressed, but retentionist and *de facto* abolitionist states continue to rely on the death penalty with scant regard to international, regional and domestic safeguards.

Paradoxically, even in those countries where the death penalty has been replaced, there have been few marked improvements to legal and social infrastructures, leaving societies with a raft of imperfections in dire need of remedies. Amongst the priorities are the alternative penalties and the inhumane circumstances in which such sentences are served.

I wish I could claim that my research, and that of too many volunteers to name, has exhausted the published material. It hasn't. The work has been made more difficult by my decision not to turn to the 'usual suspects' whose scholarship has thus far shaped the traditional discourse and the received wisdom that I am challenging. Instead I have sought out 'approaches' rather than reputations. This leaves editors of diverse collections such as this with anxieties about the gems they have missed and those they are presented with too late for inclusion! Such has been the birth of the International Library.

It is my hope to broker a sounder and broader appreciation of the complexities of capital punishment via these topics.

PETER HODGKINSON

Introduction

This first volume in *The International Library of Essays on Capital Punishment* has six parts that address the following: Legal Issues, Innocence, Race and Religious Discrimination, Gender and Sexuality Issues, Juveniles, and Victim Issues.

Part I includes, amongst others, mandatory sentencing of drug offenders in Singapore; enforcement of the rulings of the International Court of Justice; right to life in death penalty cases; the lay juror system in Japan; global capital litigation and the death row phenomenon from a legal perspective. Part II examines the authority of innocence research and the effect of the innocence phenomenon on the death penalty discourse. In Part III, Race and Religious Discrimination is examined through its link to wrongful convictions and its effect on capital punishment in Africa. The essays in Part IV cover gender in Islamic Law, capital punishment and homosexuality and chivalry in the implementation of capital punishment. Juveniles are the topic of Part V which examines juveniles as parricide offenders and those sentenced to death as juveniles. Lastly, Part VI, addresses the issue in the context of therapy for the families of the condemned, creating more victims through the capital process and questioning the rhetoric of victims and closure discourse.

Sentencing in Capital Cases

Chapters 10 and 20 address different aspects of the issue of sentencing in capital cases, with Esther Gumboh examining 'The Penalty of Life Imprisonment under International Criminal Law' and Jeffrey Fagan, dealing with the iniquitous position of juvenile offenders in the USA, asking to 'End Natural Life Sentences for Juveniles'. A fuller examination of alternatives to the death penalty, including life imprisonment, is contained in Volume II of this collection but it is important to place these essays in context with that debate.

One of many weaknesses in abolitionist campaigns is the lack of attention given to the issue of an alternative sanction to the death penalty. Demands to abolish the death penalty are all very well, but the lack of an informed discussion about alternative punishments weakens any such campaign. In its absence it is more likely that governments may opt for draconian penalties in the belief that they will placate a public hostile to abolition – for example, 75 years with hard labour in Trinidad and Tobago.

In those countries that have abolished the death penalty, the most common alternative has been a form of lengthy imprisonment frequently referred to as life imprisonment, although the term itself is a source of much confusion. In the USA, a life without parole sentence[1] is generally taken to mean exactly that. Forty-nine states, the military and the federal system

[1] Other jurisdictions may use different terminology such as 'life without the possibility of parole', 'life without the possibility of release', 'whole life tariff' and 'natural life'. For the purposes of this chapter, all terms are treated as being synonymous, unless otherwise stated.

have the option of life without parole; the exception being Alaska.[2] For certain crimes, particularly first-degree murder, life without parole is the only sentence available in states that have abolished the death penalty.[3] What is more, 41 states and the federal government apply life without parole provisions to juvenile offenders despite international consensus against such practice.[4] The result is that there are now over 2,200 juvenile offenders in the USA who will spend the rest of their lives in prison.[5] Of these, 73 were 13 or 14 years old when they committed their crimes.[6]

Currently, only a handful of countries in the Council of Europe have provisions for whole life imprisonment, including Armenia, Bulgaria, Sweden, Ukraine, the Netherlands, Estonia and Turkey.[7] Although normally a whole life tariff will only be imposed under special circumstances, such as multiple murders or prior convictions, in some cases it is possible to petition the president for a pardon (for example in Bulgaria[8] and Estonia[9]) or the court for a determinate tariff (for example in Sweden) after a certain period of time has elapsed.

England and Wales recently joined the list of those countries with whole life tariffs. Stricter penalties brought in under the 2003 Criminal Justice Act mean that for the first time for generations courts have the powers to hand down a whole life sentence, to be distinguished from the power of the executive to 'impose' whole life tariffs.[10] This is the stark reality of the decision to entomb our citizens, be they child or adult, despite the overwhelming evidence

---

2 Death Penalty Information Centre, 'Life Without Parole', available at: deathpenaltyinfo.or (last accessed September 21st 2013).

3 In Illinois, Iowa, Louisiana, Maine, Pennsylvania and South Dakota, all life sentences are imposed without the possibility of parole. See Mauer, M., King, R.S., & Young, C. (2004). The meaning of "life": Long prison sentences in context. Washington, DC: The Sentencing Project and . Appleton, C & Grover, B. 'The Pros and Cons of life without parole', Brit. J Criminology, 2007, 47, 597–615.

4 See Article 6(5) of the International Covenant on Civil and Political Rights; Article 37a of the UN Convention on the Rights of the Child; paragraph 31(a) of UN General Assembly resolution on the rights of the child, A/RES/61/146, passed by 185 votes to 1. The USA has not signed up to these provisions.

5 Human Rights Watch, *The Rest of Their Lives: Life without Parole for Child Offenders in the United States* (New York: Human Rights Watch, 2005); E. Pilkington, 'Life without Hope', *The Guardian*, 4 August 2007.

6 Equal Justice Initiative, *Cruel and Unusual: Sentencing 13 and 14 Year Old Children to Die in Prison* (Montgomery, AL: EJI, 2007).

7 Article 38.a. (New, SG 50/95) (1) of the 1968 Penal Code of Bulgaria, amended 13 September 2002; Chapter 3, Section 1 of the 1962 Swedish Penal Code, Ds 1999:36, published 1999; see Articles 51, 64 and 115 of the Criminal Code of Ukraine, entered into force 1 September 2001; Article 31 of the Dutch Penal Code, adopted 3 March 1881, updated by amendments up to 1994; Article 45 of the Penal Code of Estonia, RT I 2001, 61, 364; consolidated text RT I 2002, 86, 504, passed 6 June 2001, entered into force 1 September 2002; Articles 47(1) and 48(1) of the Criminal Code of Turkey, Law Nr. 5237, passed on 26 September 2004. Whilst every effort has been made to ensure that the correct articles and dates have been cited in this note, due to translation issues some errors might remain.

8 Article 74 of the 1968 Penal Code of Bulgaria, amended 13 September 2002.

9 Article 77 of the Penal Code of Estonia, RT I 2001, 61, 364; consolidated text RT I 2002, 86, 504, passed 6 June 2001, entered into force 1 September 2002.

10 Section 269 (4) and Schedule 21.

that offenders, however grotesque their offending, are capable of change and consequently can make future positive contributions to society.

Issues of International law, the United Nations and the Council of Europe

In Chapter 2 'The Limits of International Law: Efforts to Enforce Rulings of the International Court of Justice in U.S. Death Penalty Cases', Sandra Babcock examines the lack of opportunities to deal with breaches of globally accepted international law:

> Yet, even in the wake of favorable judgments from the Inter-American Commission of Human Rights, the Inter-American Court on Human Rights, and the International Court of Justice (ICJ), national courts have persistently refused to grant any measure of relief to condemned foreign nationals, even in cases in which the violation was undisputed. (p. 22)

It is frustrating to have the authority of the international law yet find that those who violate the law can do so with impunity. Perhaps uniquely in the *Avena* case,[11] a case that Sandra Babcock brought to the courts on behalf of the Government of Mexico concerning Article 36 violations of Mexican citizens sentenced to death in the US, President George W. Bush agreed to comply with the order of the International Court to refer all the complainants to the originating state courts for resentencing. The President's unique act of compliance with international law was followed within days by the US withdrawing from Article 36 of the Vienna Convention on Consular Relations,[12] a treaty the United States ratified in 1969.

The United Nations has provided another arena of opportunity for abolitionists and they have been able to secure majority support for their position through draft resolutions on moratoriums tabled at the UN General Assembly, most recently on 20 December 2012, when the resolution was adopted by 111 votes in favour, with only 41 votes against and 34 abstentions – this followed three earlier votes supporting similar draft resolutions. In essence, the UN's principal involvement with capital punishment is its quinquennial survey of the status of capital punishment amongst its member states, its Second Optional Protocol to the International Covenant on Civil and Political Rights (ICCPR), its periodic global seminars and its publications.[13]

It would be churlish of me not to acknowledge that such an outcome is a positive sign but I would be more impressed if the evidence showed that these voting patterns demonstrated improvements in the generic human rights records of all the signatory nations. Regretably the evidence indicates that many states voting in favour of the resolution continue to have records of appalling human rights abuses, thus calling into question the reasons why such states support the resolution.

William Schabas, in Chapter 8, 'The United Nations and Abolition of the Death Penalty', provides a comprehensive analysis of the UN's contribution to the debate and to the universal abolition of capital punishment.

---

11 *Avena and Other Mexican Nationals (Mex. v. U.S.)*, Judgment, 2004 I.C.J. 12, 71–72 (Mar. 31).

12 Vienna Convention on Consular Relations, United Nations, 24 April 1963, 21 U.S.T. 77.

13 For example, UNOHC, 'Moving Away from the Death Penalty: Lessons from National Experiences'. This publication is based on the first of a series of proposed discussions, held at the United Nations in New York on 3 July 2012. See www.ohchr.org.

As to the legitimacy of capital punishment, many in the abolitionist industry continue to assert that capital punishment is unlawful. On the contrary most international and regional human rights instruments expressly provide for it as an exemption to the right to life. A weakness of some provisions of international law is the absence of any sanctions for those who breach them, with what limited sanctions there are taking other forms – for example, censure by the UN Committee on Human Rights or the International Court of Justice, and any subsequent negative publicity that might cause embarrassment.

So it is appropriate to mention here that there are four instruments aimed at restricting or abolishing the use of the death penalty:

- The Second Optional Protocol to the International Covenant on Civil and Political Rights (ICCPR) has a worldwide scope and provides for the total abolition of the death penalty except in times of war – 36 signatories and 76 parties to.[14]
- Protocol No. 6 to the European Convention on Human Rights (ECHR) places restrictions on the use of the death penalty in peacetime, an undertaking ratified thus far by 46 of the 47 member states of the Council of Europe, with Russia being the sole exception.[15]
- Protocol No. 13 to the ECHR is the only piece of legislation to be found in regional or international human rights treaties that outlaws the death penalty under all circumstances – 43 ratifications and 2 signatories.[16]
- The Protocol to the American Convention on Human Rights to Abolish the Death Penalty provides for the total abolition of the death penalty, but allows states parties to retain it in wartime if a reservation is made to that effect. There are 32 member states to the Convention with 13 state parties to the protocol.[17]

In Chapter 5, 'The Right to Life and Abolition of the Death Penalty in the Council of Europe', Jon Yorke charts the obstacles (legal and political) to the developments that led finally to the Holy Grail of European abolitionists – Protocol 13.

Delay

Another negative outcome of the capital litigation process and its aftermath is that of delay, specifically the period between sentence and execution. This issue was addressed in the Zimbabwean case *Catholic Commission for Justice and Peace in Zimbabwe* v. *The Attorney General and Others*[18] where it was held that delay in implementation of death sentences of up to 72 months was contrary to Article 15(1) of the Zimbabwean Constitution, which provides that no person shall be subjected to 'torture or to inhuman or degrading punishment or other such treatment'. The decision relied on several US Supreme Court decisions as well

---

14 http://www.amnesty.org/en/death-penalty/ratification-of-international-treaties.

15 http://www.amnesty.org/en/death-penalty/ratification-of-international-treaties.

16 http://www.amnesty.org/en/death-penalty/ratification-of-international-treaties.

17 http://www.amnesty.org/en/death-penalty/ratification-of-international-treaties.

18 *The Catholic Commission for Justice and Peace* v. *Attorney General of Zimbabwe and Others*, 1993(4) SA 239(ZS), Zimbabwe Supreme Court, 1993.

as the opinions of Indian judges and those of the Judicial Committee of the Privy Council describing the effects of being on death row. Caycie Bradford addresses this issue in 'Waiting to Die, Dying to Live: An Account of the Death Row Phenomenon from a Legal Viewpoint' (Chapter 7). The remedies to this troublesome issue receive too little attention and when addressed there is a failure to do so in a just and consistent manner. Kerry Akers touches on this in her analysis of 'The Global Capital Litigation Landscape' (Chapter 12), which provides an assessment of global litigation strategies, highlighting the largely foreseeable if unintended negative consequences of some of the challenges. Many strategies entrench capital punishment constitutionally rather than shaking it loose. For example, the case of *Pratt & Morgan* v. *The Queen*[19] whilst determining that the death penalty itself was constitutional in Jamaica found that the delay in administering it was not. The litigation strategy relied on the dysfunctional administration of the judicial system, which failed to deal with cases expeditiously, leaving people to languish on death row. This inefficiency was capitalized upon by the litigation team, which led to a ruling that a delay of more than five years on death row invalidated the application of the death penalty. This meant that should the Jamaican judicial system evolve and develop into a robust and efficient administration, the death penalty would be a viable sentence once more. This imposition proved an obstacle to the development of the justice system and deterred what would have been healthy changes to a dysfunctional system, rendering capital defendants in a better position being tried by a faulty, protracted system than by an effective, expedient system.

More recently, the Constitutional Court of Uganda in *Attorney General* v. *Susan Kigula & 417 Others*[20] held that persons on death row for three or more years, after all appeals have been exhausted (a process that can last for up to 12 years), were entitled to have their death sentences commuted to life imprisonment.

Mandatory Sentencing

We move now to the implications of mandatory death sentencing. In Chapter 1, '*Yong Vui Kong* v. *Public Prosecutor* and the Mandatory Death Penalty for Drug Offences in Singapore: A Dead End for Constitutional Challenge?', Yvonne McDermott deals with a topic that underlines the irrationality and inconsistency of both the justification for and the implementation of the death penalty.

Trafficking varying quantities of certain drugs carries a mandatory death sentence in Malaysia, Thailand and Singapore. China, Indonesia, Laos, Taiwan and Vietnam all have provisions for the death penalty for drug traffickers though none are mandatory. The most recent comprehensive review of the practice of countries that have narcotic capital crimes was published by the International Harm Reduction Association in May 2010.[21] One of the conclusions drawn by the authors is that the link between some of these countries and the

---

[19] *Pratt & Morgan* v. *The Queen* [1993] UKPC 1.

[20] *Attorney General* v. *Susan Kigula & 417 Others*, Constitutional Appeal No. 03 of 2006, Supreme Court of Uganda at Mengo, 21 January 2009.

[21] Chapter 30 by Patrick Gallahue and Rick Lines in Volume III of this collection draws on this review.

financial assistance they receive for drug programmes from the UN and the EC amongst others is potentially compromising.[22]

Any sentencing model that fetters judicial discretion is unsafe, so challenges to all mandatory sentencing are to be applauded, but I have some concerns that the litigation strategy adopted is inadequate in many crucial respects, including a failure to address the nature of the alternative penalty and the process through which this is determined. Specifically that those who are deemed to be the beneficiaries of such judgments should be resentenced in a timely manner. Douglas Mendes' 'The Mandatory Death Penalty – An International and Comparative Perspective' (Chapter 3), presented at a seminar in the Commonwealth Caribbean, draws on the experience of the jurisprudence established and inherited from the Commonwealth from which challenges to the mandatory sentence are cut and pasted.

I have written elsewhere[23] about my concern that places lawyers and some litigation strategies are part of the problem in challenging capital punishment. Whilst it is imperative that this issue is debated it is frustrating given that it may not be possible to 'correct' the 'problems' because the causes are inherent to the litigation process and to the culture of legal education. Law is a blunt instrument and lawyers are programmed to win; winning in the field of capital litigation means avoiding the death sentence regardless of the consequences, such as life imprisonment without the benefit of parole (LWOP), which some commentators believe to be worse than execution. It is a shame that a version of the medical professions' maxim *primum non nocere* [above all do no harm] isn't available to curb the worst excesses of the lawyers' maxim 'win at any cost'.

My concerns were confirmed in three recent cases, the details of which are extracted from Chapter 12 of this collection, by Akers, firstly *Attorney General* v. *Susan Kigula & 417 Others*. As a result of the *Kigula* ruling, access to legal aid was reduced , as was an automatic appeal for capital offences. The life sentence was increased from the former statutory 20 years to whole of life and led, too, to non-capital defendants receiving increased sentences as a result of *Tigo Steven* v. *Uganda*.[24]

Secondly, *Kigula* prompted similar challenges across the region. In Malawi, the case of *Kafantayeni*[25] mimicked *Kigula* in so far as it challenged the mandatory death penalty but did not raise the issue of the death penalty's constitutionality per se. This fragmented replication of the *Kigula* challenge also neglected to address delay, which has repeatedly been identified as the most pressing issue in Malawi's homicide trials. Similar to *Kigula*, the beneficiaries of the ruling are still waiting to reap any benefit whilst whole of life imprisonment has been endorsed as the default alternative by Presidential decree.

Thirdly, an even more fragmented challenge followed in Kenya. In the case of *Godfrey Ngotho Mutiso* v. *Republic*[26] lawyers employed a strategy in the same vein as the *Kafantayeni*

---

22 *Complicity or Abolition? The Death Penalty and International Support for Drug Enforcement*, International Harm Reduction Association, 2010, available at: www.ihra.net.

23 Hodgkinson, P. (2005), 'The Unintended, Entirely Foreseeable Though Perhaps Unavoidable Consequences of Litigating the Abolition of Capital Punishment', 13 *Amicus Journal*, 2005 and the response Mendes, D. and Delzin, G. (2005), 'Using the Bill of Rights to halt executions: A reply to Peter Hodgkinson', 15 *Amicus Journal*, 18–1.

24 *Tigo Steven* v. *Uganda*, Criminal Appeal No. 08 of 2009, [2011] UGSC 7.

25 *Kafantayeni* [2007] MWHC I.

26 *Godfrey Ngotho Mutiso* v. *Republic* [2010] eKLR.

challenge, neglecting issues of delay and the constitutionality of the death penalty per se. However, the challenge was further fragmented as it only addressed the mandatory death penalty for murder, leading to the bizarre outcome of the mandatory death penalty for murder being abolished but the mandatory death penalty for armed robbery remaining intact.

There are encouraging signs that some African countries are moving away from the mandatory death sentence for certain crimes. Zambia reduced the scope of capital punishment by making it discretionary for the crime of murder. The mandatory nature of the death penalty can have a distorting effect on the criminal justice system. For example, it is the only sentence available for armed robbery in several countries in Africa, including Kenya and Nigeria. Those who call for the death penalty for those convicted of sexual offences, such as the recent Kenyan case involving a 4-year-old child, Miss X, express anger that robbery with violence is a mandatory capital offence, when other, seemingly more heinous, crimes attract lesser punishment.

Elsewhere the mandatory death penalty in Jamaica was declared unconstitutional by the Privy Council in the case of *Watson* v. *The Queen*.[27] In 2002 the Judicial Committee of the Privy Council in the case of *Fox* v. *The Queen*[28] declared the mandatory death penalty of St. Christopher and Nevis unconstitutional, followed by a similar declaration regarding that of Belize.[29]

Murder carries a mandatory death sentence in Singapore, Malaysia and Thailand – with Singapore being an anomaly in that the level of intent required for a death to be classified as murder is only the intent to injure, not to kill.

The mandatory death penalty does not exist in the Northern African region – death sentences are passed at the judge's discretion for all capital crimes. Hypothetically, the mandatory death penalty does exist in Shari'a, whereby some Hadd offences (apostasy and adultery) carry a fixed sentence of death. However, that can be mitigated through repentance.

Legal Processes and Legal Education

In her preamble to Chapter 4, 'Fair Trial Rights and their Relation to the Death Penalty in Africa', Lilian Chenwi writes:

> This article provides an overview of fair trial rights in relation to the death penalty in Africa. It begins with a discussion of fair trial standards at the regional level, including the African Charter on Human and Peoples' Rights 1981 (African Charter), and their interpretation by the African Commission on Human and Peoples' Rights (African Commission). Subsequently, some of the fair trial rights with regard to capital trials in African States are examined. (p. 56)

In my experience defendants and appellants in capital cases are by and large inadequately represented despite the fact that millions of pounds have been donated by national governments, the UN and the EC to legal NGOs supporting litigation and legal challenges. In great part explained by the failure of foreign nationals and NGOs to build capacity within their host countries, parachuting in as post- or even neo-colonialists imposing their legal solutions

27 *Watson* v. *The Queen*, Appeal No. 36 of 2003, UKPC.

28 *Fox* v. *The Queen* (St Christopher & Nevis) [2002] 2 AC 284.

29 *Mejia* v. *Attorney General*, Action No. 296 of 2000 Supreme Court; *Reyes* [2002] 2 AC 235.

and departing without dealing with the consequences of their intervention. Well-ordered initiatives working in partnership with local activists can help build sustainable capacity with a view to such activists taking full responsibility for the legal and humane advocacy services essential to the implementation of capital litigation and the transition to and the aftermath of the abolition of capital punishment.

Some 30 years ago the London Panel of Lawyers began an initiative to defend capital defendants in the Commonwealth Caribbean and in 2013 it continues to do so – surely it should not take that long to build self-sufficiency?

Thoughtfully designed projects can, however, address the issues whilst providing a vehicle for clinical legal education initiatives for donor universities in partnership with local universities. Andy Boon and Peter Hodgkinson, in 'Life and Death in the Lawyer's Office: The Internship in Capital Punishment Studies' (Chapter 9), and Joyce G. Reed and Glenn E. Rohrer, in 'Death Penalty Mitigation: A Challenge for Social Work Education' (Chapter 11), provide a glimpse of the possibilities that such programmes can offer. Since its founding in 1992 the Centre for Capital Punishment Studies has staged an annual internship programme in many countries, including the Philippines, Nigeria, Sierra Leone, the USA (Georgia, Texas, Louisiana, Oklahoma, Pennsylvania, Ohio, Tennessee, California, Arizona, South Carolina and Maryland), Malawi, Uganda, Trinidad and Tobago, Jamaica and St Christopher and Nevis. These two essays demonstrate the value to both the participating students and to those enmeshed in the capital process. They show too the many academic disciplines that can and do usefully participate.

Jury Sentencing

In Chapter 6, 'The People Decide: The Effect of the Introduction of the Quasi-Jury System (*Saiban-In Seido*) on the Death Penalty in Japan', Leah Ambler writes:

> The Japanese people will soon decide the fate of criminal defendants for the first time in over 50 years. Under the Lay Assessor Act as of May 2009, randomly selected members of the Japanese public will preside over criminal trials alongside professional judges and be responsible for determining both verdicts and sentences. Japan's retention of the death penalty means that members of the public will ultimately have to decide whether a person lives or dies. (p. 107)

Her conclusion is 'that the introduction of the lay assessor system may create the momentum for Japan to align its criminal justice system with that of other developed countries – that is, abolition of the death penalty as an available criminal sanction' (p. 107).

The evidence on which, I suspect, her optimism is based is that from the USA, where counter-intuitively (at first blush) jury sentencing leads to fewer death sentences than judge sentencing. Intuitively one might expect the positions to be reversed given that jurors, in capital cases, are carefully selected on the basis of their support for the death penalty[death qualified] and are hence more likely to favour the death option. On the other hand, as many judges are elected, there is good reason to surmise that they would turn to the death sentence in anticipation of popular electoral support. Whilst it is early days, the evidence thus far is that where the death sentence is available to lay assessor panels it is implemented in a majority of cases.[30] Can any evidence be adduced about the 'personality' of US and Japanese lay jurors? I am confident that research is being done as I write – if not, it soon will be.

Issues of Innocence and the Implementation of the Death Penalty

The pioneering research of Bedau, Radelet and Putnam identified 416 cases in which the wrong person had been convicted and sentenced to death in the United States between 1900 and 1991. By the time of publication of their book in 1992, 66 more wrongful convictions had been confirmed. According to their research, 24 death sentences were actually carried out on the wrongfully convicted[31] and that the most frequent causes of error are perjury by prosecution witnesses, mistaken eyewitness testimony, 'passion' roused against vulnerable defendants and, finally, failures in police work and overzealous prosecution.

Chapters 13 and 14 deal with the issue of innocence and the death penalty. In Chapter 13, 'The Myth of Actual Innocence', Morris Hoffman, a District Court Judge in Colorado, USA, draws on this experience in his analysis of the growth of innocence projects in the USA. He reflects on the classic film *12 Angry Men*, in particular the role played by Henry Fonda, arguing that innocence projects are the current equivalent with 'too few Henry Fondas in modern jury pools' (p. 252).

By contrast, in Chapter 14, 'The Role of the Innocence Argument in Contemporary Death Penalty Debates', Michael Radelet reviews the lessons learnt by society over the last two decades as more wrongful convictions are revealed and fewer sentences of death are imposed, arguing that the two are linked.

Disparity and Discrimination in the Administration of Capital Punishment

There is a great deal of literature dedicated to the issue of racial disparity in the application of the death penalty in the United States, but too little data on this topic from death penalty jurisdictions elsewhere in the world. There is certainly no shortage of evidence, anecdotal and even scientific, showing the presence of racism in the administration of justice in many parts

---

[30] See the Supreme Court of Japan website, which has not published its statistics data since 2011, at http://www.moj.go.jp/housei/toukei/toukei_ichiran_kensatsu.html, http://www.courts.go.jp/search/jtsp0010List1 and the Japan Federation of Bar Associations, which has not updated its data since 2010, at http://www.nichibenren.or.jp/activity/criminal/deathpenalty/shiryou.html#data02_3.

The following figures are from Japanese newspaper articles. For 2010, number of death sentences in the First Court (where lay assessors got involved): 4 and number of other sentences in the First Court: 46; number of total death sentences in this year: 9; number of total life sentences: 50. For 2011, number of death sentences in the First Court: 10; number of other sentences in the First Court: 24; number of total death sentences in this year: 23; number of total life sentences: 43. For 2012, number of death sentences in the First Court: 3; number of other sentences in the First Court: not known; number of total death sentences in this year: 9; number of total life sentences: not known. For 2013, number of death sentences in the First Court: 2; number of other sentences in the First Court: not known; number of total death sentences in this year: 6; number of total life sentences: not known.

[31] See preface to the revised edition of M. Radelet, H.A. Bedau and C. Putnam, *In Spite of Innocence* (Boston: Northeastern University Press, 1995).

of the world but it may be that more research still needs to be done. There are some obvious candidate countries such as South Africa, Australia, Canada and New Zealand where there is ample evidence of the disproportionate numbers of indigenous peoples being subject to prosecution.[32] In the sister collection to this series *Capital Punishment: New Perspectives* I commissioned research into the administration of the death penalty in colonial Canada, which unsurprisingly reveals wholesale disparity in its implementation against indigenous peoples. I am confident that the indigenous peoples of Australia and New Zealand have had similar experiences given that more recent data on sentencing outcomes in both countries reveals wholesale disparity. Other countries where examples of ethnic and/or religious disparities may exist are Singapore, Malaysia, Indonesia, Trinidad and Tobago, and Ceylon. Here too, research in the US 'laboratory' is surely of considerable universal relevance.

It is not sufficient to point out that members of ethnic or racial minorities are prosecuted and convicted in percentages far exceeding their proportion in the population of the United States; one conclusion that appears to be uncontested in the literature, is that this disparity is marked by the race of the victim.[33] In other words, the murderer of a white victim is far more likely to receive a death sentence than the murderer of an African-American victim.

The issue of racism in the US death penalty system has dominated the case law of the Supreme Court. In two cases within the last three decades, the Court has come within a hair's breadth of judicial abolition. In 1972, in *Furman*, it invalidated virtually every death penalty statute in the country, holding that capital punishment was being applied in an arbitrary and capricious manner.[34] A few years later, it outlawed the use of capital punishment for rape of an adult woman.[35] Many damning studies had indicated the role of racial bias in rape prosecutions:[36] Amnesty International reported that 89 per cent of those executed for rape between 1930 and 1967 were black.[37] In 1986, the Supreme Court considered the case of prosecutors who systematically strike blacks from jury panels, ruling this to breach the right to a fair trial.[38]

---

[32] See I. Potas and J. Walker, *Capital Punishment*, Trends and Issues in Crime and Criminal Justice, No. 3 (Canberra: Australian Institute of Criminology, 1987), fn. 3, discussing the *Sydney Morning Herald*, 1 March 1985, which shows that in 1984 'of those executed in South Africa, 2 were white, 87 black, 24 coloured and 1 Indian'; available at: http://www.aic.gov.au/publications/tandi/ti03.pdf. This is confirmed by Amnesty International, *When the State Kills: The Death Penalty v. Human Rights* (London: Amnesty International, 1989), p. 205, which argues that 'one of the most notable aspects of the use of the death penalty in South Africa is its disproportionate imposition on the black population … by an almost entirely white judiciary'. By contrast, racial breakdowns of Australian execution statistics, including the number of executions of those from the aboriginal and indigenous populations, do not appear to be available.

[33] D.C. Baldus, G.G. Woodworth and C.A. Pulaski, *Equal Justice and the Death Penalty: A Legal and Empirical Analysis* (Boston: Northeastern University Press, 1990).

[34] *Furman* v. *Georgia*, 408 U.S. 238 (1972).

[35] *Coker* v. *Georgia*, 433 U.S. 584 (1977).

[36] E. Johnson, 'Selective Factors in Capital Punishment', *Social Forces*, **35**, 2 (1957), pp. 165–69.

[37] Amnesty International USA, 'The Death Penalty' (1987), p. 11.

[38] *Batson* v. *Kentucky*, 476 U.S. 79 (1986).

Ironically, the mandatory nature of sentencing in several South East Asian countries[39] limits the possibility of discrimination regarding the implementation of the death penalty.

Chapters 15 and 16 by Greg Wallance and Hugo Bedau, respectively, reflect aspects of disparity and discrimination, and their implications.

Wallance's 'South Africa: Racism and the Death Penalty' (Chapter 15) reveals one of the chilling effects of the Pass Laws in South Africa, encapsulated by the following statistical evidence, 'Between 1947 and 1969, 288 whites were convicted of rape of non-whites, and 844 blacks were convicted of the rape of white women. Not a single white was executed. Of the convicted blacks, 121 were sentenced to death, of whom 108 were executed' (p. 307). As to murder, in 1974–75 blacks received 132 of the 136 death sentences imposed.

In 'Racism, Wrongful Convictions, and the Death Penalty' (Chapter 16), Bedau challenges the protagonists of the debate to consider whether there are

> important similarities, differences, or both, in the merits of the administrative argument from wrongful convictions and of the administrative argument from racial bias? Since most of today's opponents of the death penalty rely on both of these arguments, it is hardly surprising that we do not see these arguments distinguished and evaluated by abolitionists. (p. 318)

I hope you will allow me a moment to recognize the contribution made to death penalty scholarship by the late Hugo Bedau (1926–2012) and, of more importance, his ability to combine intellectual rigour with compassion. He gave his heart and soul to the goals of abolition. Thank you Hugo for helping me understand capital punishment.

Issues of Gender and Sexuality

The three essays in this section offer welcome insights into issues frequently overlooked and misunderstood in the debate. Barrie Sanders, in Chapter 17, 'A Nation at War with Itself: The Potential Impact of Uganda's Anti-Homosexuality Bill', charts the early period of the debate in Uganda concerning the introduction of capital punishment as a penalty for specific homosexual actors and acts. The debate still rages, and rage is an appropriate description of the dialogue between supporters and detractors of the measures nationally and internationally. The public discussion is confused by the misinformation that it attracts with near daily alleged changes to the proposed legislation. Despite the continuing outcry internationally from governments, media, faith groups and human rights organizations, the government remains determined to pass a version of the legislation.

[39] Murder and drug offences carry a mandatory death sentence in Malaysia, Singapore and Thailand.

A number of publications, including essays by Aaron Clemens,[40] Michael Shortnacy[41] and Tiffany Lebron,[42] explore gay people's experience of capital trials and suggestions that homosexuality is an aggravating factor.

Steven Shatz and Naomi Shatz's essay 'Chivalry is Not Dead: Murder, Gender and the Death Penalty' (Chapter 18) charts the influence of chivalry on criminal law from the High Middle Ages to the current implementation of the death penalty in California. Their analysis is empirically based and they 'conclude that chivalric norms may explain the disparities we identify and that when prosecutors and jurors are given unguided discretion to make life and death decisions, those enduring roles may play a significant part in determining who lives and who dies' (p. 355).

Other important essays on this topic include those by Amanda Wolf,[43] Jenny Carroll,[44] Elizabeth Reza[45] and Victor Streib.[46]

Chapter 19, 'Zina (Adultery) under Islamic law in Nigeria: The Gender Issues in Amina Lawal's Case', is Aminu Adamu Bello's account of the notorious case of a woman sentenced to death by stoning for an adultery adduced from the fact that she was pregnant. The man identified as the father denied responsibility and escaped any charges. Bello is optimistic that there is a growth in knowledge, confidence and power amongst women living under Islamic law but recognizes that many women and women's organizations believe that Shari'a is anti-women. Other sources on this topic include essays by Ogbu Kalu,[47] Sarah Crutcher[48] and Juliette Terzieff.[49]

---

40 Aaron Clemens, 'Executing Homosexuality: Removing Anti-Gay Bias from Capital Trials', *Georgetown Journal of Gender and the Law*, **6**, 1 (2005), pp. 71–104.

41 Michael B. Shortnacy, 'Sexual Minorities, Criminal Justice, and the Death Penalty', *Fordham Urban Law Journal*, **32**, 2 (March 2005), pp. 23–36.

42 Tiffany M. Lebron, 'Death to Gays – Uganda's One Step Forward, One Step Back Approach to Human Rights', *Buffalo Human Rights Law Review*, **17** (2011), pp. 173–206.

43 Amanda Wolf, 'The Hidden Arena for Gender Bias: Capital Punishment in the United States', *Dartmouth Law Journal*, **6**, 1 (Winter 2008), pp. 110–27.

44 Jenny E. Carroll, 'Images of Women and Capital Sentencing among Female Offenders: Exploring the Outer Limits of the Eight Amendment and Articulated Theories of Justice', *Texas Law Review*, **75**, 6 (1997), pp. 1413–54.

45 Elizabeth Marie Reza, 'Gender Bias in North Carolina's Death Penalty', *Duke Journal of Gender Law & Policy*, **12** (Spring 2005), pp. 179–214.

46 Victor L. Streib, 'Gendering the Death Penalty: Countering Sex Bias in a Masculine Sanctuary', *Ohio State Law Journal*, **63**, 1 (2002), pp. 433–74.

47 Ogbu U. Kalu, 'Safiyya and Adamah: Punishing Adultery with Sharia Stones in Twenty-First-Century Nigeria', *African Affairs* (London), **102**, 408 (2003), pp. 389–408.

48 Sarah Crutcher, 'Stoning Single Nigerian Mothers for Adultery: Applying Feminist Theory to an Analysis of Gender Discrimination in International Law', *Hastings Women's Law Journal*, **15** (2004), pp. 239–262.

49 Juliette Terzieff, 'In Pakistan, Those Who Cry Rape Face Jail', *WeNews*, 16 May 2004, available at: http://womensenews.org/story/incarceration/040516/in-pakistan-those-who-cry-rape-face-jail#.UhS_TZJf15c.

Juveniles' Experience of the Death Penalty

Exempting from the death penalty those under the age of 18 who commit potentially capital offences is universally accepted in law although not in practice, with frequent examples of violations recorded annually. Only the USA and Somalia have yet to ratify the Convention on the Rights of the Child, of which Article 37 (torture and deprivation of liberty) states 'Both capital punishment and life imprisonment without benefit of release are prohibited for offences committed by persons below age 18.'

Some of those countries that violate Article 37 do so with complete disregard for their legal undertakings. According to Amnesty International, since 1990, only nine countries in the world are known to have executed juvenile offenders: China, Congo, Pakistan, Iran, Saudi Arabia, Nigeria, Yemen, Sudan and the United States. Other country's violations can perhaps be explained by their failure to have in place measures that accurately identify the age of their citizens, placing too much reliance on mistaking secondary sexual characteristics as reliable indicators of chronological age. I certainly recall the claims of justice officials in Papua New Guinea that presence of underarm hair in males is proof of age over 18 years. Their criteria for assessing the age of females was less clear. The registration of demographic data in many countries is crude and unreliable.

Chapter 20, 'End Natural Life Sentences for Juveniles', by Jeffrey Fagan, and Chapter 21, 'Juvenile Parricide Offenders Sentenced to Death', by Kathleen Heide and Jessica McCurdy, both deal with different aspects of juvenile offenders convicted of serious violent crimes, including capital murder – both in the USA.

I referred earlier to Fagan's essay by way of illustrating the generic issue of life sentencing but do so here to illustrate the indefensible practice of draconian not to say unlawful sentences passed on juveniles. Fagan sets out his stall thus,

> In 2005, the U.S. Supreme Court in *Roper v. Simmons* (125 S. Ct. 1183) banned executions of persons who commit capital murder before they reach age 18. *Roper* overturned death sentences for 72 people in 18 states. Most (but not all) were resentenced to natural life or life in prison without the possibility of parole (or JLWOP). (p. 421)

Kathleen Heide and Jessica McCurdy's essay considers the dynamics of the circumstances in which children kill their parents, examining research about juveniles who were sentenced to death between 1973 and 2005. The basis for their study is a detailed analysis of one of the four cases sentenced to death for parricide in this period.

Capital Punishment and All Its Victims

I conclude this review of Volume I by addressing the important but frequently overlooked issue about the victims of the capital punishment process. I am extending the usual analysis beyond the paradigm victims of homicide and their families as my belief is that everyone associated with the machinery of death is in some respects victimized by exposure to or engagement with the process. One thing is clear and that is that at any level of the 'victim' debate too little attention has been paid to the issues. The principal 'victim' is the homicide victim and his/her family; the accused and his/her family with others, including legal counsel and the judiciary; jurors; law enforcement especially prison staff and the execution team; religious advisers; witnesses to executions who experience a number of nuanced adverse effects.

Three essays complete this volume and address a spread of the issues. Chapter 22, Walter Long's, 'Trauma Therapy for Death Row Families', describes a very important contribution to an otherwise impoverished debate. As Long puts it:

> The family members of death row inmates undergo unique suffering that includes disenfranchised grief and intense psychological trauma. In Texas, where executions occur at a rate of 1 every 2 weeks, this class of trauma victims presumably is large, a fact that should generate public mental health concern. Yet the class remains virtually unknown to the therapeutic community. Very little has been done to address the trauma healing needs of death row families. (p. 459)

Long proposes that one of the most effective means to help this population survive trauma is 'structural therapy designed to reengage attachment relationships and reempower family members' innate resources to emotionally regulate one another' (p. 459).

Chapter 23, Nancy Bern's 'Contesting the Victim Card: Closure Discourse and Emotion in Death Penalty Rhetoric', examines the victim issue and the use of the term 'closure', which is offered wholesale as a solution for the families of homicide victims and to the generality of the pro-death penalty industry – in my opinion this is a term in breach of any 'trade descriptions' legislation and somewhat concerning in that it offers false assurances to too many bereaved family members. In Chapter 24, 'Capital Punishment: Creating More Victims?', Peter Hodgkinson, Seema Kandelia and Rupa Reddy's intention was to examine the issue of why we kill in the context of capital punishment. In particular they examine justifications for the death penalty that revolve around addressing the needs of victims in homicide cases. The authors' major contention is that the death penalty, whilst purporting to help victim's families to achieve 'justice' on behalf of the deceased, and 'closure' for themselves after the trauma of homicide, in fact creates a form of 'secondary victimization'[50] and further victims, including the families of the condemned. Far from usefully addressing the aftermath of homicide for victims' families, the authors argue that the death penalty and its processes, from the initial prosecution to the end of the lengthy appeals process, reproduce and widen the scope of victimization.

In Conclusion

This volume has begun the process of broadening capital punishment's discourse, which will be built on in Volumes II and III. Contributions include some country-specific experiences with essays on race and death sentencing in South Africa (Chapter 15), mandatory death sentencing for drug offenders in Singapore (Chapter 1), gender issues in Shari'a law in Nigeria (Chapter 19), proposals for death sentencing for homosexuality in Uganda (Chapter 17), the impact of lay juror sentencing in capital cases in Japan (Chapter 6) and fair trial rights in Africa (Chapter 4).

---

[50] A term often used by rape victims when they refer to the 'aggressive and embarrassing cross-examination' to which they are subjected by police and at trial.

International law issues are examined via the United Nations (Chapter 8), the right to life and the Council of Europe (Chapter 5), the mandatory death penalty (Chapter 3), rulings of the International Court of Justice (Chapter 2), life imprisonment under international law (Chapter 10) and a summary of global capital litigation (Chapter 12).

Chivalry issues are addressed in Chapter 18; innocence in Chapter 14, the relation between race and innocence in Chapter 16 and the myth of innocence in Chapter 13. Juvenile death sentencing and juvenile parricide offending and the death penalty are covered in Chapters 20 and 21 respectively.

Some aspects of the victim debate are covered – therapy for death row families (Chapter 22), questioning victimization (Chapter 23) and finally creating more victims (Chapter 24).

These contributions are built on in Volume II, with an examination of abolition strategies, alternative sentences to the death penalty and moratoriums. To complete the collection, Volume III examines medical issues, capital punishment policy around the world, executions, executioners and the condemned, media, capital punishment and religion, drug offenders and capital punishment, war and the death penalty. I cannot conclude this volume and collection without thanking all those volunteers who have helped in the research over the past three years, especially Kerry Ann Akers and Amelia Montgomery. Thank you all for your hard work and encouragement.

Part I
Legal Issues

[1]

Yong Vui Kong v. Public Prosecutor and the Mandatory Death Penalty for Drug Offences in Singapore: A Dead End for Constitutional Challenge?

Yvonne McDermott*

ABSTRACT

This article examines constitutional challenges to the mandatory death sentence in Singapore, with particular reference to the most recent case of *Yong Vui Kong v. Public Prosecutor* (2010). It discusses whether the Court of Appeal was too hasty in disregarding more recent jurisprudence of the Privy Council, which held the mandatory death sentence as a form of inhuman treatment or punishment. It also examines the customary international law prohibition of the mandatory death penalty, and the imposition of the mandatory death penalty for drug offences as a breach of the equality guarantee in Singapore's constitution. The article reveals a dismal future for a nuanced and sensible approach towards drug crime in Singapore, in that the latest case closes off many avenues for constitutional litigation.

On 14 May 2010, the Court of Appeal in the Republic of Singapore upheld the death penalty imposed on 22-year old Malaysian national Yong Vui Kong, who was 19 years of age when he was arrested in 2008. He had been convicted of trafficking not less than 42.27g of diamorphine and sentenced to death in 2009[1] under s 5(1)(a) of the Misuse of Drugs Act,[2] which provides for a mandatory sentence of death for trafficking in 15g or more of the substance.

* Yvonne McDermott, B. Corp. Law, Diop. sa Gh., LL.B., LL.M. cum laude (Leiden) is a Ph.D. Candidate at the Irish Centre for Human Rights at the National University of Ireland Galway. The author wishes to thank Niall Mulligan for his helpful comments and suggestions on an earlier draft.

1 *Public Prosecutor v. Yong Vui Kong* [2009] SGHC 4 [hereinafter, 'Judgment'].

2 Cap 185, 2008 Rev Ed.

The appeal of the original decision related to the constitutionality of the mandatory nature of the death penalty, as provided for by the Misuse of Drugs Act. This was not the first appeal of its kind before the Singaporean courts. In 1980, an appeal against the mandatory death penalty for trafficking in drugs was dismissed in the case of *Ong Ah Chuan*,[3] while the mandatory death penalty was similarly upheld in the case of *Nguyen* in 2004.[4] Both *Ong Ah Chuan* and *Nguyen* were unsuccessful in their arguments that the mandatory death penalty violated Articles 9 and 12 of the Singaporean constitution, which cover the protection against deprivation of liberty without due process of the law and the right to equal protection of the law, respectively.

Leave to appeal the applicant's initial sentence was granted on the basis of two principal submissions made by his counsel: that the two aforementioned decisions were decided wrongly at that time, and that the circumstances had changed to such a degree that the court should now be in a position to deem the mandatory death penalty in the Misuse of Drugs Act unconstitutional.[5] Like the preceding *Ong Ah Chuan* and *Nguyen* cases, the challenge was grounded in Article 9 and Article 12 of the constitution.

As with the court's judgment, this article does not propose to deal with the issue of the legal validity of the death penalty *per se*, but rather the continuing significance and legitimacy of the mandatory death penalty for drug offences. A downward trend in the number of countries that impose the death penalty has continued over the last four decades.[6] As Amnesty International has noted, since 2007 alone, eight countries have formally abolished the death penalty for all crimes,[7] leaving the number of *de jure* abolitionist states at ninety-five. The number of countries that have *de facto* abolished the death penalty, that is those retaining capital punishment in their statute books but who have not executed anyone for ten or more years, stands at forty-five.[8] Notably, however, for those fifty-eight countries that retain the death penalty, thirty-two list drug offences as capital offences.[9]

While figures on the exact number of executions in Singapore are not freely available, concern has been raised about its high execution rates.[10] Amnesty International in 2004 estimated that over 400 prisoners had been hanged in the country since 1991, which

3 *Ong Ah Chuan v. Public Prosecutor* [1981] AC 648 [hereinafter, 'Ong Ah Chuan'].
4 *Nguyen Tuong Van v. Public Prosecutor* [2004] 1 SGCA 47 [hereinafter, 'Nguyen'].
5 Judgment (n 1) para. 5.
6 See further, Roger Hood and Carolyn Hoyle, *The Death Penalty: A Worldwide Perspective*, Oxford University Press, Oxford, 2008, pp. 18–32.
7 These are: Albania, Cook Islands, Kyrgyzstan and Rwanda (2007); Uzbekistan and Argentina (2008), and Burundi and Togo (2009). Figures from http://www.amnesty.org/en/death-penalty/abolitionist-and-retentionist-countries, (accessed 1 October 2010).
8 Roger Hood, 'Abolition of the Death Penalty: China in World Perspective', 1(1) *City University of Hong Kong Law Review* 1, 2009, p. 6.
9 Patrick Gallahue and Rick Lines, *The Death Penalty for Drug Offences: Global Overview 2010*, International Harm Reduction Association, London, 2010, p. 7.
10 European Union Annual Report on Human Rights, 2002, p. 87.

rendered it the state with 'possibly the highest execution rate in the world relative to its population.'[11] That being said, there has been a decrease in recent years, with reported executions averaging around seven per year over the past decade, compared to twenty-one hangings in 2000 alone.

Of the thirty-two countries that retain the death penalty for drug offences, Singapore is one of just thirteen to keep the mandatory death sentence for drug offences on its statute books, meaning that no mitigating circumstances can be taken into account when imposing the harshest possible sentence. Domestic law also reserves the mandatory death penalty for treason,[12] pre-meditated murder using arms[13] and armed robbery,[14] while misdemeanours such as spitting in public, chewing gum, and leaving the toilet seat up are criminalised.[15] The harsh criminal justice system, paired with the country's cleanliness, thriving economy and the material wealth of its inhabitants, has led one commentator to dub the small island nation a 'theme park with the death sentence'.[16]

The mandatory death penalty as inhuman treatment or punishment

Article 9(1) of Singapore's constitution provides that 'No person shall be deprived of his life or personal liberty save in accordance with law'. In *Yong Vui Kong*, the appellant argued that the mandatory death sentence imposed contravened this provision in two respects. First, it was argued that the mandatory nature of the sentence was inhuman and, as such, it could not be considered 'law' for the purposes of Article 9(1) and the 'in accordance with the law' proviso. Second, it was submitted that the phrase 'law' ought to include customary international law, and a customary international law norm had emerged such to find that the mandatory death penalty was inhuman treatment, and thus in contravention to international human rights law.

As regards the first strand of this argument, the definition of 'law' under Article 2 of the Singaporean constitution must be considered. Article 2(1) defines law as encompassing written law passed by the UK Parliament and having force in Singapore, and common law and custom in so far as it is in operation in Singapore. In *Ong Ah Chuan*, the appellant submitted that the mandatory death penalty invoked a presumption of guilt and, as such,

11 Amnesty International, *Singapore: The death penalty - A hidden toll of executions*, January 2004, AI Index: ASA 36/001/2004. Notably, however, Amnesty International's *Death sentences and executions in 2009* report noted that Singapore carried out one known hanging in 2009, for the second year in a row.

12 Singapore Penal Code (Cap 224, 2008 Rev Ed), section 121A.

13 Arms Offences Act (Cap 14, 2008 Rev Ed), section 4.; Singapore Penal Code (Cap 224, 2008 Rev Ed), section 302.

14 Arms Offences Act, section 4(a).

15 Vinay Lal, 'The Flogging of Michael Fay: Culture of Authoritarianism', *Economic and Political Weekly* (1994), vol. 29, no. 23, pp. 1386—1388.

16 John Clammer, 'Framing the Other: Criminality, Social Exclusion and Social Engineering in Developing Singapore', *Social Policy and Administration* (1997), vol. 31, 136–53, p. 142.

was contrary to fundamental norms of due process. In response, the Prosecutor argued that as the Misuse of Drugs Act was validly passed by Parliament, it thus fell under the rubric of 'law' under Article 9(1). The Privy Council was not convinced by this interpretation, and held that regard must be had to 'fundamental rules of natural justice',[17] ultimately finding no conflict between the Misuse of Drugs Act and these basic tenets of natural justice. Lord Diplock, rather unconvincingly, argued that a miscarriage of justice or unjust application of the written law could be avoided by recourse to executive clemency.[18]

If the protection of due process in matters concerning the deprivation of life and liberty is not to be considered a 'fundamental rule of natural justice', it is difficult to imagine what might be. The court in *Yong Vui Kong* attempted to answer this by stating *obiter* that a piece of legislation designed to act as a judgment against one individual might meet the standard set down in *Ong Ah Chuan*.[19]

However, since the decision of *Ong Ah Chuan* in 1981, the Privy Council's position on the mandatory death penalty has changed significantly. A string of cases in the intervening time held that a violation of the convicted person's rights had occurred and that the mandatory death penalty was a form of inhuman punishment.[20]

Nguyen first brought this change in the Privy Council's approach to the Court of Appeal's attention in 2004. Therein, the court summarily dealt with this argument, surmising after a brief analysis of the relevant decisions that,

> We are of the view that the mandatory death sentence prescribed...is sufficiently discriminating to obviate any inhumanity in its operation. It is therefore constitutional.[21]

This position, particularly the lack of explanation as to *why* the law was 'sufficiently discriminating', has been heavily criticised by several academics.[22] In his statement in the

17 *Ong Ah Chuan* (n 3) pp. 670—671

18 This is one of the principal arguments put forward by 'Chief Justice Truepenny' in Lon L. Fuller's *Speluncean Explorers* fable, heavily criticised by his 'fellow judges' as basing his reasoning on extraneous factors to the case at hand, when the role of the judge is to interpret and apply the law. Lon L. Fuller, 'The Case of the Speluncean Explorers in the Supreme Court of Newgarth, 4300', *Harvard Law Review* (1949), vol. 62 no.4, p.616.

19 Judgment (n 1) para. 16, referring to *Don John Francis Liyanage v. The Queen* [1967] 1 AC 259.

20 *Inter alia, Reyes v. The Queen* [2002] 2 AC 235; *Boyce and anor. v. The Queen* [2005] 1 AC 400; *Watson v. The Queen (Attorney General for Jamaica intervening)* [2005] 1 AC 472, and *Matthew v. State of Trinidad and Tobago* [2005] 1 AC 433; *R v Hughes* [2002] UKPC 12; *Fox v. The Queen* [2002] 2 AC 284, and *Bowe (Junior) & Anor. v. The Queen* [2006] 1 WLR 1623.

21 Nguyen (n 4) para. 83.

22 For an analysis, Li-ann Thio, 'The Death Penalty as Cruel and Inhuman Punishment Before the Singapore High Court? Customary Human Rights Norms, Constitutional Formalism and the Supremacy of Domestic Law in *PP v Nguyen Tuong Van*', *Oxford University Commonwealth Law Journal*, 2004, vol. 4, no.2, pp. 213—226.; Michael Hor, 'The Death Penalty in Singapore and International Law', *Singapore Yearbook of International Law*, 2004, vol. 8, pp. 105—117.; CL Lim, 'The Constitution and the Reception of Customary International Law: *Nguyen Tuong Van v. Public Prosecutor*', *Singapore Journal of Legal Studies*, 2005, pp. 218—233.

aftermath of the decision, the Special Rapporteur on extrajudicial, summary or arbitrary executions, Philip Alston, expressed his concern that the precedent laid down in *Boyce and Joseph v. The Queen*[23] had not been given due weight.[24] Therein, the majority held that the maintenance of the mandatory death penalty would 'not be consistent with the current interpretation of various human rights treaties to which Barbados is a party'.[25] Moreover, the appellants had submitted that, 'No international human rights tribunal anywhere in the world has ever found a mandatory death penalty regime compatible with international human rights norms', and this assertion was not contradicted by the court.[26]

In *Reyes v. The Queen*, Lord Bingham of Cornhill stated that,

> To deny the offender the opportunity, before the sentence is passed, to seek to persuade the court that in all circumstances to condemn him to death would be disproportionate and inappropriate is to treat him as no human being should be treated and thus to deny his basic humanity.[27]

We are of the view that respect for the offender's 'basic humanity' must surely come under the 'fundamental rules of natural justice' as underlined in the earlier decision of *Ong Ah Chuan*. It may be logical to surmise, as did Lord Bingham in the case of *Bowe v. The Queen*,

> [T]hat it took some time for the legal effect of entrenched human rights guarantees to be appreciated, not because the meaning of the rights changed but because the jurisprudence was... unfamiliar.[28]

However, the submissions to this effect made by counsel for Yong Vui Kong were met with a certain degree of hysteria, with the Court of Appeal saying that it 'borders on the fanciful' to suggest that Lord Diplock in *Ong Ah Chuan* may have incorrectly assessed the nature of the mandatory death penalty or, in the alternative, that *Nguyen* applied the wrong interpretation of the word 'law'.

Unlike *Nguyen*, which denied the Article 9(1) submission on the reasoning (however underdeveloped) that the Misuse of Drugs Act was sufficiently discriminatory to not be inhuman, the present case went to great lengths to show that the Privy Council cases were based on the relevant national constitutions, which contain a prohibition against torture,

23 *Boyce and anor. v. The Queen* (n 20).
24 Statement by Special Rapporteur on Extrajudicial, Summary or Arbitrary Executions, Philip Alston, regarding Singapore, 17 November 2005.
25 *Boyce and anor. v. The Queen* (n 20) para. 6.
26 Alston (n 24).
27 *Reyes v. The Queen* (n 20) para. 43.
28 *Bowe (Junior) & Anor. v. The Queen* (n 20) para. 42.

inhuman or degrading treatment, and that as the Singaporean constitution contains no such provision, the court was not bound to take them into consideration.[29]

After Singapore seceded from Malaysia in 1965, a temporary constitution was adopted. This was primarily based on the state constitution of Singapore, which was intended to work for the state within a federation setting, with a mix of elements from the Republic of Singapore Independence Act 1965 and portions of the Malaysian Federal Constitution imported through the Republic of Singapore Independence Act.[30] In order to ensure that minorities were duly protected in the new constitution, Chief Justice Wee Chong Jin was asked to convene a constitutional commission to consider how such protections might be included in the new constitution.[31] Among its recommendations, the Wee Commission proposed that three new articles be included: one on the prohibition against torture, one on the right to vote and one on the right to a judicial remedy.[32] The government considered these suggestions, and noted that they would be 'incorporated in some form in the new Constitution to be drawn up'.[33] However, no new constitution was ever developed, and the temporary constitution of December 1965 essentially remains the version in place today. In 1969, the Constitution (Amendment) Act 1969 was passed to give effect to one of the Wee Commission's recommendations, to date the only recommendation so adopted, on the establishment of a Presidential Council for Minority Rights.[34]

The Court of Appeal in *Yong Vui Kong* interpreted the adoption of only one of Chief Justice Wee's recommendations as an 'unambiguous' rejection of the proposed Article 13 preventing torture, inhuman or degrading treatment or punishment 'whatever the reasons for such rejection were'.[35] With respect, the explicit approval of the three proposed new articles by the Parliament must bear some weight, especially since the judgement just three paragraphs later relies on the fact that 'the Government has expressed the view that torture is wrong' in parliamentary debates to prevent the logical consequence of its reasoning, discussed below, that laws permitting torture, as well as what is widely-recognised as inhuman treatment in this case, would be regarded as 'law' for the purposes of Article 9(1).[36] In this regard, the court clearly applies double standards as regards the weight which must be given to parliamentary debates.

29 Lai J did refer to the differing constitutional traditions and human rights obligations of Belize and the United States of America, respectfully, to distinguish the cases of *Reyes and Watson* [2005] 1 AC 472 from *Nguyen*. Arun K Thiruvengadam describes this position as 'nitpicking', which fails to address the substantive issues underlying those decisions ('Comparative law and constitutional interpretation: Insights from Constitutional Theory', in Li-ann Thio and Kevin YL Tan (eds.) *Evolution of a Revolution: Forty years of the Singapore Constitution,* Routledge, London, 2009, pp. 113–152 at p. 145.

30 Kevin YL Tan, 'State and Institution Building through the Singapore Constitution, 1965-2005' in Thio and Tan (n 29), p. 54.

31 Li-ann Thio, 'The passage of a generation: Revisiting the report of the 1966 Constitutional Commission' in Thio and Tan (n 29) pp. 8—9.

32 ibid, p. 16.

33 Edmund William Barker, Minister for Law and National Development, *Singapore Parliamentary Debates, Official Report*, 21 December 1966, vol. 25, cols. 1052—1053.

34 Act 19 of 1969.

35 Judgment (n 1) para. 72.

36 ibid, para. 75.

Furthermore, in the intervening forty years, the Wee Report's other two suggestions have been recognised as 'unenumerated rights' in the Singaporean constitution.[37] The first, the right to a judicial remedy, was read into the provisions of Article 93 of the constitution (on judicial power) by the High Court in *Colin Chan v. PP*,[38] while the Attorney-General was asked to provide a report to the Parliament in 2002 on whether there was a right to vote entrenched in the constitution. On this, he opined that 'the right to vote at parliamentary and presidential elections is implied within the structure of our Constitution.'[39] In the light of this evidence that there are unenumerated rights implicit in the Singaporean constitution, the court's position that the Wee Commission only suggested a provision against torture (and for that matter, the right to vote and to a judicial remedy) 'because Article 9(1) did not deal with the same subject matter...otherwise, [it] would have been redundant',[40] must be taken with a pinch of salt.

In an attempt to copper fasten its reasoning as to why the absence of a prohibition against torture in Singapore's constitution should render the numerous Privy Council decisions on the mandatory death penalty irrelevant, the Court of Appeal invokes a cultural relativist argument in paragarph 73 of its judgment.

> In this connection, we wish to highlight Lord Bingham's observation in *Reyes* at [28]...that states are not bound to give effect in their Constitutions to norms and standards accepted elsewhere, perhaps in very different societies.

In making this argument, the Court of Appeal appeared to overlook a number of judgments passed in rather different societies – Malawi,[41] Uganda[42] and most recently Kenya[43] – which have accepted the reasoning of the Privy Council in this regard when interpreting their own domestic constitutions.

Moreover, in the case of *Mithu v. State of Punjab*,[44] the Indian Supreme Court was asked to rule on the constitutionality of Section 303 of the Indian Penal Code, which provided for the mandatory death sentence for persons serving a life sentence who committed murder while serving that sentence. Whether or not one considers India and Singapore to be 'very different societies', the fact remains that Articles 14 and 21 of the Indian constitution are

37 On this point, see Li-ann Thio, 'Protecting Rights' in Thio and Tan (n 29), pp. 202—204.
38 [1994] 3 SLR 662, p. 681
39 Thio (n 37) citing 73 *Singapore Parliamentary Reports*, 16 May 2001, col. 1720, at 1726.
40 Judgment (n 1) para. 72.
41 *Kafantayeni and Others v Attorney General*, Constitutional Case No. 12 of 2005 [2007] MWHC 1, 27 April 2007, pp. 6, 10.
42 *Attorney General v Susan Kigula & 417 Others*, Constitutional Appeal No. 3 OF 2006 [2009] UGSC 6, 21 January 2009.
43 *Godfrey Ngotho Mutiso v Republic*, Criminal Appeal 17 of 2008 [2010] eKLR, 30 July 2010, para. 32.
44 AIR 1983 SC473 [hereinafter, 'Mithu'].

almost identical to Articles 9 and 12 of the Singaporean model. Importantly, like Singapore, India's constitution contains no express prohibition on torture, inhuman or degrading treatment or punishment. The Indian Supreme Court struck down Section 303 as being 'arbitrary and oppressive', stating that 'it must go the way of all bad laws.'[45] The court stated that a 'provision of law which deprives the Court of its wise and beneficent discretion in a matter of life and death, without regard to the circumstance in which the offence was committed...cannot but be regarded as harsh, unjust and unfair.'[46]

In *Nguyen,* Liu J differentiated *Mithu* on the basis that, apparently, it was clear in that case that there was no 'rational justification' for imposing sentence against those serving life sentences, as opposed to others convicted of murder, whereas it was not as apparent that there was no rational justification for the 15g differentia.[47] He did not elaborate on that point, nor on why the rational justification was more apparent in the case of trafficking of a specific amount of a controlled substance.[48]

The Court of Appeal in *Yui Vui Kong* also rejected the precedent of *Mithu* but gave a more detailed reasoning for doing so. First, it opined, *Mithu* was decided on the grounds of the Indian constitution which uses the phrase 'according to procedure established by law'. The Indian Supreme Court stated that taking autonomy away from judges 'in a matter of life and death' was not fair, just or reasonable. Instead of the phrase 'according to procedure established by law', Article 9(1) uses the wording 'in accordance with the law'. Thus, the Court of Appeal argued, the Court need not concern itself with procedural safeguards, as the Indian courts must.[49] To draw a distinction between the phrases 'in accordance with the law' and 'according to procedure established by law' is nitpicking at best, and disingenuous at worst.

The Court further followed *Ong Ah Chuan* in holding that applying the *Mithu* test 'requires the Court to intrude into the legislative sphere of Parliament as well as engage in policy making'.[50] However, the court's reasoning here displays an excessive and unreasonable deference to the executive and legislative branches of government. Article 93 of Singapore's constitution grants judicial power onto the judiciary and confers on the judges the right of judicial review of any official power. The court's reasoning throughout, as exemplified in this rejection of the *Mithu* case, shows a worrying subservience to the legislative and executive branches.

45 ibid, para. 25.
46 ibid, para. 12.
47 *Nguyen* (n 4) para. 74.
48 Thiruvengadam (n 29) p. 146.
49 Judgment (n 1) para. 80.
50 ibid.

Further, the court took issue with what it saw as an almost renegade Indian Supreme Court which, since the 'extreme position' taken in *Mithu*, has 'expanded the scope of Article 21 even further to include...the right to education, the right to health and medical care and the right to freedom from noise pollution.'[51] Perhaps the court was concerned with the possibility that the elusive 'floodgates', often referred to in constitutional jurisprudence, would open, but each further case based on Article 21's equivalent, Article 9, would have to be decided on its individual merits. Later, unrelated jurisprudence ought to have no bearing on the weight of a case with the same facts based on almost identical constitutional provisions.

By the same token, the fact that *Mithu* was based on denying the judiciary the power to decide an appropriate sentence would, according to the Singaporean court, have the effect of declaring *all* fixed sentences proscribed by the legislature unconstitutional.[52] In fact, as in the U.S. case of *Woodson*,[53] the Indian court distinguished the finality and severity of the punishment concerned as necessitating a different, procedurally safer, position.

Thus, in comparison to its blanket rejection of Privy Council decisions post-*Ong Ah Chuan*, the Court of Appeal was forced to proffer some very specific and somewhat far-fetched reasons for rejecting the *Mithu* standard. In spite of their specific differences, there is an argument to be made that the sum of these constituent cases should add to a whole that casts doubt on the appropriateness of the mandatory death penalty as a sentence, in spite of the lack of an explicit prohibition on torture/inhuman or degrading treatment in the Singaporean constitution. This line of reasoning was put forward by the appellant in arguing that term 'law' must include customary international law, which prohibits inhuman punishment generally and proscribes the mandatory death penalty as a form of inhuman punishment specifically.

The customary international law prohibition of the mandatory death penalty

Counsel for *Yong Vui Kong* had proposed that the word 'law' in Article 9(1) be interpreted so as to include customary international law. As mentioned above, the term 'law' as defined by Article 2(1) of the constitution is to include 'any custom or usage having the force of law in Singapore'. The Court of Appeal was not convinced that sufficient reason had been given by the appellant as to why customary international law should be considered to be part of 'law' for the purposed of Article 9(1). However, even the Attorney General had conceded that 'law'

51 ibid, para. 83.
52 ibid, para. 81.
53 *Woodson et al v. North California* (1976) 428 US 280.

should indeed include customary international law.[54] The court interpreted this concession to mean that the Attorney General did not intend to aver that any customary norm should become domestic law immediately, stating,

> It seems clear enough to us that what the AG meant when he said that the expression 'law' should be interpreted to include CIL was that this expression would include a CIL rule which had already been recognised and applied by a domestic court as part of Singapore law.[55]

In this sense, it was held that rules of customary international law cannot become part of domestic law 'until and unless it has been applied as or definitively declared to be part of domestic law by a domestic court.'[56]

This reasoning is rather flimsy as regards the customary international prohibition on torture, inhuman or degrading treatment or punishment for two reasons. First, the need for a declaration or application of the customary rule by a domestic court does not logically stand as a reason why *this* domestic court could not apply a customary rule. Second, following the court's reasoning, it would mean that as long as there was no positive law or judicial pronouncement to the contrary, there could be no customary international law against torture, for example, applied in the domestic context. To counter this lacuna of logic, the court noted the fact that the Government has 'expressed the view that torture is wrong' in parliamentary debates.[57] This is a direct contradiction to its own reasoning on the need for a domestic *court* to apply a customary rule before it becomes part of domestic law and also the little weight given to parliamentary debates following the Wee Report, as mentioned above.

The court went on to deny that international legal norms or Singapore's international legal obligations could be used to read provisions into the constitution that were not expressly provided for therein, stating instead that they had a duty to interpret international obligations consistently with domestic law only insofar as is possible.[58] This strictly textualist approach in interpreting the constitution is a far cry from the decision in *Ong Ah Chuan*, which made reference to the 'fundamental rules of natural justice' and recognised that if the constitution was not interpreted as protecting certain fundamental liberties, it 'would be little better than a mockery'. It is also at odds with the court's reasoning in *Nguyen*, which,

54 Judgment (n 1) para. 44.
55 ibid, para. 44.
56 ibid, para. 91.
57 ibid, para. 75.
58 ibid, para. 59.

despite holding that it had not been firmly established that death by hanging fell under the accepted customary international law prohibition against cruel and unusual punishment, appeared open to using international law in domestic courts, explicitly accepting that Article 5 of the Universal Declaration of Human Rights constituted customary international law.[59]

The appellant, presumably expecting the Court of Appeal to show a similar openness to customary international law as it did in *Nguyen*, argued that the mandatory death penalty fell under this customary international law prohibition on torture, cruel, inhuman or degrading treatment or punishment. Justification for this position was given with reference to the numerous Privy Council decisions, as stated above, and other decisions like the case of *Woodson et al. v. North California*,[60] which ruled that the mandatory nature of the sentence was inhuman because it dehumanised individual offenders and treated them not as human beings but as a 'faceless, undifferentiated mass'.[61]

There is generally an overall trend outlawing the mandatory death sentence in the past twenty years, with the most recent Asian case being the Bangladeshi High Court's decision in *BLAST and another vs. Bangladesh and others* ['Shukur Ali' Case] of 2 March 2010,[62] which held that Section 6(2) of the Nari-O-Shishu Nirjatan (Bidesh Bidhan) Act, 1995 was unconstitutional. The court said judges should be given the opportunity to examine the circumstantial conditions and credibility of evidences and witnesses when awarding punishment. Other notable developments include a decision of the Inter-American Court of Human Rights in 2009 denouncing the mandatory death penalty,[63] a Ugandan Supreme Court ruling outlawing the practice in January of that year[64] and a similar decision of the Kenyan Court of Appeal in Mombasa in July 2010.[65]

The Attorney General of Singapore justified the continued use of the mandatory death sentence by pointing out that thirty-one states retain the mandatory death penalty for 'drug-related and other serious offences',[66] while counsel for the appellant argued that only fourteen countries apply the mandatory sentence for drug-related offences. The court followed the Attorney General's reasoning and held that there was insufficient *opinio juris* to justify a finding that a customary prohibition existed.[67] This was in spite of the fact that 93%

59 *Nguyen* (n 4) para 85.
60 *Woodson et al v. North California* (n 54).
61 ibid, pp. 303—305.
62 *BLAST and another v. Bangladesh and others ['Shukur Ali' Case]*, Writ Petition No. 8283 of 2005, High Court Division of the Supreme Court of Bangladesh, 2 March 2010.
63 *DaCosta Cadogan v. Barbados*, Judgment of September 24 2009, Inter-American Court of Human Rights.
64 *Attorney General v. Susan Kigula and 417 Others*, No. 03 of 2006, Ugandan Supreme Court, 21 January 2009.
65 *Godfrey Ngotho Mutiso v. Republic* (n 43).
66 Judgment (n 1) para. 94.
67 ibid, para. 99.

of the states in the world do not have laws which impose the mandatory death penalty for drug offences.[68]

In practice, however, only six of these states practice executions for drug offences to such a degree that they could be regarded as 'highly committed' to the practice: China, Iran, Saudi Arabia, Viet Nam, Singapore and Malaysia.[69] In fact, some of the states which retain the mandatory death penalty on their statute books are considered *de facto* abolitionist states. For example, Brunei-Darussalam, which adopted such legislation in 2001,[70] has not executed anyone since 1959, and India is thought to have never carried out an execution under its Narcotics and Psychotropic Substances Act, as amended in 1989.[71]

The mandatory death penalty as a breach of the equality provisions of Singapore's constitution

The appellant's final argument was that the differentia under which the mandatory death penalty was imposed was arbitrary, and thus incompatible with the equality provision in Article 12(1) of the Singaporean constitution. This argument (also raised in *Ong Ah Chuan*) centred on the proposition that the '15g differentia' under the Misuse of Drugs Act was arbitrary insofar as it ruled that once an individual was found to be in possession of more than 15g of diamorphine, he or she was presumed to be trafficking in that substance, and no mitigating factors could be taken into account.[72]

The 15g differentia as the benchmark for imposing the death penalty was introduced by the Misuse of Drugs (Amendment) Act, 1975. The then Minister for Home Affairs and Education, stating that the law was 'not intended to sentence petty morphine and heroin peddlers to death' declared that it was 'necessary to specify the quantity by weight, exceeding which the death penalty will be imposed.'[73] No legal or scientific justification was put forward, aside from the relative leniency apparently shown by this approach in comparison to Iran, where trafficking in 10g or more attracts a sentence of death.[74] Since the passage of this Act, Brunei's relevant legislation followed suit with the 15g differentia, while Bangladesh's Narcotics Control Act 1990 makes it possible to sentence people to death if caught with more than 25g of heroin.[75]

68 That is, UN member states, of which there are 192.
69 Gallahue and Lines (n 9).
70 Misuse of Drugs Act, 2001.
71 Gallahue and Lines (n 9) p. 41, citing US Department of State, 2009 International Narcotics Control Strategy Report, Volume 1, 27 February 2009.
72 Judgment (n 1) paras. 101—104.
73 *Singapore Parliamentary Debates, Official Report* (20 November 1975) at col 1382.
74 ibid.
75 Gallahue and Lines (n 9) p. 36.

It is difficult to determine what makes trafficking in 15g of a controlled substance so much worse than 14.99g, yet *Ong Ah Chuan* held that the 15g differentia 'bears a reasonable relation to the social object of the law'. As counsel for the appellant Yong Vui Kong pointed out, an offender can be caught multiple times with 14.99g but he who is caught once with 15 g or over will be sentenced to hanging.[76] By the same token, someone who traffics in 15g and someone who traffics in 1,500g would face the same sentence.[77] Moreover, the mandatory nature of the offence means that mitigating circumstances, such as whether there was a voluntary assumption of risk, information on the individual and their likelihood of reoffending cannot be taken into account.[78]

As Amnesty International's 2004 report points out, Clause 18 of the Misuse of Drugs Act states that if someone is caught with the keys to a vehicle or building found to contain drugs, there is a rebuttable presumption that he or she is personally in possession of that quantity of drug.[79] This means, potentially, that if a number of drug users are sharing accommodation, and one is caught with the key to the building in which they are staying which contains an accumulated amount of heroin exceeding 15g, he will be sentenced to the death penalty. This is perhaps an extreme example, but it shows the nonsensical cumulative effect of the mandatory fixed penalty based on the 15g differentia.

Ong Ah Chuan and *Nguyen* both rejected the arguments before them based on the principle of equality before the law, finding that if the dissimilarity applied bore a 'reasonable relation'[80] to the object of the law, there could be no inconsistency with the constitution. *Nguyen* declared that a differentiating measure is valid if the classification is founded on an 'intelligible' criterion.

On this question, the Court of Appeal in *Yong Vui Kong* held, unsurprisingly given the amount of autonomy it allowed the legislature in earlier findings, that it was the legislature's prerogative to determine where on the scale between large-scale traffickers and small-time users a given amount would fall. This decision to be based on the information at hand, and bearing in mind the desire to punish those whose position rests nearer to the apex of the distribution pyramid. While it can be argued whether quantity alone is an appropriate policy to differentiate between categories of persons found in possession of drugs, the court found it a 'question of social policy', and so long as it bears a rational relation to the social object, its hands are tied.[81]

76 Judgment (n 1) paras. 103—104.
77 ibid, para. 108.
78 ibid, paras. 105—108.
79 Amnesty International Report on Singapore (n 11) p. 13.
80 Or, as in the case of *Nguyen*, a 'rational relation'.
81 Judgment (n 1) paras. 112—113.

It is deference to the legislature's apparent prerogative in deciding the appropriate threshold for imposing the penalty as a policy issue, the court appears to have neglected the fact that sentencing generally falls within the remit of professional judges. Indeed, under Article 93 of the Singaporean constitution, 'The judicial power of Singapore shall be vested in a Supreme Court and in such subordinate courts as may be provided by any written law for the time being in force'. This article clearly grants judicial power to judges. The Singaporean constitution has a traditional 'separation of powers' function, yet the last three decades has seen a marked increase in 'executive sentencing', whereby the judicial function of sentencing is diluted by a number of legislative acts containing mandatory sentences for given offences.[82] This decision, showing an unquestioning approach towards legislative sentencing, paves a worrying path for the future of judicial independence in Singapore.

Deterrent Effect

Counsel for Yong Vui Kong raised a final argument in the form of an affidavit with testimony from Prof Jeremy Fagan on the minimal deterrent effect that the death penalty has on drug use and trafficking into Singapore.[83] In response, the Attorney General filed statistics from the UN Office on Drugs and Crime (UNODC) to show that Singapore has one of the lowest drug addiction rates internationally, which the court accepted.[84]

The court's reliance on this UNODC report, insofar as it relates to Singapore, is disingenuous at best. The same report clearly warns that, 'Data from Singapore are registry data and thus not directly comparably with data from other countries'.[85] This 'registry data' comes from people who are in contact with the treatment system or the judicial system of the country, and UNODC itself notes that there is often 'considerable divergence' between it and survey data.[86]

The same report provides statistical analysis of drug prices worldwide. The wholesale price of heroin in Singapore in 2006 was $5,365/kg, significantly cheaper than in neighbouring Malaysia, where the price was reported at $7,100/kg.[87] This undermines the claim of any deterrent effect of the mandatory death penalty. If less heroin had entered the country

82 *Inter alia*, the Immigration Act, Vandalism Act, Miscellaneous Offences (Public Order and Nuisance) Act, Undesirable Publications Act, Internal Security Act, the Banishment Act, the Maintenance of Religious Harmony Act, the Environmental Public Health Act, the Singapore Broadcasting Authority Act, and the Telecommunications Authority of Singapore Act, *per* Ross Worthington, 'Between Hermes and Themis: An Empirical Study of the Contemporary Judiciary in Singapore' *Journal of Law and Society* (2002), 28(4) 490—519, p. 510. Worthington also mentions some interesting statistics on judicial salaries, which are determined solely by the Minister for Finance and increased more than threefold between 1995 and 1998, p. 512.

83 Judgment (n 1) para. 116.

84 ibid, para. 117.

85 UN Office on Drugs and Crime, *World Drug Report* 2008, p. 214.

86 ibid, p. 295. For a further discussion of this critique, see Gallagher and Lines (n 9) pp. 26—27.

87 UN Office on Drugs and Crime (n 85) p. 257.

in 2006, it can be assumed that this would have had the effect of pushing up the cost per wholesale kilo. Yet according to the UNODC report relied upon by the court, this was not the case. In fact, in the East and South-East Asia region, the price per kilo was cheapest in Singapore, and most expensive in the Philippines, where the wholesale price is over $100,000/kg. Interestingly, the Philippines ceased executing people for drug-related and other offences in 2001.[88] The court's reasoning on the purported 'deterrent effect' of the punishment is therefore highly suspect.

Conclusion

Against the backdrop of an international culture tending towards abolitionism, the decision of the Court of Appeals reflects the fact that Singapore remains a country clinging tightly to its 'right' to not only execute drug offenders, but to impose a mandatory death sentence on those found to be in possession of a given quantity of a drug, with no scope for considering mitigating factors in sentencing.

The UN Human Rights Committee has criticised those states which retain the death penalty for drug offences, noting such legislation as being contrary to the threshold laid down in Article 6(2) of the International Covenant on Civil and Political Rights, which states that the sentence of death can only be applied for 'most serious crimes',[89] that is intentional crimes with lethal or other extremely grave consequences. As wryly noted in a 2007 report on this issue, although drug use can sometimes have lethal consequences, it is difficult to argue that this outcome is the intention of drug traffickers, as killing one's own customers is generally not seen as a good business model.[90]

Whilst government officials may credit a purported deterrent effect of the mandatory death penalty with saving thousands of lives,[91] no concerted effort has been made to empirically substantiate this claim. Indeed, no compelling evidence has been found in such studies, conducted elsewhere, to support the deterrent effect of either the death penalty[92] or mandatory sentencing generally.[93] In arguing against clemency, Law Minister Mr. K. Shanmugam asserted that,

88 David T. Johnson and Franklin E. Zimring, *The Next Frontier: National Development, Political Change and the Death Penalty in Asia*, Oxford University Press, Oxford, 2009, p. 104.

89 See for example, UN Human Rights Committee, *Concluding observations of the Human Rights Committee: Thailand* (8 July 8 2005) UN Doc No. CCPR/CO/84/THA, para. 14.; UN Human Rights Committee, *Concluding observations of the Human Rights Committee: The Sudan* (29 August 2007) UN Doc No. CCPR/C/SDN/CO/3, para. 19.

90 Rick Lines, *The Death Penalty for Drug Offences: A Violation of International Human Rights Law*, International Harm Reduction Association, London, 2007, p. 12.

91 Zakir Hussain, 'Tough stance on serious crimes saves lives: Minister, *The Straits Times*, 10 May 2010.

92 For example, Hugo Adam Bedau, 'Abolishing the Death Penalty even for the Worst Murderers' in *The Killing State: Capital Punishment in Law, Politics and Culture*, ed. A Sarat, Oxford University Press, Oxford, 1999, pp. 40—59.; Roger Hood, *The Death Penalty: A Worldwide Perspective 3rd edn.*, Oxford University Press, Oxford, 2003, pp. 208—232.

93 For example, David McDowall, Colin Loftin and Brian Wiersema, 'A Comparative Study of the Preventive Effects of Mandatory Sentencing Laws for Gun Crimes', *The Journal of Criminal Law and Criminology* (1992), vol. 83(2), pp. 378—394.

> Yong Vui Kong is young, but if we say, 'We let you go', what is the signal we are sending? We are sending a signal to all the drug barons out there: just make sure you choose a victim who is young, or a mother of a young child, and use them as the people to carry the drugs into Singapore.[94]

This line of reasoning proceeds from the rather dubious assumption that drug barons are more concerned for the wellbeing of their couriers than they are the integrity of their supply lines. Furthermore, its presumption that the imposition of a lengthy term of imprisonment in lieu of hanging would patently be less potent in its deterrent and incapacitatory effects must be treated with due circumspection.

For those whose primary concern is the economic development of Singapore, the most serious consequence of drug crime is really its potential economic fallout. Oehlers and Tarulevicz note that, 'What is usually identified as gravest...is the escapism that is associated with drug consumption, which if left unchecked, could potentially undermine the strength of human resources in the country, compromising the pursuit of economic development.'[95]

In Singapore, still in a state of nation-building after centuries of subjugation to foreign empire followed by a period of internal tensions, sociologists have opined that the strict criminal law acts as a tool of social control.[96] It is useful to paint Singapore and its citizens as a law-abiding and controlled. To this end, comments such as those of the then Minister for Home Affairs, speaking on the sentencing of US teenager Michael Fay to the punishment of caning for vandalism, are typical of the government's mindset.

> Unlike some other societies which may tolerate acts of vandalism, Singapore has its own standards of social order as reflected in our laws...It is because of our tough laws against anti-social crimes that we are able to keep Singapore orderly and relatively crime free. We do not have a situation where acts of vandalism are commonplace as in cities like New York, where even police cars are not spared the acts of vandals.[97]

As in the case of Yong Vui Kong, who is Malaysian, a very significant proportion of those executed for trafficking offences are nationals of other countries.[98] In this sense, harsh

94 Hussain (n 91).

95 Alfred Oehlers and Nicole Tarulevicz, 'Capital Punishment and the Culture of Developmentalism in Singapore, in Sarat (n 92) pp. 298—299.

96 Christopher Tremewon, *The Political Economy of Social Control in Singapore 2nd edn.*, Macmillan, London, 1996.

97 Philip Shenon, 'Singapore, the Tiger Whose Teeth are not Universally Scorned, *New York Times*, 10 April 1994.

98 Oehlers and Tarulevicz (n 95) p. 303, citing Amnesty International, *Amnesty International Report 2003- Singapore* which indicates that out of 174 executions recorded by Amnesty International from press reports between 1993 and 2003, the number of foreign nationals totals 93, which is more than half.

drug penalties may be seen as necessary to protect the state from 'the dark forces waiting just outside the charmed circle of Singapore's boundaries'.[99] For example, in 2007, Nigerian Iwuchukwu Amara Tochi and stateless African Nelson Malachy were hanged for drug trafficking offences.[100]

In the cultural politics of the 'war on drugs', traffickers are assigned the role of 'folk devils'.[101] They are framed by the primary definers[102] within Singaporean society, and by the mass media, as entirely 'other' and malevolent, threatening to undermine the hard-won economic vibrancy of the state. In *Yong Vui Kong*, the court implicitly suggested that drug offences were of a more serious nature than murder, referring to the Privy Council decisions on the mandatory death penalty, all of which focussed on the sentence for murder.[103] Relying on Lord Diplock's *dicta* in *Ong Ah Chuan*, the Court of Appeal distinguished between murderers and drug traffickers insofar as the latter are motivated by 'cold calculated greed', while murder can be committed in the heat of the moment.[104]

However, the realities of individuals such as Yong Vui Kong and Nguyen crucially undermine this narrative by exposing the brutal reality of the mandatory death penalty and muddying the crisp demarcation between a pure, virtuous society and the monstrous trafficker that is a *sine qua non* to the ascendency of a harsh, punitive 'criminology of the other'.[105]

> Their stories are heavy with pathos: Both came from poor backgrounds, struggled with family problems and received the death sentence while still painfully young. It could be said they were small fry, mere mules acting under the direction of shadier, more powerful drug lords who hovered out of reach of the law.[106]

In this context, it is difficult to avoid the conclusion that the significance of the mandatory death penalty resides not so much in its efficacy as a practical tool in the suppression of drug trafficking, as in its cultural and symbolic resonance. A harsh policy on drug trafficking may warrant a particular place in Singapore's developmentalist schema. However, just as the

---

99 Clammer (n 16) p. 143.
100 *Iwuchukwu Amara Tochi and Another v Public Prosecutor* [2006] 2 SLR 503.
101 Stanley Cohen, *Folk Devils and Moral Panics 3rd edn.*, Routledge, London, 2002.
102 Defined by Hall et. al. as 'accredited' sources, generally possessed of a representative status, such as politicians or organised interest groups, or particular expertise, on whose "objective and "authoritative" statements news organisations are dependent. Stuart Hall et. al., *Policing the Crisis*, MacMillan, London, 1978, p. 57.
103 Judgment (n 1) para. 48.
104 *Ong Ah Chuan* (n 3) p. 674.
105 '[the] criminology of the other, of the threatening outcast, the fearsome stranger, the excluded and the embittered ... functions to demonize the criminal, to act out popular fears and resentments, and to promote support for state punishment'. David Garland, *The Culture of Control: Crime and Social Order in Contemporary Society*, Oxford University Press, Oxford, 2001, p. 131 et seq.
106 Rachel Lin, 'Why so little data on hanging?', *The Straits Times*, 18 September 2010.

imposition of exemplary punishment bears 'surplus meanings'[107] beyond the expediencies of the particular case, so these meanings are 'always contingent, never certain' and may serve to undermine the intended purpose.[108] The problematisation of the "evil criminal" status, in particular, 'exert[s] the most leverage against...structures of legitimacy and feeling.'[109]

It is noteworthy that despite the low level of press freedom in Singapore,[110] an island where newspapers have been described as 'essentially organs of the state...instruments of only the most desirable propagation',[111] the *Yong Vui Kong* case has prompted calls for the re-introduction of judicial discretion in the imposition of the death penalty,[112] and greater transparency in its administration.[113]

Yong Vui Kong has been given leave to appeal a separate ruling from the High Court of Singapore concerning the dismissal of his appeal for judicial review of the authority to grant presidential clemency. This hearing will commence in early 2011.[114] While this development may bring some flicker of optimism on an individual level, the fact remains that there are no further avenues for him to pursue on the mandatory death penalty issue following the Court of Appeal's 14 May decision. The Court of Appeal's judgment does not bode well for advocates of due process and judicial impartiality in Singapore. Its frankly dubious ruling on several accounts not only upholds the constitutionality of the mandatory death sentence, a penalty quashed by countless decisions worldwide, it also shows a worrying reverence to the executive branch of government. It demonstrates an unwillingness to engage with international law on a domestic level, and an "eyes shut" approach to the sheer futility of the harshest punishment in deterring potential drug traffickers. By continuing to target vulnerable young drug mules like Yong Vui Kong, the legislature in complicity with the judiciary sends a message to those in the highest positions of the Singaporean drug trade can rest assured that their position remains safe for some time to come.

---

107 David Garland, 'Penal Excess and Surplus Meaning: Public Torture Lynchings in Twentieth-Century America', *Law & Society Review*, 2009, vol. 39 (4), pp. 793—833.
108 ibid, p. 827
109 Philip Smith, *Punishment and Culture*, University of Chicago Press, Chicago, 2008, p. 55.
110 Singapore was ranked as 133rd in Reporters Without Borders' Press Freedom Index for 2009.
111 William Gibson, 'Disneyland with the Death Penalty', *Wired*, September/October 1993.
112 KC Vijayan, 'Keep death penalty but allow leeway', *The Straits Times*, 11 October 2009.
113 Lin (n 106).
114 'Vui Kong's appeal set for Jan 2011', *The Online Citizen*, 31 August 2010, http://theonlinecitizen.com/2010/08/breaking-news-vui-kongs-appeal-set-for-jan-2011 (accessed 1 October 2010).

[2]

THE LIMITS OF INTERNATIONAL LAW: EFFORTS TO ENFORCE RULINGS OF THE INTERNATIONAL COURT OF JUSTICE IN U.S. DEATH PENALTY CASES

Sandra Babcock[†]

CONTENTS

INTRODUCTION 183
I. ARTICLE 36 LITIGATION PRIOR TO THE ICJ RULINGS 185
II. ARTICLE 36 LITIGATION AFTER THE ICJ'S RULINGS 187
A. *The Impact of the ICJ's Provisional Measures in* Avena... 187
B. *The Impact of* LaGrand *and* Avena *in the State of Oklahoma: A Case Study* 189
III. WHAT THE FUTURE MAY HOLD: PROSPECTS FOR COMPLIANCE WITH *AVENA* IN THE WAKE OF *MEDELLÍN V. TEXAS* 193
CONCLUSION 195

INTRODUCTION

Since the Supreme Court reinstated the death penalty in 1976,[1] the United States has executed twenty-eight foreign nationals from fifteen different countries.[2] Most of those foreign nationals were never informed of their rights to consular notification and access under Article 36 of the Vienna Convention on Consular Relations,[3] a treaty the United States ratified in 1969.[4] Violations of Article 36 in capital cases have caused consternation in foreign capitals and endless litigation in domestic courts and international tribunals. Mexico, which has the largest number of foreign nationals on death row,[5] established the

---

† Clinical Professor and Clinical Director, Center for International Human Rights, Northwestern University School of Law. I was counsel for the government of Mexico in *Avena and Other Mexican Nationals*, and subsequently represented Mexican nationals Osbaldo Torres, José Medellín, Roberto Moreno Ramos, and Humberto Leal García. I witnessed many of the events described in this essay, and could not fairly be described as an objective observer. Nonetheless, my involvement in the litigation described herein allows for a more nuanced perspective on both the successes and failures associated with our attempts to obtain legal remedies for foreign nationals whose consular rights were violated.

1. Gregg v. Georgia, 428 U.S. 153, 187, 207 (1976).

2. *Confirmed Foreign Nationals Executed Since 1976*, DEATH PENALTY INFO. CENTER, http://www.deathpenaltyinfo.org/foreign-nationals-part-ii#executed (last updated Oct. 2, 2011).

3. *Id.*; *see generally* Vienna Convention on Consular Relations, United Nations, Apr. 24, 1963, 21 U.S.T. 77.

4. Vienna Convention on Consular Relations, *supra* note 3, at 77 (entered into force Dec. 24, 1969).

5. *Reported Foreign Nationals Under Sentence of Death in the U.S.*, DEATH PENALTY INFO. CENTER, http://www.deathpenaltyinfo.org/foreign-nationals-and-death-penalty-

Mexican Capital Legal Assistance Program in 2000 to assist its nationals facing the death penalty and to ensure that Vienna Convention claims were aggressively litigated.[6] Several foreign governments have filed briefs in state and federal courts describing the nature of the assistance they could have provided if their nationals had been promptly notified of their consular rights.[7] In dozens of cases, appellate lawyers have argued that consular assistance could have made the difference between life and death. Yet, even in the wake of favorable judgments from the Inter-American Commission of Human Rights,[8] the Inter-American Court on Human Rights,[9] and the International Court of Justice (ICJ),[10] national courts have persistently refused to grant any measure of relief to condemned foreign nationals, even in cases in which the violation was undisputed. As of September 2011, domestic courts have overturned death sentences on the basis of Article 36 violations in only two cases.[11]

In light of these statistics, it is tempting to conclude that Article 36 litigation has had negligible effects on the application of the death penalty in the United States. And indeed, under no circumstances could

---

us#Nationality (last updated Oct. 2, 2011).

6. Michael Fleishman, *Reciprocity Unmasked: The Role of the Mexican Government in Defense of its Foreign Nationals in United States Death Penalty Cases*, 20 ARIZ. J. INT'L & COMP. L. 359, 393-94 (2003) (describing Mexico's consular assistance in capital cases in Texas and elsewhere over the last several decades).

7. *See, e.g.*, Paraguay v. Allen, 949 F. Supp. 1269, 1273 (E.D. Va. 1996); Complaint at ¶¶ 70, 76, United Mexican States v. Woods (D. Ariz. 1997) (No. CIV 97-1075-PHX SMM); *see generally* Brief of the Gov't of the United Kingdom of Great Britain & N. Ireland as Amicus Curiae in Support of Petitioner-Appellant & Reversal, Carty v. Quarterman, 345 Fed. Appx. 897 (5th Cir. 2009) (No. 08-70049).

8. *See, e.g.*, Martínez Villareal v. United States, Case 11,753, Inter-Am. Comm'n H.R., Report No. 52/02, OEA/Ser.L/V/II.117, doc. 1 rev. ¶ 64 (2003), *available at* http://www.cidh.oas.org/annualrep/2002eng/USA.11753.htm.

9. *See* The Right to Information on Consular Assistance in the Framework of the Guarantees of the Due Process Law, Advisory Opinion OC-16/99, Inter-Am. Ct. H.R. (ser. A) No. 16, ¶¶ 121-22 (Oct. 1, 1999), *available at* http://www1.umn.edu/humanrts/iachr/A/OC-16ingles-sinfirmas.html.

10. *See* Avena and Other Mexican Nationals (Mex. v. U.S.), Judgment, 2004 I.C.J. 12, 71-72 (Mar. 31).

11. *See* Torres v. Oklahoma, 120 P.3d 1184, 1189-90 (Okla. Crim. App. 2005); Valdez v. Oklahoma, 46 P.3d 703, 709-11 (Okla. Crim. App. 2002). In *Valdez*, the court's decision to vacate the death sentence of Gerardo Valdez was based on its finding that trial counsel was ineffective for failing to contact the Mexican consulate and make use of the resources consular officers would have provided. *Valdez*, 46 P.3d at 710. Although the court found the petitioner's Vienna Convention claim to be procedurally barred, the court's decision to grant relief was based on its conclusion that the Mexican consulate would have provided extensive assistance if it had been notified of Valdez's detention. *Id.* at 709-10. For that reason, I include it among the cases in which Vienna Convention claims have prevailed—although I recognize that others may quibble with this assessment.

even the most optimistic internationalist claim that Article 36 litigation has been a resounding success. But it would be similarly misguided to say that Article 36 litigation has had no effect on domestic legal culture. As an initial matter, the United States complied with the ICJ's provisional measures order in *Avena and Other Mexican Nationals*,[12] leading to a five-year moratorium on the execution of Mexican nationals in the United States.[13] In addition, the death sentences of two Mexican nationals were vacated in direct response to the ICJ's final judgment in *Avena*; one of those cases is examined in greater detail below. And finally, litigation over violations of the Vienna Convention in U.S. death penalty cases has attracted substantial public commentary calling on the courts and Congress to comply with their international obligations. Although it is too soon to say whether the United States will ultimately comply with the ICJ's *Avena* judgment in the cases of Mexican nationals who remain on death row, there can be little question that litigation in domestic and international tribunals has led to increased awareness of the United States' obligations under the Vienna Convention, which in turn has led to greater compliance with Article 36 at the trial level.

I. ARTICLE 36 LITIGATION PRIOR TO THE ICJ RULINGS

Twenty years ago, few in the United States had heard of the Vienna Convention on Consular Relations.[14] Ratified by the United States in 1969, the treaty had been all but forgotten by the judges, lawyers, police and court personnel who came into contact with foreign nationals in the criminal justice system. In the first two decades after its ratification, the few courts to consider the rights established in Article 36 limited their analysis to the validity of deportation orders.[15] In the

12. Avena and Other Mexican Nationals (Mex. v. U.S.), Provisional Measures, 2003 I.C.J. 6 (Feb. 5).

13. *See Confirmed Foreign Nationals Executed Since 1976*, *supra* note 2. After Mexico filed its application instituting proceedings in the ICJ in January 2003, no Mexican national whose case was addressed in the ICJ proceedings was executed until August 5, 2008, when Texas executed José Medellín Rojas. *Id.*

14. The first law review article on the topic was published in 1994. *See generally* Gregory Dean Gisvold, *Strangers in a Strange Land: Assessing the Fate of Foreign Nationals Arrested in the United States by State and Local Authorities*, 78 MINN. L. REV. 771 (1994).

15. *See* United States v. Calderon-Medina, 591 F.2d 529, 531 & n.6 (9th Cir. 1979) (holding defendants could challenge indictments for illegal re-entry following deportation on the grounds that they were denied the right to consular notification during earlier deportation proceedings); *see also* United States v. Rangel-Gonzales, 617 F.2d 529, 530 (9th Cir. 1980) (establishing consular notification as a personal right and reversing a conviction of illegal re-entry following deportation on the grounds that the indictment should have been

1990s, litigation over violations of Article 36 became increasingly common.[16] Defense lawyers and prosecutors began to grapple with the consequences of consular rights violations, and state and federal officials began to study and implement means to ensure greater compliance with Article 36. This period of increasing awareness coincided with the executions of more than a dozen foreign nationals. At least eleven of these nationals raised an Article 36 violation prior to being executed,[17] but in most of these cases the courts determined that the issue had been waived by the defendants' failure to raise it in a timely manner.[18]

Nonetheless, there were some signs that the domestic and international litigation had some effect. In California, legislators passed a bill in 1999 implementing, at least in part, the notification provisions of Article 36.[19] The bill's legislative history referred specifically to the case of Canadian national Joseph Stanley Faulder,[20] which had led to a decision from the Fifth Circuit Court of Appeals implying that individuals had enforceable rights under Article 36 of the Vienna Convention.[21] In Texas, the Attorney General's Office published a manual on consular notification, which it distributed to law enforcement agencies and courts.[22] In federal courts around the country, magistrates began to notify known foreign nationals of their rights under Article 36.[23] The U.S. Department of State undertook a massive educational campaign in response to litigation in *Faulder* and other cases in an attempt to teach local law enforcement officers their obligations under Article 36.[24] Through these efforts, compliance with Article 36, at least

---

dismissed after defendant was denied the right to consular notification in the underlying deportation proceeding).

16. *See, e.g.*, Faulder v. Johnson, 81 F.3d 515, 517 (5th Cir. 1996); Breard v. Pruett,134 F.3d 615, 618-19 (4th Cir. 1998).

17. *Confirmed Foreign Nationals Executed Since 1976*, *supra* note 2.

18. *See, e.g.*, *Breard*, 134 F.3d at 619, 620; LaGrand v. Stewart,133 F.3d 1253, 1261-62 (9th Cir. 1998); Murphy v. Netherland, 116 F.3d 97, 100 (4th Cir. 1997).

19. CAL. PENAL CODE § 834c (West 2008).

20. *Arrest of Foreign Nationals: Hearing on S.B. 287 Before the S. Comm. on Pub. Safety*, 1999-2000 Reg. Sess. (Cal. 1999), *available at* http://www.leginfo.ca.gov/pub/99-00/bill/sen/sb_0251-0300/sb_287_cfa_19990316_125225_sen_comm.html.

21. Faulder v. Johnson, 81 F.3d 515, 520 (5th Cir. 1996).

22. *Magistrate's Guide to the Vienna Convention on Consular Relations*, ATT'Y GEN. OF TEX. (Jan. 2006) *available at* http://www.oag.state.tx.us/AG_Publications/pdfs/vienna_guidebook.pdf.

23. U.S. DEP'T OF STATE, CONSULAR NOTIFICATION AND ACCESS 16 (3d ed. 2010), *available at* http://travel.state.gov/pdf/cna/CNA_Manual_3d_Edition.pdf.

24. Counter-Memorial of the United States of America, Avena and Other Mexican Nationals (Mex. v. U.S.), 2003 I.C.J. Pleadings 1, ¶ 2.31 (Nov. 3, 2003), *available at* http://www.icj-cij.org/docket/files/128/10837.pdf.

in some parts of the nation, began to improve.[25]

II. Article 36 Litigation After the ICJ's Rulings

In 1998, Paraguay was the first state to initiate proceedings in the ICJ over violations of Article 36 in the case of Angel Breard, a Paraguayan national condemned to death in Virginia.[26] The following year, Germany initiated proceedings on behalf of nationals Karl and Walter LaGrand, leading to the *LaGrand* judgment in 2001.[27] And in 2003, Mexico initiated proceedings on behalf of fifty-four Mexican nationals sentenced to death by the United States in *Avena and Other Mexican Nationals*.[28] In both *LaGrand* and *Avena* the ICJ held that foreign nationals whose Article 36 rights were violated and who were subjected to "severe penalties" or prolonged incarceration, were entitled to "review and reconsideration" of their convictions and sentences.[29] In *Avena*, the ICJ made clear that the required "review and reconsideration" must be judicial in nature and that the courts must not invoke procedural bars to prevent review of Article 36 claims on the merits.[30]

A. The Impact of the ICJ's Provisional Measures in Avena

Each of the nations that initiated proceedings in the ICJ sought and received provisional measures to prevent the execution of their nationals during the pendency of proceedings before the international court.[31] Prior to the *LaGrand* judgment, however, there was no uniform consensus regarding the legal effect of the ICJ's provisional measures. In proceedings before the U.S. Supreme Court leading up to Walter LaGrand's execution, the United States argued that such measures were

25. *See id.* ¶ 2.33.

26. Vienna Convention on Consular Relations (Para. v. U.S.), Application of the Republic of Paraguay, ¶¶ 3, 28 (Apr. 3, 1998), *available at* http://www.icj-cij.org/docket/files/99/7183.pdf. Paraguay ultimately withdrew its case from the ICJ after its national, Angel Breard, was executed by the United States. Vienna Convention on Consular Relations (Para. v. U.S.), 1998 I.C.J. 426, 427 (Nov. 10).

27. LaGrand Case (Ger. v. U.S.), 2001 I.C.J. 466, ¶¶ 1, 10, 128 (June 27).

28. Application Instituting Proceedings (Mex. v. U.S.), 2003 I.C.J. No. 128, ¶ 1 (Jan. 9), *available at* http://www.icj-cij.org/docket/files/128/1913.pdf.

29. *LaGrand*, 2001 I.C.J. at 46 ¶ 125; Avena and Other Mexican Nationals (Mex. v. U.S.), Judgment, 2004 I.C.J. 12, ¶¶ 138, 140 (Mar. 31).

30. *Avena*, 2004 I.C.J. ¶¶ 112, 113, 140.

31. *See, e.g.*, Vienna Convention on Consular Relations (Para. v. U.S.), Provisional Measures, 1998 I.C.J. 248, ¶¶ 6, 9, 41 (Apr. 9); LaGrand Case (Ger. v. U.S.), Provisional Measures, 1999 I.C.J. 9, ¶¶ 6, 9, 29 (Mar. 3); Avena and Other Mexican Nationals (Mex. v. U.S.), Provisional Measures, 2003 I.C.J. 14, ¶¶ 9, 13, 59 (Feb. 5).

not directly binding on parties to the litigation.[32] In both *Breard* and *LaGrand*, the Supreme Court refused to stay the executions notwithstanding the existence of provisional measures.[33]

In its 2001 *LaGrand* judgment, the ICJ determined for the first time that provisional measures were binding on the parties to proceedings before the court.[34] The effect of this determination was to be tested two years later when Mexico initiated proceedings in the *Avena* case and sought provisional measures to prevent the executions of its nationals while the court considered the merits of Mexico's claims.[35] In February 2003, the ICJ issued provisional measures directing the United States to take "all measures necessary" to ensure that three Mexican nationals—Cesar Roberto Fierro Reyna ("Fierro"), Roberto Moreno Ramos ("Moreno"), and Osbaldo Torres Aguilera ("Torres")—were not executed while the Court considered Mexico's claims.[36] At the time, none of the Mexican nationals had been scheduled for execution, but all had exhausted (or had nearly exhausted) their post-conviction appeals and were in imminent danger of receiving execution dates.[37]

Two of the three nationals facing execution, Fierro and Moreno, were on death row in the state of Texas; the third, Torres, was in Oklahoma. Texas had the nation's busiest execution chamber, and at the time, Oklahoma executed more individuals per capita than any other state.[38] The judiciaries in both states were renowned for their conservative bent and hostility toward criminal defendants. And politicians in Texas and Oklahoma at times seemed to revel in their tough-on-crime reputations.

When Mexico initiated proceedings in the ICJ, Moreno appeared to be at greatest risk of execution. Prosecutors had sought to schedule his execution at a court hearing in November 2002, but before the trial court could consider the prosecution's request the Inter-American Commission on Human Rights issued precautionary measures calling

32. *See* Germany v. United States, 526 U.S. 111, 113 (1999) (Breyer, J., dissenting) (noting that the Solicitor General of the United States filed a letter with the Court opposing a stay of execution for Walter LaGrand on the grounds that a provisional measures order from the International Court of Justice is not binding).

33. *See* Breard v. Greene, 523 U.S. 371, 374, 378-79 (1998); *see also*, LaGrand v. Arizona, 526 U.S. 1001, 1001 (1999).

34. *LaGrand*, 2001 I.C.J. ¶ 109.

35. *Avena*, 2003 I.C.J. ¶¶ 9, 13.

36. *Id.* ¶ 59.

37. *Id.* ¶ 11.

38. *State Execution Rates*, DEATH PENALTY INFO. CENTER, http://www.deathpenaltyinfo.org/state-execution-rates (last updated Aug. 2, 2011).

on the United States not to execute Moreno while they considered a complaint filed by his lawyers.[39] The prosecution and the trial judge agreed temporarily to defer consideration of when to schedule Moreno's execution. Three months later, the ICJ issued its provisional measures order.[40]

Through counsel, Mexico contacted the prosecutors assigned to the cases of Moreno, Fierro, and Torres. All agreed to defer the setting of execution dates while the ICJ considered Mexico's application. In the case of Torres in Oklahoma, Attorney General Drew Edmondson filed an unprecedented notice with the Oklahoma Court of Criminal Appeals recommending that the court refrain from scheduling his execution while the ICJ considered Mexico's claims.[41] Although Oklahoma law does not provide for any grounds under which the court can defer the setting of execution dates,[42] the court nonetheless refrained from scheduling Torres' execution for over fourteen months while the ICJ proceedings were pending.

For observers unfamiliar with the politics of capital punishment in Texas and Oklahoma, these actions may seem unremarkable. But for capital litigators, the prosecutors' decisions to comply with the order of an international court were nothing short of extraordinary. Although Texas prosecutors could have sought execution dates for both Fierro and Moreno under state law,[43] they did not. From the time Mexico filed its application at the ICJ in January 2003 until the ICJ issued its final judgment in March 2004, none of the Mexican nationals subject to provisional measures were executed.

B. The Impact of LaGrand *and* Avena *in the State of Oklahoma: A Case Study*

At the time the ICJ issued its judgment in March 2004, a May 17th execution date had already been scheduled for Torres. Shortly after the ICJ issued its judgment, Torres filed a clemency petition with the Oklahoma Board of Pardons and Paroles and a post-conviction application before the Oklahoma Court of Criminal Appeals arguing that the *Avena* judgment was binding on the United States courts.[44]

39. Moreno Ramos v. United States, Case 12.430, Inter-Am. Comm'n H.R., Report No. 1/05, OEA/Ser.L./V/II.124, doc. 5 ¶¶ 1, 76 (2005).

40. *Avena*, 2003 I.C.J. at 6.

41. Adam Liptak, *Mexico Awaits Hague Ruling on Citizens on Death Row*, N.Y. TIMES, Jan. 16, 2004, at A1.

42. *See* OKLA. STAT. tit. 22, § 1001.1 (2003).

43. *See* TEX. CODE CRIM. PROC. ANN. art. 43.141 (West 2006).

44. *See* Torres v. Oklahoma, 120 P.3d 1184, 1186 (Okla. Crim. App. 2005).

On May 7, 2004, the clemency board considered Torres' bid for commutation of his death sentence.[45] The Ambassador of Mexico to the United States, Carlos de Icaza, attended the clemency hearing at the maximum security prison in McAlester, Oklahoma and appealed to the board for clemency based on the *Avena* decision.[46] Surviving relatives of the victims asked that Torres' sentence be carried out.[47] The five-member Board listened, then voted, one by one. Two voted in favor of commutation, and two were against.[48] The deciding vote was cast by Susan Loving, a former Attorney General and the Board's chairperson.[49] Loving cited the ICJ's decision in *Avena* and stated that she believed Torres "may very well have been prejudiced" by the Article 36 violation.[50] She then stated:

> I worry a great deal about Americans who may be overseas, whose rights are violated under an international treaty, and who, and the country that makes the decision as to what happens because of those rights being violated is the same one who violated those rights. We have many Americans overseas whose lives are in jeopardy as we speak, and that is one very important reason for my vote today.[51]

The Board's vote, however, was simply a recommendation to the Oklahoma Governor Brad Henry.[52] Henry was free to accept or reject the Board's recommendation—and indeed, on the previous three occasions when the Board had recommended clemency during Henry's tenure as Governor, he disagreed with the Board's decision and refused to grant clemency.[53] One of those cases involved a consular rights violation in the case of Vietnamese national, Hung Thanh Le, where the Board had voted unanimously in favor of clemency.[54] Henry had already presided over eighteen executions as Governor by the time the

45. Transcript of Clemency Hearing of Osvaldo Torres at 1, 2 (May 7, 2004) (on file with author).
46. *Id.* at 1, 2-7.
47. *Id.* at 101-04.
48. *Id.* at 116-17.
49. *Id.* at 1, 117.
50. Transcript of Clemency Hearing, *supra* note 45, at 117.
51. *Id.* at 118-19.
52. *Id.* at 119.
53. Ernesto Londoño, *Oklahoma Parole Board Urges Life Term for Mexican*, DALLAS MORNING NEWS, May 8, 2004, at A6; *see also David Jay Brown*, CLARKPROSECUTOR.ORG, http://www.clarkprosecutor.org/html/death/US/brown901.htm (last visited Oct. 25, 2011); *Bobby Joe Fields*, CLARKPROSECUTOR.ORG, http://www.clarkprosecutor.org/html/death/US/fields832.htm (last visited Oct. 25, 2011); *Hung Thanh Le: Case Overview*, INT'L JUST. PROJECT, http://www.internationaljusticeproject.org/nationalsTLe.cfm (last visited Oct. 25, 2011).
54. *Hung*, *supra* note 53.

Board recommended clemency for Torres.[55] Within an hour of the Board's vote, the Governor issued a press release indicating that he would not stay Torres' execution.

Henry agreed to meet with counsel for Torres and for Mexico only days before the scheduled execution. He told them they had no more than thirty minutes to make their case. The conversation quickly turned to the ICJ's judgment in *Avena*, and Henry removed his jacket and rolled up his sleeves. His assistant entered the room to advise that the thirty minutes were up, but Henry decided he needed more information. He asked whether the United States had a legal obligation to comply with the ICJ's judgment, and whether Oklahoma was bound to comply. The meeting lasted over an hour. At the end, Henry was non-committal.

Meanwhile, Torres' post-conviction application and request for stay of execution was pending in the Oklahoma Court of Criminal Appeals. Four days before his scheduled execution, on May 13, 2004, the Oklahoma court issued a stay of execution in a brief, unpublished order. In his concurrence, Judge Chapel elaborated on the majority's reasoning, and opined that the *Avena* judgment was binding on United States courts:

> There is no question that this Court is bound by the Vienna Convention and Optional Protocol . . . . At its simplest, this is a matter of contract. A treaty is a contract between sovereigns. The notion that contracts must be enforceable against those who enter into them is fundamental to the Rule of Law.[56]

The court remanded Torres' case for an evidentiary hearing to consider the effect of the Article 36 violation on his capital murder prosecution.[57] Two hours after the Oklahoma court issued its historic decision, Henry decided to commute Torres' death sentence to life imprisonment without the possibility of parole. The Governor's press release stated that "[u]nder agreements entered into by the United States, the ruling of

55. DEATH PENALTY INFORMATION CENTER, SEARCHABLE EXECUTION DATABASE, http://www.deathpenaltyinfo.org/views-executions?exec_name_1=&exec_year%5B%5D=2003&exec_year%5B%5D=2004&sex=All&state%5B%5D=OK&sex_1=All&federal=All&foreigner=All&juvenile=All&volunteer=All (last visited Oct. 31, 2011).

56. Torres v. Oklahoma, No. PCD-04-442, 2004 WL 3711623, slip op. at 2 (Okla. Crim. App. May 13, 2004) (order granting stay of execution and remanding case for evidentiary hearing) (Chapel, J., specially concurring).

57. Torres ultimately received an evidentiary hearing on the Article 36 violation, and the trial court determined that he had been prejudiced by the violation. On appeal, the Oklahoma Court of Criminal Appeals concurred that Torres had demonstrated prejudice at the penalty phase of his capital murder trial, but concluded that the Governor's grant of clemency rendered any determination of prejudice moot. Torres v. Oklahoma,120 P.3d 1184, 1188 (Okla. Crim. App. 2005).

the ICJ is binding on U.S. courts."[58]

After the Oklahoma court's historic decision in *Torres,* other courts began to address the implications of the ICJ's judgment. In the case of Rafael Camargo, a Mexican national sentenced to death in Arkansas, prosecutors agreed to reform his death sentence to life imprisonment after learning of the *Avena* judgment.[59] In response to media inquiries, they characterized the *Avena* judgment as the "primary motivation" for their decision to stipulate that Camargo was mentally retarded and therefore ineligible for the death penalty.[60] The federal district court for the Western District of Arkansas subsequently issued a decision finding that the agreement to modify Camargo's sentence to life imprisonment remedied "any and all potential prejudice caused by the denial of petitioner's rights under the Vienna Convention."[61] In *Ex parte Medellín* , however, the Texas Court of Criminal Appeals refused to adhere to the ICJ's judgment, even after President George W. Bush directed state courts to provide the review and reconsideration mandated by *Avena.*[62]

The constitutional issues raised by Texas' defiance of the President's directive were addressed by the U.S. Supreme Court in *Medellín v. Texas.*[63] In *Medellín* , the Supreme Court determined that the ICJ's *Avena* judgment was not self-executing, and that the decision did not therefore preempt states from applying procedural default rules to bar review of Article 36 claims.[64] Although all nine justices agreed that the United States had an international legal obligation to comply with the ICJ's judgment,[65] the Court held that only Congress could

58. *Gov. Henry Grants Clemency to Inmate Torre*, OFFICE OF THE GOVERNOR BRAD HENRY (May 13, 2004), *available at* http://www.eurunion.org/legislat/deathpenalty/TorresVOklaGovMess.htm.

59. Jeff Arnold, *Deal Gives Killer Life*, TIMESRECORD, Aug. 13, 2004, http://swtimes.com/news/article_6c2fa457-f4b3-5bfe-9e29-c29ef6a52789.html. The prosecution agreed to this outcome shortly after the defense filed a motion to vacate Camargo's conviction and death sentence based on the ICJ's *Avena* ruling. *See* Petitioner's Motion to Vacate His Convictions and Death Sentences and for a New Trial, Camargo v. Norris, Civ. No. 02-2188 (W.D. Ark. Jul. 19, 2004).

60. *Id.*

61. Camargo v. Norris, Civ. No. 02-2188, slip op. at 5 (W.D. Ark. Aug. 12, 2004).

62. Memorandum for the U.S. Attorney General Regarding Compliance with the Decision of the International Court of Justice in Avena (Feb. 28, 2005) 44 I.L.M. 964, *available at* http://georgewbush-whitehouse.archives.gov/news/releases/2005/02/20050228-18.html. The President's written directive was attached to an *amicus curiae* brief submitted by the Solicitor General of the United States in *Medellín v. Dretke*. 544 U.S. 660 (2005).

63. 552 U.S. 491, 498-99 (2008).

64. *Id.* at 525, 527, 530.

65. *Id.* at 504.

transform this international obligation into binding federal law.[66] The President, acting unilaterally, could not compel Texas to review Medellín's Article 36 claim.[67]

III. What the Future May Hold: Prospects for Compliance with *Avena* in the Wake of *Medellín v. Texas*

Although *Medellín* left open the possibility that states could choose to enforce *Avena*, and although Justice Stevens exhorted the states to follow Oklahoma's example in his concurring opinion,[68] no state has done so apart from Oklahoma. Only the California Supreme Court has addressed the issue in the wake of *Medellín*, and the court refused to set aside its procedural default rules to allow for review and reconsideration of the appellant's Article 36 claim.[69] As of this writing, a second case is pending in the Nevada Supreme Court; a ruling is expected in early 2012.[70]

Congress has been slow to respond to the *Medellín* decision. In July 2008, several members of Congress introduced "The Avena Case Implementation Act."[71] The bill would have implemented the *Avena* judgment and would have provided judicial remedies, both civil and criminal, for foreign nationals whose Article 36 rights had been violated.[72] Mexican national José Medellín sought to stay his execution on the basis of the pending legislation, arguing that he had a due process right to remain alive until Congress enacted legislation to implement his right to review and reconsideration.[73] The Supreme Court denied the stay, noting that the Executive Branch had not indicated its support for the pending legislation.[74] Medellín was executed on August 4, 2008, without receiving the judicial review mandated by *Avena*.[75]

---

66. *Id.* at 520.

67. *Id.* at 525.

68. *Medellín*, 552 U.S. at 536-37 (Stevens, J., concurring).

69. *In re* Martínez, 209 P.3d 908, 911 (Cal. 2009).

70. Gutierrez v. State, No. 53506 (Nev. Dec. 22, 2010) (order granting oral argument), *available at* http://www.nevadajudiciary.us/index.php./oralarguments/1011-gutierrez-carlos-vs-state-death-penalty.

71. The Avena Case Implementation Act, H.R. 6481, 110th Cong. (2008), *available at* http://www.gpo.gov/fdsys/pkg/BILLS-110hr6481ih/pdf/BILLS-110hr6481ih.pdf.

72. *Id.*

73. Application for Stay of Execution Pending Disposition of Motion to Recall and Stay the Mandate and Petition for Writ of Certiorari or Writ of Habeas Corpus at 2, *Medellín*, 552 U.S. 491 (2008) (No. 06-984).

74. Medellín v. Texas, 554 U.S. 759, 760, 761 (2008).

75. The ICJ subsequently held that by executing Medellín, the United States had violated its obligations under the *Avena* Judgment. *See* Request for Interpretation of the Judgement of 31 March 2004 in the Case concerning Avena and Other Mexican Nationals (Mex. v. U. S.), Judgment, 2009 I.C.J. 139 (Jan. 19).

In late 2010, legislation intended to implement *Avena* was again introduced in the U.S. Senate as part of an omnibus appropriations bill.[76] The appropriations bill failed to pass by the end of the congressional term.[77] In June 2011, Vermont Senator Patrick Leahy introduced the Consular Notification Compliance Act (CNCA),[78] remarking that "[g]iven the long history of bipartisan support for the VCCR, there should be unanimous support for this legislation to uphold our treaty obligations."[79] Secretary of State Hillary Clinton and Attorney General Eric Holder immediately announced their support for the legislation.[80] In the interim, Texas had set an execution date for Humberto Leal García, another Mexican national who had not yet received the review mandated by the ICJ in *Avena*.[81] Leal, like Medellín, petitioned the U.S. Supreme Court to stay his execution, arguing that Congress was poised to implement his right to review and reconsideration.[82] The United States filed an amicus curiae brief in support of Leal's motion for stay, informing the Court that Leal's case "implicate[d] United States foreign-policy interests of the highest order."[83] Prominent international leaders, including the United Nations High Commissioner for Human Rights, the Special Rapporteurs for Torture and Extrajudicial, Summary and Arbitrary Executions, and the Inter-American Commission on Human Rights, all issued statements calling for a stay in light of the United States' unfulfilled obligations under the *Avena* judgment.[84] Leal cited the Obama Administration's strong support for the Leahy Bill as a critical fact that distinguished his case from *Medellín*,[85] but the Court was unpersuaded. On July 7, the Court denied the stay over a strong dissent by Justices Breyer, Ginsburg, Kagan, and Sotomayor.[86] Leal was executed less than two

76. Department of State, Foreign Operations, and Related Programs Appropriations Act of 2011, S. 3676, 111th Cong. (2010).

77. *Id.*

78. Consular Notification Compliance Act, 112th Cong. (1st Sess. 2011).

79. 157 CONG. REC. S3780 (2011).

80. 157 CONG. REC. S4216 (2011).

81. Avena and Other Mexican Nationals (Mex. v. U.S.), Judgment, 2004 I.C.J. 12, ¶ 106, 121 (Mar. 31).

82. Motion for Stay of Execution at 10, García v. Texas, 131 S. Ct. 2866 (2011).

83. Brief for the United States as Amicus Curiae in Support of Motions for a Stay at 11, *García*, 131 S. Ct. 2866 (2011).

84. *U.S. Urges Supreme Court to Halt Mexican's Execution*, AGENCE FRANCE-PRESSE (July 1, 2011), *available at* http://ph.news.yahoo.com/un-agency-urges-texas-halt-execution-mexican-135001141.html.

85. Petition for Writ of Certiorari at 20, *García*, 131 S. Ct. 2866 (2011) (No.11-5001), 2011 WL 2743200, at *20.

86. *García*, 131 S. Ct. at 2868-71 (2011).

hours later.[87]

Within the next year, at least two other Mexican nationals whose cases were addressed in the *Avena* judgment are likely to face execution in Texas.[88] Unless Congress enacts the CNCA by mid-2012, both men may be executed without receiving the review required by the *Avena* judgment, and still others face the possibility of execution within the next year.

Despite the poor prospects for compliance with *Avena* in the short term, the long-term outlook is slightly more encouraging. Most of the Mexican nationals affected by the judgment are incarcerated on California's death row.[89] The great majority of these nationals will not face execution for at least a dozen years, so they could eventually benefit from state or federal legislation designed to implement *Avena*. In addition, some will have an opportunity to litigate their Article 36 claims in federal court, unencumbered by the procedural default ruling that proved fatal for Medellín. After all, *Medellín* did not bar the federal courts from reviewing Article 36 claims on their merits—it simply held that *Avena* was not binding federal law that preempted the application of state procedural default rules.[90]

CONCLUSION

Six years after the ICJ's *Avena* judgment, we can only begin to assess the effects of the litigation. By one measure, the litigation has been a tremendous success: in the eight years since Mexico initiated proceedings in the ICJ, only two Mexican nationals named in the judgment have been executed, whereas in the eight years preceding the ICJ litigation, four Mexican nationals were executed.[91] This de facto moratorium was initiated by the ICJ's issuance of provisional measures, and continued during the litigation of *Medellín*. Although more executions may be carried out in the near future, the significance of the

87. Chris McGreal, *Humberto Leal García Executed in Texas Despite White House Appeal*, THE GUARDIAN (July 7, 2011), http://www.guardian.co.uk/world/2011/jul/08/humberto-leal-garcia-executed-texas.

88. Félix Rocha Díaz and Virgilio Maldonado Rodríguez have both filed petitions for writ of certiorari with the U.S. Supreme Court raising violations of the Vienna Convention. Those petitions were denied by the Court on October 3, 2011. Petition for Writ of Certiorari, Maldonado v. Thaler, 132 S. Ct. 124 (2011), (No. 10-9511), 2011 WL 4530498, at *1; Petition for Writ of Certiorari, Rocha v. Thaler, 132 S. Ct. 397 (2011), (No. 10-9659), 2011 WL 1060963, at *1.

89. *See* Avena and Other Mexican Nationals (Mex. v. U.S.), Judgment, 2004 I.C.J. 12, ¶15 (Mar. 31).

90. Medellín v. Texas, 552 U.S. 491, 498-99 (2008).

91. *Confirmed Foreign Nationals Executed Since 1976*, *supra* note 2.

moratorium should not be understated. In a field where victories are rare, capital litigators often measure success by their ability to extend their clients' lives as long as possible. Two Mexican nationals—Torres and Camargo—have been permanently removed from death row as a result of the ICJ's judgment.

All nine justices in *Medellín* recognized that non-compliance with the ICJ's judgment could have serious consequences for the United States' standing in the international community and for its relations with Mexico.[92] But in the wake of *Leal García*, it is clear that the Supreme Court will not stay the executions of Mexican nationals whose cases were addressed by the *Avena* judgment unless and until Congress enacts implementing legislation.

The prospects for future compliance with *Avena* are closely linked to political and legal perspectives on the value of international law. Some politicians are clearly hostile to the notion that the United States should comply with the decision of an international tribunal such as the ICJ—even where the United States consented to the court's jurisdiction.[93] Even politicians who are not overtly hostile to international law may have little to gain by supporting legislation that benefits a group of foreign nationals on death row. Congress is more likely to act, however, if its members recognize the reciprocal nature of the rights to consular notification and access. Accounts of U.S. citizens detained abroad—particularly when they are imprisoned by nations perceived as repressive and undemocratic—arouse a great deal of public sympathy.[94] In the weeks leading up to the execution of Humberto Leal, multiple commentators called on Congress and the Supreme Court to stay the execution out of concern for the welfare of U.S. citizens who rely on the protections afforded by Article 36 when traveling abroad.[95]

---

92. *Medellín*, 552 U.S. at 523-24.

93. *See, e.g.*, *Fulfilling Our Treaty Obligations and Protecting Americans Abroad: Hearing Before the S. Comm. on the Judiciary*, 112th Cong. (2011) (Statement of Senator Chuck Grassley) (webcast), *available at* http://judiciary.senate.gov/hearings/hearing.cfm?id=3d9031b47812de2592c3baeba62c686d; Ted Cruz, *Scotus Rejects Authority of World Court*, HUMAN EVENTS (Apr. 2, 2008), http://www.humanevents.com/article.php?id=25783.

94. *See, e.g.*, Editorial, *Iran's Release of American Hikers is "Wonderful News,"* SEATTLE TIMES, Sept. 22, 2011, at A15; Nicholas Kristoff, *Laura Ling, Euna Lee, and North Korea*, N.Y. TIMES BLOG (June 22, 2009, 12:35 PM), http://kristof.blogs.nytimes.com/2009/06/22/laura-ling-euna-lee-and-north-korea/.

95. *See, e.g.*, Editorial, *The World is Watching*, N.Y. TIMES, July 6, 2011, at A22; Editorial, *Another Chance for Justice*, WASH. POST, July 5, 2011, at A12, *available at* http://www.washingtonpost.com/opinions/another-chance-for-justice/2011/07/05/gHQA7LmkzH_story.html; Editorial, *The Law, Even on Death Row*, L.A. TIMES, July 2, 2011, at 24.

Politicians may not gain many votes by enacting legislation to benefit foreign nationals on death row, but they are unlikely to lose popular support if their constituents understand the relationship between domestic compliance with Article 36 and consular access abroad, and if they appreciate the limited nature of the remedy mandated by the ICJ. Review and reconsideration is not a "get out of jail free" pass. Even if the courts provided review and reconsideration to every Mexican national named in the judgment, they would need to find evidence of "actual prejudice" before vacating a conviction or sentence—in which case the national would be subject to retrial, not release.[96]

The Oklahoma example demonstrates that international legal arguments founded on reciprocity do resonate, even in the conservative heartland. Even in the wake of *Medellín,* the Oklahoma Court of Criminal Appeals has continued to provide judicial remedies for Article 36 violations.[97] And in 2011, the Massachusetts Supreme Judicial Court accepted its obligation to provide review and reconsideration under the ICJ's ruling in the case of a foreign national seeking to vacate a guilty plea based on an Article 36 violation.[98] It remains to be seen whether these cases are interesting anomalies, or whether they presage an era of increasing concern for the international rule of law.

---

96. Consular Notification Compliance Act, S. Res. 1194, 112th Cong. § 4(a)(3)(2011). As of the time of this writing, the legislation had not yet passed.

97. *See* Duenas-Flores v. Oklahoma, No. C-2005-1, slip op. at 5 (Okla. Crim. App. June 28, 2007).

98. Commonwealth v. Gautreaux, 941 N.E.2d 616, 625 (Mass. 2011).

[3]

The Mandatory Death Penalty – An International and Comparative Perspective

Douglas L Mendes SC

I. Introduction

Upon conviction for murder, death is the only penalty which the law allows a Trinidad and Tobago judge to impose.[1] There is no room for taking into account the personal circumstances of the accused or the motivations which may have led to the killing. Such considerations are irrelevant because in any event the judge is not empowered to select any other sentence but death. Traditionally, before pronouncing the sentence, the judge would ask the offender whether he or she has anything to say but this may be to give him or her the opportunity to refer to circumstances which in law might preclude the imposition of the death sentence, such as his or her young age at the date the murder was committed, or the fact that she is pregnant or that he or she is so mentally impaired as to obviate the death sentence. Other than these exceptional cases, however, it is not expected that the accused would seek to mitigate the death sentence.

Death was the mandatory sentence for murder at common law. Section 4 of the Offences Against the Person Act, enacted in 1925, incorporated the common law rule. When the 1962 Constitution came into force, the mandatory death sentence was an existing law and saved from challenge on the constitutional grounds by an uncompromising savings law clause which declared that the Bill of Rights did not apply to existing law.[2] For the next four decades, no one conceived that the mandatory death sentence was challengeable on the ground that it violated the human rights provisions in the constitution[3] despite rulings

---

[1] Section 4 of the Offences Against the Person Act provides that "Every person convicted of murder shall suffer death."

[2] Section 3 of the 1962 Constitution provided that: "Sections 1 and 2 of this Constitution shall not apply in relation to any law that is in force in Trinidad and Tobago at the commencement of this Constitution." Sections 1 and 2 contained the human rights provisions.

[3] ***de Freitas v Benny*** [1976] AC 239.

in the 1970's by the United States Supreme Court[4] that depriving a person convicted of murder of the opportunity to mitigate the death sentence was an inhuman punishment violative of the 8th amendment of the United States Constitution. The same applied across the Caribbean where general savings laws clauses in Jamaica, Barbados, the Bahamas and Guyana[5] precluded the mandatory death penalty from being held to be inconsistent with the human rights provisions[6] and savings clauses specific to the prohibition against inhuman and degrading punishment in the Eastern Caribbean Constitutions[7] protected punishments which were authorised under existing law. Only in Belize was existing law left unprotected by any savings law clause after a five year grace period, but the point was not taken there until the 21st century.

The turning point came with the ground-breaking decisions of the Eastern Caribbean Court of Appeal in ***Spence*** and ***Hughes***[8] at the turn of the century declaring the mandatory death penalty to be an inhuman and degrading punishment under the Constitutions of St Lucia and St. Vincent and the Grenadines. This led to appeals to the Privy Council, joined by an appeal from Belize, resulting in the landmark decisions in the first of a trilogy of cases, ***Reyes***, ***Hughes*** and ***Fox***[9]. The Privy Council held that, while the death penalty as a punishment was sanctioned by the Constitutions themselves in provisions which envisioned that life could be taken away as long as it was done pursuant to a judicial sentence, the mandatory aspect of the death penalty was an inhuman

[4] ***Woodson v North Carolina*** (1976) 428 US 280; ***Roberts v Louisiana*** (1977) 431 US 633

[5] For example, section 26(1) of the Barbados Constitution provides that:
"Nothing contained in or done under the authority of any written law shall be held to be inconsistent with or in contravention of any provision of sections 12 to 23 to the extent that the law in question—(a) is a law (in this section referred to as 'an existing law') that was enacted or made before 30 November 1966 and has continued to be part of the law of Barbados at all times since that day; (b) repeals and re-enacts an existing law without alteration; or (c) alters an existing law and does not thereby render that law inconsistent with any provision of sections 12 to 23 in a manner in which, or to an extent to which, it was not previously so inconsistent."

[6] ***Director of Public Prosecutions v Nasralla*** [1967] 2 AC 238.

[7] For example, section 17 of the Jamaican Constitution provides that :
(1) No person shall be subjected to torture or to inhuman or degrading punishment or other treatment.
(2) Nothing contained in or done under the authority of any law shall be held to be inconsistent with or in contravention of this section to the extent that the law in question authorise the infliction of any description of punishment which was lawful in Jamaica immediately before the appointed day.

[8] ***Spence v The Queen; Hughes v The Queen*** (unreported) 2 April 2001; Eastern Caribbean Court of Appeal (Saint Vincent and the Grenadines and Saint Lucia) (Criminal Appeals Nos 20 of 1998 and 14 of 1997)

[9] ***Reyes v The Queen*** [2002] 2 AC 235; ***R v Hughes*** [2002] 2 AC 259; ***Fox v The Queen*** [2002] 2 AC 284.

treatment, not saved by the special savings law clauses. These clauses, which had to be construed narrowly, saved existing law which merely *authorised* the death sentence. They did not save an existing law which *required* the death sentence to be imposed. Accordingly, the mandatory death sentence was inconsistent with the constitution and pursuant to what are referred to as modification clauses[10], stood to be modified by the courts to bring them into conformity with the constitution. This was achieved by making the death sentence a punishment which could be imposed in the discretion of the judge, but no longer the only sentence which could be imposed.

It was not immediately apparent that these developments applied to Trinidad and Tobago. Although, the Trinidad and Tobago Constitution Act contains a modification clause similar to those pressed into service in the first trilogy of cases there was no similarly malleable special savings law clause protecting the mandatory death sentence. Rather, section 6 of the Republican Constitution provided that the human rights provisions shall not invalidate existing law, albeit that this represented a change from the language used under the Independence Constitution. But it was this change in language which spurred the argument, first rejected by the Court of Appeal of Trinidad and Tobago, but later accepted by a 3 to 2 majority of the Privy Council in ***Roodal***[11], that by interpreting the modification clause generously but the general savings law clause narrowly, it was permissible to modify the mandatory death penalty to make it conform to the human rights provisions, as long as the court stopped short of invalidating the death penalty. So the law in Trinidad and Tobago was declared to be on par with the remainder of the Eastern Caribbean.

This proved to be short lived. A matter of a few weeks later, an appeal from Barbados was before a differently constituted Privy Council, the members of which no doubt had concerns about the correctness of the ***Roodal*** decision. Accordingly, the appeal was

[10] For example, section 5(1) of the Trinidad and Tobago 1976 Constitution Act provides that :
"Subject to the provisions of this section, the operation of the existing law on and after the appointed day shall not be affected by the revocation of the Order in Council of 1962 but the existing laws shall be construed with such modifications, adaptations, qualifications and exceptions as may be necessary to bring them into conformity with this Act."
[11] [2005] 1 AC 328.

adjourned to be heard by a reconstituted panel of nine Privy Councillors, including one Caribbean judge, to be joined by pending appeals from Trinidad and Jamaica. This lead to the second trilogy of ***Matthew***, ***Boyce*** and ***Watson***[12] in which, by another bare 5 to 4 majority, with the Caribbean judge joining the majority, the savings law clauses in Trinidad and Tobago and in Barbados were held to be a complete bar to any challenge to existing law for inconsistency with the human rights provisions. The legality of the mandatory death sentence was accordingly restored for Trinidad and Tobago and confirmed for Barbados.

Jamaica, on the other hand, had amended its existing law by establishing the mandatory death penalty to provide for certain classes of murder, with the mandatory death sentence being reserved for the more serious offences. The alteration of the existing law made the general saving law clause inapplicable with the result that, consistent with the first trilogy, the mandatory death penalty, even for the most atrocious murders, was held to be an inhuman punishment and modified accordingly.

Despite the setback in Barbados and Trinidad and Tobago, it was significant that the nine member panel was unanimous in finding that the mandatory death penalty violated the right not to be subjected to an inhuman or degrading punishment and it would have been modified out of existence but for the operation of the savings law clauses. But more than that, as I will attempt to show, the mandatory death penalty in Trinidad and Tobago sits disharmoniously with basic principles which lie at the core of our legal system, with developments in other countries and in the region, and with our international obligations.

[12] ***Boyce v The Queen*** [2005] 1 AC 400; ***Matthew v State of Trinidad and Tobago*** [2005] 1 AC 433; ***Watson v The Queen (Attorney General for Jamaica intervening)*** [2005] 1 AC 472.

II. Core Principles of Justice

One of the core principles which underpins our judicial system is that there must be a proportionate relationship between the punishment meted out to a convicted person and the gravity of the crime that he or she has been found guilty of. This principle can be traced back to Magna Carta. Its vintage and significance were captured by Saunders J.A (as he then was) in ***Spence*** and ***Hughes*** when he observed that

> "It is and has always been considered a vital precept of just penal laws that the punishment should fit the crime."

The principle was thought to be embodied in the 1689 Bill of Rights prohibition against cruel and unusual punishment which has been viewed by the United States Supreme Court since 1892 as being directed, not only at punishments which inflict torture "but against all punishments which by their excessive length or severity are greatly disproportional to the offences charged."[13]

The principle that the punishment should fit the crime is pertinent particularly to the offence of murder which, of all offences, is unique in the multifarious ways in which it may be committed and the variety of motivations which might give rise to it. The Royal Commission on Capital Punishment (1949-1953) catalogued the infinite variety of circumstances in which murder is committed in a passage which, though long, deserves quotation in full:

> Convicted persons may be men, or they may be women, youths, girls, or hardly older than children. They may be normal or they may be feeble-minded, neurotic, epileptic, borderline cases, or insane; and in each case the mentally abnormal may be differently affected by their abnormality. The crime may be human and understandable, calling more for pity than for censure, or brutal and callous to an almost unbelievable degree. It may have occurred so much in the heat of passion as to rule out the possibility of premeditation, or it may have been well prepared and carried out in cold blood. The crime may be committed in order to carry out another crime or in the course of committing it or to secure escape after its commission.

[13] ***O'Neil v Vermont*** (1892) 144 US 323, 339-340.

> Murderous intent may be unmistakable, or it may be absent, and death itself may depend on an accident. The motives, springing from weakness as often as from wickedness, show some of the basest and some of the better emotions of mankind, cupidity, revenge, lust, jealousy, anger, fear, pity, despair, duty, self-righteousness, political fanaticism; or there may be no intelligible motive at all.

To similar effect is this passage from the judgment of the Privy Council in ***Reyes*** (at para 11)

> (The crime of murder) covers at one extreme the sadistic murder of a child for purposes of sexual gratification, a terrorist atrocity causing multiple deaths or a contract killing, at the other the mercy-killing of a loved one suffering unbearable pain in a terminal illness or a killing which results from an excessive response to a perceived threat. All killings which satisfy the definition of murder are by no means equally heinous.

Given the vastly differing circumstances in which a murder can occur, the imposition of one invariable penalty for anyone convicted of the crime, irrespective of his or her personal circumstances or the circumstances in which the crime was committed, is wholly incongruous with the basic principle that the punishment must fit the crime.

It is not surprising therefore that in every country which at one time had, or still retains the death penalty, including countries where the mandatory death penalty is still on the statute books, mechanisms are put in place to ensure that death is reserved only for those who deserve it. Some countries classify murder by degrees. Others abolish the mandatory death penalty altogether, allowing courts to take account of mitigating circumstances. In recognition of the notion that not everyone convicted of murder deserves to die, all of the Constitutions of the Commonwealth Caribbean mandate that the case of every person sentenced to death be referred to a committee charged with the responsibility of advising the Head of State on the power of pardon. In practice, this system has resulted in the reprieve of significant numbers of condemned prisoners. In the Bahamas, for example, there is evidence that "the proportion of those reprieved has been greater than the proportion of those executed."[14] In Trinidad and Tobago, before the spate of constitutional challenges following upon the Pratt and Morgan decision 1993,

[14] See ***Bowe v The Queen*** [2006] 1 WLR 1623, para 34.

more than half those convicted of murder had their death sentences commuted to life imprisonment.[15] In ***Bowe***, the Privy Council could find no evidence of "any jurisdiction in which, by 1973, the mandatory death sentence was retained and it was considered just to execute all who were convicted." As much as the law required the death sentence to be imposed in every case, the fact is that as a matter of practice, not every condemned prisoner was actually executed.

Another core principle which permeates all democratic societies is that decisions concerning the appropriate punishment which should be imposed are for the judiciary, not the executive, to make. As the Supreme Court of Ireland said[16] "the selection of punishment is an integral part of the administration of justice and, as such, cannot be committed to the hands of the executive." This principle has been recognised ever since Coke CJ in the early 17th century declared in the ***Prohibitions del Roy*** case[17] that

> "no King after the Conquest assumed to himself to give any judgment in any cause whatsoever, which concerned the administration of justice within this realm, but those were solely determined in the courts of justice."

But the mandatory death sentence deprives the judiciary of the duty to consider the individual circumstances of the offenders in order to determine the appropriate sentence. And our Constitution compounds the error by allowing the Executive to decide who should live and who should die. The fact that the actual punishment which a person convicted of murder is to suffer is actually determined by the executive in the exercise of the prerogative of mercy can only be reconciled with the notion that sentencing is a quintessential judicial function by emphasising that what the executive does when it commutes a sentence of death is to dispense mercy, not justice. As Lord Diplock said in ***De Freitas v Benny***, "Mercy begins where legal rights end."

[15] Commission of Enquiry into the Death Penalty – Report on the Death Penalty whether it should be retained for offences under the Criminal Law of Trinidad and Tobago.
[16] ***Deaton v Attorney General and Revenue Commissioners*** [1963] IR 170, 183-3.
[17] (1607) 12 Co. Rep. 63, 64.

But it was only a matter of time before these basic truths, that the punishment should fit the crime, that culpability for murder varies widely, that not everyone convicted of murder deserves death and that the appropriate sentence for murder should be determined by the judiciary, would result in the mandatory death penalty coming under constitutional scrutiny.

III. Developments in the Untied States of America

In response to the decision of the United States Supreme Court in ***Furman v Georgia***[18] that the vesting of an unbridled discretion in a jury to determine whether the death sentence should be imposed constituted a violation of the 8th and 14th amendments, North Carolina made the death penalty mandatory for first degree murder, defined as any murder perpetrated by means of poison, lying in wait, imprisonment, starving, torture, or any other kind of wilful deliberate and pre-meditated killing or which is perpetrated in the preparation of the attempt to commit arson, rape, robbery, kidnapping, burglary or any other felony. In a constitutional challenge before the Supreme Court[19] the sole issue was whether the mandatory death penalty constituted a cruel and unusual punishment. The Court held that the mandatory death penalty "treats all persons convicted of a designated offence not as uniquely individual human beings, but as members of a faceless, undifferentiated mass to be subjected to the blind infliction of the penalty of death." Noting that "consideration of both the offender and the offence in order to arrive at a just and appropriate sentence has been viewed as a progressive and humanising development", the Court took the view, particularly having regard to the qualitatively different nature of the penalty of death, differing from all other penalties in its finality, that there was accordingly a greater need to consider the character and record of the individual offender and the circumstance of the offence in order to ensure that "death is the appropriate punishment in a specific case."[20]

---

[18] 408 US 238.
[19] ***Woodson v North Carolina*** (1976) 428 US 280.
[20] Ibid. pp. 303-305.

Neither is the mandatory death sentence justifiable in relation to offences which are presumptively the worst of the worst. In Louisiana, first degree murder was defined as including any killing in connection with the commission of certain felonies; killing of a fireman or a peace officer in the performance of his duties; killing for remuneration; killing with the intent to inflict harm on more than one person; and killing by a person with a prior murder conviction or under a current life sentence. The Supreme Court virtually held that any mandatory death penalty constituted a cruel and unusual punishment irrespective of the category into which the murder fell. The Court said:[21]

> There is a special interest in affording protection to these public servants who regularly must risk their lives in order to guard the safety of other persons and property. But it is incorrect to suppose that no mitigating circumstances can exist when the victim is a police officer. Circumstances such as the youth of the offender, the absence of any prior conviction, the influence of drugs, alcohol, or extreme emotional disturbance, and even the existence of circumstances which the offender reasonably believed provided a moral justification for his conduct are all examples of mitigating facts which might attend the killing of a peace officer and which are considered relevant in other jurisdictions.

The Supreme Court of India reached a similar conclusion in ***Mithu v State of Punjab***[22] in relation to murder committed while the offender was under sentence of imprisonment for life. The Court concluded that "so final, so irrevocable and so irrestitutable is the sentence of death that no law which provides for it without involvement of the judicial mind can be said to be fair, just and reasonable. Such a law must necessarily be stigmatised as arbitrary and oppressive."[23]

IV. The United Nations System

Trinidad and Tobago is a member of the United Nations and is accordingly bound by the provisions of the Universal Declaration of Human Rights. Article 5 of the Declaration prohibits cruel, inhuman and degrading treatment or punishment, while Article 3 protects

[21] ***Roberts v Louisiana*** (1977) 431 US 633, 636-637
[22] [1983] 2 SCR 690.
[23] Ibid., p. 713.

the right to life and Article 10 entitles everyone to a criminal trial before an independent and impartial tribunal. On 21 December 1978, Trinidad and Tobago acceded to the International Covenant for Civil and Political Rights, Articles 7 and 14(1) of which mirror Articles 5 and 10 of the Universal Declaration. Article 6(1) provides that "Every human being has the inherent right to life. This right shall be protected by law. No one shall be arbitrarily deprived of his life" and Article 14(5) provides that "Everyone convicted of a crime shall have the right to his conviction and sentence being reviewed by a higher tribunal according to law."

On November 14th 1980, Trinidad and Tobago acceded to the Optional Protocol to the ICCPR giving citizens the facility to petition the Human Rights Committee to complain of violations of the Covenant. However, Trinidad and Tobago withdrew from the Optional Protocol altogether on 27th March 2000, after its attempt to withdraw and re-accede with a reservation precluding persons under sentence of death from petitioning, was rejected as invalid by the Human Rights Committee. The concern was that the delay caused while petitions were being processed would trigger the ***Pratt and Morgan***[24] principle, namely that a delay in execution of five years or more after conviction for murder constitutes inhuman and degrading punishment. As such, Trinidad and Tobago remains a party to and is bound by the Covenant but citizens are denied the right to complain about violations to the HRC.

In ***Thompson v Saint Vincent and the Grenadines***[25], the Human Rights Committee held that the mandatory death penalty in St. Vincent violated the right not to be arbitrarily deprived of life. The Committee felt that provision for pardon by the executive was an insufficient substitute for a judicial determination of the appropriate sentence. The Committee said:

> The committee considers that such a system of mandatory capital punishment would deprive the author of the most fundamental of rights, the right to life, without considering whether this exceptional form of punishment is appropriate in the circumstances of his or her case. The

[24] ***Pratt v Attorney General for Jamaica*** [1994] 2 AC 1.
[25] (2000) UN Doc CCPR/C/70/D/906/1998.

existence of a right to seek pardon or commutation, as required by article 6, paragraph 4, of the Covenant, does not secure adequate protection to the right to life, as these discretionary measures by the executive are subject to a wide range of other considerations compared to appropriate judicial review of all aspects of a criminal case. The committee finds that the carrying out of the death penalty in the author's case would constitute an arbitrary deprivation of his life in violation of article 6, paragraph 1, of the Covenant.

The Committee came to the same conclusion in ***Kennedy v Trinidad and Tobago***[26], on a petition which was lodged before Trinidad and Tobago denounced the Covenant.

V. The Inter-American System

Trinidad and Tobago joined the Organisation of American States on 14th March 1967 and thereby became bound by the American Declaration of Human Rights. Article 1 thereof protects the right to life and Article 26 provides that

> "Every person accused of an offense has the right to be given an impartial and public hearing, and to be tried by courts previously established in accordance with pre-existing laws, and not to receive cruel, infamous or unusual punishment."

Trinidad and Tobago ratified the Inter-American Convention on Human Rights on 28 May 1991 and simultaneously recognised the compulsory jurisdiction of the Inter-American Court of Human Rights whose judgments are binding. However, on May 26th 1999 Trinidad and Tobago denounced the Convention and the jurisdiction of the Court but not before a number of condemned prisoners had filed a petition challenging the mandatory death penalty. Nevertheless, Trinidad and Tobago remains a member of the OAS and the Inter-American Commission has held[27] that the Declaration is binding on members of the OAS, whether or not they have ratified the Convention.

[26] (March 26th 2002) CCPR/C/74/D/845/1998.
[27] Case No. 2141 (United States), 6 March 1981.

In ***Edwards v The Bahamas***[28], the Inter-American Commission held that the mandatory death penalty violated Article 26 of the Declaration by which Trinidad and Tobago is still bound. The Commission said:

> "147. The mandatory imposition of the death sentence, however, has both the intention and the effect of depriving a person of their right to life based solely upon the category of crime for which an offender is found guilty, without regard for the offender's personal circumstances or the circumstances of the particular offense. The commission cannot reconcile the essential respect for the dignity of the individual that underlies articles XXV and XXVI of the Declaration, with a system that deprives an individual of the most fundamental of rights without considering whether this exceptional form of punishment is appropriate in the circumstances of the individual's case."

In ***Hilare, Constantine and Benjamin v Trinidad and Tobago***[29], the Inter-American Court held that the mandatory death penalty violated the prohibition against the arbitrary depravation of life, in contravention of Article 4(1) and 4(2) of the Convention. The Court held that:

> (Section 4 of the Offences of the Person) Act prevents the judge from considering the basic circumstances in establishing the degree of culpability and individualising the sentence since it compels the indiscriminate imposition of the same punishment for conduct that can be vastly different…… and is arbitrary according to the terms of article 4(1) of the Convention…..
>
> The court concurs with the view that to consider all persons responsible for murder as deserving of the death penalty, 'treats all persons convicted of a designated offence not as uniquely individual human beings, but as members of a faceless, undifferentiated mass to be subjected to the blind infliction of the death penalty'.

The Court ordered Trinidad and Tobago to institute legislative reforms which would "include the introduction of different categories (criminal classes) of murder, in keeping with the wide range of differences in the gravity of the act, so as to take into account the

---

[28] Report No. 48/01 4 April 2001

[29] (Ser C) No 94 (2002), 21 June 2002, Inter-American Court of Human Rights.

particular circumstances of both the crime and the offender' and to introduce a system of graduated levels which would "ensure that the severity of the punishment is commensurate with the gravity of the act and the criminal culpability of the accused." To date Trinidad and Tobago has not complied with the order of the Court. In fact it had already withdrawn from the American Convention of Human Rights and thus from the jurisdiction of the Court.

Unlike Trinidad and Tobago and Jamaica, Barbados has not taken the drastic step of withdrawing from the jurisdiction of the Inter-American Court. It too was subject to a ruling by the Inter-American Court in ***Boyce and Joseph v Barbados*** that the mandatory death penalty violated Articles 4(1) and (2) of the Convention[30]. The Court reiterated that

> "the reference to "arbitrary" in Article 4(1) of the Convention and the reference to "the most serious crimes" in Article 4(2) render the imposition of mandatory death sentences incompatible with such provisions where the same penalty is imposed for conduct that can be vastly different, and where it is not restricted to the most serious crimes.... A lawfully sanctioned mandatory sentence of death may be arbitrary where the law fails to distinguish the possibility of different degrees of culpability of the offender and fails to individually consider the particular circumstances of the crime."

In response to the argument that "the unique circumstances of the individual and of the crime are taken into account by the executive branch" when deciding whether a pardon should issue, the Court emphasized that sentencing is a judicial function and noted that while "the executive branch may grant pardon or commutation of a sentence already imposed .... the judicial branch may not be stripped away of its responsibility to impose the appropriate sentence for a particular crime."

Furthermore, appreciating that the mandatory death penalty would be held to be in violation of the Barbados Constitution, but for the savings law clause, the Court ruled that the savings law clause itself violated Article 2 of the Convention since it embodied a

[30] Judgment of November 20, 2007 Series C. No. 169

failure by the State of Barbados to take steps to bring its laws into compliance with the Convention. The Court ordered Barbados to:

> "adopt such legislative or other measures as may be necessary to ensure that the .... death penalty ..... is not imposed through mandatory sentencing" and to "remove the immunizing effect of section 26 of the Constitution of Barbados on its "existing laws"..."

Caribbean States have not been known to comply with orders, far less recommendations of international human rights bodies, or if they have done so, they do not make such compliance public. It was therefore with great surprise and admiration that human rights lawyers received the news that Barbados has notified the Court that in compliance with its orders it intends to abolish the mandatory aspect of the death penalty and to repeal the general savings law clause in its Constitution.

VI. The Caribbean

The ruling by the Privy Council in first trilogy of cases (see page 2 above) has brought members of the Eastern Caribbean States and Belize in compliance with their international obligation. The Privy Council held that the mandatory death penalty violated the prohibition against inhuman and degrading punishment was accordingly modified to make the death penalty discretionary. The Board held that "To deny the offender the opportunity, before sentence is passed, to seek to persuade the court that in all the circumstances to condemn him to death would be disproportionate and inappropriate is to treat him as no human being should be treated and thus to deny his basic humanity, the core of the right which (the prohibition against inhuman and degrading punishment) exists to protect."

Jamaica amended its laws to categorise murder into capital and non-capital murder. Death was the only penalty for capital murders and for non-capital murders where the offender has been convicted of murder on a previous occasion or on the same occasion.

The Privy Council in ***Watson v The Queen*** held nevertheless that attempts to confine the mandatory death sentence to those categories of murder that are most reprehensible will always fail to meet the objective of giving the offender the opportunity to persuade the Court that in the circumstances of his case the penalty is disproportionate or inappropriate.[31] "Basic humanity", the Board said

> "requires that the appellant should be given an opportunity to show why the sentence of death should not be passed on him. If he is to have that opportunity, it must be open to the judge to take into account the facts of the case and the appellant's background and personal circumstances. The judge must also be in a position to mitigate the sentence by imposing, as an alternative, a sentence of imprisonment. The mandatory sentence flies in the face of these requirements, as it precludes any consideration of the circumstances."

VII. The African Continent

The trend towards abolition of the mandatory death sentence has found momentum on the African continent due in no small part to the efforts of the organisers of this conference. On January 21st 2009 the Supreme Court of Uganda[32]struck down the mandatory death penalty holding that it violated the right to a fair trial by denying the offender the right to persuade a court that death is not the appropriate sentence, the right to equality of treatment since persons convicted of crimes other than murder are given the opportunity to mitigate and that it violated that part of the Constitution which vested judicial power in the judiciary since it deprived the judiciary of the right to determine the appropriate sentence. The Supreme Court of Malawi had come to a similar decision.[33]

---

[31] ***Watson v The Queen*** [2005] 1 AC 490.
[32] ***A.G. of Uganda v Kigala*** Constitution Appeal No. 3 of 2006, 21st January 2009
[33] ***Kiafantanyeni v AG of Malawi*** (Case No. 12 of 2005).

VIII. Conclusion

The picture which emerges is not a flattering one for Trinidad and Tobago. Maintaining the mandatory death penalty has put us in violation of our obligations under the International Covenant for Civil and Political Rights and the American Declaration on the Rights of Man. We are in default of a specific order of the Inter-American Court requiring us to abolish the mandatory death penalty while our neighbour just to the north has undertaken to comply with a similar order. We are now one of two CARICOM countries which maintain the mandatory death penalty. Guyana is the other country. I have left Barbados out of account since it has undertaken to amend its laws. The mandatory death penalty contravenes one of the rights considered by the international community to be a core fundamental right, namely the right not to be subjected to cruel and unusual punishment. This is the unanimous view of a nine member panel of the Privy Council. The mandatory death penalty subsists only because of the savings law clause which was included in our constitutions in the first place to preserve the status quo and to give the legislature the opportunity to take steps to bring colonial laws into conformity with the fundamental rights and freedoms. More than four decades after independence, successive Parliaments have failed to pass the necessary legislation. The mandatory death penalty is inconsistent with the bias principle that the punishment must fit the crime and that appropriate sentences must be determined by the judiciary. It violates basic human decency by precluding the individualisation of the sentencing process. It is not that we intend that all persons who are convicted of murder should suffer death. The vast majority of death sentences are commuted by the executive, thus usurping the judicial function. And, as the study conducted by Professor Hood and Dr. Seemungal demonstrates, the overwhelming majority of persons involved in the criminal justice system favour the abolition of the mandatory death sentence. In his letter to me apologising for not being able to attend this conference, the Honourable leader of the Opposition said

> "I would like to say that I am against the mandatory death penalty, for the simple reason that 'murder' as defined by our law occurs in a variety of circumstances with varying levels of moral guilt/turpitude and,

> consequently, should not be treated as if they were the same. I would like to suggest that we amend the law to allow for a verdict of guilty of varying degrees of murder, for example, first, second and third degree murders with appropriate sentences for each."

It is high time that we bring our law into harmony with the core principles which underpin our system of justice.

[4]

FAIR TRIAL RIGHTS AND THEIR RELATION TO THE DEATH PENALTY IN AFRICA

LILIAN CHENWI*

I. INTRODUCTION

A fair trial is a basic element of the notion of the rule of law,[1] and the principles of 'due process' and 'the rule of law' are fundamental to the protection of human rights.[2] At the centre of any legal system, therefore, must be a means by which legal rights are asserted and breaches remedied through the process of a fair trial in court, as the law is useless without effective remedies.[3] The fairness of the legal process has a particular significance in criminal cases, as it protects against human rights abuses. Hence, constitutional due process and elementary justice require that the judicial functions of trial and sentencing be conducted with fundamental fairness, especially where the irreversible sanction of the death penalty is involved.[4]

To a great extent, increased concern about the use of the death penalty in Africa is as a result of the death penalty being imposed after trials that do not conform to international and national fair trial standards. For instance, as discussed below, trials are conducted after excessive delay and, in some cases, defendants have no access to legal assistance and lack proper defence. Adherence to fair trial (due process) rights in death penalty cases is essential. The United Nations (UN) General Assembly has pointed out in some of its resolutions the importance of fair trial standards being respected by all countries in death penalty cases.[5] This is imperative, as the non-existence of due

* Researcher, Community Law Centre, University of the Western Cape, and Research Associate of the Centre for Human Rights, University of Pretoria, South Africa. This article is partly based on research conducted for my doctoral thesis titled 'Towards the abolition of the death penalty in Africa: A human rights perspective' (2005) University of Pretoria, South Africa.

[1] C Ovey and R White *The European Convention on Human Rights* (OUP New York 2002) 139.

[2] R Clayton and H Tomlinson *Fair Trial Rights* (OUP New York 2001) 2.

[3] H Davis *Human Rights and Civil Liberties* (Willan Publishing Devon 2003) 146.

[4] American Civil Liberty Union 'The case against the death penalty' <http://www.aclu.org/deathpenalty/deathpenalty.cfm?ID=9082&c=17>.

[5] UNGA Res 2393 (XXIII) (26 Nov 1968) and UNGA Res 35/172 (15 Dec 1980). The European Court of Human Rights has also emphasized how imperative it is to respect fair trial rights. In *Delcort v Belgium* (1970) 1 EHRR 355, the Court stated that 'in a democratic society within the meaning of the Convention, the right to a fair administration of justice holds such a prominent place that a restrictive interpretation of Art 6(1) would not correspond to the aim and purpose of that provision' (para 25). The Court has, in subsequent cases, pointed out the imperative nature of fair trial rights (see for example *Öcalan v Turkey* (2003) 7 Amicus Journal 24; and *Soering v United Kingdom* ECHR (1989) Series A, No 161.

process of law within the jurisdiction of a State weakens the efficacy of the remedies provided under domestic law to protect the rights of individuals.[6] In addition, in Resolution 1996/15 of 23 July 1996, the UN Economic and Social Council (ECOSOC) encouraged UN Member States in which the death penalty has not yet been abolished to ensure that defendants facing a possible death sentence are given all guarantees to ensure a fair trial.

Considering the above, it is imperative that fair trial standards for the imposition of the death penalty are met. Failure to respect fair trial standards in capital trials increases the likelihood of innocent defenders being sentenced to death, and subsequently executed. Moreover, it can also lead to abuse of the whole trial process. This article provides an overview of fair trial rights in relation to the death penalty in Africa. It begins with a discussion of fair trial standards at the regional level, including the African Charter on Human and Peoples' Rights 1981 (African Charter), and their interpretation by the African Commission on Human and Peoples' Rights (African Commission). Subsequently, some of the fair trial rights with regard to capital trials in African States are examined.

II. THE AFRICAN CHARTER

Procedural safeguards for a fair trial have been enumerated in Article 7 of the African Charter.[7] The due process rights provided for in Article 7 are, first, the right to an appeal to competent national organs against acts violating fundamental rights as recognized and guaranteed by conventions, laws, regulations and customs in force (Article 7(1)(a)). Secondly, the right to be presumed innocent until proved guilty by a competent court or tribunal (Article 7(1)(b)). Thirdly, the right to defence, including the right to be defended by counsel of the defendant's choice (Article 7(1)(c)). Lastly, the right to be tried within a reasonable time by an impartial court or tribunal (Article 7(1)(d)).

The fair trial (due process) rights provided for in Article 7 are not as exhaustive as those, for example, in Article 14 of the International Covenant on Civil and Political Rights 1966 (ICCPR). The right to an interpreter, which is an aspect of a fair trial, is omitted. Nevertheless, as seen below, this has been stated in some of the African Commission's resolutions on the right to a fair trial. Article 6 of the African Charter, dealing with the right to liberty and

[6] This view was expressed by the Inter-American Commission on Human Rights (S Davidson *The Inter-American Human Rights System* (Dartmouth Aldershot 1997) 296). Also, the Inter-American Court of Human Rights has indicated that the concept of due process of law is a necessary prerequisite to ensure the adequate protection of persons whose rights and obligations are pending determination before a court or tribunal (Inter-American Court of Human Rights Advisory Opinion OC-9/87 (6 Oct 1987) Judicial guarantees in states of emergency, para 29).

[7] It should be noted that Arts 3 and 5 of the African Charter are also relevant to the right to a fair trial. Art 3 guarantees equality before the law and Art 5 provides for the right to the respect of the dignity inherent in a human being and to recognition of his legal status.

security of the person, is also of relevance with regard to the pre-trial phase in ensuring a fair trial. It prohibits arbitrary arrests and detentions. However, Article 6 has been criticized as not having sufficiently dealt with the pre-trial phase of the criminal process, and Article 7 as being incomplete.[8]

III. OTHER FAIR TRIAL STANDARDS AT THE REGIONAL LEVEL

The African Commission has adopted some resolutions on fair trial rights, which incorporate and expand on the fair trial rights contained in the African Charter. They supplement the provisions of the African Charter.[9] In 1992 the Commission adopted its Resolution on the Right to Recourse and Fair Trial.[10] The Commission's adoption of this resolution was aimed at deepening the understanding of substantive rights guaranteed by the African Charter.[11] The preamble highlights the imperative nature of fair trial rights in the words 'the right to a fair trial is essential for the protection of fundamental human rights and freedoms'. This resolution restates the fair trial rights contained in Articles 6 and 7, and the right to equality before the law provided for under Article 3 of the African Charter. The resolution goes further to provide for fair trial rights that are not contained in the African Charter, for example, the right of individuals to have the free assistance of an interpreter if they cannot speak the language used in court, and the right of individuals to have adequate time and facilities for the preparation of their defence.[12]

In 1999 the African Commission adopted 'Resolution on the Right to a Fair Trial and Legal Assistance in Africa'.[13] As can be deduced from the preamble of this resolution, its adoption was a means to emphasize the importance of the right to a fair trial and the need to strengthen the provisions of the African Charter relating to this right. This resolution adopts the Dakar Declaration and Recommendations on the Right to a Fair Trial in Africa, which states that

> the right to a fair trial is a fundamental right, the non-observance of which undermines all other human rights. Therefore, the right to a fair trial is a non-derogable

[8] F Viljoen 'Introduction to the African Commission and the regional human rights system' in C Heyns (ed) *Human Rights Law in Africa* (Martinus Nijhoff Publishers Leiden 2004) 404. Generally, detention and trial, which are often the areas where systematic violations of civil and political rights occur, are not dealt with adequately in the African Charter (C Heyns 'Civil and political rights in the African Charter' in M Evans and R Murray (eds) *The African Charter on Human and Peoples' Rights: The System in Practice, 1986–2000* (CUP Cambridge 2002) 155.

[9] Art 66 of the African Charter provides that, if necessary, special protocols or agreements may supplement the provisions of the Charter.

[10] Adopted at its Eleventh Session held in Tunis, Tunisia, 2–9 Mar 1992; reproduced in C Heyns (ed) *Human Rights Law in Africa* (Martinus Nijhoff Publishers Leiden 2004) 526.

[11] *Fifth Annual Activity Report: 1991–1992* para 22.

[12] Para 2(e)(I) & (IV) of the Resolution.

[13] Adopted at its Twenty-sixth Session held in Kigali, Rwanda, 1–15 Nov 1999; reproduced in Heyns (n 10) 584.

right, especially as the African Charter does not expressly allow for any derogations from the rights it enshrines.[14]

In addition, in 2003, the Commission adopted 'Principles and Guidelines on the Right to a Fair Trial and Legal Aid in Africa'.[15] The general principles include the right to a fair and public hearing by a legally constituted competent, independent and impartial judicial body. The above principles and guidelines identify essential elements of a fair hearing, which include: equality of all persons before any judicial body; the right to consult and be represented by a legal representative or other qualified persons of one's choice at all stages of the proceedings; the right to the assistance of an interpreter if a defendant cannot understand the language used; the right to a determination of the defendant's rights and obligations without undue delay; and the right to an appeal to a higher judicial body. Thus, the principles and guidelines incorporate fair trial standards in the ICCPR and the African Charter and elaborate on them.

IV. JURISPRUDENCE OF THE AFRICAN COMMISSION

Although the African Commission's position with regard to the death penalty remains unclear,[16] it has addressed the issue of fair trial rights in a number of death penalty cases, in which the issue of the death penalty was raised in the context of the deprivation of fair trial rights during the trial process. The Commission has had more impact where the issue of the death penalty was raised on procedural grounds, than on the right to life. Its decisions on fair trial rights have been progressive, and can be seen as procedural benchmarks in capital cases.[17] In *Amnesty International (on behalf of Orton and Vera Chirwa) v Malawi*,[18] the African Commission found a violation of Article 7(1)(c), the right to defence, on the ground that the trial of the Chirwas took

[14] Heyns (n 10) 585.

[15] Adopted at its 33rd Ordinary Session held in Niamey, Niger in May 2003, *Final Communiqué* of the Session and *Seventeenth Annual Activity Report: 2003–2004* (hereinafter referred to as African Commission's principles and guidelines). The Preamble points out the need for these fair trial standards to become known to everyone in Africa, and urged that these standards be promoted and protected by civil society organizations, judges, lawyers, prosecutors, academics, and be incorporated into domestic legislation by state parties to the African Charter and respected by them.

[16] The Commission has not pronounced itself on the death penalty as such. However, some Commissioners have openly stated their opposition to the death penalty or that they favour abolition (see L Chenwi 'The African Commission and the death penalty' (2005) 11 Amicus Journal 13). Recently, the death penalty has been included in the Commission's agenda.

[17] However, implementation of its decisions depends largely on the political will of African States.

[18] Communications 68/92 and 78/92 *Eighth Annual Activity Report: 1994–1995*, para 10. In this case, the Southern Regional Traditional Courts had sentenced Orton and Vera Chirwa to death, after a trial that did not meet fair trial standards. After international protest, the sentences were commuted to life imprisonment (paras 1–5).

place before a Traditional Court consisting of five chiefs who had no legal training, and the Chirwas were tried without being defended by counsel.

The Commission has subsequently elaborated on the meaning of the right to defence. The right to defence, including the right to be defended by counsel of one's choice, guaranteed under Article 7(1)(c), as seen in the Commission's decision in *Constitutional Rights Project (in respect of Lekwot) v Nigeria*,[19] requires that the counsel representing the accused should not be intimidated or harassed during the trial. Intimidation and harassment of counsel to the extent that they withdraw from a case would amount to a violation of this right. If after such withdrawal, the accused is not given the opportunity to procure the services of another counsel; his right to be represented by counsel of his choice is violated.[20]

Further, the severity of sentence (the death sentence) is a relevant consideration in establishing whether denial of the right to appeal constitutes a violation, as was the Commission's position in *Constitutional Rights Project (in respect of Akamu) v Nigeria*.[21] The Commission found a violation of Article 7(1)(a) in this case on the ground that special tribunals created in 1984 in Nigeria foreclosed any avenue of appeal to 'competent national organs' in criminal cases bearing such penalties.[22] The Commission further found a violation of Article 7(1)(d) due to the fact that an appearance of partiality had been created by the composition of the special tribunals.[23] The character of the individual members of the tribunal was immaterial in deciding whether the right to be tried by an impartial court or tribunal has been violated.

Similarly, in *International Pen (on behalf of Saro-Wiwa) v Nigeria*,[24] the

[19] Communication 87/93 *Eighth Annual Activity Report: 1994–1995*; (2000) AHRLR 183 (ACHPR 1995) para 12. In this communication, the individuals concerned had been sentenced to death under the Civil Disturbances (Special Tribunal) Decree No 2 of 1987. The decree does not provide for any judicial appeal against the decisions of the Special tribunals and prohibits the courts from reviewing any aspect of the operation of the tribunal. The Communication also alleged that the accused and their counsels were constantly harassed and intimidated during the trial, ultimately forcing the withdrawal of the defence counsel (paras 1 and 2).

[20] ibid.

[21] Communication 60/91 *Eighth Annual Activity Report: 1994–1995*; (2000) AHRLR 180 (ACHPR 1995).

[22] ibid, para 13. The individuals in this communication had been sentenced to death under the Robbery and Firearms (Special Provision) Decree No 5 of 1984, which created special tribunals, composed of one serving or retired judge, one member of the armed forces and one member of the police force. The Decree does not provide for any appeal of sentences, but merely subjects them to confirmation or disallowance by the Governor of the state (para 1).

[23] ibid, para 12. Similarly, the Inter-American Commission on Human Rights has found the appearance of impartiality to constitute a violation of the right to be tried by an impartial tribunal in, eg, *Andrews v United States* Case 11.139, Report No 57/96 (6 Dec 1996); OEA/Ser.L/V/II.98 Rev 6 (13 Apr 1998).

[24] Communication 137/94, 139/94, 154/96, and 161/97 *Twelfth Annual Activity Report: 1998–1999*; (2002) AHRLR 212 (ACHPR 1998) paras 90 and 95. The case concerned the detention and trial of Mr Saro-Wiwa and the human rights violations suffered by him. During detention, he was denied access to a lawyer. The trial took place before a tribunal established under the Civil Disturbances Act. He was later sentenced to death together with his co-defendants. Although the African Commission requested a stay of execution, he was executed together with the others in secret (paras 1–10).

Commission found special tribunals with an appearance of partiality to be in violation of Article 7(1)(d), and consequently, Article 26 of the African Charter, as the Government did not guarantee the independence of the judicial bodies in question. As well, Article 7(1)(a) would be violated if accused persons have no possibility of appealing their sentences to competent national organs.[25] Also, to openly pronounce an accused guilty prior to and during the trial, will constitute a violation of the accused's right to be presumed innocent.[26]

In *Amnesty International v Sudan*,[27] the Commission found a violation of Article 7(1)(d); first, as the composition of special courts in Sudan create the impression, or indicate the reality, of lack of impartiality (the courts consisted of 'three military officers or other persons of integrity and competence' appointed by the president, his deputies and senior military officers); second, on the basis that the Government dismissed judges opposed to the formation of these courts. The Commission saw the dismissal as depriving courts of the personnel qualified to ensure that they operate impartially, thus denying individuals the right to have their case heard by such body.[28] Further, giving a tribunal the power to veto the choice of counsel of defendants is an unacceptable infringement of the right to freely choose one's counsel under Article 7(1)(c), which is essential to the assurance of a fair trial.[29]

The African Commission, in the recent case of *Interights (on behalf of Bosch) v Botswana*,[30] did not find a violation of fair trials rights. One of the issues raised was whether the misdirection of the trial judge with regard to the onus of proof was so fatal as to negate the right to a fair trial in the circumstances of the case, amounting to a violation of Article 7(1)(b) of the African Charter, which guarantees the right of every individual to be presumed innocent until proved guilty by a competent court or tribunal. The Commission noted that there is no general rule or international norm to the effect that any

[25] ibid, para 93.

[26] ibid, para 96.

[27] Communications 48/90, 50/91, 52/91, 89/93 *Thirteenth Annual Activity Report: 1999–2000*; (2000) AHRLR 297 (ACHPR 1999), para 68. In this communication, it was alleged that in Sudan, legal representation is denied at new trials and there is no appeal of a death sentence (see paras 1–20 for a summary of the facts).

[28] ibid, para 69.

[29] ibid, para 64 and 66.

[30] Communication 240/2001 *Seventeenth Annual Activity Report: 2003–2004* (African Commission). The High Court of Botswana convicted Mariette Bosch of murder on 13 Dec 1999 and sentenced her to death. An appeal to the Court of Appeal of Botswana in 2001 was unsuccessful (para 2). A petition was submitted on her behalf to the Commission alleging violations of her rights in the African Charter. The Chairman of the African Commission, after receiving the petition, wrote to the President of Botswana on 27 Mar 2001, appealing for a stay of execution pending consideration of the communication by the Commission (paras 7–10). The President did not respond to the appeal, and Bosch was executed by hanging on 31 Mar 2001 (para 11). For an evaluation of this case, see L Chenwi 'What future for the death penalty in Africa? An appraisal of the case of *Interights et al (on behalf of Mariette Sonjaleen Bosh) v Botswana*' (2005) 12 Amicus Journal 13.

misdirection by itself vitiates a verdict of guilt, and that a breach of Article 7(1) would only arise if the conviction had resulted from such misdirection.[31] Drawing inspiration from, inter alia, the case law of the European Court of Human Rights, and based on the fact that Bosch's conviction for murder did not result from the misdirection but from the evidence presented, the Commission concluded that there had not been a violation.[32]

According to the Commission's decision, there could be a basis for finding a violation of Articles 4 and 7(1) of the African Charter, if it is shown that the Courts' (the High Court and Court of Appeal of Botswana) evaluation of the facts was manifestly arbitrary or amounted to a denial of justice.[33] However, this was not the case. A reversal of the presumption of innocence is a fundamental violation of Article 7(1)(b) of the African Charter. The presumption of innocence is essential to ensure a fair trial. Since, as seen from the jurisprudence of the African Commission, the rights under Article 7 are mutually dependent, the Commission should have been bold enough in finding a violation of Article 7(1), as there was a clear violation of Article 7(1)(b)—presumption of innocence—by placing the burden of proof on Bosch.[34]

Nevertheless, with the exception of the *Bosch* case, the jurisprudence of the African Commission shows that the mere appearance of partiality alone would suffice to find a violation of Article 7(1)(d). It is also clear from the Commission's jurisprudence that where the right to be heard is infringed, other violations may occur, such as an execution becoming arbitrary (thus, a violation of Article 4), and violations of Article 26, as governments have a duty to provide structures necessary for the exercise of the right to be tried by an independent (and impartial) court. The Commission has therefore taken an approach similar to that of the UN Human Rights Committee, with regard to the relation between the right to life and fair trial rights. The Human Rights Committee is also of the view that imposition of the death penalty following an unfair trial is a breach not only of procedural standards but also of the right to life.[35] The Inter-American Commission on Human Rights has adopted a similar position with regard to the relationship between fair trial rights and the right to life.[36]

[31] ibid, paras 24 and 26. [32] ibid, paras 27 and 28. [33] ibid, para 29.

[34] Notwithstanding, the Commission acknowledged the evolution of international law and the trend towards abolition of the death penalty. It further conceded its support of this trend by its adoption of the 1999 resolution, and encouraged all states party to the African Charter to take all measures to refrain from exercising the death penalty (para 52).

[35] For a discussion of the Committee's jurisprudence, see W Schabas *The Abolition of the Death Penalty in International Law* (CUP Cambridge 2002) 112–13.

[36] It is clear from the Inter-American Commission's jurisprudence that since a violation of due process invalidates a conviction and sentence, an execution pursuant to flawed criminal proceedings would amount to an arbitrary deprivation of life, thus a violation of the right to life under Article I of the American Declaration (see, eg, *Graham v United States* Case 11.193, Report No 97/03 (29 Dec 2003)). Similarly, the Inter-American Court of Human Rights has adopted the same approach, finding the imposition of capital punishment without respect for due process to constitute an 'arbitrary' deprivation of life (see Inter-American Court of Human Rights Advisory Opinion OC-16/99 (1 Oct 1999)).

V. RESPECT FOR FAIR TRIAL RIGHTS IN CAPITAL TRIALS

As long as the reality pertains that the death penalty exists in Africa, it is imperative that it is imposed only in exceptional circumstances, and that fair trial standards for its imposition are met so as to undo or mitigate its possible effects, such as conviction of the innocent. If such fair trial standards cannot be met, the death penalty should not be imposed since, as mentioned above, constitutional due process and elementary justice require that the judicial functions of trial and sentencing be conducted with fundamental fairness, especially where the irreversible sanction of the death penalty is involved.

Fair trial rights have been enumerated in the national constitutions of most African States.[37] However, some of the provisions are very inadequate, or not in conformity with the norms and standards of the relevant UN instruments[38] or those at the regional level. For example, despite the fact that Sierra Leone has ratified the ICCPR and African Charter, accused persons have no right to a lawyer at the appeal stage of the trial.[39]

A. The right to be tried within a reasonable time

The purpose of the right of an accused to be tried within a reasonable time is to prevent undue and oppressive incarceration prior to trial, to minimize anxiety and concern accompanying public accusation and to limit the possibilities that long delay will impair the ability of an accused to defend him or herself.[40] The object of this right therefore is to give effect to the principal right to a substantively fair trial, thus preventing injustice resulting from delays. The

[37] eg Arts 1 and 3 of the Constitutions of Central African Republic 1994; Art 10 of the Constitution of Djibouti 1992; Arts 19 and 20 of the Constitution of Ethiopia 1995; s 32 of the Constitution of the Republic of Sudan 1998; Art 13 of the Constitution of Tanzania 1995; Art 18 of the Constitution of Zambia 1996; the Preamble of the Constitution of the Republic of Cameroon 1996; ss 35 and 36 of the Constitution of the Federal Republic of Nigeria 1999; s 19 of the Constitution of Ghana 1996; s 28 of the Constitution of Uganda 1995; and s 23 of the Constitution of Sierra Leone 1996. It should be noted that the Constitution of Morocco 1996 has nothing on fair trial rights. Somalia and Swaziland have no constitution at present. The Constitution of Somalia was suspended on 27 Jan 1991. For the sections of the various African constitutions that deal with fair trial rights, see Heyns (n 11) 854–5. Further, the years of the constitutions referred to in this article are the years the constitutions were last amended as at Mar 2005.

[38] A Adeyemi 'United Nations human rights instruments and criminal justice norms and standards' in M Bassiouni and Z Motala (eds) *The Protection of Human Rights in African Criminal Proceedings* (Martinus Nijhoff Publishers Dordrecht 1995) 4.

[39] Report of the national coordinator of Sierra Leone, Abdul Tejan-Cole, presented at the 'First International Conference on the Application of the Death Penalty in Commonwealth Africa' held in Entebbe, Uganda from 10 to 11 May 2004. The reports presented at this conference are available at web site <http://www.biicl.org/deathpenalty>.

[40] M Code *Trial Within a Reasonable Time: A short history of recent controversies surrounding speedy trial rights in Canada and the United States* (Carswell Thomson Professional Publishing Scarborough Ontario 1992) 9; N Steytler *Constitutional Criminal Procedure: A commentary of the Constitution of the Republic of South Africa* (Butterworths Durban 1998) 272.

right of an accused to be tried within a reasonable time runs through the pre-trial, trial and post-trial phases of a trial. That is, this right relates not only to the time by which a trial should commence, but also the time by which it should end and judgment be rendered; and all stages must take place 'without undue delay' (within a reasonable time).[41] For this right to be effective, a procedure must be available in order to ensure that the trial will proceed 'without undue delay' both in the first instance and on appeal.[42]

In establishing whether this right has been violated (or whether there has been undue delay), factors such as the nature and complexity of the case, the availability of state resources with regard to the investigation or prosecution of the case, and the kind of prejudice suffered by the accused, have to be considered.[43] The above factors have to be taken into account as it is difficult to establish undue delay, for example, where there are insufficient resources to carry out investigations, or the case is very complex, or the accused has not suffered any prejudice. For example, a case in which an accused had not been brought to trial two years after his first appearance was held not to constitute a violation of the right to a trial within a reasonable time.[44]

The right to be tried within a reasonable time is a constitutional value of supreme importance that must be interpreted in a broad and creative manner.[45] Trials held within a reasonable time have an intrinsic value. If innocent, the accused should be acquitted with a minimum disruption to his social and family relationships. If guilty, the accused should be convicted and an appropriate sentence be imposed without unreasonable delay.[46] Regrettably, most capital trials in Africa take many years, as accused persons are not brought before a court within a reasonable time. In Sierra Leone, for example, the main problem with capital trials is that of massive pre-charge and pre-trial delays, and moreover, suspects are most often, not informed of the reasons for their arrest until they are about to be charged in court, contrary to Section 17(2)(a) of the Constitution of Sierra Leone 1996.[47] In Zambia, trials take very long,

[41] UN Human Rights Committee, General Comment No 13: Equality before the courts and the right to a fair and public hearing by an independent court established by law (Art 14 of the ICCPR) (13 Apr 1984) para 10.

[42] ibid.

[43] The Inter-American Commission on Human Rights has laid down, in a case against Argentina, three criteria to be used to determine what constitutes a reasonable time, namely: the duration of imprisonment; the nature of the acts that led to criminal proceedings; and the difficulties or judicial problems encountered when conducting trials (Davidson (n 6) 288). In this case, the Inter-American Commission relying on these criteria, found a pre-trial detention period of four years in this case not to be unjustifiable delay in the administration of justice (*Case 10.037 v Argentina* (1989) IAYHR 52, 100). This goes to show that there is no set period of time to be considered as unreasonable, as this will depend on the circumstances of each case.

[44] *Sanderson v A-G* [1997] 12 BCLR 1675.

[45] *Smyth v Uhsewokunze* [1998] 4 LRC 120, 129b.

[46] *Re Mlambo* (1993) 2 LRC 28, 34e–f (Supreme Court of Zimbabwe).

[47] A person arrested for treason, murder or robbery with aggravation may spend an average between three and six months in police custody despite the fact that s 17(3) of the Constitution of Sierra Leone 1991 specifically states that persons arrested for capital offences have to be brought

often more than three years from the date of arrest.[48] In Nigeria, the pre-trial time in detention for capital offenders, which is rarely less than five years in some states and in some cases over 10 years, has been a matter of serious concern.[49] Also in Lesotho, although Section 12(1) of the Constitution provides that the accused person be afforded hearing within a reasonable time, the law enforcement agencies more often than not, do not comply with this provision.[50]

Trials that take too long can lead to injustice, as it becomes difficult to procure the presence of witnesses due to the long trials. This has been the case in Cameroon where capital trials take a very long time. Some lawyers in Cameroon have stated that one of the difficulties they face with regard to capital trials is the fact that the trials are lengthy, with many adjournments; and that the consequence of trials not done within a reasonable time is that it makes it difficult to secure the presence of witnesses.[51] It is difficult to guarantee a fair hearing under such circumstances.

Such delays above are clearly in violation of fair trial rights in the ICCPR, African Charter, national constitutions of the above States, and other UN and African Commission standards for a fair trial. The African Commission held in *Pagnoulle (on behalf of Mazou) v Cameroon*[52] that two years without any hearing or projected trial date constitutes a violation of Article 7(1)(d) of the African Charter dealing with the right to be tried within reasonable time. The Commission's finding was based on the fact that no reason had been given for the delays. Although the case was not related to the death penalty, it sets precedence for capital cases.[53]

It is worth noting that some of the delays are caused by deficiencies in the criminal justice systems of some African States. In Ghana, for example, the

before a court of law within 10 days from the date of arrest (Report of the national coordinator of Sierra Leone (n 39)).

48 International Commission of Jurists 'Zambia: Attacks on Justice' <http://www.icj.org/news>.

49 Amnesty International 'Nigeria: The death penalty and women under the Nigerian penal systems' AI Index: AFR 44/007/2004 (10 Feb 2004).

50 Initial report of Lesotho submitted under Art 40 of the ICCPR, UN Doc CCPR/C/81/Add 14 (16 Jan 1998) para 101.

51 The author is from Cameroon, and became aware of these difficulties from a discussion with some defence lawyers in Apr 2004 in Cameroon, in which I asked them of the difficulties they experience in preparing capital cases.

52 Communication 39/90 *Tenth Annual Activity Report: 1996–1997*; (2000) AHRLR 57 (ACHPR 1997) para 19. See also the following cases involving African States: *Birindwa and Tshisekedi v DRC*, Communication 241/1987, UN Doc CCPR/C/37/D/241/1987 (29 Nov 1989) para 13, in which the Human Rights Committee found a violation of Art 9(3) of the ICCPR because Tshisekedi was not brought before a judge within a reasonable time and consequently, not tried within reasonable time; *Muteba v DRC* Communication 124/1982, UN Doc CCPR/C/22/D/124/1982 (24 July 1982), in which the Committee found a violation of the right to be brought promptly before a judge and to be tried within reasonable time.

53 As can be deduced from the above case, the burden is on the State to justify lengthy detentions or delays in bringing an accused before a court within reasonable time. Otherwise such detentions will amount to a violation of the right to be tried within a reasonable time.

police service is ill equipped and lacks adequate training, coupled with corruption impacting negatively on the pre-trial phase of the criminal justice system.[54] In Lesotho, delays are as a result of the lack of resources and shortage of qualified staff particularly at the investigative and preparatory stages.[55] The justice system in Burundi suffers from inadequate resources and training, corruption, lack of belief in the rule of law and a lack of political will to end impunity.[56] The difficulty with respecting the right to be tried within a reasonable time in Uganda is that

> [t]he administration of justice in Uganda is painfully slow. The Judiciary...[is] understaffed and under funded. It cannot effectively respond to the rising rate of crime. Courts of judicature are understaffed. . . . This problem is compounded by irregular High Court sessions. The Director of Public Prosecutions, which is responsible for prosecuting cases, is inadequately staffed and under funded which has contributed to the delay of [j]ustice.[57]

When the human rights of individuals are at stake, deficiencies in the criminal justice system cannot be used to justify violations of such rights. It is clear from the UN Human Rights Committee's decision in *Lubuto v Zambia* that a State cannot use its economic situation to justify violations of minimum human rights standards (including violations of fair trial rights).[58] It is imperative that accused persons be tried within a reasonable time. Delays must not exceed a few days;[59] otherwise, it will constitute a violation of the above right. Nonetheless, as long as these deficiencies continue to exist in some African states, it is without doubt that accused persons in such states would not receive a fair trial.

B. The right to be presumed innocent until proven guilty by a court of law

In any system of criminal justice, the presumption of innocence is fundamental to the protection of human rights.[60] The right to be presumed innocent until proven guilty by a court of law is directly linked to the right to be tried within

[54] Report of the national coordinator of Ghana, Kristine Lartey, presented at the 'First International Conference on the Application of the Death Penalty in Commonwealth Africa'.

[55] Report of the national coordinator of Lesotho, Moses Owori, presented at the 'First International Conference on the Application of the Death Penalty in Commonwealth Africa'.

[56] *Amnesty International Report* (Amnesty International Secretariat London 2005) <http://web.amnesty.org/report2005>.

[57] Initial report of Uganda submitted under Art 40 of the ICCPR, UN Doc CCPR/C /UGA/2003/1 (25 Feb 2003) para 242.

[58] Communication 390/1990, UN Doc CCPR/C/55/D/390/1990/Rev 1 (31 Oct 1995) para 7.3. In this case, the Human Rights Committee found a period of eight years between arrest and final decision of the court to be incompatible with the requirements of Art 14(3)(c) of the ICCPR.

[59] See UN Human Rights Committee, General Comment No 8: Right to liberty and security of persons (Art 9 of the ICCPR), 30 June 1982, paras 2–3. The Human Rights Committee is of the opinion that pre-trial detention should be an exception and as short as possible, thus ensuring conformity with the right 'to trial within a reasonable time or to release'.

[60] General Comment No 13 (n 41) para 7.

a reasonable time, because to give effect to the former, an accused has to be tried within a reasonable time. Respect for the latter right mitigates the tension between the presumption of innocence and the publicity of the trial, thus rendering the criminal justice system more coherent and fair.[61] Unfortunately, as seen above, the right to be tried without undue delay has not been respected in some African States. Consequently, the presumption of innocence of an accused person is not upheld in such cases.

The right to be presumed innocent is not respected in, for example, Nigeria, Cameroon and other Commonwealth African States, as suspects are tortured and treated by the police and the society at large as guilty before the trial.[62] Non-respect for the right to be presumed innocent in a country like Morocco could be attributed to the fact that there is no provision on this right in the Constitution or the Code of Criminal Procedure.[63] The UN Human Rights Committee has expressed concern over this, and recommended that the Government adopt appropriate legislation so as to guarantee the presumption of innocence, as required under Article 14(2) of the ICCPR.[64]

Since the burden is generally on the prosecution to prove the guilt of an accused person, a court has to conduct the trial without previously forming an opinion on the guilt or innocence of the accused. It, therefore, follows that the right to be presumed innocent by a court of law requires that the prosecution or respondent State should not make open statements prior to and during the trial in press conferences or public gatherings pronouncing an accused guilty of the crime. In *International Pen and Others (on behalf of Saro-Wiwa) v Nigeria*, the African Commission found the Government of Nigeria to be in violation of the right to be presumed innocent under Article 7(1)(b) of the African Charter because the Government pronounced the accused guilty of the crimes in question at various press conferences and before the UN.[65]

In addition, the requirement that an accused be released on bail pending trial is important, as it gives effect to the right of every accused to be presumed innocent until proven guilty according to law.[66] Yet, the most restriction placed upon a pre-trial defendant is the requirement of bail. Generally speaking, it is rare in most jurisdictions for a person accused of a capital offence to get bail. For example, despite provisions for bail, some judges are reluctant to grant bail in capital cases, as is the situation in Cameroon.[67] In Uganda, it is

[61] Steytler (n 40) 273.

[62] Country reports presented at the 'First International Conference on the Application of the Death Penalty in Commonwealth Africa'.

[63] Concluding observations of the Human Rights Committee on the fourth periodic report of Morocco submitted under Art 40 of the ICCPR, UN Doc CCPR/C/79/Add 113 (1 Nov 1999) para 18.

[64] ibid.

[65] (n 24) para 96.

[66] Art 7(1)(b) of the African Charter.

[67] This was brought to the author's attention during a research conducted by the author in Apr 2004 in Cameroon, when defence lawyers were asked about the position in law regarding the granting of bail to those accused of capital offences. Section 118(1) of the Criminal Procedure Ordinance makes provision for bail in all criminal cases.

rare for those accused of capital offences to get bail.[68] Section 23(6)(a) of the Ugandan Constitution (1995) dealing with bail uses the word 'may', which implies that bail can be denied. Worse of all, the Ugandan Military Courts do not accord accused persons bail, they are detained until such time that the court is ready to hear the case.[69] This amounts to a violation of the right to liberty of accused persons and their right to be presumed innocent. In Lesotho, bail can be refused where an accused is charged with capital murder, unless the accused adduces evidence that satisfies the court that exceptional circumstances exist, which in the interest of justice permit his or her release.[70] However, it is not clear what is considered to be in the 'interest of justice' and the criteria used to determine this.

Further, bail can be refused to persons charged with murder and treason in Ghana.[71] As seen in the cases below, the courts have been lenient in applying this provision. It would appear that where it can be established that there has been, or would be, unreasonable delay in bringing an accused to trial, or where the applicants allege without any objection from the prosecution, that they did not commit the offence in question, bail could be granted. In *Republic v Arthur*,[72] the applicants who had been charged with murder filed for bail pending trial, arguing that there was no likelihood of their case being heard within reasonable time. The Court held that what constituted unreasonable time had to be determined within the particular context, and therefore dismissed the application on the ground that the applicants had failed to show that there had been unreasonable delay in bringing them to trial. Also, in *Prah and Others v The Republic*,[73] the applicants, who had been charged with murder, applied for bail on the ground that they did not commit the offence charged. The Court held that although under Section 96(7)(a) bail could not be granted, the applicants could be granted bail, as the prosecution did not oppose the affidavit in which the applicants denied committing the crime.[74]

In other jurisdictions, bail is refused to those charged with capital offences regardless of the fact that the law makes provision for it. For example, despite the provision for bail in Section 71 of the Criminal Procedure Act 1965 of Sierra Leone, it has become standard practice not to admit to bail persons accused of treason, murder or aggravated robbery which are capital offences.[75] In Sudan, bail is prohibited for crimes punishable with the death penalty,

[68] Report of the national coordinator of Uganda, Emmanuel Kasimbazi, presented at the 'First International Conference on the Application of the Death Penalty in Commonwealth Africa'.

[69] Initial report of Uganda (n 57) para 296.

[70] Criminal Procedure and Evidence Act No 10 of 2002.

[71] Section 96(7)(a) of the Criminal Procedure Code of Ghana (Act 30) 1960. Murder and treason are punishable by death under ss 46 and 180 of the Criminal Code of Ghana 1960 respectively. See also Art 21(d)(i) of the Constitution of Liberia 1984.

[72] (1982–3) GLR 249.

[73] (1976) 2 GLR 278.

[74] ibid; *Dogbe v The Republic* (1976) 2 GLR 82, with regard to bail in murder cases.

[75] Report of the national coordinator of Sierra Leone (n 39).

provided that if the arrest continues for more than six months, the record is submitted to the head of the Judicial Authority, who then makes whatever order is deemed appropriate.[76] This provision is open to abuse, as it does not specify a list of the appropriate measures that could be made.

In a nutshell, the refusal of bail to accused persons in capital cases could impact negatively on the right of accused persons to be presumed innocent. The situation is exacerbated by the deficiencies in criminal justice systems, such as the manner an investigation is carried out.

C. The right to have adequate time for the preparation of his or her defence

The right of an accused to have adequate time for the preparation of his or her defence implies that an accused should have access to materials necessary for the preparation of his or her defence.[77] It should be noted that what is adequate time depends on the circumstances of each case, but the facilities must include access to documents and other evidence that the accused requires to prepare his or her case, as well as the opportunity to engage and communicate with counsel.[78] However, this has not been the case in some African States. In Nigeria, for example, the prosecution is always reluctant to share information with the defence lawyers, and in some cases there have been allegations of the prosecution suppressing information favourable to the accused.[79]

Implicit in this right is the need for an accused to be notified of the date and place of the trial, if the accused is going to be tried in absentia. In *Mbenge v Zaïre*, no steps were taken to inform the accused before hand of the proceedings against him, as required under Article 14(3)(a) of the ICCPR.[80] It was alleged that the accused learned of the death sentences through the press.[81] The Human Rights Committee held that judgment in absentia requires that, despite the absence of the accused, all due notification has to be made to inform the accused of the trial date and place and to request the accused's attendance. Otherwise, it amounts to a violation of Article 14(3)(b) of the ICCPR as the accused, in particular, is not given adequate time and facilities for the preparation of his or her defence.[82]

Furthermore, the right of an accused to have adequate time for the preparation of his or her defence is also related to the right to be tried within a reason-

[76] Section 106(1) of the Criminal Procedures Act of 1991.

[77] Guideline N(3) of the African Commission's principles and guidelines.

[78] General Comment No 13 (n 41) para 9.

[79] Report of the national coordinator of Nigeria, Jude Ilo, presented at the 'First International Conference on the Application of the Death Penalty in Commonwealth Africa'.

[80] Communication 16/1977, UN Doc CCPR/C/18/D/16/1977 (25 Mar 1983).

[81] ibid, para 2.2.

[82] ibid. The HRC also found the above circumstance to be in violation of Art 14(3)(d), as the accused cannot defend himself through legal assistance of his choice and Art 14(3)(e), as the accused does not have the opportunity to examine, or have examined, the witnesses against him and to obtain the attendance and examination of witnesses on his behalf.

able time. The fact that an accused has to be tried without undue delay, does not mean that the accused should not be given adequate time to prepare his or her defence or does not preclude the carrying out of a full investigation. In Uganda, in 2002, two soldiers were executed after an Emergency Field Court Martial, which reportedly lasted just 2 hours and 36 minutes, and did not allow for a full investigation of the circumstances surrounding the case.[83] It cannot be said that the trial of the soldiers was fair, without a full investigation into the circumstances of the case, which could have revealed information that could have been relevant in deciding the case.

D. The right to a fair hearing by an independent and impartial court established by law

The right to a fair hearing by an independent and impartial court established by law means that all parties before the court have to be subjected to the same standards of hearing. This will enable everyone before a court to have a fair hearing, without any discrimination. Nevertheless, it should be noted that the true test of fair hearing in a given case is whether from the observation of a reasonable person present at the trial, justice has been done.[84]

In order to clarify the above right, provided for under Article 7(1)(d) of the African Charter, the African Commission adopted 'Resolution on the Respect For and Strengthening of the Independence of the Judiciary'.[85] In addition, most jurisdictions in Africa have constitutional provisions that guarantee anyone charged with a criminal offence, the right to a fair hearing by an independent and impartial court established by law.[86]

However, with regard to military and other special tribunals, it is questionable whether these tribunals can be independent and impartial. The UN Human Rights Committee has noted that the existence of military and special courts that try civilians in many countries could present problems as far as the equitable, impartial and independent administration of justice is concerned.[87] Further, the African Commission's principles and guidelines provides that if such tribunals do not use the duly established procedure of the legal process, they shall not be created to displace the jurisdiction of the ordinary judicial bodies.[88]

[83] *Amnesty International Report* (Amnesty International Secretariat London 2003) 258.

[84] M Owoade 'Some aspects of human rights and the administration of criminal justice in Nigeria' in M Bassiouni and Z Motala (n 38) 181.

[85] Adopted at its Nineteenth Session held in Ouagadougou, Burkina Faso, 26 Mar–4 Apr 1996 *Ninth Annual Activity Report: 1995–1996* Annex V, 5; reproduced in Heyns (n 10) 558.

[86] eg Art 4 of the Constitution of Burkina Faso 2000, Art 42(2)(f)(i) of the Constitution of Nigeria 1999, Art 19 of the Constitution of Togo 1992, and Art 18(2) of the Constitution of Zimbabwe 2000.

[87] General Comment No 13 (n 41) para 4. The Committee's doubt about the impartiality and independence of these courts stems from the fact that quite often, the reason for their establishment is to enable exceptional procedures to be applied that do not comply with normal standards of justice.

[88] Guideline A(4)(e).

Some African States have empowered special or military courts to pass death sentences without affording full fair trial safeguards. In Sudan, Tunisia, Egypt, and Eritrea, for example, as discussed below, capital trials have taken place before special courts that could not be seen as competent, independent or impartial, as the presence of military judges or untrained judges in such courts raises doubts regarding their independence, competence, and impartiality.

Special Criminal Courts in the Darfur region, Sudan, continue to impose death sentences after summary trials that failed to meet fair trial standards.[89] The fact that the Special Courts were created by presidential decree raises questions regarding their independence. This raises questions regarding the Sudanese Government's commitment to respecting its duties under Article 26 of the African Charter, which gives state parties the duty to guarantee the independence of courts. As discussed above, the African Commission in *Amnesty International and Others v Sudan*, has found such tribunals to be in violation of Article 7(1)(d), first, by reason of their composition, and second, on the basis that the Government's dismissal of judges opposed to the formation of these courts deprives courts of the personnel qualified to ensure that they operate impartially, thus denying individuals the right to have their case heard by such a body.[90] Similarly, as discussed above, the African Commission has found the establishment of military courts and special tribunals in Nigeria, to be in violation of Article 7(1)(d) of the African Charter due to their composition.[91]

Furthermore, capital trials take place in Egypt before exceptional courts such as state security courts, established under emergency legislation, in which trial procedures fall short of international and regional fair trial standards.[92] For example, it is not possible for defendants before such courts to have a fair trial as they do not have the right to a full review before a higher tribunal, amounting to a violation of Article 14(5) of the ICCPR, which Egypt has ratified. The fact that these courts are established by emergency decree casts doubts on their independence. The Human Rights Committee has noted that the independence of military and state security courts in Egypt is not guaranteed.[93]

[89] Amnesty International (n 56). It should be noted that the imposition of the death sentences by the Special Courts is a violation of Art 4 of the African Charter, especially if they are, or were, subsequently executed.

[90] *Amnesty International and Others v Sudan* (n 27) paras 68–9.

[91] For further discussion of this right and how it has been addressed by the African Commission and the Inter-American Commission, see R Barnidge 'The African Commission on Human and Peoples' Rights and the Inter-American Commission on Human Rights: Addressing the right to an impartial hearing on detention and trial within a reasonable time and the presumption of innocence' (2004) 4 AHRLJ 108.

[92] Amnesty International (n 56).

[93] Concluding observations of the Human Rights Committee on the third and fourth periodic reports of Egypt submitted under Art 40 of the ICCPR, UN Doc CCPR/CO/76/EGY (28 Nov 2002) para 16(b). Also in Eritrea, trials before Special Courts are unfair, with the accused having

Generally, the independence of the judiciary is questionable in some African countries. For example, the Human Rights Committee has expressed concern at the judiciary's lack of independence in the Republic of Congo, due to first, the lack of any independent mechanism responsible for the recruitment and discipline of judges, and second, the many pressures and influences, including those of the executive branch, to which judges are subjected.[94] The Committee found this to be in violation of Article 14(1) of the ICCPR and recommended that the government take appropriate steps to ensure the independence of the judiciary, in particular, by amending the rules concerning the composition and operation of the Supreme Council of Justice and its effective establishment.[95] The Committee has also expressed concern over the independence of the judiciary in Sudan, stating that

> the Committee is concerned that in appearance as well as in fact the judiciary is not truly independent, that many judges have not been selected primarily on the basis of their legal qualifications, that judges can be subject to pressure through supervisory authority dominated by the Government. . . .[96]

Thus, if the independence or impartiality of the judiciary is not guaranteed, it is very unlikely that defendants would receive a fair trial. As a result, it is imperative that retentionist African States consider abolishing the death penalty, as it cannot be guaranteed that defendants facing such serious and irreversible punishment (the death penalty) would receive a fair trial.

E. The right to be present at the trial

Every accused person has the right to be present at his or her trial. Although the African Charter makes no reference to this right, Guideline N(6)(c) of the African Commission's principles and guidelines provides that in criminal proceedings, the accused has the right to be tried in his or her presence. In most African States, for example in Egypt, Gabon, and Sudan, there is provision for an accused to be present at the trial.[97] Generally, an accused person can be removed from the courtroom during trial, due to misconduct on the part

no right to defence counsel. It is also unlikely that such special courts could be independent, competent, and impartial due to the presence of military judges, which is exacerbated by the fact that they have little or no legal training (see *Amnesty International Report* (2003) 100).

[94] Concluding observations of the Human Rights Committee on the second periodic report of Congo submitted under Art 40 of the ICCPR, UN Doc CCPR/C/79/Add 118 (27 Mar 2000) para 14.

[95] As above.

[96] Concluding observations of the Human Rights Committee on the second periodic report of Sudan submitted under Art 40 of the ICCPR, UN Doc CCPR/C/79/Add 85 (19 Nov 1997) para 21.

[97] Combined third and fourth periodic reports of Egypt submitted under Art 40 of the ICCPR, UN Doc CCPR/C/EGY/2001/3 (15 Apr 2002) para 404(d); Second periodic report of Gabon submitted under Art 40 of the ICCPR, UN Doc CCPR/C/128/Add 1 (14 June 1999) para 32, hereinafter referred to as second periodic report of Gabon; and second periodic report of Sudan submitted under Art 40 of the ICCPR, UN Doc CCPR/C/75/Add 2 (13 Mar 1997) para 115(h).

of the accused, and the court can proceed with the trial in his or her absence.[98] An accused person may, however, voluntarily waive the right to be present at his or her hearing.[99]

Although an accused person may not be tried in absentia,[100] the UN Human Rights Committee has noted that proceedings in absentia are in some circumstances (for instance, when the accused person, although informed of the proceedings sufficiently in advance, declines to exercise his or her right to be present) permissible in the interest of proper administration of justice.[101] Where an accused person does not waive this right, any trial in absentia would not only be a violation of the right to be tried in his or her presence, but also a violation of the right to have adequate time for the preparation of his or her defence, the right to legal representation, and the right to examine witnesses. Accordingly, in *Mbenge v Zaïre*, where no steps were taken to inform the accused before hand of the proceedings against him as required under Article 14(3)(a) of the ICCPR, the Human Rights Committee held:

> Judgment in absentia requires that, notwithstanding the absence of the accused, all due notification has to be made to inform him of the date and place of his trial and to request his attendance. Otherwise, the accused, in particular, is not given adequate time and facilities for the preparation of his defence (art. 14 (3) (b)), cannot defend himself through legal assistance of his own choosing (art. 14 (3) (d)) nor does he have the opportunity to examine, or have examined, the witnesses against him and to obtain the attendance and examination of witnesses on his behalf (art. 14 (3) (e)) . . . In the view of the Committee, therefore, the Sate party has not respected D. Monguya Mbenge's rights under article 14 (3) (a), (b), (d) and (e) of the Covenant.[102]

F. The right to legal assistance and proper defence

The right to legal assistance (representation) and proper defence is central to the realization of a fair trial; it is a fundamental pillar of the administration of justice.[103] It guarantees an accused person three rights: to defend himself or herself in person, to defend themselves through legal assistance of their choice, and on certain conditions, to be given free legal assistance. Generally, free legal assistance is dependent on the interest of justice and insufficient means to procure the services of counsel. However, the term 'interest of justice' is vague and there are no generally accepted established criteria to determine if it is in the interest of justice that an accused person be given legal aid; thus, leaving the right to legal assistance open to abuse.

[98] eg this is the case in Kenya (W Mutunga *The Rights of an Arrested and an Accused Person* (OUP Press Nairobi 1990) 57).
[99] Guideline N(6)(c)(3), African Commission's principles and guidelines.
[100] Guideline N(6)(c)(2), African Commission's principles and guidelines.
[101] *Mbenge v Zaïre* (n 80) para 14.1.
[102] ibid, paras 14.1–14.2.
[103] M Finkelstein *The Right to Counsel* (Butterworths Toronto 1988) 1-1.

The constitutions of some African States explicitly provide that an accused person be provided with legal representation at State or public expense if he or she cannot afford one. For example, Article 20(5) of the Constitution of Ethiopia 1995 provides that if an accused cannot afford legal counsel and miscarriage of justice will result, the accused has to be provided with legal representation at the expense of the State.[104] Article 24(3)(d) of the Constitution of The Gambia 2001 is more specific as it states that if an accused is charged with a capital offence, the accused shall be entitled to legal representation at the expense of the State.[105]

In addition, the UN Human Rights Committee has stated that in capital trials 'unavailability of legal aid amounts to a violation of Article 6 *juncto* Article 14 of the Covenant'.[106] Unavailability of legal aid will also amount to a violation of Article 7(1)(c) of the African Charter. However, as seen below, capital trials have been conducted in some African States in which the accused had no legal representation, was refused one, or was provided with inadequate defence counsel.

It is undisputable that capital trials are very expensive and that most people charged with capital offences cannot afford the fees of experienced counsel. As a result, they are assigned inexperienced counsel or article clerks who are not well versed with the issues in capital trials. Without effective representation, an accused can hardly be said to have had a fair trial.[107] For example, in 2003 in Sudan, 24 people were sentenced to death by a Special Court, in which they were tried without adequate legal representation.[108] This constitutes a violation of Articles 6 and 14 of the ICCPR and Article 7(1)(c) of the African Charter.

Furthermore, the right of an accused person to legal assistance entitles the accused to proper defence. The African Commission's principles and guidelines provide that the lawyer appointed shall be qualified to represent and defend the accused and shall have the necessary training and experience corresponding to the nature and seriousness of the matter.[109] The UN Special Rapporteur on extrajudicial, summary or arbitrary executions has reiterated

[104] See also, Art 42 (2)(f)(v) of the Constitution of Malawi 2001.

[105] Upon ratification of the ICCPR, The Gambia entered a reservation in respect of Art 14(3)(d) to the effect that 'for financial reasons free legal assistance for accused persons is limited in our constitution to persons charged with capital offences only' (Heyns (n 10) 53. Art 28(3)(e) of the Constitution of Uganda 1995 has a similar provision with regard to capital offences.

[106] Concluding observations of the Human Rights Committee on the second periodic report of Jamaica submitted under Art 40 of the ICCPR, UN Doc CCPR/C/79/Add 83 (19 Nov 1997) para 14.

[107] J Hatchard and S Coldham 'Commonwealth Africa' in P Hodgkinson and A Rutherford (eds) *Capital Punishment: Global Issues and Prospects* (Waterside Press Winchester 1996) 164.

[108] Amnesty International 'Sudan: 24 sentenced to death after unfair trial' AI Index: AFR 54/027/2003 (29 Apr 2003). Also, in Nigeria, a *Shari'a* court in Bauchi sentenced Jibrin Babaji to death by stoning on 14 Sept 2003 after a trial in which he was not represented by a lawyer (*Amnesty International Report* (Amnesty International Secretariat London 2004) 68).

[109] Guideline H(e)(1) and (2), African Commission's principles and guidelines.

that 'all defendants facing the imposition of capital punishment have to benefit from the services of a competent defence counsel at every stage of the proceedings'.[110] However, in some African States like Botswana and Malawi, as seen below, inexperienced lawyers have defended capital offenders.

In Botswana, for example, Kobedi, a South African, was sentenced to death and executed in July 2003 after a trial that did not meet the standards for a fair trial.[111] Kobedi was represented, in his original hearing, by a lawyer who was unfamiliar with trying death penalty cases, and who failed to raise important legal and factual issues on his behalf. Due to the fact that his lawyer did not have the necessary training and experience corresponding to his case, Kobedi could, therefore, not be said to have benefited from the services of a competent defence counsel at every stage of the proceedings as required under international human rights law.

Likewise, in Malawi, some defence lawyers are inexperienced, and lack the necessary resources to enable them prepare their cases. By 2002 the Malawi Legal Aid Department had seven lawyers, including three new graduates with no experience in handling capital cases.[112] The lawyers lack up to date law books, have problems with transport, and have neither the time nor budget for tracing and interviewing witnesses.[113] These lawyers cannot be said to be in a position to offer proper defence.

In addition, the remuneration given to some defence lawyers affects their ability and commitment to effectively defend an accused person, thus not fully affording an accused person the right to legal assistance and proper defence. In *Republic v Mbushuu and Another*, it was stated that most poor persons in Tanzania do not obtain good legal representation, as lawyers on dock briefs who are paid very little defend them. As a result of such poor remuneration, the defence counsel may not exert enough effort in such a case.[114] Thus, it is likely that most poor persons in Tanzania charged with a capital offence will get the death sentence. In such cases, the defendants' right to legal assistance and proper defence is violated. Similarly, due to resource constraints in Botswana, the amount paid to state-funded lawyers is minimal, and often, the result is that lawyers who lack the skills, resources and commitment to handle such serious matters handle most *pro deo* cases.[115]

[110] Report by the Special Rapporteur on extrajudicial, summary or arbitrary executions, UN Doc E/CN.4/1997/60 (24 Dec 1996) para 81.

[111] Hands Off Cain *The Death Penalty Worldwide: 2004 Report* (Quaderni Radicali Rome 2004) 37–8.

[112] 'The quality of justice: Trial observations in Malawi' <http://www.penalreform.org/english/dp_malawi.htm>.

[113] ibid.

[114] *Republic v Mbushuu and Another* (1994) 2 LRC 349, 353.

[115] 'Death penalty in Botswana' <http://www.ditshwanelo.org.bw>.

G. The right to appeal to a higher judicial body

An accused person has the right to appeal against his or her conviction or sentence or both. The right to appeal is provided for in Article 7(1)(a) of the African Charter and Article 14(5) of the ICCPR. ECOSOC safeguard No 6 requires that anyone sentenced to death shall have the right to appeal to a court of higher jurisdiction, and steps should be taken to ensure that such appeals become mandatory. This right is also provided for in the national constitutions of most African States.[116] The right to appeal or review to a higher court at the minimum implies the opportunity to have adequate re-appraisal of every case and an informed decision on it.[117] Of relevance in deciding whether denial of the right to appeal constitutes a violation of Article 7(1)(a) of the African Charter, is the severity of the sentence.[118] Thus, denial of the right to appeal in capital trials will amount to a violation of the above provision due to the severity of the death sentence.

Despite the above provisions, in some African States, there is no automatic right of appeal, while in others, there is no provision in some cases for a formal appeal with sentences merely being confirmed or otherwise by a higher body.[119] As noted above, the African Commission has found the procedure in special tribunals in Nigeria, where sentences are subject to confirmation or disallowance by the governor of a state, with no provision for judicial appeal against the decisions of the tribunals or where courts are prohibited from reviewing any aspect of the operation of such tribunals, to constitute a violation of the African Charter.[120] From the Commission's decision, it is clear that the governor of a state is not a higher judicial body or 'competent national organ' (as used in the African Charter). Thus, subjecting sentences to confirmation by such a body or others of similar character cannot be seen as a genuine appeal procedure.

The right to appeal is denied to those convicted of capital offences in other African States. Those who face trial in Egypt before exceptional courts, such as State Security Courts, established under emergency legislation do not have the right to a full review of their sentence before a higher tribunal.[121] In Sierra Leone, people have been tried, convicted and executed after being denied the right to appeal to a higher tribunal, which the African Commission has found to be in breach of Article 7(1)(a) of the African Charter.[122] For instance, in

[116] See eg Art 17(7) of the Constitution of Eritrea 1997, Art 20(6) of the Constitution of Ethiopia 1995, and Art 42(2)(f)(VIII) of the Constitution of Malawi 2001.

[117] *S v Ntuli* (1996) 1 BCLR 141.

[118] *Constitutional Rights Project (in respect of Akamu and Others) v Nigeria* (n 21) para 13.

[119] Hatchard and Coldham (n 107) 168.

[120] *Constitutional Rights Project (in respect of Akamu and Others) v Nigeria* (n 21) para 13; and *Constitutional Rights Project (in respect of Lekwot and Others) v Nigeria* (n 19) para 11.

[121] Amnesty International (n 56).

[122] Communication 223/98, *14th Annual Activity Report: 2000–2001*; (2000) AHRLR 293 (ACHPR 2000) para 20.

Forum of Conscience v Sierra Leone, the execution of 24 soldiers by a Court Martial without the right to appeal was found to be in violation of Article 7(1)(a) of the African Charter, which provides for the right to appeal.[123] Generally, the Commission's decisions emphasize that the right to appeal must be respected in cases involving serious offences.

Furthermore, the death sentence cannot be carried out until the expiration of the time for appeal in some African States, for example, Sierra Leone.[124] In others, despite the existence of a provision for the right to appeal, those convicted of capital offences have been executed without given adequate time to appeal, or despite the fact that they were still trying to appeal, or their appeals were still pending. The above amounts to a violation of the right to appeal. In *Mansaraj and Others v Sierra Leone*,[125] the Human Rights Committee found a violation of Article 14(5) of the ICCPR because the complainants did not have a right to appeal the conviction by a court martial, *a fortiori* in a capital case. ECOSOC safeguard No 8 prohibits execution where an appeal against the death sentence is pending or an appeal for pardon or commutation of sentence is pending. Yet, in Chad, for example, four men sentenced to death on 25 October 2003 after a three-day trial, were executed while the defence counsel was trying to appeal the sentence.[126] This does not only amount to a denial of the right to appeal, but also a violation of the right to a fair trial.

H. The right to seek pardon or commutation

Pardon (clemency) or commutation is the last hope for a prisoner under sentence of death. It is important in that it can be used to mitigate the harshness of punishment, correct possible errors in the trial or to compensate for the rigidity of the criminal law by giving consideration to factors relevant to an individual case for which the law makes no allowance.

In most States, pardon or commutation is exercised by the chief executive (the president) of the country in which the death sentence was imposed. In some States, other bodies could be empowered to exercise pardon or commutation. In Zimbabwe, in addition to the president having the power to pardon convicted persons or exercise the prerogative of mercy and commute a death sentence, parliament is empowered to consider a petition for pardon submitted to it by an offender sentenced to death.[127] In Libya, general amnesties are

[123] ibid. See also, *International Pen and Others (on behalf of Saro-Wiwa) v Nigeria* (n 24) para 93.

[124] Report of the national coordinator of Sierra Leone (n 39).

[125] Communications 839/1998, 840/1998, and 841/1998, UN Doc CCPR/C/72/D/839/1998 (30 July 2001) para 5.6.

[126] 'Chad: First executions by firing squad in more than a decade' <http://www.irinnews.org/report.asp?ReportID=37687&SelectRegion=West_Africa&SelectCountry=CHAD>.

[127] Initial report of Zimbabwe submitted under Art 40 of the ICCPR, UN Doc CCPR/C/74/Add 3 (29 Sept 199), paras 68–70.

proclaimed by the 'General People's Congress'.[128] The president or other body in charge acts on its own initiative or on the presentation of a petition by the convicted person to be considered for pardon or clemency. Through the exercise of clemency, a death sentence can be set aside, which usually takes the form of a decision to commute the sentence to a lesser punishment.

The right to seek pardon or commutation is guaranteed under Article 6(4) of the ICCPR and ECOSOC safeguard No 7. Furthermore, the UN ECOSOC has recommended that UN Member States provide for 'mandatory appeals or review with provisions for clemency or pardon in all cases of capital offences'.[129] This right is also provided for in national constitutions and laws of African States. In Congo, a person sentenced to death may not be executed unless the president has refused to grant a pardon.[130] In Tanzania, a person sentenced to death can appeal to the president to commute the sentence under Section 325(3) of the Criminal Procedures Act of 1985. The president relies on the judgment and notes of evidence taken during the trial to arrive at a decision.[131] Also, Article 121(4) of the Constitution of Uganda 1995, dealing with the prerogative of mercy, gives the president the power, on the advise of the Advisory Committee on the prerogative of mercy, to grant any person convicted of an offence a pardon either free or subject to lawful conditions.[132] The fact that the Attorney General is part of this Committee, and that the president partly controls the process by appointing the six prominent Ugandans raises a lot of concerns.

The power to grant pardon or commutation is discretionary and the chief executive is not obliged to follow the recommendations of the Advisory Committee or the trial judge.[133] The extent to which this discretion is exercised is questionable. Further, generally, the clemency process varies from country to country. Some apply a more generous standard while others exercise clemency or pardon on very limited grounds. In some African States, for example in Zambia, the president controls the whole process. He appoints

[128] Third periodic report of Libya submitted under Art 40 of the ICCPR, UN Doc CCPR/C/102/Add 1 (15 Oct 1997) para 129.

[129] ECOSOC Res 1989/64, 24 May 1989, Implementation of the Safeguards Guaranteeing Protection of the Rights of Those Facing the Death Penalty, para 1(b).

[130] Second periodic report of Congo submitted under Art 40 of the ICCPR, UN Doc CCPR/C/63/Add 5 (5 May 1997) para 19.

[131] Third periodic report of Tanzania submitted under Art 40 of the ICCPR, UN Doc CCPR/C/83/Add 2 (7 Oct 1997) para 49.

[132] The only successful appeal during the past five years is that of Nassur, who had been on death row for 20 years, and was pardoned by the president in 2001. Initial report of Uganda (n 57) para 139–40.

[133] It should be noted that pardons are not only an executive issue, as it can be granted by way of renouncing retribution or pardon from the victim or the victim's family in countries that apply Islamic law. In Libya, renunciation of the right to retribution in return for payment of blood money or for any other reason is equivalent to commutation of the death penalty (Third periodic report of Libya (n 128) para 129. In Sudan, the death penalty can be commuted with pardon of the victim or the victim's relative, and such pardon cannot be retracted from if made expressly by consent (s 38(1) of the Penal Code of Sudan 1991).

members of the Advisory Committee on the prerogative of mercy, is entitled to preside at its meetings and determine the procedure.[134] In Ghana, Lesotho, Uganda, and Zimbabwe, the president does not have total control over the process, as he acts on the advice of the Advisory Committee.[135] Also in Togo, the granting of pardon by the president is exercised in the light of an opinion given to him by the Supreme Judicial Council.[136]

Respect for the right to pardon or clemency ensures that any possible errors in the trial are corrected, thus, reducing the risk of executing the innocent. However, in practice, there is very little information as to the extent to which the prerogative is exercised, since the process is shrouded in secrecy. Reports prepared are confidential in, for example, Zimbabwe, Zambia and other countries in southern Africa.[137] Such secrecy allows for arbitrariness in the exercise of clemency and disparity in the granting of pardon or clemency. It is possible that innocent persons that are convicted and sentenced to death may not be able to exercise this right to correct such wrong conviction due to the arbitrariness and disparity in the whole process. There is, therefore, the need for the clemency process to be more accountable.

VI. CONCLUSION

Fair trial rights have, observably, been provided for at the international and national levels. Their imperative nature has been emphasized by various human rights bodies—the UN Human Rights Committee, the European Court, the Inter-American Commission and Court, and the African Commission. The above bodies have also adopted a similar approach with regard to the relation between fair trial rights and the right to life, finding the imposition of the death penalty after an unfair trial to constitute a violation of the right to life.

Considering the irreversible nature of the death penalty, it is of grave concern that the death penalty is continuously being used without respect for fair trial rights, without any guarantee that judicial error or arbitrariness in its imposition can be eliminated. There have been reports of persons from countries in Africa, for example, Malawi, being released from prison, sometimes after many years in custody, on the grounds of their innocence.[138] Also, persons have been sentenced to death in Uganda and released after many years on grounds of their innocence. For example, Mpagi was on death row for 19 years in Luzira Maximum Security Prison for murder. It later turned out that the man he was accused of murdering was alive. Mpagi said court officials

[134] Hatchard and Coldham (n 107) 169. Also in Kenya and Tanzania.

[135] ibid 169. See also Initial report of Zimbabwe (n 127) para 68–71.

[136] Third periodic report of Togo submitted under Art 40 of the ICCPR, UN Doc CCPR/C/TGO/2001/3 (5 July 2001) para 110.

[137] Hatchard and Coldham (n 107) 169.

[138] R Hood *The Death Penalty: A worldwide perspective* (OUP New York 2002) 132.

refused to try him in the district where the murder was alleged to have been committed. His conviction was the result of an irresponsible justice system and indifferent investigators.[139]

Notwithstanding, due to the imperfections inherent in criminal trials, it is difficult or almost certainly not possible to design a system that avoids arbitrariness, judicial error and delays in carrying out the death sentence. These imperfections include the lack of rights consciousness among lawyers, the public at large and, in some instances, in the judiciary and the state organs, inadequate training of police officers, lawyers and judges, lack of resources to carry out proper and swift investigations, understaffed and under funded courts, and failure of the legal system as a whole. In *S v Makwanyane*, Justice Chaskalson acknowledged the fact that such arbitrariness cannot be eliminated completely, as it is difficult or almost certainly not possible to design a system that avoids arbitrariness and delays in carrying out the sentence.[140]

Therefore, African States have to take steps to remedy shortcomings in the administration of justice. Judges and lawyers have to be given effective legal training, so that they can apply and use fair trial standards appropriately. The Human Rights Committee, noting that the provisions of the ICCPR have not be invoked in any case before the Constitutional Court or ordinary courts in Togo, recommended that training be provided for judges, lawyers and court officers concerning the content of the ICCPR and other human rights instruments.[141] Availability of resources for the conduction of investigations will help prevent delays in capital trials. It is also important that national fair trial standards that are not in conformity with international standards be revised so as to ensure such conformity. Overall, there is the need for empirical research to establish not only the nature and magnitude of the problems but, more importantly, to find solutions based on a thorough research leading to a political decision on the abolition of the death penalty.

139 'Foes of death penalty making gradual gains in Africa' *The New York Times* (New York 20 Oct 2004).

140 *Makwanyane* 1995 (3) SA 391 (CC) paras 54–5.

141 Concluding observations of the Human Rights Committee on the third periodic report of Togo submitted under Art 40 of the ICCPR, UN Doc CCPR/CO/76/TGO (28 Nov 2002) para 7.

[5]

The right to life and abolition of the death penalty in the Council of Europe

Jon Yorke*

LT Council of Europe; Death penalty; Right to life

This article investigates the prima facie paradox of the endorsement of the death penalty in Art.2(1) of the European Convention on Human Rights, with the "abolition" of the punishment provided by Protocol No.6 and Protocol No.13. It will analyse the evolution of the Council of Europe's abolitionist discourse which led to this juxtaposition, and identify whether there are unified or heterogeneous approaches to the punishment by the Committee of Ministers, the Parliamentary Assembly, and the judicial organs of the Commission and Court. What emerges is a conflict between the radical expansion of the boundaries of human rights by the Assembly, with the Committee's demonstration that the shadow of state sovereignty constantly attempts to thwart progress. Consequently, the Court has bowed to the need for Member State acceptance of provisions for amendment of Art.2(1) and has not applied any purposive application of the "living instrument" doctrine. However, the gradual solidification of the Council's abolitionist position has produced the possibility of legislative abolition through the Protocols, but the text of Art.2(1) remains. So is the death penalty abolished or not? As contemporary practice within Member States affirms that it is, is textual amendment now a moot issue?

Introduction

Article 2(1) of the European Convention on Human Rights 1953 (hereinafter "Convention") states:

> "Everyone's right to life shall be protected by law. No one shall be deprived of his life intentionally save in the execution of a sentence of a court following his conviction of a crime for which his penalty is provided by law."[1]

Although, as A.H. Robertson noted, the text was "careful to protect the legality of capital punishment",[2] from the early life of the Council of Europe there were stalwart parliamentarians who would not allow the human rights organisation to completely

* Dr Jon Yorke, Visiting Fellow in Law, School of Law, University of Birmingham; Lecturer in Law, School of Law, University of Surrey. Email: j.yorke@surrey.ac.uk. I would like to thank Professor Panos Koutrakos, and the two anonymous referees, for their constructive comments. All errors remain my own.

[1] Convention for the Protection of Human Rights and Fundamental Freedoms CETS No.5 (1953).

[2] A.H. Robertson, "The Contribution of the Council of Europe to the Development of International Law" (1965) 59 Am. Soc'y Int'l L. Proc. 201, 205.

reject the anti-death penalty sentiments which had emerged from the Enlightenment.[3] Over the proceeding 30 years, the Council held numerous debates and gradually the arguments against the punishment solidified and instruments were adopted for restriction and abolition. The first regional curtailment of the punishment occurred in 1983, when Art.1 of Protocol No.6 to the Convention provides for the removal of the death penalty in times of peace, but Art.2 concedes that states may, "make provision in its law for the death penalty in respect of acts committed in time of war or of imminent threat of war".[4] More debates followed as the wartime exception proved problematical and so the abolitionist discourse became more complex with techniques employed to encourage regional abolitionism which would be extended to new Member States from Central and Eastern European countries post-1994. Then in 2002, Protocol No.13 to the Convention was adopted and Art.1 decrees that in all circumstances, "[t]he death penalty shall be abolished. No one shall be condemned to such penalty or executed."[5]

With such clear wording it would appear that the denunciation of the punishment is now incontrovertible. However the problem of the punishment has not completely gone away, as although both Protocols provide for "abolition", neither specifically amend the text of Convention Art.2(1). Thus the question remains as to whether the resultant juxtaposition furnishes a coherent discourse on abolition and the right to life, and whether a satisfactory human rights position can be identified. If it can be, the amendment of Art.2(1) is not of immediate necessity. But if an ambiguity, or ambivalence, is present then amendment should still be viewed as an exigent human rights quest. The analysis which follows questions whether the Council of Europe has adequately resolved the interpretive difficulties.

The dialogue between the Parliamentary Assembly and the Committee of Ministers

To isolate the right to life and attempt to provide an interpretation of what it means is no easy task. James Griffin has observed that this right does not have a "clear boundary" because what "starts off as the least problematic of rights becomes, on reflection, distinctly problematic",[6] and Torkel Opsahl affirmed:

> "Article 2 of the Convention and the context in which it operates will show that what at first seemed simple may have problematic points."[7]

[3] The Enlightenment humanist Cesare Beccaria, and his principled position against the sovereign possessing a "right" of the death penalty, has been referred to during the debates on the punishment within the Council of Europe. For example see, M. Ancel, *The Death Penalty in European Countries* (Strasbourg: Council of Europe Press, 1962), p.3; *Report on the abolition of capital punishment* (Doc 4509, 2nd and 3rd sittings, April 22, 1980), p.2.

[4] Protocol No.6 to the Convention for the protection of human rights and fundamental freedoms concerning the abolition of the death penalty, Strasbourg, April 28, 1983.

[5] Protocol No.13 to the Convention for the protection of human rights and fundamental freedoms concerning the abolition of the death penalty in all circumstances, Vilnius, May 3, 2002.

[6] J. Griffin, *On Human Rights* (Oxford: Oxford University Press, 2008), p.213. For an analysis of Griffin's contribution to the human rights discourse, see, B. Bowring, *The Degradation of the International Legal Order? The Rehabilitation of Law and the Possibility of Politics* (Abington: Routledge-Cavendish, 2008), pp.115–116.

[7] T. Opsahl, "The Right to Life" in R. St. J. Macdonald et al. (eds), *The European System for the Protection of Human Rights* (Netherlands: Kluwer Academic Publishers, 1993), p.207.

To investigate the problem is to firstly engage with the complicated past-half century dialogue between the Parliamentary Assembly and the Committee of Ministers. Secondly, it is necessary to analyse the European Commission of Human Rights and European Court of Human Rights' interpretation of the instruments which have emerged from this dialogue. Several questions arise which require analysis including: what was the role of each Council organ in the initial evolution of the abolitionist discourse? How has the Council approached the question of the amendment of Art.2(1)? Are all the organs unified or are there differences of opinion on the appropriate way to further the abolitionist agenda?

1950–1982: Uncertainties and frictions

In reviewing the early work of the Council of Europe, Frank Dowrick stated that the various, "organs of the Council of Europe [were] very much alive to the need to revise and extend the basic doctrine of human rights".[8] From its early stage, there were those within the Council who displayed a firm dissatisfaction that the "basic doctrine" preserved the death penalty within Convention Art.2(1), and in 1958 various subordinate committees were created to investigate the problematical human rights issues of the time. One of these committees was the European Committee on Crime Problems which in turn established sub-committees including the Sub-Committee on the Death Penalty.[9] The Sub-Committee agreed that the death penalty was a problem,[10] and so in 1961 Marc Ancel led a study compiling information on Member State implementation or rejection of the punishment. A quantitative analysis was provided of Member State practices focusing upon judicial and administrative practice, sociological and criminological factors, proposed legislative reform and crime policy. Ancel did not seek to extend the investigations to formulate a human rights perspective. He stated that the purpose was to focus on the implementation of criminal law, and other aspects of the punishment were, "outside the scope of the study".[11] As a result the early initiatives did not demonstrate how human rights arguments could be formulated to tackle the punishment, and so by 1966, only four years after the publication of the Ancel report, the Committee decided to cease the investigations.[12]

Then in 1973, Astrid Bergegren, a Swedish parliamentarian, presented a Motion for a resolution on the abolition of capital punishment.[13] This first specific proposition

[8] F.E. Dowrick, "Juristic Activity in the Council of Europe: 25th Year" (1974) 23(3) I.C.L.Q. 610, 616.

[9] Ancel, *The Death Penalty in European Countries*, 1962, p.3. Hans Christian Krüger stated, "barely four years after the entry into force of the Convention, there was a move at expert level of the Council of Europe to study the problem of capital punishment in Europe": Krüger, "Protocol No.6 to the European Convention on Human Rights" in Council of Europe, *Death Penalty—Beyond Abolition* (Strasbourg: Council of Europe Publishing, 2004), p.87. See also, M. Ancel, "The Problem of the Death Penalty" in T. Sellin, (ed.), *Capital Punishment* (New York: Harper and Row, 1967).

[10] A.H. Robertson, "The Legal Work of the Council of Europe" (1961) 1 I.C.L.Q. 143, 159–160; Hans Christian Krüger also noted that the death penalty was a "problem"; see, "Protocol No. 6 to the European Convention on Human Rights" in Council of Europe, *Death Penalty*, 2004, pp.87–88.

[11] Ancel, *The Death Penalty in European Countries*, 1962, p.3.

[12] See, W.A. Schabas, *The Abolition of the Death Penalty in International Law*, 3rd edn (Cambridge: Cambridge University Press, 2002), p.280.

[13] Committee on Legal Affairs, Motion for a resolution on the abolition of capital punishment (8th Sitting, May 18, 1973), Doc.3297.

calling for the Parliamentary Assembly to renounce the death penalty relied upon theories of utilitarianism and humanism, and stated, inter alia, that capital punishment is irrevocable,[14] that the punishment does not possess any special deterrent quality,[15] that the use of the punishment for retribution is no longer representative of a civilised society,[16] and consequently, called for abolition in all Member States and for the Assembly to develop initiatives to achieve this penological change.[17] However, Bergegren's motion did not find favour within the Assembly and it was sent back to the Committee on Legal Affairs where it was stalled. Then, a newly appointed rapporteur, Bertil Lidgard, reignited the debates and presented a report. After lengthy discussions at several meetings in January 1975, the Committee on Legal Affairs evaded the issue when it decided "not to submit the report to the Parliamentary Assembly",[18] but some parliamentarians refused to back-down and in April 1975, the rapporteur presented an unpublished report identifying that the,

> "debate on the death penalty ought [to be carried on]. Attention should be drawn to various new developments as well as certain familiar arguments which militate strongly in favour of the abolition cause".[19]

This stalwart effort was stonewalled by the Committee on Legal Affairs in 1976, and it stated that the question of the death penalty should be "deferred".[20] So Lidgard resigned as rapporteur.[21]

However, this was not the end. In 1978 the European Ministers of Justice considered the issue at their Conference held in Copenhagen,[22] and the Austrian Minister of Justice, Christian Broda, championed Resolution No.4 which recommended that the Committee of Ministers, "refer questions concerning the death penalty to the appropriate Council of Europe bodies for study as part of the Council's work programme".[23] After further examination, the Ministers of Justice reiterated their position and were more pointed declaring, "Article 2 of the European Convention on Human Rights does not adequately reflect the situation actually attained with regard to the death penalty in Europe". They suggested that the Parliamentary Assembly, "study the possibilities for the elaboration of new and appropriate European standards concerning abolition of the death penalty".[24]

[14] Committee on Legal Affairs, Motion for a resolution on the abolition of capital punishment, point 2.

[15] Committee on Legal Affairs, Motion for a resolution on the abolition of capital punishment, point 3.

[16] Committee on Legal Affairs, Motion for a resolution on the abolition of capital punishment, point 4.

[17] Committee on Legal Affairs, Motion for a resolution on the abolition of capital punishment, points 8–9.

[18] Unpublished report submitted to the Committee on Legal Affairs in 1975, cited in *Report on the abolition of capital punishment* (2nd and 3rd sittings, April 22, 1980), Doc.4509, p.2.

[19] Unpublished report submitted to the Committee on Legal Affairs in 1975, cited in *Report on the abolition of capital punishment*, p.3.

[20] Unpublished report submitted to the Committee on Legal Affairs in 1975, cited in *Report on the abolition of capital punishment*, p.3. See also, Parliamentary Assembly, *Official Report of Debates* (32nd Ordinary Session, "Abolition of capital punishment, Debate on the report of the Committee on Legal Affairs", 2nd and 3nd Sittings, April 22, 1980), Doc.4509 and amendments, address during debate by Mr Stoffelen, p.60.

[21] During the debates, Mr Grieve of the United Kingdom revealed the rapporteur's emotion when he described Bertil Lidgard as "sorrowful" after the Committee on Legal Affairs voted against the report: Parliamentary Assembly, *Official Report of Debates*, Doc.4509 and amendments, p.86.

[22] European Ministers of Justice, 11th Conference (Copenhagen: June 21–22, 1978).

[23] Resolution No.4 of the 11th Conference of European Ministers of Justice on the death penalty (Copenhagen: June 21–22, 1978).

[24] European Ministers of Justice, 12th Conference (Luxembourg, May 20–21, 1980).

Carl Lidbom, the next Committee on Legal Affairs rapporteur, firmly grasped the abolitionist mantel and authored a pioneering report in 1980.[25] He forcefully explained to the Assembly that,

> "there is no doubt that abolition of capital punishment is one of the most controversial topics we can tackle, and at the same time one of the most important subjects for an organisation whose calling is to further liberty and human rights".[26]

The published records of the drafting debates on the report in the Parliamentary Assembly reveal a similar outline of the anti-death penalty arguments put forward by Bergegren in 1973. Numerous parliamentarians accepted the prominence of the discourse which led to *de facto* abolition of the death penalty within Western European Member States by 1981, including the punishment's lack of special deterrent effect,[27] the renunciation of retribution and the *lex talionis*,[28] the probability that innocent people have and will be executed,[29] that the punishment brutalises society,[30] but the methods of execution by hanging and guillotine were not debated.

Lidbom restricted the abolition strategy to times of peace because he thought it "realistic to proceed by stages".[31] He held the view that the death penalty should be abolished because it was barbaric, but he maintained that,

> "it is an illusion to believe that in the present state of the world we can put an end to barbarism in times of war. Unfortunately times of war are, by definition, times of barbarism and cruelty."[32]

So in peacetime, the death penalty was no longer to be seen as an exclusive issue for the state and a centralised challenge to the sovereign's monopoly over the death penalty was beginning to be formulated. Mr Ruperez Rubio of Spain declared,

> "we believe that nobody in this world should have a monopoly or claim the right to put an end to the life of others, not even the state".[33]

[25] Committee on Legal Affairs, *Report on the abolition of capital punishment*.

[26] Parliamentary Assembly, *Official Report of Debates*, Doc.4509 and amendments, p.52 Mr. Koehl of France agreed when he stated that the "abolition of capital punishment is ... one of the greatest issues of our time": p.84.

[27] Parliamentary Assembly, *Official Report of Debates*, Doc.4509 and amendments, as argued by: Mr Lidbom of Sweden, p.53; Mr Flanagan of Ireland, p.56; Mr Stoffelen of the Netherlands, p.60; Mr Meier of Switzerland, pp.60–61; Mr Bacelar of Portugal, p.62; Mrs Hawlicek of Austria, p.63; Mr Reddemann of the Federal Republic of Germany, p.65; Mr Batliner of Liechtenstein, p.66; Mrs Aasen of Norway, p.67; Mr Bardens of the Federal Republic of Germany, p.74; Mr Beith of the United Kingdom, p.80; Mr Belin of France, p.84; Mr Koehl of France, p.84.

[28] Parliamentary Assembly, *Official Report of Debates*, Doc.4509 and amendments, as argued by: Mr Lidbom of Sweden, p.53; Mr Aksoy of Turkey, p.57; Mrs Hawlicek of Austria, p.63; Mr Batliner of Liechtenstein, p.66; Mrs Aasen of Norway, p.67.

[29] Parliamentary Assembly, *Official Report of Debates*, Doc.4509 and amendments, as argued by Mr Lidbom of Sweden, p.53; Mr Mercier of France, p.55; Mr Flanagan, p.56; Mr Stoffelen of the Netherlands, p.60; Mr Meier of Switzerland, p.61; Mrs Hawlicek, p.63; Mrs Aasen of Norway, p.67; Mr Urwin of the United Kingdom, p.69.

[30] Parliamentary Assembly, *Official Report of Debates*, Doc.4509 and amendments, as argued by Mr Lidbom of Sweden, p.54; Mr Stoffelen of the Netherlands, p.60.

[31] Committee on Legal Affairs, *Report on the abolition of capital punishment*, 1980, p.5.

[32] Committee on Legal Affairs, *Report on the abolition of capital punishment*, 1980, p.5.

[33] Parliamentary Assembly, *Official Report of Debates*, Doc.4509 and amendments, p.71.

The renunciation of this sovereign state right was then affirmed through recourse to the individual's right to life. As Mrs Lindquist of Sweden reasoned,

> "[i]f we really mean what we say, we cannot deprive human beings of the most fundamental human right, namely, the right to life",[34]

and Mrs Meier of Switzerland affirmed,

> "we set the right to life in the first place on the list of human rights because without this all other rights are meaningless".[35]

These arguments were used as the basis for the Parliamentary Assembly's adoption of Resolution 727 which called for abolition in peacetime,[36] and Recommendation 891 to the Committee of Ministers to, "amend Article 2 of the European Convention on Human Rights".[37] As Lidbom stated, "[l]egally speaking ... the European Convention on Human Rights does not preclude capital punishment. Article 2 even allows it *expressis verbis*",[38] and so this was the central legislative problem to be rectified. Lidbom attempted to map out the amendment process when he identified, "[a]ny decision to amend the Convention can be taken solely by the Committee of Ministers of the Council of Europe".[39] But a conflict of opinion arose as to whether it was appropriate for the Parliamentary Assembly to endorse such a provision. Mr Grieve of the United Kingdom, the Chairman of the Committee on Legal Affairs, argued that the Committee of Ministers could not change the Convention text, but only draft an additional protocol, "which would require the consent of every one of the...countries that make up our Assembly".[40] It was then argued that the Parliamentary Assembly could not recommend this amendment mechanism and so the proposals should be rejected. In essence, Mr Grieve and others sought to elevate state sovereignty and renounce any perceived centralised encroachment upon the right of the death penalty. As Mr Smith of the United Kingdom argued, "[i]t is up to each individual country at the end of the day to make its own decision",[41] that the states themselves should grapple with the penological questions and the Parliamentary Assembly "should stop interfering".[42] Mr Grieve continued,

> "in the end it is for each country to decide what is right for its own society and whether a reserved power which, after all, has been kept by nearly all human societies since the beginning of time, should be withdrawn. I respectfully suggest that it is not for this Assembly to say that countries that still believe that it is right to retain that power are wrong."[43]

[34] Parliamentary Assembly, *Official Report of Debates*, Doc.4509 and amendments, p.65.
[35] Parliamentary Assembly, *Official Report of Debates*, Doc.4509 and amendments, p.61.
[36] Resolution 727 on the abolition of capital punishment, text adopted by the Parliamentary Assembly (3rd sitting, April 22, 1980).
[37] Recommendation 891 on the abolition of capital punishment, text adopted by the Parliamentary Assembly (2nd and 3rd sittings, April 22, 1980), point 3.
[38] Committee on Legal Affairs, *Report on the abolition of capital punishment*, 1980, p.13.
[39] Parliamentary Assembly, *Official Report of Debates*, Doc.4509 and amendments.
[40] Parliamentary Assembly, *Official Report of Debates*, Doc.4509 and amendments, p.87.
[41] Parliamentary Assembly, *Official Report of Debates*, Doc.4509 and amendments, p.58.
[42] Parliamentary Assembly, *Official Report of Debates*, Doc.4509 and amendments, p.59, and this position was supported by Mr Karamollaoglu of Turkey, p.68.
[43] Parliamentary Assembly, *Official Report of Debates*, Doc.4509 and amendments, p.87. See also, Mr Michel of Belgium, pp.58–59; Mr Banks of the United Kingdom, pp.78–79; Mr Beith of the United Kingdom, pp.80–81; Mr Grieve of the United Kingdom, pp.86–86; Mr Michel of Belgium, p.59.

These propositions maintained that the Member State sovereign right of the punishment was not evanescent. But such impaired political logic did not deter the majority of the Parliamentary Assembly as it adopted the report, resolution and recommendation. Hence, Lidbom's initiatives should be seen as a significant moment in the history of the Parliamentary Assembly's formulation of a human rights discourse against the punishment. In many ways, the time was now ripe to make such an argument, as, in Western Europe in 1980, France was the only country who would be likely to impose executions in peacetime.[44] In this geo-political region, Denmark[45] had removed the death penalty from its statutes for ordinary criminal offences in peacetime in 1933, and so had (West) Germany (which abolished the punishment for all crimes in 1949, and East Germany had done so in 1978), Italy (1947), the Netherlands (1870), Norway (1905), Portugal (1978), Spain (1976), Sweden (1921), and the United Kingdom (suspended in 1965, and confirmed in 1969).

The Parliamentary Assembly had a strong political basis to approach the Committee of Ministers and request that it formulate these principles of abolitionism within new legislation.[46] Then in 1981 the Committee of Ministers gave direction to the Steering Committee for Human Rights to prepare, "a draft additional protocol to the European Convention on Human Rights abolishing the death penalty in peacetime".[47] William Schabas notes that in 1982 the Parliamentary Assembly asked the Committee of Ministers for a progress report, and they indicated that the European Committee on Crime Problems and the Steering Committee for Human Rights had been instructed to draw up the protocol, and the joint committees were of the opinion that a protocol would be a "possible solution".[48] For the first time a substantial meeting-of-the-minds occurred between the Committee of Ministers and the Parliamentary Assembly on what would become Protocol No.6. This would create the first regional human rights treaty to call for a restriction of the death penalty to wartime application.

The impact of Protocol No.6 of the Convention

The "possible solution" quickly became reality. Protocol No.6 was adopted in 1983, and it mandated a restriction of the prima facie unconfined scope of Convention Art.2(1) through formulating abolition of the death penalty in peacetime. As such this Protocol provided an opportunity for abolitionist Member States to confirm their commitment to a centralised regional instrument, and at the same time establish an ideological platform from which the Council of Europe could encourage those Member States which had not yet restricted the death penalty to do so. The commentary on Protocol No.6 Art.1 states that the article should be read in conjunction with Art.2 and that the two articles, "affirm

[44] France abolished the death penalty in 1981, and Belgium still had the punishment on its statute books but had not executed anyone since 1950.

[45] Denmark had administered the death penalty for wartime offences in 1950.

[46] Resolution 727; Recommendation 891; and Committee on Legal Affairs, *Report on the abolition of capital punishment*, 1980.

[47] Council of Europe, *Explanatory Report on Protocol No.6 to the Convention for the Protection of Human Rights and Fundamental Freedoms concerning the Abolition of the Death Penalty* (Strasbourg: Council of Europe Publishing, 1983), "Introduction", p.5.

[48] Schabas, *The Abolition of the Death Penalty in International Law*, 2002, p.286.

the principle of abolition of the death penalty".[49] However, the mechanism which the Protocol utilised was not specifically a "human rights" mandate to reduce the punishment, but a centralised affirmation of an already existent state practice. But Protocol No.6 did provide the genesis for a regional principle of European constitutionalism and should be seen as the first time that the Convention human rights discourse attempted to reflect, and influence, Member State public law on the punishment. The Council had for the first time attempted to rectify the inadequate position created by the inability of the drafters of the Convention to deal with the relationship of state sovereignty and the punishment: as through Art.2(1) they had conceded too much ground on the state's side and not enough to the human rights of the individual. Of course, the state may decide not to impose a death penalty in wartime but Art.2(1) allowed the possibility of the punishment to remain in the state's arsenal.

Even though Protocol No.6 reflected the position of Western European governments post-1981, the dark shadow of state sovereignty lingered as some states were reluctant to sign and ratify a document which would symbolise an acceptance that this anti-death penalty position was evolving into a regional public law norm.[50] By 1989, of the then 22 Member States, 14 had ratified Protocol No.6, including Austria (1984), Denmark (1983), France (1986), Germany (1989), Iceland (1987), Italy (1988), Luxembourg (1985), Netherlands (1986), Norway (1988), Portugal (1986), San Marion (1989), Spain (1985), Sweden (1984), Switzerland (1987). However, there were still eight Member States which had not posted their ratifications at that time including Belgium, Cyprus, Greece, Ireland, Liechtenstein, Malta, Turkey and the United Kingdom.[51] This displayed insecurity on the part of these members in relinquishing their monopoly to decide whether or not to impose the death penalty. The lack of majority ratifications revealed that even though the centralising of the discourse reflected what the states had already decided individually, some were cautious about the process facilitated through Protocol No.6. The regional codification was perhaps thought more significant than individual states renouncing the punishment by themselves and remaining separate and autonomous in their decision making.

A comparative example can be seen from a resolution adopted in the European Community. In 1985 the European Commission spoke against a reluctance of some Member States to sign and ratify Protocol No.6.[52] Of the 12 Member States of the European Community in 1985, the Resolution noted that Ireland and the United Kingdom had not signed the Protocol,[53] and Belgium, Germany, Greece, Italy, the Netherlands and Portugal, had not posted their ratifications.[54] Point 3 states that the European Parliament "[e]xpresses its misgivings over the delay", and Preamble E noted a regret that,

[49] *Explanatory Report on Protocol No.6*, 1983, p.6.

[50] See, S. Rosena and S. Journey, "Abolition of the Death Penalty: An Emerging Norm of International Law" (1993) Hamline J. Pub. L. & Pol'y 163, 166–169; and S. Bae, *When the State no Longer Kills: International Human Rights Norms and Abolition of the Death Penalty* (New York: State University of New York Press, 2007), pp.1–12.

[51] Belgium ratified Protocol No.6 in 1998, as did Greece (1998), Ireland (1994), Liechtenstein (1990), Malta (1991), Turkey (2003), and the United Kingdom (1999).

[52] Resolution on the abolition of the death penalty and the accession to the Sixth Protocol to the Convention for the Protection of Human Rights and Fundamental Freedoms [1986] OJ C36.

[53] Resolution on the abolition of the death penalty [1986] OJ C36 point 1.

[54] Resolution on the abolition of the death penalty point 3.

"the procedures for the ratification...are being carried out very slowly, which might be considered as an expression of some hesitation on the part of those States over being bound by an international undertaking to abolish the death penalty".[55]

Hence, the 1980s can be seen as a significant, but not yet universal, Member State acceptance of the evolving Convention human rights discourse.

The drafting of Protocol No.13 of the Convention

Following the Vienna Summit in 1993 and the adoption of the Vienna Declaration,[56] greater emphasis was placed upon the development of policies to intensify abolitionism for all circumstances and thus strengthen the regional position. Roger Hood described the Vienna Summit's condition of acceptance of the Convention system as the "most important political decision"[57] for the furtherance of human rights. Only one year after the Vienna Declaration, Hans Göran Franck, the new rapporteur to the Committee on Legal Affairs, took the opportunity and inspired further change.[58] He authored a report which focused upon clearing up the existing capital laws within Member States, as at this time although the Western Member States had removed the death penalty for ordinary crimes, Protocol No.6 still had not been signed and ratified by all of them.[59] Franck argued that a "control mechanism" should be set up under the Secretary General to analyse the remaining retentionist Member State's capital laws. He advised,

"all states whose legislation still provides for the death penalty to set up a commission as soon as possible in their country with a view to abolishing capital punishment".[60]

A regionalised abolition position would lay the foundation for the expectation that new Member States should follow suit and so a draft resolution was included in the report.[61] In 1994, Resolution 1044 was adopted which stated that the "willingness to ratify the protocol be made a prerequisite for membership",[62] and to bolster the Resolution, Recommendation 1246 was sent to the Committee of Ministers inviting it to implement the outlined provisions.[63] In its interim reply, the Committee of Ministers noted that it would examine the Parliamentary Assembly's recommendations, and also emphasised that it would encourage,

[55] Resolution on the abolition of the death penalty preamble E.

[56] Vienna Declaration Decl-09.10.93E, October 9, 1993.

[57] R. Hood, "Introduction: The Importance of Abolishing the Death Penalty" in Council of Europe, *The Death Penalty—Beyond Abolition,* 2004, p.16.

[58] See, H.G. Franck, *The Barbaric Punishment: Abolishing the Death Penalty* (edited by W.A. Schabas) (The Hague: Martinus Nijhoff, 2003), p.64.

[59] *Report on the abolition of capital punishment* (September 15, 1994), Doc.7145. These countries are listed here and the ratification dates are in brackets: Belgium (1998), Estonia (1998), Greece (1998), Ireland (1994), Romania (1994), Russia (still to ratify), Slovenia (1994), and United Kingdom (1999).

[60] *Report on the abolition of capital punishment*, Doc.7145, para.6 (ii)(a).

[61] *Report on the abolition of capital punishment*, Doc.7145, Part II: Draft Resolution, paras 5–6.

[62] Resolution 1044 on the abolition of capital punishment, text adopted by the Parliamentary Assembly (25th sitting, October 4, 1994), para.6.

[63] Recommendation 1246 on the abolition of capital punishment, text adopted by the Parliamentary Assembly (25th sitting, October 4, 1994).

> "member states which have not abolished the death penalty to operate de facto or de jure a moratorium on the execution of death sentences".[64]

The Committee of Ministers had been nuanced in its response to the Parliamentary Assembly and it began to promote the initiation of moratoriums as a kind of political middle-ground between the role of the sovereign Member States in abolition and the radical expansion of the human rights boundaries by the Assembly. Danny Nicol noted this intricate legislative friction and argued that the Parliamentary Assembly was more "enthusiastic" in its legislative transcriptions and the Committee of Ministers displayed a more "cautious" approach.[65]

Consequently, a difficult dialogue resulted between the Parliamentary Assembly and the Committee of Ministers. The Committee did not initially deal with the 1994 provisions and so in 1996 the Assembly adopted a further Recommendation calling on the Committee to respond.[66] It welcomed the Committee's encouragement of moratoria, but regretted it had "not yet taken any action on the most important proposals".[67] The Assembly was not satisfied with the Committee dragging its feet on the new protocol, and called for complete abolition and a greater monitoring of Member States which imposed the punishment. Following its preference of moratoria over explicit calls for signature and ratification of Protocol No.6, the Committee instructed the Rapporteur Group on Human Rights to examine both Recommendations with a view to proposing a draft reply.[68] The Assembly was again dissatisfied as it viewed the Committee's actions as another stalling tactic, but the determined efforts of the Assembly finally forced their hand. In 1997, the Committee put forward an interim reply to Recommendation 1302,[69] stating that it "fully shares the concern voiced by the Parliamentary Assembly", but equanimously explained that the "parliaments and governments share responsibility regarding the abolition of the death penalty", and that the Committee,

> "considers that the process of monitoring compliance with commitments accepted by *member States of the Council of Europe can contribute, in a spirit of dialogue and co-operation*, to the process of putting an end to capital punishment. It also considers that the Parliamentary Assembly has an important role to play in this regard." (Emphasis added.)[70]

This may be read as the Committee of Ministers attempting to distance itself as the final arbiter to determine the Parliamentary Assembly's stream of recommendations. The

[64] Interim reply to Recommendation 1246 on the abolition of capital punishment, Doc.7466, adopted on January 22, 1996.

[65] D. Nicol, "Original intent and the European Convention on Human Rights" (2005) P.L. 152, 154.

[66] Recommendation 1302 on the abolition of the death penalty in Europe, text adopted by the Parliamentary Assembly (24th sitting, June 28, 1996). This Recommendation was adopted following the *Report on the abolition of the death penalty in Europe*, Doc.7589, text adopted by the Parliamentary Assembly (24th sitting, June 28, 1996).

[67] Recommendation 1302 para.2.

[68] See, Notes on the Agenda; Reference Documents (628/4.6), "Abolition of the death penalty in Europe: Draft Reply to Recommendation 1246 and 1302 of the Parliamentary Assembly".

[69] Reply to Recommendation 1246 and 1302 of the Parliamentary Assembly, 555th meeting (January 1996) and 588th meeting (April 1997); Interim Reply to Recommendation 1302, "Abolition of the death penalty in Europe", Communication from the Committee of Ministers Doc.7798, April 25, 1997, adopted April 9, 1997, 588th Meeting of the Minister's Deputies.

[70] Reply to Recommendation, point D.

Committee demonstrated that it sought to share the burden with the national parliaments, and identified the importance of "dialogue" for this abolition process. It emphasised that the Parliamentary Assembly played a crucial role in this dialogue, but this was stating nothing new to the Assembly: it already possessed an acute sense of the importance of its work. So this manoeuvre by the Committee appears to indicate that there was a heavy uncertainty on how to balance a new protocol and the possibility of amending Art.2(1), with the impact of this process on the sovereign Member States. It appears that "dialogue" was the buffer for remedying any difficulties. However, the Assembly displayed no uncertainty, or ambivalence, and boldly reaffirmed its position in Resolution 1097 which stated,

> "the Assembly reminds applicant states to the Council of Europe that the willingness to sign and ratify Protocol No. 6 to the European Convention on Human Rights and to introduce a moratorium upon accession *has become a prerequisite for membership* of the Council of Europe on the part of the Assembly". (Emphasis added.)[71]

Clearly the Assembly did not want to wait any longer for specific affirmation from the Committee on the reach of its abolitionist agenda, and therefore developed its own membership criteria. The language had markedly shifted from the Resolution 1044 invitation that states display a "willingness" to adopt the specified penal changes, to a position that it has become "a prerequisite for membership" under Resolution 1097. The Assembly was not acquiescing with the legislative mire created by the Committee, it sought to map out new boundaries for the human rights discourse against the punishment. In the battle for abolition in all circumstances the Assembly was leading the way and the Committee then, again, felt compelled to reaffirm its nuanced position stating that it, "considers that the priority is to obtain and maintain moratoria on executions, to be consolidated by complete abolition of the death penalty".[72] Even though the Committee had the fundamental responsibility as the "legislator in this field",[73] it still did not simply endorse the Assembly's position, and shifted the deliberations to the Second Summit held in Strasbourg on October 10–11, 1997.[74] It sidestepped the call to require prospective Member States to ratify Protocol No.6, and reemphasised instead the, "maintenance, in the meantime, of existing moratoria of executions in Europe".[75] But this prevarication was not the end, as the European Ministerial Conference on Human Rights held in Rome on November 3–4, 2000 changed the legislative tide.[76] A further Resolution was drafted inviting the Committee of Ministers to adopt a,

[71] Resolution 1097 on the abolition of the death penalty in Europe, text adopted by the Parliamentary Assembly (24th Sitting, June 28, 1996), para.6.

[72] See, Notes on the Agenda; Reference Documents (628/4.6), "Abolition of the death penalty in Europe: Draft Reply to Recommendation 1246 (1994) and 1302 (1996) of the Parliamentary Assembly", 555th meeting (January 1996) and 588th meeting (April 1997).

[73] Abolition of capital punishment, reply to Recommendation 1246; Abolition of the death penalty in Europe, reply to Recommendation 1302, adopted April 16, 1998 at the 628th meeting of the Minister's Deputies (Doc.8079, April 21, 1998).

[74] Second Summit of Heads of State and Government of the Council of Europe (Strasbourg, October 10–11, 1997), Final Declaration.

[75] Second Summit of Heads of State and Government of the Council of Europe, 1997, Final Declaration.

[76] For the draft documents see, Steering Committee for Human Rights (49th meeting, October 3–6, 2000), CDDH (2000) 025 Addendum (Strasbourg: October 11, 2000); and for the adopted text, see, Proceedings: European Ministerial Conference on Human Rights and Commemorative Ceremony of the 50th Anniversary of the European Convention on Human Rights (Rome, November 3–4, 2000).

> "new additional protocol to the Convention which would exclude the possibility of maintaining the death penalty in respect of acts committed in time of war or of imminent threat of war".[77]

The Foreign Ministers produced a Declaration for a European Death Penalty-Free Area, which identified that the achievement of abolition of all Member States was "our common goal".[78] This was not quite the same as specifically stating that the Committee would formulate a protocol in order to abolish the death penalty in wartime, or that, even, Art.2(1) would be amended. Resolution II was then adopted at the Ministerial Conference and the section on the death penalty, inter alia, invited Member States to consider the possibility of the abolition of the death penalty in all circumstances, which would in effect make abolition a condition of membership.[79] This was a departure from the singular focus on moratoria as a stepping stone to abolition. However, the wording of the Draft Declaration was restricted as it stated that the Committee of Ministers considered, "the signing and the ratification of Protocol No. 6 by all member states [is] highly advisable".[80] Making ratification a "highly advisable" position, as opposed to a "prerequisite for membership", was a tentative step in the Parliamentary Assembly's direction. The subsequent text did not simply state that Member States should ratify Protocol No.6, but requested that the,

> "member states ratify as soon as possible, if they have not yet done so, Protocol No.6 and in the meantime, respect the moratoria on executions".[81]

Again this was not a specific affirmation of the Parliamentary Assembly's position. However the Committee of Ministers should be viewed as providing a certain freedom, and discretion, to the Assembly. The Committee was not opposing the Assembly's prerequisites for future Member States, but it did not plainly endorse them either. As a result, the Committee's promotion of moratoria can be seen as a minimal requirement and the Assembly's position provided a higher human rights threshold.

Then in 2001, the Rapporteur Group on Human Rights submitted to the Committee of Ministers the Draft Protocol for the abolition of the death penalty in all circumstances.[82] The text called for complete abolition but, as with Protocol No.6, there were no provisions specifically amending Art.2(1). It considered and accepted the Draft Protocol, and it was then presented with an Explanatory Report to the Assembly for opinion.[83] In her Explanatory Memorandum to the Draft Protocol, Renate Wohlwend, the next rapporteur

[77] European Ministerial Conference, para.14 (ii) of Resolution IIB (2000).

[78] Declaration for a Death Penalty-Free Area adopted by the Committee of Ministers, November 9, 2000, 107th session.

[79] Proceedings, Resolution II: B, "Abolition of the death penalty in times of war and times of peace", para.14(ii), "invites the Committee of Ministers to consider the feasibility of a new additional protocol to the Convention, which would exclude the possibility of maintaining the death penalty in respect of acts committed in time of war or imminent threat of war".

[80] Draft Declaration on the European Death Penalty-Free Area COM(2000) 163 (Restricted) (728th meeting (October 30, 2000)), para.5.

[81] Declaration for a European Death Penalty-Free Area, para.4.

[82] Draft Protocol No.13 to the Convention for the Protection of Human Rights and Fundamental Freedoms, concerning the abolition of the death penalty in all circumstances, Ministers' Deputies Meeting (773rd meeting, November 21, 2001).

[83] Parliamentary Assembly, European Convention on Human Rights—Draft Protocol No.13 on abolition of the death penalty in all circumstances, (December 14, 2001), Doc.9291.

to the Committee on Legal Affairs, reiterated that the unsatisfactory situation of Art.2(1) remained under the draft and that amendment was required to match "theory with reality".[84] Wohlwend proposed a seemingly reasonable legislative mechanism to remedy the deficiency when she argued that a provision should be included in the new protocol according to which:

> "When this Protocol has come into force in all States Parties to the Convention, the second sentence of Article 2 paragraph 1 of the Convention shall be replaced with the text of Article 1 of this Protocol, and in the first sentence of Article 47 of the Convention, after the words 'provision of the Convention' the words 'except for Article 2, paragraph 1' shall be added."[85]

Wohlwend argued that Protocol No.13 was a great opportunity for textual abolition. She proposed that, when universal ratification occurs, the Member States should be viewed as signalling a collective affirmation of amendment of the article.[86] A legislative mechanism would fall into place which alters the specific text by deleting the second sentence and inserting the replacement wording, "[t]he death penalty shall be abolished. No one shall be condemned to such penalty or executed". However, the Committee of Ministers, in the final drafting of Protocol No.13, did not include Wohlwend's provisions and so the perplexed rapporteur strongly questioned,

> "are we then going to draw up another (the third!) Protocol on the same subject—the abolition of the death penalty—in order to at long last amend Article 2 of the Convention itself? In treaty law, this is a very inelegant solution ... I would suggest a 'hybrid' Protocol, which starts out as an additional Protocol, and becomes an amending Protocol when it has entered into force in all State Parties to the Convention."[87]

This unimpeachable approach of constructing a hybrid protocol was not followed by the Committee of Ministers as they would not "think the unthinkable",[88] and the exchange of opinions between the Assembly and the Committee on the status of Art.2(1) reveals the frustration that was present at this time. Indeed, Wohlwend's exclamation of the need for "the third!" protocol, and sighing "at long last", exposes the historical tensions between the Parliamentary Assembly and the Committee of Ministers. Following this exchange, the Assembly's efforts were again thwarted, and, in response to Wohlwend, the Rapporteur Group on Human Rights stated:

> "With regards to the Assembly's Opinion the Group, whilst welcoming its strong political support for such a protocol, came to the conclusion that it was not advisable to accede to the Recommendation ... In the Group's view such an amendment would present only limited interest given that the purported legal effect in respect of Article 2, ECHR will in practice also be achieved through an additional protocol.

[84] Explanatory Memorandum, by Mrs Renate Wohlwend, rapporteur, point 1, in Draft Protocol to the European Convention on Human Rights concerning the abolition of the death penalty in all circumstances, Doc.9316, January 15, 2002.

[85] Opinion No.233, Draft Protocol to the European Convention on Human Rights concerning the abolition of the death penalty in all circumstances (1st Sitting, Assembly Debate, January 21, 2002), paras 5–6.

[86] See, Explanatory Memorandum in Draft Protocol, Doc.9316, paras 1–12.

[87] Explanatory Memorandum in Draft Protocol, Doc.9316, paras 9–10.

[88] Explanatory Memorandum in Draft Protocol, Doc.9316, para 2.

Furthermore, the amendment could, in the opinion of the [Rapporteur Group on Human Rights], give rise to some legal questions, not least with regard to territorial declarations and reservations, extending beyond the scope of the consideration of the protocol itself, which could delay unduly the adoption of this important text."[89]

The Rapporteur Group on Human Rights were advancing complex legal arguments but displayed a notable ambivalence in that it recognised the importance of abolition in all circumstances, and at the same time allowed for the preservation of the punishment in the text of Art.2(1). However, the Group was of the opinion that Protocol No.13 would provide amendment by implication, and that the "purported legal effect" will be achieved "in practice". But such an interpretation seems to be irreconcilable with Protocol No.13 Art.5 on the relationship of the protocol with the Convention as it stated that the "Protocol shall be regarded as additional articles to the Convention", and not that it amends the Convention. Also, the final Protocol commentary on Art.5, confusingly states:

"As an additional Protocol, it does not, as far as the Parties to the Protocol are concerned, supersede Article 2 of the Convention, since the first sentence of paragraph 1 and the whole of paragraph 2 of that article still remain valid ... It is clear that the second sentence of paragraph 1 is no longer applicable in respect of the States Parties to this Protocol."[90]

Although the Commentary endorsed the inapplicability of the second sentence of Art.2(1), the Protocol nevertheless preserved the possibility of the death penalty within the main text of the Convention. The Committee allowed this complex human rights position because of some undisclosed "legal questions", and again the issue of state sovereignty raised its ugly head. The Group considered two reasons which, in their view, rendered amendment unnecessary, and both related to the preservation of Member State's opinions. First, it presumed that the amendment would only be of "limited interest" to the signatories, and secondly, that the proposal may attract unwanted considerations of "territorial declarations and reservations". However, territorial considerations have been a central factor of the sovereignty of European states since their legal articulation following the Treaty of Westphalia in 1648, and the *travaux préparatoires* reveal that the sovereignty issue was hegemonic within the 1949–1950 drafting debates of the Convention and can be seen as directly contributing to the preservation of the death penalty within Art.2(1).[91] So the importance of the recognition of state issues should not have been underestimated. Indeed the death penalty has an intricate genealogy which reveals that the punishment has been considered within the annals of European history to be an essential element of sovereign power.[92] And although the vast majority of

[89] Reference documents: European Convention on Human Rights, Draft Protocol No.13 on the abolition of the death penalty in all circumstances, Ministers' Deputies Meeting (784th meeting, February 21, 2002), sixth unnumbered paragraph.

[90] Protocol No.13 to the Convention for the Protection of Human Rights and Fundamental Freedoms, concerning the abolition of the death penalty in all circumstances (Vilnius: May 3, 2002); Commentary on the provisions of the Protocol Art.5: Relationship to the Convention.

[91] See J. Yorke, "The Evolving Human Rights Discourse of the Council of Europe: Renouncing the Sovereign Right of the Death Penalty" in *Against the Death Penalty: International Initiatives and Implications* (Aldershot: Ashgate Publishing, 2008).

[92] M. Foucault, *Discipline and Punish: The Birth of the Prison* (London: Penguin, 1976); P. Spierenburg, *The Spectacle of Suffering: Executions and the Evolution of Repression* (Cambridge: Cambridge University

Member States have ratified Protocol No.13,[93] the preservation of the text of Art.2(1) still, theoretically at least, allows such power to be legitimately applied. This was the result of the Committee endorsing the Group's opinions over the Parliamentary Assembly's analysis of the final wording of Protocol No.13, and as with Protocol No.6, we see the manifestation of a political middle-way.

The Interpretation of Article 2(1) of the Convention

The Preamble to Protocol No.13 states that,

> "everyone's right to life is a basic value in a democratic society and that the abolition of the death penalty is essential for the protection of this right".

The right to life is stated twice in the Preamble, although not in the Protocol articles, and reminiscent of the internal conflict detailed above, the Convention Art.2(1) is not specifically referred to. The important question remains as to why Art.2(1) was not amended if the right to life is such an intrinsic aspect of the Protocol? The Explanatory Report point 1 refers to the European Court of Human Rights' judgment in *Streletz, Kessler and Krenz v Germany*, which held that the right to life is "an inalienable attribute of human beings", and that this right possesses "supreme value in the international hierarchy of human rights".[94] Nowhere is it stated that "life" itself is inalienable, only that it is an "inalienable attribute". An attribute is an aspect of something and not the essence of it, and here we see the root issue. Can the right to life be used as an *end* to eradicate the sovereign use of the death penalty, or is it only a *means* with which to challenge the punishment? The case law that attempts to provide an answer to this fundamental question is considered below.

1957–1983: The literal endorsement of Article 2(1) of the Convention

The early decisions of the European Commission of Human Rights and the European Court of Human Rights suggest that the judicial bodies accepted the textual affirmation of the death penalty in Art.2(1). In 1957, the European Commission of Human Rights considered *Greece v United Kingdom*,[95] and a special Sub-Committee of the Commission was established with an investigatory mandate restricted to scrutinising the emergency situation of the British colonial control in Cyprus.[96] The punishment was indirectly

Press, 1984); J.Q. Whitman, *Harsh Justice: Criminal Punishment and the Widening Divide between America and Europe* (New York: Oxford University Press, 2003).

[93] See below for the ratification process.

[94] Application No.34044/96 *Streletz v Germany* (2001) 33 E.H.R.R. 31 at [72], [85], [87] and [94].

[95] Council of Europe, *Application by the Government of the Kingdom of Greece, lodged against the Government of the United Kingdom of Great Britain and Northern Ireland*, App. No.176/56, *Application of the European Convention of Human Rights and Fundamental Freedoms to the Island of Cyprus, Report of the European Commission of Human Rights*, Doc. No.A 42.048, (Art.31 of the Convention) (Strasbourg, September, 26, 1958), in A.H. Robertson et al. (ed.), *European Commission on Human Rights: Documents and Decisions 1955–1956–1957* (The Hague: Martinus Nijhoff, 1959), pp.48–49.

[96] R. Holland, *Britain and the Revolt in Cyprus, 1954–1959* (Oxford: Clarendon Press, 1998), p.133. For a detailed analysis of the two cases brought by Greece against the United Kingdom, see A.W.B. Simpson, *Human Rights and the End of Empire: Britain and the Genesis of the European Convention* (Oxford: Oxford University Press, 2004), pp.924–1052.

affirmed as the fundamental issue it determined was that the British Government had legitimately used its powers of derogation under Convention Art.15, and in derogation the death penalty had been implemented. Article 2(1) appeared to legitimise the colonial use of the death penalty in legally mandated capital crimes, and following the emergency in 1956, regs 52, 53, 53A and 53B considerably extended its scope and introduced the mandatory application of the punishment in terrorist cases.[97] These draconian laws were applied to administer the executions of two Cypriots, Andreas Demetriou on May 10, 1956 and Evagoras Pallikarides on March 14, 1957. Demetriou was found guilty of wounding, and Pallikarides, who was only 18 years old, was arrested in December 1955 when an army patrol came across an armed EOKA group making its way to their winter hide-out. Pallikarides's companions escaped but he surrendered without resistance and following a trial was executed.[98] Nancy Crawshaw observed concerning the two executions of Demetriou and Pallikarides, that in the former case under normal criminal law he would have been liable for only a maximum sentence of life imprisonment, and in the later case no severe charges would have been possible.[99] The *Second Cyprus Case* was to consider the specific allegations of human rights violations. There was an outcry by the Greek government against the application of the death penalty, and although Art.2(1) allows for the use of the punishment, it had not eradicated the problems presented by its application. However, after many legal petitions by the British Government which argued against judicial scrutiny, the case was discontinued.[100]

Following this, the next cases to consider the death penalty were in the early 1980s where there was further judicial acceptance of the punishment. In *Deweer v Belgium*, the Court noted in an obiter statement that the "Convention permits under certain conditions some very serious forms of treatment, such as the death penalty",[101] and in *Kirkwood v United Kingdom*,[102] the United Kingdom government had argued that extradition circumstances where the person transferred would face a capital trial could not violate Art.2(1).[103] The Commission stated that, "the provisions of Article 2(1) of the Convention ... expressly recognises the ending of life through the death penalty following appropriate criminal conviction".[104] *Deweer* and *Kirkwood* endorsed a literal application of the text of Art.2(1), but this was not the only interpretative mechanism open to the Court at this time. In *Tyrer v United Kingdom*,[105] the Court held that the Convention must not be viewed in

[97] Supplement to *Cyprus Gazette* No.4001, November 22, 1956, cited in A.W. B. Simpson, "Round Up the Usual Suspects: The Legacy of British Colonialism and the European Convention on Human Rights" (1996) 41 Loy. L. Rev. 629, 658, fn.264. For arguments against the mandatory death penalty, see, David Pannick, who stated, it is "neither fair nor reasonable, and lacks the procedural safeguards demanded by the rule of law" in *Judicial Review of the Death Penalty* (London: Duckworth, 1983), p.114.

[98] *Times of Cyprus*, March 14, 1957, cited in Holland, *Britain and the Revolt in Cyprus*, 1998, p.173.

[99] N. Crawshaw, *The Cyprus Revolt: An Account of the Struggle for Union with Greece* (London: George Allen & Unwin, 1978), pp.232–233.

[100] See Simpson, *Human Rights and the End of Empire*, 2004, pp.924–1052; Robertson, *European Commission on Human Rights*, 1959, pp.48–49.

[101] Application No.6903/75, *Deweer v Belgium* (1979–80) 2 E.H.R.R. 439 at [53].

[102] Application No.10479/83, *Kirkwood v United Kingdom* (1984) 6 E.H.R.R. CD373. In Application No.5961/72, *Amekrane v United Kingdom*, not yet reported, July 19, 1974, the United Kingdom reached a friendly settlement with Mrs Amekrane, as it had extradited her husband back to Morocco for a capital crime and he was executed.

[103] *Kirkwood v United Kingdom* (1984) 6 E.H.R.R. CD373 at [183]–[184].

[104] *Kirkwood v United Kingdom* at [188], [190].

[105] Application Nos 5856/72; 5775/72, *Tyrer v United Kingdom*, not yet reported, December 14, 1976.

a vacuum because the document is a "living instrument", which "should be interpreted in the light of present day conditions".[106] By the time of *Deweer* in 1980, only France would be seen to possibly apply the death penalty, and four years later in *Kirkwood* every Western European state had renounced the punishment for peacetime offences. Hence, an evolution of municipal law was occurring within Western Europe, but at the time it was not considered to be constitutive of a uniform "present day condition". In fact, the *Kirkwood* decision would mark the beginning of a judicial reluctance to apply the living instrument doctrine to specifically amend the text of Art.2(1).

The interpretation of Protocol No.6 of the Convention

The judicial interpretation evolved following the adoption of Protocol No.6 and the introduction of the possible prohibition against the death penalty in peacetime. In 1989 the Commission considered the application of Art.2(1) to extradition proceedings in *Soering v United Kingdom*.[107] Hans Soering was detained in the United Kingdom and the Virginian government requested his extradition to stand trial for capital murder. The Commission considered that Soering was only 18 at the time of the purported crime, that he suffered from the mental condition "*folie à deux*" and the extreme conditions of death row in the State of Virginia were enhanced by prolonged incarceration of up to eight years. However, the Commission relied on the interpretation of Art.2(1) that it established in *Kirkwood*, and held that Soering could be extradited to face a capital trial. The Commission did not venture to apply any evolutive interpretation to move away from the *Kirkwood* decision, but on appeal to the European Court of Human Rights, the question arose as to how Art.2(1) was to be interpreted against Protocol No.6.[108] The Court considered the issue at length and stated:

> "Subsequent practice in national penal policy, in the form of a generalised abolition of capital punishment, could be taken as establishing the agreement of the Contracting States to abrogate the exception provided for under Article 2(1) . . . However, Protocol No. 6, as a subsequent written agreement, shows that the intention of the Contracting Parties as recently as 1983 was to adopt the normal method of amendment of the text in order to introduce a new obligation to abolish capital punishment in time of peace and, what is more, to do so by an optional instrument allowing each State to choose the moment when to undertake such an agreement."[109]

The political debates and jurisprudence concerning Art.2(1) reveals that the locus of the authority to dictate the final decision of whether or not to apply the death penalty

[106] *Tyrer v United Kingdom* at [31]. Furthermore, it should be noted that the Court should interpret the Convention and any bilateral or multilateral treaties following the rules in the Vienna Convention on the Law of Treaties 1969 Arts 31–33, which call for inter alia interpretation in, "good faith in accordance with the ordinary meaning to be given to the terms of the treaty in their context and in the light of its object and purpose". Although the Vienna Convention was not specifically referred to in *Deweer* (1979–80) 2 E.H.R.R. 439, *Kirkwood* (1984) 6 E.H.R.R. CD373 or App. No.14038/88, *Soering v United Kingdom* (1989) 11 E.H.R.R. 439 , the Court appears to have followed the "ordinary meaning" of Art.2(1) of the Convention.

[107] Application No.14038/88, *Soering v United Kingdom* (1989) 11 E.H.R.R. 439.

[108] *Soering v United Kingdom* at [103]. The then 13 ratifying states were: Austria, Denmark, France, Germany, Iceland, Italy, Luxembourg, the Netherlands, Norway, Portugal, (San Marino), Spain, Sweden, Switzerland.

[109] *Soering v United Kingdom* at [103].

manifests through a three-layered political process of Committee of Ministers legislating protocols and then the acceptance or rejection of the provisions of the protocols by the Member States, and finally the Court's adjudication on the state signature and ratification process. As the dialogue between the Committee of Ministers and Parliamentary Assembly displayed, it is a sensitive political project to engage the sovereign state in relinquishing such an historically legitimised right, even when it was just applied in wartime. In his 1980 report for the Parliamentary Assembly, Carl Lidbom had stated that it was the Committee of Ministers who could only provide for the possibility of the amendment of the Convention text itself,[110] and *Soering* agreed that this legislative offering is then accepted or rejected by the Member State governments. Alastair Mowbray has cogently observed that the Court was careful to display a legitimate basis for its decision and this is why it gave prominence to the actions of the states and adopted a "limitation on the use of the 'living instrument' doctrine".[111] But Judge De Meyer held the view that the *Soering* Court should have gone further and he stated in his concurring opinion that:

> "The second sentence of Article 2(1) of the Convention was adopted nearly forty years ago, in particular historical circumstances, shortly after the Second World War. In so far as it still may seem to permit, under certain conditions, capital punishment in times of peace, it does not reflect the contemporary situation, and is now overridden by the development of legal conscience and practice."[112]

Judge De Meyer's concurring opinion is more strongly worded than the majority's and it echoed the determined Parliamentary Assembly resolutions and recommendations. In effect, he was arguing that the Member States had over a 39-year period, arrived at a better understanding of the penal issues concerning the death penalty. George Letsas views the importance of Member States endeavouring to develop "better" legislation as he argues,

> "it is not enough to there being a different understanding evolved, this understanding must also be better, i.e., towards the truth of the substantive protected right".[113]

Even though the *Soering* Court did not hold that the Member States had agreed to amend Art.2(1), it is evident that the states were formulating a collective understanding of more effective and humane penal policy. Judge De Meyer thought that there had been a significant ideological shift, but whilst the Court did observe this development, it did not see that it had a judicial function in furthering this new penal perspective through specific textual amendment. It delineated what was happening in 1989, and as Mowbray observed, left any subsequent advances to the Member States.[114]

[110] *Report on the abolition of capital punishment*, Doc.4509 (2nd and 3rd sitting, April 22, 1980), p.22.

[111] A. Mowbray, "The Creativity of the European Court of Human Rights" (2005) 5(2) H.L.R. Rev. 57, 66.

[112] *Soering* (1989) 11 E.H.R.R. 439 at [51].

[113] G. Letsas, *A Theory of Interpretation of the European Convention on Human Rights* (Oxford: Oxford University Press, 2007), p.79; Michel Foucault has observed that in the Enlightenment the European governments were searching for ways to not "punish less, but to punish better", in *Discipline and Punish*, 1976, p.73. It appears that this is an ever-evolving European governmental quest.

[114] Mowbray, "The Creativity of the European Court of Human Rights" (2005) 5(2) H.L.R. Rev. 57, 66.

The juxtaposition of Art.2(1) with Protocol No.6 did not provide the only interpretive difficulty. A further issue was presented by the balancing of Art.2(1) with Art.3, which prohibits, inter alia, inhuman punishment. *Kirkwood* first considered this intricate question and held that there was a "certain disharmony between Articles 2 and 3 of the Convention", resulting in the death penalty not being denounced as it stated:

> "Whereas Article 3 prohibits all forms of inhuman and degrading treatment and punishment without qualification of any kind, the right to life is not protected in an absolute manner. Article 2(1) expressly envisages the possibility of imposing the death penalty."[115]

The Commission established a rule concerning the parameters of the right to life and what this seems to mean in a practical sense is that there will be some (unspecified) circumstances where the death penalty was not considered to be an Art.3 violation. As such, the Commission was demonstrating that there were pragmatic issues to this evolving discourse with which the Assembly had not adequately engaged and which it had not resolved. The *Soering* Court then persisted with this reasoning and affirmed that, with the presence of Art.2(1), "article 3 cannot be interpreted as generally prohibiting the death penalty".[116] William Schabas has observed that the Court viewed this interpretive conundrum as a, "matter for the States parties to resolve by amendment to the Convention and not something to be tackled by the judiciary".[117] Protocol No.13 would provide a significant opportunity for this specific amendment procedure.

The interpretation of Protocol No.13 of the Convention

In 2002 the Chamber of the European Court of Human Rights considered *Öcalan v Turkey*.[118] Turkey had imposed a death sentence on Abdullah Öcalan, the leader of the PKK (Kurdistan Worker's Party),[119] for the Kurdish uprisings aimed at destroying the "integrity of the Turkish state."[120] This was the first case to come before the Chamber which involved a Member State's application of the death penalty within its municipal territory.[121] Following the ratifications of Protocol No.6 and Protocol No.13, it was argued

[115] *Kirkwood* (1984) 6 E.H.R.R. CD373.

[116] *Soering* (1989) 11 E.H.R.R. 439 at [103]–[104].

[117] W. A. Schabas, *The Death Penalty as Cruel Treatment and Torture: Capital Punishment in the World's Courts* (Boston: Northeastern University Press, 1996), p.9.

[118] Application No. 46221/99, *Öcalan v Turkey* (2005) 41 E.H.R.R. 45.

[119] For an outline of the history of the Kurdistan Worker's Party see, H. Chiapetta, "Rome, 11/15/1998: Extradition or Political Asylum for the Kurdistan Worker's Party Leader Abdullah Öcalan" (2001) 13 Pace Int'l L. Rev 117. For a review of the legal and political polices adopted by Turkey in an attempt to join the European Union, see D. Kanarek, "Turkey and the European Union: The Path to Accession" (2003) 9 Colum. J. Eur. L. 457.

[120] M. Trilsh and A. Rüth, "Case Comment: *Öcalan v. Turkey*" (2006) 100 A.J.I.L. 180; A. Sherlock, "Case Comment: *Öcalan v. Turkey* (46221/99) (unreported, December 14, 2000)" (2001) E.L. Rev. 133. Sherlock's note analysed the admissibility stage of the trial, and see also, Schabas, *The Abolition of the Death Penalty in International Law*, 2002, pp.277–279.

[121] Sir Sydney Kentridge, one of the lawyers for Abdullah Öcalan, pointed out in his opening statement, "this is one of the most significant and high-profile cases ever to come before the European Court of Human Rights ... it is a case in which the passing and proposed implementation of the death penalty within a signatory state has resulted in litigation before the court", cited by Colin Wells, who was an observer at the trial; see, "Human Rights in Turkey: Death by State Hanging" (2003) 9 *Amicus Journal* 8, 9.

for the applicant that the practice of the contracting states in this area can be taken as establishing an agreement to abrogate the exception provided for in the second sentence of Art.2(1). The Chamber noted the Parliamentary Assembly's Opinion on the Draft Protocol No.13, and engaged with the dialogue between the Parliamentary Assembly and the Committee of Ministers. However, it adopted the *Soering* reasoning that the normal method of Convention amendment is through state practice in signing and ratifying optional protocols,[122] and asked,

> "whether it is necessary to await [complete] ratification of Protocol No. 6 . . . before concluding that the death penalty exception in Article 2 has been significantly modified".[123]

It thought it was, and consequently it looked for Member State unanimity to enable it to present an interpretation that Art.2(1) had been amended. The Chamber then applied this interpretive methodology to Protocol No.13 and held:

> "In expressing this view, the Court is aware of the opening for signature Protocol 13 which provides an indication that the Contracting States have chosen the traditional method of amendment of the text of the Convention in pursuit of their policy of abolition. However this Protocol seeks to extend the prohibition by providing for the abolition of the death penalty in all circumstances—that is to say both in times of peace and in times of war. This final step toward complete abolition of the death penalty can be seen as a confirmation of the abolitionist trend established by the practice of the Contracting States. It does not necessarily run counter to the view that Article 2 has been amended in so far as it permits the death penalty in times of peace."[124]

The Chamber does observe a development towards possible amendment, but ultimately its language is imprecise and does not say simply and categorically, that Art.2(1) *is* amended. Mowbray observed that the Chamber, "would not unequivocally rule that the State's contemporary practice had modified Article 2(1)",[125] and this decision outlines the fact that the development of abolition in Member States, "could" and "can" but "does not necessarily run counter" to the signalling to "abrogate" Art.2(1). The Chamber explained that "it can" be said that the death penalty is "unacceptable" in peacetime, and so, if Art.2(1) is now interpreted judicially to be amended to reflect this specific prohibition, this does not mean that there is a textual change. The Chamber held that the ratifications of Protocol No.13 did not yet create a per se rule for Member States, as by the date of the judgment (March 12, 2003), only eight countries had posted their ratifications, which were: Bulgaria, Croatia, Cyprus, Denmark, Liechtenstein, Malta, Switzerland and the Ukraine. The Partly Dissenting Opinion of Judge Türmen furthers the argument when he stated that the specific amendment, "would require clear evidence over and above the uniform amendment of penal policy in favour of abolition. Such evidence is, however, lacking".[126] The judge then affirmed that it is for the states to specifically decide, and,

[122] *Öcalan* (2005) 41 E.H.R.R. 45 at [191].
[123] *Öcalan* at [196].
[124] *Öcalan* at [197].
[125] Mowbray, "The Creativity of the European Court of Human Rights" (2005) 5(2) H.L.R. Rev. 57, 67.
[126] *Öcalan* (2005) 41 E.H.R.R. 45 partly dissenting Opinion of Judge Türmen.

in his opinion, Protocol No.13 only strengthened Protocol No.6, and it did not directly provide textual amendment as:

> "In reality there is no basis for the view that this new Protocol represents the treaty confirmation of any previous agreement between the States to complete abrogation—only partially achieved in Protocol No. 6—of the exception contained in Article 2(1). Against such a clear background, the conclusion reached in the judgment that the exception in Article 2(1) is abrogated is not tenable. Accordingly, Article 2(1) must still be read as permitting the imposition of the death penalty."[127]

Judge Türmen is correct in his literal application of the current text of Art.2(1), but he has not given enough judicial credence to the practical application of Protocol No.6 and Protocol No.13 and that in reality there is a current abolition position in practice. It also appears that Judge Türmen is not completely clear on his interpretation of the majority judgment, as it does not specifically state that Art.2(1) *is* abrogated, only that it "could" and "can", not that it *does*.[128] However, this decision identifies a theoretical loophole, as, even with the presence of Protocol No.6 and Protocol No.13, the death penalty is still possible pursuant to the text of Art.2(1). By implication, this judicial reasoning severely questions the Rapporteur Group on Human Rights' position on the extent of Protocol No.13 as detailed above. It appears that the lack of express reference to Art.2(1) is the "clear evidence" which Judge Türmen required, but which the Group had mistakenly thought was not necessary. Furthermore, he made reference to the Preamble, noting that "the final step"[129] has not yet been taken. But it is difficult to see how the final step could be taken if the Committee does not legislate for this possibility. The Committee must open the door and then it will be for the states to step in.

The *Öcalan* Chamber judgment was appealed to the Grand Chamber, and it stated that the applicant asked it to take its jurisprudence,

> "a stage further by concluding that the States had, by their practice, abrogated the exception set out in the second sentence of Article 2(1)".[130]

This confirms that the Chamber had not abrogated Art.2(1) and Öcalan was trying to persuade the Grand Chamber to adopt an "evolutive" interpretation of the Convention, and in effect create European policy. But echoing *Kirkwood*, the Grand Chamber held that,

> "if Article 2 is to be read as permitting capital punishment, notwithstanding the almost universal abolition of the death penalty in Europe, Article 3 cannot be interpreted as prohibiting the death penalty since that would nullify the clear wording of Article 2(1)".[131]

This displays the difficulty the Grand Chamber had in dealing with the prima facie theoretical loop-hole left by Protocol No.13 and so, following the Chamber, it deferred

[127] *Öcalan* at [70].
[128] *Öcalan* at [196].
[129] *Öcalan* partly dissenting Opinion of Judge Türman.
[130] *Öcalan* at [175].
[131] *Öcalan* at [162].

the question to the practice of the Member States.[132] It appears that the Grand Chamber is waiting for unanimity, as by the time of the Grand Chamber judgment, 16 Member States had not posted their ratifications,[133] and as of December 2008, Armenia, Azerbaijan, Italy, and Latvia have not yet posted their ratifications, and Russia is the only Council Member State who has not signed the Protocol.[133a] The majority clearly thought that the ratifications of these countries is required, but such implementation of judicial restraint did not find favour from all on the Court, as a partly concurring, partly dissenting, Opinion from Judge Garlicki displays. He stated:

> "Today the Court, while agreeing that 'it can be said that capital punishment in peacetime has come to be regarded as an unacceptable ... form of punishment which is no longer permissible under Article 2,' seems to be convinced that there is no room for the death penalty even in the original text of the Convention. But, at the same time, it has chosen not to express that position in a universally binding manner. In my opinion, there are some arguments suggesting that the Court could and should have gone further in this case."[134]

The judge then cited the Opinion of the Parliamentary Assembly and could not give, in his mind, "a good reason" why the Court did not follow the Opinion as he held that the Court did have jurisdictional competence.[135] He stated:

> "The only problem is: who shall have the power to declare, in a binding manner, that such modification has taken place? So this is a problem not of substance, but of jurisdiction (competence)."[136]

In effect, Judge Garlicki was asking, *where does the authority to amendment lie*? And he further stated:

> "I am not convinced by the majority's replication of the *Soering* approach. I do not think that there are any legal obstacles to this Court's taking a decision with respect to the nature of capital punishment."[137]

If Judge Garlicki had considered Lidbom's 1980 report and the subsequent Parliamentary Assembly recommendations to the Committee of Ministers, he would have been able to identify the apparent prominent legislative position of the Committee of Ministers. It would have been useful if Judge Garlicki had distinguished the observation that the Committee of Ministers is the only Council organ which can offer the specific amendment of the text of the Convention. In 1980, Lidbom had pointed out that the amendment authority resided within the Committee, and the Grand Chamber's judgment displayed

[132] *Öcalan* at [164]. With regards to Art.3 of the Convention, the Court has evolved its interpretation to hold that on death row the prison conditions should not be constructed to infringe "human dignity", see App. No.38812/97, *Poltoratskiy v Ukraine* (2004) 39 E.H.R.R. 43 at [132].

[133] See *Öcalan* (2005) 41 E.H.R.R. 45 at [164]; the 16 Member States who had not posted their ratifications were: Albania, Armenia, Azerbaijan, France, Italy, Latvia, Luxembourg, Moldova, Monaco, Netherlands, Norway, Poland, Russia, Slovakia, Spain, and Turkey.

[133a] Russia is also the only Council Member who has not ratified Protocol No.6.

[134] *Öcalan* partly concurring, partly dissenting Opinion of Judge Garlicki at [2].

[135] *Öcalan* at [3]–[7].

[136] *Öcalan* at [3].

[137] *Öcalan* at [5].

an acceptance of this amendment mechanism. It appears that the current Council of Europe three-layered process for amendment still holds strong. If this is correct, the European Court of Human Rights must adhere to the wording of the Protocol. In this case, neither Protocol No.6 nor Protocol No.13 expressly amends Art.2(1), so it would appear that, in strict literal application, the Grand Chamber did not have jurisdiction at this time.

The European Court of Human Rights has considered cases post-*Öcalan* and, although specific amendment has not occurred, an evolution of the jurisprudence has been apparent. Peter Hodgkinson had predicted in 2000 that the "Court will probably be obliged to go beyond the principles laid down in the Soering judgment",[138] and Mirja Trilsh and Alexandra Rüth note that in *Öcalan* the "Court's interpretation of Article 2 was ... too narrow".[139] Post *Öcalan*, the Court has not reconsidered its decisions of the complicated balancing of the textual amendment of Art.2(1) with Protocol No.13, because no other Member State has sought to directly impose the death penalty. But it has considered the parameters of the right to life of condemned prisoners during moratoriums and in extradition circumstances where a suspect may be transferred by a Member State to a receiving state to face a capital charge.[140] In between the two *Öcalan* judgments, the Court considered *G.B. v Bulgaria*,[141] where the applicant was convicted and sentenced to death in 1989. Then a moratorium was put in place and Bulgaria abolished the death penalty in 1998 and ratified Protocol No.6 in 1999. No Art.2(1) violation was held, and this reasoning was followed in *Iorgov v Bulgaria*.[142] In *Mamatkulov and Askarov v Turkey*,[143] the Court held unanimously that in extradition circumstances, if a death penalty would be applied then there is a violation of Art.3 under *Soering*, and so it does not need to consider the case under Art.2(1).[144] This decision was handed down in February 2005, and two months later in *Shamayev v Georgia and Russia*,[145] the Court confirmed that extradition would not expose the applicants to a real risk of extra-judicial execution, contrary to Art.2(1).

Then, in November 2005 the Court modified its jurisprudence. *Bader v Sweden*,[146] concerned the deportation of a suspect to Syria with the possibility of facing a capital trial. The Court considered that Art.2(1) may be implicated if a Member State deports an alien who has suffered or risks suffering a flagrant denial of a fair trial in the receiving state, "the outcome of which was or is likely to be the death penalty".[147] It found that, "the deportation of the applicants to Syria, if implemented, would give rise to [a violation

[138] P. Hodgkinson, "Europe-A Death Penalty Free Zone: Commentary and Critique of Abolitionist Strategies" (2000) 26 Ohio N.U.L. Rev. 625, 630.

[139] Trilsh and Rüth, "Case Comment: *Öcalan v. Turkey*" (2006) 100 A.J.I.L. 180, 182.

[140] See, J. Yorke, "Europe's Judicial Inquiry in Extradition Cases: Closing the Door on the Death Penalty" (2004) 29(4) E.L. Rev. 546.

[141] Application No.42346/98, *G.B. v Bulgaria*, not yet reported, March 11, 2004.

[142] Application No.40653/98, *Iorgov v Bulgaria* (2005) 40 E.H.R.R. 7.

[143] Applications Nos 46827/99 and 46951/99, *Mamatkulov v Turkey* (2005) 41 E.H.R.R. 25, where the assurances against the death penalty are sufficient, Art.2 of the Convention is not violated. See also, App. No.62806/00, *S.R. v Sweden*, not yet reported, April 23, 2002; App. No.58128/00, *Ismaili v Germany*, not yet reported, March 15, 2001; *Bahaddar v Netherlands* (1998) 26 E.H.R.R. 278 at [75]–[78].

[144] *Mamatkulov* (2005) 41 E.H.R.R. 25 at [78].

[145] Application No.36378/02, *Shamayev v Georgia and Russia*, not yet reported, April 12, 2005.

[146] Application No.13284/04, *Bader v Sweden* (2008) 46 E.H.R.R. 13.

[147] *Bader v Sweden* at [42].

of article 2]".[148] As such, the Court was extending its jurisprudence on the right to life and the death penalty, and it now declared that there are some circumstances where an execution does not have to take place to initiate an Art.2(1) violation. Only the potential of an execution is required, and the determining factor in this case was the possibility of an arbitrary deprivation of life. Judge Cabral Barreto stated in his concurring opinion that this was the first time,

> "the Court has plainly stated that the extradition or deportation of a person to a country where he or she risks an unfair trial followed by capital punishment will violate Article 2 of the Convention".[149]

Conclusion

The essential question for the amendment of Art.2(1) is to determine whether an alteration of the text would provide clarity for the abolitionist position. The answer to this question is not as simple as it first may appear to be, and the debates between the Committee and Assembly, and the uncomfortable jurisprudence of the Court, represent this fact. It is perhaps true that this question can only be answered with the benefit of hindsight, and if this is the case, the abolition of the death penalty in the Council of Europe should be viewed as an on-going legal and political project, and not exclusively determined by the event of amendment. If the current mechanisms through Protocol No.6 and Protocol No.13 keep the death penalty at bay, then amendment would not appear to be necessary. But this is not to forget that in 1957, Albert Camus argued,

> "in the unified Europe of the future the solemn abolition of the death penalty ought to be the first article of the European Code we all hope for",[150]

and this abolitionist cry has been echoed in the Parliamentary Assembly. Wohlwend has explained that the fulfilment of this goal is constantly on the parliamentarian's hearts as she stated, "[i]t is taking a long time to bring about abolition of the death penalty" and revealed, "the anxieties felt by the Assembly . . . remain".[151] Furthermore, in 2006 René van der Linden, the President of the Parliamentary Assembly, declared:

> "Capital punishment must be totally removed once and for all from the legislation of all countries which strive to uphold democracy, the rule of law and human rights."[152]

The anxieties felt by these contemporary parliamentarians reveal the constant fight in which human rights is engaged against the sovereign power to implement the death

[148] *Bader v Sweden* at [48].

[149] *Bader v Sweden* concurring opinion of Judge Cabral Barreto.

[150] A. Camus, "Reflections on the Guillotine" in Justin O'Brien (trans.), *Resistance, Rebellion, and Death* (New York: Vintage Press, 1988) p.230. Renate Wohlwend noted that Camus's phrase was quoted in some reports presented to the Parliamentary Assembly, and that some parliamentarians recited it in debates; see R. Wohlwend, "The Role of the Council of Europe's Parliamentary Assembly" in Council of Europe, *Death Penalty—Beyond Abolition*, 2004, p.84.

[151] Position of the Parliamentary Assembly as regards the Council of Europe member and observer states which have not abolished the death penalty, Doc.10911 (April 21, 2006), paras 1, 49–50.

[152] "Capital punishment must be totally removed once and for all from the legislation of all countries which strive to uphold democracy, the rule of law and human rights": Press Release (Strasbourg: October 10, 2006).

penalty. They are attempting to ensure that municipal law no longer, and never in the future, reflects the possibility of the punishment. It is the stalwart proposition that law does *not* have to reach its lethal potential to rule situations and promote legitimate governmental action. At the moment, Protocol No.6 and Protocol No.13 constitute hegemonic advances towards total abolition, and in the current practice of the Member States, textual amendment will perhaps not alter the abolitionist position. However, the danger may arise if states begin to want to pull-out of Protocol No.6 and Protocol No.13, as Andrew Clapham has observed, "we cannot absolutely discount the possibility that states may in the future try to denounce [the Protocols]".[153] If this happens, the current text of Art.2(1) may provide a legal loophole for rogue states to implement the death penalty. As such, in order to provide a uniform expression of abolitionism it still appears necessary to do away with the second sentence of this problematical provision.

[153] A. Clapham, "Symbiosis in International Human Rights Law: The Öcalan case and the Evolving Law on the Death Sentence" (2003) 1 J.I.C.J. 475, 483.

[6]

The People Decide: The Effect of the Introduction of the Quasi-Jury System (*Saiban-In Seido*) on the Death Penalty in Japan

Leah Ambler*

I. Introduction

The Japanese people will soon decide the fate of criminal defendants for the first time in over 50 years.[1] Under the Lay Assessor Act as of May 2009, randomly selected members of the Japanese public[2] will preside over criminal trials alongside professional judges and be responsible for determining both verdicts and sentences.[3] Japan's retention of the death penalty means that members of the public will ultimately have to decide whether a person lives or dies.[4]

This article examines the potential impact of the new lay assessor system, or *saiban-in seido*, on capital punishment in Japan, and considers whether it may reduce death sentences to the point of effectively abolishing them at trial stage in the District Court. The article posits that the introduction of the lay assessor system may create the momentum for Japan to align its criminal justice system with that of other developed countries—that is, abolition of the death penalty as an available criminal sanction.[5]

I approach questions about the lay assessor system and abolition of the death penalty from a normative perspective linked to current trends in international law and human rights law.[6] Accordingly, this article argues that abolition of the death penalty—*de facto* or *de jure*—is the most desirable outcome of the introduction of lay participation in Japan. It explores the possibilities of a shift in the public conscience from passively

---

* I would like to thank Professor Kent Anderson for his guidance, patience and support. Thanks also to Japanese prosecutors, defense lawyers and abolitionists who provided views on the new system and to family and friends for their encouragement. Please note that this article reflects the author's personal views and not those of the Commonwealth Department of Foreign Affairs and Trade, or the Australian Government. This paper is dedicated to Kazutoshi Takahashi whose death sentence was confirmed by the Supreme Court of Japan, 28 March 2006.

1 See Kent Anderson & Mark Nolan, Lay Participation in the Japanese Justice System: A Few Preliminary Thoughts Regarding the Lay Assessor System (saiban-in seido) from Domestic Historical and International Psychological Perspectives, 37 VAND. J. TRANSNAT'L L. 935, 937 (2004) (noting that Japan had a jury system between 1923 and 1943).

2 *Id.* at 954; Saiban-in no sanka suru keiji saiban ni kansuru horitsu [Act Concerning Participation of Lay Assessors in Criminal Trials], Law No. 63 of 2004, art. 13 [hereinafter Lay Assessor Act], *translated in* 6 ASIAN-PAC. L. & POL'Y J. 233, 243 (2005) (noting lay assessors must be selected from Japanese citizens who are eligible to vote); Koshoku senkyo ho [Public Election Act], Law No. 100 of 1950, art. 9 (providing requirements for eligibility to vote).

3 *Id.* at art 6, *translated in* 6 ASIAN-PAC. L. & POL'Y J. 233, 240-41 (2005).

4 *See* Keiho [Penal Code], Law No. 45 of 1907, art. 9 (listing the available criminal penalties, namely death, imprisonment with hard labour, imprisonment, fine, detention or fine with added forfeiture).

5 *See* WILLIAM A. SCHABAS, THE ABOLITION OF THE DEATH PENALTY IN INTERNATIONAL LAW 14-15 (3d ed. 2002).

6 *See, e.g., id.*; ROBERT BADINTER ET AL., DEATH PENALTY – BEYOND ABOLITION (2004).

pro-capital punishment to abolitionist through active participation in the judicial system. It is without doubt that any outcomes will depend upon the roles played by each of the parties involved in the criminal justice system: the ministry of justice, judiciary, prosecutor's office, defendant and defense lawyers. This article will examine the development and possible impact of these roles through an analysis of the vested interests of each of the parties, from the staunchly pro-capital punishment to the violently opposed, and perhaps most importantly, to the fence-sitters.

Part One of this article describes developing international norms that are moving towards *de jure* abolition of the death penalty under all circumstances. Part Two describes the current capital punishment system in Japan—from arrest to execution—and the reasons used to justify its retention. Part Three explores Japan's twenty-year jury system in the pre-World War II period in light of the future role of lay assessors in deciding verdicts and sentences. Part Four considers how the lay assessor system may impact Japan's current attitude towards the death penalty and may even lead to a suspension of death sentences or *de facto* abolition. In assessing its impact, the article analyses the vested interests of each party involved. It concludes that the introduction of the *saiban-in seido* may prove a vital first step towards eventual *de facto* abolition of the death penalty in Japan, provided each party abides by rules of fairness and justice.

II. ABOLITION OF THE DEATH PENALTY IN INTERNATIONAL LAW

A. Background

Since the end of the Second World War, the international stance on capital punishment has shifted from retentionist to abolitionist—more than half the countries in the world have instated either *de facto* or *de jure* abolition of the death penalty. As of December 2001, only seventy-one countries and territories had retained the death penalty.[7] Of these, thirty-four had *de facto* abolition, that is, no executions were carried out in the previous decade.[8] Currently seventy-five countries and territories are *de jure* abolitionist and fourteen are *de jure* abolitionist for all but exceptional crimes, such as war crimes.[9] The overwhelming trend towards *de facto* and *de jure* abolition in state practice, along with a growing body of international and regional instruments urging abolition, suggest that abolition of the death penalty is on the way to becoming a customary rule of international law.[10]

B. Abolition in International Instruments

Modern developments in international law and capital punishment began with the proclamation of the right to life in the 1948 Universal Declaration of Human Rights.[11] This right encompasses the right to protection of one's life from arbitrary deprivation by

---

[7] ROGER HOOD, THE DEATH PENALTY: A WORLDWIDE PERSPECTIVE app. 1, table A1.1 (3d ed. 2002)
[8] *Id.* at app. 1, table A1.2.
[9] *Id.* app. 1, tbls. A1.3, A1.4.
[10] *See, e.g.*, William A. Schabas, *International Law and the Death Penalty*, *in* CAPITAL PUNISHMENT: STRATEGIES FOR ABOLITION 36 (Peter Hodgkinson & William A. Schabas eds., 2004); SCHABAS, *supra* note 5; BADINTER ET AL., *supra* note 6.
[11] Universal Declaration of Human Rights, G.A. Res 217A, at art. 3, U.N. GAOR, 3d Sess., 1st plen. mtg., U.N. Doc A/810 (Dec. 10, 1948).

the State.[12] The 1966 International Covenant on Civil and Political Rights[13] further espoused the right to life[14] and specifically referred to the death penalty and its abolition.[15] The ICCPR also established a prohibition on cruel, inhumane or degrading treatment and torture. In addition, it codified the doctrine of due process, the presumption of innocence and the right to review.[16] However, it did not impose any specific obligation to abolish or suspend capital punishment upon the ratifying States.[17]

Several scholars have argued that by separating the death penalty from the right to life, provisions of the ICCPR render the former an exception to the latter. However, the adoption in July 1991 of the Second Optional Protocol to the International Covenant on Civil and Political Rights Aiming at the Abolition of the Death Penalty casts doubt on the validity of such arguments.[18] The Second Optional Protocol came after a raft of UN Resolutions on abolition,[19] and although Japan opposed the Draft Protocol, it voted in favor of the resolution that mandated its drafting.[20]

C. Abolition in Regional Organizations

Even before the Second Optional Protocol entered into force, regional developments towards abolition began with the 1985 Council of Europe Protocol No. 6 to the Convention for the Protection of Human Rights and Fundamental Freedoms Concerning the Abolition of the Death Penalty.[21] Subsequently in 1991, the Organization of American States adopted the Protocol to the American Convention on Human Rights to Abolish the Death Penalty.[22] Most recently and perhaps most controversially on May 3, 2002, the Council of Europe opened for signature a further Protocol No. 13 to the Convention for the Protection of Rights and Fundamental Freedoms Concerning the Abolition of the Death Penalty in All Circumstances.[23] Signed by all member states except Azerbaijan and Russia and ratified by all but seven states,[24] Protocol No. 13

---

[12] For approaches considered by the drafters, see SCHABAS, *supra* note 5, at 24.
[13] International Covenant on Civil and Political Rights, 21 U.N. GAOR Supp. (No. 16) at 52, U.N. Doc. A/6316 (1966), 999 U.N.T.S. 171 (entered into force 23 March 1976), [hereinafter ICCPR].
[14] *Id.* at art. 6(1).
[15] *Id.* at arts. 6(2), 6(4)-(6).
[16] *Id.* at arts. 7, 14.
[17] Japan ratified the ICCPR on September 21, 1979. *See e.g.,* Office of the United Nations High Commissioner for Human Rights, *Status of Ratifications of the Principal International Human Rights Treaties as of 09 June 2004*, 6, http://www.unhchr.ch/pdf/report.pdf.
[18] Second Optional Protocol to the International Covenant on Civil and Political Rights, aiming at the abolition of the death penalty, opened for signature Dec. 15, 1989, G.A. res. 44/128, annex, 44, U.N. GAOR Supp. (No. 49) at 207, U.N. Doc. A/44/49 (entered into force July 11, 1991).
[19] SCHABAS, *supra* note 5, at 156-167.
[20] *See id.* at 176 (Japan (UN Doc. A/C.3/37/SR.32, para. 44, UN Doc. A/C.3/37/SR.53, para. 4, UN Doc. A/C.3/37/SR.67, para. 84)).
[21] Protocol No. 6 to the Convention for the Protection of Human Rights and Fundamental Freedoms Concerning the Abolition of the Death Penalty, Apr. 28, 1983, Europ. T.S. No. 114.
[22] Protocol to the American Convention on Human Rights to Abolish the Death Penalty, June 8, 1990, O.A.S. T.S. No. 73, 29 I.L.M. 1447.
[23] Protocol No. 13 to the Convention for the Protection of Rights and Fundamental Freedoms Concerning the Abolition of the Death Penalty in All Circumstances, May 3, 2002, Europe. T.S. No. 187.
[24] Armenia, Azerbaijan, Italy, Latvia, Poland, Russia, Spain. *See* Council of Europe Treaty Office, *Protocol No. 13 to the Convention for the Protection of Human Rights and Fundamental Freedoms Concerning the Abolition of the Death Penalty in All Circumstances CETS No. 187 - Status as of: Nov. 9, 2007*, http://conventions.coe.int/Treaty/Commun/ChercheSig.asp?NT=187&CM=&DF=&CL=ENG.

permits neither reservations nor derogations and calls for outright abolition of the death penalty in all circumstances.[25] The strongly abolitionist Parliamentary Assembly of the Council of Europe has passed recommendations and resolutions calling on Japan, as a country with observer status, to institute a moratorium on executions and take the necessary steps towards abolition of the death penalty.[26]

D. *Abolition in Asia*

The death penalty is most widely used in Asia. Only Nepal,[27] Hong Kong,[28] Cambodia[29] and Timor Leste have established *de jure* abolition.[30] Other attempts at abolition have met with little success. For example, after becoming the first country in Asia to abolish the death penalty in 1987, the Philippines reintroduced it in 1994.[31] The prospect for eventual *de jure* abolition exists in many countries which maintain *de facto* abolition of the death penalty, including Laos (no executions since 1993), Myanmar (1989), Brunei Darussalam (1957) and Bhutan (1964).[32] The abolition debate is also gaining traction in Taiwan and South Korea.[33]

On May 17, 1998, the Hong Kong-based Asian Human Rights Commission pushed for abolition at the regional level by drafting and declaring Article 3.7 of the Asian Charter on Human Rights.[34] Article 3.7 specifically calls for the abolition of the death penalty in all states and sets out minimum standards to be complied with in countries

---

[25] *See* Peter Hodgkinson, *Capital Punishment: improve it or remove it?*, *in* CAPITAL PUNISHMENT: STRATEGIES FOR ABOLITION, *supra* note 10, at 21-22.

[26] Abolition of the Death Penalty in Council of Europe Observer States, EUR. PARL. ASS. 17th Sitting, Res. 1253 (June 25, 2001), *available at* http://assembly.coe.int/Documents/AdoptedText/ta01/eres1253.htm#_ftn1 (last visited Nov. 9, 2007); EUR. PARL. ASS., 17th Sitting, Rec. 1522 (June 25, 2001), *available at* http://assembly.coe.int/Main.asp?link=http://assemb ly.coe.int/Documents/AdoptedText/TA01/EREC1522.htm; EUR. PARL. ASS., 30th Sitting, Res. 1349 (Oct. 1, 2003), *available at* http://assembly.coe.int/Main.asp?link=http://assembly.coe.int/Documents/AdoptedText/ta03/ERES1349.htm; Eur. Parl. Ass., 30th Sitting, Rec. 1627 (Oct. 1, 2003), *available at* http://assembly.coe.int/Main.asp?link=http://assembly.coe.int/Documents/AdoptedText/ta03/EREC1627.htm.

[27] *See* HOOD, *supra* note 7, at 43 (Nepal abolished capital punishment in 1990 through insertion of Article 12 of the Constitution of the Kingdom of Nepal).

[28] *Id.* (Hong Kong abolished capital punishment in 1993 while under British administration and maintains it abolished under the 'one nation two systems' form of government under China).

[29] *Id.* (Cambodia abolished capital punishment in 1993 through insertion of Article 32 of the Constitution).

[30] *Id.* (East Timor abolished capital punishment on declaring independence from Indonesia in December 2001).

[31] Law Reimposing the Death Penalty for Heinous Crimes, Republic Act 7659 (1994). Hodgkinson, *supra* note 25, at 25; HOOD, *supra* note 7, at 44.

[32] *Id.* at 45.

[33] Hodgkinson, *supra* note 25, at 26. In particular, a Special Bill on Abolishing the Death Penalty was introduced to the seventeenth South Korean National Assembly in February 2005; however, the legislation is still under consideration. *See* Submission of the New South Wales Council for Civil Liberties to the Joint Standing Committee on Foreign Affairs, Defense and Trade: Inquiry into Australia's Relationship with Korea (Oct. 3, 2005), *available at* http://www.nswccl.org.au/docs/pdf/south%20korea%20and%20death%20penalty.pdf.

[34] Asian Human Rights Commission, *Asian Human Rights Charter*, art. 3.7, May 17, 1988, *available at* http://material.ahrchk.net/charter/pdf/charter-final.pdf.

where it still exists.[35] The Charter is an unofficial document that was used initially as a lobbying tool to urge countries in the Asian region to protect fundamental human rights.[36]

III. THE DEATH PENALTY IN JAPAN

Against this international backdrop of declining use, Japan is an outlier in retaining the death penalty. It has continuously maintained an active system of capital punishment excepting two periods of *de facto* abolition.[37] Japan suspended death sentences for three and a half centuries during the *Heian* period from 818 A.D until 1156,[38] and for three years from November 1989 until March 1993.[39]

This section describes current legal authority, procedures and practices for the death penalty in Japan. It then examines the varying justifications made by Ministers of Justice and the Public Prosecutors Office, along with references to public opinion polls, which serve to promote Japan's retentionist policy.

A. Capital Offences, Charges and Sentencing

Article 9 of the Penal Code lists the death penalty as one of six possible criminal punishments.[40] Eighteen crimes are punishable by death under the Penal Code and other special laws.[41] In practice though, death sentences have been limited to convictions of murder, robbery-murder and rape-murder.[42]

Despite the availability of the death penalty, prosecutors and judges lack guidelines for determining when to seek and impose it.[43] One formula for prosecutorial charges and judicial sentencing that was developed by a Japanese defense lawyer provides: [44]

---

35 *Id.*

36 Seth R. Harris, *Asian Human Rights: Forming a Regional Covenant*, 1 ASIAN-PAC. L. & POL'Y J., at 4 (2000). Japanese groups and individuals—such as the Catholic Human Rights Committee, the International Human Rights Centre, the Japan Union of Civil Liberty, and academics from Sophia University Institute of International Relations and Kanagawa University—participated in the drafting of the charter.

37 *See* PETRA SCHMIDT, CAPITAL PUNISHMENT IN JAPAN 9-31 (2002).

38 Except for two occasions. *See* Daniel Foote, *"The Door that Never Opens"?: Capital Punishment and Post-Conviction Review of Death Sentences in the United States and Japan*, 19 BROOK. J. INT'L L. 367, 376 (1993); SCHMIDT, *supra* note 37, at 11-12.

39 Foote, *supra* note 38. at 376.

40 Penal Code, *supra* note 4, at art. 9.

41 *Id.*, at art. 77(1) (Insurrection); art. 81 (Instigation of Foreign Aggression); art. 82 (Assistance to the Enemy); 108 (Arson of Inhabited Buildings); art. 117 (Detonating by Explosives); art. 119 (Damage to Inhabited Buildings by Flood); art. 126 (Overturning of Trains); art. 127 (Endangering Traffic by Overturning a Train); art. 146 (Pollution of Water Supplies with Poisonous Materials and Causing Death Thereby); art. 199 (Homicide); art. 240 (Robbery Causing Death or Injury); art. 241 (Rape at the Scene of the Robbery; Causing Death Thereby); *see also* SCHMIDT, *supra* note 37, at 30 (use of explosives; causing death as a result of a duel; causing death as a result of an aeroplane crash; causing death by hijacking an aircraft; killing a hostage); Yoshihiro Yasuda, *The Death Penalty in Japan, in* DEATH PENALTY, *supra* note 6, at 215, 217.

42 Foote, *supra* note 38, at 380.

43 Joachim Herrmann, *The Death Penalty in Japan: An "Absurd" Punishment*, 67 BROOK. L. REV. 827, 830 (2002).

44 David T. Johnson, *The Death Penalty in Japan: Secrecy, Silence and Salience*, *in* THE CULTURAL LIVES OF CAPITAL PUNISHMENT: COMPARATIVE PERSPECTIVES 251, 262-63 (Christian Boulanger & Austin Sarat eds., 2005).

(i) Single murders without prior convictions do not result in death charges or convictions;
(ii) Double murders without prior convictions may result in a sentence of life imprisonment instead of a death sentence; and
(iii) Triple murders will definitely result in a death charge and sentence.[45]

Other criteria often used to impose the death penalty have been derived from the 1983 Supreme Court decision in the famous Nagayama trial[46] and include the circumstances of the crime, motive, number of victims and effect on society.

The new Lay Assessor Act contains nothing in the way of sentencing guidelines for lay assessors or judges. Whether the yet-to-be-drafted Supreme Court Rules will provide such guidance remains to be seen.

B. Appeals

Once sentenced to death at the trial stage in a District Court, a convicted person may lodge a direct appeal to the High Court for review of the original judgement, and subsequently to the Supreme Court on constitutional matters or precedential consistency.[47] Once a second appeal fails and the sentence is confirmed, the convicted person may seek retrial, pardon, amnesty or extraordinary appeal, all of which are granted at the discretion of the Cabinet.[48] Such requests do not guarantee a stay of execution.[49]

Although this article focuses on the effect of lay participation on the death penalty at the trial phase, subsequent High Court and Supreme Court review of *saiban-in* decisions will ultimately decide whether death sentences will continue to be handed down.

C. Executions

Seven detention centers are equipped for executions, which are carried out by hanging under Japanese law.[50] Executions must be carried out within six months of the judgment becoming final[51] and within five days of the issuance of an order by the Minister of Justice.[52] However, the lengthy nature of appeals and applications for retrial usually extends the period between confirmation of sentence and execution to fifteen to twenty years.[53]

---

[45] *Id.*
[46] Nagayama v. Japan, 37 Keishu 6, 609 (Sup. Ct., Jul. 8, 1983). *See also* SCHMIDT *supra* note 37, at 50.
[47] Yasuda, *supra* note 41, at 220.
[48] Nihonkoku Kenpo [Constitution of Japan], art. 73, para. 2 [hereinafter Kenpo] ("The Cabinet shall . . . decide on general amnesty, special amnesty, commutation of punishment, reprieve, and restoration of rights"); SCHMIDT, *supra* note 37, at 123.
[49] Shikei Haishi Henshu Iinkai, *2004 Nenpo: Mujitsu no shikeiin tachi* [*2004 Annual Report: The Innocent Condemned*] 88 (2004) (Teruo Ono was executed 17 December 1999 with a pending request for retrial).
[50] Keiji soshoho [Code of Criminal Procedure], Law No. 131 of 1949, art. 475.
[51] *Id.* at art. 476.
[52] *Id.* at art. 475.
[53] SCHMIDT, *supra* note 37, at 196.

Table 1. Death Sentences and Executions Since 1988[54]

Year	88	89	90	91	92	93	94	95	96	97	98	99	00	01	02	03	04
District Court Decisions	10	2	2	3	1	4	8	11	1	3	7	8	14	10	18	13	14
High Court Decisions	4	5	2	4	4	1	4	4	3	2	7	4	6	16	4	17	15
Supreme Court Decisions	7	5	7	4	4	5	2	3	4	4	5	4	3	4	2	0	13
Newly confirmed sentences	11	5	6	5	5	7	3	3	3	4	7	4	6	5	3	2	15
Executions	2	1	0	0	0	7	2	6	6	4	6	5	3	2	2	1	2
Number of people with confirmed sentences	38	40	46	51	56	56	57	54	51	51	52	50	53	56	57	56	68

D. Justification for Japan's Retention of the Death Penalty

1. The Ministry of Justice

The Japanese Minister of Justice is responsible for signing execution orders (*shikei shikko meirei*) and has ultimate control over the continuation of executions. I have classified Japanese Ministers of Justice into three categories of approaches to signing execution orders. The first is the "Sheriff"-- a Minister of Justice who exercises his duties in the pursuit of social stability. For example, Minister Masaharu Gotoda justified signing three execution warrants, which ended a forty-month moratorium from November 1989 to March 1993 by stressing his obligation as Minister of Justice to "protect law and order."[55]

The second category consists of the "Servants," or Ministers of Justice who prioritize their official duties above any contrary personal beliefs. For instance, at current Minister of Justice Seiken Sugiura's first press conference upon taking office, he announced that he would not sign an execution order for philosophical and religious reasons.[56] The very next day, speaking in his official capacity, he retracted that statement:

> The statement I made at yesterday's press conference in relation to executions was an expression of my individual sentiments and not a statement in relation to the performance of my role as Minister of Justice and guardian of the law. In this respect I regret that there has been a misunderstanding and seek to rectify it.[57]

---

[54] Shikei Haishi Henshu Iinkai, *supra* note 49, at 141.
[55] Johnson, *supra* note 44, at 257.
[56] Minister of Justice Seiken Sugiura, Homu daijin hatsutochogo kisha kaiken no gaiyo [Overview of press conference after the Minister of Justice first took up office] (Oct. 31, 2005).
[57] *Id.* (Nov. 1, 2005).

The final group are the "Samaritans," those Ministers of Justice who refuse to sign executions on principle. Minister Akama Bunzo was perhaps the first of these; he reportedly refused to sign any execution orders presented to him during his term from November 1967 until November 1968.[58] Other Samaritans include Ministers Hasegawa, Kajiyama, Sato and Tahara who held office between November 1989 and March 1993.[59] During this period, not a single execution took place, effectively resulting in a forty-month moratorium on executions.

2. The Judiciary and the Public Prosecutors Office

While Ministers of Justice play the decisive role in finalizing death sentences, prosecutors initiate the process by deciding whether to seek the death penalty at the trial stage and whether to continue to seek it on appeal. In turn, decisions by prosecutors to seek death sentences place pressure on judges to grant them, as Japanese judges tend to give weight to the exercise of prosecutorial discretion.[60] Due in large part to judges and prosecutors sharing similar social and educational backgrounds,[61] judges rely heavily on evidence of confessions extracted by prosecutors for convictions.[62] This reliance results in a seemingly concerted effort between prosecutors and judges in criminal cases. A further factor contributing to the judiciary's pro-retentionist stance is its conservatism.[63] Trained and nurtured by the Ministry, the judiciary demonstrates a strong tendency to defer to government policy. Death sentences prove no exception.[64] The greatest imperative on judges to continue death sentencing is, however, a perception of public pressure. High profile cases attract extensive media attention which arouses public sentiment and creates a perceived obligation on the judiciary to give defendants in more violent crimes the ultimate penalty.[65]

3. Public Opinion Polls

The most frequently cited reason for continued sentencing and execution in Japan is public support for capital punishment. The Japanese government has relied on public opinion polls to respond to criticism and justify its stance both domestically and

[58] SCHMIDT, *supra* note 37, at 63.
[59] Shikei Haishi Henshu Iinkai, *supra* note 49, at 205.
[60] *See, e.g.,* DAVID T. JOHNSON, THE JAPANESE WAY OF JUSTICE: PROSECUTING CRIME IN JAPAN 62 (2002) (Judges not only convict what prosecutors charge, but they also impose sentences which prosecutors seem to like).
[61] *Id.*
[62] SCHMIDT, *supra* note 37, at 152.
[63] There is general consensus among Japanese and foreign academics on the conservatism of the Japanese judiciary. However, different reasons are identified. *See, e.g.*, Setsuo Miyazawa, *Administrative control of Japanese Judges, in* LAW AND TECHNOLOGY IN THE PACIFIC COMMUNITY 263 (Philip S.C. Lewis, ed., 1994); J. Mark Ramseyer, *Judicial (In)dependence in Japan, in* UNIV. OF CHICAGO LAW SCHOOL RECORD 1993-1995 at 4 (volume 39 Fall) (1993); John O. Haley, *Judicial Independence in Japan Revisited,* 25 *Law in Japan* 1, 2, 8-18 (1995), *in* JAPANESE LAW IN CONTEXT: READINGS IN SOCIETY, THE ECONOMY AND POLITICS 89 (Curtis J. Milhaupt et al., eds., 2001).
[64] 'Courts,' *infra* Part III. E(a).
[65] SCHMIDT, *supra* note 37, at 122; *see also*, Mayumi Negishi and Kaho Shimizu, *Young killers at the heart of capital punishment fight*, THE JAPAN TIMES, May 20, 2006, http://search.japantimes.co.jp/print/nn20060520f2.html (last visited Nov. 9, 2007).

internationally.[66] Linking the will of the people to retention of capital punishment gives such sentences a certain democratic legitimacy.

Public opinion polls regularly demonstrate widespread support for capital punishment. In the most recent poll conducted in 2004 by the government, an unprecedented 81.4% of people surveyed agreed with the statement that in certain circumstances the death penalty is unavoidable.[67] Arguably, public opinion polls are relatively more empirical and form a more rational and universal basis[68] for retention.[69]

Table 2. Public opinion poll results concerning the death penalty in the last 50 years[70]

Year	Implementing Agency	Retentionist	Abolitionist
1953	Prime Minister's Office	65.0%	18.0%
1967	Prime Minister's Office	70.5%	16.0%
1975	Prime Minister's Office	56.9%	20.7%
1980	Prime Minister's Office	62.3%	14.3%
1989	Prime Minister's Office	66.5%	15.7%
1990	Tokyo Newspaper	53.0%	34.0%
1993	Asahi Television	62.1%	20.6%
1993	Yomiuri Newspaper	63.9%	28.3%
1994	Japan Broadcasting Corporation (NHK)	62.8%	17.2%
1994	Prime Minister's Office	73.8%	13.6%
1994	Forum 90	58.3%	22.2%
1999	Prime Minister's Office	79.3%	8.8%
2003	Asahi Television	45.7%	32.0%
2004	Cabinet Office	81.4%	6.0%

Critics point out many deficiencies in the public opinion polls, including a lack of cross-sectional quality in the audience surveyed; problematic phrasing of questions; and the political motivations of the agency conducting the poll.[71] Nonetheless, overall support for Japan's system of capital punishment is undeniably high.

Judging from the normative perspective grounded in international law that the death penalty should be abolished under all circumstances, one argument may be that the Japanese public is wrong in its support of the death penalty. This article asserts instead that the Japanese public is uninformed. Due to their relative ignorance about the system of capital punishment in their own country, the Japanese are ill-equipped to make judgments required in these opinion polls. This lack of information permeates every

[66] *See* ICCPR Human Rights Committee, *Fourth Periodic Reports of States Parties Due in 1996: Japan. 01/10/97,* CCPR/C/115/Add.3 art. 6, para. 62 (Jan. 10, 1997) ('under present conditions, the majority of the Japanese people insist that capital punishment should be maintained to punish those who commit extremely atrocious offences'), *available at* http://www.unhchr.ch/tbs/doc.nsf/0/9afe294abf7c3f628025663900556e44?Opendocument; *see, e.g.*, SCHMIDT, *supra* note 37, at 61-62; NOEL WILLIAMS, THE RIGHT TO LIFE IN JAPAN 44 (1997).

[67] *See* Government Publications Office, Department of the Minister for the Cabinet Office, *Kihonteki ho seido ni kansuru yoronchosa* [*Public opinion poll in relation to the basic legal system*] (Dec, 2004), http://www8.cao.go.jp/survey/h16/h16-houseido/index.html (last visited Nov. 9, 2007).

[68] *See* SCHMIDT, *supra* note 37, at 160.

[69] *Id.* at 158.

[70] *Id.* at 117.

[71] *Id.* at 157-188.

stage of the process—from interrogation of suspects[72] to post-trial detention[73] to most importantly, execution.[74]

Up until now the direct impact of this judgment has been minimal. However, the introduction of the lay assessor system in May 2009 will require the Japanese public to determine whether to sentence individual defendants to death, not whether to retain or abolish the death penalty as a system. Already future lay assessors have indicated that they do not want to be involved in the system; in one public opinion poll, 46.5 percent of those surveyed did not want to become lay assessors because they did not want to judge people. Another 46.4 percent responded that they did not wish to participate because of the difficulty in determining guilt or innocence.[75] For the first time, the new *saiban-in seido* will educate and equip the public with the necessary tools to make an informed decision about the future of capital punishment in Japan. While predictions about the nature of this decision are difficult, a certain shift in the public's stance on the death penalty is foreseeable.

E. Abolition of the Death Penalty in Japan

Despite overwhelming support for retention of the death penalty in the judiciary, legislature and general public, abolitionist groups do exist in each of these sectors. This section applies an institutional analysis to attempts thus far as well as plans in the future to abolish Japan's system of capital punishment.

1. The Courts

To date, challenges to the constitutionality of the death penalty have been few and unsuccessful. By the end of the 1950s, the Supreme Court had ruled on almost all major constitutional challenges to capital punishment and made no subsequent revisions thereafter.[76]

Perhaps the most unequivocal of judicial precedents on the death penalty is the Japanese Supreme Court's 1948 decision[77] that considered whether capital punishment contravenes the right to life[78] and the prohibition on cruel punishment.[79] The court found

---

[72] A suspect may be detained and questioned for twenty-three days between arrest and indictment without any form of mandatory recording of the interrogation process. *See id.*, at 152.

[73] Once a death sentence is confirmed, all communication with the outside world is severed, except brief, supervised meetings with lawyers and close family. *See, e.g.*, Herrmann, *supra* note 43; Yasuda, *supra* note 41.

[74] Most executions take place when Parliament is not sitting and the practice of publishing the number and date of executions has only been in place since November 1998. *See, e.g.*, Johnson, *supra* note 44, at 258; SCHMIDT, *supra* note 37, at 75.

[75] *See* Government Publications Office, Department of the Minister for the Cabinet Office, *Saiban-in seido ni kansuru yoron chôsa* [*Public opinion poll in relation to the Lay Assessor System*] (Feb. 2005), http://www8.cao.go.jp/survey/h16/h16-saiban/.

[76] SCHMIDT, *supra* note 37, at 100.

[77] A v. Japan, 2 Keishu 3, 191 (Sup. Ct., 1948).

[78] Constitution of Japan, art. 13, provides, "All of the people shall be respected as individuals. Their right to life, liberty, and the pursuit of happiness shall, to the extent that it does not interfere with the public welfare, be the supreme consideration in legislation and in other governmental affairs." KENPO, *supra* note 48, at art. 13.

[79] *Id.* at art. 36 ("The infliction of torture by any public officer and cruel punishments are absolutely forbidden").

that the Constitution protects an individual's right to life only to the extent that that right does not interfere with the public welfare. Therefore, in eliminating threats to the public welfare, the death penalty trumped the right to life.[80] The Court also held that capital punishment does not contravene the prohibition of cruel punishment contained in article 36.[81] Although the four judges in the minority allowed scope for reconsideration of this doctrine in the event of a shift in public opinion against the death penalty, this remains the definitive stance on the issue.[82]

In the final constitutional challenge to capital punishment, *Ichikawa et al v. Japan*,[83] defense counsel argued that the current method of execution violates Article 31's requirement that criminal penalties be imposed according to procedure established by law. Defense counsel claimed that the Act concerning the Validity of Provisions which were in Force at the Time of Enactment of the Japanese Constitution[84] rendered ineffective Cabinet Order No. 65 of 20 February 1873,[85] which created the framework for executions; hence, the death penalty was not being carried out according to procedure established by law. The Court rejected this argument and with no further successful challenges to capital punishment's constitutionality as of June 2006, has unequivocally excluded a judicially-driven abolition of the death penalty.

Nevertheless, there are judges opposed to the death penalty, including former Justice of the Supreme Court of Japan Shigemitsu Dando.[86] Yet even Dando spoke of death sentencing as unavoidable during his term as Supreme Court Justice,[87] as prosecutors continue to press for the death penalty where it remains a legal form of punishment.[88] Accordingly, legislative change alone can remove this constraint, which ultimately requires a shift in the official government stance.

2. The Legislature

The official position of the Japanese government is retentionist. Apart from an unofficial three-year moratorium on the death penalty by virtue of individual Ministers of Justice choosing not to sign execution orders, there has been at least one execution annually.[89] Bills on abolition were presented to the Diet four times in 1901, 1902, 1906 and 1956. None of these bills passed.

---

[80] *See* SCHMIDT, *supra* note 37, at 99.
[81] *Id.* at 91.
[82] *Id.*
[83] Ichikawa et al v. Japan, 15 KEISHU 7, 1106 (Sup. Ct., July 19, 1961), *translated in* THE CONSTITUTIONAL CASE LAW OF JAPAN: SELECTED SUPREME COURT DECISIONS, 1961-70, at 161-164 (Hiroshi Itoh & Lawrence Ward Beer eds., 1978).
[84] Nihon koku kenpo shiko no sai ni gen ni koryoku wo yusuru meirei no kitei no koryokuto ni kansuru horitsu [Act Concerning the Validity of Provisions which Were in Force at the Time of Enactment of the Japanese Constitution], April 18, 1947.
[85] Dajokan fukoku [A Revised Chart of Hanging Equipment], Cabinet Order No. 65 of 1873, *available at* http://hourei.ndl.go.jp/help/ilabhelp.html#dajyoukan.
[86] *See* Shigemitsu Dando, *Toward the Abolition of the Death Penalty*, 72 IND. L.J. 7 (1996).
[87] *See id.* at 15.
[88] *See id.* at 16.
[89] Shikei Haishi Henshu Iinkai, *supra* note 49, at 169 ("It is considered that abolition of the death penalty would be inappropriate." (quoting *Chieko Nono, Item 9, Minutes of the Justice Committee*, 161st Sess. of the H. of Councillors (7 November 2004) (response of former Minister of Justice))).

In 1994, however, several members of the Diet formed an all-party Diet Members' League for the Abolition of the Death Penalty (Parliamentary Union for the Abolition of the Death Penalty).[90] As of 2003 the League had 122 members, the equivalent of one-sixth of the Diet.[91] In conjunction with the Japan Federation of Bar Associations (JFBA),[92] in November 2004 the League drafted an Act for a Moratorium on Executions. The League considered the passage of this Act to be the best first step towards abolition, based on advice from Parliamentary Assembly members of the Council of Europe who attended a Justice and Human Rights Seminar hosted by the Diet Members' League on May 17, 2002.[93] The subsequently established JFBA Committee on the Realization of a Moratorium on Executions[94] produced the first draft of the Act, which also incorporated the establishment of a House of Councillors Committee on the Death Penalty on May 17, 2005.[95] As of June 2006, the Bill has yet to be presented to parliament. Nevertheless, increased abolitionist activity at a governmental level suggests that if the momentum continues, *de jure* abolition may be possible.

3. The People

Around two dozen abolitionist groups have established themselves in Japan, [96] the largest of which is Forum 90.[97] Forum 90 was set up in 1990 as a collaboration among Amnesty International's Japan Section, private citizens, community organizations, lawyers, politicians, academics, members of religious groups and convicted persons. Originally established to support Japan's ratification of the Second Optional Protocol, Forum 90 now has over 5,000 members. It conducts seminars, holds interviews with the Minister of Justice, and cooperates with abolitionist movements in Korea and the United States.[98] Forum 90, along with other organizations such as Amnesty International and the Japan Civil Liberties Union, has submitted NGO reports on the death penalty in Japan to the United Nations Human Rights Committee.[99]

Despite gradually changing attitudes towards capital punishment in Japan, the legislature, judiciary, administration and the populace continue to support the death penalty. The following section examines Japan's previous jury system, the new lay assessor system, and their past and future impact on the death penalty in Japan.

---

[90] *Shikei haishi giin renmei.*
[91] Yasuda, *supra* note 41, at 229.
[92] *Nihon bengoshi rengokai* (*nichibenren*).
[93] *See* Shikei Haishi Henshu Iinkai, *supra* note 49, at 184.
[94] *Nichibenren shikei shikko teishi jitsugen iinkai.*
[95] Shikei seido chosakai no secchi oyobi shikei shikko no teishi ni kansuru horitsu [Act Concerning the Establishment of the Committee on the Death Penalty and a Moratorium on Executions], First Draft of the Committee 17 May 2005.
[96] *See* Shikei Haishi Henshu Iinkai (2004) Mujitsu no shiheishu-tachi. Tokyo Impakuto Press, 177-186 (for a list of these groups).
[97] Shikei haishi kokusai joyaku no hijun wo motomeru Forum 90.
[98] Shikei Haishi Henshu Iinkai, *supra* note 49, at 179.
[99] *See, e.g.*, FORUM 90, ALTERNATE REPORT ON ARTICLE 6 OF THE ICCPR WITH REGARD TO THE FOURTH PERIODIC REPORT OF THE GOVERNMENT OF JAPAN (Sept. 1998); AMNESTY INT'L, JAPAN: THE DEATH PENALTY: SUMMARY OF CONCERNS, AI INDEX: ASA 22/01/97 (1997); INT'L FED'N FOR HUMAN RIGHTS, THE DEATH PENALTY IN JAPAN: A PRACTICE UNWORTHY OF A DEMOCRACY, REPORT NO. 359/2, at 8-9 (2003), http://www.fidh.org/IMG/pdf/jp359a.pdf (citing JAPAN CIVIL LIBERTIES UNION, 1998 REPORT CONCERNING THE PRESENT STATUS OF HUMAN RIGHTS IN JAPAN (Oct. 1998)).

IV. Lay Participation and the Death Penalty in Japan

The concept of lay participation in the criminal justice system in Japan is not new. For example, civil conciliation proceedings (*chotei*) involved lay persons during the Tokugawa period,[100] in the pre-WWII jury system that lasted for twenty years[101] and in prosecutorial review commissions (*kensatsu shinsa kai*).[102] This section briefly describes the twenty-year jury system that was suspended in the midst of World War II and examines its outcomes relative to the new lay assessor system and its role in potential abolition of the death penalty. It then describes the new lay assessor system and its future shape and influence as the greatest grant of judicial decision-making power to the Japanese people to date.

A. The Japanese Jury (1923-1943)

1. Background

Japan's pre-war jury system (*baishin seido*) was introduced by the 1923 Jury Act,[103] which, like the Lay Assessor Act,[104] imposed a five-year grace period before the Act entered force. After taking effect in 1928, the jury system was then suspended in 1943.[105] The pre-war jury system was based on systems for lay participation in France, Germany, England and the United States.

In the pre-war system, a jury presided over death or life imprisonment trials unless the accused chose otherwise.[106] In all other cases, juries were only empanelled if specifically requested by the defendant,[107] in which case the defendant had to bear the costs of the jury.[108] Only Japanese males over the age of thirty who paid three yen or more in taxes over the previous two years were eligible to serve as jurors.[109] Rather than returning a verdict of guilty or not guilty, the jury deliberated and formulated responses to questions of fact posed by the judge.[110] A simple majority of the twelve jurors[111] determined the responses, which were ultimately not binding on the outcome of the case.[112] The Jury Act did not allow for objections to the judge's jury instructions.[113]

---

[100] The Tokugawa period ran from 1603 to 1868. Lester W. Kiss, *Reviving the Criminal Jury in Japan*, 62 LAW & CONTEMP. PROBS. 261, 280 (1999); *See also* DAN FENNO HENDERSON, CONCILIATION AND JAPANESE LAW: TOKUGAWA AND MODERN, VOLUMES I AND II (1965).
[101] *See* 'The Japanese Jury', *infra* Part IV. A.
[102] *See, e.g.*, Mark West, *Prosecution Review Commissions: Japan's Answer to the Problem of Prosecutorial Discretion*, 92 COLUM. L. REV. 684, 695 & n.61 (1992).
[103] Baishin ho [Jury Act], Law No. 50 of 1923 [hereinafter Jury Act].
[104] Lay Assessor Act (Supp. 2004), art. 1, *supra* note 2, at 280.
[105] Baishin ho no teishi ni kansuru horitsu [Act to Suspend the Jury Act], Law No. 88 of 1943.
[106] *Id.* at art. 3.
[107] *Id.*
[108] Takashi Maruta, *The Criminal Jury System in Imperial Japan and the Contemporary Argument for Its Reintroduction*, 72 INT'L REV. PENAL L. 215, 216 (2001) (Fr.).
[109] *Id.*
[110] *Id.*
[111] *Id.*
[112] *Id.* at 217.
[113] Jury Act, *supra* note 103, at art. 78.

2. Death Sentences and the Japanese Jury

In contrast to jurors in the future Japanese *saiban-in seido*, pre-war jurors in Japan did not have to decide directly whether to sentence a particular defendant to death. Nevertheless, the experience of those jurors offers a glimpse into how jurors in the new lay assessor system may act when called upon to sentence a criminal. Data collected from Japan's original jury system suggests that lay people are more lenient than professional judges in criminal sentencing. Juries returned significantly more acquittals than modern judge-only trials across the board and despite wartime mobilization and other impediments.[114] For example, a study of the criminal courts in Sendai between 1928 and 1943 indicates a certain leniency in the overall jury decisions; of sixteen defendants tried by juries, ten were acquitted and three were found guilty of a lesser charge.[115] A second study found that juries acquitted sixty-three percent of murder suspects and accused arsonists, while judges acquitted only .07% of persons accused of those crimes during the same period.[116] Scholars argue that this dramatic difference in outcomes resulted from jurors' heavier reliance on physical evidence, replacing the traditional judicial reliance on prosecutorial dossiers and written confessions in convictions.[117] If the new lay assessors act similarly to their predecessors, this may allow room for *de facto* abolition in the form of lesser sentences or acquittals and may even create a momentum for *de jure* activism.

B. The New Lay Assessor System

While not the first form of lay participation in Japanese history, the *saiban-in seido* is the first of its kind in Japan and the world.[118] A hybrid of the classic common law jury system and the mixed courts of the civil system, this model for a new lay assessor system significantly reconstructs criminal justice in Japan and thereby may change Japan's fundamental approach to capital punishment. This section highlights areas for potential development and change through an analysis of articles in the Lay Assessor Act related to the role of *saiban-in* in death sentencing.

1. Purpose

The Lay Assessor Act was enacted on May 28, 2004, as one of a suite of judicial reforms proposed by the Justice System Reform Council (*shiho seido kaikaku shingikai*) in its 2001 report.[119] The main goals of the *saiban-in seido* are to deliver better justice and promote a more democratic society through citizen involvement in the judicial process.[120] The explicit purpose of the Lay Assessor Act is "to contribute to the

---

[114] *See* Anderson & Nolan, *supra* note 1, at 964.
[115] Maruta, *supra* note 108, at 217.
[116] *Id.*
[117] *Id.*
[118] For a detailed background of the political lead-up to the drafting of the law, see generally Anderson & Nolan, *supra* note 1.
[119] *See generally* JUSTICE SYSTEM REFORM COUNCIL, RECOMMENDATIONS OF THE JUSTICE SYSTEM REFORM COUNCIL—FOR A JUSTICE SYSTEM TO SUPPORT JAPAN IN THE 21ST CENTURY, ch. IV, pt. 1(1), 88-92 (June 12, 2001), *available at* http://www.kantei.go.jp/foreign/judiciary/2001/0612report.html.
[120] Anderson & Nolan, *supra* note 1, at 941-44.

promotion of the public's understanding of the judicial system and thereby raise their confidence in it."[121] From the outset, even before the Act was drafted, there was no consideration of the protection of defendants' rights as a reason for reform.[122] Neither the drafters nor the text itself envisage the introduction of the new system as a catalyst for reform and ultimate abolition of capital punishment in Japan. Any such reform must therefore begin at a grassroots level upon implementation of the system.

2. Lay Assessor Trials

In a typical lay assessor trial, six *saiban-in* will sit on a panel with three judges and determine both the verdict and sentence in criminal cases.[123] To this end, lay assessors and judges will make joint decisions in recognizing the facts, applying the laws to those facts and determining sentences.[124] Decisions of the mixed panel will be made on the basis of a simple majority, which must include the vote of one judge.[125] Lay assessors are to be selected by lottery[126] from a list of eligible voters in each district[127] and will preside over all capital trials.[128] In 2004, 3,308 trials would have been eligible for lay assessment. Notably, prosecutors could have sought capital punishment in up to two-thirds of those trials.

Table 3. 2004 Trials Eligible for Lay Assessment (by offence)[129]

Offence	Number of Trials
Robbery causing bodily injury	890
Murder	795
Arson of an inhabited structure	297
Bodily injury causing death	277
Robbery and rape causing death	270
Forcible Indecency resulting in death or injury	141
Robbery causing death	126
Robbery and rape	105
Offences against the Special Drugs Act	83
Offences against the Stimulant Drug Control Act	80
Currency forgery	79
Dangerous driving causing death	50
Offences against the Possession of Firearms and Weapons Control Act	40
Money laundering	24

121 Lay Assessor Act, art. 1, *supra* note 2, at 236.
122 The Justice System Reform Council, *Recommendations of the Justice System Reform Council - For a Justice System to Support Japan in the 21st Century*, June 12, 2001, *available at* http://www.kantei.go.jp/foreign/policy/sihou/singikai/990612_e.html.
123 *See id.* at art. 2, at 237, art. 6, at 240.
124 *See id.* at art. 6, at 240-241 (in relation to interpretation of relevant law, lay assessors may comment but do not have a vote).
125 *Id.* at art. 66, at 273.
126 *Id.* at art. 26, at 252.
127 *See id.* at art. 13, at 243.
128 *Id.* at art. 2, at 237.
129 Supreme Court of Japan, Zaimei betsu ni mita taisho jikensu (heisei 16 nen) [Number of subject cases by offence (2005)] (2005) Saiban-in Seido [Lay Assessor System], http://www.saibanin.courts.go.jp/shiryo/pdf/06.pdf.

Capture and imprisonment resulting in death	15
Kidnap and ransom	15
Others	21
Total	**3,308**

3. Qualification of Lay Assessors

Lay assessors will initially be selected at random from the general public. They must be eligible to vote; that is, they must be Japanese citizens who are twenty years of age or more.[130] Certain persons are prohibited or disqualified from service, namely lawyers, quasi-lawyers and politicians, and persons who have not completed compulsory education, were subject to imprisonment, or for whom lay assessor duties would be a burden.[131] Lay assessor candidates may decline service if they are elderly, members of local councils, students, or have recently served as a lay assessor or on a Prosecutorial Review Commission.[132]

Lay assessors who have difficulty executing their duties due to illness, carers' duties, potential damage to business, or attendance at a parent's funeral or important social obligation are also excused from service.[133] These allowances for declining service leave significant leeway for self de-selection by those who oppose the death penalty and/or do not wish to be involved in sentencing a defendant to death, even as a minority vote.[134]

Another provision of the Lay Assessor Act pertaining to capital punishment is Article 18, which grants courts discretion to disqualify lay assessor candidates whom the court deems may act unfairly in a trial.[135] This provision may effectively eliminate lay assessor candidates identified as being opposed to the death penalty. Arguably, as long as the death penalty remains a valid sentence under the Penal Code, an abolitionist lay assessor is incapable of acting fairly in determinations of whether to sentence a defendant to death.

4. Dismissal

The Lay Assessor Act contains a procedure similar to the American voir-dire, whereby the prosecutor, defendant or defense counsel may invoke a number of grounds to request dismissal of lay assessors.[136] In particular, a request for dismissal may be based on "fear that any lay assessors or reserve lay assessors would conduct a trial unfairly,"[137] but only where the causes have already arisen or are learned after the appointment of the particular lay assessor. Pursuant to this provision, the court is entitled

---

130 *See* Anderson & Nolan, *supra* note 1, at 992.

131 Lay Assessor Act, art. 14-15, *supra* note 2, at 243-246.

132 *Id.* at art. 16, at 246-247

133 *See id.*

134 *See id.*

135 *Id.* at art. 18, at 249.

136 *See id.* at art. 41, at 260-261 (allowing for dismissal of lay assessors for failure to take the oath, failure to attend or appear, failure to carry out their obligations, falling under a ground for disqualification, fear that they would conduct a trial unfairly, false entries on the lay assessor questionnaire, and inappropriate behavior).

137 *Id.* at art. 41, at 261.

to conduct a questionnaire of lay assessors before the Lay Assessor Selection Proceeding[138] and to question them at the Proceeding itself.[139] The court may do this to ascertain whether the person is someone who may conduct the trial unfairly.[140] Given the open-ended nature of this provision, a lay assessor's stance on capital punishment could be the subject of such questioning and prosecutors could seek their dismissal on the basis of their response.[141]

This criterion therefore leaves the door open for American-style death qualification by prosecutors in capital cases. In *Lockhart v McCree*,[142] the United States Supreme court addressed the practice of death qualification in Arkansas courts where jurors decide upon both the verdict and sentence in capital cases. The trial judge removed eight prospective jurors on the basis of their statements that they could not vote to impose the death penalty under any circumstance. The Court upheld the practice as coming within the "representative cross-section" interpretation of a defendant's constitutional right to an impartial jury.[143] The selection of death-qualified jurors has ramifications beyond an increased likelihood of death sentences, especially in models for lay participation that involve concomitant deliberation on verdict and sentence, such as the new Japanese lay assessor system. Specifically, death qualified jurors are more likely to convict and influence the dynamics of deliberations.[144]

How often and under what circumstances the death-qualification procedure will be used is unclear. However, the "simple majority plus judge"[145] rule for verdict and sentencing, as opposed to the traditional requirement of unanimity, largely allays the risk of biased jurors threatening procedural integrity. This safeguard renders the voir dire-like procedure somewhat superfluous. Furthermore, considering its potential to draw out proceedings and enlarge workload, prosecutors may be reluctant to request a dismissal. While worth noting then, the death-qualification system is unlikely to affect criminal justice rendered in *saiban-in* courts given that unanimous verdicts are not required.

5. Powers, Duties and Penalties

In addition to imposing affirmative duties on lay assessors to attend trial,[146] deliberations,[147] and verdict,[148] the Lay Assessor Act also penalizes those who leak secrets,[149] make fraudulent statements,[150] or fail to appear.[151] In the execution of their

---

138 *Id.* at art. 30, at 254-255.
139 *Id.* at art. 34, at 256-257.
140 *Id.* at art. 30, at 254-255.
141 It is also possible that defense lawyers may seek to have jurors removed on the basis of an avowed propensity to vote for the death penalty in all cases in which it is sought. It is, however, unlikely that such requests will succeed.
142 Lockhart v. McCree, 476 U.S. 162 (1986).
143 *Id.* at 173.
144 *See generally* Claudia L. Cowan, William C. Thompson & Phoebe C. Ellsworth, *The Effects of Death Qualification on Jurors' Predisposition to Convict and on the Quality of Deliberation*, 8 LAW & HUM. BEHAV. 1/2 (1984).
145 'Deliberation, Verdict and Sentencing', *infra* Part IV. B(f).
146 Lay Assessor Act, art. 52, *supra* note 2, at 266.
147 *Id.* at art. 66, at 273.
148 *Id.* at art. 63, at 269.
149 *Id.* at art. 79, at 277.
150 *Id.* at art. 81, at 279.

duties, lay assessors have the authority to question witnesses,[152] victims[153] and defendants.[154] In mock lay assessor trials currently being conducted across Japan, lay assessors prove unhesitant to exercise this authority.[155] The possibility of personal interaction between lay assessors and defendants, victims and eyewitnesses will bring the Japanese public closer to criminal trials than they have ever been before. This signals a shift away from the traditional format for criminal trials in Japan, in which judges had little room for exploring evidence independent of prosecutorial influence. Both the Japanese Supreme Court and the Supreme Court Public Prosecutors Office have drafted reports aimed at minimizing voluminous trial paperwork and introducing a more interactive, verbal trial to facilitate greater lay involvement.[156] Because lay assessors, unlike judges, have no legal training and are unaccustomed to the routine of the criminal justice system, prosecutors will have to work harder to validate their cases through admitted evidence and live witness testimony, rather than complicated dossiers.

6. Deliberation, Verdict and Sentencing

Although the Act does not specify that verdict deliberations should take place before sentencing deliberations, there is speculation among academics studying the new system that, despite the fact that verdict and sentence will be determined in the single sitting, verdict deliberations will take place prior to sentencing. In whichever order they occur, deliberations on one will undoubtedly influence the shape of deliberations on the other. No specifications for deliberation procedure exist other than that a verdict must be determined on the basis of a simple majority and that it "shall include both an empanelled judge and a lay assessor holding that opinion."[157] While relatively simple for deciding guilt or innocence, this decision formula becomes complicated when applied to sentencing.

Given the range of possible sentences for any one crime, sentencing deliberations will likely yield a confusing range of different opinions as to which sentence is most appropriate in a particular case; a distinct majority comprising both lay assessors and judges will be unlikely. In this situation, the law requires:

> [T]he number of opinions for the option most unfavourable to the defendant will be added to the number of opinions for the next favourable option, until a majority opinion of the members of the judicial panel which includes both an empanelled judge and a lay assessor holding that opinion is achieved.[158]

---

[151] *Id.* at art. 83, at 279.
[152] *Id.* at art. 56, 267.
[153] *Id.* at art. 58, 268.
[154] *Id.* at art. 59, 268.
[155] *See* e.g., Supreme Court of Japan, *Summary of Minutes of the Fifth Meeting of the Matsuyama District Court Committee* (2005) (a report on the mock trials conducted by the Matsuyama District Court, August 3-4th, 2005) (on file with author).
[156] *See* Yusuke Yoshino & Fumio Tanaka, *Cut in Trial Paperwork Eyed, Yomiuri Shimbun*, (Apr. 2006) (on file with author).
[157] *See* Lay Assessor Act, art. 67, *supra* note 2, at 273-274.
[158] *Id.* at 274.

The formula is a windfall for *de facto* abolition. In the likely absence of a majority opinion for the death penalty in a capital case, the vote of those in favor of the harshest sentence will be added to those in favor of the second harshest, and so forth, until the requisite majority is attained. Therefore, votes in favor of the death penalty, if not constituting the requisite simple majority, will be added to the next harshest penalty and capital punishment will be eliminated from the equation.

The requirements that each lay assessor express an opinion at verdict and sentence deliberations,[159] and that the chief judge sitting on the mixed panel facilitate such expressions of opinion,[160] further mitigate the likelihood that a suspect will receive the death penalty. Given its controversial nature and profundity, a decision to condemn a defendant to death will likely result in a wide spread of opinion in mixed panel deliberations, and hence, a greater range within which to apply the above-described formula.

The success of the lay assessor system will depend upon how the various members of the *saiban-in* court play their roles. The following section identifies each of the parties involved in the new system, their vested interests, and how the overall dynamics among the parties may produce a shift towards *de facto* abolition.

V. Abolition and the *Saiban-in Seido*

A. The Saiban-in Court

Moving from a closed system in which capital cases were largely dominated by prosecutors and judges[161] to the *saiban-in seido* will open the Japanese court system to the closest public scrutiny it has ever had. Beginning in May 2009, with six lay assessors sitting on mixed panels with three judges, the public will potentially be the most represented party in the courtroom. This revolutionary change in dynamics between the parties will largely dictate the outcomes of the system and thus the potential for *de facto* abolition. This section examines the varying perspectives and expectations of prosecutors, judges, defendants and defense lawyers, and future lay assessors regarding the *saiban-in seido*.

1. Prosecutors

As long as the death penalty remains a valid form of punishment, prosecutors have the duty to charge and pursue the sentence in applicable cases. Regardless of the introduction of the lay assessor system then, prosecutors are first and foremost interested in obtaining a conviction and death sentence in every case for which they seek it. Once the lay assessor system commences, prosecutors will face difficulties in successfully pursuing these interests.

The predictability of the system up until now means that a prosecutor often brings charges in accordance with what he expects the outcome to be in a case.[162] Scholars have

---

159 *Id.* at art. 66, at 273.
160 *Id.*
161 Only 0.3% of Japan's 18,000 lawyers are willing to defend prisoners sentenced to death. *See* Yasuda, *supra* note 41, at 229.
162 *See* Johnson, *supra* note 44, at 45.

argued that this is one principal reason for Japan's extraordinarily high conviction rate.[163] The unpredictability associated with lay involvement in the system carries with it the potential for prosecutors to lose their power to anticipate outcomes. Given that acquittals are regarded as a threat to prosecutors' legitimacy,[164] the introduction of lay participation may lead prosecutors to bring more moderate charges and fewer capital cases than previously.

Versed and rehearsed in a largely inquisitorial system involving little oral evidence or cross-examination at trial phase, prosecutors working with the lay assessor system will need to focus on developing advocacy skills that are appropriate in a much less formal, adversarial proceeding. In preparation for this new role, prosecutors are undergoing training both in Japan and abroad to become educated in the art of trial advocacy.[165]

The Supreme Court Public Prosecutors Office has finalized a draft report proposing a reduction in trial documentation to better facilitate the introduction of the new system.[166] Still, the report falls short of abolishing the system of written records of investigators' questioning of defendants. Thus, courts may continue to rely on written confessions in determining guilt or innocence. In failing to exclude such written confessions, prosecutors reveal their intent for lay assessors to also rely on written confessions obtained during initial investigation rather than verbal statements given by defendants in court.[167] However, the Minister of Justice indicated in recent statements that even this shady area of Japanese criminal procedure will soon become more transparent as prosecutors prepare to make audio and video recordings of suspect interrogations on a trial basis.[168] Although the Public Prosecutors Office states that not every stage of the interrogation process would be recorded, this change in documentation demonstrates willingness on the part of the procuracy to increase transparency, give greater credibility to evidence of confessions, and facilitate more easily understandable trials in anticipation of lay involvement.

2. Judges

Judges face the same dilemma as prosecutors in interacting with members of the public, but to a much greater extent. First, where a prosecutor must persuade, a judge must cooperate with other judges and lay assessors during verdict and sentence deliberations. In the lay assessor system, judges—noted for their conservatism and reputation for being out-of-touch with society[169]—may no longer maintain an arms-length relation to jurors. Instead, they must aim to explain the relevant laws in a more easily understandable fashion and facilitate the participation of each lay assessor.[170]

---

[163] *Id.*
[164] *Id.* at 46.
[165] *See* Tim Winkler, *ANU Opens Export Market: Training Japanese Lawyers*, (Jan. 21, 2004), http://info.anu.edu.au/mac/Media/Media_Releases/_2004/_210104Japaneselawyers.asp (explaining that Japanese prosecutors have participated in a cooperative training program being conducted in both Japan and Australia through the Australian National University's Legal Workshop).
[166] Yusuke Yoshino & Fumio Tanaka, *supra* note 156.
[167] *Id.* ("If a suspect confessed, investigators' records of oral statements is [sic] easier to understand in many cases.").
[168] Yomiuri Shimbun, *Prosecutors plan to try recording interrogations*, May 10, 2006 (on file with author).
[169] *See* SCHMIDT, *supra* note 37, at 122.
[170] Lay Assessor Act, art. 66, *supra* note 2, at 273.

Accordingly, they must exhibit a degree of empathy and patience, a much greater change in conduct than for prosecutors.

Second, the *saiban-in-seido* will pose new ethical challenges to judges in light of the significant amount of discretionary power that the Lay Assessor Act grants the judiciary. For example, judges will have power, directly or at counsel's request, to dismiss lay assessors on the basis of a belief that they will act unfairly.[171] An even more important ethical challenge, though the Act does not consider it, is that judges may have to exercise personal discretion to avoid unduly influencing lay assessors during deliberations, since judges are predisposed to relying on confessions and entering judgments imposing the death penalty.[172] It is of significant concern that, because the content and procedure of deliberations are to be kept secret,[173] the degree of judicial influence on the outcomes of lay assessor trials will not be ascertainable. The judiciary is, however, taking measures in the lead-up to the system's introduction to make participation as accessible and worthwhile as possible for future lay assessors.

Some of the suggested improvements may indirectly pave the way for *de facto* abolition, and to some extent alleviate fears of undue judicial influence in deliberations mentioned above. For example, in contrast to the draft report of the Supreme Public Prosecutors Office,[174] a Supreme Court draft report published in November 2004 emphasized the importance of relying principally on oral submissions during trial and considering written statements from pre-trial proceedings only when necessary for clarification purposes.[175] In formulating this proposal, the Supreme Court considered the risk that professional judges, who are accustomed to dealing with such written statements, will instruct lay assessors on how to decide whether a particular defendant is guilty.[176]

3. Defendants and Defense Lawyers

Defendants and defense lawyers have the greatest interest in seeing the new system pave the way for *de facto* and eventual *de jure* abolition of the death penalty. Certain obstacles, however, may impede progress toward those goals. First, defense lawyers are as disadvantaged as prosecutors in terms of a lack of advocacy experience and training. Their access to the same or similar training schemes as Japanese prosecutors will determine how level the playing field will be post-introduction of the system. If the JFBA and the defense counsel committees of its regional counterparts (*keiji bengo iinkai*) cannot prepare defense lawyers for their new roles in the same way that the Supreme Public Prosecutors Office and Ministry of Justice are doing for prosecutors, the introduction of the lay assessor system could prove very detrimental to the defense.

Second, depending on the prosecution's use of the so-called voir dire procedure, defense lawyers will need to learn to play the game of jury stacking to their benefit. However, recent trends towards both recording pre-trial interrogations and reducing

---

[171] *Id.* at art. 18, at 249.
[172] SCHMIDT, *supra* note 37, at 152.
[173] Lay Assessor Act, art. 70, *supra* note 2, at 274.
[174] Shimbun, *supra* note 168.
[175] *Id.*
[176] *Id.*

reliance on written confessions give hope to defendants and defense lawyers whose clients face the ultimate penalty.

4. Lay Assessors

Surveys and forums held prior to and after the enactment of the Lay Assessor Act reveal a general reluctance among the Japanese public to participate as a lay assessor.[177] This reluctance appears to stem not only from a desire to avoid disruption to daily life and business, but also from a general feeling that it lacks the education and qualifications necessary to fulfil the role.[178] Another reason for this reluctance is the public's hesitance to be directly involved in harsh sentencing.[179] During the question and answer session of a Ministry of Justice-sponsored forum on the introduction of the *saiban-in seido*, members of the public voiced a reluctance to vote for the death penalty even in the most heinous crimes.[180] Satoru Shinomiya, a lawyer presiding over the "Town Meeting in Kanazawa," responded by stating that the new lay assessor system would provide a good opportunity for those Japanese people who previously supported capital punishment, but left its administration to lawyers and the government, to review their stance and reconsider the issue. He concluded with the hope that public debate on capital punishment would further deepen as a result of the public's newly imposed obligation to grapple with the issue.[181]

B. The Potential Outcomes

Although the drafting of the Lay Assessor Act expressly excluded abolition of capital punishment as a reason for reform, each party in the new *saiban-in* court since then has appeared to directly or indirectly contemplate the prospect of *de facto* abolition of the death penalty. At least three avenues for *de facto* abolition exist, though the possible outcomes of the new lay assessor system are multitudinous. The first scenario may happen where prosecutors seek the death penalty and it is outvoted in accordance with the simple majority formula. The second may occur when prosecutors seek the death penalty and it is outvoted upon applying the complex sentence reduction formula, despite some members of the mixed panel voting for it. Finally, prosecutors may very well not seek the death penalty in some cases, due to the unpredictability of success, and instead seek a lesser penalty for which they have greater chances of success.

Of course much will depend upon the interaction among each of the parties involved. However, procedural changes in place and under consideration that are aimed at facilitating the *saiban-in seido* indicate positive first steps towards achieving some form of abolition.

---

177 Government Publications Office, *supra* note 75.
178 *Id.*
179 *Id.*
180 Koizumi Cabinet, *Shihô seido kaikaku: Town Meeting in Kanazawa* [*Justice System Reform: Town Meeting in Kanazawa*] (June 25, 2005), http://www8.cao.go.jp/town/kanazawa170625/index.html (the Minister of Justice Chieko Nôno, Chairman of the Justice Reform Promotions Office Criminal Investigation Council Masahito Inoue, and Waseda University Professor and Lawyer Satoru Shinomiya presided over the meeting).
181 *Id.*

VI. CONCLUSION

Japan, like any other democracy, grounds its national policies in the will of its people. This is especially so in the case for retention of the death penalty. With *de jure* abolition of the death penalty close to becoming a norm of customary international law, and absent affirmative steps by the Japanese ministry, judiciary or procuracy towards abolition, the task will fall to the people to effect the change necessary to bring Japan in line with its international legal obligations and to set an example in Asia.

The introduction of the lay assessor system in May 2009 will place Japan's system of capital punishment squarely within the public domain and provide the Japanese public with the tools to initiate a change towards *de jure* abolition. For the first time, the Japanese people will make decisions on capital sentencing, which may play an essential role in abolition at a grassroots level. Many factors will influence the decisions of lay assessors, not the least of which are the roles played by the prosecutors, judges, defendants and defense lawyers in the new system. Each of these members of the future *saiban-in* courtroom is surely anxious about how the introduction of the new system will affect their interests. However, attempts already made and currently under consideration to make the system more transparent, accessible and efficient suggest that any change will be positive for the criminal justice system overall.

From the perspective that *de jure* abolition of Japan's system of capital punishment is desirable if not imperative, the *saiban-in seido* may well prove to be the necessary first step towards that end. Allowing the people to decide may turn out to be the necessary catalyst for a shift in conscience away from support of capital punishment. Although the Japanese government ultimately will decide whether to pass legislation abolishing the death penalty once and for all, the decisions that the Japanese people make as participants in the *saiban-in seido* will surely inform that decision.

[7]

WAITING TO DIE, DYING TO LIVE

An Account of the Death Row Phenomenon from a Legal Viewpoint

*Caycie D. Bradford**

Across the globe, the death penalty is being abolished under theories of human rights. The United States is the only country left in the Americas that regularly performs executions. The Death Row Phenomenon has been coined to be an inhumane and degrading punishment. The long-term effects of the Death Row Phenomenon have been determined to be a second punishment inflicted upon Death Row inmates. While awaiting their executions, inmates are deteriorating physically and mentally. Overall, the Death Row Phenomenon is a violation of fundamental human rights guaranteed to all individuals, even prisoners.

"Despair is not greater
than you find it on death row.
You have been abandoned
by even the most loyal of souls."[1]

I. INTRODUCTION

Far from the view of the public are the "cages"[2] that house the nation's inmates on death row. It's a cemetery that continues to grow every year with those that are not quite dead, but surely not alive.

The topic of beheadings, electrocutions, hangings, lethal injections, shootings, and stoning sounds much like a history lecture regarding something of the past. Perversely, even during the twenty-first century, these horrific events are still happening. This type of carnage occurs around the world under the guise of capital punishment ("the death penalty"). The use of death as a punishment or penalty for a crime an individual has committed continues to be used in fully developed countries with modern societies. More than two-thirds of the countries in the world

---

* J.D. Candidate, University of La Verne College of Law, Ontario, CA, 2011; M.A., Communications and Culture with an emphasis in Human Rights, Trinity Law and Graduate School, Santa Ana, CA, 2009; B.A., Political Science, Northern Arizona University, Flagstaff, AZ, 2006. I would like to thank my mother and father for giving me every opportunity to pursue my dreams; I would not be where I am today without them. I would also like to thank Ms. Gloria Killian for being such an inspiration and her continuous fight for the cause. Lastly, I would like to thank a specific professor at La Verne Law who has inspired me to be the individual I am today. Thank you Professor Chaney. For the countless number of individuals currently serving on death row in the world, this article was written with you and your families in mind. To all the people and organizations fighting for abolition of the death penalty—thank you, keep fighting.

[1] Frank P. Whyte, *Death Row*, 16 March 2005, *available at* www.authorsden.com/visit/viewPoetry.asp?id=132479 (last accessed 11 November 2009).

[2] Tony Medina, inmate on Texas Death Row, http://www.tony-medina.info//index.php?option=com_content&task=view&id=43&Itemid=191.

have abolished the death penalty.[3] The laws of 58 countries allow for this form of punishment, but only 25 are actively executing detainees.[4] In 2008, 2,390 executions were performed.[5] In 2009, 17,118 people were living under a sentence of death in the world.[6] In 2009, the highest number of executions, approximated to be in the thousands, occurred in China.[7] Following not far behind China was the Middle East. In Iran, where stoning and hanging are the preferred forms of capital punishment, 388 individuals were subjected to this type of "punishment."[8] In Saudi Arabia, where the method of death is public beheading and crucifixion, more than 69 lives were ended in this manner.[9] In the United States, where lethal injection and electrocution are the means of death, 52 individuals were executed.[10] In the same year, 106 individuals were sentenced to death, and nine individuals were released for innocence.[11] The majority of executions in 2009 occurred within five countries: China, Iran, Saudi Arabia, Pakistan, and the United States of America. These five states accounted for 93 percent of all executions that year.[12]

The United States is the only country left in the Americas that is regularly committing executions.[13] Texas alone has executed 16 individuals in 2010.[14] The United States purportedly protects individuals from "cruel and unusual punishments,"[15] yet remains one of the top five countries executing inmates. In 2010, the United States had nine executions scheduled for the month of October among five states, three more scheduled deaths in November among three states, and executions scheduled to occur throughout the months until March 2011.[16] The only explanation for such a civilized country to continue this barbaric practice is that the citizens of the United States seem to gain some type of illusion of finality and justice from the imposition of this drastic penalty. It appears that the people of the United States have been misled into believing either that those inmates on death row deserve the harm that they suffer as a payment for their wrongs or that inmates do not suffer as they await their execution.[17]

---

[3] Amnesty International, *Death Sentences and Executions in 2008*, ACT 50/003/2009, 5 (2009).

[4] Amnesty International, *Death Sentences and Executions in 2009,* ACT 50/001/2010, 24 (2010).

[5] *Id.* at 8.

[6] Amnesty International, *supra* note 4, at 7.

[7] *Id.* at 12.

[8] *Id.* at 7.

[9] *Id.* at 24.

[10] Death Penalty Information Center, *The Death Penalty in 2009: Year End Report* (2009), www.deathpenaltyinfo.org/documents/2009YearEndReport.pdf (last visited 15 September 2010).

[11] *See id.*

[12] Amnesty International, *supra* note 4, at 2.

[13] *See id.*

[14] *See id.*

[15] U.S. CONST. amend. VIII.

[16] Death Penalty Information Center, Upcoming Executions, http://www.deathpenaltyinfo.org/upcoming-executions (last visited 15 September 2010)

[17] Amy Smith, *Not "Waiving" But Drowning: The Anatomy of Death Row Syndrome and Volunteering for Execution,* 17 PUB. INT. L. REP. 237, 238 (2008).

Further, it appears that despite the rest of the world's efforts, the United States holds fast to the ethical relativist view that the death penalty is correct in the U.S., even though it may not be internationally. When an individual is sentenced to death, they are sentenced to exactly that, death; not to be tortured while they await their execution. However, what most citizens fail to recognize is that death row is not the punishment; the loss of the inmate's life is the punishment. "The one consideration that must not be forgotten in all of this is that prisoners are human beings. They have to be regarded as subjects not objects."[18] Inmates are still humans, entitled to respect; no matter what crime they may be accused or convicted of, they remain persons.

In an effort to understand the circumstances of confinement for death row inmates, including the mental and physical experience, the terms "death row phenomenon" and "death row syndrome" have been adopted. These terms describe the harsh conditions of confinement (the death row phenomenon) and the psychological harms that result (the death row syndrome). This paper explores the definitions of both the death row phenomenon and the death row syndrome and the effects that they have on U.S. and international human rights law.

II. THE DEATH ROW PHENOMENON

"Our punishment is the loss of our lives, the execution, not the process."[19]

A. Death Row Phenomenon Defined

The term "death row phenomenon" has been used to define the circumstances that are found on death row and the physical deterioration in prisoners who are serving death sentences and awaiting their execution.[20] The death row phenomenon is commonly analyzed by looking at two components: a temporal one (the length of time that an inmate spends on death row) and a physical one (the harsh conditions that an inmate is subjected to on death row).[21] This phenomenon is a direct result of the ruthless and cruel conditions that an inmate will experience while on death row, the length of time that such conditions are experienced, and, finally, the anxiety of awaiting one's own execution.[22]

The concept of the death row phenomenon is frequently used internationally to prevent extradition of individuals who are facing the death penalty to the United States.[23] The term was first introduced to the

---

[18] Institut International des Droits de l'Homme, *Conferences introductive et cours thematique: Education et droit international des droits de l'homme,* 40th Session annuelle d'enseignement Vol. 1, 93, 94 (6-31 Julliet 2009).

[19] Medina, *supra* note 2.

[20] Elisabeth Hanowsky, Representing Human Rights Advocates through University of San Francisco School of Law's International Human Rights Clinic, *The Death Row Phenomenon is a Violation of the Limitations Placed on Capital Punishment Under International Human Rights Law* 3, *available at* www.humanrightsadvocates.org/.../HRC_Hanowsky_Death-Row-Phenomenon.doc.

[21] Patrick Hudson, *Does the Death Row Phenomenon Violate a Prisoner's Rights Under International Law,* 11 EJIL 833, 834-36 (2000).

[22] *See id.*

[23] Smith, *supra* note 17.

international realm in the court case of *Soering v. United Kingdom*.[24] In the *Soering* case, the court was posed with the issue of whether an extradition to a country (in particular, the United States) who still utilized the death penalty would be a violation of Article 3 of the European Convention for the Protection of Human Rights and Fundamental Freedoms (ECHR).[25] The major difficulty posed was that Article 3 provides that "no one shall be subjected to torture or to inhuman or degrading treatment or punishment."[26] Under the laws protecting international human rights, the death penalty itself might not be a direct violation of Article 3 of the ECHR, but the question of "whether its administration constituted 'inhuman or degrading treatment of punishment'" was left for the court to decide.[27] The *Soering* court held that "the condemned prisoner has to endure for many years the conditions on death row and the anguish and mounting tension of living in the ever-present shadow of death," and this extradition would be a violation of the protections afforded under Article 3.[28]

The death row phenomenon was later expanded in 1993, with the case of *Pratt v. Jamaica* by Great Britain's Judicial Privy Council. The *Pratt* court dealt with prisoners who were deteriorating for 16 years on Jamaica's death row in terrible conditions.[29] The court held that "there is an instinctive revulsion against the prospect of hanging a man after he has been under sentence of death for many years. What gives rise to this instinctive revulsion? The answer can only be our humanity; we regard it as an inhuman act to keep a man facing the agony of execution over a long extended period of time."[30] This concept, that an extreme length of time can constitute cruel and unusual punishment, has not gained the sympathy of Americans. In the United States, an inmate's appeal may take several years, if not a decade. Yet, this concept has gained great understanding in the international courts and plays an integral part of the international pressure against the United States maintaining the death penalty.[31]

B. Death Row Phenomenon and the Implications for Capital Punishment within the United States

There is a strong debate among scholars on whether the concept of death row phenomenon has any implications for capital punishment within the United States, particularly with reference to constitutional issues.[32] One of the major difficulties in applying the death row phenomenon concept as internationally developed to cases that occur in

---

[24] *Soering v. United Kingdom*, (1989) App. No. 14038.88, II Eur. H.R. Rep.

[25] Smith, *supra* note 17.

[26] European Convention on Human Rights art. 3, 4 Nov. 1950, E.T.S. No. 11, 213 U.N.T.S. 222.

[27] Alan W. Clarke, THE BITTER FRUIT OF AMERICAN JUSTICE: INTERNATIONAL AND DOMESTIC RESISTANCE TO THE DEATH PENALTY 36 (Northeastern University Press Boston ed., University Press of New England 2007).

[28] *Soering v. United Kingdom*, *supra* note 24.

[29] Clarke, *supra* note 27.

[30] *See id.*

[31] *See id.*

[32] Smith, *supra* note 17, at 240.

the United States is that the *Soering* case "failed to specify which circumstances in the case constituted 'death row phenomenon' and which were anomalous to Jans Soering himself."[33]

To date, the American courts have still refused to adopt the theory of death row phenomenon. The closest that the courts have come was the abolition of the death penalty in California in 1972.[34] In the case of *People v. Anderson,* the court held that "the cruelty of capital punishment lies not only in the execution itself and the pain incident thereto, but also in the dehumanizing effects of the lengthy imprisonment prior to execution during which the judicial and administrative procedures essential to due process of law are carried out."[35] Further, the court supported its argument by stating that "penologists and medical experts agree that the process of carrying out a verdict of death is often so degrading and brutalizing to the human spirit as to constitute psychological torture."[36] In recent years, Supreme Court Justices Breyer and Stevens have held fast to the possibility of the phenomenon in several opinions. In the dissenting opinion of *Foster v. Florida,* Justice Breyer stated, "the combination of uncertainty of execution and long delays is arguably cruel."[37] Further, Justice Breyer referenced the 1890 decision of *In Re Medley,* in which the court held that long delays "inflict horrible feelings" and "in immense mental anxiety amounting to a great increase of the offender's punishment."[38] In effect, Breyer argued that the prisoner is facing two punishments: "punishment by death and also by more than a generation spent in death row's twilight."[39] Justice Stevens pushed lower courts to inquire into the idea that there was a possibility that the growing delay between sentencing and execution of inmates is a violation of the cruel and unusual punishment clause of the Eighth Amendment.[40] Dissenting in *Knight v. Florida,* Justice Breyer wrote about the "delays in administration of the death penalty in the United States,"[41] and how he believed it was "difficult to deny the suffering inherent in a prolonged wait for execution."[42] Even further, in their dissent, Justice Breyer and Justice Marshall stated, "the death penalty is in all circumstances cruel and unusual punishment prohibited by the Eighth and Fourteenth Amendments."[43]

The concept of the death row phenomenon has at least been brought to the attention of the United States courts, but has still failed to receive the type of recognition the international realm has given it. It is important to note, however, that there is one major difference between the American cases and that of *Soering.* In the *Soering* court, the decision was "based on

---

[33] Smith, *supra* note 17, at 241.
[34] *People v. Anderson,* 493 P.2d 880, (Cal. 1972).
[35] *Id.* at 894-95.
[36] *See id.*
[37] *Foster v. Florida,* 123 S. Ct. 470, 471 (2002) (Breyer, J., dissenting).
[38] *See id.* (quoting *In Re Medley,* 134 U.S. 160, 172 (1890)).
[39] *Foster v. Florida, supra* note 37.
[40] *Lackey v. Texas,* 514 U.S. 1045 (1995).
[41] *Knight v. Florida* and *Moore v. Nebraska,* 120 S. Ct. 459, 461 (1999) (Breyer, J., dissenting).
[42] *Id.* at 462.
[43] *See id.*

the potential for harm to an individual in the future (a breach of international law by reason of its foreseeable consequences)."[44] An American court would require specific proof of harm in order to make the determination that there was an Eighth Amendment violation.[45] In the American system, to simply state the horrors that occur on death row leading to the death row phenomenon is not enough; there must be "a persuasive constitutional claim," showing evidence that the inmate has experienced some particular harmful consequence of the death row phenomenon.[46]

III. THE DEATH ROW SYNDROME

A. Death Row Syndrome Defined

The concept of the death row phenomenon explores the effects of the physical experience of confinement, as well as the harsh conditions in which inmates are housed on death row. The current analysis of the death row phenomenon has moved towards the psychological effects that an inmate experiences while on death row. The term "death row syndrome" has been analogized to the resulting psychological harms that arise from such an experience. Professor Atul Gawande of the Harvard Medical School points out that "holding prisoners in long-term solitary confinement is a mechanism of torture. 'It wasn't always like this; the wide-scale use of isolation is, almost exclusively, a phenomenon of the past twenty years...' America now holds at least twenty-five thousand inmates in isolation in supermax prisons."[47]

B. Death Row Syndrome Appears in the United States

The concept of death row syndrome first appeared in a 1986 article by Dr. Stuart Grassian, in which he depicted the lives of 14 inmates who were in solitary confinement.[48] These fourteen inmates were living in a six by nine foot cell with no windows and a single 60-watt light bulb. There was a single steel bed, steel table and stool, and a steel open toilet in the cell. These inmates had no televisions, radios or books, except for the Bible. There was a solid steel door locking these inmates into this solitary confinement, which was unbroken for 23 hours of the day.[49] In his article, Dr. Grassian describes the drastic psychological and psychiatric reactions

---

[44] Smith, *supra* note 33.

[45] *See id.*

[46] *See id.*

[47] Atul Gawande, *Hellhole: Is Solitary Confinement Torture,* The New Yorker, March 30, 2009, www.newyorker.com/reporting/2009/03/30/090330fa_fact_gawande (last visited 11 November 2009).

[48] Stuart Grassian, *Psychopathological Effects Of Solitary Confinement*, 140 AM. J. PSYCHIATRY 1450–54, (1983). Stuart Grassian & N. Freidman, *Effects of Sensory Deprivation in Psychiatric Seclusion and Solitary Confinement,* 8 INT'L. J. L. & PSYCHIATRY 49 (1986). Grassian is an expert who testified in the Ross competency hearing. He developed the concept based on a study of inmates at Walpole prison in the late seventies.

[49] *See id.*

that inmates have experienced from being held in such conditions, which in the legal sphere has become known as death row syndrome.

Despite its lack of scientific support and evidence to authenticate its existence, death row syndrome gained dramatic awareness in America in February 2005 with the postponed Connecticut execution of Michael Ross.[50] Ross was a sadistic serial killer and rapist housed on Connecticut's death row for eighteen years before being executed.[51] Allegedly, Ross attempted suicide three times before deciding to abstain from further state and federally mandated appeals and "volunteered" for his execution.[52] The Judge in the case advised counsel to investigate the competency of this voluntary decision, stating that it must be given "voluntary, knowingly and intelligently."[53] Ross's attorneys argued that Ross's voluntary execution was not valid because he was suffering from death row syndrome or at the very minimum "a negative psychological response to long-term incarceration on death row under difficult conditions, in combination with the psychological uncertainty of living under a sentence of death."[54] In the end, counsel's argument failed and "the much anticipated death row syndrome or segregated housing unit syndrome never materialized in this case," and Ross was found competent and executed.[55]

The United States court system has failed to hear arguments on a right to life basis. Generally, the United States courts do not refer to international law when making decisions; however, in this particular instance, international law would be highly influential. While international law has outlawed the death penalty, the United States has not ratified a single treaty enforcing such law. Therefore, opponents to the death penalty in the U.S. cannot rely on international law as a basis for overcoming the death row phenomenon and must solely utilize domestic law. Currently, proponents of the death row phenomenon argue that it is a violation of the cruel and unusual punishment provisions. So far, arguments brought to the courts on the grounds of the death row phenomenon have been unsuccessful. Recently, in April of 2009, the United States Supreme Court refused to hear the appeal of death row inmate and political prisoner[56] Mumia Abu-Jamal on a death row phenomenon basis.[57]

The attempt to shift the terminology from death row phenomenon to death row syndrome is an attempt at changing social policy through the use of a psychiatric disorder. The use of the term "syndrome" implies a medical diagnosis with a set of recognizable signs or symptoms, whereas

---

50 Harold I. Schwartz, *Death Row Syndrome and Demoralization: Psychiatric Means to Social Policy Ends*, 33 J. AM. ACAD. PSY. LAW 153-155 (2005), *available at* www.jaapl.org/cgi/content/full/33/2/153 (last accessed 12 November 2009).

51 Death Penalty Information Center, www.deathpenaltyinfo.org/michael-ross (last visited 12 November 2009); *Id.*

52 Smith, *supra* note 17, at 242.

53 *Miller v. Stewart,* 231 F.3d 1248 (9th Cir. 2000) (Fisher, J., concurring).

54 Smith, *supra* note 17, at 242.

55 *State v. Ross,* 2005 Conn. Super. LEXIS 1116 at *11 (Conn. Super Ct. 22 Apr. 2005)

56 A political prisoner is a person who has been imprisoned for holding or advocating dissenting political views.

57 C. Clark Kissinger, *Supreme Court Rejects Mumia Appeal* (19 Apr. 2009), http://revcom.us/a/162/mumia-en.html (last visited 12 November 2009).

the word "phenomenon" simply implies an experience of an incident. Despite the differing meanings some scholars use the terms interchangeably. However, if this death row condition becomes labeled as a mental illness and the use of that illness is to reach a finding of incompetence, what is really being procured is the change of social policy—the abolition of the death penalty—on the basis of psychiatry.[58]

While the term alone indicates that there is a medically recognizable syndrome, neither the concept of death row phenomenon nor of death row syndrome is accepted in the medical health field.[59] Currently both the American Psychiatric Association and the American Psychological Association do not accept these terms.[60] Further, neither term appears in the *Diagnostic and Statistical Manual of Mental Disorders-IV* (DSM-IV).[61] It seems that the use of these terms has gained quicker recognition in the legal realm than in the psychological world due to the lack of scientific research on the topic. Even though they are relevant in the legal world, the terms are not even defined in Black's Law Dictionary.[62] The definitions come out of case law and reference articles mainly from an international perspective. In spite of the lack of psychological support, there is some casual link between the long delays, harsh conditions, and psychological effects that death row inmates' experience, scientific data would aid in the confirmation of the concept of death row syndrome.[63]

IV. THE LONG DELAYS

"The wait times amount to prisoners getting two distinct punishments: the death sentence and the years in solitary confinement."[64]

A. The Temporal Component (Inmates Spend Extreme Lengths of Time on Death Row)

In some countries death row inmates wait to be executed for more than a decade. A century ago, death row inmates could expect to wait only days or possibly weeks between sentencing and execution.[65] However waiting merely days is a thing of the past. The length of time that prisoners spend on death row in the United States has nearly doubled over the last two decades.[66] In 2006, the average wait time rose to 12 years from the 1986 average wait of seven years.[67] In California, the wait time is

---

[58] Schwartz, *supra* note 50.

[59] Smith, *supra* note 17, at 243.

[60] Smith, *supra* note 52.

[61] AM. PSYCHIATRIC ASSOCIATION, DIAGNOSTIC AND STATISTICAL MANUAL OF MENTAL DISORDERS-IV, (4th ed., 1994). New update will not come out until 2012, revised edition released in 2000.

[62] BRYAN A. GARNER, BLACK'S LAW DICTIONARY, (West Group ed., West Publishing Co., 1996).

[63] Smith, *supra* note 59.

[64] Kevin Johnson, *Prisoners' Time Spent on Death Row Doubles*, USA TODAY, 7 June 2008, www.usatoday.com/news/nation/2008-07-23-Death-row-time_N.htm (last visited 12 November 2009).

[65] Smith, *supra* note 17, at 248.

[66] Johnson, *supra* note 64.

[67] *See id.*

approximately 20 years between sentencing and execution.[68] However, these long waits are not a characteristic of only the death row inmates in the United States. Nigerian death row prisoners have an average wait of twenty years on death row.[69] Japanese inmates will spend more than 10 years awaiting execution, and in one reported case, a prisoner had spent more than 38 years waiting for execution.[70] A prisoner in Yemen was sentenced in 1996 to death and in 2005 was still awaiting execution.[71] Clearly, the length of time that a death row inmate will wait for execution has changed over the past several decades, making the temporal nature of the death sentence process much different than that of even a decade ago. Long delays, often decades long, are the customary practice on death rows across the world.

1. Delays alone are enough to support a finding of death row phenomenon

The argument has been posed that this extreme delay in time, irrespective of prison conditions and anxiety over the sentence, is enough to be the source of the death row phenomenon. Proponents of this argument claim that this delay in execution alone is enough to violate the prohibition on torture, cruel, inhuman or degrading punishment.[72] The Judicial Committee of the Privy Council in the case of *Pratt v. Jamaica*, held that "the delay alone in the implementation of a death sentence can warrant a finding of the death row phenomenon—and that a delay of fourteen years was enough alone to constitute a violation of cruel punishment."[73] Further, the Privy Council found the death row phenomenon to be present under a delay of four years and 10 months because the delay is outside of the prisoner's control.[74]

Although legal scholars emphasize the importance of this component in procuring the death row phenomenon, there is a "lack of understanding regarding the psychological effects of the amount of time spent on death row."[75] Further, the Human Rights Committee (Committee) has declined to accept that the delay alone is enough to affirm a finding of the death row phenomenon and a violation based on torture or cruel punishment.[76]

[68] UNITED STATES BUREAU OF JUSTICE, Statistics Bulletin, *Capital Punishment, 2005*, published Dec. 2006 www.ojp.usdoj.gov/bjs/pub/pdf/cp05.pdf. (last visited 11 November 2009).

[69] Hanowsky and Newman, *supra* note 20, at 7.

[70] Amnesty International, *Amnesty International Report 2005 - Japan*, 25 May 2005, *available at*, http://www.unhcr.org/refworld/docid/429b27e82.html, *see* case of Hakamada Iwao.

[71] *See id.*

[72] *Johnson v. Jamaica*, (No. 588/1994), UN Doc. CCPR/C/56/D/588/1994 (1996).

[73] *Pratt v. The Attorney General for Jamaica*, Privy Council Appeal No. 10, 22 (1993).

[74] *See id.*

[75] Smith, *supra* note 65.

[76] *Johnson v. Jamaica* , *supra* note 72.

2. The delays are not the fault of the prisoners

Despite the fact that the Committee has found that a prisoner who has spent seven years on death row is a cause for concern, there is still no violation of Article 7 of the International Covenant on Civil and Political Rights (ICCPR).[77] The Committee has expressed concern that these cases are delayed in part because of the prisoners' themselves. However, the Committee believes "that these concerns are inapplicable in cases of extreme delay as the prisoners are often not at fault for the delay and cases of extreme delay do not interfere with prohibitions against undue haste."[78] Further, "a prisoner should not be faulted for taking advantage of the legitimate appeals process offered by the state when the prisoner is fighting to save his or her own life."[79] An inmate might be pushing the appeal process to its limits in this fight, but such a struggle to remain alive is an essential part of human nature. Any country that makes this struggle delayed must be held accountable for their actions.[80] The European Court of Human Rights (ECHR) took the position that "even if the delay was the result of the inmate's actions they were not to be blamed for pursuing life as the fact remained that they were pursuing life under death row conditions with mounting tensions over their own death."[81]

The delays in execution fall on the hands of the state. Internationally, the Privy Council has stated that the delays that prisoners experience are not due to their own causing, but are a result of the failure of the judicial system.[82] Various judicial systems across the globe prolong death penalty proceedings for indeterminable periods of time. In the United States a judge critiqued the delays caused by the appeals process by stating that "the process has become unacceptably cruel to defendants...who spend long years under the sentence of death while the judicial system conducts seemingly interminable proceedings which remind many observers of a cruelly whimsical cat toying with a mouse."[83] As a result, death row inmates are waiving their rights to appeals and choosing to volunteer for execution to avoid these long delays. Between 1976 and 2003, 10 percent of those executed in the United States were volunteers.[84]

Lastly, with the recent hasty execution of Saddam Hussein it must be noted that hasty executions are not a solution to the delays. The death row phenomenon only encompasses those delays that are extreme in length, not all delays that occur. Reasonable amounts of time are predictable, however prisoners are waiting decades, even lifetimes to be executed. These extreme delays have become the average wait time and are no longer the exceptional cases. The temporal component of long delays in awaiting

---

[77] International Convention on Civil and Political Rights art. 7, G.A. Res. 2200A, U.N. Doc. A/RES/2200 (16 Dec. 1966).

[78] Hanowsky and Newman , *supra* note 20, at 8.

[79] Hanowsky and Newman , *supra* note 20 at 9.

[80] *See id.*

[81] *Soering v. United Kingdom* , *supra* note 24.

[82] *Guerra v. Baptiste,* (1986) ac 397; (1995) 3 WLR 891; (1995) at ALL ER 583.

[83] Hanowsky and Newman, *supra* note 78.

[84] Stephen Blank, *Killing Time: The Process of Waiving Appeal The Michael Ross Death Penalty Case,* 14 J. L. POLY. 735, 749.

one's execution alone may not be sufficient to warrant a finding of the death row phenomenon but it is certainly a key component. The psychological effects a death row inmate experiences is not the punishment that these individuals were sentenced to; their sentence was execution.

B. The Physical Component of the Long Delays

Inmates not only spend vast amounts of time waiting for their executions to be carried out, they do so in unacceptable conditions. Inmates on death row have depicted the conditions as a living hell; a graveyard behind high walls far from the eye of the public. Under these deplorable conditions, the physical state of inmates deteriorates rapidly. According to Amnesty International's (AI) annual report, generally, prisoners are denied the basic human comforts.[85] Death row circumstances around the world include: inmates being denied hobbies or meaningful ways to entertain themselves, lights that are left on at all times—including during sleep, temperature extremes, inadequate nutrition and sanitation, lack of exercise, loss of contact with the outside world and sometimes cells are so constricting that inmates cannot even stand in them. Two different scientific studies have shown that after being subjected to a few hours of solitary confinement, prisoners' brain waves shift to a pattern of "stupor and delirium," and that complete sensory deprivation causes hallucinations in as little as 48 hours.[86] One scholar has even characterized this type of confinement as "no-touch torture."[87] In the United States, prisoners are subjected to solitary confinement for months and years prior to their execution dates.[88]

These physical conditions are found in death rows across the globe. In Japan, death row inmates are subjected to severe physical conditions while awaiting their executions: they are prohibited from speaking to other prisoners, allowed only infrequent and supervised visits from their families and attorneys, prohibited from having hobbies, prohibited from having televisions, subjected to sleeping with a bright light on without the ability to cover their faces, subjected to extreme temperatures, and receive inadequate nutrition.[89] In Uzbekistan, death row inmates are "regularly beaten and denied outdoor exercise."[90] Death row inmates in China are subjected to physical beatings, kept in chains from the moment of arrest

---

85 Amnesty International Report 2005, *supra* note 70; Amnesty International Report 2006, *available at* www.amnesty.org/en/library/asset/POL10/001/2006/en/52433fd0-d46f-11dd-8743-d305bea2b2c7/pol100012006en.html.

86 Jeffrey Kluger, *Are Prisons Driving Prisoners Mad*, TIME MAGAZINE, 26 Jan. 2007, *available at* www.time.com/time/magazine/article/0,9171,1582304,00.html (last visited 13 October 2009).

87 ALFRED W. MCCOY, A QUESTION OF TORTURE: CIA INTERROGATION FROM THE COLD WAR TO THE WAR ON TERROR (American Empire Project ed., Metropolitan Books, 2006).

88 Kluger, *supra* note 86.

89 Bruce Wallace, *Japanese Death Row an 'Affront to Human Decency'*, SUNDAY INDEPENDENT, 12 March 2006, *available at* www.independent.co.uk, and Amnesty International, *supra* note 70.

90 HRA commends the action of Uzbekistan, by Presidential Decree, to abolish the death penalty starting1 January 2008.

until their execution, and are subjected to sleep and food deprivation.[91] In Mongolia, prisoners are subjected to overcrowding, temperature extremes, inadequate nutrition and isolation.[92] In the Komotini prison in Greece, solitary confinement prisoners are subjected to cells with a putrid smell, poor ventilation, no bed, no washbasin, and minimal access to natural light.[93] Solitary confinement inmates in Serbia are forced to sleep on a wooden platform, receive a wooden box for personal belongings and access to artificial and natural light is at best mediocre.[94] In Iran, solitary confinement prisoners are placed in basement cells measuring about one meter by two meters with a ceiling of four meters with a light on 24 hours a day; some inmates are allowed outside for 20 minutes while others never see the open air.[95] In drastic contrast are the conditions in which prisoners in Europe are treated. While there is currently no death row in Europe, the existing death row countries could learn from the conditions in which the prisoners with life sentences in Europe are housed.

The United Nations Minimum Standard Rules (MSR) and the European Prison Rules (EPR) established a standard in which European prisoners should be treated. Such standards include: proper cell size and accommodations within the cell, no use of all dark cells as well as no use of permanently lit cells,[96] sanitary conditions sufficient to health standards, good ventilation, low noise levels, privacy and an alarm button. In addition, under these standards prisoners are allowed access to outside exercise for at least one hour out of the day,[97] and access to hobbies and activities.[98] Prisoners are given access to written and broadcast media.[99] Further, prisoners are allowed contact with the outside world; this has held to be "crucial" to inmates, especially those detained for long periods of time.[100] While prisoners lose their right to free movement, they retain other rights as a human being.[101] One right in particular is the right to contact with their families, and prison authorities have a duty to assist them in this.[102]

---

[91] Amnesty International *People's Republic of China Executed "According to law – The Death Penalty in China*. Doc. 17/003/2004, *available at* http://web.amnesty.org/library/index/engasa170032004 (last visited 11 November 2009).

[92] Amnesty International, *supra* note 85.

[93] Sharon Shalev, *Sourcebook on Solitary Confinement*, 39, 41-44 (2008), *available at* www.solitaryconfinement.org/sourcebook (last visited 12 November 2009).

[94] *See id.*

[95] *See id.*

[96] Inmates are to have the ability to control the artificial light within their cell. In no case should the cells be lighted at all times of the day. Further, there shall be no lighting situation in which to cause harm to an inmate's eyesight.

[97] Shaley, *supra* note 93.

[98] The Close Supervision Centre (CSC) at Whitemoor prison (UK) has a communal area with table tennis and pool tables, a classroom equipped with a computer, a trolley of books and a stock of board games, and a workshop. It also has a well equipped fitness suite with free weights and an outside exercise yard which contains a greenhouse and a secure garden.

[99] Shaley, *supra* note 93.

[100] *See id.*

[101] Andrew Coyle, *Minimum International Standards for the Treatment of Prisoners*, Institut International des Droits de l'Homme 93, 94 (July 2009).

[102] This is not just what is right for the prisoner but also what is right for the families. This right is protected under Article 17 of the ICCPR: "no one shall be subjected to arbitrary

The physical conditions that death row inmates are being subjected to worldwide are a violation of international law (discussed below). The United Nations Human Rights Committee (HRC) has expressed concern over the "living conditions of inmates on death row in terms of visits and correspondence, cell size, food, exercise, extreme temperatures, lack of ventilation, insects, and lack of time outside of cells."[103] The physical conditions that a death row inmate faces for an indefinite period of time are a factor that plays into the death row phenomenon. The conditions on death rows worldwide are so unfortunate that no individual could expect to physically survive. In June 2005, the UN Special Rapporteur on torture even declared the conditions on Mongolia's death row to be so poor that they may amount to torture.[104]

C. The Experimental Component of the Long Delays

In his essay *Reflections on the Guillotine*, Albert Camus writes "as a general rule, a man is undone by waiting for capital punishment well before he dies. Two deaths are inflicted on him, the first being worse than the second."[105] Supplementing the long extenuating periods of time and deplorable conditions, inmates must also face the unimaginable anxiety over their own imminent death. There are three subcategories that arise from the anxiety created while an inmate awaits his/her own death: the lack of notice as to the date and time of the execution, public executions, and mistakes in administering the penalty. These conditions all factor into the mental trauma that death row inmates' face since they create further confusion, humiliation, and fear in the inmates.

1. Lack of notice as to the date and time of execution

In some countries, death row inmates, their families and their attorneys are denied advance notice of the date and time of the execution. This is a violation of a basic human right resulting in inhuman and degrading treatment under the procedural safeguards surrounding the right to life.[106] In Japan,[107] Uzbekistan,[108] and Iran[109] inmates and their families are deprived of advance notice of the time and place of the

---

or unlawful interference with his privacy, family, home or correspondence..." The right to family life is also protected by Article 11 of the American Convention on Human Rights and Article 8 of the European Convention on Human Rights.

[103] *See generally*, Concluding Observations of the Human Rights Committee; Japan, UN Document CCPR/CO/79/Add. 102, 19 Nov. 1998, para 21; Concluding Observations of the Human Rights Committee: Uzbekistan, UN Doc. CCPR/CO/71/UZB, 26 Apr. 2001, para 10; *Safarmo Kurbanova v. Tajikistan*, views of the Human Rights Committee, Communication No. 1096/2002, UN Cod. CCPR/C/79/D/1096/2002, 12 Nov. 2003.

[104] 2006 Commission on Human Rights Mission to Mongolia at E/CN.4/2006/6/Add/.4 on 20 Dec. 2005.

[105] Smith, *supra* note 17, at 250.

[106] Report of the Special Rapporteur on Extrajudicial, Summary or Arbitrary Executions, Philip Alston – *Transparency and the Imposition of the Death Penalty*, E/CN.4/2006/53/Add.3, at para. 32 (24 March 2006).

[107] Amnesty International, *supra* note 92, and Alston, *supra* note 106.

[108] Amnesty International, *supra* note 92.

[109] Alston, *supra* note 106.

execution. In Thailand, death row inmates are given sixty minutes notice before their executions are carried out.[110] Inmates in Saudi Arabia are not only denied advance notice but some inmates are unaware that they are even subject to the execution.[111] In extreme cases such as Thailand, the inmates find out about their execution only moments prior to the ending of their life. Inmates on death row as a result wait in constant, unrelenting fear of not knowing when their day to die has come.

2. *Public executions*

Public executions also disgrace prisoners and are "incompatible with human dignity."[112] China, Japan, the Democratic People's Republic of Korea (North Korea), Uzbekistan, and Saudi Arabia still hold public executions when utilizing the death penalty.[113] In a report done by Amnesty International in 2004 regarding China's death row inmates it was reported that prisoners are placed in an open truck and paraded through the busy streets to the execution site with a placard strung around their neck with their name crossed out in red.[114] The use of public executions in the administration of the death penalty is a form of humiliation that is inconsistent with the basic fundamental human rights and human dignity a society should have and promote.

3. *Errors in the administration of the execution*

The administration of the execution itself can increase the anxiety of an inmate. Again, the punishment is death, not the pain that they should suffer while being executed. An improperly administered execution constitutes a violation of the cruel and inhumane provisions of both the U.S. Constitution and international treaties. In a 2006 trial, Dr. Mark Heath, of Columbia University, stated the belief that at least two California inmates may have been conscious when executed: Robert Massie[115] and Stanley Williams.[116] Further, Dr. Heath stated that the medical logs of San Quentin State Prison indicate that there were mistakes in the mixtures of the drugs leading some inmates to "be conscious longer than supposed" during their executions.[117] The United States District Judge Fogel believed that there was "substantial evidence in past medical logs to suggest that as many as the last six men executed in San Quentin State Prison might have

---

[110] Statement by the Thailand Union for Civil Liberties, *Thailand: Civil Libertarians Condemn* Executions (25 August 2009*), availble at* http://asiadeathpenalty.blogspot.com/ (last accessed 12 November 2009).

[111] Amnesty International, *supra* note 92.

[112] Concluding Observations of the Human Rights Committee: Democratic People's Republic of Korea, UN Doc. CCPR/CO/72/PRK, 27 Aug. 2001.

[113] Amnesty International, *supra* note 92.

[114] Amnesty International *People's Republic of China Executed "According to Law – The Death Penalty in China"* Doc. 17/003/2004, *available at* http://web.amnesty.org/library/index/engasa170032004.

[115] Executed in 2001, www.ojp.usdoj.gov/bjs/cp.htm (last visited 11 November 2009)

[116] Executed in 2005, www.ojp.usdoj.gov/bjs/cp.htm (last visited 11 November 2009)

[117] David Kravets, *Logs Show Some Inmates May Have Been Conscious During Executions* (28 Sept. 2006), *available at* www.sfgate.com/cgi-bin/article.cgi?f=/n/a/2006/09/27/state/n162151D44.DTL (last accessed 12 November 2009).

been conscious because they were still breathing after the paralyzing agent was given."[118] In another United States execution,[119] allegedly improperly done, an inmate continued to move and retain consciousness for more than 24 minutes. Most executions are completed within 15 minutes with the inmate losing consciousness in approximately three minutes.[120] In attempting to execute Romell Broom, the inmate was pricked by a needle 18 times in an effort to find a vein before being returned to Ohio's death row.[121] In an Alabama execution administered by electrocution, flames erupted from the electrode attached to a prisoner's leg and even after his flesh burned doctors found a heartbeat.[122] The process of administering the execution is not always a smooth process without harmful or drastic errors. The punishment is not the pain, but death itself and the knowledge that this type of pain can be endured increases an inmate's anxiety.

In sum, the lack of notice, administration of public executions, and the faulty process of the execution itself increase the already enormous anxiety of death an inmate faces on death row. This anxiety leads to the development of the death row phenomenon.

V. DEATH ROW PHENOMENON IS A VIOLATION OF INTERNATIONAL LAW

The concept of the death row phenomenon and of death row syndrome depicts a brutal picture of suffering; both psychological and physical. It is argued that this suffering is a form of torture under international standards. Torture is a violation of the ICCPR—articles 6, 7, and 10. Further, the Convention Against Torture, Cruel or Other Inhuman or Degrading Treatment or Punishment (CAT) is violated by this phenomenon. Lastly, this form of torture violates other safeguards—such as the disallowance of the execution of any person suffering from a mental disorder, and the prohibition on excessive suffering—provided and affirmed by the HRC.

A. The Long Delays Are a Violation of International Law

The long delays in both sentencing and execution that inmates face are a violation of international law. Under Article 14(3)(c) of the International Covenant on Civil and Political Rights (ICCPR) it is required that "in the determination of any criminal charge against him, everyone shall be entitled to the following minimum guarantees, in full equality: (c) to be tried without undue delay."[123] States that impose the death penalty and death sentences must strictly adhere to the procedural requirements of

---

[118] *See id.*

[119] The execution took place in Florida and the inmate required two injections of the lethal serum before the execution was completed.

[120] *Lethal Injection Comes Under Fire in Florida and California* 15 Dec. 2006, *available at* www.msnbc.msn.com/id/16227702/ (last visited 11 November 2009).

[121] Alonzo, *Man Survives Execution Attempt, Case Highlights Cruelty of Methods* (3 Oct. 2009), www.democracyforums.com/frontpage/?p=vB34199 (last visited 12 November 2009).

[122] *See id.*

[123] Clarke, *supra* note 27.

Article 14.[124] The length of time that individuals are spending on death row is anywhere from ten years to 20 years or more.[125] In interpreting the phrase "without undue delay," the UN HRC determined that a violation of the right to be tried without undue delay was present where there was a 45 month delay while waiting for an appeal on a death sentence.[126] Further, the HRC found that Article 14(5) which requires that "everyone convicted of a crime shall have the right to his conviction and sentence being reviewed by a higher tribunal according to law,"[127] must be read in conjunction with 14(3)(c), "so that the right to review of conviction and sentence must be made available without undue delay."[128] Therefore, the imposition of death sentences that are excessive in duration are a violation of an individual's right to be tried without undue delay.

B. Violation of the Right to Life

Article 6 of the Covenant "transformed the laconic 'right to life' provision found in Article 3 of the Universal Declaration of Human Rights (UDHR). Under Article 6 of the ICCPR, "every human being has the inherent right to life. This right shall be protected by law. No one shall be arbitrarily deprived of life."[129] While Article 6 does not explicitly require the abolition of the death penalty, it highly favors such a result.[130] Article 6 takes the protection of the fundamental right to life a step further by limiting the circumstances in which the death penalty may be employed; (1) it disallows the arbitrary deprivation of life, (2) disallows the execution of juveniles, and (3) the death penalty may only be imposed "for the most serious crimes."[131] Three regional conventions have enacted similar provisions recognizing the right to life: the European Convention on Human Rights (ECHR), the American Convention on Human Rights (ACHR), and the African Charter of Human and Peoples' Rights (ACHPR).[132]

---

[124] Hanowsky and Newman, *supra* note 20, at 11.

[125] California Department of Corrections and Rehabilitation Division of Adult Operations, Death Row Tracking System, http://www.cdrr.ca.gov (last accessed 11 November 2009) and Texas Department of Correctionsm www.tdcj.state.tx.us/stat/deathrow.htm (last accessed 11 November 2009).

[126] *Pratt and Morgan v. Jamaica*, (Nos. 210/1986 and 225/1987), UN Doc. A/44/40 222 (1989).

[127] International Covenant on Civil and Political Rights Art. 14(5), 19 Dec. 1966, 999 U.N.T.S. 171, 6 I.L.M. 368.

[128] *Pratt v. The Attorney General for Jamaica*, Privy Council Appeal No. 13.3 (1993).

[129] ICCPR, *supra* note 127, at Article 6.

[130] It was not until the Second Optional Protocol to the International Covenant on Civil and Political Rights, aiming at the abolition of the death penalty was put into force that the death penalty was abolished under international law. Currently, the United States has not signed or ratified this optional protocol requiring, "that article 6 of the International Covenant on Civil and Political Rights refers to the abolition of the death penalty in terms that strongly suggest that abolition is desirable, convinced that all measures of abolition of the death penalty should be considered as progress in the enjoyment of the right to life." ICCPR, Optional Protocol General Assembly resolution 44/128 December 1989.

[131] ICCPR, *supra* note 129.

[132] Stephen Garvey, BEYOND REPAIR: AMERICA'S DEATH PENALTY 184 (Duke University Press) (2003).

The HRC stated, "The right to life is the supreme right, because without it, no other rights can be enjoyed".[133] Further, "scrupulous" attention must be given to the principles affected by the death penalty when applied to the right to life.[134] The unjustified placing of an individual on death row for an unknown period of time is crucial in determining the death penalty regarding one's right to life. "Because death row inmates are subjected to severe mental torture [of not knowing when their sentence will be fulfilled] their right to life has been violated."[135] The right to life under Article 6 is interpreted broadly, and "it must be construed to prevent the imposition of extreme psychological torture while awaiting one's punishment."[136] A person's right to life is not taken away until the last decision is handed down and therefore the conditions of death row are a violation of the individual's right to life. While Article 6 does allow for the death penalty under narrow circumstances,[137] it does not allow for the psychological implications of the death row phenomenon, which are affecting the inmates' right to life.

C. Violation of the Prohibition against Torture

Article 7 of the ICCPR provides that "no one shall be subjected to torture or to cruel, inhuman or degrading treatment or punishment."[138] The HRC has stated that the imposition of the death penalty must be conducted "in such a way as to cause the least possible physical and mental suffering."[139] The HRC determined in its decision of *Ng v. Canada*, that "execution by gas asphyxiation...constitutes cruel and inhuman treatment in violation of Article 7."[140] The Committee found that execution by lethal injection (when properly administered) is not a breach of Article 7, because lethal injection does not amount to the type of torture required.[141]

Further, CAT defines torture to mean "any act by which severe pain or suffering, whether physical or mental, is intentionally inflicted on a person."[142] Torture does not have to come in the form of only physical punishment, but can also amount from the effects of psychological punishment. The United States ratified this definition with the reservation that "the United States understands that, in order to constitute torture, an act must be specifically intended to inflict severe physical or mental pain or suffering and that mental pain or suffering refers to prolonged mental harm caused by or resulting from (1) the intentional infliction or

[133] Alston, *supra* note 106, at para. 11 and 18.

[134] *See id.*

[135] Hanowsky and Newman, *supra* note 20, at 14.

[136] *See id.*

[137] The second optional protocol to the ICCPR completely outlawed the death penalty but the United States is not a signatory.

[138] ICCPR, *supra* note 127, at Article 7.

[139] *See id.*

[140] Ng v. Canada, Communication No. 469/1991, U.N. Doc. CCPR/C/49/D/469/1991 (1994).

[141] Cox v. Canada, Communication No. 539/1993, U.N. Doc. CCPR/C/52/D/539/19930. (1994).

[142] Convention Against Torture, Cruel or Inhuman or Other Degrading Treatment or Punishment Art. 1.1, 9 Dec. 1975, 999 U.N.T.S. 171, 6 I.L.M. 368.

threatened infliction of severe physical pain or suffering..."[143]The sentencing of individuals to long drawn-out incarcerations under the conditions of death row has been shown to have prolonged psychological effects on the inmates. Accordingly, those that are sentenced to unending death sentences are being tortured under both definitions. These actions are a violation of the provision set forth in Article 7 of the ICCPR and the provisions of CAT.

D. Violation of Humane Treatment while in Custody

Article 10 of the ICCPR requires that all prisoners be treated humanely while in custody. Article 10(1) provides that "all persons deprived of their liberty shall be treated with humanity and with respect for the inherent dignity of the human person."[144] Under the basic principles for the treatment of prisoners, adopted and proclaimed by the General Assembly, it is proclaimed "all prisoners shall be treated with the respect due to their inherent dignity and value as human beings."[145] The individuals that are being housed under the conditions of this phenomenon are not being treated humanely. The long delays in the process, the conditions of confinement and the anxiety of awaiting one's death, make the confinement and treatment of the prisoners in conflict with Article 10.

E. Violation of Other United Nations Safeguards

The death row phenomenon is a violation of an international prohibition against excessive suffering. The international realm has provided for safeguards guaranteeing the protection of the rights of those facing the death penalty.[146] Under resolution 2004/67, "where capital punishment occurs, it shall be carried out so as to inflict the minimum possible suffering."[147] The United Nations has asked under this resolution for the protections to be afforded to those individuals that are facing the death penalty in the countries that have not abolished the death penalty.[148] The United Nation's Economic and Social Council has advocated that states keep the suffering of death row prisoners to a minimum and to avoid exacerbating the suffering.[149] This resolution is another example of how the death row phenomenon is a violation of international law and standards. Death row inmates that are subjected to these long delays, appalling and inhumane conditions, along with other circumstances surrounding executions, are being subjected to severe psychological and physical trauma. This trauma increases the suffering of the inmate on death row and is a violation of the requirement that the sentence be carried out with as little suffering as possible.

---

143 Convention Against Torture, Cruel or Inhuman or Other Degrading Treatment or Punishment, U.S. Reservations, 9 Dec. 1975, 999 U.N.T.S. 171, 6 I.L.M. 368.

144 ICCPR, *supra* note 127, at Article 10.

145 Institut International des Droits de l'Homme, *supra* note 18.

146 *Id.* at 80.

147 U.N. Human Rights Commission Resolution 2004/67 of 21 April 2004, para.4(*i*).

148 Institut International des Droits de l'Homme, *supra* note 18, at 80.

149 U.N. Economic and Social Council resolution 1996/15 of 22 Feb. 1996.

In addition, international law does not provide for the execution of an individual with a diminished mental capacity. The United Nations requests that all states which still maintain and impose the death penalty "not to impose the death penalty on a person suffering from any form of mental disorder or to execute such person."[150] Under resolution 1989/64 of the Economic and Social Council, states are called to "eliminate the death penalty for persons suffering from mental handicap or extremely limited mental capacity."[151] These safeguards further impose the duty on states not to execute individuals who have become insane.[152] The conditions of death row and of being sentenced to death greatly affect the psychological functioning of an individual. Further, these circumstances can even lead to insanity and a diminished mental capacity. Under the international resolutions, an individual who has become a victim of the factors that cause the death row phenomenon should not be executed. Such an execution violates this prohibition against the execution of one suffering from a mental disorder.

F. United States Ratification of the ICCPR

The U.S. government regularly condemns the human rights abuses around the world but has failed to implement international human rights law into the domestic law of the United States. The United States ratified the ICCPR in 1992 with five reservations, five understandings, and four declarations; stating that Articles 1-27 of the covenant are not self-executing.[153] Where a treaty or covenant is not self-executing and where Congress has not acted to implement the agreement with legislation, no private right of action is created by ratification.[154] Therefore, as a matter of international law, the ICCPR is binding upon the United States but the ICCPR does not form part of the domestic law of the nation. So while the above discussion explains how the death row phenomenon and death row syndrome are violations of the ICCPR, the United States is not bound by this law domestically. However, the HRC urges the United States to begin implementing these standards into the United States' domestic law when dealing with death row inmates.

VI. IN THE END PRISONERS ARE STILL HUMAN BEINGS WITH THE BASIC RIGHTS TO HUMAN LIFE

"Persons deprived of their liberty retain all rights that are not lawfully taken away by the decision sentencing them or remanding them in custody"[155]

---

[150] U.N. Human Rights Commission Resolution 2004/67, *supra* note 147 and U.N. Human Rights Commission resolution 2003/67 of 24 April 2003.

[151] Alston, *supra* note 106.

[152] *See id.*

[153] ICCPR, *supra* note 127, at Articles 1-27.

[154] *See Fujii v. State* 38 Cal.2d 718, 242 P.2d 617 (1952); also see *Buell v. Mitchell* 274 F.3d 337 (6th Cir., 2001) (discussing ICCPR's relationship to death penalty cases, citing to other ICCPR cases).

[155] Institut International des Droits de l'Homme, *supra* note 18, at 95.

No matter the culture or society, humans are humans, even if they come in the form of a prisoner in an orange jumpsuit. "We are not a perfect society but we do not have compassion for other people."[156] Extreme delays in the imposition of death sentences, the deplorable conditions on death row, and the anxiety created by the threat of one's own imminent death are inflicting a great psychological pressure and trauma on death row inmates.[157] Death row inmates are no longer sentenced to just death, they are subjected to two sentences—one of death and one of torture. The three components making up the death row phenomenon result in a psychological breakdown of death row inmates, which results in violation of international law. The concept of death row phenomenon is a violation against the prohibitions of torture and protections for humane treatment, a violation of the right to life, a violation of executing those with mental incapacity, and a violation of limiting the suffering of prisoners in custody.

In order to find a universal ethical context in which to view the rights of all humans, countries will need to compile a body of international law and no longer live under the guise of ethical relativism. What is right for one human being is right for all, no matter the circumstances. The conditions and trauma of death row phenomenon should be applied equally to all humans.

Note from the Editor:

On 11 November 2010, as this article went to press, the Third Committee of the United Nations General Assembly adopted a resolution calling for a moratorium on capital punishment. This is the third such resolution since 2007. There may be some changes when the Plenary General Assembly takes the final vote in December.[158]

---

[156] Gloria Killian, speaking event at the University of La Verne College of Law on 13 September 2010.

[157] Hanowsky and Newman, *supra* note 20, at 16.

[158] William Schabas, "Success for Death Penalty Resolution in General Assembly." Blog entry, 13 November 2010, http://humanrightsdoctorate.blogspot.com/

[8]

The United Nations and Abolition of the Death Penalty

William A. Schabas

As diplomats were labouring in San Francisco to create the United Nations in 1945, a parallel exercise was underway in London to establish the first international tribunal for the prosecution of serious violations of international law. The institution that resulted, the International Military Tribunal, which sat in Nuremberg and tried several of the Nazi leaders, was a creation of the four 'great' powers, and was independent of the United Nations. Nevertheless, the principles established at Nuremberg were endorsed by the United Nations General Assembly at its first session, in December 1946.[1] Only a few weeks earlier, the Tribunal had completed its work with the execution by hanging of eleven leading Nazis.[2] Although the General Assembly of the United Nations did not then speak specifically to the use of capital punishment for the punishment of Nazi war criminals, the matter was, at the time, entirely uncontroversial. A report on the death penalty prepared by the Secretariat of the United Nations more than thirty years later noted that 'the post-war years were not conducive to allowing Member States to come to an unequivocal position on the issue. Some countries with a long abolitionist tradition argued for barring the death penalty during times of war, while other members proposed an exception for offenders guilty of crimes against mankind'.[3]

Not quite half a century later, the United Nations Security Council established two international criminal tribunals, to deal with atrocities committed in the former Yugoslavia and Rwanda.[4] In at least one major respect, the new institutions contrasted with their ancestor at Nuremberg: the tribunals could only impose terms of imprisonment.[5] During the Security Council debate on the *Statute of the International Criminal Tribunal for Rwanda,* the representative of New

1 GA Res. 95(I).

2 *Agreement for the Prosecution and Punishment of Major War Criminals of the European Axis, and Establishing the Charter of the International Military Tribunal (I.M.T.),* annex (1951) 82 UNTS 279, art. 27.

3 UN Doc. A/CONF.87/9, para. 4.

4 UN Doc. S/RES/827 (1993); UN Doc. S/RES/955 (1994).

5 *Statute of the International Criminal Tribunal for the former Yugoslavia,* UN Doc. S/RES/827 (1993), annex, art. 24(1); *Statute of the International Criminal Tribunal for Rwanda,* UN Doc. S/RES/955 (1994), annex, art. 23(1). See also: *Statute of the Special*

Zealand stated that '[f]or over three decades the United Nations has been trying progressively to eliminate the death penalty. It would be entirely unacceptable – and a dreadful step backwards – to introduce it here'.[6] Indeed, over the forty-nine years since the beginning of the United Nations, world opinion and national practice with respect to capital punishment had shifted dramatically, and this was reflected in the policy of the organisation. This chapter endeavours to chart the evolution of the death penalty debate within the United Nations.

Standard Setting: The Universal Declaration of Human Rights and the International Covenant on Civil and Political Rights

The *Charter of the United Nations,* adopted in San Francisco in June 1945, provided several references to human rights, and declared that 'promoting and encouraging respect for human rights and for fundamental freedoms for all without distinction as to race, sex, language, or religion' was among the purposes of the United Nations.[7] To the dismay of many, however, the major powers reneged on earlier commitments to include a declaration of human rights within the *Charter* itself (Lauren 2003). The compromise at San Francisco was to make ample reference to human rights in the *Charter* but to postpone adoption of anything substantive. In early 1947, the Commission on Human Rights began work on two documents, a general declaration of human rights principles of a non-binding nature and a full-blown treaty or 'covenant' to which States could adhere if they so decided. Three years later, on 10 December 1948, the United Nations General Assembly adopted the *Universal Declaration on Human Rights.*[8] Work on the proposed covenant took considerably longer, and a final text was only adopted in 1966.[9] Important debates about capital punishment figured in the preparation of both instruments, principally within the context of discussion about the 'right to life'.

The issue of capital punishment was debated at considerable length by the Commission on Human Rights and the General Assembly in the course of adoption of the *Universal Declaration of Human Rights,* during 1947 and 1948. This was the first significant consideration of the death penalty within the United Nations. In its final version, article 3 of the *Universal Declaration* states: 'Everyone has the right to life, liberty and security of person'. However, the original draft of this provision, prepared by John P. Humphrey in early 1947, recognised a right to life that 'can be denied only to persons who have been convicted under general

Court for Sierra Leone, art. 19(1); *Statute of the Special Tribunal for Lebanon,* UN Doc. S/RES/1757 (2007), Attachment, 11, art. 24(1).

6 *ibid.,* p. 5.

7 *Charter of the United Nations,* TS 67 (1946), Cmd. 7015, P. (1946-7) XXV 1, 145 BSP 805.

8 *Universal Declaration of Human Rights,* GA Res. 217 A (III) UN Doc. A/810.

9 GA Res. 44/128.

law of some crime to which the death penalty is attached'.[10] Eleanor Roosevelt, who chaired the Drafting Committee of the Commission on Human Rights, cited movement underway in some states to abolish the death penalty, and suggested that it might be better not to make any explicit mention of capital punishment as an exception to the right to life.[11] René Cassin reworked Humphrey's draft and removed the reference to the death penalty.[12]

Although Cassin's proposal found its way, virtually unchanged, into the final version of the *Universal Declaration,* when the text was being studied by the Third Committee of the General Assembly in late 1948 there was an important debate about the death penalty. The Soviet Union proposed an amendment calling for abolition of the death penalty in peacetime.[13] In the ensuing debate, nary a voice was raised to defend the use of capital punishment in peacetime, although some delegates conceded that their governments had not yet abolished the death penalty.[14] Many participants in the debate said only that the proposal was inopportune[15] or premature.[16] The United Kingdom representative said that its inclusion in the declaration might make it difficult for some states to accept,[17] and a number of delegates said they would abstain in the vote for this reason.[18]

Several Latin American delegates were unhappy with the Soviet amendment because it did not go far enough. They were opposed to the death penalty entirely, even in wartime. Costa Rica's delegation said it would abstain from voting on the Soviet amendment because it restricted abolition to times of peace.[19] The Venezuelan delegate said he could not support the Soviet proposal on the death penalty, because it implied that such punishment was legal in times of war, and this was contrary to his country's laws.[20] He said that he would have been able to vote in favour of the proposal, if it had envisaged the complete abolition of the death penally.[21] Uruguay's delegate proposed an amendment aimed at total abolition,

10 UN Doc. E/CN.4/AC.1/3; reprinted in UN Doc. E/CN.4/21, Annex A.

11 UN Doc. E/CN.4/AC.1/SR.2, 10.

12 UN Doc. E/CN.4/AC.l/W.2/Rev.l; UN Doc. E/CN.4/AC.l/W.2/Rev.2.

13 UN Doc. A/C.3/265.

14 e.g., Belgium: UN Doc. A/C.3/SR.103, 9 (Belgium). Although Belgium had not actually carried out executions since the nineteenth century, with a few exceptions following the Second World War, it did not formally abolish capital punishment until the 1990s, and Belgian courts continued to pronounce death sentences until that time.

15 UN Doc. A/C.3/SR.105, 5; Norway (UN Doc. A/C.3/SR.104, 12); Pakistan (UN Doc. A/C.3/SR.105, 8); Haiti (UN Doc. A/C.3/SR.105, 2); New Zealand (UN Doc. A/C.3/SR.105, 10); Australia (UN Doc. A/C.3/SR.103, 2); Turkey (UN Doc. A/C.3/SR.103, 11).

16 UN Doc.A/C.3/SR.102, 4–5.

17 *ibid,* 9.

18 Pakistan: UN Doc. A/C.3/SR.105, 8; Peru: UN Doc. A/C.3/SR.104, 10.

19 UN Doc.A/C.3/SR.105, 6.

20 UN Doc. A/C.3/SR.102, 10–11.

21 UN Doc.A/C.3/SR.104, 10.

although it was never put to a vote.[22] The Soviet amendment was defeated, on a roll call vote, by twenty one votes to nine, with eighteen abstentions.[23] Uruguay actually voted against the amendment, and other proponents of abolition abstained. The United Kingdom delegate expressed the view that the vote on the Soviet proposal aimed at abolition could in no way be interpreted as a vote for or against capital punishment.[24]

After adoption of the *Universal Declaration,* work proceeded in the Commission on Human Rights and subsequently in the Third Committee of the General Assembly on the more detailed provisions of the proposed covenant. With respect to the death penalty, the result was article 6 of the *International Covenant on Civil and Political Rights,* the final text of which was agreed by the Third Committee in 1957.[25] Article 6 of the *Covenant* states as a general principle that nobody shall be deprived arbitrarily of the right to life, but goes on to recognise capital punishment explicitly as an exception or limitation on the right to life.[26] Article 6(2) of the *Covenant* declares:

> In countries which have not abolished the death penalty, sentence of death may be imposed only for the most serious crimes in accordance with the law in force at the time of the commission of the crime and not contrary to the provisions of the present Covenant and to the Convention on the Prevention and Punishment of the Crime of Genocide. This penalty can only be carried out pursuant to a final judgment rendered by a competent court.[27]

The provision goes on to state that anyone sentenced to death is entitled to seek amnesty, pardon or commutation of sentence, and to prohibit the death penalty for persons under eighteen at the time of commission of the crime (see Schabas and Sax 2006)[28] and for pregnant women. A final paragraph, really more programmatic

22 UN Doc. A/C.3/274/Rev.1.

23 UN Doc. A/C.3/SR.107, 6. *In favour*: Byelorussian Soviet Socialist Republic, Cuba, Czechoslovakia, Dominican Republic, Mexico, Poland, Ukrainian Soviet Socialist Republic, Union of Soviet Socialist Republics, Yugoslavia. *Against:* Afghanistan, Australia, Brazil, Canada, Chile, China, France, Greece, Guatemala, Haiti, Luxembourg, Panama, Philippines, Siam, Syria, Turkey, Union of South Africa, United Kingdom, United States of America, Uruguay, Yemen. *Abstained*: Argentina, Belgium, Burma, Costa Rica, Denmark, Ecuador, Egypt, Ethiopia, Honduras, India, Lebanon, Netherlands, New Zealand, Norway, Peru, Saudi Arabia, Sweden, Venezuela.

24 UN Doc. A/C.3/SR.103, 12.

25 UN Doc. A/C.3/SR.820, para. 27.

26 *International Covenant on Civil and Political Rights* (1976) 999 UNTS 171, art. 6.

27 *ibid.*, art. 6(2).

28 *ibid.*, art. 6(5). The *Convention on the Rights of the Child,* GA Res. 44/25, annex, art. 37(a), adopted by the General Assembly in 1989, also prohibits execution for crimes committed under the age of eighteen. It has been ratified by 192 countries, and signed but

than normative, proclaims: 'Nothing in this article shall be invoked to delay or to prevent the abolition of capital punishment by any State Party to the present Covenant'.[29] This was the marker placed in article 6 by abolitionist States. There is a tension between paragraphs (2) and (6) of article 6. It is a relationship that testifies to a conservative reality in terms of State practice, at the time the text was adopted, but at the same time it manifests a progressive vision. The 1957 text remained unchanged in the final version of the *Covenant,* which was adopted by the United Nations General Assembly in 1966, and which entered into force a decade later.

The *Covenant* is currently ratified by approximately 155 States, and its principles are therefore approaching near-universal acceptance. In accordance with dynamic principles of treaty interpretation, the meaning given to article 6 has evolved considerably since its adoption. The primary body charged with implementation of the *Covenant,* the Human Rights Committee, has recently taken the view that the prohibition on arbitrary deprivation of the right to life, affirmed in article 6(1) of the *Covenant,* means that the death penalty is fundamentally incompatible with the right to life. The exception, set out in article 6(2), is to be applied narrowly and can only be invoked by States that still retain capital punishment. The inevitable conclusion is that States that have abolished the death penalty are permanently foreclosed from reinstating it.[30] Moreover, they cannot participate indirectly in its implementation by, for example, extraditing or otherwise transferring individuals to places where they might be at risk of execution.[31]

Positioning the Issue on the United Nations Agenda

Although the issue of capital punishment had been debated as part of United Nations standard-setting in the area of human rights, it was far from obvious, in the early years of the organisation, that the death penalty should be part of the organisation's regular agenda. Some States took the view that this was solely an issue of domestic criminal law, with no claim to the organisation's activity. They invoked, in this respect, article 2(7) of the *Charter of the United Nations;* 'Nothing contained in the present Charter shall authorise the United Nations to intervene in matters which are essentially within the domestic jurisdiction of any state'. Thus, merely positioning capital punishment as an issue with which the United Nations should be concerned, outside the context of human rights standard-setting, was no small accomplishment.

not ratified by the United States of America. On the relevant provision, see, Schabas and Sax 2006.

29 *ibid,* art. 6(6).

30 *Piandong et al.* v. *Philippines* (no. 869/1999), UN Doc. CCPR/C/70/D/869/1999, para. 7.4.

31 *Judge* v. *Canada* (No. 829/1998), UN Doc. CCPR/C/78/D/829/1998.

The 1957 debate in the Third Committee of the General Assembly during adoption of article 6 of the *International Covenant on Civil and Political Rights* had the consequence of stimulating abolitionist States to further action. In 1959, Austria, Ceylon, Ecuador, Sweden, Venezuela, and Uruguay proposed a resolution in the General Assembly inviting the Economic and Social Council to begin a study on the question of capital punishment.[32] These countries managed to rally support from a spectrum of United Nations Member States, including Ghana, India, Israel, Japan, Pakistan, the Philippines and the United Kingdom. The proposed study was to be based on the relevant provisions of the *Universal Declaration of Human Rights* and on article 6 of the draft covenant.[33] Pursuant to a resolution adopted by the General Assembly, Marc Ancel, an eminent French jurist and Director of the Criminal Science Section of the Institute of Comparative Law in Paris, was engaged to prepare the study.[34] Discussing the consequences of abolition and the issue of deterrence, Ancel observed that 'all the information available appears to confirm that such a removal [of the death penalty] has, in fact, never been followed by a notable rise in the incidence of the crime no longer punishable with death' (Ancel 1962, 54). According to Ancel, the 'modern tendency' was towards a discretionary and not a mandatory death penalty, the latter being used only in exceptional cases, such as capital murder or crimes against the external security of the state (Ancel 1962, 12). Ancel also concluded that most legal systems protected juveniles and pregnant women from the death penalty and that, in practice, a stay of execution for pregnant women nearly always led to commutation of the sentence (Ancel 1962, 13, 25).

A resolution proposed in the 1968 session of the Commission on Human Rights noted, in its preamble, that 'the major trend among experts and practitioners in the field is towards the abolition of capital punishment', and affirmed a number of safeguards respecting appeal, pardon and reprieve, and delay of execution until the exhaustion of such procedures.[35] During the brief discussion in the Commission on Human Rights,[36] some voices opposed the mention of a general trend towards abolition, agreeing however with the idea that there was a trend to reducing the number and categories of offences.[37] There were also objections to what one delegate termed the 'pejorative nuance' that states that had not abolished the death penalty were in breach of article 3 of the *Universal Declaration of Human Rights.*[38]

32 UN Doc. A/C.3/L.767. The idea of such a study had originally been suggested by Sweden, during the 1957 debate on article 6 of the draft *Civil Rights Covenant:* UN Doc. A/C.3/SR.813.

33 UN Doc. A/4250, para. 55.

34 GA Res. 1396(XIV), by fifty-seven to zero, with twenty-two abstentions, UN Doc. A/SR.841.

35 UN Doc. E/4475, UN Doc. UN Doc. E/CN.4/972, 134–136, 162–164.

36 UN Doc. E/4475, UN Doc. UN Doc. E/CN.4/972, 265–269.

37 France, India, Poland, Union of Soviet Socialist Republics.

38 UN Doc. E/CN.4/SR.990, 267.

The United States supported the resolution, noting a trend in its country towards reducing the number of executions and the federal government's contemplation of abolition of the death penalty.[39] After Sweden toned down the draft resolution slightly, it was adopted by the Commission.[40]

In 1971, the Secretary-General prepared a note on information received from member states on the subject of the death penalty which in effect updated the Ancel report, and a subsequent one by Norval Morris (Morris 1967).[41] The note was submitted to the Economic and Social Council, together with a draft resolution reminding states of the principle of progressive restriction of the number of offences for which capital punishment should be imposed, and of the desirability of full abolition.[42] Operative paragraph 3 of the draft stated that the 'main objective to be pursued is that of progressively restricting the number of offences for which capital punishment might be imposed with a view to total abolition of this punishment in all countries, so that the right to life, provided for in article 3 of the *Universal Declaration* may be fully guaranteed'. During debate in the Social Committee of the Economic and Social Council, the sponsors agreed to change the term 'total abolition' to 'desirability of abolishing'.[43] The resolution was adopted in the Economic and Social Council by fourteen votes to zero with six abstentions.[44] After addition of an operative paragraph requesting the Secretary-General to prepare a separate report on practices and statutory rules which may govern the right to petition for pardon, commutation, or reprieve, the resolution[45] was adopted by the General Assembly, with a lone negative vote, Saudi Arabia, and a large number of abstentions.[46]

---

39 *ibid.,* 266.

40 *ibid.,* by nineteen votes to none, with three abstentions.

41 UN Doc. E/4947, UN Doc. ST/SOA/SD/9, U.N. Doc. ST/SOA/SD/10.

42 UN Doc. E/AC.7/L.578, proposed by Italy, Norway, United Kingdom, Uruguay. Amendments were proposed by the Soviet Union: UN Doc. E/AC.7/L.579.

43 UN Doc. E/4993, para. 6.

44 ESC Res. 1574(L); UN Doc. E/SR.1769.

45 U.N. Doc. A/C.3/L.1908, sponsored by Austria, Costa Rica, Italy, Netherlands, New Zealand, Norway, Sweden, United Kingdom, Uruguay, Venezuela.

46 GA Res. 2857(XXVI), UN Doc. A/PV.2027, by fifty-nine votes to one, with fifty-four abstentions. In the Third Committee, a separate vote was taken on the term 'total abolition' in the first preambular paragraph, UN Doc. A/C.3/SR.1905, para. 69, and it was retained by twenty-four votes to eight, with sixty-one abstentions. A separate vote was taken on the term 'total abolition' in operative paragraph four, UN Doc. A/C.3/SR. 1905, para. 69, and it was retained by twenty-three votes to nine, with sixty-two abstentions. The request for a new report from the Secretary-General was also accepted on a separate vote, UN Doc. A/C.3/SR. 1905, §69, adopted by thirty-three votes to none, with sixty-two abstentions. In the Third Committee, the resolution was adopted, UN Doc. A/C.3/SR. 1905, para. 69, by thirty-three votes to none, with sixty-two abstentions.

The Secretary-General's report on capital punishment was presented to the Economic and Social Council in February 1973.[47] Citing article 3 of the *Universal Declaration of Human Rights* and suggesting it implied limitation and abolition of the death penalty,[48] the report observed that 'the United Nations has gradually shifted from the position of a neutral observer concerned about, but not committed on, the issue of capital punishment to a position favouring the eventual abolition of the death penalty'.[49] The Economic and Social Council called on the Secretary-General to prepare similar reports every five years.[50] It also asked the Committee on Crime Prevention and Control and the United Nations Social Defence Research Institute to study the Secretary-General's report and propose appropriate areas for further scientific examination (see Leone 1987).[51] The resolution, 'with a view to the desirability of abolishing this punishment in all countries', reaffirmed that progressive restriction of capital offences was the main objective to be pursued. Indonesia suggested deletion of the phrase 'in all countries' from this paragraph,[52] and this was accepted on a separate vote.[53]

In 1975, the Economic and Social Council reaffirmed the commitment to progressive restriction and the desirability of abolition.[54] It requested the United Nations Committee on Crime Prevention and Control, with the cooperation of the United Nations Social Defence Research Institute, to study appropriate ways of analysing existing trends towards the restriction of the number of capital offences. The resolution also asked the Secretary-General to proceed with a report on practices and statutory rules which might govern the right to petition for pardon, commutation, or reprieve, and to include this information in its next report, due in 1980.[55]

At the General Assembly session of 1977, a draft resolution on capital punishment adopted the formulation of several earlier Economic and Social Council resolutions, affirming that the main objective in the field of capital punishment was progressive restriction of the number of offences for which it might be imposed,

---

47 UN Doc. E/5242 and Add.1. See also UN Doc. E/AC.57/12 and Corr.1, paras. 1–6; UN Doc. E/AC.57/18.

48 UN Doc. E/5242, para. 11.

49 *ibid.,* para. 16.

50 UN Doc. E/5298.

51 UN Doc. E/AC.7/L.624, sponsored by Italy, Austria, Finland, the Netherlands, New Zealand, Sweden and Venezuela. For the Secretary-General's communication with the Committee on Crime Prevention and Control, see UN Doc. E/AC.3/18. On the work of the Social Defence Research Institute.

52 UN Doc. E/AC.7/L.624/Rev.2.

53 UN Doc. E/5298, para. 16, by twenty-five votes to ten, with seven abstentions.

54 UN Doc. E/AC.7/L.678/Rev.1, sponsored by Italy, Austria, Ecuador, Norway, the Netherlands and Venezuela.

55 ESC Res. 1930(LVIII), UN Doc. E/SR. 1948, by twenty-seven votes to zero with nine abstentions. See also: UN Doc. A/10003, paras. 296–302.

with the desirability of overall abolition.[56] It urged Member States to cooperate with the Secretary-General in providing information for his five-year study and called upon the 1980 United Nations Congress on the Prevention of Crime and the Treatment of Offenders to consider the matter. The General Assembly undertook to consider the question of capital punishment at its 1980 session, which would follow the Congress by a few weeks, 'with high priority'.[57]

The Congress was held from 25 August to 5 September 1980, in Caracas. At the Congress, more time was devoted to the issue of capital punishment than to any other question.[58] The report of Committee II noted that many delegations representing countries which still retained capital punishment 'expressed their interest in the attainment of its abolition as a possible final goal'.[59] But there were also strong voices raised in support of the death penalty, something which had not previously featured in United Nations debates on the subject.[60] A draft resolution called for restriction and eventual abolition of the death penalty and added that abolition would be 'a significant contribution to the strengthening of human rights, in particular the right to life'.[61] States retaining the death penalty were invited to respect the terms of articles 6 and 14 of the *Civil Rights Covenant,* which codified 'generally accepted international human rights standards'. A controversial provision urged states which had not abolished capital punishment to 'consider establishing a moratorium in its application, or creating other conditions under which capital punishment is not imposed or is not executed, so as to permit those States to study the effects of abolition on a provisional basis'.

Egypt challenged the draft resolution with an 'amendment', which added preambular paragraphs stressing the importance of general deterrence in providing for penalties, including capital punishment, and referred to 'the importance of providing for capital punishment in order to instil the necessary fear in the hearts of people...'.[62] Faced with stiff opposition and inadequate time to complete the discussions, the sponsors withdrew the revised draft resolution.[63] For abolitionists,

56 UN Doc. A/C.3/32/L.21, sponsored by Austria, Costa Rica, Denmark, Ecuador, Finland, Honduras, Italy, Netherlands, New Zealand, Norway, Portugal, Senegal, Sweden. Venezuela. See also UN Doc. A/C.3/32/SR.40, paras. 46–47.

57 GA Res. 32/61. UN Doc. A/PV.98, adopted without a vote. In the Third Committee: UN Doc. A/C.3/SR.49, para. 35.

58 See comments of the Chief, Crime Prevention and Criminal Justice Branch, UN Doc. A/C.3/35/SR.74, para. 40.

59 UN Doc. A/CONF.87/14/Rev. 1, para. 98.

60 *ibid.*, paras. 99–100.

61 UN Doc. A/CONF.87/C.1/L.1. Sponsored by Austria, Ecuador, the Federal Republic of Germany, Sweden. It was revised following informal discussions (UN Doc. A/CONF.87/14/Rev.l, para. 111; UN Doc. A/CONF.87/C.l/L.l/Rev.l). The resolution is reproduced as an Annex to the Congress Report (UN Doc. A/CONF.87/14/Rev.1, 58–60).

62 UN Doc. A/CONF.87/C. 1/L.9. The amendment is reproduced as an Annex to UN Doc. A/CONF.87/14/Rev.l, 60.

63 UN Doc. A/CONF.87/14/Rev.1, para. 111.

the results of the desultory discussion were disappointing, although, had the resolution proceeded to a vote and been defeated, the movement might have been seriously set back.[64]

The debates at the 1980 Congress were in many ways the culmination of an evolution that had begun in 1957, when the General Assembly adopted article 6 of the *Covenant.* Progressively, the debate on capital punishment had advanced from one of neutral studies, in the 1959 General Assembly resolution, to calls for the restriction of the death penalty and suggestions that abolition was the only view consistent with modem scientific thought, in the late 1960s and throughout the 1970s. A technique of reporting on the subject had been developed, and it seemed to discern a trend towards abolition. The time was now ripe to take the debate a step further. Although the Congress failed to adopt a resolution on the issue of capital punishment that expressed the goal of 'further restriction in the application of capital punishment',[65] in its report it 'took note' of the draft resolution and agreed that it should be considered further by United Nations legislative bodies (United Nations 1983, 781, 783).[66] The immediate result was the preparation of 'safeguards' concerning use of the death penalty, aimed at those countries that still retained capital punishment.

The 'Safeguards'

In 1981 the General Assembly assigned the Committee on Crime Prevention and Control to examine how to delineate summary execution from 'legitimate' capital punishment in accordance with article 6 of the *International Covenant on Civil and Political Rights.*[67] The Secretary-General subsequently prepared a report on summary and arbitrary executions,[68] based on a questionnaire sent to Member States, and in 1982 the Committee on Crime Prevention and Control issued a series of draft 'guidelines' or 'safeguards' that were to be respected where the death penalty was being imposed.[69] According to the draft, capital punishment could only be imposed for the most serious crimes, in accordance with the law in

64 Later that year a draft resolution in the General Assembly was aimed at the same moratorium on the death penalty that had failed in Caracas (UN Doc. A/C.3/35/L.67, sponsored by Austria, Costa Rica, Denmark, Ecuador, Federal Republic of Germany, Italy, Norway, Panama, Papua New Guinea, Portugal, Spain, Sweden, Venezuela). It was criticised for reviving the Caracas debate, and effectively shelved by procedural motions from two retentionist states, Morocco and India: UN Doc. A/C.3/35/SR.76, UN Doc. A/C.3/35/SR.84.

65 UN Doc. A/CONF.87/C.1/L.1.

66 UN Doc. A/CONF.87/14/Rev. 1.

67 GA Res. 36/22.

68 UN Doc. E/AC.57/1982/4 and Add.l.

69 UN Doc. E/CN.5/1983/2, chap. I, sect. A, para. 1, draft resolution I; also chap. V, para. 174.

force at the time of commission of the crime, and not for crimes committed while under eighteen or by pregnant women, and always pursuant to a final judgment by a competent court, for which legal assistance should be available at all stages of the proceedings. The death penalty must be suspended pending any appeal or proceedings relating to pardon or commutation, there must be a right to appeal and a right to apply for pardon or commutation, and there must be the possibility of seeking amnesty, pardon, or commutation at all stages.

The United Nations Secretariat proposed a number of changes to the text. It suggested expanding the guideline referring to 'the most serious crimes', mentioning that the scope of this term be limited to intentional lethal offences and that it exclude political offences.[70] On the guideline prohibiting the death penalty for juveniles and pregnant women, the report urged the addition of new mothers and persons over seventy years of age,[71] groups that had not been included in article 6(5) of the *Covenant* but that appeared in other instruments drafted subsequently.[72] Returning to an old proposal,[73] the Secretary General recommended a temporary stay of the death penalty, following sentencing, that could vary from two to six months.[74] The Secretary-General also urged that the guidelines specify that an appeal procedure be automatic in capital cases.[75]

The Committee adopted the 'Safeguards Guaranteeing Protection of the Rights of those Facing the Death Penalty' at its March 1984 session, proposing they be entrenched in an Economic and Social Council resolution.[76] Many of the changes suggested by the Secretary-General were accepted, but the Committee made some innovations of its own. For example, in article 1, providing that the death penalty

70 UN Doc. E/AC.57/1984/16, para. 43: '...it being understood that their scope should be limited to intentional lethal ofences. Accordingly, it should be excluded for offences which are considred to be of a merely political nature, or for cases in which the political nature of the offence exceeds its criminal aspects'.

71 UN Doc. E/AC.57/1984/16, para. 49.

72 The elderly, in article 4(5) of the *American Convention on Human Rights* (1979) 1144 UNTS 123, OASTS 36, adopted in 1969; 'mothers having dependent children' in article 76(3) of *Protocol Additional I to the 1949 Geneva Conventions and Relating to The Protection of Victims of International Armed Conflicts* (1979) 1125 UNTS 3, adopted in 1977; 'mothers of young children' in article 6(4) of *Protocol Additional II to the 1949 Geneva Conventions and Relating to The Protection of Victims of Non-International Armed Conflicts* (1979) 1125 UNTS 609, adopted in 1977.

73 GA Res. 2393(XXIII), art. 1(b).

74 UN Doc. E/AC.57/1984/16, para. 55: '...and in any case, not until a specific minimum period of time has elapsed, ranging on average betrween two and six months, and established in accordance with the legal practice and social circumstances of each non-abolitionist country, after all the legal remedies in capital proceedings have been exhausted and taking into account the physical and mental health condition of the condemned person'.

75 UN Doc. E/AC.57/1984/16, para. 87.

76 'Draft resolution VII', UN Doc. E/1984/16, UN Doc. E/AC.57/1984/18.

could only be imposed for 'the most serious crimes', the Committee welcomed the suggestion that it refer to crimes with lethal consequences but added a rather large loophole with the addition of the phrase 'or other extremely grave consequences'.[77] Article 2 essentially provided for the rule against retroactive imposition of the death penalty and for the benefit of the lesser penalty where the law has been changed.

Other significant additions to restrictions on the use of capital punishment that had not previously figured in the debates about standard-setting included article 4, dealing with the burden of proof in capital cases. It declared that capital punishment could not be imposed unless there was 'clear and convincing evidence leaving no room for an alternative explanation of the facts'. Article 6 of the Safeguards took up the suggestion of the Secretary-General that appeals should be mandatory (see Strafer 1983; Urofsky 1984; White 1991, 164–185).[78] Article 9 added that capital punishment should be carried out so as to inflict the minimum possible suffering, a point which had previously received little attention in the international law debate on the death penalty.[79]

After adoption by the Committee, the Safeguards were submitted to the Economic and Social Council. There were concerns that they might appear to legitimise capital punishment, and an amendment from staunchly abolitionist states replaced, in article 3, the more neutral phrase 'not to be interpreted as affecting the consideration of the question of the abolition or retention of capital punishment' with the abolition-leaning 'not to be invoked to delay or to prevent the abolition of capital punishment'.[80] In the Council, an oral amendment proposed by the United States calling for reinstatement of the original article 3 was rejected.[81] The phrase '[i]n countries which have not abolished the death penalty,' borrowed from article

77 According to Nigel Rodley, who attended the meeting as an observer for Amnesty International, the term 'or other extremely grave' was added upon the representations of a member of the Committee, who said that some acts, such as provision of secret information to an enemy in wartime, could result in large scale loss of life, although the lethal results of the offence might not easily be proven (see Rodley 1987, 174).

78 Several cases in the United States courts have raised the problem of persons condemned to death who refuse to exhaust their appeals, in effect welcoming execution and renouncing to any right of appeal, even if the right is mandatory. See: *Gilmore* v. *Utah,* 429 U.S. 1012 (1976); *Commonwealth* v. *McKenna,* 476 Pa. 428, 383 A.2d 174 (1978); *Lenhard as next friend of Bishop* v. *Wolf,* 100 S.Ct. 3 (1979); *Betty Evans, as next friend of John Evans* v. *Bennett,* 440 U.S. 1301 (1979).

79 See: *General Comment No. 20(44),* UN Doc. CCPR/C/21/Rev. l/Add.3, para. 6; *Ng* v. *Canada* (No. 469/1991), UN Doc. CCPR/C/49/D/469/1991, UN Doc. A/49/40, Vol. II, 189.

80 UN Doc. E/1984/C.2/L.8, sponsored by Austria, Costa Rica, Italy, Netherlands, Sweden, Uruguay. The amendment was adopted by twenty-nine votes to one, with seventeen abstentions.

81 UN Doc. E/1984/SR.21, para. 22, by twenty-three votes to six, with sixteen abstentions.

6(2) of the *Covenant,* was added at the beginning of paragraph 1 of the Safeguards. Its value is twofold, recalling that abolition is the goal and suggesting that states which have already abolished the death penalty may not revive it.

After adoption by the Economic and Social Council,[82] the Safeguards were endorsed by the General Assembly[83] and by the Seventh United Nations Congress on the Prevention of Crime and the Treatment of Offenders, held in Milan in 1985,[84] which called in a resolution for their widespread dissemination and implementation.[85]

The Safeguards may be said to constitute an authoritative development of the content of article 3 of the *Universal Declaration of Human Rights.* Because of the circumstances of their adoption and the importance of their subject matter, it is also arguable that they constitute a statement of norms of customary international law, a sort of common denominator of acceptable behaviour applicable even to States that have not ratified the *International Covenant on Civil and Political Rights.*[86] In its consideration of State reports as part of the new universal periodic review, it is likely that the United Nations Human Rights Council, which replaced the Commission on Human Rights in 2006, will rely upon the 'Safeguards' when dealing with States for whom the treaty norms are not directly applicable.

Subsequent resolutions have effected minor improvements to the Safeguards. In 1988, building upon a study of the death penalty by criminologist Roger Hood (Hood 1989),[87] the Committee on Crime Prevention and Control adopted a resolution dealing with implementation of the Safeguards that expanded upon their content. The resolution declared that not only must there be adequate assistance of counsel, as found in article 5 of the Safeguards, but also this must go 'above and beyond the protection afforded in non-capital cases'.[88] The resolution also stated that a maximum age should be established above which the death penalty cannot be imposed or carried out.[89] However, the 1988 resolution did not set a specific

82 ESC Res. 1984/50, adopted without a vote.

83 GA Res. 39/118, UN Doc. A/PV. 101, para. 79, without a vote.

84 UN Doc. A/CONF.121/22/Rev.l, 83–84, 131–132.

85 UN Doc. A/CONF.121/C.1/L.9, sponsored by Austria, Denmark, France, Greece, India, Italy, Norway, Uruguay and Yugoslavia. Adopted by consensus at the fifteenth meeting of Committee I, UN Doc, A/CONF.121/22/Rev.l, para. 195; adopted by the Congress at its fourteenth plenary meeting, UN Doc. A/CONF.121/22/Rev.1, para. 214. The resolution adopted at the Congress had been drafted at the Varenna preparatory meeting for the Congress, held in 1984: UN Doc. A/CONF.121/IPM/3, para. 61–68. A Secretariat note on capital punishment had been submitted to the Varenna meeting: UN Doc. A/CONF.121/CRP.2.

86 'Capital punishment and implementation of the safeguards guaranteeing protection of the rights of those facing the death penalty', UN Doc. E/2005/3.

87 UN Doc. E/AC.57/1988/CRP.7. See: E/1988/20, para. 72.

88 UN Doc. E/1988/20, UN Doc. E/AC.57/1988/17, 28-29. Draft resolution E/AC.57/1988/L.19, art. 1(a).

89 *ibid.*, art. 1(c).

age, as had been proposed, unsuccessfully, in 1984. The 1984 'Safeguards' had excluded the insane from the death penalty; the 1988 resolution added 'persons suffering from mental retardation or extremely limited mental competence'.[90] The change in emphasis was due to developments in Washington, where the issue of execution of the mentally disabled was before the Supreme Court at the time.[91] The new resolution, entitled 'Implementation of the Safeguards Guaranteeing Protection of the Rights of Those Facing the Death Penalty', was adopted by the Economic and Social Council.[92]

The Second Optional Protocol to the International Covenant on Civil and Political Rights

The late 1970s were very much of a turning point within the international debate on capital punishment. Amnesty International took on the issue as one of its core campaigns. An important international conference, held in Stockholm, built momentum for abolition. The result of these developments was a series of initiatives in both regional organisations, such as the Council of Europe, and in the United Nations itself. Development of the Safeguards was one manifestation. But of perhaps more enduring importance was the effort to enhance the *International Covenant on Civil and Political Rights* by in a sense correcting its original compromise on the death penalty, which is reflected in article 6. Here, the idea was to devise a subsidiary treaty or 'protocol' that would amend or repeal the references to capital punishment, making the instrument truly abolitionist. A similar effort undertaken in Strasbourg led to the adoption, in 1983, of *Protocol No. 6 to the European Convention on Human Rights.*[93]

The first universal treaty abolishing the death penalty was submitted in draft form to the United Nations General Assembly at its 1980 session. Annexed to a draft resolution was the 'Second Optional Protocol to the International Covenant on Civil and Political Rights'.[94] There was no preamble, although space had been left to add some paragraphs later. Of the nine operative paragraphs in the protocol, article 1 quickly established the substance:

---

90 *ibid.*, art. 1(d).

91 *Penry* v. *Lynaugh,* 492 US 302, 331, 109 SCt 2934, 2953, 106 LEd.2d 256 (1989). Subsequently reversed: *Atkins* v. *Virginia,* 122 SCt 2242 (2002).

92 ESC Res. 1989/64, adopted without a vote.

93 *Protocol No. 6 to the Convention for the Protection of Human Rights and Fundamental Freedoms Concerning the Abolition of the Death Penalty,* ETS No. 114.

94 UN Doc. A/C.3/35/L.75. Submitted by Austria, Costa Rica, Dominican Republic, Federal Republic of Germany, Italy, Portugal, Sweden. Another draft resolution, UN Doc. A/C.3/35/L.80, dealt with summary executions.

> *Article 1*
>
> 1. Each State party shall abolish the death penalty in its territory and shall no longer foresee the use of it against any individual subject to its jurisdiction nor impose nor execute it.
>
> 2. The death penalty shall not be re-established in States that have abolished it.

Article 2 provided that article 1 would be regarded as an additional article to the *International Covenant on Civil and Political Rights* 'as between the States parties'. Furthermore it stated that no derogation whatsoever could be permitted from article 1. The remainder of the draft dealt with such matters as communications to the Human Rights Committee and the formalities of signature, ratification, or accession, federal states, and coming into force. The sponsors of the draft protocol advanced with considerable caution, admitting that their proposal was 'breaking new ground' and that it might be years before any action was taken. Their real goal, they said, was for the Secretary-General to take note of the proposal and seek information from member states, with a view to a more thorough discussion the following year.[95]

The General Assembly decided to seek further submissions from member states, with a view to a full debate on the subject in the 1982 session.[96] Sixteen governments replied to the Secretary-General, with the responses being almost equally divided between abolitionist and retentionist states.[97] In 1982, the General Assembly assigned the issue to the Commission on Human Rights.[98] It, in turn, transmitted the draft second protocol to its Sub-Commission on Prevention of Discrimination and Protection of Minorities.[99] At its August 1984 session, the Sub-Commission assigned Belgian academic Marc Bossuyt to prepare an analysis of the question.[100] Bossuyt's 1987 report to the Sub-Commission[101] included a review of the international law provisions dealing with the death penalty, the decisions of the Human Rights Committee under the *Optional Protocol to the International Covenant on Civil and Political Rights,* the periodic reports submitted to the Committee pursuant to article 40 of the *International Covenant on Civil and Political Rights,* the comments of the Committee on those reports, and the case law of the Inter-American Commission and Court of Human Rights.[102]

---

95 UN Doc. A/C.3/35/SR.74, para. 56.

96 U.N.Doc. A/C.3/36/L.33/Rev.l, sponsored by Austria, Costa Rica, Dominican Republic, Ecuador, Federal Republic of Germany, Italy, Netherlands, Nicaragua, Norway, Panama, Peru, Portugal, Sweden, Uruguay.

97 See: UN Doc. E/CN.4/Sub.2/1987/20, para. 83.

98 GA Res. 37/192, UN Doc. A/37/PV.111.

99 CHR Res. 1984/19, UN Doc. E/1984/14.

100 S.-CHR Res. 1984/7, UN Doc E/CN.4/Sub.2/1984/L.8, UN Doc. E/CN.4/1985/3.

101 UN Doc. E/CN.4/Sub.2/1987/20.

102 UN Doc. E/1985/43.

Bossuyt's analysis and revised draft protocol were accepted by the Sub-Commission and transmitted to the Commission on Human Rights on 1 September 1988.[103] The draft was approved by the Commission[104] and the Economic and Social Council[105] early the following year and then submitted to the General Assembly at its forty-fourth session in the autumn of 1989. The *Second Optional Protocol to the International Covenant on Civil and Political Rights, Aiming at the Abolition of the Death Penalty* was adopted by the General Assembly on 29 December 1989, with fifty-nine votes in favour, twenty-six votes against and forty-eight abstentions.[106] The numbers were such that supporters of capital punishment might well have blocked adoption using procedural gambits. Perhaps they were simply not sufficiently organised. Possibly, also, adoption was influenced by the heady atmosphere that accompanied the end of the Cold War, and that seemed to inaugurate a new era for the promotion of human rights by the United Nations. The *Second Optional Protocol* entered into force on 11 July 1991, following its tenth ratification. As of 1 September 2007, it had obtained 60 ratifications.[107]

The 1989 session of the United Nations General Assembly was the scene of another important initiative respecting capital punishment, the adoption of the *Convention on the Rights of the Child.* Article 6(5) of the *International Covenant on Civil and Political Rights* prohibits execution of persons for crimes committed while under the age of eighteen. The norm also appears in the 'Safeguards Guaranteeing the Rights of Those Facing the Death Penalty'. This prohibition on execution of individuals for crimes committed while under the age of eighteen is reaffirmed in article 37(a) of the *Convention on the Rights of the Child.*[108] Because the *Convention* has attained near-universal ratification, there is a strong claim that the norms it sets out are customary in nature. Following a 2005 judgment of the Supreme Court of the United States, the practice of execution for juvenile offenders appears to have been totally eradicated, with the possible exception of Iran. The Committee on the Rights of the Child has said it is 'seriously disturbed' at the application of the death penalty for crimes committed under the age of eighteen by the Iranian authorities.[109] In 2007, the special *rapporteur* on summary, arbitrary and extrajudicial executions said that Iran was the only country in the world from which he continued to receive credible reports of juvenile executions (United Nations 2007a, 63).

103 S-CHR Decision 1988/22, UN Doc. E/CN.4/Sub.2/1987/28.

104 CHR Res. 1985/25, UN Doc. E/1989/20, 83–84.

105 ESC Res. 1989/139.

106 GA Res. 44/128, UN Doc. A/44/824, UN Doc. A/44/PV.82, 11.

107 When this figure is combined with the ratifications of the abolitionist instruments of the Council of Europe and Organisation of American States, a total of 80 States are bound to abolition of the death penalty by international treaty.

108 *Convention on the Rights of the Child,* GA Res. 44/25, annex.

109 UN Doc. CRC/C/15/Add.123, para, 29; UN Doc. CRC/C/SR.617, paras. 46–47.

As Momentum Grows, the Opponents Mobilise

In 1989 Amnesty International published a seminal study, *When the State Kills,* that offered a statistical portrait of capital punishment in the modern world (Amnesty International 1989). It showed that 70 States had abolished capital punishment, either in law or in practice, while 100 still retained it. Many in the latter category only used capital punishment occasionally. Perhaps of greatest importance, the statistics showed an unmistakable trend towards universal abolition. Each year, two to three countries abolished capital punishment. There was only isolated evidence of movement in the other direction. Nevertheless, three of the five permanent members of the Security Council, Russia, China and the United States, made generous use of the death penalty. A fourth, France, had held its last execution barely a decade earlier, and had only abolished capital punishment in 1981. The fifth, the United Kingdom, had not executed anyone since 1964, but its Conservative Party government led by Margaret Thatcher was profoundly negative about efforts to advance an abolitionist agenda at the international level.

Alongside this somewhat precarious situation, there was an increasingly active caucus of Islamic states within the United Nations, who espoused a reactionary interpretation of Islamic law and maintained that capital punishment was actually required by their religion (see Schabas 2000a). As a result, while the abolitionist agenda continued to advance throughout the 1990s and into the twenty-first century, debates were increasingly rancorous and difficult.

At the 1990 Congress on the Prevention of Crime and the Treatment of Offenders, held in Havana, a resolution on capital punishment was proposed that returned to the idea of a moratorium on the death penalty, 'at least on a three year basis'.[110] Promoted by the Italian delegation, the resolution was adopted in Committee by forty votes to twenty-one, with sixteen abstentions,[111] but was rejected in plenary session because it failed to obtain a two-thirds majority (Clarke 1990, 518–519).[112] The issue of capital punishment was absent from the agenda of the 1995 Congress, held in Cairo.

In 1994, Italy attempted to take the issue to a new level, proposing a resolution in the United Nations General Assembly that called for a moratorium on the death penalty.[113] Italy's efforts began with a request addressed to the Office of the Presidency of the General Assembly that the item 'capital punishment' be added to

110 UN Doc. A/CONF. 144/C.2/L.7, as amended orally.

111 UN Doc. ACONF. 144/28/Rev. 1, para. 350.

112 UN Doc. A/CONF. 144/28/Rev. 1, para. 358.

113 UN Doc. A/49/234 and Add. 1 and Add.2 (1994), later revised by UN Doc. A/C.3/49/L.32/Rev.1 (1994). The resolution originated from a newly-formed non-governmental organisation, 'Hands Off Cain – the International League for Abolition of the Death Penalty Before the Year 2000', which had obtained the support of the Italian Parliament for the draft resolution.

the agenda. Pakistan opposed modification of the agenda to include the item.[114] The representative of Sudan described capital punishment as 'a divine right according to some religions, in particular Islam'.[115]

A series of preambular paragraphs referred to earlier General Assembly resolutions on the death penalty, the 1984 'Safeguards', relevant provisions, in the *Universal Declaration of Human Rights,* the *International Covenant on Civil and Political Rights* and the *Convention on the Rights of the Child,* the Statutes of the *ad hoc* criminal tribunals for the former Yugoslavia and Rwanda, and the draft statute of the proposed International Criminal Court. The first of three operative paragraphs invited States that still maintain the death penalty to comply with their obligations under the *International Covenant* and the *Convention on the Rights of the Child,* and in particular to exclude pregnant women and juveniles from execution. The second paragraph invited states which had not abolished the death penalty to consider the progressive restriction of the number of offences for which the death penalty may be imposed, and to exclude the insane from capital punishment. The final paragraph 'encourage[d] states which have not yet abolished the death penalty to consider the opportunity of instituting a moratorium on pending executions with a view to ensuring that the principle that no state should dispose of the life of any human being be affirmed in every part of the world by the year 2000'.

Italy eventually obtained forty-nine co-sponsors for the resolution.[116] During debate in the Third Committee of the General Assembly, Singapore took the initiative in attacking the draft resolution. According to Singapore's representative, ' it strongly opposed efforts by certain States to use the United Nations to impose their own values and system of justice on other countries'. He added that it was evident, from the wording of the *International Covenant on Civil and Political Rights,* that no universal consensus held capital punishment to be contrary to international law.[117]

Singapore initially attempted to block the resolution by proposing a 'no action' motion, which is often an effective procedural technique to block such initiatives. This attempt was rejected, sixty-five States voting in favour to seventy-four against, with twenty abstentions. Singapore then proposed an 'amendment' that in effect distorted the original purpose of the resolution, by adding the following

114 UN Doc. A/BUR/49/SR.6, para. 2.

115 UN Doc. A/BUR/49/SR.5, para. 13.

116 Andorra, Argentina, Australia, Austria, Belgium, Bolivia, Cambodia, Cape Verde, Chile, Colombia, Costa Rica, Cyprus, Czech Republic, Denmark, Dominican Republic, Ecuador, El Salvador, Finland, France, Germany, Greece, Haiti, Honduras, Hungary, Iceland, Ireland, Liechtenstein, Luxembourg, Malta, Marshall Islands, Micronesia, Monaco, New Zealand, Nicaragua, Norway, Panama, Paraguay, Portugal, Romania, San Marino, São Tomé and Principe, Slovak Republic, Solomon Islands, Spain, Sweden, Uruguay, Vanuatu and Venezuela.

117 UN Doc. A/C.3/49/SR.33, paras. 23–27.

preambular paragraph: 'Affirming the sovereign right of states to determine the legal measures and penalties which are appropriate in their societies to combat serious crimes effectively'.[118] In order to save the resolution, Italy then modified its original text by incorporating the Singapore amendment, while at the same time adding a reference to the *Charter of the United Nations* and to international law, aimed at making Singapore's reactionary appeal to 'state sovereignty' subject to some recognition of international norms.[119] By a close vote, seventy-one to sixty-five, with twenty-one abstentions, Singapore's amendment was adopted. The amendment made the resulting text unacceptable to many abolitionist States. Italy continued to support the resolution, even with the Singapore amendment, but most of its co-sponsors had deserted the camp and abstained in the final vote (a total of seventy-four States abstained). The remainder, essentially retentionist states, tended to divide: thirty-six voted in favour and forty-four voted against.[120]

While the debate was underway in the Third Committee of the General Assembly, a dispute erupted within the Security Council about the death penalty in the course of creation of the International Criminal Tribunal for Rwanda. The draft statute excluded the death penalty as a possible sanction for crimes of genocide, war crimes and grave breaches of international humanitarian law concerning non-international armed conflicts.[121] The draft statute was modelled on a similar instrument adopted by the Security Council in May, 1993, creating the *ad hoc* tribunal for the former Yugoslavia.[122] The provision excluding the death penalty in the case of the Yugoslav tribunal does not appear to have provoked any controversy whatsoever. The draft statute for a permanent International Criminal Court, proposed in 1994 by the International Law Commission, also excluded any use of the death penalty.[123]

Rwanda, which by pure chance was itself a member of the Security Council at the time, opposed the prohibition on capital punishment. It claimed there would be a fundamental injustice in exposing criminals tried by its domestic courts with execution if those tried by the international tribunal – presumably the masterminds of the genocide – would only be subject to life imprisonment, while those prosecuted by the country's national courts would be liable to execution.[124] 'Since it is foreseeable that the Tribunal will be dealing with suspects who devised, planned and organised the genocide, these may escape capital punishment whereas those who simply carried out their plans would be subjected to the harshness of

118 UN Doc. A/C.3/49/L.73.

119 UN Doc. A/C.3/49/L.74.

120 UN Doc. A/C.3/49/SR.61.

121 *Statute of the International Tribunal for Rwanda,* UN Doc. S/RES/955 (1994) annex, art. 23(1).

122 *Statute of the International Tribunal for the Former Yugoslavia,* UN Doc. S/RES/827 (1993), annex, art. 24(1).

123 UN Doc. A/49/10 (1994), art. 47.

124 UN Doc. S/PV.3453, 16.

this sentence', said Rwanda's representative. 'That situation is not conducive to national reconciliation in Rwanda'.[125]

Eventually, when the International Criminal Tribunal for Rwanda offered to transfer some of its backlog of cases back to Rwanda for trial by national jurisdictions, Rwanda promised the death penalty would not be applicable in such cases.[126] Some months later, it took its position to its logical conclusion, and abolished capital punishment throughout the country (United Nations 2007b). Thus, the insistence by the Security Council that the International Criminal Tribunal refrain from capital punishment ultimately promoted abolition within the country itself.

It took a few years for the abolitionists to regroup after the 1994 setback in the General Assembly. A resolution was adopted at the fifth session of the Commission on Crime Prevention and Criminal Justice in 1996, following up on the quinquennial report of the Secretary-General.[127] The resolution was subsequently endorsed later that year by the Economic and Social Council.[128] In March 1997, a resolution on capital punishment was presented to the annual session of the Commission on Human Rights.[129] The resolution welcomed the exclusion of capital punishment from the statutes of the *ad hoc* international criminal tribunals, took note of the Human Rights Committee's General Comment noting that article 6 of the *International Covenant on Civil and Political Rights* refers to abolition of the death penalty in terms which strongly suggest that abolition is desirable, and said the Commission was '[c]onvinced that abolition of the death penalty contributes to the enhancement of human dignity and to the progressive development of human rights'. It called upon States parties to the *Covenant* that had not yet ratified or acceded to the *Second Optional Protocol* to consider doing so, urged States that still maintain the death penalty to comply fully with their international treaty obligations on the subject to observe the Safeguards guaranteeing protection of the rights of those facing the death penalty, to progressively to restrict the number of offences for which the death penalty may be imposed and to make available to the public information on imposition of the death penalty. It 'called upon' such

125 *ibid.*

126 UN Doc. S/PV.5594, 31; UN Doc. S/PV.5697, 15.

127 UN Doc. E/CN.15/1996/19.

128 UN Doc. E/RES/1996/15.

129 In addition to the annual resolutions, which began in 1997, the Commission on Human Rights has also condemned the manner in which the death penalty is used in its geographic or country resolutions. For example, in 1998 it expressed its concern that use of the death penalty by military tribunals in the Democratic Republic of Congo as being contrary to the provisions of the *International Covenant on Civil and Political Rights*. See: CHR Res. 1998/61, para. 2(b)(ii); also CHR Res. 1999/56, para. 2(b)(iv). Similarly, on death row conditions in Burundi: CHR Res. 1998/82, para. 12; on lapidation and public executions, and the scope of crimes for which the death penalty is imposed in Iran: CHR Res. 1998/80, para. 3(a)(j); CHR Res. 1999/13, para. 4(b); on arbitrary imposition of capital punishment in Iraq: CHR Res. 1999/14, para. 2(b).

States 'to consider suspending executions, with a view to completely abolishing the death penalty'.[130] The resolution was adopted by a roll-call vote of twenty-seven votes to eleven, with fourteen abstentions.[131]

The subject returned to the agenda of the Commission on Human Rights the following year.[132] The call for a moratorium was worded somewhat more robustly, 'urging' States that still maintain the death penalty '[t]o establish a moratorium on executions, with a view to completely abolishing the death penalty'.[133] The results of the voting were about the same: twenty-six to thirteen, with twelve abstentions, once again on a roll-call vote. Reacting to this development, fifty-one States filed a letter with the president of the Commission on Human Rights, on 31 March 1998, asserting that there was no international consensus calling for abolition of the death penalty, citing differences linked to religion and judicial systems in various countries.[134] The successful resolution in the Commission may also have helped provoke efforts a few months later to make the issue of the death penalty a 'deal breaker' during the Rome Diplomatic Conference where the *Statute of the International Criminal Court* was adopted (Schabas 2000b).

The 1999 resolution in the Commission on Human Rights was proposed by the fifteen-member European Union.[135] The preamble of the 1999 resolution 'welcomed' the exclusion of capital punishment from the *Rome Statute,* a jab at the retentionist States who, at the Rome Diplomatic Conference, had negotiated ambiguous statements that might suggest the *Statute* was neutral on the subject. The draft resolution went considerably further than the 1997 and 1998 version, calling upon States that still maintain the death penalty not to impose it 'for non-violent financial crimes or for non-violent religious practice or expression of conscience' or 'on a person suffering from any form or mental disorder', and '[n]ot to execute any person as long as any related legal procedure, at international or at national level, is pending'. The draft resolution also urged States not to enter any reservations to article 6 of the *Covenant,* and to withdraw any existing reservations (at the time, the only State with reservations to article 6 was the United States of

130 UN Doc. E/CN.4/1997/L.40.

131 Retentionist states later complained to the Economic and Social Council: UN Doc. E/CN.4/1997/L.20, UN Doc. E/1997/196.

132 UN Doc. E/CN.4/1998/L.12.

133 'The question of the death penalty', E/CN.4/RES/1998/8.

134 UN Doc. E/CN.4/1998/156. It was signed by: Algeria, Antigua and Barbuda, Bahamas, Bahrein, Bangladesh, Barbados, Bhutan, Brunei Darussalam, Burundi, China, Congo, Egypt, Ghana, Guyana, Indonesia, Iran, Iraq, Jamaica, Japan, Jordan, Kuwait, Lesotho, Lebanon, Liberia, Libya, Malaysia, Malawi, Maldives, Mauritania, Mongolia, Myanmar, Nigeria, Oman, Philippines, Qatar, Rwanda, St. Kitts and Nevis, St. Lucia, St. Vincent and the Grenadines, Saudi Arabia, Singapore, Sudan, Swaziland, Syria, Tadjikistan, Tanzania, Trinidad and Tobago, United Arab Emirates, Vietnam, Yemen, Zimbabwe.

135 UN Doc. E/CN.4/1999/L.91. There were seventy-two cosponsors of the 1999 resolution, compared with sixty-five in 1998.

America).[136] The addition of a reference to extradition, and a request for States to reserve explicitly the right to refuse extradition in the absence of effective assurances that the death penalty would not be carried out, drove Canada, at least temporarily, off the list of the resolution's sponsors.[137] Compromise language was ultimately developed that managed to woo Canada back to the camp of those supporting the resolution. It was adopted in the final days of the Commission's annual session, on 28 April 1999, by a roll call vote of thirty votes to eleven, with twelve abstentions.[138]

The European Union was emboldened by this success in the Commission, and developed a strategy to conquer the General Assembly, where efforts had failed in 1994. Finland held the European Union presidency, and to it fell the initiative to submit the proposal. The Finnish delegation's draft, circulated on 7 October 1999, called on States to apply international safeguards in the application of death sentences, urged ratification of the *Second Optional Protocol* by States parties to the *International Covenant on Civil and Political Rights,* progressive restriction of the death penalty and establishment of a moratorium, all with a view to complete abolition.[139]

Opposition mobilised, with Egypt and Singapore – both of them subject to international criticism for death penalty practice[140] – in the lead. As in the past, the strategy was not to vote down the resolution but rather to use so-called 'wrecking amendments' to make it unpalatable for the abolitionists. Two draft amendments were tabled, adding language stating that the death penalty was not prohibited under international law, as there is no global consensus on the issue, invoking article 2(7) of the *Charter of the United Nations,* asserting that capital punishment is primarily a criminal justice issue, not a human rights one, 'in the context of the rights of victims and the community to live in peace', and recalling that not all rules are suitable for application in all places at all times because of diversity of socio-legal and economic conditions in each country.[141]

---

136 UN Doc. E/CN.4/1999/L.91.

137 UN Doc. E/CN.4/1999/SR.58, para. 40.

138 CHR Res. 1999/61. See: UN Doc. E/CN.4/1999/SR.58, paras. 61–62. A separate vote was held on paragraphs 3(f), 4(b) and 5, adopted by twenty-seven to thirteen with thirteen abstentions.

139 UN Doc. A/C.3/54/L.8.

140 On Singapore: UN Doc. E/CN.4/1997/60/Add.l, para. 438; on Egypt: UN Doc. E/CN.4/1999/39, para. 57.

141 On Singapore: UN Doc. E/CN.4/1997/60/Add.l, para. 438; on Egypt: UN Doc. E/CN.4/1999/39, para. 57; UN Docs. A/C.3/54/L.31 and A7C.3/54/L.32. These amending principles were signed by Afghanistan, Algeria, Antigua and Barbuda, Bahamas, Bahrain, Bangladesh, Barbados, Belize, Benin, Botswana, Brunei, Burkina Faso, Burundi, Cameroon, Chad, China, Comoros, Cuba, North Korea, Congo, Dominica, Egypt, Equatorial Guinea, Eritrea, Ethiopia, Gabon, Ghana, Guatemala, Guyana, India, Indonesia, Iran, Jamaica, Japan, Jordan, Kazakhstan, Kenya, Kuwait, Kyrgyzstan, Laos, Lebanon, Lesotho, Liberia, Libya, Malawi, Malaysia, Maldives, Mauritania, Mongolia, Morocco, Myanmar, Niger, Nigeria,

Humiliated, the European Union decided to withdraw the resolution rather than see it transformed beyond recognition. Speaking to the European Parliament some time afterwards, Commissioner Chris Patten said it had been necessary 'to freeze our resolution on the death penalty or risk the passing of a resolution that would have incorporated wholly unacceptable arguments that asserted that human rights are not universally applicable and valid' (Patten 2000a). He explained that 'following intensive negotiation, we decided at last year's General Assembly in November that no resolution was better than a fatally flawed text, and that therefore the EU should not pursue its initiative in UNGA'. Patten said that 'hardline retentionists' now seem resigned to resolutions in the Commission on Human Rights, but that they will continue to resist strongly any efforts to secure a General Assembly resolution. 'This would lead to further divisive debate', he noted. Consequently, the European Union has decided 'it would not be either advisable or timely to table a resolution on the death penalty' at the 2000 session of the General Assembly (Patten 2000b).

Any nervousness that the setback in the General Assembly would ricochet on what had become a tradition in the Commission on Human Rights, with its progressively more exigent annual resolutions, proved to be misplaced. In 2000, the Commission resolution was adopted by twenty-seven votes to thirteen, with twelve abstentions, essentially comparable to the voting pattern in the previous three years (Dennis 2001, 214).[142] It welcomed the fact that many countries were in fact applying a moratorium on executions, repeating the principles of the 1999 resolution. In 2001, the result was twenty-seven votes to eighteen, with seven abstentions. The number in favour was essentially comparable to results over the previous four resolutions, but the number against was the highest ever.[143] The resolution repeated its request to the Secretary-General to prepare annual updates to the quinquennial reports, a practice since the first Commission resolution in 1997. The resolution 'welcomed' a resolution adopted the previous August by the Sub-Commission on the Promotion and Protection of Human Rights, that had described the prohibition of juvenile executions as a norm of customary international law.[144] At the Commission's final working session, in 2005, the death penalty resolution was the strongest ever adopted. It called for states to abolish the death penalty completely and, in the meantime, to establish a moratorium on executions. Those that retain the death penalty were requested to progressively restrict the number

Oman, Pakistan, Philippines, Qatar, South Korea, Rwanda, St. Kitts Nevis and Anguilla, St. Lucia, St. Vincent and Grenadines, Saudi Arabia, Sierra Leone, Somalia, Sudan, Surinam, Swaziland, Syria, Tajikistan, Thailand, Togo, Trinidad and Tobago, Tunisia, Uganda, United Arab Emirates, Tanzania, Uzbekistan, Vietnam, Yemen, Yugoslavia, Zambia. Zimbabwe and Turkey.

142 UN Doc. E/CN.4/RES/2000/65.

143 UN Doc. E/CN.4/RES/2001/68, based on UN Doc. E/CN.4/2000/L.93. For the vote, see: UN Doc. E/CN.4/2001/SR.78, paras. 17–18.

144 UN Doc. E/CN.4/Sub.2/RES/2000/17. The resolution is discussed below.

of offences for which the death penalty may be imposed and, at the least, not to extend its application to crimes to which it did not apply. They were also to ensure also that the notion of 'most serious crimes' does not go beyond intentional crimes with lethal or extremely grave consequences and that the death penalty is not imposed for non-violent acts such as financial crimes, religious practice or expression of conscience and sexual relations between consenting adults, nor as a mandatory sentence. The resolution, which was adopted by twenty-six votes to eighteen, with seven abstentions, garnered the largest number of co-sponsors since the process had begun, in 1997.[145]

The Commission on Human Rights, where the first discussion on capital punishment within the United Nations had taken place in 1947, was dissolved in 2006 and replaced by the Human Rights Council.[146] A resolution on capital punishment has yet to appear on the agenda of the body. Because the composition of the Council is somewhat different than that of the Commission, the pattern in the earlier body cannot be mechanically transposed. Nevertheless, if members of the Council vote in the same way that they did in the Commission, a death penalty resolution would almost certainly succeed. There was a brief discussion of the death penalty at the March 2007 session of the Council. On that occasion, one sign of evolution was a statement by the representative of China, La Yifan, who said: 'The death penalty's scope of application was to be reviewed shortly, and it was expected that this scope would be reduced, with the final aim of abolishment' (United Nations 2007c, 9).

Initiatives aimed at restriction and abolition of the death penalty have also arisen in other United Nations organs. In 1999, the United Nations Sub-Commission on the Promotion and Protection of Human Rights adopted a resolution condemning 'unequivocally the imposition and execution of the death penalty on those aged under eighteen at the time of the commission of the offence' (United Nations, 1999a). At the same session, the Sub-Commission also adopted a resolution expressing concern at denunciation of human rights treaties, referring specifically to the death-penalty related denunciation of the *Optional Protocol to the International Covenant on Civil and Political Rights* by Trinidad and Tobago and by Guyana.[147] The Sub-Commission returned to the issue in 2000, this time managing to adopt a resolution by consensus. The resolution claimed that execution for juvenile offences was contrary to customary international law. It adopted a draft decision for the Commission on Human Rights stating 'that international law concerning the imposition of the death penalty in relation to juveniles clearly establishes that the imposition of the death penalty on persons aged under 18 years at the time of the offence is in contravention of customary international law'.[148]

145 UN Doc. E/CN.4//RES/2005/59.

146 UN Doc. A/RES/60/251.

147 SCHR Res. 1999/5.

148 UN Doc. E/CN.4/Sub.2/RES/2000/17, para. 6.

Much of the human rights monitoring work of the United Nations is carried out by special *rapporteurs* and similar institutions known generically as special procedures. Capital punishment issues have been addressed by several of the thematic *rapporteurs,* including the special *rapporteur* on violence against women (United Nations 1998a), on religious intolerance[149] and on independence of judges.[150] The Working Group on Arbitrary Detention has also considered death penalty cases.[151] Similarly, concerns about the death penalty have been expressed by the geographic *rapporteurs* with respect to Nigeria,[152] Democratic Republic of Congo,[153] Myanmar,[154] Sudan,[155] Iraq,[156] Burundi[157] and the former-Yugoslavia,[158] as well as by the special representative on Iran (United Nations 1997a, 19–21, 65; 1998b 4, 27–29). But the special *rapporteur* on Equatorial Guinea, noting that capital sentences imposed for murder had no political connotation, said that there was no violation of international law and that it did not fall within his mandate to issue opinions about the application of capital punishment.[159]

The mechanism with particular responsibility for capital punishment is the special *rapporteur* on extrajudicial, summary and arbitrary executions. The position of special *rapporteur* on summary and arbitrary executions was created by the Economic and Social Council in 1982,[160] on the recommendation of the Commission on Human Rights.[161] Addition of the word 'extrajudicial' to the title, in 1992, signalled adoption of a broader approach to the mandate, and implied this to include the subject of capital punishment (see United Nations 1993, 42–68).[162] The Commission on Human Rights has specifically charged the special *rapporteur* with 'monitor[ing of] the implementation of international standards, including safeguards and restrictions, relating to the imposition of capital punishment'.[163] On a regular basis, the special *rapporteur* protests the non-respect of international standards concerning implementation of the death penalty (United Nations 2005, 19(a)). The special *rapporteur* has also made visits, to countries such as the United

149 UN Doc. E/CN.4/1998/6, para. 62(A).

150 UN Doc. E/CN.4/1998/39, paras. 96, 122, 170.

151 UN Doc. E/CN.4/1998/44/Add.1, para. 5; UN Doc. E/CN.4/1998/44/Add.2, para. 33.

152 UN Doc. E/CN.4/1998/62, paras. 31, 81, 91, 109(g) and (x).

153 UN Doc. E/CN.4/1998/65, paras. 102, 126.

154 UN Doc. E/CN.4/1998/70, para. 24.

155 UN Doc. E/CN.4/1998/66, paras. 7, 8, 9, 10, 11, 16

156 UN Doc. E/CN.4/1998/67, paras. 1–5, 12. 18, 32, 34, 37.

157 UN Doc.E/CN.4/1998/72, paras.45–46.

158 UN Doc. E/CN.4/1998/13, paras. 72–75, 159–160; UN Doc. E/CN.4/1998/15, paras. 16, 17, 19, 38.

159 UN Doc. E/CN.4/1998/73, para. 43.

160 ESC Res. 1982/35.

161 CHR Res. 1982/29.

162 CHR Res. 1992/72, ESC Res. 1992/242.

163 UN Doc. E/CN.4/RES/2000/31; UN Doc. E/CN.4/RES/2003/53.

States (United Nations 1998c) and Jamaica (United Nations 2004, 21), with the purpose of monitoring death penalty practice.

The special *rapporteur* on extrajudicial, summary and arbitrary executions has made certain authoritative statements about the interpretation of article 6 of the *International Covenant,* and other applicable norms. In annual reports to the Commission on Human Rights, the special *rapporteur* has expressed the view that 'given that the loss of life is irreparable ... the abolition of capital punishment is most desirable in order fully to respect the right to life', adding that 'where there is a fundamental right to life, there is no right to capital punishment'.[164] According to the special *rapporteur,* the extension of capital punishment to new crimes is contrary to article 6 of the *Covenant* (United Nations 1997b, 176). The special *rapporteur* has complained that laws that reverse the onus of proof upon a person found in possession of a substantial quantity of narcotic drugs, requiring that person to negative charges of trafficking in dangerous drugs, may violate not only the presumption of innocence but also the right to life in capital cases (United Nations 1995, 212; 1997b, 306–307, 436, 438). Transparency in its application is required, and this dictates the availability of accurate statistics in States where capital punishment is still practiced (United Nations 2005, 57–59). The special *rapporteur* has also complained about the practice of public executions in some countries (United Nations 2004, 53). The special *rapporteur* has said that 'the death penalty should be abolished for economic and drug-related crimes' (United Nations 1997b, 473; 2007) and that it should never be mandatory as punishment for a specific offence (United Nations 2005, 63–64; 2007, 54–62). But the special *rapporteur* has been hesitant to argue that the 'death row phenomenon' is contrary to international norms, expressing concern that this might encourage governments to carry out executions more rapidly (United Nations 1994, 682; 1995, 382).

The High Commissioner on Human Rights, who is the primary executive officer within the United Nations with responsibility for human rights, opposes capital punishment and regularly calls for its suspension, for a moratorium and for abolition.[165] A representative of the High Commissioner has noted that considering the death penalty within the United Nations exclusively as a human rights issue, rather than one of criminal justice, could be considered to be progress in promoting human rights.[166] In February 1998, the High Commissioner, Mary Robinson, condemned the execution of Carla Fay Tucker by the State of Texas (United Nations, 1998d). In April 1998, she protested Rwanda's execution of twenty-two persons convicted for their role in the 1994 genocide. Indeed, she regularly issued statements condemning capital executions in various countries of the world (1999b).

---

164 UN Doc. E/CN.4/1997/60 (1996); UN Doc. E/CN.4/1996/614, paras. 507–517, paras. 540–557.

165 UN Doc. E/CN.4/1998/61, paras. 38, 81.

166 UN Doc. E/CN.4/Sub.2/1998/19, para. 66.

Success in the General Assembly, however, remains the big prize. The failures in 1994 and 1999 continue to haunt the abolitionist camp, and create doubt about the claim that an international consensus on the subject is being established. In December 2006, abolitionist countries in the General Assembly tried a somewhat innovative approach. Instead of a resolution, some eighty-five Member States delivered a 'statement' to the General Assembly within the context of the presentation of the report of the Third Committee.[167] The statement said:

> The right of everyone to life was universally affirmed in article 3 of the Universal Declaration of Human Rights and reaffirmed in other international instruments, such as article 6 of the International Covenant on Civil and Political Rights and articles 6 and 37 (a) of the Convention on the Rights of the Child. Over the past decade, the Commission on Human Rights adopted in all consecutive sessions a resolution on the question of the death penalty, expressing deep concern at its continuing use around the world and calling upon States that still maintain the death penalty to abolish it completely and, in the meantime, to establish a moratorium on executions. We firmly believe that the abolition of the death penalty contributes to the enhancement of human dignity and the progressive development of human rights. The death penalty provides no added value in terms of deterrence. Any miscarriage or failure of justice is irreversible when, in a cruel and inhumane way, the punishment deprives one of his or her right to life. The signatories of this statement are pleased to note that the trend towards the worldwide abolition of the death penalty continues, and they welcome the abolition of capital punishment in three States over the past year, together with positive developments towards its complete abolition in many other countries. However, despite these developments, there is still cause for great alarm. The signatories of this statement remain deeply concerned about the resort to the death penalty all over the world. The signatories of this statement commit themselves to working towards the abolition of the death penalty and, where the death penalty still exists, call for its use to be progressively restricted, insist that it be carried out according to minimum standards such as those set out in Economic and Social Council resolution 1984/50, and, in the meantime, call for the establishment of a moratorium on executions. The signatories call upon the General Assembly to be seized of this matter in the future.[168]

167 Albania, Andorra, Angola, Argentina, Armenia, Australia, Austria, Belgium, Bolivia, Bosnia and Herzegovina, Brazil, Bulgaria, Cambodia, Canada, Cape Verde, Chile, Colombia, Costa Rica, Côte d'Ivoire, Croatia, Cyprus, the Czech Republic, Denmark, the Dominican Republic, Ecuador, El Salvador, Estonia, Finland, France, Georgia. Germany, Greece, Guatemala, Guinea-Bissau, Haiti, Honduras, Hungary, Iceland, Ireland, Israel, Italy, Latvia, Liechtenstein, Lithuania, Luxembourg, Macedonia, Malta, Marshall Islands, Mauritius, Mexico, Micronesia, Moldova, Monaco, Montenegro, Nepal, the Netherlands, New Zealand, Nicaragua, Norway, Palau, Panama, Paraguay, the Philippines, Poland, Portugal, Romania, San Marino, São Tomé and Principe, Senegal, Serbia, Seychelles, Slovakia, Slovenia, Solomon Islands, Spain, Sweden, Switzerland, Timor-Leste, Turkey, Tuvalu, the United Kingdom, Ukraine, Uruguay, Vanuatu and Venezuela.

168 UN Doc. A/RES/61/PV.81, 33.

The statement was actually a prelude to a renewed effort within the General Assembly planned for the 2007 session.

In November 2007, there was a vigorous and quite unpleasant debate in the Third Committee when the European Union, with broad support from many regions of the world, tried yet again to secure the adoption of a draft resolution with the General Assembly.[169] The text reads as follows

Moratorium on the use of the death penalty

The General Assembly,

Guided by the purposes and principles contained in the Charter of the United Nations,

Recalling the Universal Declaration of Human Rights, the International Covenant on Civil and Political Rights and the Convention on the Rights of the Child,

Recalling also the resolutions on the question of the death penalty adopted over the past decade by the Commission on Human Rights in all consecutive sessions, the last being its resolution 2005/59,4 in which the Commission called upon States that still maintain the death penalty to abolish it completely and, in the meantime, to establish a moratorium on executions,

Recalling further the important results accomplished by the former Commission on Human Rights on the question of the death penalty, and envisaging that the Human Rights Council could continue to work on this issue,

Considering that the use of the death penalty undermines human dignity, and convinced that a moratorium on the use of the death penalty contributes to the enhancement and progressive development of human rights, that there is no conclusive evidence of the

169 *In favour*: Albania, Algeria, Andorra, Angola, Argentina, Armenia, Australia, Austria, Azerbaijan, Belgium, Benin, Bolivia, Bosnia and Herzegovina, Brazil, Bulgaria, Burkina Faso, Burundi, Cambodia, Canada, Cape Verde, Chile, Colombia, Costa Rica, Côte. d'Ivoire, Croatia, Cyprus, Czech Republic, Denmark, Dominican Republic, Ecuador, El Salvador, Estonia, Finland, France, Gabon, Georgia, Germany, Greece, Guatemala, Haiti, Honduras, Hungry, Iceland, Ireland. Israel, Italy, Kazakhstan, Kyrgyzstan. Latvia, Liechtenstein, Lithuania, Luxembourg, Mali, Malta, Marshall Islands, Mauritius, Mexico, Micronesia (Federated States of), Moldova, Monaco, Montenegro, Mozambique, Namibia, Nepal, Netherlands, New Zealand, Nicaragua, Norway, Panama, Paraguay, Philippines, Poland, Portugal, Romania, Russian Federation, Rwanda, Samoa, San Marino, São Tomé and Principe, Serbia, Slovakia, Slovenia, South Africa, Spain, Sri Lanka, Sweden, Switzerland, Tajikistan, The former Yugoslav Republic of Macedonia, Timor-Leste, Turkey, Turkmenistan, Tuvalu, Ukraine, United Kingdom, Uruguay, Uzbekistan, Vanuatu, and Venesuela.

death penalty's deterrent value and that any miscarriage or failure of justice in the death penalty's implementation is irreversible and irreparable,

Welcoming the decision taken by an increasing number of States to apply a moratorium on executions, followed in many cases by the abolition of the death penalty,

1. Expresses its deep concern about the continued application of the death penalty;

2. Calls upon all States that still maintain the death penalty to:

(a) Respect international standards that provide safeguards guaranteeing the protection of the rights of those facing the death penalty, in particular the minimum standards, as set out in the annex to Economic and Social Council resolution 1984/50 of 25 May 1984;

(b) Provide the Secretary-General with information relating to the use of capital punishment and the observance of the safeguards guaranteeing the protection of the rights of those facing the death penalty;

(c) Progressively restrict the use of the death penalty and reduce the number of offences for which it may be imposed;

(d) Establish a moratorium on executions with a view to abolishing the death penalty;

3. Calls upon States which have abolished the death penalty not to reintroduce it;

4. Requests the Secretary-General to report to the General Assembly at its sixty-third session on the implementation of the present resolution;

5. Decides to continue consideration of the matter at its sixty-third session under the same agenda item.

As in the past, so-called 'wrecking amendments' were proposed in an attempt to derail the process. None of these was successful, however. When the vote on the resolution was taken in the Third Committee, the result was 99 in favour to 52 against, with 33 abstentions. Confirmation of the vote in the plenary General Assembly was little more than a formality. On 18 December 2007, the resolution was passed by a vote of 104 in favour to 54 against, with 29 abstentions.[170] Mexico,

170 *In favour*: Albania, Algeria, Andorra, Angola, Argentina, Armenia, Australia, Austria, Azerbaijan, Belgium, Benin, Bolivia, Bosnia and Herzegovina, Brazil, Bulgaria, Burkina Faso, Burundi, Cambodia, Canada, Cape Verde, Chile, Colombia, Congo, Costa Rica, Côte d'Ivoire, Croatia, Cyprus, Czech Republic, Denmark, Dominican Republic, Ecuador, El Salvador, Estonia, Finland, France, Gabon, Georgia, Germany, Greece, Guatemala, Haiti, Honduras, Hungary, Iceland, Ireland, Israel, Italy, Kazakhstan, Kiribati, Kyrgyzstan,

spoke on behalf of the 87 co-sponsors of the resolution, expressing the wish that this text would impel the Assembly to move forward in the struggle to improve human rights. The matter had been a source of concern in the international community, and the co-sponsors were pleased, after so many years, that the Assembly was adopting the resolution to establish a moratorium on the death penalty. Several delegations who opposed the resolution took the floor to register their discontent. Antigua and Barbuda spoke on behalf of the thirteenth Caribbean Community states who had voted against the draft as a bloc. Singapore said the vote demonstrated that the issue was not universally accepted and was, in fact, quite divisive. Nigeria, China, Syria and Malaysia made comments along similar lines. Egypt said it had voted against because the resolution was contrary to 'religious, practical and legal norms', and that the death penalty was only imposed 'according to the provisions of Islamic law'. Bangladesh conceded that the resolution was representative of the growing trend against the death penalty but said 'the time was not right for its total abolition'.

Early in the year, on 2 January 2007, United Nations Secretary-General Ban Ki Moon held his first press conference upon taking office. Saddam Hussein had been executed in a barbaric and undignified manner only a few days earlier. Perhaps predictably, the matter was at the top of the list of questions from the assembled press corps:

Latvia, Liechtenstein, Lithuania, Luxembourg, Madagascar, Mali, Malta, Marshall Islands, Mauritius, Mexico, Micronesia (Federated States of), Moldova, Monaco, Montenegro, Mozambique, Namibia, Nauru, Nepal, Netherlands, New Zealand, Nicaragua, Norway, Palau, Panama, Paraguay, Philippines, Poland, Portugal, Romania, Russian Federation, Rwanda, Samoa, San Marino, São Tomé and Príncipe, Serbia, Slovakia, Slovenia, South Africa, Spain, Sri Lanka, Sweden, Switzerland, Tajikistan, The former Yugoslav Republic of Macedonia, Timor-Leste, Turkey, Turkmenistan, Tuvalu, Ukraine, United Kingdom, Uruguay, Uzbekistan, Vanuatu, Venezuela; *Against:* Afghanistan, Antigua and Barbuda, Bahamas, Bahrain, Bangladesh, Barbados, Belize, Botswana, Brunei Darussalam, Chad, China, Comoros, Democratic People's Republic of Korea, Dominica, Egypt, Ethiopia, Grenada, Guyana, India, Indonesia, Iran, Iraq, Jamaica, Japan, Jordan, Kuwait, Libya, Malaysia, Maldives, Mauritania, Mongolia, Myanmar, Nigeria, Oman, Pakistan, Papua New Guinea, Qatar, Saint Kitts and Nevis, Saint Lucia, Saint Vincent and the Grenadines, Saudi Arabia, Singapore, Solomon Islands, Somalia, Sudan, Suriname, Syria, Thailand, Tonga, Trinidad and Tobago, Uganda, United States, Yemen, Zimbabwe; *Abstain:* Belarus, Bhutan, Cameroon, Central African Republic, Cuba, Democratic Republic of the Congo, Djibouti, Equatorial Guinea, Eritrea, Fiji, Gambia, Ghana, Guinea, Kenya, Lao People's Democratic Republic, Lebanon, Lesotho, Liberia, Malawi, Morocco, Niger, Republic of Korea, Sierra Leone, Swaziland, Togo, United Arab Emirates, United Republic of Tanzania, Viet Nam, Zambia; *Absent:* Guinea-Bissau, Peru, Senegal, Seychelles, Tunisia.

Q: Should Saddam Hussein have been executed, Mr. Secretary-General?

SG: Saddam Hussein was responsible for committing heinous crimes and unspeakable atrocities against the Iraqi people. We should never forget the victims of his crimes. The issue of capital punishment is for each and every Member State to decide. As a Secretary-General, at the same time, while I am firmly against impunity, I also hope that the members of the international community should pay due regard to all aspects of international humanitarian laws. During my entire tenure, I will try my best to help Member States, the international community, to strengthen the rule of law.

Q: Will his death help in bringing stability to Iraq in your opinion, with the death of Saddam Hussein in this way, or might it break a civil war there?

SG: The Iraqi people and Government have taken steps to address their past, and I hope that the international community should also understand the stakes and try to build the rule of law nationally and internationally.

...

Q: [inaudible on death penalty, moratorium]

SG: I said that capital punishment, the death penalty, is the issue for each and every Member State to decide. At the same time, I would hope that the international member states would pay due regard to all aspects of international humanitarian laws.

The answer was perhaps spontaneous, and seemed to reflect the personal views of the Secretary-General rather than those of the organisation. It was particularly disturbing that they seemed to echo the reaction of the President of the United States. But almost immediately, damage control was underway. At the 11 January 2007 news conference, the Secretary-General made it clear that life is precious and that he believed the death penalty should be eliminated. He called on the government of Iraq to suspend the execution of those who were already sentenced to die. The Secretary-General endorsed the position taken by the High Commissioner for Human Rights, which was one of unequivocal condemnation of the Hussein execution. The initial statement by the Secretary-General was disconcerting, but the subsequent rectification provided an unplanned continuation of the unwavering position of the United Nations with respect to the abolition of capital punishment. On 18 December 2007, Ban Ki Moon enthusiastically welcomed the success of the resolution on capital punishment in the General Assembly.

Bibliography

Amnesty International (1989), *When the State Kills...* (New York: Amnesty International).

Ancel, M. (1962), *Capital Punishment,* UN Doc. ST/SOA/SD/9, Sales No. 62.IV.2 (New York: United Nations).

Clark, R.S. (1990), 'The Eighth United Nations Congress on the Prevention of Crime and the Treatment of Offenders, Havana, Cuba, August 27–September 7, 1990' (1990) 1 *Criminal Law Forum* 513.

Dennis, M.J. (2001), 'The Fifty-sixth Session of the UN Commission on Human Rights' (2001) 95 *AJIL* 213.

Hood, R. (1989), *The Death Penalty: A World-wide Perspective* (Oxford: Clarendon Press).

Lauren, P.G. (2003), *The Evolution of International Human Rights, Visions Seen,* 2nd Edition (Philadelphia: University of Pennsylvania Press).

Leone, U. (1987), 'UNSDRI's Activities Related to the Death Penalty Issue', 58 *Revue Internationale de droit pénal* 325.

Morris, N (1967), *Capital Punishment: Developments, 1961–1965,* Sales No. E.67.IV.15.

Patten, C. (2000a), 'Excerpts from a Statement Delivered by the Rt. Hon. Christopher Patten,' EU Commissioner for External Relations to the European Parliament, 16 February 2000.

_______(2000b), 'Speech to European Parliament', 25 October 2000.

Rodley, N. (1987), *The Treatment of Prisoners Under International Law* (Oxford: Clarendon Press).

Schabas, W.A. (2000a), 'Islam and the Death Penalty', 9 *William & Mary Bill of Rights Journal* 223.

______(2000b) 'Life, Death and the Crime of Crimes: Supreme Penalties and the ICC Statute', 2 *Punishment & Society* 263.

Schabas, W.A. and Sax, H. (2006), 'Article 37, Prohibition of Torture, Prohibition of Death Penalty and Life Imprisonment and the Deprivation of Liberty', in Alen, A. et al. (eds) *A Commentary on the United Nations Convention on the Rights of the Child* (Leiden / Boston: Martinus Nijhoff Publishers).

Strafer, M. (1983), 'Volunteering for Execution: Competency, Voluntariness and the Propriety of Third Party Intervention', 74 *J. Criminal Law and Criminology* 860.

United Nations (1983), *Yearbook of the United Nations, 1980* (New York: United Nations).

______(1993), 'Extrajudicial, Summary or Arbitrary Executions, Report of the Special Rapporteur', UN Doc. E/CN.4/1993/46.

______(1994), 'Report by the Special Rapporteur, Mr. Bacre Waly Ndiaye, submitted pursuant to Commission on Human Rights resolution 1993/71', UN Doc. E/CN.4/1994/7.

______(1995), 'Report by the Special Rapporteur, Mr. Bacre Waly Ndiaye, submitted pursuant to Commission on Human Rights resolution 1994/82', UN Doc. E/CN.4/1995/61.

______(1997a), 'Report on the situation of human rights in the Islamic Republic of Iran, prepared by the Special Representative on the Commission on Human Rights, Mr. Maurice Copithorne, pursuant to Commission resolution 1996/84 and Economic and Social Council decision 1996/287', UN Doc. E/CN.4/1997/63.

______(1997b), 'Report of the Special Rapporteur, Mr. Bacre Waly Ndiaye, submitted pursuant to Commission on Human Rights resolution 1996/74', UN Doc. E/CN.4/1997/60/Add.l.

______(1998a), 'Report on the mission to Rwanda on the question of violence against women in situations of armed conflict', UN Doc. E/CN.4/1998/54/Add.l; UN Doc. E/CN.4/1998/54.

______(1998b), 'Interim report on the situation of human rights in the Islamic Republic of Iran, prepared by the Special Representative of the Commission on Human Rights in accordance with General Assembly Resolution 51/107 and Economic and Social Council Decision 1997/264', UN Doc. A/52/472, E/CN.4/1998/59.

______(1998c), 'Report of the Special Rapporteur on extrajudicial, summary or arbitrary executions, Mr. Bacre Waly Ndiaye, submitted pursuant to Commission resolution 1997/61', Addendum, Mission to the United States of America, UN Doc. E/CN.4/1998/68/Add.3.

______(1998d),'Statement by Mary Robinson, United Nations High Commissioner for Human Rights', UN Doc. HR/98/6, 4 February 1998.

______(1999a), 'The death penalty, particularly in relation to juvenile offenders', UN Doc. E/CN.4/Sub.2/RES/1999/4.

______(1999b), 'Daily Press Briefing of Office of Spokesman for Secretary-General', 16 June 1999.

______(2004), 'Extrajudicial, summary or arbitrary executions, Report of the Special Rapporteur, Asma Jahangir', UN Doc. E/CN.4/2004/7.

______(2005), 'Extrajudicial, summary or arbitrary executions, Report of the Special Rapporteur, Philip Alston', UN Doc. E/CN.4/2005/7.

______(2007a), 'Extrajudicial, summary or arbitrary executions, Report of the Special Rapporteur, Philip Alston', UN Doc. A/HRC/4/20.

______(2007b), UN Press Release, 'High Commissioner for Human Rights Hails Abolition of Capital Punishment in Rwanda', 27 July 2007.

______(2007c), 'Human Rights Council Opens Fourth Session', HRC/07/3, 12 March 2007.

Urofsky, M.L. (1984), 'A Right to Die: Termination of Appeal for Condemned Prisoners', 75 *J. Criminal Law and Criminology* 553.

White, W.S. (1991), *The Death Penalty in the Nineties* (Ann Arbor: University of Michigan Press).

[9]

LIFE AND DEATH IN THE LAWYER'S OFFICE: THE INTERNSHIP IN CAPITAL PUNISHMENT STUDIES

By ANDY BOON and PETER HODGKINSON*

CLINICAL PROGRAMMES generally have one or more underlying goals: an exposure to welfare cases which harnesses student motivation and idealism; an exposure to 'real life casework' which enhances a broader understanding of the operation of law in context;[1] or the development of the skills associated with the practice of law.[2] What these aims share is "a belief in and quest for an alternative to a curriculum dominated by propositional knowledge for its own sake".[3] As the aims of clinical programmes have become more concrete and diverse the traditional conception of the clinical experience in law—the tyro lawyer conducting welfare cases—has expanded.[4] This article describes the Internship in Capital Punishment Studies, a programme which places students, for a brief period of their studies, in the teams of organisations struggling to save convicted prisoners from execution. The main foci are the ethical issues raised by the involvement of students in this kind of clinical programme. This is a fortuitous linking of the two strongest themes to emerge from the *First Report on Legal Education and Training* by the Lord Chancellor's Advisory Committee on Education and Conduct (ACLEC). The report both endorsed clinical legal education[5] and expressed concern that, with changes in the market for legal services, "there are real dangers that professional standards will be threatened unless counter-balancing steps are taken to reinforce ethical values".[6]

* Peter Hodgkinson is the Director of the Centre for Capital Punishment Studies (CCPS) based at the University of Westminster School of Law and is responsible for the operation of the internship programme. Andy Boon is Head of the School of Law at the University of Westminster and advised on the design of the internship module and the assessment methods used. We are grateful to Austin Sarat and Stuart Scheingold for providing copies of unpublished papers, to John Flood and Chris Stanley for comments on an earlier draft of this article, to the Human Rights budget line of the European Commission for its financial support and to all the interns who have helped to establish this project.

1 H. Brayne, "Law Students as Practitioners: developing an undergraduate clinical programme at Northumbria University" (1996) in *Teaching Lawyers' Skills* (eds Webb, J. and Maughan, C.) Butterworths: London, p. 167.

2 These include the capacity to solve real life problems whereby students learn how to use resources and develop independence. D. A. Cruickshank, "Problem Based Learning in Legal Education" in *Teaching Lawyers' Skills'* (1996) (eds Webb, J. and Maughan, C.) Butterworths: London, p. 55.

3 J. Webb, "Approaches to Skills Teaching" (1996) in *Teaching Lawyers' Skills* (eds. Webb J. and Maughan, C.) Butterworths: London, p. 55.

4 See generally A. Boon, M. Jeeves, and J. Macfarlane, 'Clinical Anatomy: Towards a Working Definition of Clinical Legal Education' (1987) *21 Law Teacher 61*, and R. Grimes, 'The Theory and Practice of Clinical Legal Education' (1996) in *Teaching Lawyers' Skills* (eds Webb, J. and Maughan, C.) Butterworths: London.

5 (1996) para. 3.39.1 at p. 54 recommends that universities take into account, *inter alia*, 'the distinctive features of clinical legal studies' in allocating their block grant.

6 Id. at para. 1.19 at p. 17.

The relationship of these issues will be considered in the context of the ethics of 'cause lawyering' and of assessment.

Despite their great strengths as a practicum in which to learn, assessment of the clinical experience presents perennial problems: the challenge of providing an adequate foundation of skills and knowledge to allow the student to play a useful role in the clinical process; the balance to be struck between the student's interest in a rewarding educational experience and the client's interest in receiving competent advice and representation; the task of ensuring the availability of adequate cases at the right times and, particularly when assessment is an issue, of comparable difficulty. The internship magnifies these problems by adding physical distance, cultural difference and psychological pressure to the burdens on staff and student. In addressing these issues we move from a brief description of context to an empirical account. Our data from the field derives from students' oral and written reports of their experience. Through these data we illustrate the range of dilemmas, anxieties and confusion faced by neophytes in the field and the considerations which dictate our choice of assessment model.

The internship programme

In the internship module, students negotiate a learning contract with the module leader, and/or the Director of a Capital Defence Team, work as an active member of this team, and present written records of their experience in which they analyse their experience from both a substantive and a practical perspective.[7] The module is divided into three broad phases: preparation, placement and assessment.[8]

Preparation

Students study preliminary modules in criminal justice[9] and lawyers' skills'[10] and complete core modules in criminal law.[11] Prospective

7 (1996) University of Westminster Student Handbook, module outline for Internship in Capital Punishment.

8 Students receive academic credit for completing the module of which the internship forms a part. The LL.B is a 360 credit programme which full-time students complete by studying 120 credits, or 8 modules, a year. The Internship in Capital Punishment Studies is a 15 credit module.

9 These include the causes of crime, the aims of a penal system and the role of the police, the prisons, the probation service, the effectiveness of sentencing and the issue of discrimination in the legal and criminal justice system, capital punishment and mentally disordered offenders.

10 The Lawyers' Skills module is studied in the second semester of year 2 in the case of full time students and is described in A. Boon, "Skills in the initial stage of legal education: theory and practice for transformation" (1996) in *Teaching Lawyers' Skills* (eds Webb, J. and Maughan, C.) Butterworths: London, pp. 99–136.

11 Exceptionally, equivalent knowledge or experience is acceptable.

interns must demonstrate satisfactory commitment and aptitude[12] and are interviewed as part of the selection process. Learning is partly self-directed, supplemented by lectures by the module leader and visiting speakers.[13] We are able to draw on the expertise of Visiting Professors,[14] Advisory Board members,[15] the Internship Programme Management Committee[16] and members of the London Panel. During the second semester prior to the internship,[17] students familiarise themselves with the legal system of either the USA or Caribbean Commonwealth, the countries where the internships are presently located, with particular reference to the capital trial and appeal process.[18] Former interns share information with prospective interns both informally and as part of the formal orientation programme during this phase.

Placement

The overriding aim of the programme is that students are involved in the process of representation in capital cases. Through this involvement, and opportunities to meet academics active in the field, they develop an understanding of the context in which the death penalty is used through exposure to the police, the courts, the prison system and the socio-political systems in the jurisdiction in which they are located.[19] A subsidiary aim is to develop students' library and IT

12 It is not uncommon for CPE students to undertake the programme, but these students do not receive academic credit for their work.

13 The internship module includes legal process, the political process, the role of the criminal justice agencies, the range of research techniques relevant to the area and the social and cultural influences affecting the administration of justice. The Centre for Capital Punishment studies holds materials specific to the work of the various centres providing placements. Two recent additions to the collection have been produced by the CCPS. 1] "Capital Punishment: Global Issues and Prospects" (1996) eds: P. Hodgkinson and A. Rutherford. Waterside Press: Winchester; 2] P. Hodgkinson, H. A. Bedau, M. Radelet, G. Dunmall & K. Massey, "Capital Punishment in the United States of America: a review of the issues", (1996) *Report for the UK Parliamentary Human Rights Committee.*

14 The CCPS has three Visiting Professors: Hugo Adam Bedau, Austin Fletcher Professor of Philosophy at Tufts University, Massachussetts, USA; Andrew Rutherford, Professor of Law, University of Southampton, England; Michael Radelet, Professor of Sociology, University of Florida at Gainesville.

15 In addition to the three Visiting Professors there are three other Advisory Board members: William Schabas, Professor of International Law, University of Quebec at Montreal, Canada; Dr James MacKeith, Consultant Forensic Psychiatrist, Bethlem Royal and Maudsley Hospitals, London; Victor Strieb, Professor of Law, Cleveland-Marshall College of Law, Cleveland, Ohio, USA.

16 The three members of the Management Committee are: Clive Stafford-Smith, Attorney and Director, Louisiana Crisis Assistance Center, New Orleans; Saul Lehrfreund, Human Rights Adviser, Simons Muirhead Burton (solicitors) London; David Marshall, Barrister, 5 Kings Bench Walk.

17 February to June.

18 We are currently developing two new projects, the first of which is to increase the opportunities for placements within the Caribbean Commonwealth, and develop a network of placements with member firms of the London Panel of Solicitors, and the second is to establish links with cause lawyering projects in Eastern Europe, and the former USSR, as locations in which to place interns and to find internships for practitioners and students from these countries in projects in the UK and the USA.

19 In 1993 six of the interns were able to attend a major conference on the death penalty in Boston funded by the University's Enterprise in Higher Education fund.

research skills and build on their existing interpersonal or applied legal skills, particularly in areas such as interviewing.[20] The work placement is in an organisation—governmental, state, private practice or voluntary sector—with substantial involvement in capital trials and appeals. While students are assisted in this process of finding a host organisation, there is no guarantee that an internship will be available. Since the programme was established four years ago all the work placements have been located in the USA and Jamaica.[21] Seven students were placed in 1993, 16 in 1994, 17 in 1995 and 13 so far in 1996.[22] A typical placement lasts for approximately eight to ten weeks. The majority of interns bear the full cost of placement, which varies between £1,500 to £2,000 for eight to ten weeks,[23] but recently the scheme has attracted bursaries[24] and scholarships.[25] Interns receive support and supervision from the Director of the project or his/her representative.[26] In most cases a job description is agreed with host agencies.[27].

Assessment

Workplace assessments raise the problem of combining evaluation by work place assessors with academic assessment, requiring grading and

20 The views of the hosts, confirmed by the interns, suggest that the following skills and abilities are necessary for successful participation:
- Research and analysis skills
- Good communication skills—interview, negotiation, diplomatic
- Developed writing skills
- Ability to use initiative and to accept responsibility
- Experience of working in an office—work experience in general
- Word processing skills
- Capacity to work alone and in a team
- Time management skills
- Ability to work under pressure
- Emotional resilience
- Adaptability and flexibility
- Sensitivity, understanding and awareness.

21 Students going to the USA benefit from the visa waiver scheme. Those interns who have visited Jamaica have not needed any particular visa.

22 Some interns have come from other universities (and from disciplines other than law), the Bar and the Legal Practice Course.

23 Students are advised to start the search for funding at least a year in advance. Occasionally, the host organisation is able to help cushion the cost by offering to have interns as house guests, find house-watches or at least arrange low-cost safe accommodation.

24 In 1995, £25,000 was received from the European Commission as a result of which Westminster students received travel bursaries of £500. Joyti Manjdadria, a Westminster LL.B and LPC graduate undertook an internship with the Jamaica Council of Human Rights in 1994, which was endowed with a grant of £2,000 by Lovell White Durrant, a large City law firm.

25 The Andrew Lee Jones Fund provides annual scholarships of £1,000 to help towards the cost of one Westminster intern's placement to the USA. This fund is in memory of Andrew Lee Jones who was executed in Louisiana: it has already helped support two British students, one a graduate of Westminster, through law school in the USA and onto practice in capital litigation.

26 The module leader maintains contact with the interns and their supervisors by telephone throughout the summer months and visited some of the interns at their placements in 1993 and 1995.

27 Interns usually undergo an orientation programme on their arrival. Where a job description has already been agreed with an agency this provides a useful focus for the preparation phase.

classification. Our own assessment methodology was adopted following analysis of student activity, the context in which the activity takes place and the practical limitations imposed by that context. Recent work on skills based and active learning identify theoretical models which are rooted, at one end of a scale of possibilities, in a behaviourist tradition and, at the other, to methods which are more holistic in nature.[28] The impact of these underlying philosophies has a profound effect on every aspect of learning. Differences of approach are particularly acute in relation to assessment.[29] Where the emphasis is on 'learning the skill' pedagogy is more likely to involve reproduction of behaviour.[30] Where programme aims are diverse and open-ended, as in the internship module, assessment methods tend to reflect this.

The holistic model of teaching and assessment applied in the internship module derives from the tradition of the UK undergraduate clinical programmes of the 1970s and 1980s. The assessment method does not assess students' capacity to perform specific clinical tasks but rather their capacity for analysis and critical reflection. We see this as a key element of understanding and improving on performance.[31] Students often develop a full appreciation of their clinical experience some time after the event. In the internship module seminars they are encouraged to rigorously analyse their performance and develop a richer perception of the ways in which their legal education, including their introduction to legal skills, merged into the task of 'learning through work experience'. One student explained:

> "My tasks varied. They included legal research and statistical collation, court record searches, regular use of on-line services such as Lexis and Westlaw, visits to the prison to meet clients, interviewing witnesses, filing of briefs in both state and federal courts, participation at staff meetings, photocopying and attending the phones when the pressure was on and generally any other task that came along and needed quick attention. With each of these tasks I had to maintain a level of commitment to getting the task done and at the same time I had to be flexible. Often I would start one job and be pulled off it in order to complete something that was more pressing. The other task did not go away however so keeping track of one's work was crucial. Accuracy and clarity was imperative as the conclusions from one's legal research would often find their way into a brief. This required

28 J. Webb, "Why theory matters" (1996) and A. Boon, "Skills in the Initial Stage of Legal Education: Theory and Practice for Transformation" (1996) both in *Teaching Lawyers' Skills* (eds Webb, J. and Maughan, C.). Butterworths: London.

29 A. Boon, "Conveying Meaning in Formal Contexts: Advocacy and Negotiation" *(1996) IALS Research Report* (forthcoming).

30 See D. Cruickshank "Skills demonstrations: Where 'show' works better than 'tell'" (1994) *Law Teacher* 14–21.

31 See, for example, G. S. Gildin, "Testing Trial Advocacy: A Law Professor's Brief Life as a Public Defender" (1994) 44 Journal of Legal Education 199.

> the need to fully understand the task ahead, so it was no good suffering in silence if confused. If in doubt, *ASK*."[32]

This extract underlines the fact that students have to adapt to working in an office environment. While their experience was not of the kinds of tasks they might undertake in the UK, much of the research, investigation and other tasks they describe require skills which are transferable to other walks of life including more conventional legal practice. The development of a committed and motivated attitude to legal work is also a discernible effect of most students' experience of the programme.

> "Investigation is an important aspect in capital post-conviction work and I was fortunate enough to be involved in extensive investigation for one particular client who expected an execution date to be set each morning he woke up. Investigation can be important for a number of reasons but probably none more so than the need for good mitigating evidence. At the sentencing stage of any capital offence trial the consideration of any aggravating factors, such as previous convictions or that the killing was performed in a particularly cruel, heinous or depraved way, will go to deciding whether the defendant shall receive the death penalty. To counteract this the defence is allowed to adduce mitigating evidence, such as mental illness and intoxication. If the evidence is sufficient to outweigh the aggravating factors the defendant should not be death qualified. My investigation work was a quest for mitigating evidence and the search took me to court houses, hospitals and health clinics, library records, newspaper records, into witnesses homes and consultant's offices. Sometimes unsuccessful but mostly successful I soon learnt that if this type of investigation had been done for all the 123 inmates of Arizona's death row then the project would probably be made redundant, as nearly all those on the 'row' should have been able to present substantial mitigating evidence to the sentencing court."[33]

Students are expected to maintain a detailed log of their work and experiences. When they return from the internship they attend fortnightly seminars of two hours' duration and use the intervening weeks to complete their log or a project on an aspect of their internship.[34] All interns participate in the Internship Conference which is held towards the end of the first semester.[35] One of the tasks of the seminars

32 Jasmine Danity who graduated LL.B from Westminster in 1996 worked with Denise Young, Attorney and Director at the Arizona Post-Conviction Defender Organization in Tempe.

33 Id.

34 The project is an academic essay on a topic negotiated prior to the internship phase, so allowing time and opportunity for research during the placement.

35 The first semester runs from September to January.

is to help prepare the interns for the conference and interns are assessed both on the content of, and on the presentation of, their papers.[36]

The Student Experience

Context

Although the internship programme locates students in both the USA and Jamaica the available literature relates mainly to practice in the USA where the work of capital punishment lawyers in the USA has changed over time.[37] During the 1970s lawyers were motivated by a commitment to abolish capital punishment. This goal seemed attainable when, in 1972, the US Supreme Court ruled in *Furman* v. *Georgia*[38] that the death penalty, as then applied, was unconstitutional. Furman held that execution violated the Eighth Amendment protection against 'cruel and unusual punishment' because its application was arbitrary and discriminatory. The Supreme Court were influenced by what they perceived to be a climate of public opinion against the death penalty. The Furman judgment led to approximately 600 inmates on death row having their sentences reversed and all existing death penalty legislation being struck down. The effect was to galvanise the pro-capital punishment lobby, whose natural supporters were traditionally to be found in the southern states of the US. Southern State legislatures drafted new capital statutes which attempted to remedy the 'arbitrary and capricious' characteristics of capital punishment, by regulating the criteria and procedures by which defendants were selected for the death penalty.

In 1976 the Supreme Court ruled in three related cases [*Gregg* v. *Georgia; Jurek* v. *Texas; Proffitt* v. *Florida*][39] that the death penalty was not *per se* a cruel and unusual punishment, and that the new death penalty statutes, with their 'guided discretion', addressed the problems of arbitrariness and discrimination. Since then there has been an incremental erosion in the procedural protection of death row inmates culminating in the Federal Death Penalty Act [1994] and the more recent Comprehensive Terrorism Prevention Act and the Effective Death Penalty Act [1996]. Sarat argues that the accused's lawyers were

36 The conference in November 1996 will be the fourth in the series. The 1995 Conference attracted an audience of over 100 many of whom were students from universities other than Westminster, lawyers representing the London Panel, academics and human rights activists.

37 See generally A. Sarat "Between (The Presence of) Violence and (The Possibility of) Justice: Lawyering Against Capital Punishment" (Amherst College, USA, August 1994). Paper prepared for the Conference on Cause Lawyers (Amherst College, USA, August 1994). An abbreviated version of the paper appears under the title "Bearing Witness and Writing History in the Struggle Against Capital Punishment" (1996) 8 *Yale Journal of Law and the Humanities*.

38 408 US 238 [1972].

39 *Gregg* v. *Georgia* 428 US 153 [1976]; *Jurek* v. *Texas*, 428 US 262 (1976); *Proffitt* v. *Florida*, 428 US 242 (1976).

demonised as part of this process. In one notable case, an appellant's lawyers were criticised for "abusive delay, which has been compounded by last minute attempts to manipulate the judicial process".[40] Thus, Sarat and Scheingold suggest that, in this changed climate, death penalty lawyers in the USA no longer litigate to abolish capital punishment but to delay execution, often for short periods of time, and to "invest those whose lives they cannot save with dignity".[41]

This, then, is the context in which interns operate. They invariably come into contact with representatives of the legal and criminal justice system and are confronted with the realisation that they are working in a hostile environment where most people are 'friends' of the death penalty. In contrast, the lawyers in their host organisation are dedicated to postponing the execution of sentence for as long as possible thereby frustrating the apparent will of the courts. This tension in the relationship between host lawyers and the State underlines the political nature of the work undertaken by the interns.[42] While this usually involves interviewing jurors, victims' families, witnesses, prisoners' families and death row inmates, and collecting evidence of mitigating circumstances in medical, social, educational and psychiatric dossiers, on occasions they participate in campaigns to have execution delayed or commuted.[43]

The Interns' Perceptions

The establishment of federally funded resource centres in the 1980s enabled lawyers to make a relatively meagre living out of capital punishment work.[44] This may explain why many of the lawyers interviewed for Sarat's qualitative research perceived the issues raised by the death penalty to be substantive rather than moral; the execution of the death penalty remains "fraught with arbitrariness, discrimination, caprice and mistake".[45] This was a perspective adopted by many interns. One student observed, in support of the suggestion that the sentence of death was arbitrary, that:

> "In particular, I became acutely aware of just how few murders lead to the death penalty being sought, let alone imposed. The cases in which sentence had already been passed showed me that juries' decisions on the death penalty cannot be predicted, and seem to bear no rational explanation, as to why some people receive it, and others

40 *Gomez* v. *US* 112 S.Ct. 1652, 1653 (1992) discussed by Sarat *op. cit.* note 36.
41 See A. Sarat and S. Scheingold "Contexts and Conditions of Cause Lawyering" (Forthcoming).
42 See, for example, D. Luban, "Lawyers and Justice: An Ethical Study" (1988) and D. L. Rhode, "Institutionalising Ethics" (1994) 44 *Case Western Reserve Law Review* pp. 665–736.
43 For further examples of interns' work see *Internship in Capital Punishment Studies Report* 1995. Copies of this report are available from the Centre for Capital Punishment Studies, School of Law, University of Westminster, Red Lion Square, London WC1R 4SR.
44 *Op. cit.* note 37 at p. 16.
45 Id. at p. 19 citing Justice Harry Blackmun in *Callins* v. *Collins* 114 S.Ct. 1127 (1994).

not. Even worse was seeing the people against whom the District Attorneys (DA) chose to seek the death penalty, and those who they decided did not deserve it. It was painfully obvious that those facing the death penalty would be those the DA believed would be unable to defend themselves, and whose sentencing to death would gain the DA some more votes. MPD's [Multicounty Defenders' Office] monitoring of the death penalty across the state showed clearly how an individual DA could make a massive difference in the number of death penalty trials."[46]

Another developed the theme of discrimination.

> "Where the crime is black on white, it may be considered that more political mileage can be gained from seeking the death penalty. Indeed, in all the cases that we studied over a two month period, if sufficient aggravating circumstances were present or the crime was particularly heinous the death penalty was always sought."[47]

Frequently, the students' experience of the operation of law is heightened by direct contact with clients. This generally underlines academic and empirical points regarding the victims of capital punishment. For, as one of Sarat's respondents suggests, the death penalty is a "microcosm of everything that's wrong in society. There are poverty issues, race issues, classism, everything that's wrong in society at some point ends up in capital punishment".[48] A student's account of a visit to death row reinforces this view:

> "The next client is Bobby Shaw. Tall. Lanky. Black. Thud. Thud. [sound of client's feet on the floor] He shakes my hand limply. He does not look me in the eye. He sits down in a corner. He talks behind his hand. Between his fingers I can see that the top right half and the bottom left half of this teeth are missing. He is unresponsive. Sean tries to start a conversation.
> 'How are they treating you?'
> 'You know . . . OK'
> 'Did you get the money?'
> 'Um'. He moves his head from side to side. 'Yeah'. Silence.
> 'I see you got your Converse All Start'.
> 'I . . . um . . . want to get some new shoes . . . these are, you know . . . hard . . . on the floors'.
> Bobby is clearly in a poor mental state. He needs psychiatric care. He is no longer on death row. The Governor of Missouri granted

46 Clive Baldwin was a CPE student at City University who worked with Michael Mears, Attorney and Director of the Multicounty Public Defenders office in Atlanta, Georgia, USA. He has a training contract with Bindman & Co.

47 Kendal Travis, who graduated LL.B at Westminster in 1996, worked with Clive Stafford-Smith, Attorney and Director of the Louisiana Crisis Assistance Centre in New Orleans. She is going on to do the BVC.

48 *Op. cit.* note 37 at p. 22.

clemency on the grounds of insanity. Bobby Shaw killed a prison guard. The prison officers beat him up as execution-substitution. Sean checks him. He asks questions. He looks at him close up without getting close up. No signs of physical damage. Bobby's mental shape is worse. He needs care. He will not receive it. Thud. Thud."[49]

Often students become deeply involved in a single case and follow it through the stages which take place during their internship. They are rapidly required to understand the nature of the work and the steps necessary to mount a defence or to prosecute an appeal.

"Some weeks before our arrival in this small parish, a murder had been committed. An elderly white male had been beaten to death. The weapon? Allegedly the carcass of a frozen racoon. The motive? Robbery. The arrest had been an extravagant operation. Helicopters circled the area, the assistance of the state troopers was sought, the sheriff's department was enlisted and of course the local armed police supervised the whole event.

A middle aged indigenous black man, homeless at the time, was arrested and charged with first degree murder. A man well known to the locals. A man that, had he been asked, would probably have voluntarily gone to the police station to help with enquiries—but then the public and the police department would have been deprived of the spectacle.

This man was our client. The Louisiana Crisis Assistance Centre [LCAC] represented other clients in this judicial district, all of whom had been charged and indicted with first degree murder, all of whom potentially faced the death penalty.

The work of the LCAC is mainly trial based. This differs from the other resource centres who deal primarily with appeals. Our investigation was multi-faceted. We were to assemble a file of all the homicides that had been committed in this district over the past ten years. We had to identify the race, sex and age of both the defendant and the victim. The pre-indictment charge had to be contrasted with the indicted charge in every case. Particulars of the offence had to be specified and the aggravating and mitigating factors of each case had to be recorded. Any media coverage was to be copied. Autopsy reports studied. Was a sanity commission appointed? What did they conclude? Rap sheets had to be found. Defence and prosecution attorneys had to be named, motions filed and responses to the same had to be considered. Was there a trial or did the defendant plead?

49 Andrew Lorie, a CPE student at Westminster, worked with Sean O'Brien, Attorney and Director of the Missouri Post-Conviction Defender Organization. He completed the BVC in 1996.

Did the parties appeal, and if so what was the disposition after appeal?"[50]

As can be imagined, this kind of work can be disturbing and, in many cases students found that their experience of the internship had a profound effect on them personally. This, however, was often seen to stimulate cognitive and affective development.

> "The knowledge you acquire is incalculable. Not just practical but personal. You are at times pushed to your maximum. There will be times when you want to leave it all behind you and get on the next plane home. Other times you will be wanting to defer your course and stay for the year. The work can be hard and seemingly incomprehensible. It is fascinating. It can be harrowing and sometimes tedious. Your beliefs and attitudes are tested and stretched to the limits."[51]

Most interns acquired a highly developed sense of the importance of the work and the ways in which it was necessary to adapt in order to conduct it. A student serving an internship in Jamaica wrote:

> "A successful intern requires diplomacy, common sense, determination, self advocacy, a willingness to work, and a genuine interest in the work of the council. Above all, one needs respect for this young, independent, struggling country in which violence in all its manifestations from physical attack to verbal intolerance is a way of life for many from the ghettos up to the educated elite and which is arguably and regrettably a product of our own historical design."[52]

Typically, the host lawyers were extremely busy and depended on interns to carry out important research and case preparation. This underlined how the work of the intern, like that of the lawyer, involved extremely high degrees of responsibility and accountability.

> 'MPD [Multicounty Defenders' Office] was typically American in that they assumed that because you had volunteered to work, that you wanted to do as much work as possible. In return they offered a significant amount of responsibility early on. This could be alarming as I soon realised when I was left to prepare a client's entire mitigation case in my first week. However, I almost always received adequate help if I asked for it, and, most importantly, only spent one morning photocopying ... The final major piece of work I did was the legal research for a client's petition to the US Supreme

50 *Op. cit.* note 47.

51 Laban Leake, a CPE student at Westminster, worked with Florizel O'Connor at the Jamaica Council for Human Rights in Kingston. He completed the BVC in 1996 and is registered for a Ph.D at Essex University.

52 Id.

Court. Neither of the lawyers working on this case were around when I was doing this, so I was left entirely on my own."[53]

Students were also aware that the weapons in the armoury of capital punishment lawyers typically exceeded those used by most lawyers. This was because their goals were different. As Sarat and Sheingold suggest, they were keeping clients alive hoping for a change in political climate. Their colleagues in the organisations for which they worked were extremely committed to a cause and used political pressure, as well as the law, in order to further this objective.

"There are about 50 employees at CCR—it is like a large family and there is always a happy and jovial atmosphere, except when there is a warrant. Suddenly there was a tense and serious mood, nobody went home at weekends and people were called to come back to the office to start work immediately on appeals. The case attracted huge media attention, which was mostly positive, a bonus when most of the population wants your client to die. Whilst the lawyers were working round the clock putting appeals together I was writing to the Governor urging him to grant clemency and to the newspapers trying to get some more coverage. It was then that I realised playing the appalled English visitor was a good move. Any international criticism is taken seriously."[54]

Thus, interns saw that the professional role of the lawyers with whom they worked went beyond a traditional legal role. Often they were implicated in activities which cut across lawyers' duties to 'the system' to wider duties which were humanitarian in nature. Some students were fortunate in that their placement gave them a specific role in relation to human rights abuses. A student serving in the Jamaican Commission on Human Rights (JCHR) wrote:

"Not surprisingly, an internship with the JCHR is challenging. The organisation is understaffed and underfunded. Its remit is to cover all human rights violations in Jamaica, not simply those associated with Death Row, which nevertheless occupy a large portion of time and energy. A six day working week of 11 hours a day is not uncommon for the intern, whose duties include; visiting inmates of the euphemistically labelled St Catherine's Adult Correctional Centre, or the more realistically named General Penitentiary, serving Privy Council papers, taking model UN questionnaires, responding to letters smuggled out of either institution, complaining of beatings, riots, ill health, shootings or psychological torture, court attendance, time spent responding to requests for information from one of the 44 solicitors' firms carrying out Death Row work here in the UK, visits

53 *Op. cit.* 46.

54 Joanne Kearsley who graduated LL.B from Westminster in 1996 worked at the Capital Collateral Representative in Tallahassee, Florida.

to attorneys seeking information, interviews with the press and the occasional meeting with a diplomat."[55]

Despite the deep involvement in many of the stages of a case, interns also found that they needed to maintain a psychological distance from the client, sometimes called a 'professional attitude', in order to cope with the physical and psychological pressure of the field of practice.

> "... I would like to note that I had some extra duties to perform because of the unfortunate fact that one of the inmates was executed while I was there. I was asked to get people to sign petitions to stop the execution and actively try to get people involved in our cause. This was a genuine race against the clock and we lost. Of course, sadness was all around. Personally, based on this particular experience, I would like to remark that I believe it is a bad idea to get too involved in either personal contact with inmates or in the fight against capital punishment. Although a strong motivation is a prerequisite to do a good job, don't get there thinking you are going to change things. Your contribution will be valuable, but you can only do so much in a few months. Be aware of that and your disappointment and frustration will be limited."[56]

As these accounts illustrate, students often work in a setting where the tenets of ethical legal practice are abrogated in favour of a moral commitment on behalf of clients. Moreover, interns are often subject to heavy physical and psychological demands which may impede their ability to resist indoctrination into the value system of the 'cause lawyers' who are their hosts. Is this exposure, this risk, justified and how does it relate to the growing commitment to ethics in legal education in both the USA and UK?[57] The ACLEC, in advancing its argument for an ethical component in undergraduate legal education suggests that "no amount of external regulation of professional practice will serve as an adequate substitute for the personal and professional values and standards that lawyers should internalise from the earliest stages of their education and training."[58] It is not clear what these values and standards are. Here we critically examine the arguments against exposing students to the values of cause lawyers.

55 *Op. cit.* note 51.
56 Anne Marie Geelen, ERASMUS student at the University of Westminster School of Law from the University of Limburg at Maastricht, Netherlands.
57 This is reflected in both the ACLEC document and in the report of the McCrate Commission which examined legal education in the USA for the American Bar Association (see R. McCrate, "Preparing Lawyers to Participate Effectively in the Legal Profession" 44 *Journal of Legal Education* 89 and I. J. Costonis, "The McCrate Report: Of Loaves, Fishes and the Future of American Legal Education" 43 *Journal of Legal Education* 157 for lively discussions of McCrate's proposals).
58 ACLEC (1996) para. 1.19 p. 17.

Discussion

In terms of preparation for the ethics of legal practice we argue that the risks that students will internalise a distorted view of the role of lawyers is balanced by the advantages of their exposure to this area of practice. Before pursuing this argument, however, it is necessary to explore the ways in which capital punishment lawyers may present a model of 'unethical lawyering' to interns. We explore two principles which underpin the role morality of lawyers; neutrality and partisanship.[59] Neutrality, manifest in the bar's 'cab rank rule', requires that lawyers offer their services to all those that seek them. Partisanship requires that the lawyer devotes herself to her client's cause and offers 'zealous advocacy' within the limits of the law.

As regards the principle of neutrality, capital punishment lawyers reject the notion that they are 'hired guns' available to anyone able to pay for their services in favour of 'a vision of the Good' whereby they confront the law as 'the daily reality of violence'.[60] They refuse to fulfil the morally neutral role assigned to them by professional ethics choosing instead to "self consciously politicize their professional lives, and make lawyering a vocation of Justice rather than technique, or moral engagement rather than moral neutrality".[61] In this, their commitment to one kind of client is, arguably, no more than the practical reality of lawyering in other contexts where the principle of lawyer neutrality is increasingly undermined. Its vulnerability is seen in the right of solicitors to refuse to represent a particular client,[62] the ability of commercial clients to monopolise the customised services offered by large City firms and the decision of the Bar to re-examine the applicability of the 'cab rank rule' in legal aid cases.[63]

The second charge against death penalty lawyers is that their use of legal means, such as groundless applications, and extra-legal means, such as organising petitions to State governors, in order to delay the legal process and, therefore, the execution of their clients, exceeds the boundaries of legitimate partisanship. By these actions, it could be argued, they undermine the principle that lawyers have a responsibility to society to uphold the rule of law, and, therefore, that they fail in both their social and professional obligations. This is a substantial claim and one which can only be rebutted by an argument that a lawyer's wider duties might transcend their own code of ethics. Such an argument can

59 See W. L. Simon, "The Ideology of Advocacy: Procedural Justice and Professional Ethics" (1978) *Wisconsin Law Review* pp. 30–144 and D. L. Rhode, "Institutionalizing Ethics" 44:2 *Case Western Reserve Law Review* pp. 665–736 at 669.

60 *Op. cit.* note 37 at p. 3.

61 Id.

62 Principle 12.01 of the Guide to the Professional Conduct of Solicitors (6th ed. (1993) (Taylor, N. ed).

63 See J. Malpas, "Bar Council to Confront Cab Rank Rule". (1996) *The Lawyer* vol. 10 issue 28 p. 1.

be made, although the examples given may seem extreme. Thus, for Sarat, "to oppose the death penalty in the United States in the 90s is not unlike fighting against apartheid in the courts of South Africa in the 1970s, or litigating on behalf of Palestinian rights in the occupied territories in the 1980s".[64]

The argument that ends justify means may seem unattractive and yet partisanship itself has extremely unclear boundaries. Lawyers, in more mundane areas of work than capital cases, frequently transgress the legitimate boundaries of partisan action on behalf of their clients. Codes of professional conduct barely address the issue.[65] Why do cause lawyers' actions excite criticism while the actions of other lawyers are barely noticed? The public may be broadly mystified by the lawyers' ethic of zealous advocacy but it is mainly when zealousness is deployed on behalf of convicted murderers that the results are held up to scrutiny and criticism. We argue that it is the political and human stakes, and in particular the implicit denial of the accused's right to 'justice',[66] rather than the unusual deviancy of their actions, which expose capital punishment lawyers to criticism on ethical grounds.

The moral relativism which pervades professional codes is, we argue, the weakness of the ACLEC's call for higher ethical standards. In the examples we cite of the threat to the principle of lawyer neutrality, we see evidence for Abel's assertion that professional codes of conduct merely legitimate economic activity[67] and for Stanley's argument that the normative boundaries between legitimate and illegitimate economic activity are, in market economies, essentially negotiable.[68] While professional bodies may seek to represent professions as homogeneous, and their ethics as universal, the workplace is the most powerful determinant of ethical norms and, in the workplace, professionals develop quite different norms and ideologies in order to legitimatise their work.[69] Capital punishment lawyers, particularly in the current climate, lack political leverage within their profession. The norms of their workplace are, at the extremes, contrary to those chosen as a model of professional conduct. The commitment of cause lawyers and the denial of their neutral role has, at least, a justification on moral rather

64 *Op. cit.* note 37 at p. 9.

65 The general issue of partisanship in an adversarial system is discussed in Luban, *op. cit.* note 42. See particularly the procedural abuses detailed at p. 14. For a discussion of the limits of partisanship under the solicitors' rules of conduct see A. Boon, 'Ethics and Strategy in Personal Injury Litigation' (1995) 22:3 *Journal of Law and Society* pp. 353–373.

66 C. Douzinas and R. Warrington "'A Well-founded fear of Justice': Law and Ethics in Postmodernity" (1991) *Law and Critique* Vol. 2:2 pp. 115–147.

67 R. Abel, "Why Does the ABA Promulgate Ethical Rules?" (1981) 59:4 *Texas Law Review* pp. 639–688.

68 C. Stanley, "Speculations of the Conflict of Discourses: Finance, Crime and Regulation" (1996) 4:3 *Journal of Financial Regulations and Compliance* pp. 239–254.

69 R. L. Nelson, and D. M. Trubeck, "Arenas of Professionalism: The Professional Ideologies of Lawyers in Context" (1994) in *The Ethics of Lawyers* (ed. Luban, D.) Dartmouth Publishing Co. Ltd.

than financial grounds. Moreover, it can be argued that the professional deviance of cause lawyers is balanced by their ideological commitment to higher values. Therefore, while, on the one hand, cause lawyers represent a 'deviant strain' in the legal profession they have the capacity to 'reconnect law and morality, and make tangible the idea that law is a public profession . . .' thereby, 'serving the purpose of legitimising the profession but undermining the legitimation of law'.[70]

Interns frequently reflect on the ethical dilemmas which confront them. They are, to some extent, attuned to the issues by their in-course preparation. Yet we acknowledge that the internship programme offers a process of sensitisation to ethical issues rather than a programme of systematic instruction. It is intended to reinforce the learning in relation to these dimensions of the students' clinical experience in the future.[71] The implementation of ACLEC's proposals for ethics teaching in degree courses generally would, however, provide a more adequate foundation for students exposed to profound ethical dilemmas in practice. The internship programme offers an experience which is formative on several levels affecting both an understanding of the role and limitations of law in a particular context and an understanding of the relative importance of law, skills and political action. It may be suggested that an intern's experience offers them a distorted view of legal practice or the career or conduct of lawyers. However, it is an experience of practice which cannot be had in the UK. Most interns are moved to critically evaluate the 'value neutral' approach to legal study with which they are most familiar and move to confront ethical issues in a meaningful way. Most importantly, perhaps, they are encouraged to think about their role, as lawyers, in the legal process.

Conclusion

In this article we have confronted some of the practical and ethical issues raised by the internship programme. We have shown that interns can and do play a useful role in their host organisations and discussed some of the arguments against offering them this opportunity. The ethical dilemmas to which they are exposed go to the heart of the lawyer's role. It is clear from the extracts from interns' work that students appreciate possible disjunctions between ethics and rules of conduct. By the methods of assessment we have adopted students are given the opportunity to reflect on these fundamental issues from a perspective of engagement and experience, rather than as a hollow

70 *Op. cit.* n. 41.

71 See J. E. Molinerno, "On the Future of Integration Between Skills and Ethics Teaching: Clinical Legal Education in the Year 2101" (1996) *Journal of Legal Education* 46:1 pp. 67–78 for discussion of developing relationships between clinic and ethics.

academic exercise. This makes concrete an implicit agenda of the ACLEC report which asserts, appropriately in this context, that "students must be made aware of the values that legal solutions carry, and of the ethical and humanitarian dimensions of law as an instrument which affects the quality of life".[72]

A more explicit recognition of the educational value of the work of interns is found in the ACLEC report's assertion that the legal profession has a role in "protecting the rights of minorities within society and promoting the welfare of the disadvantaged".[73] By encouraging students to consider moral issues connected with the representation of the poor and those denied access to adequate legal services, we address one of the fundamental ethical failures of legal education[74] and perhaps, on occasions, reverse the inexorable drift of students into comfortable and profitable practice.[75] There can be no more concrete example of a commitment to the disadvantaged than that demonstrated by death penalty lawyers. Frequently they know that the sentence of death on their clients followed a trial at which that client was incompetently represented. They know that the death penalty is a judgment which reflects the background of the accused, whether racial, class or medical. They also know that the appellate court may refuse to review the decision on any of these grounds.[76] Their practice is often a moral commitment as well as a living. As to whether it is appropriate to expose students to the reality of the law and, its potential for extreme violence, is there a 'good time' to confront issues of life and death in the lawyer's office?

72 ACLEC Report para 1.19.
73 Id. at para. 1.20.
74 H. T. Edmunds, 'The Role of Legal Education in Shaping the Professions' (1988) 38 *Journal of Legal Education* pp. 285–293.
75 A. Sherr and J. Webb, "Law Students, the External Market, and Socialisation: Do We Make Them Turn to the City?" (1989) 16:2 *Journal of Law and Society* 225–249.
76 There is an abundance of literature illustrating the extent of Ineffective Assistance of Counsel claims, prosecutorial bias, race discrimination and the prosecution and execution of the mentally ill and retarded. See "Capital Punishment in the United States of America: a review of the issues", Hodgkinson *et al.* see note 13.

[10]

The penalty of life imprisonment under international criminal law

Esther Gumboh[*]

Doctoral Candidate; Teaching and Research Assistant, University of Cape Town, South Africa

Summary

In light of the global trend towards the abolition of the death penalty and the stand of the United Nations on the matter, it is not surprising that the maximum penalty available under international criminal law is life imprisonment. However, during the negotiations for the penal aspects of the Rome Statute, some delegates contended that life imprisonment is a violation of human rights such as human dignity and the prohibition against cruel, inhuman and degrading treatment or punishment. On the other hand, some delegates felt that excluding life imprisonment from the International Criminal Court's competence where the death penalty was not available would handicap its mandate to punish gross human rights violators. Adopting a human rights perspective, the article revisits this debate by critically examining the penalty of life imprisonment under international criminal law. It argues that no clear justification has been given for the imposition of life imprisonment and that the release mechanism for lifers needs to be improved. Focusing on the International Criminal Tribunal for Rwanda, the International Criminal Tribunal for the Former Yugoslavia and the International Criminal Court, the article analyses the relevant statutes and rules and the manner in which life imprisonment has been imposed by these tribunals. Further consideration is given to the enforcement of sentences with respect to the prospect of release for 'lifers'. The article concludes by stressing the need for a more focused and cautious approach to life imprisonment and the enforcement of sentences under international criminal law.

* LLB (Hons) (Malawi), LLM (Cape Town); egumboh@yahoo.com

1 Introduction

> The concept of life imprisonment destroys human dignity, reducing a prisoner to a number behind the walls of a gaol waiting only for death to set him free. The fact that he may be released on parole is no answer. [F]or a judicial officer to impose any sentence with parole in mind is an abdication by such officer of his function and duty ....[1]
>
> Levy J, Namibia High Court

Although most states that have abolished the death penalty have accepted life imprisonment as an appropriate alternative,[2] the compatibility of the latter with human rights has been an ongoing debate both at national and international levels.[3] Nevertheless, life imprisonment has been accepted as the maximum penalty under international criminal law. With specific reference to the International Criminal Tribunal for Rwanda (ICTR), the International Criminal Tribunal for the Former Yugoslavia (ICTY) and the International Criminal Court (ICC),[4] the article examines how this penalty has been applied under international criminal law. It commences with an overview of the human rights debate *vis-à-vis* life imprisonment, then investigates how the penalty has been imposed and the prospect of release for lifers.

Life imprisonment means different things in different countries. In some jurisdictions, it literally means that a prisoner spends the rest of his natural life in prison without the possibility of parole. In other jurisdictions, prisoners are sentenced to life imprisonment on the understanding that they will be considered for parole after serving a set number of years. In this essay, the emphasis is on life imprisonment as prescribed under international criminal law, that is, life imprisonment with the possibility of parole.

2 Life imprisonment and human rights

Life imprisonment without the possibility of parole is criticised as a violation of human rights. Below is a summary of some arguments against this kind of punishment.

---

1 *S v Tjijo* 4 September 1991 (NM), unreported – but reproduced substantially in *S v Tcoeib* (2001) AHRLR 158 (NaSC 1996), previously reported as 1996 1 SACR 390 (NmS), para 16.

2 R Stokes 'A fate worse than death? The problems with life imprisonment as an alternative to the death penalty' in J Yorke (ed) *Against the death penalty: International initiatives and implications* (2008) 282.

3 D van Zyl Smit 'Life imprisonment as the ultimate penalty in international law: A human rights perspective' (1999) 9 *Criminal Law Forum* 5 26-45.

4 The Special Court for Sierra Leone is excluded because art 19(1) of its Statute demands imprisonment for a specific number of years.

2.1 Human dignity

Human beings should always be treated as ends in themselves;[5] hence, an offender should not be turned into an object of 'crime prevention to the detriment of his constitutionally-protected right to social worth and respect'.[6] Even the vilest offender remains possessed of human dignity.[7] In this context, life imprisonment has been criticised as a violation of the right to human dignity in that it is imposed as a deterrent to potential offenders, hence the instrumentalisation of offenders.

Moreover, it is doubtful whether deterrence can be achieved by life imprisonment or indeed long terms of imprisonment. The underlying causes of gross human rights violations, some of which lie within the political system, cannot be curbed by the threat of imprisonment. Indeed, not even the prospect of death can deter the commission of such crimes.

2.2 Cruel, inhuman and degrading punishment

It has been argued that life imprisonment presents 'an intolerable threat to the human dignity' of the offender because it is a cruel, inhuman and degrading punishment.[8] At the heart of the prohibition of such punishment lies the concept of proportionality of punishment to the crime.[9] In addition to being a form of cruel, inhuman and degrading punishment,[10] disproportionate sentences are generally regarded as violations of other human rights.[11] The indeterminacy of life imprisonment and the potential loss of liberty until the offender dies lend it to criticism that it is a grossly disproportionate and arbitrary sentence. Certainty is a crucial element of the rule of law as recognised in the principle of legal certainty.[12] It is in the interests of justice to quantify sentences so that a prisoner knows exactly what his punishment is.[13] Life sentences leave the quantification of punishment to death itself, hence they are arbitrary.

---

5 The second premise or maxim in Emanuel Kant's *Categorical imperative*.

6 BVerfGE 45, 187 227-228 (1977), translated in R Miller 'The shared transatlantic jurisprudence of dignity' (2003) 4 *German Law Journal* 925 930.

7 *Gregg v Georgia* 428 US 153 (1976).

8 Van Zyl Smit (n 3 above) 29.

9 *S v Dodo* 2001 1 SACR 594 (CC) para 37.

10 D van Zyl Smit *Taking life imprisonment seriously in national and international law* (2002) 198.

11 See D van Zyl Smit & A Ashworth 'Disproportionate sentences as human rights violations' (2004) 67 *Modern Law Review* 541.

12 Van Zyl Smit (n 3 above) 29.

13 *Tjijo* (n 1 above).

2.3 Right to rehabilitation

Life imprisonment denies the prisoner any hope of rehabilitation and reintegration into society.[14] Sentenced prisoners have a right to be given an opportunity to rehabilitate themselves[15] and re-establish themselves in the community.[16] Some judges have expressed the view that the mere possibility of parole does not in itself mitigate the fact that life imprisonment infringes the right to rehabilitation. As eloquently put by Levy J:[17]

> When a term of years is imposed, the prisoner looks forward to the expiry of that term when he shall walk out of gaol a free person ... Life imprisonment robs the prisoner of this hope. Take away his hope and you take away his dignity and all desire he may have to continue living ... [E]ven though [he] may be out of gaol on parole, [he] is conscious of his life sentence and conscious of the fact that his ... debt to society can never be paid ... Life imprisonment makes a mockery of the reformative end of punishment.

It is recognised that not all prisoners need rehabilitation. In such contexts, the right argued for here is the right to be returned to a free society.[18] The essential content of the right to human dignity is seriously compromised 'if the prisoner, notwithstanding his personal development, must abandon any hope of ever regaining his freedom'.[19]

2.4 A death sentence?

It has been stated that life imprisonment is a death sentence[20] and that it amounts to 'putting an individual in a waiting room until his death'.[21] It is therefore akin to death and results in a denial of dignity, because 'a human life involves not just existence and survival, but [also] the unique development of a personality, creativity, liberty, and unfettered social intercourse'.[22]

Whether or not life imprisonment is a lesser punishment than the death penalty is a 'legal-philosophical question'.[23] Poor conditions of

---

14 G de Beco 'Life sentences and human dignity' (2005) 9 *The International Journal of Human Rights* 411 414.

15 Art 10(3) of the International Covenant on Civil and Political Rights, 1966 (ICCPR) states that 'the penitentiary system shall comprise treatment of prisoners the essential aim of which shall be their reformation and social rehabilitation'.

16 *Lebach* BVerfGE 35, 187 235-236 (1973).

17 *Tjijo* (n 1 above).

18 Van Zyl Smit (n 3 above) 34.

19 BVerfGE 45, 187 245.

20 See *Tjijo* (n 1 above) reproduced in *Tcoeib* (n 1 above).

21 De Beco (n 14 above).

22 LS Shellef *Ultimate penalties: Capital punishment, life imprisonment, physical torture* (1987) 138.

23 GA Knoops *Theory and practice of international and internationalised criminal proceedings* (2005) 275.

detention can make it worse than death itself.[24] Life sentences without parole have also been equated to death sentences.[25] It is possible to argue that the *possibility* of parole does not diminish this proximity since there is no guarantee that the maximum sentence for life will not be served.[26]

3 Life imprisonment under international criminal law

3.1 International Criminal Tribunal for Rwanda

The ICTR is empowered to impose a life sentence pursuant to Rule 101(A) of its Rules of Procedure and Evidence (RPE).[27] The Trial Chamber in *Kayishema* attempted to distinguish life imprisonment from a sentence of 'imprisonment for a term up to and including the remainder of [a defendant's] life' as phrased in the Rule.[28] This resulted in four concurrent 'remainder-of-life' sentences being imposed, with the Chamber holding that the sentence should be given its 'plain meaning' and distinguished from a 'life sentence' as understood in national law.[29] The Appeals Chamber has also noted that, unlike life imprisonment, 'imprisonment for a term up to and including the remainder of [a defendant's] life' as envisaged in Rule 101A 'is *always* subject to possible reductions'.[30] This rather peculiar interpretation is 'suspicious' and 'reveals some of the judges' intention that a full life sentence be imposed', an equivalent of the American life without parole sentence.[31] Read in this manner, Rule 101A would violate international human

---

24 Stokes (n 2 above) 288.

25 D van Zyl Smit 'Life imprisonment: Recent issues in national and international law' (2006) 29 *International Journal of Law and Psychiatry* 405.

26 Van Zyl Smit (n 10 above) 199.

27 Rule 101A reads: 'A convicted person may be sentenced to imprisonment for a term up to and including the remainder of the convicted person's life.'

28 *The Prosecutor v Kayishema and Ruziandana*, ICTR-95-1-T, judgment, 21 May 1999 para 31.

29 *Kayishema* (n 28 above), para 32. On appeal, a single life sentence was imposed. See *Prosecutor v Kayishema*, ICTR-95-1, appeals judgment (Reasons), 1 June 2001.

30 *Kambanda v Prosecutor*, ICTR-97-23-A, appeals judgment 19 October 2000, n 144 (emphasis in original). See, generally, JD Mujuzi 'Is there a need for the ICTY to clarify the difference(s) between life imprisonment and imprisonment for the remainder of the offender's life? The *Galić* and *Lukić* decisions' (2010) 10 *International Criminal Law Review* 855.

31 Van Zyl Smit (n 10 above) 186 187. See also *Kigula v Attorney-General* Constitutional Petition 6 of 2003, Constitutional Court of Uganda (unreported) 140-142, where Twinomujuni J remarked: 'Life imprisonment is a realistic alternative to a death penalty and it can only be a viable alternative if it means imprisonment for life, and not a mere 20 years.'

rights norms which regard life imprisonment without parole as a violation of human rights.[32]

The ICTR has not clearly justified its imposition of life imprisonment. Instead, undue emphasis has been placed on the gravity of the offence. It has been held that life imprisonment can be imposed even if there are mitigating circumstances so long as 'the gravity of the offence requires the imposition of a life sentence provided for'.[33] Alas, there is no threshold of gravity that unambiguously deserves such a sentence. The obscurity of this guideline is further compounded by the assertion that[34]

> mitigation of punishment does not ... reduce the degree of the crime, it is more a matter of grace than of defence. [T]he punishment assessed is not a proper criterion to be considered in evaluating the findings of the court with reference to the degree of magnitude of the crime.

In *Kambanda*, the gravity of the crimes and the defendant's senior position led the court to impose a life sentence despite his plea of guilty and substantial co-operation with the prosecutor.[35] A similar sentence was imposed in *Akayesu* after the court emphasised that a 'heavy penalty' was warranted.[36] However, there is no knowing why the only appropriate 'heavy penalty' was life imprisonment. In *Ndindabahizi*, the Trial Chamber specifically mentioned that it had taken into account the defendant's prospects of rehabilitation, but did not state its conclusion on the matter that justified the imposition of a life sentence.[37] A challenge against this sentence on the grounds that it did not give credit to the mitigating circumstances was unsuccessful.[38] The ICTR has since held that life imprisonment should generally not be imposed

32 *Tcoeib* (n 1 above) para 22: Life sentence without parole treats a prisoner as a 'thing' instead of a human being; *S v Bull* 2001 2 SACR 681 (SCA) para 23; *Kafkaris v Cyprus*, application 21906/04, judgment 12 February 2008, ECHR; Van Zyl Smit (n 10 above) 183-185; JD Mujuzi 'Why the Supreme Court of Uganda should reject the Constitutional Court's understanding of imprisonment for life' (2008) 8 *African Human Rights Law Journal* 163-185.

33 *Musema v Prosecutor*, ICTR-96-13-A, appeals judgment 16 November 2001, para 396.

34 *Prosecutor v Akayesu*, ICTR-96-4-T, sentencing judgment 2 October 1998 8.

35 *Prosecutor v Kambanda*, ICTR 97-23-S, judgment and sentence, 4 September 1998, paras 44 & 61-62. This sentence was upheld on appeal. See *Kambanda v Prosecutor*, ICTR-97-23-A, appeals judgment 19 October 2000, para 126. See also *Prosecutor v. Ferdinand Nahimana, Jean-Bosco Barayagwiza, Hassan Ngeze*, ICTR-99-52-A, appeals judgment 28 November 2007, para 1038(3). (The existence of mitigating circumstances does not automatically preclude the imposition of life imprisonment.)

36 *Akayesu* (n 34 above) 8; see also *Rutaganda v Prosecutor*, ICTR-96-3-T, judgment and sentence, 6 December 1999, paras 455-473.

37 *Prosecutor v Ndindabahizi*, ICTR-2001-71-I, judgment and sentence 15 July 2004, para 498.

38 *Ndindabahizi v Prosecutor*, ICTR-01-71-A, appeals judgment 16 January 2007, paras 124-142; see also *Prosecutor v Ngiyitegeka*, ICTR-96-14-A, appeals judgment, 9 July 2004, para 267; *Ngiyitegeka*, appellant's brief, 23 December 2003, para 215.

where one has pleaded guilty 'in order to encourage others to come forward'.[39]

The ICTR also appears to impose life imprisonment in lieu of the death penalty[40] in the name of 'recourse to the general practice' in Rwanda.[41] Since the imposition of the death penalty in Rwanda was dependent on the circumstances of the offence,[42] there can be no absolute certainty as to its imposition in any case. Therefore, while bearing in mind the practice in Rwanda, the court should focus on the circumstances of the case before it in determining the appropriate sentence. The ICTR has noted that life imprisonment is reserved for those who planned and ordered atrocities and who participated in them with 'particular zeal and sadism',[43] irrespective of the formal position held.[44]

3.2 International Criminal Tribunal for the Former Yugoslavia

Controversy surrounds the imposition of life sentences by the ICTY pursuant to Rule 101(A) of the RPE because the courts of the former Yugoslavia were not allowed to impose life sentences; they could only impose the death penalty or a maximum term of 20 years' imprisonment.[45] Under article 24 of the ICTY Statute, the Trial Chamber must 'have recourse to the general practice regarding prison sentences in the courts of the former Yugoslavia'. In its defence, the ICTY has stated that it is not bound by the maximum penalty in the national courts;[46]

39 *Prosecutor v Serugendo*, ICTR-2005-84-I, judgment and sentence, 12 June 2006, paras 57 & 89.

40 See eg *Akayesu* (n 34 above).

41 Art 23(1) Statute of the International Criminal Tribunal for Rwanda (ICTR Statute).

42 *Simba v Prosecutor*, ICTR-01-76-T, judgment and sentence 13 December 2005, para 434. Rwanda abolished the death penalty in 2007.

43 *Simba* (n 42 above), para 434; See also *Prosecutor v Nchamihigo*, ICTR-01-63-T, judgment and sentence, 12 November 2008, para 388; *Prosecutor v Muvunyi*, ICTR-00-55A-T, judgment and sentence, 12 September 2006, para 538; *Prosecutor v Seromba*, ICTR-2001-66-I, judgment 13 December 2006, para 403; *Prosecutor v Ntagerura*, ICTR-99-46-T, appeals judgment 25 February 2004, para 815; *Ngiyitegeka v Prosecutor*, ICTR-96-14-T, judgment and sentence 16 May 2003, para 486; *Prosecutor v Muhimana*, ICTR- 95-1B-T, judgment and sentence 28 April 2005, paras 604-616; *Prosecutor v Kamuhanda*, ICTR-99-54A-T, judgment and sentence, 22 January 2004, paras 6, 764 & 770; *Ndindabahizi* (n 37 above) paras 505, 508 & 511; *Musema* (n 33 above) para 388.

44 *Karera v Prosecutor*, ICTR-01-74-T, judgment and sentence 7 December 2007, para 583; *Prosecutor v Musema*, ICTR-96-13-T, judgment and sentence 27 January 2000, paras 999-1008; *Rutaganda* (n 36 above) paras 466-473.

45 WA Schabas 'Perverse effects of the *nulla poena* principle: National practice and the *ad hoc* tribunals' (2000) 11 *European Journal of International Law* 521 525.

46 *Prosecutor v Tadić*, IT-94-1-T, sentencing judgment, 14 July 1997, para 21.

that life imprisonment is the natural alternative to the death penalty;[47] and that its imposition is supported by the *travaux préparatoires*.[48]

These justifications are not convincing. Firstly, they reduce article 24 'to a mere statement of general principle of international law, providing only that the death penalty and punishments other than imprisonment may not be imposed'.[49] This undermines the legal certainty that the drafters of the article sought to create by their reference to the practice in the former Yugoslavia.[50] Secondly, the ICTY should seriously consider the acceptability of life imprisonment as an alternative to the death penalty; more so since the latter, and not the former, was imposed in the former Yugoslavia.[51] Thirdly, it is debatable whether reliance on the *travaux préparatoires* was appropriate.[52] Had the Security Council intended to make life imprisonment available to the ICTY, it would have been in the interests of legal certainty for the Statute to have stated so explicitly.[53]

Rule 101(A) is yet another example of the inherent power of the ICTY to regulate itself, a weakness rooted in article 15 of the ICTY Statute that makes it 'alarmingly simple' to amend the RPE.[54] The ICTY 'simply invoked its power to make' the RPE in including life imprisonment as an applicable penalty.[55] However, the RPE being subordinate to the Statute, the imposition of life imprisonment is *ultra vires* the Statute.[56]

---

47 *Prosecutor v Erdemovic*, IT-96-22-T, sentencing judgment 29 November 1996, paras 33-39; *Tadić* (n 46 above) para 9.

48 The statement relied on was that of Madeline Albright, the United States representative at the Security Council. See Provisional Verbatim Record of the 3217th meeting.

49 Van Zyl Smit (n 10 above) 181.

50 Van Zyl Smit (n 10 above) 181. In *Erdemovic* (n 47 above) para 38, the ICTY recognised that the reference to 'general practice' arose because of concerns about legal certainty but refused to give effect to the intention of the drafters, stating that its application did 'not recognise the criminal nature universally attached to crimes against humanity'; MC Bassiouni & P Manikas *The law of the International Tribunal for the Former Yugoslavia* (1996) 701-702 hold the opinion that Rule 101A also violates the prohibition of *ex post facto* laws; See also WA Schabas 'Sentencing and the international tribunals: For a human rights approach' (1997) 7 *Duke Journal of Comparative and International Law* 461 482, who avers that the principle of legal certainty can be respected without the need for the tribunals following 'in a strict sense' the practice of Yugoslavia or Rwanda.

51 Van Zyl Smit (n 10 above) 181-182.

52 D van Zyl Smit 'Punishment and human rights in international criminal justice' (2002) 2 *Human Rights Law Review* 1 8.

53 As above.

54 See J Laughland *Travesty: The trial of Slobodan Milosevic and the corruption of international justice* (2007) 90-91 who argues that the RPE can even be amended by an exchange of e-mails by the judges.

55 Van Zyl Smit (n 52 above).

56 Van Zyl Smit (n 52 above). This question does not arise in the ICTR since life imprisonment is imposed in Rwandan courts.

The ICTY has imposed three life sentences to date.[57] However, the lengthy terms that have been imposed in other cases are arguably tantamount to tacit life sentences.[58]

3.2.1 The case of *Galić*

An example of the manner in which life imprisonment has been imposed by the ICTY is borne out by the case of *Galić*.[59] In that case, the ICTY Appeals Chamber held that the Trial Chamber had abused its discretion by imposing a sentence of 20 years on the accused,[60] which it described as having been taken from 'the wrong shelf' in light of the aggravating factors.[61] Without further ado whatsoever, the sentence was substituted with life imprisonment. In his dissenting opinion, Pocar J was sceptical about the Appeals Chamber's power to increase a sentence against which there would be no right of appeal,[62] arguing that the case should have been remitted to the Trial Chamber for reconsideration in order to reserve the right to appeal.[63]

Meron J, also dissenting, contended that there was no basis for tampering with the sentence. He noted that it was not 'so low that it demonstrably shocks the conscience' and had been imposed after

57 *Prosecutor v Galić*, IT-98-29-A, appeals judgment 30 November 2006; *Prosecutor v Stakić*, IT-97-24-T, appeals judgment 31 July 2003; *Prosecutor v Lukić*, IT-98-32/1-T, judgment 20 July 2009. Stakić's sentence was reduced to 40 years' imprisonment on appeal. See *Prosecutor v Stakić*, IT-97-24-A, appeals judgment 22 March 2006, para 428.

58 See *Prosecutor v Krištić*, IT-98-33-T, judgment 2 August 2001 (46 years) – reduced to 35 years in *Prosecutor v Krištić*, IT-98-33-A, appeals judgment 19 April 2004, para 275; *Prosecutor v Blaškić*, IT-95-14-T, judgment 3 March 2000 (45 years) – reduced to nine years in *Prosecutor v Blaškić*, IT-95-14-A, appeals judgment 29 July 2004, 258; *Prosecutor v Jelišić*, IT-95-10-T, judgment 14 December 1999 (40 years). In his partially dissenting opinion to the confirmation of Jelišic's sentence in *Prosecutor v Jelišić*, IT-95-10-A, appeals judgment 5 July 2001, para 2, Wald J stated that the 40-year term imposed on the accused, who was 31 years old at the time of sentencing, was 'in effect a life sentence'.

59 *Galić* (n 57 above).

60 *Galić* (n 57 above) para 456.

61 *Galić* (n 57 above) para 455.

62 See the partially dissenting opinion of Pocar J in *Galić* (n 57 above) paras 2-4 186-187.

63 The question of whether or not an Appeals Chamber can competently increase a sentence is beyond the scope of this paper. Suffice to say that art 14(5) of ICCPR guarantees the right to appeal against sentence.

careful consideration of the circumstances of the case.[64] He concluded thus:[65]

> The majority's decision to increase Galić's sentence to life imprisonment may satisfy our sense of condemnation. But this increase disserves the principles of procedural fairness on which our legitimacy rests. As the highest body in our court system, we are not readily accountable to any other authority and thus have a particular obligation to use our power sparingly. We should not substitute our own preferences for the reasoned judgement of a Trial Chamber. A sound method for assuring that we have not fallen prey to such preferences is to measure our choices fully and comprehensively against those made in prior cases. Although precise comparisons may be of limited value, the radically different approach adopted by the majority in this case requires at least some explanation. Rather than undertaking such an analysis, however, the majority simply offers conclusory statements. I cannot accept the majority's approach. No matter what he has done, Galić is entitled to due process of law — including a fair application of our standard of review.

It is submitted that by imposing such an extreme punishment without proper justification, the Appeals Chamber itself abused its discretion. It is unfortunate that life sentences are imposed in this manner without due regard for an accused person's right to appeal.[66] Surely if it falls within the Trial Chamber's discretion to impose life imprisonment,[67] it also falls within its discretion to impose a lighter sentence provided all circumstances are considered? Even more unfortunate is the view expressed by Shahabuddeen J that the ICTY is not a state, hence it cannot be bound to uphold all fair trial rights.[68]

3.3 International Criminal Court

Article 77(1)(b) of the Rome Statute of the ICC (ICC Statute) restricts the imposition of life imprisonment to cases where it is 'justified by the extreme gravity of the crime and the individual circumstances of the convicted person'. Although the ICC is expected 'to try nothing

---

64 Separate and partially dissenting opinion of Meron J in *Galić* (n 57 above) paras 9 & 10 205-208. The gist of Meron J's argument was that the Trial Chamber had not committed a 'discernible error', hence the Appeals Chamber had no power to intervene on the sentence. (See *Prosecutor v Tadić* IT-94-1-A and IT-94-1-Abis, judgment in sentencing appeals 26 January 2000, para 22.) The Trial Chamber had in fact noted that a 20-year sentence was the maximum prison term available in the former Yugoslavia Courts. See *Prosecutor v Galić*, IT-98-29-T, judgment 5 December 2003, para 761. It is arguable, therefore, that it was imposed as a comparably heavy penalty, short only of the death penalty itself.

65 Separate and partially dissenting opinion of Meron J (n 64 above) para 13.

66 See also *Gacumbitsi v Prosecutor*, ICTR-2001-64-A, appeals judgment 7 July 2006, where the ICTR Appeals Chamber increased a 30-year sentence to life imprisonment.

67 *Prosecutor v Jelišić*, IT-95-10-A, appeals judgment 5 July 2001, para 100.

68 See separate and partially dissenting opinion of Shahabuddeen J in *Jelišić* (n 67 above) paras 25 & 26 55-56, asserting that the ICTY Statute is equivalent to a reservation to ICCPR.

but crimes of extreme gravity' and 'the most heinous offenders',[69] the restriction implies that life imprisonment should be the exception rather than the rule. Clear distinctions will have to be made to justify a life sentence.[70] It is hoped that, unlike the case in the *ad hoc* tribunals, this restriction, coupled with the provision for distinct sentencing hearings in article 76(2) of the ICC Statute, will bolster a more comprehensive approach to sentencing. Of some concern, however, is the manner in which the Statute limits the Court's discretion to a choice between a fixed term of 30 years' imprisonment or less and life imprisonment. While the limitation may influence the ICC to reduce its sentence in order to avoid a life sentence, it may also tilt in favour of a life sentence where a longer prison term would have otherwise sufficed.

4 Prospect of release

In order to pass the test of human dignity, life imprisonment should offer a 'real and tangible prospect' of release.[71] It should be noted that the decision to release a prisoner under international criminal law is final and irreversible.[72] None of the tribunals have supervisory powers over the offender after his release, a feature which can be attributed to the lack of an international police force. The inevitable reliance on states for the enforcement of sentences is therefore a setback in the development of a universal system of international criminal sentencing and enforcement proceedings.[73] This section considers the release system in the courts under discussion.

4.1 The *ad hoc* tribunals

The ICTR and ICTY cannot grant early release *proprio motu*. Their Statutes provide that pardon or commutation of sentences will only be considered '[i]f pursuant to the applicable law of the state in which the convicted person is imprisoned, he or she is eligible for pardon or commutation of sentence'.[74] The state of enforcement is required to notify the tribunal if the prisoner is so eligible. However, it is the president of the tribunal, in consultation with the judges, on 'the basis of the interests of justice and the general principles of law',[75] who is to make the final decision. Factors that must be taken into account include the

69 WA Schabas *An introduction to the International Criminal Court* (2003) 317.

70 Van Zyl Smit (n 52 above) 14.

71 *De Boucherville v The State of Mauritius* (2008) UKPC 37, para 23; *Kafkaris* (n 32 above) para 6 of the joint dissenting judgment of Tulkens, Cabral Barreto, Fura-Sandström, Spielmann and Jebens JJ.

72 Schabas (n 69 above) 142.

73 Knoops (n 23 above) 274.

74 Arts 27 & 28 of the ICTY and ICTR Statutes respectively.

75 As above.

gravity of the crime, the treatment of similarly-situated offenders, the demonstration of rehabilitation by the offender, and any substantial co-operation with the prosecutor.[76]

4.1.1 Evaluating the tribunals' release system

It would be interesting to see how these tribunals would consider reducing a sentence on the basis of a factor which is in fact a mitigating factor in sentencing but which was 'negated' during sentencing. It is submitted that it would be paradoxical to grant release on the same factors that were evident during trial but which, for one reason or another, were considered insufficient to warrant a lenient sentence in the first place. For instance, would Kambanda benefit from his co-operation with the prosecutor at this stage?[77]

A major weakness of this system is that the eligibility for pardon or commutation lies primarily with the state of enforcement.[78] This does not only put prisoners on an unequal footing due to differences in national laws,[79] but also renders the system susceptible to manipulation by states.[80] There is no guarantee that a lifer, or indeed any other prisoner, has a real prospect of release. Secondly, some of the criteria cannot be applied equally to all prisoners. For instance, co-operation is not possible in some crimes.[81] In addition, not all prisoners may have the same potential for co-operation, such as being witnesses in other cases. This factor may also pressurise prisoners to co-operate with the prosecutor in the hope of increasing their chance of early release. Thirdly, consideration of the gravity of the crime at this stage may amount to 'double jeopardy' against prisoners whose crimes are very grave.[82] Conversely, prisoners who committed less serious offences may benefit twice, both at sentencing and release.

While appreciating the need for equality in the treatment of prisoners, taking into account the treatment of 'similarly-situated prisoners' is not appropriate. It is unrealistic to expect all international prisoners to be considered for pardon at the same time, more so since the criteria for such pardon are subject to national law. Furthermore, it is not clear

---

76 Rules 125 & 126 of the ICTY and ICTR RPE respectively.

77 Kambanda provided 'invaluable information' to the prosecutor and agreed to testify in other cases. See *Prosecutor v Kambanda,* ICTR 97-23-S, judgment and sentence 4 September 1998, para 47.

78 Van Zyl Smit (n 52 above) 9. The criteria for pardon are not always public knowledge. See JD Mujuzi 'The evolution of the meaning(s) of penal servitude for life (life imprisonment) in Mauritius: The human rights and jurisprudential challenges confronted so far and those ahead' (2009) 53 *Journal of African Law* 242-244.

79 Van Zyl Smit (n 3 above) 51.

80 A Hoel 'The sentencing provisions of the International Criminal Court' (2005) 30 *The International Journal of Punishment and Sentencing* 37-66.

81 Van Zyl Smit (n 10 above) 195.

82 Van Zyl Smit (n 10 above) 184.

whether the phrase 'similarly-situated' is confined to prisoners serving in the same country or those who committed similar crimes or indeed those tried jointly. It would be unfair to deny release to a prisoner on the ground that his 'counterpart' has not been given an opportunity for the same; when there is no uniform or alternative release system.

Fifthly, the Statute does not clarify what is meant by the 'interests of justice' or 'general principles of law'. The former notion gives too much discretion to the Court.[83] It is a fluid concept capable of accommodating a wide variety of factors. This can, of course, act either in favour of or against the prisoner. However, it would have been better to explicitly list the factors.[84]

Of great concern, in the context of this paper, is the fact that the system does not have special considerations for lifers. It is the possibility of release that saves life imprisonment from being a cruel, inhuman, and degrading punishment.[85] It is ironic that the *ad hoc* tribunals which have no release mechanism of their own have the power to deny release contemplated by the state of enforcement, leaving no guarantee that release may be considered again. In the absence of an independent release system, it is best that the tribunals not impose life imprisonment at all.[86]

A solution to some of these problems may be the introduction of a rule providing for release pursuant to articles 27 and 28 of the ICTY and ICTR Statutes respectively, which vest the tribunals with supervisory powers over the enforcement of sentences.[87] Alternatively, review may be provided for in the sentencing judgment.[88] However, the latter measure would not satisfy the principle of equality. Moreover, whether such measures would in fact be *intra vires* the Statutes is debatable.[89]

4.2 International Criminal Court

The ICC Statute reserves the right to reduce sentences to the Court itself.[90] The hearings on reduction of sentence are mandatory and are to be heard by three judges of the Appeals Chamber or a judge delegated by it.[91] Article 110(3) mandates the ICC to review the sentence after 'the person has served two-thirds of the sentence, or 25 years in the case of life imprisonment'. Subsequent hearings on reduction may

83 Schabas (n 50 above) 513.
84 The listing in the RPE (n 76 above) is not exhaustive.
85 *Bull* (n 32 above).
86 Schabas (n 50 above) 516.
87 Schabas (n 50 above) 510.
88 As above.
89 As above.
90 Art 110.
91 Rule 224(1) of the ICC RPE.

be scheduled every three years or at any time stipulated in the first hearing.[92]

Reduction may be granted if the ICC is satisfied that the offender was either willing to co-operate with the Court from an early stage and continues to be so willing;[93] or rendered voluntary assistance in the enforcement of Court judgments and orders;[94] or if there are other factors 'establishing a clear and significant change of circumstances sufficient to justify the reduction of sentence'.[95] Rule 223 of the ICC RPE expounds the last condition by listing the following criteria: genuine dissociation from the crime; prospect of resocialisation; impact of release on social stability and victims; significant action taken by the prisoner for the benefit of the victims; and the individual circumstances of the prisoner, such as age or poor physical or mental health.

4.2.1 Evaluating the International Criminal Court release system

The ICC release mechanism attempts to balance the interests of the offender, the victims and society at large.[96] While is worth applauding as a considerable improvement on the *ad hoc* tribunals' system, it is not without its flaws. Firstly, there is concern with the set minimum term of 25 years for lifers. Though this period is reasonable because the maximum fixed term is 30 years,[97] it is rather harsh as a minimum and is in fact sufficient for retribution.[98] Further, it is questionable how two-thirds of a fixed sentence has been parallelled to 25 years.[99] The indeterminacy of life imprisonment means that 25 years can be any fraction of the sentence, indeed more than two-thirds of it.

The inclusion of article 110(4)(c) mitigates legal certainty of release.[100] The change of circumstances was initially intended to cater for a change in the political circumstances under which the original offence was committed.[101] However, it now gives room for a fragmented release mechanism where one set of factors is fixed in the ICC Statute itself while the other is articulated in the RPE, hence subject to change at any time.[102] To make matters worse, the Statute gives

---

92 Rule 224(3) of the ICC RPE. A sentenced person may also apply for an earlier subsequent hearing.

93 Art 110(4)(a).

94 Art 110(4)(b).

95 Art 110(4)(c). Art 27 expressly proscribes the consideration of official capacity as a factor 'in and of itself'.

96 Hole (n 80 above).

97 Art 77(1)(a).

98 Van Zyl Smit (n 52 above) 16.

99 Van Zyl Smit (n 3 above) 52 observes that the determination of this period is 'inevitably arbitrary'.

100 Van Zyl Smit (n 10 above) 195.

101 As above.

102 As above. As at 10 December 2009, the ICTY had amended its RPE 44 times.

room for the application of different criteria in subsequent hearings.[103] Consequently, the criteria in Rule 223 may be applied independently.

Interestingly, the factors set out in the ICC Statute and RPE do not bear a direct connection to the purposes of punishment. On the contrary, some of them render the reduction process an award ceremony. Reduction may be awarded for co-operating with the Court or assisting victims. There is no clarity as to when such co-operation or assistance should be made. However, from the wording of the Statute, which states 'early and continuing willingness' to co-operate, it can be said that co-operation before conviction may also be considered. This clearly puts offenders who plead guilty at a great advantage. Since there is nothing to preclude such an offender from benefiting from his plea both at the sentencing and reduction stages,[104] the ICC will have to distinguish its treatment of such factors at the two stages.[105] Other factors, such as assisting victims and the prisoner's dissociation from the crime, erroneously assume that prisoners generally accept their being guilty after conviction by a court of law.[106]

The extent to which a prisoner may assist victims is greatly limited by the very fact of imprisonment itself. Prisoners with good connections outside the prison and sufficient finances would undoubtedly be better placed to offer such assistance. This would influence a positive attitude from victims, hence it would increase the chances of release for the concerned prisoner even more. It is not clear what action should be taken for the benefit of victims to qualify as 'significant'. Would an apology suffice? The Court may look to the impact of the action on the victims in order to assess its significance. The major challenge with such an assessment is the identification of victims, who may be countless.

The problem of taking into account the acknowledgment of the offence or dissociation therefrom is illustrated by the case of *Leger v France*, where the applicant's claim of innocence throughout his incarceration following a conviction of murder was seen as evidence of a lack of 'serious effort to readjust to society'.[107] This factor may also face evidential challenges. Would it be appropriate for the Court to look to the prisoner's communications with other people? I think not. It would be improper for a prisoner's friends or therapists to testify against him on this score based on his conversations with them. It is therefore submitted that acknowledgment of the offence should not be a major consideration, if at all.

---

103 Art 110(5) allows the Court to apply 'such criteria as provided in the Rules' in subsequent hearings.

104 Hoel (n 80 above) 65.

105 See the discussion at 4.1.1 above.

106 An offender can have less reason for assisting victims if he or she does not accept responsibility for their victimisation.

107 *Leger v France*, Aapplication 19324/02, judgment 11 April 2006, ECHR. For a detailed analysis of this case, see Stokes (n 2 above).

The prospect of resocialisation and successful resettlement can be criticised as having no relation with the punishment of the prisoner in the first place, save perhaps for its remote connection to rehabilitation. Resocialisation is dependent on a wide variety of factors, most of which are beyond the control of the prisoner. These include the attitude of the community towards the prisoner and the prospect of securing a job. Chances for success in these matters for the class of perpetrators to be tried by the ICC are indeed slim.

Continued detention based on the perceptions of victims would tend to be arbitrary. Some victims are more vengeful than others, while some take more time to heal. This is in turn related to the impact of the atrocities in the first place. Such considerations may also lead to the unequal treatment of prisoners. It would be inappropriate to detain a person simply because the victims concerned are still aggrieved, hence against the idea of his early release.

It is foreseeable that the determination of social instability would pose a great difficulty to the Court. It would be an affront to justice to deny release because it may cause social upheaval,[108] a situation over which the prisoner has no control. Such incarceration would not be 'punishment', but rather an abuse of imprisonment for convenience. This would result in arbitrary detention and degrading treatment. After all, the reactions of society are not considered in assessing the guilt of an accused person.

The individual circumstances of the prisoner, as envisaged in Rule 223, appear to be more appropriate. However, the problem is that such consideration is only possible after the prescribed period. A prisoner may be in a critical health or mental condition before the minimum period has elapsed. It is submitted that a more reasonable position would be achieved by the inclusion of a general proviso to article 110(3), to the effect that a reduction of sentence may be considered at any time after sentencing on medical, humanitarian or other compelling grounds.[109] There is no reason for consideration of age at this stage when the age of the prisoner at that point can be deduced during sentencing. A prisoner can be spared the turmoil of being a lifer if due account of his age is taken during sentencing.

4.3 Final observations on release systems

The ICC has tacitly set the preventive element of life imprisonment at 25 years. Once this has been served, the grounds for continued detention must be based upon considerations of risk and dangerousness; any other grounds would necessarily carry the risk of arbitrariness.[110] While considerations of dangerousness can be accommodated into the

108 Van Zyl Smit (n 3 above) 48.
109 Van Zyl Smit (n 3 above) 52.
110 Stokes (n 2 above) 293.

'interests of justice' category in the *ad hoc* tribunal system, they can hardly be read into the ICC's article 110(4) or Rule 223. In any case, predictions of recidivism are 'notoriously hard to make', especially in politically-motivated crimes.[111] Indeed, do convicts like Rutaganda, Akayesu, Kambanda and other lifers pose a danger to society? Can they reoffend in the absence of the social conditions and political climate that facilitated their actions that have been characterised as international crimes? It is unfortunate that criminal law at times decontextualises offences from the circumstances in which they were committed.[112] Gross human rights violations are essentially group crimes; one can hardly commit them singly. Neither are they necessarily connected to previous criminal conduct that may predict future dangerousness.[113] Therefore, the real question should not be whether the prisoner will be able to live a law-abiding life, but whether it is abusive to continue to detain him further.[114] In the long run, despite the possibility of release, continued detention beyond a certain period will raise other issues of fundamental rights.[115]

5 Conclusion

This article has examined life sentences under international criminal law. Save for rehearsing aggravating and mitigating factors,[116] the tribunals have paid little attention to justifying the imposition of life imprisonment. No wonder their sentencing judgments have been criticised as 'repetitive and ground-clearing exercise[s]'.[117] There is a need for a more cautious approach to life imprisonment because of its potential to deny liberty indefinitely, especially where no independent release system is in place.

The uncertainty of release weighs heavily on lifers,[118] and its denial has 'as much an impact on an offender as the initial sentencing decision'.[119] Legal certainty as to the possibility of such release is therefore imperative. It is recommended that the criteria for release

---

111 Van Zyl Smit (n 10 above) 194; see generally N Padfield (ed) *Who to release? Parole, fairness and criminal justice* (2007).

112 P Allot 'Deliver us from social evil' Guest Lecture Series of the Office of the Prosecutor, 11 August 2004, The Hague, para 2.68.

113 AL Smeulers 'What transforms ordinary people into gross human rights violators?' in SC Carey & SC Poe (eds) *Understanding human rights violations: New systematic studies* (2004) 239-256.

114 De Beco (n 14 above). There can be no guarantee that any individual will live a law-abiding life.

115 Fura-Sandström J, dissenting, in *Leger* (n 107 above) para 14.

116 Pursuant to arts 23 & 24 of the ICTR and ICTY Statutes respectively.

117 Van Zyl Smit (n 52 above) 9.

118 United Nations Crime Prevention and Justice Branch *Life imprisonment* (1994) 20.

119 Van Zyl Smit (n 3 above) 52.

should be clearly spelt out in the Statutes of the *ad hoc* tribunals. The ICC regime promises better treatment of life imprisonment. However, its release mechanism is quite inflexible, with the Court only able to consider reduction of a sentence after 25 years in the case of lifers. Further, the manner of its implementation, particularly considerations of eligibility for release, raises significant challenges.

The position taken by international criminal law with regard to life imprisonment is undoubtedly in need of revision in light of the challenges raised in the article. It is hoped that this will be done in the near future to promote the protection of the human rights of offenders facing trials before international tribunals.

[11]

Death Penalty Mitigation: A Challenge for Social Work Education

Joyce G. Reed
Glenn E. Rohrer

ABSTRACT. Recent literature suggests that the preparation of students for changing practice environments requires the establishment of non-traditional field placement opportunities through creative university-agency partnerships. This article describes a field education/capital mitigation project developed by a school of social work and the state death penalty resource center. The project provides an example of a unique, collaborative educational effort; it reflects the increasing recognition by the courts of the contribution of social work to the understanding of human behavior; and it illustrates the role of the profession in the expanding field of forensic social work. *[Article copies available for a fee from The Haworth Document Delivery Service: 1-800-342-9678. E-mail address: <getinfo@haworthpressinc.com> Website: <http://www.haworthpressinc.com>]*

KEYWORDS. Capital mitigation, capital sentencing, death penalty mitigation, death penalty sentencing, field education, forensic social work, mitigation, mitigation specialist

In this last decade of the millennium, the social work profession must seek innovative ways to educate students for practice in a world far

---

Joyce G. Reed, JD, LLM, is Assistant Professor, and Glenn E. Rohrer, MDiv, MSW, PhD, is Associate Professor, School of Social Work and Criminal Justice Studies, East Carolina University, Ragsdale Hall, Greenville, NC 27858-4353.

The authors wish to acknowledge the contributions of Lena W. Carawan, MSW, ABD, Associate Director of Field Education, and the students who participated in this project.

A version of this paper was presented at the Annual Program Meeting of the Council on Social Work Education, February, 1996, Washington, DC.

more complicated, violent, and problematic than most of us would have imagined a generation ago (Schneck, Grossman, & Glassman, 1991, p. 16). As social and human problems become increasingly complex, the continuing challenge for social work educators is to prepare students with the latest intervention strategies and to develop appropriate field placement settings designed to implement these strategies in diverse practice environments. The field education office is called on to explore creative university-agency linkages, to "reach out and develop learning opportunities that reflect changing consumer groups, new practice interventions, and current social issues" (Ruffolo & Miller, 1994, p. 311).

"Forensic social work" is a relatively new term applied to practice that focuses on the interface between the legal and human service systems (Barker & Branson, 1993, p. 1). The legal/justice system, however, does not present an entirely new practice arena. Many early social workers served the courts by investigating child abuse and providing expert testimony of their findings. They also worked in prisons and courts as probation officers and in crime-infested neighborhoods with youth gangs (Barker & Branson). During the last decade, courts and attorneys have recognized a need for social evaluation of defendants and professional assistance in preparing mitigation evidence in death penalty cases. This emerging area of forensic practice places social workers on capital defense teams and creates opportunities for social workers committed to social/criminal justice. This article describes a field education/mitigation project designed to assist appointed counsel in capital cases and to train students as mitigation specialists.

CAPITAL PUNISHMENT AND THE LEGACY OF LOCKETT

Mitigation in Death Penalty Cases

Since the reinstatement of the death penalty in the United States, the Supreme Court has struggled to provide guidance to juries charged with the ultimate life-or-death decision in capital cases. In 1978, the Court determined that our Constitution requires that jurors be given the opportunity to consider, as a *mitigating factor*, any aspects of the defendant's character, record, or circumstances of the crime that might provide a basis for a sentence less than death (*Lockett v. Ohio,* 1978). The Court concluded that the death penalty is so "profoundly different" from other criminal penalties, that individualized determinations are critical; each capital defendant must be treated with "that degree of respect due the uniqueness of the individual" (*Lockett v. Ohio,* 1978, p. 605). Through *Lockett* and its progeny, the Court has left little doubt as to the significance of presenting for the jury's evaluation any and all potentially mitigating factors.

The individualized determination mandated by *Lockett* requires that counsel present information to the jury that goes beyond merely portraying the defendant as a human being. It must include a showing of *what kind* of a human being the defendant is and *how* he or she got to be that way (Stebbins, 1988). A death penalty case is tried in two parts: during the first, or judgment phase, the jury determines the guilt or innocence of the defendant; if the defendant is found guilty, and there is evidence of at least one aggravating factor, the court will go forward with the second part, the sentencing phase. During the second part of the trial, the jury will weigh aggravating and mitigating factors and decide whether the defendant should be sentenced to life in prison or be executed. Death penalty statutes typically specify a number of mitigating factors such as age or mental disturbance. Most include, as well, a "catch-all" subsection allowing for the introduction of *any evidence* "stemming from the diverse frailties of humankind" (*Woodson v. North Carolina,* 1976, p. 304) that a jury might find mitigating. Thus, the evidence that might be appropriately introduced in mitigation arguably embraces the full range of human behavior and experience.

The presentation of mitigating evidence is not limited to the sentencing phase of trial. Properly introduced during the guilt or judgment phase, mitigating evidence serves a dual purpose: First, it may lead a jury to convict the defendant of a lesser offense than first-degree murder; and second, it provides the groundwork for the penalty phase by presenting the jury with compelling reasons for imposing a life sentence rather than death. Thus, the ultimate defense objective is not to excuse culpable behavior, but to convince the jury that the defendant's life should be spared. Presenting the particularized and human [hi]story of the defendant and the crime provides the best hope of winning a life sentence (Hudson, Core & Schorr, 1987; Logan, 1989; Stebbins, 1988). The jury must be able to "see the world from [the defendant's] perspective, i.e., to appreciate his subjective experience" (Blume, 1995, p. 10). Stebbins (1988) urges that in order to succeed, the defense team must explain the crime to the jury and the court:

> Unless one accepts the theory of inherent evil, there is an explanation for every crime . . . The 'typical' defendant has not spent his entire life plotting to commit this one murder or murders. Influences beyond the control of the defendant, impacting on his ability to control himself, have been working on him since he was born and even before. *It is the collection of data on these influences and an explanation of how these added up to develop the psychological makeup of the individual that is the process of mitigation* [italics added]. (p. 34)

Social Workers as Mitigation Specialists

Social work expertise is particularly relevant to the task of developing mitigation evidence. Social workers are trained to look at problems from the viewpoint of a social systems perspective and to examine individual behavior within the larger social context. Those elements of the defendant's history that may assist the defense in its life-preserving effort are the kinds of problems that family members are not eager to reveal to strangers, even when the life of a loved one is at stake. Sometimes they are "middle-class" problems that are simply not adequately addressed for the poor: health, mental health, special educational needs, or disabilities. Often, more serious issues exist: family criminal activity; physical, mental or sexual abuse; substance abuse; post-traumatic stress syndrome; organic brain damage; . . . the list includes practically all physical, mental, and psycho-social injuries and deficiencies. Social workers possess the interviewing and investigative techniques required to gather this information, even when people are hesitant to reveal it. In addition, they have the evaluation/assessment skills required to prepare for the jury a comprehensive and comprehensible view of the individual within the environment that has shaped his or her life.

A historical commitment to social justice and to working with disenfranchised populations (Rogge, 1993; Ruffolo & Miller, 1994; Schneck, 1991) further qualifies social workers to provide assistance in death penalty cases and strongly suggests mitigation as an appropriate area for social work practice and education. Capital defendants are disproportionately poor and black (Kleck, 1981; Mann, 1993; NAACP-LDF, 1992; Reiman, 1990; Schaefer, 1993; Vito, 1995). Indigent defendants are frequently inarticulate and unable to aid in their own defense. Further, since their only option is court-appointed counsel, "they tend to be suspicious, hostile, and critical toward their attorney from the beginning of the case" (Mann, 1993, p. 177, citing Skolnick, 1967). Minority defendants, especially, distrust and criticize their public defenders or court-appointed attorneys because they are generally white, middle-class professionals. To these defendants, appointed attorneys appear to have more in common culturally with the lawyers and judges than with their clients, the majority of whom are poor, minority, and of a different socio-economic class (Mann, 1993, citing NMAC, 1980). Social workers, by education, experience, and cultural sensitivity, are able to provide invaluable assistance to the defense team in ameliorating the interface of capital defendants with their attorneys and the legal system.

The Capital Defense Team

In capital cases, the team approach has proven the best method of increasing the chances of a life sentence (Blume, 1995; Hudson, Core & Schorr, 1987). The attorneys appointed to represent the defendant assemble the team and retain ultimate responsibility for the development and presentation of the case. The remainder of the defense team generally consists of criminal investigators, mitigation specialists, psychologists, psychiatrists, and includes, as well, the defendant and other witnesses. Because the defendant's story is crucial to the development of the case for both parts of the trial, several authors suggest that the selection of a defense team should begin with a social worker as a mitigation specialist (Blume; Hudson et al.; Stebbins, 1988). According to Blume (p. 9), "it is critical [to] obtain a social worker . . . to assist in compiling and understanding the social and medical history," and to begin organizing and interpreting the data into coherent themes. When the initial investigation reveals a need for additional evaluation of the defendant, the mitigation specialist helps identify other experts. Depending upon the nature of the findings and the unique features of the case, professionals from other fields may be brought in to explain the effects of problems beyond the expertise of the social worker/mitigation specialist or psychologist (Stebbins). Seeking assistance from experts in the medical/mental health fields has become routine; and increasingly, social scientists are being called upon to explain the effects of poverty, racism, homelessness, etc.

As the defense team works toward trial, each expert prepares an independent report. Most experts rely on the social history, which provides an essential foundation for their evaluations (Andrews, 1991) and corroborating data to support their testimony (Stebbins, 1988). During the trial, the expert witnesses function as impartial educators whose testimony provides information that the jury can use to evaluate the facts of the case (Andrews). Since the mid-1980s, social workers have been accepted by the courts as having sufficient knowledge and skill to be qualified as expert witnesses in several fields of practice (Gothard, 1989). More recently, as their contributions in the area of sentence mitigation have been recognized by the courts, social workers have begun to provide expert testimony as to their findings. Social workers who are members of a capital defense team do not always testify as experts at trial, however. In many cases, the greater value of social worker/mitigation specialists lies in the application of their assessment techniques, practice experience, and organizational skills to the development of the mitigation case. If not testifying, they frequently assist counsel in the selection of jurors and in preparing witnesses for trial. Throughout the case, from initial interview until the final verdict, the social worker/mitigation specialist functions as a team coordinator and as a liaison between the attorney/defense team and the defendant and his or her family.

FIELD EDUCATION IN DEATH PENALTY MITIGATION

Field Education in Non-Traditional Environments

According to CSWE Curriculum Policy Statements, social work education is intended "to prepare competent and effective social work professionals who are committed to practice that includes services to the poor and oppressed, and who work to alleviate poverty, oppression, and discrimination" (CSWE, 1992a; CSWE, 1992b). In order to achieve that goal, the literature suggests that the field education component of the social work program must create opportunities for students to engage in practice with diverse populations, especially those with special needs (Cohen, 1990; McClelland, 1991; Ruffolo & Miller, 1994, citing Bennett, Maddox & Lager, 1992). Indigent capital defendants present just such a population: They are typically poor and black, often with little social support and multiple social problems. What Cohen (1990) said of student service to the homeless mentally ill applies equally to work with capital defendants:

> Social work's historic commitment to poor and vulnerable client populations provides a knowledge and value base upon which practice with [these clients] rests. There is a need to build on this foundation, to develop and teach particular practice approaches and specific skills geared to work with this extremely disadvantaged and disaffiliated population. (p. 4)

Involvement in death penalty cases provides an excellent opportunity for students to apply classroom learning to a societal problem and to use newly-acquired professional skills in a unique and appropriate practice environment.

Social work practice is not static; it adapts problem-solving interventions to new combinations of issues, populations, and settings (Rogge, 1993). The preparation of students for practice in the twenty-first century will require field coordinators to investigate placements in which students may move beyond traditional assignments. It will be essential to explore opportunities for students to extend new services and resources, or to develop innovative models for approaching client problems (Schneck, 1991). Current literature suggests that the changing environment of social work practice challenges educators to create new paradigms and fresh approaches to advocacy, service, and the education and training of our students (Jarman-Rhode, McFall, Kolar & Strom, 1997). The importance of developing creative university-agency partnerships to meet this challenge has been the focus of several authors (Bennett et al., 1992; Bogo & Globerman, 1995; Grossman, 1991; Marshack & Glassman, 1991; Mokuau & Ewalt, 1993; Rogge; Ruffolo & Miller, 1994; Schneck). Most recently, Jarman-Rhode et al. describe a number of projects connecting schools with agencies inside and outside the profession. They take the position that preparing social work students for practice in the future demands such collaborative efforts.

Field Education/Mitigation Project

The field education/mitigation project described here is the result of a partnership between the East Carolina University School of Social Work and Criminal Justice Studies and the North Carolina Resource Center. The university is located in an area of the state that is predominantly rural and poor, showing income levels well below the statewide average (ECU, 1993, p. 47). Homicide presents a serious regional problem, and the state is one of five states with the highest numbers of executions (Vito, 1995). Unfortunately, legal services available to indigent clients in the region are very limited. Only two counties in the judicial division are served by public defender offices; indigent defendants in the remaining thirty counties are represented by court-appointed counsel (AOC, 1992). As is true in many states, appointed counsel are most often solo practitioners and lack experience in capital cases. Further, due to decreases in government funding, the Resource Center has been limited in its ability to extend legal assistance and technical support to attorneys in the far rural corners of the state. Prior to the establishment of the field education/mitigation project, school faculty had worked with Resource Center staff on issues related to death penalty litigation. Subsequent appointment as mitigation specialists in two local cases afforded an opportunity for faculty to involve students in capital mitigation and to provide service to the legal community in the eastern part of the state.

An important objective of the project was to train selected students in the investigation and preparation of mitigation evidence. In the initial term of the project, a graduate social work student and an undergraduate criminal justice student completed their field education under the supervision of project faculty. Project faculty included a social work professor/mitigation specialist and a criminal justice professor/attorney. They were responsible for instructing and guiding students in gathering data and in applying fundamental social work techniques to capital sentencing investigations. The students selected for placement became part of a capital defense team. They assisted appointed counsel in the discovery of potentially mitigating evidence and its development for trial. Under the guidance of faculty, professional staff, and defense attorneys, student involvement in cases included the following: interviewing defendants, witnesses, relatives, employers, teachers and other community members; reviewing school, military and medical records; compiling social histories; constructing genograms; identifying appropriate experts; and assisting in the preparation of questions for potential jurors and in their selection at trial. The students worked together on all aspects of the project. Generally, the social work student collected data and assisted in compiling social histories; the criminal justice student assisted in investigations and conducted supportive legal research.

Evaluation of the Project

"Schools of social work have a tripartite mission consisting of the transmission of knowledge (teaching), the development of knowledge (scholarship), and the application of knowledge to societal problems (service)" (Mokuau & Ewalt, 1993, p. 328, citing Task Force on Quality in Graduate Social Work Education, 1984, pp. 11-12). According to Mokuau and Ewalt, the integration of the three dimensions of that mission is "requisite to the enrichment of social work education" (p. 336). The mitigation project provided such integration. Consistent with its established educational objectives, the project supported the teaching mission of the school from both a theoretical and an applied base. Project faculty employed case studies and practice situations as the basis for class discussion and analysis in a variety of teaching contexts. Further, project students were able to integrate classroom knowledge with their practicum experiences, which were then shared with classmates. As one of the participating students wrote in her evaluation:

> I put the education I have received . . . to practical use, and it all came together and made sense. Very often you learn something during a semester, then completely forget it. This internship served as a refresher course for practically EVERYTHING that I had learned in my classes.

In regard to scholarship, the project presented a number of research possibilities from both pedagogical and substantive perspectives. The service component was advanced by the very nature of student and faculty involvement in the project. As members of various capital defense teams, project participants applied their professional expertise to a social problem of life-and-death proportions.

Many human problems encountered in social work practice are actually, or potentially, very serious. Few, however, hold the dramatic implications for the client that are presented in capital mitigation. The practice is, therefore, quite tedious and carries with it tremendous responsibility. In addition, it embraces ethical and philosophical concerns that are generally not present in other areas. Imposition of the death penalty continues to be a controversial issue, often evoking intense and emotional responses. Inasmuch as the social worker/mitigation specialist is obligated to serve without reservation the client who wants to live, one who is ambivalent about the process should not serve on a capital defense team (Andrews, 1991). For the welfare of students and the integrity of the program, participants in this type of field setting must be selected with great care. Interviews with the applicant and recommendations of advisors or major professors are essential.

It is not unusual for students entering the field to experience anxiety related to the assumption of professional responsibility (Grossman, Levine-Jordano & Shearer, 1991, citing Towle, 1954). These feelings may be exacerbated for the student selected for placement with a mitigation team. The normal apprehensions about their readiness for practice and the quality of their skills may be compounded by fears about working with extremely vulnerable clients or entering unfamiliar practice settings (Cohen, 1990). Field educators should consider these subjective reactions within a framework that helps students recognize, cope with, and use their emotional responses to meet the needs of clients and further the students' goals as learners (Grossman et al.). Mitigation is an area where students may also experience very strong positive or negative reactions toward their clients or to the practice setting. Few students have had any contact with people in prison; fewer still with anyone charged with first-degree murder. Even a student who has self-selected, and who has been carefully screened by faculty for a mitigation internship, may respond uncharacteristically to this particular client population. Other problems encountered by students may relate to the necessity of traveling in unfamiliar communities and working in surroundings that are often unpleasant or possibly dangerous.

Just as placement with a capital defense team is not appropriate for all students, such a project may not be suitable for all programs or at all times. Non-traditional placements often depend upon the existence of an independent faculty-agency relationship or the leadership of a faculty-based field instructor with special skills. As observed by Bogo and Globerman (1995) and Mokuau and Ewalt (1993), subsequent availability of these unique field situations may require the continued involvement of a particular faculty member. His or her retirement or departure from the program may mean the elimination of the placement. While such factors may present planning difficulties for field education coordinators, these creative partnerships are worth cultivating. They present exciting possibilities for enriching the professional educational experience-for students and faculty.

CONCLUSION

This innovative field education project demonstrates the increasing recognition by the legal community of the social work profession as a legitimate contributor to the understanding of human behavior. The logical fit between the mitigation task and the social work perspective makes it clear that the profession has much to offer to the courts and to the pursuit of social justice. While mitigation in capital murder cases is a very narrow field and will not become a major area of practice, it is representative of the expanding opportunities in the field of forensic social work. The mitigation project offers, further, an example of the non-traditional, collaborative efforts that will be necessary to educate and prepare social work students for practice in the next century. As the literature suggests, and this project affirms, such creative university-agency partnerships provide opportunities for students and faculty to explore unique professional liaisons, to extend services to changing or emerging client populations, and to develop new protocols for approaching and responding to contemporary problems.

REFERENCES

Administrative Office of the Courts. (1994). *The judicial system in North Carolina*. Raleigh, NC: Author.

Andrews, A. B. (1991). Social work expert testimony regarding mitigation in capital sentencing proceedings. *Social Work 36(5)*, 440-45.

Barker, R. & Branson, D. (1993). *Forensic Social Work*. New York: The Haworth Press, Inc.

Bennett, C., Maddox, K., & Lager, P. (1992). *Foundation training for community based field instructors*. Paper presented at the 37th Annual Program Meeting of the Council on Social Work Education, New Orleans, LA.

Blume, J. (1995). Mental health issues in criminal cases: The elements of a competent and reliable mental health examination. *The Advocate, 17*(4), 4-12.

Bogo, M., & Globerman, J. (1995). Creating effective university-field partnerships: An analysis of two inter-organization models for field education. *Journal of Teaching in Social Work, 11*(1/2), 177-92.

Cohen, M. B. (1990). Practice with homeless mentally ill clients: A challenge for field education. *Journal of Teaching in Social Work, 4*(2), 3-18.

Council on Social Work Education. (1992a). *Curriculum policy statement for baccalaureate degree programs in social work education.* Alexandria, VA: Author.

Council on Social Work Education. (1992b). *Curriculum policy statement for master's degree programs in social work education.* Alexandria, VA: Author.

East Carolina University [ECU] Regional Development Institute. (1993). *Project EAST Profiles.* Greenville, NC: Author.

Gothard, S. (1989). Power in the court: The social worker as an expert witness. *Social Work, 34*, 65-67.

Grossman, B. (1991). Themes and variations: The political economy of field instruction. In D. Schneck, B. Grossman, & U. Glassman (Eds.). *Field education in social Work: Contemporary issues and trends* (pp. 36-46). Dubuque, IA: Kendall/Hunt Publishing Company.

Grossman, B., Levine-Jordano, N., & Shearer, P. (1991). Working with students' emotional reactions in the field: An education framework. In D. Schneck, B. Grossman, & U. Glassman (Eds.). *Field education in social Work: Contemporary issues and trends* (pp. 205-216). Dubuque, IA: Kendall/Hunt Publishing Company.

Hudson, J., Core, J., & Schorr, S. (1987, June). Using the mitigation specialist and the team approach. *the CHAMPION*, 33-36.

Jarman-Rhode, L., McFall, J., Kolar, P. & Strom, G. (1997). The changing context of social work practice: Implications and recommendations for social work educators. *Journal of Social Work Education, 33*(1), 29-46.

Kleck, G. (1981). Racial discrimination in sentencing: A critical evaluation of the evidence with additional evidence on the death penalty. *American Sociological Review, 43* 783-805.

Lockett v. Ohio, 438 U.S. 586 (1978).

Logan, D. (1989, Sept./Oct.). Is it mitigation or aggravation? Troublesome areas of defense evidence in capital sentencing. *CACJ/Forum*, 14-20.

Mann, C. (1993). *Unequal justice: A question of color.* Bloomington, IN: University Press.

Marshack, E., & Glassman, U. (1991). Innovative models for field instruction: Departing from traditional methods. In D. Schneck, B. Grossman, & U. Glassman (Eds.). *Field education in social work: Contemporary issues and trends* (pp. 84-95). Dubuque, Iowa: Kendall/Hunt Publishing Company.

McClelland, R. (1991). Innovation in field education. In D. Schneck, B. Grossman, & U. Glassman (Eds.). *Field education in social work: Contemporary issues and trends* (pp.177-184). Dubuque, IA: Kendall/Hunt Publishing Company.

Mokuau, N., & Ewalt, P. (1993). School-agency collaboration: Enriching teaching, scholarship, and service in state hospital placements. *Journal of Social Work Education, 39*(3), 328-337.

National Association for the Advancement of Colored People-Legal Defense Fund [NAACP-LDF] (1992, Spring). *Death row U.S.A.* New York: NAACP Legal Defense and Educational Fund, Inc.

National Minority Advisory Council on Criminal Justice [NMAC]. (1980). *The inequality of justice.* Washington, DC: U. S. Department of Justice.

Reiman, J. (1990). *The rich get richer and the poor get prison* (3d ed.). New York: Macmillan.

Rogge, M. (1993). Social work, disenfranchised communities, and the natural environment: Field education opportunities. *Journal of Social Work Education, 29*(1) 111-120.

Ruffolo, M., & Miller, P. (1994). An advocacy/empowerment model of organizing: Developing university-agency partnerships. *Journal of Social Work Education, 30(3)*, 310-116.

Schaefer, R. (1993). *Racial and ethnic groups* (5th ed.). New York: Harper Collins.

Schneck, D. (1991). The leadership opportunity in fieldwork for responding to change. In D. Schneck, B. Grossman, & U. Glassman (Eds.). *Field education in social work: Contemporary issues and trends* (p.78-79). Dubuque, IA: Kendall/ Hunt Publishing Company.

Schneck, D., Grossman, B. & Glassman, U. (Eds.). (1991). *Field education in social work: Contemporary issues and trends.* Dubuque, IA: Kendall/Hunt Publishing Company.

Skolnick, J. (1967). Social control and the adversary system. *Journal of Conflict Resolution, 11*, 53-70.

Stebbins, D. (1988, April). Psychologists and mitigation: Diagnosis to explanation. *the CHAMPION*. 34-38.

Task Force on Quality in Graduate Social Work Education (1984). *Toward excellence in graduate social work education in the United States.* New York: National Conference of Deans and Directors of Schools of Social Work.

Towle, C. (1954). *The learner in education for the professions.* Chicago: University of Chicago Press.

Vito, G. (1995). The penalty of death in the next century. In J. Klofas & S. Stojkovic (Eds.). *Crime and justice in the year 2010* (pp. 254-257). Belmont, CA: Wadsworth.

Woodson v. North Carolina. 428 U.S. 280 (1976).

[12]

The Global Capital Punishment Litigation Landscape

Kerry Ann Akers

Over the past twenty years, the global capital punishment landscape has altered considerably; the abolition movement has garnered unprecedented momentum, with the number of countries which implement the death penalty at an all-time low, there is much to celebrate. The abolition movement itself has also evolved in this time, in its holistic quarters, to facilitate developments in the expanding human rights sphere, and in its litigation quarters, to facilitate post-colonial judicial change. Although, when it comes to measuring success, much of the abolition debate remains static, measuring the movement's success narrowly, and ignoring the wider ramifications of many abolition strategies. Evolution of the abolition debate is welcome, but corresponding recalibration of the measures of success is also required. Disturbing patterns have emerged following litigation-based abolition strategies, largely led by foreign lawyers. Patterns such as the introduction of whole of life sentences, neglect of beneficiaries, entrenching conservative constitutional interpretations, and stifling of sustainable local capacity building, all serve as worrying examples of a damaging pattern, ignored by the propagators. The fallout from such litigation strategies is further bolstered by advocacy groups who choose to ignore such ramifications in order to present the facts about abolition in a consistently positive light. This short-sighted approach to advocacy reinforces bad practice in order to demonstrate the success of the abolition movement, rather than detract from the progress made in such cases with a pragmatic analysis which would ultimately serve to further a holistic human rights based approach to abolition.

Most pressingly, given the rate of abolition paired with the large audiences receptive to major advocacy groups, is the persistent silence on the issue of alternative sanctions to the death penalty. Despite the number of supporters for advocacy groups such as Amnesty International, which have tirelessly campaigned for abolition of the death penalty, it is a subject which very few abolition activists, let alone supporters of such groups have even considered, as major advocacy groups like Amnesty remain silent on the alternative sanction with which to replace the death penalty. Whilst life without parole sentences are advocated as viable options by foreign lawyers litigating across the Commonwealth, where prison conditions violate the most basic of human rights and prison systems are ill-equipped to manage lifers, in the UK the sentence has been challenged in the European Court of Human Rights (*Cases of Vinter and Others v. The United Kingdom* (Applications nos. 66069/09 and 130/10 and 3896/10)). Although refreshing to finally see attention being paid to the subject, the European Court's decision in this case upheld the practice of life without parole, despite mounting research and numbers of advocates acknowledging the non-reviewable sentence as a violation of the prohibition of inhuman and degrading treatment. To accept the replacement of the death penalty, with another practice which violates the same human rights that the death penalty does, only bolsters the practice and principles which underpin capital punishment and negates efforts at holistic change for a humane justice system.

Many of the major cases celebrated in the abolition sphere demonstrate the maintenance of the damaging patterns propagated through litigation strategies. The most troubling element of this pattern is undoubtedly the regularity with which such damaging strategies have been replicated repeatedly over the last twenty years.

***Pratt & Morgan v. The Queen*, [1993] UKPC 1**

Led by London-based lawyers, the case of Pratt determined the death penalty itself was constitutional in Jamaica, but the delay in administering it was not. A delay of more than five years in administering capital punishment constitutes inhuman treatment and warrants a commutation of the death sentence to life imprisonment. The litigation strategy relied on the dysfunctional administration of the judicial system, which failed to deal with cases expeditiously, leaving people to languish on death row. This inefficiency was capitalised upon by the litigation team, which led to a ruling that a delay of more than five years on death row invalidated the application of the death penalty. This meant that should the Jamaican judicial system evolve and develop into a robust and efficient administration, the death penalty would be a viable sentence once more. This imposition proved an obstacle to the development of the justice system and deterred what would have been healthy changes to a dysfunctional system, rendering capital defendants in a better position being tried by a faulty, protracted system, than by an effective, expedient system.

This litigation challenge stifled progress in Jamaica's justice system and eventually led to a restriction of rights beyond that prior to Pratt. The justice sector remained underfunded, as rights proponents were now unlikely to want to streamline the appeals system, lest they jeopardise death row prisoners. In addition to this, the Jamaican government resisted the Privy Council decision at the first opportunity, not only voiding Pratt and Morgan but actually prohibiting the Courts from questioning the constitutionality of any pre-existing punishment and restricting the right to appeal through drafting a new constitution. The case prompted the removal of the protections afforded by the 1st Optional Protocol of the International Convention on Civil and Political Rights (ICCPR) by withdrawing from them. This in turn prompted the same reaction in Trinidad & Tobago, followed by Guyana. This has had the effect of denying to all citizens of these countries the right to individual petition of the monitoring body of the ICCPR, the Human Rights Committee [HRC], if they believe that any of their human rights under the ICCPR have been violated. Not only did the litigation strategy in *Pratt* lead to the entrenching of the death penalty, it also caused further reaching consequences abroad, denying all citizens protection against violations of any human right.

Similarly, alongside a host of celebrated litigation challenges which London Panel lawyers initiated in the wake of *Pratt*, such as challenges to the mandatory death penalty which qualified the use of life imprisonment as an alternative (*Fox v. The Queen* (St Christopher & Nevis) [2002] 2 AC 284; *Roodal v. The State* (Trinidad & Tobago) [2004] 2 WLR 652), *Pratt* facilitated the implementation and validation of alternatives to the death penalty such as natural life with hard labour across the Caribbean.

Attorney General v. Susan Kigula & 417 Others, Constitutional Appeal No. 03 of 2006, Supreme Court of Uganda at Mengo, Jan. 21, 2009

Shortly after the decision in *Roodal* was overturned in *Matthew -v- The State (Trinidad & Tobago) [2004] 64 WLR 412*, reinstating the mandatory death penalty, lawyers set about replicating the same challenge in Uganda. The decision in Kigula abolished the mandatory death penalty, but confirmed the constitutionality of the death penalty in Uganda. The litigation strategy in *Kigula* replicated those employed in the Caribbean with regards to the issue of the mandatory death penalty and the issue of delay. With regards to the issue of delay, the decision differed to the Caribbean jurisprudence and rendered the utility of the challenge effectively futile. The fallout from the decision was predictably damaging and reflected the lack of consideration for country-specific nuance.

As a result of the *Kigula* ruling, access to legal aid was diminished, as was an automatic appeal system for capital offences. The meaning of a life sentence was increased from the statutory twenty years, to mean whole of life and led to non-capital defendants receiving increased sentences as a result (*Tigo Steven v Uganda*, Criminal Appeal No. 08 of 2009, [2011] UGSC 7).

Similar to *Pratt*'s ripple effect cross the Caribbean, *Kigula* prompted a host of similar challenges across the region. In Malawi, the case of *Kafantayeni*, [2007] MWHC I mimicked *Kigula* in so far as its challenge to the mandatory death penalty, but did not raise the issue of the death penalty's constitutionality per se, nor did it raise the question of delay. This fragmented replication of the *Kigula* challenge neglected to address delay, which has repeatedly been identified as the most pressing issue in Malawi's homicide trials. Similar to *Kigula,* the beneficiaries of the case are still waiting to reap any benefit from the case and life imprisonment has been endorsed as the alternative to death.

Further to this, an even more fragmented challenge in Kenya followed. The case of *Godfrey Ngotho Mutiso v. Republic* [2010] eKLR assisted by foreign lawyers in the same vein as the *Kafantayeni* challenge, neglecting issues of delay and the constitutionality of the death penalty per se. However, the challenge was further fragmented, only addressing the mandatory death penalty in cases of murder, leading to the bizarre result of the mandatory death penalty for murder being abolished, but the mandatory death penalty for armed robbery remaining intact.

Yong Vui Kong v PP, My 2010

Following almost twenty years of challenges with chequered results in the Caribbean and Africa a similar strategy was embarked on, challenging Asia's mandatory death penalty. The Singapore Court of Appeal was unwilling to accept the merit of the challenge, upholding the constitutionality of the mandatory death penalty.

However, the negative impact of the challenge went beyond mere confirmation of the constitutionality of the mandatory death penalty and replicated the retaliatory approach taken by many of the Caribbean jurisdictions subjected to similar challenges, creating a wide-reaching negative effect for all of Singapore's citizens. The Court declared that the Singapore Constitution does not provide for a right against inhuman treatment or cruel punishment. In addition to this sweeping statement, the Court of Appeal ruled that customary international law not only has no legal validity in the domestic Singaporean legal sphere, but that it is also not to be treated as automatically incorporated into Singapore common law. Instead, a rule of customary international law can become part of Singapore law only if it has been domesticated directly through statute or judicial decision. The judgement thus effectively insulates the Singaporean legal sphere from all developments, trends and customs occurring internationally.

Twenty Years of Global Litigation – Case Summaries

Bahamas

Bowe and Davis v. The Queen [2006] 1 W.L.R. 1623
The Judicial Committee of the Privy Council (JCPC) struck down the mandatory death penalty as inhuman and degrading punishment on the grounds that the lack of discretion results in disproportionate and unfair sentencing. Although the 1973 Constitution prohibits fundamental rights-based challenges to pre-existing laws, which could have prevented a rights-based appeal of the pre-existing mandatory death penalty, the 1963 and 1969 constitutions of the Bahamas permitted fundamental rights-based challenges to pre-existing laws. The JCPC found that prior constitutions controlled the pre-existing constitutional ambit of the death penalty.

Bangladesh

BLAST and Sukur Ali v Bangladesh (2010) 30 BLD (HDC) 194
In February 2010, the High Court ruled the mandatory death penalty in Bangladesh unconstitutional on the grounds of it breaching the right to life and liberty. Further to this, it was ruled that the mandatory nature of the penalty interfered with the discretion of the judge and hence judicial independence

Barbados

Dacosta-Cadogan v. Barbados, Series C No. 204, Inter-American Court of Human Rights (IACrtHR), 24 September 2009
In *Cadogan*, the IACHR confirmed the ruling in *Boyce* and emphasized that psychiatrists, not trial judges, are competent to inform the jury as to a defendant's mental state at the time of the offence. The IACHR held that Barbados must inform a defendant of the right to psychiatric evaluation and permit expert testimony as to the accused person's mental state at the time of the offence.

Boyce et al v The Queen, Inter-American Commission on Human Rights, Case 12.480. Lennox Boyce, Jeffrey Joseph, Frederick Benjamin Atkins and Michael Huggins. Barbados. February 28, 2006
The IACHR struck down the mandatory death penalty on the grounds that it violates the right to life due to its arbitrary application and its failure to be applied to only the most serious crimes.

Belarus

Constitutional Court Decision No. 3-171/2004
On 11 March 2004, the Constitutional Court, following a request by the House of Representatives of the National Assembly to assess the compatibility of the Constitution of Belarus and the international treaties ratified by Belarus with the Criminal Code provisions providing for the death penalty, found that articles 48(1) (11) and 59 of the Criminal Code were inconsistent with the Constitution due to their lack of reference to the temporary character of the death penalty. The court also found that article 24(3) of the Constitution of Belarus, which allows the death penalty to be applied only until its abolition, makes both complete abolition and a moratorium on executions equally permissible.

Belize

Trimmingham v. The Queen [2009] UKPC 25
The JCPC ruled that the death sentence should only be imposed in the most extreme and exceptional cases, and only where there is no reasonable prospect of reform and the object of punishment can only be achieved by the death penalty.

Pipersburgh v. The Queen, [2008] UKPC 11
In 2007, the JCPC held that Belize's subsequent practice of placing the burden on defendants to prove why they should not be executed is inhuman and thus unconstitutional, ruling that the prosecution rebut any presumption of mitigating factors and show why the murder was 'most exceptional and extreme'.

Reyes [2002] 2 AC 235, Hughes and Fox [2002] 2 AC 284
In 2002, the Judicial Committee of the Privy Council ruled the mandatory death penalty inhuman and thus unconstitutional in Belize.

Mejia v. Attorney General, Action No. 296 of 2000 Supreme Court
In *Mejia v. Attorney General*, the Belize Supreme Court adopted *Pratt & Morgan v. The Queen, [1993] UKPC 1,* as constitutional principle, establishing the presumption that those held under sentence of death for five or more years have been subjected to inhuman treatment and must have their sentences commuted to life imprisonment.

Benin

Adrien Kolle Bamigbade, DCC 99-051, Constitutional Court of Benin, 1999
In the 1999 Bamigbade case, the Constitutional Court of Benin upheld the constitutional validity of all the death penalty provisions in Beninese legislation. The death penalty was challenged on the basis of Articles 8 of the Constitution, which enshrines the 'sacred and inviolable' nature of the human person, and article 15, protecting the right to life, liberty, security and the integrity of the person. The Constitutional Court held these articles to be compatible with the death penalty and in line with the African Charter on Human and Peoples'

Rights, which prohibits only arbitrary deprivations of the right to life. The Court held that properly legislated death penalty provisions were not arbitrary and were thus constitutional.

Botswana

Ntesang v. State, Criminal Appeal no. 57 of 1994, BWCA 12, Ct. of Appeal of Botswana, Jun. 1, 2010
The Court of Appeal acknowledged that the death penalty was increasingly recognized as 'torture, inhuman or degrading punishment or treatment', but ultimately decided that the Court did not have jurisdiction to alter the Constitution.

Kobedi v. State, Criminal Appeal no. 25 of 201, BWCA 22, Ct. of Appeal of Botswana, Mar. 19, 2003
In *Kobedi v. State*, in 2003, the Court of Appeal affirmed its response to the constitutionality of the death penalty in *Ntesang*, and indicated that the death penalty is not mandatory in Botswana. The Court also recommended the president consider clemency in this case.

Dominica

Balson v. The State, Appeal No. 26 of 2004
The JCPC struck down the mandatory death penalty as inhuman treatment and thus invalid under Dominica's Constitution. The Court upheld and extended the jurisprudence of the Eastern Caribbean Supreme Court in *Trimmingham v. The Queen [2009] UKPC 25*, which mandated that only in the most extreme and exceptional cases should the death penalty be considered.

Grenada

Queen v. Knights, Case No. GDAHCR1994/0212
National courts applied the ruling in *Pratt & Morgan v. A.G. of Jamaica, Appeal No. 10 of 1993, JCPC, Nov. 2, 1993,* that any prisoner under sentence of death for longer than 5 years had presumptively been subjected to cruel and unusual punishment necessitating commutation of her/his death sentence.

Hughes and Spence v. Queen, Appeals No. 14 of 1997 and 20 of 1998, ECSC Court of Appeals, Apr. 2, 2001
The Eastern Caribbean Supreme Court (Court of Appeals division), confirmed by the JCPC, determined that the mandatory death penalty contravened protections against arbitrariness and cruel and unusual treatment or punishment, protected by Grenada's Constitution. Further to this it ruled that the death penalty may only be imposed in only the most exceptional and appropriate circumstances.

India

Swamy Shraddananda v. State of Karnataka, AIR 2008 SC 3040
In 2008 the Supreme Court observed that an earlier aggravated murder formulation (*Machhi Singh v. State of Punjab, 3 SCC 470*) had undermined discretionary sentencing by encouraging application of the death penalty for offences falling under that formulation. The Court's 2008 decision emphasized mitigating factors and outlined a number of cases in which the death penalty was deemed inappropriate.

Indonesia

Sianturi v. State No. 2-3/PUU-V/2007
The Constitutional Court considered the appeal of members of the Bali Nine and held that the death penalty for drug offences was constitutional. The Court held that Article 28 (protecting the right to life) not only prohibits the government from taking life but also obliges the government to regulate in order to protect life, and found that drug trafficking is a crime that threatens the lives of citizens. The Court also considered whether the constitutional provision that the right to life cannot be curtailed 'under any circumstances' made the death penalty unconstitutional. The Court considered that language to refer to derogation, and turned to Indonesia's obligations under international treaties and customary law, holding that the non-derogable right to life is currently considered consistent with the application of the death penalty for serious crimes.

Nurhasyim v. State, 21/PUU-VI/2008 IDCC 32
The Constitutional Court held that execution by shooting was not torture under Indonesia's Constitution. The Court found that pain is inherent to execution and that the infliction of pain during execution is not presumptively torture and that death by shooting allows the condemned to retain dignity. The Court suggested that the legislature should consider adopting methods of execution that are less painful, but declined to rule that the choice to execute by shooting rather than by some other less painful method amounts to inflicting pain as torture.

Jamaica

Watson v. The Queen, Appeal No. 36 of 2003, UKPC
The JCPC reiterated earlier Commonwealth jurisprudence holding that the mandatory death penalty constitutes unconstitutional inhuman treatment. The JCPC further determined that because Jamaica had altered its laws on murder, the JCPC could not apply the Constitution's saving clause (which could potentially protect Jamaica's murder laws from a fundamental human rights-based challenge).

Dougal v. R, [2011] JMCA Crim 13
In Dougal, the Jamaican Court of Appeal adopted the rule in *Trimmingham v. The Queen*, a JCPC case on appeal from the Eastern Caribbean Court of Appeal for Saint Vincent and the Grenadines, restricting the death penalty for only 'the worst of the worst' or the 'rarest of the rare' murderers.

Japan

Judgment Concerning the Validity of the Withdrawal of Appeal Made by a Defendant against Whom a Sentence of the Death Penalty Was Rendered, Case 1995(Shi) no.173, Supreme Court of Japan
The Supreme Court determined that the mentally ill cannot withdraw their appeals.

Kenya

Mutiso v. Republic, Criminal Appeal No. 17 of 2008
The Court of Appeal determined that the mandatory death penalty for murder violates the protections against arbitrariness and inhuman treatment. The Court did not rule on whether treason, robbery with violence, or attempted robbery with violence could carry the mandatory death penalty, but stated that its reasoning in Mutiso may apply and doubted whether different arguments could be raised in respect of other capital offenses.

Laos

Orobator v. Lao PDR, Orobator v. HPM Holloway, CO/9527/2009, U.K. High Court of Justice, Jan. 20, 2010
The People's Court sentenced a pregnant defendant to life imprisonment rather than the death penalty for trafficking 680 grams of heroin, an offence which is believed to carry the mandatory death penalty.

Madagascar

Supreme Court of Madagascar Criminal Chamber, Case No. 87/96-PEN
In March 2003, the Madagascar Supreme Court reversed the trial court's conviction of a defendant for murder, an offence which is punishable by death or life imprisonment. The defendant had originally been charged with a lesser, non-capital crime, and was not notified of the new and more serious charge, before the trial court convicted him. The Supreme Court of Madagascar found that the conviction violated the right to a defence and ordered a retrial.

Malawi

Kafantayeni and Others v. Attorney General, Constitutional Case 12 of 2005, High Court, 2007
In 2007, the Malawi High Court struck down the mandatory death penalty ruling that the automatic nature of the death penalty in Malawi for murder violated the right to life and amounted to inhuman punishment, as it did not provide the individuals concerned with an opportunity to mitigate their death sentences.

Nigeria

Onuoha Kalu Vs. The State, (1998) 13 N.W.L.R 531
The Supreme Court upheld the constitutionality of the death penalty, as long as it is imposed for a criminal offence by a Nigerian court of law.

Papua New Guinea

Ume v. State, para. 74, SCRA 10 of 1997, Supreme Court of Justice, May 19, 2006
In Ume, the Court reduced the death sentences of the petitioners whose death sentences had been pronounced by a trial court judge who had failed to make adequate factual determinations regarding aggravating factors and who had ignored the possibility of mitigating factors. The court outlined the legislative history of the death penalty in Papua New Guinea, illustrating that the death penalty in Papua New Guinea is beyond question a discretionary penalty. The Court determined that the death penalty can apply only for seriously aggravated offences where mitigating factors or extenuating circumstances are insufficient to suggest leniency is appropriate in light of the gravity of the offence.

Russia

Constitutional Court of the Russian Federation, Decision No. 1344-O-R/2009
The Court extended the moratorium passed in the Constitutional Court of the Russian Federation, in Decision No. 3-P/1999, observing that even though the Russian Federation had put a jury system in place across all of its regions, questions about the Federation's international commitments precluded application of the death penalty. European law excludes the death penalty in peacetime and abolition of the death penalty had been one of the conditions of the country's accession to the Council of Europe in 1996.

Saint Kitts and Nevis

Fox v. The Queen, paras. 8, 10, Privy Council Appeal no. 66 of 2000
In 2002, the JCPC adopted the principles set out in *Reyes [2002] 2 AC 235* for Saint Kitts and Nevis, stating that the mandatory death penalty violates constitutional protections against inhuman or degrading treatment or punishment. In Saint Kitts and Nevis, these decisions limit application of the death penalty to the worst aggravated murders.

Pratt and Morgan v. Jamaica Privy Council Appeal No. 10 of 1993
Similarly, the decision in *Pratt and Morgan* is applied in Saint Kitts and Nevis, ruling a five-year delay of execution after sentencing is presumptively inhuman and degrading punishment.

Saint Lucia

Reyes v. The Queen, Privy Council Appeal No. 64 of 2001
In *Reyes* the JCPC determined in a ruling that affected Saint Lucia that the mandatory death penalty constituted cruel, inhuman or degrading punishment.

Hughes and Fox [2002] 2 AC 284
The JCPC in *Hughes* held that Saint Lucia's savings clause did not prevent a constitutional challenge to the mandatory nature of the death penalty, and extended *Reyes* to hold that the mandatory death penalty constitutes inhuman and degrading treatment under Saint Lucia's Constitution. The JCPC directed Saint Lucia's courts to sentence capital defendants with 'regard to all the relevant circumstances', thus striking down the mandatory death penalty.

Pratt & Morgan v. The Queen, [1993] UKPC 1
In *Pratt v. Morgan v. Attorney General of Jamaica* (adopted for Saint Lucia in 2005), the JCPC held that whenever a prisoner has been held more than five years on death row, he has presumptively been subjected to cruel, inhuman or degrading treatment. Under this decision, death row prisoners in Saint Lucia are entitled to commutation of their death sentences if they are not executed within five years of sentencing.

Saint Vincent and Grenadines

Spence & Hughes v. The Queen, Criminal Appeals Nos. 20 of 1998 & 14 of 1997, ECSC Ct. of Appeal, Apr. 2, 2001
The Eastern Caribbean Court of Appeals held that the mandatory death penalty is unconstitutionally arbitrary and that courts must consider the circumstances of the offence and the offender in determining an appropriate sentence.

Wilson v. The Queen, Criminal Appeal No. 30 of 2004, ECSC Ct. of Appeal, Nov. 28, 2005
In *Wilson*, the defendant's death sentence was overturned because of his past history of nonviolence, potential instability related to his relationship with the victim, and potential for reform. The decision demands that the sentencing Judge 'pay due regard' to every mitigating factor presented at trial.

Trimmingham v. The Queen [2009] UKPC 25
The ECCA upheld a death sentence against Trimmingham's appeal, as the killing of an elderly man in the course of a robbery was particularly gruesome, but the JCPC reversed that decision because, although the killing was cold-blooded, it was not 'the worst of the worst'.

Pratt & Morgan v. The Queen, [1993] UKPC 1
The JCPC ruled that prisoners who serve five years on death row must have their sentence commuted to life imprisonment, on the grounds that five years spent waiting for execution constitutes 'inhuman or degrading punishment or other treatment'.

Singapore

Yong Vui Kong v Public Prosecutor [2010] 2 SLR 192

The Singapore Court of Appeal upheld the constitutionality of the mandatory death penalty. The Court of Appeal ruled that customary international law not only has no legal validity in the domestic Singaporean legal sphere, but that it is also not to be treated as automatically incorporated into Singapore common law. Instead, a rule of customary international law can become part of Singapore law only if it has been 'translated' by statute or judicial decision. Additionally, the Court stated that the Singapore Constitution does not provide for a right against inhuman treatment or cruel punishment. The judgement thus effectively insulates the Singaporean legal sphere from developments, trends and custom occurring internationally.

Nguyen Tuong Van v. Public Prosecutor, CA 5/2004, Ct. of Appeal, Oct. 20, 2004

This case involved an Australian citizen who received the mandatory death penalty for drug trafficking despite a number of mitigating factors and factors that called into question his criminal responsibility. The Appeals Court upheld the High Court's conviction and sentence, holding that the mandatory death penalty did not violate Singapore's Constitution.

South Africa

S v Makwanyane and Another (CCT 3/94)

The Constitutional Court established that capital punishment was inconsistent with the commitment to human rights expressed in the Interim Constitution as the right to life and dignity were the most important of all human rights and the source of all the other personal rights. The court also prohibited the government from executing any prisoners awaiting execution, ruling that they should remain in prison until new sentences were imposed. Further to this, the court was not satisfied that it had been shown that capital punishment would be more effective as a deterrent than a life sentence.

South Korea

Hun-Ka 13, Constitutional Court of Korea, 2010

The Constitutional Court of Korea upheld the constitutionality of the death penalty on the grounds that the text of the Constitution does not recognize fundamental rights as absolute and that even a person's right to life may be subject to general statutory reservation when necessary for national security, the maintenance of law and order, and the public welfare.

Sri Lanka

Weerawardane v. State , Appeal No. 52 of 1998, Court of Appeal, Oct. 21, 1999

The court rejected a guilty plea on the basis that the death penalty for a murder conviction is mandatory; as otherwise the Court would not be able to consider whether excuses (such as provocation, intoxication or lack of shared intent or knowledge) would justify a conviction on lesser charges, including culpable homicide. The courts in Sri Lanka do not consider mitigation for the offence of murder.

Sudan

Abdulrahaman Zakaria Mohammed, December 2008 Sudanese Supreme Court
The Supreme Court decision confirmed the death sentence for Abdulrahaman Zakaria Mohammed, a juvenile offender, based in part on a conclusion that the prohibition of the death penalty for children did not extend to hudud offences – crimes seen as being 'against God'. The Court held that an individual could be executed for a hudud offence committed while under the age of 18.

Taiwan

Interpretation No. 476 (1999) Constitutional Court of Taiwan
The Constitutional Court determined that Article 15 of the Constitution protects the right to life and requires a proportionality test if the state is to exercise the death penalty, but ultimately decided that the state's interest in preventing drug trafficking was important enough that the discretionary death penalty was a proportional response against individuals who purchase drugs for their personal use.

Interpretation No. 551 (2002) Constitutional Court of Taiwan
The Court indirectly struck down the death penalty for false accusation of a capital drug crime. Previously, drug laws had allowed the court to sentence a false accuser of a drug offence to the penalty the accused would have faced; the Court found this to be disproportionate.

Tanzania

Mbushu and Anor vs Republic (1995) 1LRC, 216
The Court of Appeal ruled that lengthy delays in executions constitute inhumane treatment and violate the prohibition against torture. Furthermore, although the death penalty was found to be inherently cruel, inhuman and degrading, it was not declared unconstitutional due to Article 30(2) of the Constitution which provides that the Constitution does not invalidate existing legislation with the purpose of ensuring public safety or public order, or execution of a judgment or order of a court given or made in any criminal matter.

Tonga

Rex v. Ake, Case No. Cr. 140/05, Supreme Court of Tonga, Feb. 3, 2006
A sentencing decision of the Supreme Court explained (in dicta, as the only issue in the appeal before the court was whether the court had discretion to award a sentence lesser than life imprisonment) that the death penalty is applied as an exception for extremely grave murders that can be characterized as the 'rarest of rare'.

Trinidad and Tobago

Matthew v. State, No. 12 of 2004, Judicial Committee of the Privy Council, 2004
The JCPC held that, despite the international consensus that the mandatory death penalty is cruel and unusual and violates due process, Article 6(1)(a) of the Constitution of the Republic of Trinidad and Tobago precludes a challenge to the mandatory death penalty. Because the mandatory death penalty in Trinidad and Tobago is a law that predates the formation of its Constitution, Article 6(1)(a) precludes a human rights-based challenge to the mandatory death penalty. This overturned the decision in *Roodal v. State, No. 18 of 2003, Judicial Committee of the Privy Council, 2003,* which abolished the mandatory death penalty.

Khan v. State, para. 17-19, No. 28 of 2003, Judicial Committee of the Privy Council, 2003
During *Roodal's* brief tenure as controlling precedent, the JCPC determined in *Khan* that the mandatory death penalty for felony murder was unconstitutional. Even though *Roodal*, the basis for that ruling, was overturned by *Matthew*, *Khan* may still be good law, as the JCPC has declined to extend Matthew to overrule Khan, despite having some opportunity to do so.

Pratt & Morgan v. The Queen, [1993] UKPC 1
This JCPC decision means that death row prisoners in Trinidad and Tobago who experience a delay in execution of five or more years are to have their sentences commuted to life, on the grounds that the delay constitutes inhuman and degrading treatment.

Uganda

Attorney General v. Susan Kigula & 417 Others, Constitutional Appeal No. 03 of 2006, Supreme Court of Uganda at Mengo, Jan. 21, 2009
In this case, the Supreme Court of Uganda ruled that the mandatory death penalty was unconstitutional because it prevented a judge from exercising discretion and rendered the application of the mandatory death sentence an arbitrary deprivation of life.

The Court also ruled that a delay in execution for more than three years following confirmation of a prisoner's death sentence by the highest appellate court (which usually takes around 9 years) would constitute 'unreasonable delay' and is unconstitutional. Prisoners who remained on death row for three years after their final judicial appeal without being executed would have their sentences commuted to whole of life imprisonment.

Tigo Stephen Vs. Uganda, Criminal Appeal No. 08 of 2009
Tigo ruled that due to the *Kigula* decision, life imprisonment no longer meant twenty years, as prescribed in the Penal Code. Life imprisonment is now interpreted to mean whole of life.

Uganda Law Society v. Attorney General, Constitutional Petitions Nos. 2 of 2002 & 8 of 2002, Constitutional Court of Uganda, 2009
The Constitutional Court determined that a under Article 22 of the Ugandan Constitution a soldier's right to life demands that the soldier have an appeal as of right to the Supreme Court and the possibility of clemency from the President. Previously, there had been disagreement

over whether the UPDF Act would permit individuals tried by a Field Court Martial to appeal their sentence to a civilian court.

Ukraine

Kyiv, December 29, 1999 Case 1-33/99 N
It was ruled that the criminal code advocating the death penalty conflicted with the constitution's non-derogable right to life. The Constitutional Court ruled the death penalty an 'arbitrary deprivation of life'. The decision was also taken in light of Ukraine's accession to the Council of Europe which makes abolition of the death penalty a prerequisite to membership.

USA

Atkins v. Virginia, 536 U.S. 304 (2002)
The Supreme Court rules that individuals with intellectual disabilities cannot be executed because they are categorically less culpable than other criminals and constituted cruel and unusual punishment.

Roper v. Simmons, 543 U.S. 551 (2005)
The Supreme Court ruled that the execution of people who were under the age of eighteen at the time they committed the crime in question, violates the federal constitutional guarantee against cruel and unusual punishments.

Kennedy v. Louisiana, slip opinion, No. 07-343, U.S. Supreme Court, Oct. 1, 2008
The Court revisited *Coker* and established that rape of a minor cannot be punished by death under civilian law. Furthermore, the Court effectively prohibited the expansion of the application of the death penalty to ordinary crimes not resulting in loss of human life. The Court also highlighted the prohibition of execution of the insane, mentally retarded and juveniles, relying on *Trop v. Dulles, No. 70, U.S. Supreme Court, Mar. 31, 1958,* which implored interpretation of the Constitution in line with evolving standards of decency.

Zambia

Mudenda v. People, Judgment No. 19 of 2002, Supreme Court of Zambia, Sep. 3, 2002
The Court ruled that in cases of murder, discretionary sentencing is to be allowed in extenuating circumstances.

Zimbabwe

The Catholic Commission for Justice and Peace v. Attorney General of Zimbabwe and Others, 1993(4) SA 239(ZS), Zimbabwe Supreme Court, 1993
The legislature was quick to amend the Constitution so as to nullify the decision in this case, but the Court initially held that extended periods on death row lead to the death row phenomenon, which constitutes inhuman and degrading punishment.

Part II
Innocence

[13]

THE MYTH OF FACTUAL INNOCENCE

MORRIS B. HOFFMAN*

INTRODUCTION

Almost all criminal defendants plead guilty, and almost all of them do so because they are guilty. The ones who take their cases to trial are also overwhelmingly guilty, at least in the sense that there is no issue about whether they committed the charged acts. The relatively few felony cases that actually go to trial in America are typically about moral guilt, not factual guilt. That is, they are about the level of the defendant's culpability and therefore the level of the crime of which he will be convicted.[1]

Yet the picture of the American criminal justice system painted in *12 Angry Men* is of a truth-finding system so feeble that it must depend, in the end, on the instincts of a single courageous dissenting juror—in this case Juror #8, played by Henry Fonda.[2] True, it wouldn't have been much of a movie if the young unnamed Puerto Rican defendant had actually been guilty of killing his father and pleaded guilty to a lesser offense, or if Henry Fonda and his colleagues spent all that time[3] arguing about what real juries argue about—the meaning of phrases like "with intent and after deliberation," "knowingly," "recklessly" or "beyond a reasonable doubt"[4]—in de-

* District Judge, Second Judicial District (Denver), State of Colorado. The views expressed here do not necessarily reflect the views of the Second Judicial District or any of my colleagues on that Court.

1. These categorical pronouncements about the rates of factual innocence are based not just on my own sixteen years of experience on the bench but also on the best data we have about these questions, discussed in Part I. The panic, both in the academy and in the popular press, about the sweeping tide of wrongful convictions is, alas, part of the myth of factual innocence discussed in this essay.

2. 12 ANGRY MEN (Orion-Nova Productions 1957). One of the admirable things about the movie is that viewers—at least this viewer—are left with mixed feelings about the defendant's factual guilt or innocence. The $64,000 question, of course, is whether those "mixed feelings" rise to the level of reasonable doubt, and the movie does a poor job of exploring that question. *See infra* note 4.

3. One of the unrealistic things about the movie is that the jury deliberations, which consume all but a few minutes of the film at the beginning and end, are presented in continuous real time, yet they take only 90 minutes. There is no effort to employ time compression or other artistic devices to convey the sense that this wrenching process—in which Henry Fonda single-handedly sways all eleven of his fellow jurors—takes more than about an hour and a half.

4. There was a brief discussion of reasonable doubt in the middle of the deliberations, and the phrase was mentioned a few times after that as more and more jurors joined Fonda's position. But, interestingly, the entirety of the brief discussion about reasonable doubt consisted of the immigrant watchmaker (Juror #11, played by George Voskovec) asking the impatient baseball fan (Juror #7,

ciding whether the defendant was guilty of first degree murder, second degree murder, or criminally negligent homicide.

Innocence projects are in some ways the modern post-conviction equivalent of *12 Angry Men*. Because there are just too few Henry Fondas in modern jury pools—or so the innocence project orthodoxy goes—vast seas of wrongfully-convicted defendants must today rely on law students and their clinical faculty advisors to do what Fonda-less juries have chronically failed, and continue to fail, to do.[5]

I don't mean to suggest that innocence projects are a bad thing, or that courageous individual jurors whose efforts result in the acquittal of innocent defendants (or, for that matter, courageous individual jurors whose efforts result in the conviction of guilty defendants) are some kind of naive joke we sophisticated insiders should cluck at. On the contrary, I have gained a deep respect for jurors since coming to the bench and seeing so many trials. There is something almost mystical in their collective ability to find the truth about a case, both factual and moral.[6] It is my respect for jurors and the jury system that puts me at odds with the Chicken Littles of Innocence who think wrongful conviction is, if not the rule, then at least a very common exception.

True, innocence projects have been instrumental in suggesting points in the system that are particularly vulnerable to truth-detection errors, especially cross-racial eyewitness identifications[7] and interrogation-induced false confessions.[8] Quite apart from the rates of these errors, it is critical for anyone who cares about maximizing the reliability of the system to identify common sources of error in an effort to reduce them. Unfortunately, the

played by Jack Warden) whether he knows what reasonable doubt means, and the impatient baseball fan getting angry that an immigrant would ask such an apparently obvious question. But several times during the deliberations Henry Fonda asks, "Yes, but it is *possible*?" with reference to his interpretation of a particular piece of evidence, suggesting that the movie's writer, director, and legal consultants did not understand the difference between reasonable inferences and speculation, or between reasonable doubt and speculative doubt.

5. For those of you who think this description of the assumptions behind some innocence projects is exaggerated, I refer you to these comments by Rob Warden, the Executive Director of the Center for Wrongful Convictions at Northwestern University School of Law: "You hear the lofty pronouncement that better 10 guilty men go free than one innocent man suffer. . . . But as a nation, we've never believed that. It's the other way around." Chip Rowe, *False Justice: Are 100,000+ Innocent Men in U.S. Prisons?*, PLAYBOY, July 2002, *available at* http://www.chiprowe.com/ articles/false-justice.html. That is, Mr. Warden believes that we "as a nation" think it is better to send ten innocent people to prison than let one guilty person go free, a goal that, if achieved by the criminal justice system, would result in a wrongful conviction rate of approximately 91%.

6. *See infra* Part II for a discussion of the difference between factual and moral guilt.

7. *See* John P. Rutledge, *They All Look Alike: The Inaccuracy of Cross-Racial Identifications*, 28 AM. J. CRIM. L. 207 (2001).

8. *See* Steven A. Drizin & Richard A. Leo, *The Problem of False Confessions in the Post-DNA World*, 82 N.C. L. REV. 891 (2004) (documenting and analyzing more than 125 false confessions).

political subtext of the average innocence project is not that infrequent wrongful convictions must be detected and remedied, but rather that the system as a whole is profoundly unreliable and that the factual innocence revealed by the projects is just the tip of an iceberg of injustice.[9]

But the phenomenon of *12 Angry Men* and the explosion of innocence projects are not just about melodramatic license or extreme political pedagogy. Their resonance with lawyers, legal scholars, law students, and even ordinary citizens summoned for jury duty transcend their caricatures of the system. Myths, after all, are myths precisely because their oversimplifications, and even misrepresentations, try to teach us something important about the world and our place in it. In the best myths, what we lose in empirical truth we gain in a kind of transcendent insight.

Does *12 Angry Men* really deserve the label "transcendent"? Probably not. It was not the first, or last, movie about wrongful (or almost wrongful) convictions. There has been a continuous stream of them since at least 1943.[10] *12 Angry Men* does not seem to have had nearly the broad cultural impact lawyers assume. It was a financial disaster, despite its low budget.[11] It was (horror of horrors!) originally a teleplay, and although it was nominated for three academy awards (none for Henry Fonda), it didn't win any, losing out in all three nominated categories (Best Picture, Best Director (Sidney Lumet) and Best Adapted Screenplay) to *Bridge on the River Kwai*.[12] I'm afraid its popularity among the lawyering classes is akin to the popularity of kung fu movies among teenage boys.[13]

9. *See supra* note 5. In a claim typical of innocence projects, Northwestern's Center on Wrongful Convictions says in its mission statement that one of its purposes is to raise public awareness of the "prevalence" of wrongful convictions. Center on Wrongful Convictions, Northwestern University School of Law, http://www.law.northwestern.edu/depts/clinic/wrongful/mission.htm (last visited July 8, 2007).

10. To name just a few: AFTER INNOCENCE (American Film Found. 2005), LIFE (Imagine Entm't 2000), THE HURRICANE (Azoff Entm't 1999), A MAP OF THE WORLD (Cinerenta Medienbeteiligungs KG 1999), BROKEDOWN PALACE (Twentieth Century Fox Film Corp. 1999), SNOW FALLING ON CEDARS (The Kennedy/Marshall Co. 1999), IN THE BLINK OF AN EYE (Odyssey Video 1996), INDICTMENT: THE MCMARTIN TRIAL (Abby Mann Prods. 1995), IN THE NAME OF THE FATHER (Hell's Kitchen Films 1993), PRESUMED INNOCENT (Mirage 1990), TRUE BELIEVER (Columbia Pictures Corp. 1989), AN INNOCENT MAN (Interscope Commc'ns 1989), A CRY IN THE DARK (Cannon Entm't 1988), AMERICAN GIGOLO (Paramount Pictures 1980), . . . AND JUSTICE FOR ALL (Columbia Pictures Corp. 1979), THE WRONG MAN (Warner Bros. Pictures 1956), CALL NORTHSIDE *777* (Twentieth Century Fox Film Corp. 1948), THE OX-BOW INCIDENT (Twentieth Century Fox Film Corp. 1943).

11. It was filmed in only nineteen days at a total cost of just $349,000. *See* BlinkBits, 12 Angry Men Wikipedia RSS Feed, http://www.blinkbits.com/bits/viewtopic/12_angry_men_wikipedia_rss_feed?t=2616855 (last visited July 8, 2007) (citing SIDNEY LUMET, MAKING MOVIES (1995)).

12. *Id.*

13. By some admittedly very rough objective measures, *12 Angry Men* has had little lasting impact either in the public consciousness generally or in the halls of the legal academy. A recent (March 29, 2007) Google search of *12 Angry Men* yielded 617,000 hits, compared to 639,000 for *Bridge on the River Kwai*. An identical query in the text and periodicals database of Westlaw, restricted to the title

As of March 29, 2007, *12 Angry Men* was not among the top 100 movies rented from NetFlix.[14] Even in the NetFlix "classic" category, it is a modest #21, right below *The Sound of Music* and seven spots below its nemesis *Kwai*.[15] It is true that it has enjoyed a rather consistently high reputation among the filmerati,[16] but the notion that the movie is an important cultural icon seems itself to be largely an echo of the myth of innocence.

On the other hand, transcendent myths can be tricky things. Maybe the best measure of their vitality is in their retelling. But alas, unlike what seems to be every other movie made in the last fifty years, including *Kwai*,[17] *12 Angry Men* has never been remade on the big screen or been the subject of a sequel or prequel. No Tom Hanks as the brooding Juror #8, or Freddie Prinze, Jr., as the defendant. No sequel following the wrongfully accused youngster on to college then law school, or the courageous holdout into political office. No prequel showing the real perpetrator committing the murder.[18]

field, generated only four hits, compared to an astonishing three hits for *Kwai*. (Maybe not that astonishing, because all three articles are about a reported federal case arising out of trademark litigation over the distribution of an unauthorized sequel, *Return from the River Kwai*. *See* Tri-Star Pictures, Inc. v. Unger, 14 F. Supp. 2d 339 (S.D.N.Y. 1998). In this sense, *Kwai* has had some direct impact on the law that *12 Angry Men* never has.) Expanding the Westlaw searches for the presence of the movie titles anywhere in the text of the article generated 199 references to *12 Angry Men* and 62 for *Kwai*. To give some context to the way these searches might measure the cultural diaspora of a piece of fiction, the same Westlaw text search yielded 1,110 hits for *Alice in Wonderland*. Now *that's* cultural resonance.

14. Netflix, Top 100, http://www.netflix.com/Top100 (last visited March 29, 2007).

15. Netflix, Classics Top 25, http://www.netflix.com/Top25?sgid=306 (last visited March 29, 2007).

16. For example, in June 2003 the American Film Institute named Henry Fonda's character the twenty-eighth greatest movie hero of the twentieth century, finishing behind such dubious winners as James Bond, Dirty Harry, Indiana Jones and Bob Woodward/Carl Bernstein. *See AFI's 100 Years . . . 100 Heroes & Villains* (CBS television broadcast June 3, 2003). The list of fifty greatest heroes and fifty greatest villains is available at AFI's 100 Years . . . 100 Heroes & Villains, http://www.afi.com/tvevents/100years/handv.aspx (last visited March 29, 2007). *12 Angry Men* finished an impressive fourteenth in the Internet Movie Database's top 250 movies as voted by its users. *See* IMDb Top 250, http://www.imdb.com/chart/top (last visited March 29, 2007).

17. *See supra* note 13.

18. I do not count the mini-versions in shows like *Veronica Mars* and *Monk*, *see* Nancy S. Marder, *Introduction to* The 50th Anniversary of *12 Angry Men*, 82 CHI.-KENT L. REV. 557, 574 (2007), since they are neither full-blown remakes nor spoofs. It is not hard to imagine why Hollywood moguls might not be jumping on the bandwagon for a remake or spin-off: is the Britney Spears generation really ready for a movie that takes place almost entirely inside the four walls of one room, and not a bedroom at that? Other media have been more willing. It was remade for television in 1997, with Jack Lemmon as Juror #8. *See* BlinkBits, *supra* note 11. It was also adapted to the London stage in 1964, in a production starring Leo Genn as Juror #8, and has undergone several theatrical adaptations since, the more modern ones using actresses on the jury and retitling the work *12 Angry Jurors* or even versions called *12 Angry Women*. *Id.* Don't ask how twelve women manage to navigate the gender bias prohibited by J.E.B. v. Alabama, 511 U.S. 127, 129 (1994).

If parody is the second sincerest form of flattery, then I should mention that there have been only three parodies of *12 Angry Men* that I've been able to discover: one in 1959 on the weekly BBC sitcom *Hancock's Half Hour*;[19] one in a 1994 episode of *The Simpsons*;[20] and one in a 1998 episode of *King of the Hill*.[21]

Even if *12 Angry Men* itself has not become a transforming cultural icon, its central message has: the criminal justice system nabs innocent people just about as often (and maybe more often) as it nabs guilty ones, and as a result, the primary, and very difficult, job of jurors is to determine whether the accused is guilty as a factual matter. Of course, this notion was hardly invented by Sidney Lumet. The myth of factual innocence has a long and interesting pre-1957 history, both on and off the screen.

In this essay I examine the differences between factual and moral guilt, the long history and benefits of the myth of factual innocence, and, finally, the costs of the myth in our modern, plea-bargain-dominated era. But first, some definitional and empirical clarifications.

19. *Hancock's Half Hour: Twelve Angry Men* (BBC television broadcast Oct. 16, 1959). In a complete reversal from the movie, Hancock plays the foreman of the jury in an open-and-shut case in which the defendant is unquestionably guilty. But he delays the guilty verdict because he is making more from the daily jury fee (30 bob) than he can at work. So he pontificates throughout deliberations—for example, at one point he chides, "Does Magna Carta mean nothing to you? Did she die in vain? Brave Hungarian peasant girl who forced King John to sign the pledge at Runnymede and close the boozers at half past ten?" *Id.* For highlights from this episode, see Hancock's Half Hour—"Twelve Angry Men," http://www.phespirit.info/hancock/hancock_41.htm (last visited July 8, 2007).

20. *The Simpsons: The Boy Who Knew Too Much* (Fox television broadcast May 5, 1994). I was sure I'd seen almost every episode of *The Simpsons*, but this one did not come to mind. My thanks to Naomi Mezey & Mark C. Niles for alerting me to it in their article *Screening the Law: Ideology and Law in Popular American Culture*, 28 COLUM. J.L. & ARTS 91, 131–32 (2005). In this episode, Freddy Quimby, the nephew of the Kennedy-esque mayor of Springfield, is charged with assaulting a waiter, after a very public argument they were having over the correct pronunciation of the word "chowder." (The waiter insists on a faux-French pronunciation—"show-dair"—while Freddy argues for the Boston blue blood version—"chowdah."). *The Boy Who Knew Too Much*, *supra*. But no one witnessed the assault other than a truant and hiding Bart. What actually happened was that the waiter slipped on a Rice Krispies Square. Bart is silent because he knows if he admits he was there he'll get in trouble with Principal Skinner. The holdout juror is Homer, who is hoping, à la Hancock, not for justice but for a few more nights of free cable in the Springfield Palace Hotel, where the jury is sequestered. Homer, unlike Henry Fonda, is unable to persuade his fellow jurors of the defendant's innocence, but justice is nevertheless done when the judge allows Bart's untimely testimony, saying, "Even though reopening the trial at this point is illegal and grossly unconstitutional, I just can't say no to kids." *Id.* I suppose this makes the judge an "ordered liberty" kind of guy, rather than a textualist.

21. *King of the Hill: Nine Pretty Darn Angry Men* (Fox television broadcast Nov. 17, 1998). Hank and eight others participate in a focus group about the Mason 5500 lawnmower. Originally, Hank is the only one who prefers the old model, the Mason 1500. Hank eventually convinces seven of the others that the 1500 is superior, with arguments such as the 5500's seat warmer will warm the beer between the rider's legs. Only Hank's father, Cotton, remains a holdout for the 5500. Hank's dispute with Cotton over the lawnmowers is a thinly disguised proxy for their feelings about Cotton "trading in" Hank's mother for a newer model. *Id.* For a summary of the episode, see FOX Broadcasting Company: King of the Hill, http://www.fox.com/kingofthehill/episodes/0308.htm (last visited July 8, 2007).

I. IS FACTUAL INNOCENCE REALLY A MYTH?

It is important to frame this question with some precision. The "myth" of factual innocence is, I contend, a myth about the *frequency* with which innocent people are caught in the net of the criminal law, to be freed, if at all, only by the determination and insight of conscientious jurors, highly paid superstar lawyers, innocence project students, or, if all else fails, courageous governors. Of course, factually innocent people *are* wrongly arrested and wrongly convicted, as many innocence projects have demonstrated, and as humans have known since the dawn of time.[22] Systemic error is an unavoidable consequence of underlying, and irreducible, human error. But the important core of the myth of factual innocence holds that wrongful conviction is a regular occurrence, that prisons are full of innocent people, and in fact that graveyards are full of innocent capital defendants wrongfully executed.

Sadly, the empirical literature on wrongful convictions is itself woefully infected with the mythology of factual innocence. Part of the problem, of course, is definitional. How does one determine factual innocence after the system—whose whole purpose is supposed to be truth-finding—has determined, whether by plea or trial, that a defendant is in fact guilty? This is the mother of all confirmation bias problems.[23]

Before the advent of DNA testing, there were only a few narrow circumstances in which we could confidently assess a defendant's factual guilt by any method other than the trial itself. In the era before the *corpus delicti* rule was vigorously enforced, "victims" of "murder" occasionally resurfaced very much alive.[24] Fingerprints and some other kinds of pre-DNA forensic evidence discovered after trial could sometimes do the trick.

22. Even God sometimes has trouble distinguishing the guilty from the innocent, or at least caring about the difference. He was just about to wipe out the entire population of Sodom when Abraham managed to convince him that it would be wrong to have the innocent Sodomites perish with the guilty. *Genesis* 18:23–32. For a fascinating narrative of examples of wrongful executions in England from 1640 through 1790, see Bruce P. Smith, *The History of Wrongful Execution*, 56 HASTINGS L.J. 1185 (2005).

23. There have even been a handful of studies where judges are asked after trials whether the jury reached the right result. We almost always say that they did. *See, e.g.*, C. RONALD HUFF, ARYE RATTNER & EDWARD SAGARIN, CONVICTED BUT INNOCENT: WRONGFUL CONVICTION AND PUBLIC POLICY 60 (1996) (concluding by this deeply flawed method that a surprisingly high 2% of all convicted defendants may be innocent).

24. *See, e.g.*, Smith, *supra* note 22, at 1190–92 (discussing the case of the Gloucestershire wife, son, and servant of one William Harrison, all hanged for his murder in 1660, and all exonerated post-mortem when Mr. Harrison returned in 1661 from what he claimed had been his abduction by Turkish slavers).

Confessions by the "real" criminal could also prove convictions wrongful, though, of course, there is that problem of false confessions.[25]

But a shocking segment of the literature in this area is based on wholly unreliable evidence, and even anecdote and conjecture, to label convicted defendants "innocent." For example, one of the earliest, and most oft-cited, works on wrongful convictions was a 1987 study done by Hugo Bedau and Michael Radelet claiming that 23 of the 350 capital defendants whose cases they examined (including Sacco and Vanzetti) were executed despite their factual innocence.[26] Yet the method by which Bedau (a philosopher) and Radelet (a sociologist) determined whether the executed defendants were actually innocent was essentially to reconstruct from the trial record, and contemporaneous newspaper reports,[27] a quite one-sided narrative from which some doubt about factual guilt might plausibly be argued.

Other scholars immediately criticized this methodology and challenged Bedau and Radelet to come up with a single case of a demonstrably innocent person executed in America in the modern era.[28] Bedau and Radelet have not only been unable to do so, one of them has recently admitted that their label "innocent" was really just a way of saying there were errors in the trial, that factual guilt seemed to them to be a "close call," and

25. An argument could be made that the second confession is more reliable than the first, because it's typically made without any police pressure and under the cover of an already convicted defendant. *See* Stephanos Bibas, *The Right to Remain Silent Helps Only the Guilty*, 88 IOWA L. REV. 421, 426–27 (2003) (arguing that Miranda v. Arizona, 384 U.S. 436 (1966), has hurt the innocent by reducing confessions by the guilty). But, of course, the circumstances of each individual case matter very much on this issue, and it is not at all difficult to imagine reasons for a false second confession—for example, to protect a family member rightly arrested or even convicted.

26. Hugo Adam Bedau & Michael L. Radelet, *Miscarriages of Justice in Potentially Capital Cases*, 40 STAN. L. REV. 21, 73 tbl.10 (1987).

27. *Id.* at 29.

28. *See, e.g.*, Stephen J. Markman & Paul G. Cassell, *Protecting the Innocent: A Response to the Bedau-Radelet Study*, 41 STAN. L. REV. 121 (1988); *see also* FRANKLIN E. ZIMRING, THE CONTRADICTIONS OF AMERICAN CAPITAL PUNISHMENT 163–64 (2003). Judge Cassell has called the idea that innocent people have been executed in America under the modern death penalty system an "urban legend." Paul G. Cassell, *We're Not Executing the Innocent*, WALL ST. J., June 16, 2000, at A14. Of course, there is the now infamous case of Roger K. Coleman, executed for raping and killing his nineteen-year-old sister-in-law. Anti-death-penalty activists across the country put considerable political pressure on Virginia Governor Mark Warner to order post-execution DNA tests—the first governor ever to do so—in an effort to identify the modern era's first wrongfully executed person. *See* Maria Glod & Michael D. Shear, *DNA Tests Confirm Guilt of Executed Man*, WASH. POST, Jan. 13, 2006, at A1. The tests confirmed Coleman's guilt. *See id.* Of course, it would be just as wrong to conclude from this one story that innocence project clients are almost all guilty and the students in those projects all gullible do-gooders, as it would be to conclude that almost all innocence project clients are innocent and their student representatives all modern day Henry Fondas. These high publicity stories may catalyze issues and inject them into the public consciousness, but they cannot tell us anything more than we already know: the systems—both trial and post-trial exoneration—are not perfect.

that some of those close calls must surely, as a statistical matter, have involved some factually innocent people.[29]

It is also not unheard of for academics—or more often reporters or activists misquoting academics—to conflate trial error rates with wrongful conviction rates. Studies showing astonishingly high error rates in capital trials[30] have very little to do with the question of the rate at which factually innocent people are being convicted. It is a giant leap from an erroneous trial ruling to reversible error, and another giant leap from reversible error to factual innocence.

A similar categorical mistake was arguably made by former Illinois Governor George Ryan in 1993, when he commuted all 167 pending death sentences in Illinois, in part because the Northwestern Innocence Project had identified thirteen innocent Illinois death row inmates.[31] Among the prisoners whose death sentences were commuted were many whose factual guilt was not at all in doubt.[32] Why did those deserving to die get the benefit of this kind of twentieth-century version of the Blackstone Ratio?[33] Indeed, much of the empirical confusion about wrongful conviction rates has been driven by histrionics over the death penalty. To a large and unfortu-

29. *See* Hugo Adam Bedau et al., *Convicting the Innocent in Capital Cases: Criteria, Evidence, and Inference*, 52 DRAKE L. REV. 587, 590 (2004) ("Close calls, by themselves, do not provide evidence sufficient to enable us to point to the innocence of a particular individual defendant who was executed."). I sympathize with the so-far unsuccessful hunt for even a single wrongfully executed person in the modern era, and even with the argument that such persons almost certainly exist, given the most recent data from innocence projects. But even with a numerator other than zero, we still need a denominator to estimate the *rates* of wrongful executions, and it is the *rates* that matter in assessing imperfect systems. *See infra* text accompanying notes 34–38.

30. *See, e.g.*, James S. Liebman et al., *Capital Attrition: Error Rates in Capital Cases, 1973-1995*, 78 TEX. L. REV. 1839, 1850 (2000) (claiming overall capital trial error rate of 68%).

31. Gov. Ryan commuted 164 death sentences to life, and 3 to 40 years (consistent with the sentences received by their co-defendants). *See* Abdon M. Pallasch et al., *Gov. Ryan Empties Death Row of All 167*, CHI. SUN-TIMES, Jan. 12, 2003, at 2A. The day before, he pardoned four death row inmates whom he determined had been tortured into confessing. *Id.*

32. This included Jacqueline Williams, who wanted a baby so much that she and her confederates broke into a pregnant woman's apartment, shot and stabbed her, cut her open and removed her fetus, then killed her ten-year-old and eight-year-old children to eliminate them as witnesses. *See* James Taranto, Best of the Web Today, http://www.opinionjournal.com/best/?id=110002904 (last visited March 29, 2007). Governor Ryan admitted not all of the 167 were innocent: "Hell, I know some of those people are guilty. But you can't pick and choose. That's what drove us to mass commutations. How many more cases of wrongful convictions have to occur before we can all agree that this system in Illinois is broken?" Pallasch et al., *supra* note 31 (quoting Gov. Ryan). In his January 13, 2003, online column for the Wall Street Journal, James Taranto called the mass commutations "an act of stunning moral vanity." Taranto, *supra*.

33. One might also ask why Gov. Ryan merely commuted the death sentences of all Illinois death row inmates instead of pardoning them, since he'd admitted only "some" of them were factually guilty. That is, the "wrongful conviction" rationale is both too strong and too weak to justify Gov. Ryan's mass commutations.

nate extent, the debate about wrongful convictions in a capital context has become a proxy for arguments in favor of and against the death penalty.[34]

And then there is the biggest empirical problem of all—what I call the problem of the missing denominator. Because the myth of innocence is a myth if we have exaggerated the *frequency* of wrongful convictions, it does us no good to wring our hands over the number of wrongful convictions if we cannot associate that number with the number of rightful convictions. We need a denominator. It is true that innocence projects across the country have identified, through DNA, some 500 rape and homicide defendants over the last two decades who were wrongfully convicted at trial.[35] But over that period, more than forty million felony cases were filed.[36]

The data emanating from innocence projects never, and perhaps for ethical reasons could never, tell us how many clients had their guilt confirmed by DNA analysis.[37] Despite this lack of a denominator, most reporters and some scholars have jumped to the unsupportable conclusion that the system is in chaos and that innocent defendants are being convicted at an alarmingly high, even if never mentioned, rate.[38]

Even when they mention a rate, these leaps of faith ignore the difference between pleading guilty and being found guilty after trial, and thus

34. *Compare* Paul G. Cassell, *In Defense of the Death Penalty*, *in* DEBATING THE DEATH PENALTY: SHOULD AMERICA HAVE CAPITAL PUNISHMENT? 183 (Hugo Adam Bedau & Paul G. Cassell eds., 2004), *with* HELEN PREJEAN, THE DEATH OF INNOCENTS: AN EYEWITNESS ACCOUNT OF WRONGFUL EXECUTIONS (2005).

35. Even this number is just an educated guess, because innocence projects have sprouted at a rate that has not kept up with their reporting. It does appear that in the seventeen-year period 1989–2003 a total of 340 rape and homicide convicts were exonerated by innocence projects. Samuel R. Gross et al., *Exonerations in the United States, 1989 through 2003*, 95 J. CRIM. L. & CRIMINOLOGY 523, 523–24 (2005). I am therefore using a conservative (that is, high) extrapolated figure of 500 exonerations for the twenty-year period 1986–2005.

36. In the mid-point year of that period, 1997, there were roughly two million felony filings in state courts. NAT'L CTR. FOR STATE COURTS, EXAMINING THE WORK OF STATE COURTS, 2003, at 38 (2003), *available at* http://www.ncsconline.org/d_research/csp/2003_Files/2003_Criminal.pdf. Federal criminal filings were comparatively negligible, amounting to only 60,000 in fiscal year 1997. BUREAU OF JUSTICE STATISTICS, U.S. DEP'T OF JUSTICE, COMPENDIUM OF FEDERAL JUSTICE STATISTICS, 1997, at 16 tbl.1.2, *available at* http://www.ojp.usdoj.gov/bjs/pub/pdf/cfjs9902.pdf. Thus, I use the figure of two million felony cases per year, or forty million over the twenty-year period from 1986–2005.

37. *See* Ellen Yankiver Suni, *Ethical Issues for Innocence Projects: An Initial Primer*, 70 UMCK L. REV. 921, 949 (2002) (discussing the problem of disclosing facts learned from a guilty innocent project client).

38. *See, e.g.*, Rodney Uphoff, *Convicting the Innocent: Aberration or Systemic Problem?*, 2006 WIS. L. REV. 739. Despite its ambitious title, this article makes no effort to approximate wrongful conviction *rates* and, like virtually every other scholarly contribution to the myth of innocence, uses single cases to prove what no serious person disputes: that the system is not perfect. In fact, the title of this article itself reflects the confused thinking about this problem. Wrongful convictions can be, and I suggest probably are, both systemic and exceedingly rare. *See also* Adam Liptak, *Study Suspects Thousands of False Convictions*, N.Y. TIMES, Apr. 19, 2004, at A15.

assume with absolutely no basis that the error rates are the same for both.[39] But even if we assume a high and unacceptable trial error rate—say 20%—no serious scholar believes that two out of every ten defendants who plead guilty are innocent.[40]

It is nevertheless possible, with some careful examination of charge rates, trial rates, and data from innocence projects, coupled with some modest assumptions and extrapolations, to estimate a lower and upper bound of the wrongful conviction rate. On the upper bound side, we know wrongful *trial* convictions are exceedingly rare, as a percentage of all criminal cases, for no other reason than that criminal trials themselves are exceedingly rare. The average federal plea bargaining rate is 96.3%.[41] The average state rate is 95%.[42] That means that even if juries were only 80% right (an assumption at which even the most radical of trial critics would surely cringe), the overall wrongful conviction rate would still be only around 1%, assuming all defendants who plead guilty are guilty.

Do innocent people plead guilty? Of course. Innocent people sometimes even preempt their false guilty pleas by falsely confessing, both with and without overbearing interrogation. But, again, at what *rates* do factually innocent people confess or plead guilty?[43] Even if 1 out of 100 pleading defendants is factually innocent, the upper bound for the overall wrongful conviction rate would still be just 1.95%.[44]

39. *See, e.g.*, Andrew E. Taslitz, *Convicting the Guilty, Acquitting the Innocent: The ABA Takes a Stand*, CRIM. JUST., Winter 2005, at 18, 19 (concluding that even if the error rate is small, "tens of thousands" of innocent people are in prison or otherwise under supervision). But this very much depends on how small the wrongful conviction rate is. If it is only 0.0016%, *see infra* text accompanying notes 43–48, and even if every wrongfully convicted defendant is in prison, then of the roughly two million people in U.S. prisons today only thirty-two are innocent.

40. The only study of false guilty pleas that I am aware of was done in England in the early 1980s, and it concluded that 2.2% of a sample 500 guilty pleas in the city of Birmingham appeared unjustified based on independent reviews of the committal papers. *See* MICHAEL MCCONVILLE & JOHN BALDWIN, COURTS, PROSECUTION, AND CONVICTION 66–67 (1981).

41. In 2003 (the latest year for which these statistics are available), 74,850 federal criminal cases were filed (and not dismissed) and 72,110 of them were disposed of by guilty plea. BUREAU OF JUSTICE STATISTICS, U.S. DEP'T OF JUSTICE, SOURCEBOOK OF CRIMINAL JUSTICE STATISTICS 2003, at 423 tbl.5.22 [hereinafter BJS SOURCEBOOK], *available at* http://www.albany.edu/sourcebook/.

42. BJS SOURCEBOOK, *supra* note 41, at 450 tbl.5.46.

43. The increasingly pervasive myth of false confessions is a kind of corollary to the myth of innocence. But like the data on wrongful convictions, the data of false confessions has been exaggerated beyond all statistical recognition. *See* Paul G. Cassell, *The Guilty and the "Innocent": An Examination of Alleged Cases of Wrongful Conviction from False Confessions*, 22 HARV. J.L. & PUB. POL'Y 523 (1999) (concluding that in a recent study of false confessions a substantial fraction of defendants labeled "innocent" were in fact guilty, that the problem of false confessions does not appear to be pervasive, and that it is concentrated among the mentally retarded).

44. That is, the 1% of tried defendants wrongfully convicted, plus the wrongfully-pleading defendants, whose percentages are calculated as 95% x 1/100 = 0.95%. I can't imagine the "innocent-but-pleading" rate is anywhere near 1 out of 100, although I say this with great trepidation and humility. There is no doubt that the plea bargain machinery puts tremendous pressure on criminal defendants—

As for the lower bound, innocence project data allow us to do some estimates. In the twenty years in which innocence projects have identified roughly 500 people wrongfully convicted after trial,[45] there were roughly two million trials.[46] Even assuming 25% of those two million trials resulted in acquittals (and ignoring, as legal academics are wont to do, the problem of wrongful acquittals), that would yield a wrongful trial conviction rate of only 0.033%.[47] Since, as mentioned above, only 5% of cases are tried, that yields a lower bound for the overall error rate of the system at around 0.0016%.[48]

Now, where between these two estimated bounds—1.95% and 0.0016%—does the real wrongful conviction rate lie? No one knows, but we do know wrongful convictions are not anywhere near the 50/50 kind of proposition that infects the popular culture.

When I say that the myth of innocence infects the popular culture, I may well be doing a disservice to the general public by attributing the myth so completely and broadly to them. In fact, I suspect the average person has a great deal of confidence in the reliability of the system in ordinary kinds of cases for ordinary sorts of purposes. For example, I doubt a prospective employer's first reaction to an applicant's disclosure of a prior felony conviction is to assume the conviction was wrongful and that the applicant was factually innocent. And where have the mavens of wrongful conviction been in the slew of corporate scandals that have spilled into the criminal

guilty and innocent alike—to plead guilty to avoid the risk of a much more drastic result. And, in fact, the myth of innocence—which, to a charged defendant, makes the system look incapable of distinguishing the guilty from the innocent—only increases the pressure for the innocent to plead guilty, as discussed in Part IV(D). The confluence of these forces could mean that innocent defendants plead guilty at a higher rate, but there are other forces that reduce this likelihood. Political pressures on prosecutors will limit how sweet their offers will be to very serious charges. Trial judges can reduce the risk by refusing to accept waivers of the factual basis even when state versions of the Federal Rule of Criminal Procedure 11 allow waivers, and by refusing to take so-called *Alford* pleas. *See* North Carolina v. Alford, 400 U.S. 25, 37–38 (1970) (guilty plea by defendant who insists on his factual innocence, and says he is pleading guilty to avoid the risk of wrongful conviction and execution, is not an "involuntary" plea).

45. *See supra* note 35.

46. I reach this conclusion by applying a 5% trial rate to the roughly forty million criminal cases filed in that twenty-year period. *See supra* note 36.

47. An acquittal rate of 25% applied to a total of two million trials yields 1.5 million trial convictions. If only 500 of those trial convictions were wrongful, that represents a wrongful conviction rate of 0.00033 (500 ÷ 1,500,000).

48. It is a lower bound because we can safely assume that not all wrongfully convicted defendants in this period have been identified (that is, the real numerator is likely higher). This number also assumes all people who plead guilty are in fact guilty, and we know that's not true. *See supra* note 40 and accompanying text.

law? My guess is that not many ordinary people think Kenneth Lay was railroaded by a deeply unreliable trial system.[49]

In the end, the myth of innocence seems to be driven more by legal academics, wrongful conviction advocates, and journalists than by the available data. But as with all editorials dressed in the sheep's clothing of fact, the myth of innocence at least threatens to become accepted liturgy, and that acceptance could, paradoxically, do substantial damage to the reliability of the criminal justice system.

Before addressing the costs and benefits of the myth, let me pause to emphasize the difference between factual guilt and moral guilt. I do this because in my judgment the most significant cost of the myth of innocence is an overemphasis on factual guilt and a corresponding neglect of moral guilt.[50]

II. Factual Guilt and Moral Guilt

When I use the phrase "factual guilt" I mean to describe the situation in which a criminal defendant did in fact commit the act charged, whether or not he had the required mental state. When I use the phrase "moral guilt" I mean the conclusion the fact finder makes about the mental state of a factually guilty defendant, as well as the broader, though related, question of what punishment is just.

Mens rea, which is Latin for "guilty mind," has been part of our criminal law from its English inceptions.[51] In fact, virtually every civilization that has left a record on the subject—including the Babylonians, Jews, Egyptians, Greeks, and Romans—recognized the idea that both the act and intention must be judged by the law.[52] Indeed, the notion that punishable

49. I recognize the myth of innocence does not adhere as tightly to the rich and well-represented, which of course is just part of the central racist and classist assumptions upon which the myth has always been built. *See infra* text accompanying notes 84–86.

50. *See infra* Part IV(E).

51. It comes from the English legal precept "*actus non facit reum nisi mens sit reat*" (the act is not guilty unless the mind is guilty), which dates from at least the time of Henry I in the early 1100s, and which was likely based on the writings of St. Augustine. *See* Francis Bowes Sayre, *Mens Rea*, 45 HARV. L. REV. 974, 974 (1932); Paul Robinson, *Mens Rea* 3 (Univ. Penn. Law Sch., Working Paper No. 35, 1999), *available at* http://lsr.nellco.org/cgi/viewcontent.cgi?article=1038&context=upenn/wps.

52. *See* Morissette v. United States, 342 U.S. 246, 243 & n.4 (1952) (citing 8 ENCYCLOPEDIA OF THE SOCIAL SCIENCES 126 (1932)). It is true that this general rule had some strict liability exceptions, such as the quite common ancient rule that a man was strictly liable for the acts of his slaves, and even a strict liability view of homicide. *See* 2 FREDERICK POLLOCK & FREDERIC WILLIAM MAITLAND, THE HISTORY OF ENGLISH LAW: BEFORE THE TIME OF EDWARD I 470–73 (Lawyers' Literary Club 2d ed. 1959) (1895). But these exceptions did not displace the rule that even in ancient times—when access to the workings of the mind was so limited, at least by modern standards—civilized people cared both about the wrongdoer's acts and his intentions.

crimes must be non-accidental appears to be a human universal.[53] Holmes famously noted that even a dog knows the difference between being stumbled over and kicked.[54]

And yet mens rea also seems to be one of a handful of legal precepts that simply does not resonate with the general public.[55] True, the public's reaction to the notion that a criminal's state of mind should have something to do with his guilt has no doubt waxed and waned over time.[56] Many people's current skepticism about mental state defenses (including the general defense that the defendant did not have the required mental state) seems grounded on a perfectly appropriate and healthy skepticism of psychiatry and psychology.[57] But there also seems to be a deeper, and perhaps more longstanding, belief that serious criminal acts should be punished regardless of the actor's state of mind, simply because we can never be sure of what was in the actor's mind. Everyone understands that a Mafia hit and a hunting accident should generate different responses from the criminal law, but refinements beyond that seem troubling.[58]

53. *See* Stephen Morse & Morris B. Hoffman, *The Uneasy Entente Between Insanity and Mens Rea: Beyond* Clark v. Arizona, J. CRIM. L. & CRIMINOLOGY (forthcoming fall 2007) (manuscript at 7, *available at* http://lsr.nellco.org/cgi/viewcontent.cgi?article=1147&context=upenn/wps). *But see* Deborah W. Denno, *Criminal Law in a Post-Freudian World*, 2005 U. ILL. L. REV. 601, 610 & n.58 ("Commentators generally agree that primitive English law, developed during the fifth century, was basically grounded in strict liability.") (citing 2 POLLOCK & MAITLAND, *supra* note 52, at 470–73); Guyora Binder, *The Rhetoric of Motive and Intent*, 6 BUFF. CRIM. L. REV. 1, 15 (2002) (suggesting that "the supposedly ancient concept of mens rea as evil motive is really a modern polemical construct"). This confusion about the historical pedigree of mens rea may have something to do with the fact that the criminal law itself—in the modern sense of the state punishing free-riders—is relatively recent. *See* Morse & Hoffman, *supra*, at 55–56. This confusion may also explain why the United States Supreme Court has described principles of mens rea as being "essential" to the criminal law, *Morissette*, 342 U.S. at 273–74, but has never held that they are so fundamental as to be required by substantive due process. *Compare* Herbert L. Packer, *Mens Rea and the Supreme Court*, 1962 SUP. CT. REV. 107 (suggesting constitutional limits to the legislative abolition of mens rea) *with* Louis D. Bilionis, *Process, the Constitution, and Substantive Criminal Law*, 96 MICH. L. REV. 1269, 1278–79 (1998) (calling the notion that "individualized moral blameworthiness" is central to the criminal law a myth). The ambivalence of the Court and commentators on this constitutional question is no doubt framed by the emergence of the regulatory state and its increasing reliance on newly-created strict liability crimes.

54. OLIVER WENDELL HOLMES, JR., THE COMMON LAW 3 (Dover Publ'ns 1991) (1881).

55. The others that come to mind are the doctrines of complicity (and its cousin felony murder) and, in the civil arena, employment-at-will. The general public's uneasiness with these doctrines often emerges in jury selection. In my experience, it is not at all uncommon for prospective jurors to express disbelief that someone who did not pull the trigger could be guilty of murder, or that an employer can fire employees for almost any (or no) reason (at least in states, like Colorado, that remain employment-at-will states).

56. This vacillation seems to have corresponded roughly to a similar vacillation in the public's acceptance of the insanity defense. John Hinckley's acquittal did much to drive recent skepticism about insanity. *See* Morse & Hoffman, *supra* note 53, at 59–60.

57. *See, e.g.*, *id.* at 63 (criticizing the "over-sciencing" of mens rea and insanity).

58. This skepticism about super-refinements of intentionality has been expressed by several commentators who have argued that the four flavors of intentionality recognized by the Model Penal Code—intentional, knowing, reckless, and negligent—in fact collapse into one another. *See, e.g.*, Larry

Indeed, human brains have likely been built by evolution to give their owners a strong presumption that other humans' misbehaviors are intentional and not accidental. It is not difficult to imagine that a strong neural presumption of intentionality would have been highly adaptive. It is unlikely that our ancestors would have survived to be our ancestors had they not been equipped with powerful assumptions that the stranger coming over the hill was equipped with the same capacity for intentionality (e.g., murder) as they were.[59]

This leaves us with an impossible neural paradox. We have a deeply embedded sense that we should not punish accidents the same as non-accidents, yet an equally powerful sense that most human actions are intentional and a corresponding skepticism about protestations by the wrongdoer that the wrong was an accident. In fact, these questions have a normative content incapable of scientific assessment. Despite all of neuroscience's recent advancements, it still cannot discriminate, or indeed even define, the differences between, for example, acting intentionally and acting knowingly. Some of us have argued not only that these categories are logically indistinct,[60] but that they mask a normative continuum that really just boils down to one question: how bad was this behavior?[61] Jurors, not brain scanners, must answer that question.

In any event, this generalized resistance to the mens rea inquiry—at least to any form of the inquiry more refined than accident versus non-accident—may explain, in part, why so many people, including Sidney Lumet, wrongly assume that the focus of criminal trials is on factual

Alexander, *Insufficient Concern: A Unified Conception of Criminal Culpability*, 88 CAL. L. REV. 931 (2000); Morris B. Hoffman, Booker, *Pragmatism, and the Moral Jury*, 13 GEO. MASON L. REV. 455, 473–74 (2005); *see also* Douglas N. Husak & Craig A. Callender, *Wilful Ignorance, Knowledge, and the "Equal Culpability" Thesis: A Study of the Deeper Significance of the Principle of Legality*, 1994 WIS. L. REV. 29 (discussing the "problem" of willful ignorance and the unsatisfactory treatment of that mental state by courts); Kimberly Kessler Ferzan, *Opaque Recklessness*, 91 J. CRIM. L. & CRIMINOLOGY. 597, 597–60 (2001) (arguing that this culpable mental state does not fit into the current framework of the Model Penal Code). The same skepticism about our ability to assess mental states has driven five state legislatures to abolish the insanity defense altogether, and others to channel all mental state evidence into the insanity issue and to forbid it as a negation of mens rea. It has also driven the Supreme Court's deference to those legislative decisions. *See infra* note 62.

59. *See, e.g.*, Morris B. Hoffman & Timothy H. Goldsmith, Commentary, *The Biological Roots of Punishment*, 1 OHIO ST. J. CRIM. L. 627 (2004). Of course, I do not mean to commit the naturalistic fallacy by suggesting that the fact we may have an evolutionary predilection to assume intentionality means that the law should reflect that predilection. But such a built-in prejudice would explain the difficulties legislators, judges, and jurors have with mens rea. *See generally* Owen D. Jones, *Time-Shifted Rationality and the Law of Law's Leverage: Behavioral Economics Meets Behavioral Biology*, 95 NW. U. L. REV. 1141 (2001).

60. *See supra* note 58.

61. *See* Hoffman, *supra* note 58, at 474.

guilt.[62] At least in my experience, factual guilt is seldom a genuine trial issue,[63] and what most jurors end up struggling over is not "whodunit" but rather "what was that guy thinking?"

III. A Brief History of the Myth

Truth has always been an important human idea. The Egyptians, Sumerians, and Hindus (as just a small cross-section) all worshipped deities devoted to truth.[64] Cicero's first division of moral goodness was "the knowledge of truth."[65] The significance of the association between the good and the true is that it simultaneously recognizes the human capacity to lie and the categorical, or at least social, value of resisting the temptation to do so in most circumstances.[66]

In ancient systems, the unity of God and ruler meant that "truth-finding" wasn't any more complicated than a matter of accessing revealed truth. The myth of innocence was not necessary, or even conceivable, in

62. Even the United States Supreme Court has at times exhibited some hostility toward mens rea, driving it to the same sort of confusion between mens rea and excuse exhibited by jurors and legislators. For example, despite acknowledging the common law and pre-common law pedigree of mens rea, the Court has never found that mens rea is so fundamental as to be required by substantive due process. *See supra* note 53. To be fair, this result probably has more to do with the Court's deference to states on these issues of defining crimes than with its own hostility toward mens rea. *See, e.g.*, Montana v. Egelhoff, 518 U.S. 37, 56 (1996) (upholding Montana statute prohibiting introduction of evidence of voluntary intoxication to negate mens rea); Patterson v. New York, 432 U.S. 197, 206–07 (1977) (upholding New York statute shifting to defendant the burden of proving defense of "extreme emotional disturbance"); Powell v. Texas, 392 U.S. 514, 535–37 (1968) (upholding Texas public drunkenness law, even as applied to chronic alcoholics who allegedly cannot "control" their behavior). Moreover, in Clark v. Arizona. 126 S. Ct. 2709 (2006), the Court not only upheld Arizona's truncated insanity definition, *see id.* at 2718–25, but also upheld the Arizona case-based rule channeling most mental health evidence into insanity and away from mens rea, *see id.* at 2725–29, making it extremely difficult, if not impossible, to show already skeptical jurors that a sane but mentally disturbed defendant may nevertheless have lacked the required mens rea because of his mental condition.

63. There are, of course, cases in which factual guilt is very much at issue, and even some categories of cases that seem more likely to raise questions about factual guilt, such as sex assaults on children, where there is often no forensic evidence. But they are the exception and not the rule.

64. The Egyptian goddess of truth and justice was Maat, who represented "the order which rules the world through balance." PATRICIA TURNER & CHARLES RUSSELL COULTER, DICTIONARY OF ANCIENT DEITIES 298 (Oxford Univ. Press 2001) (2000). The Sumerian god of truth was Kittu, but, interestingly, his job title did not include justice; that job was his brother's, Misharu. *See* James W. Bell, Sumerian Gods, Demons & Immortals Whose Names Start with "K", http://www.jameswbell.com/geog0050knames.html (last visited March 29, 2007). Addanari is the Hindu goddess of truth, nature, and religion. TURNER & COULTER, *supra*, at 14. Shiva, among her many other jobs, is also associated with truth. *Id.* at 427.

65. M. TULLIUS CICERO, DE OFFICIIS 18–19 (Walter Miller trans., Harvard Univ. Press 1961) (1913).

66. There may be biological roots to our deepest notions of right and wrong, including our imperfect worship of the true, grounded in the fact that we evolved as highly social animals in relatively small groups. *See, e.g.*, Morris B. Hoffman, *The Neuroeconomic Path of the Law*, *in* LAW AND THE BRAIN (Semir Zeki & Oliver Goodenough eds., 2006); Edward O. Wilson, *The Biological Basis of Morality*, THE ATLANTIC MONTHLY, Apr. 1998, at 53.

these systems because God told us—directly or through his anointed ruler—what was true and what was false, what was right and what was wrong, and who was guilty and who was innocent.[67] But as civilizations became more complex and as the reach of absolute divine rule was diluted by bureaucracy (and, in the West, by the Church), systems had to be developed as proxies for the unerring truth-detecting abilities of individual god-kings. A certain lack of trust in the divine proxies was understandable, and more forgivable than a lack of trust in the divine itself. Justice and truth-finding became forever infected with the imperfections of man.

Thus, for example, even the Babylonians, for whom the concepts of law and justice played such an early and central role, and who identified justice with two different gods, Marduk and Shamash, developed a court system in which cases were heard by up to four judges, whose verdicts were reviewable by the king.[68] The Babylonians recognized that justice systems administered by non-divine but divinely-appointed judges might be infected with human error correctible only by the divine king himself.[69]

Another complication is that as the gods began to take on more and more characteristics of man—the gods of the Greeks fighting and lying and philandering and otherwise acting thoroughly human—gods needed their own dispute resolution system, and mythical justice began to be administered in two discrete systems, one for gods and one for men. Thus, the Greek goddess Dike was the goddess of human justice, but her mother Themis was the goddess of divine justice.[70]

But "justice" has always been much broader than mere "truth-finding." Indeed, the image of justice with the balanced scales—probably first represented by Greek depictions of Dike and Themis, and later copied by the Roman goddess Justicia—may well have been meant to reflect the

67. Although as already mentioned, in one of the Old Testament's quintessentially anthropomorphic visions of God, even He occasionally gets confused between guilt and innocence. *See supra* note 22.

68. MSN Encarta Encyclopedia, Babylonia, http://encarta.msn.com/encyclopedia_761571780_2___8/Babylonia.html#s8 (last visited March 29, 2007); Gateways to Babylon, Marduk, http://www.gatewaystobabylon.com/gods/lords/marduk1.html (last visited March 29, 2007).

69. This notion of justice by divine intervention seems to be a human universal, often expressed in the form of trial by battle or ordeal, discussed in the text accompanying notes 71–77. Where, you might ask, were the interventionist powers of Marduk (or Apollo) to prevent the errors in the first place? The answer, in part, is probably grounded in the nature of polytheistic systems, in which individual gods had limited, and competing, powers. Marduk and Apollo may have been divine, but their ability to prevent injustice in the human world was compromised by the meddling influences of dozens of other powerful gods, who cared about things other than justice.

70. In some ways this distinction may have mimicked the distinction ancients made between public and private wrongs.

balanced and proportionate approach to *punishment*, not the weighing of evidence of factual guilt, as in the modern symbolism.

Still, the ancients were well aware of the fallibility of man, and indeed even of the increasing fallibility of their anthropomorphic gods. As forms of democracy and republican government erupted onto the human stage and replaced infallible kings, even if temporarily, ancient systems begin to worry about factual guilt along with the divine challenge of just punishment. Thus, classical and post-classical trial systems were very much interested in the problem of wrongful conviction. By the time of the always practical Romans, trial systems were being designed as much for truth-finding as punishment, which was still left largely to the Senate or emperor, or their magisterial representatives.[71]

But all this began to change with the ascendancy of the Church. All-knowing god-kings, with their potentially fallible human agents, and classical trial systems designed to check fallible but powerful rulers, began to be replaced with a single all-knowing God, just interventionist enough to take worries about factual innocence back off the table. Thus, medieval truth-finding systems, both on the continent and in England, were once again based on revealed truth, in the form of reconstituted theological versions of the ancient rights of trial by battle and trial by ordeal.[72] The guilty man lost the trial by battle because God intervened to cause him to lose. The guilty were burned in the ordeal of hot iron because God intervened to cause that just result.

The jury, though long in existence in Europe, and likely imported to England during the Conquest, was nevertheless exceedingly rare from the time of Charlemagne through the mid-1200s.[73] For most serious crimes,

71. Indeed, most ancient, classical, and even medieval juries were presentment juries, that is, they typically acted as modern-day grand juries, screening cases for probable cause before the ultimate guilt or innocence, and punishment, was determined later by other methods. WILLIAM FORSYTH, HISTORY OF TRIAL BY JURY 106 (2d ed. 1971). It took the English presentment jury several centuries to evolve first from mere presentment, then to a mixed system of presentment and trial before a subset of the presentment jurors, then to a completely separate system of non-overlapping presentment and trial juries. *Id.* at 125–38.

72. Trial by battle and trial by ordeal both have rich pre-medieval histories, reaching back as far as recorded civilizations. There is evidence that the Israelites, pre-Roman era Germanic tribes, and Swedish Goths all practiced a form of trial by battle, which then spread to Europe through the Vikings. EDWARD J. WHITE, LEGAL ANTIQUITIES: A COLLECTION OF ESSAYS UPON ANCIENT LAWS AND CUSTOMS 109–12 & n.10 (1913). Various forms of the ordeal are just as old, appearing to have been practiced by the Egyptians (from the time of Ahmase II), ancient Greeks, Israelites, and even Hindus. *Id.* at 141–43 & n.4.

73. *See* THOMAS ANDREW GREEN, VERDICT ACCORDING TO CONSCIENCE: PERSPECTIVES ON THE ENGLISH CRIMINAL TRIAL JURY 1200–1800, at 11 (1985); 1 FREDERICK POLLOCK & FREDERIC WILLIAM MAITLAND, THE HISTORY OF ENGLISH LAW: BEFORE THE TIME OF EDWARD I 37–40 (2d ed. 1898). Some legal historians have even argued that the jury trial began as a procedural antecedent of the ordeal, with the role of proto-jurors limited to deciding which ordeal a given defendant should face. *See*,

trial by ordeal and, to a lesser extent, trial by battle, remained the Crown's and Church's trial method of choice.

The worm of revealed truth began to turn yet again in the early part of the thirteenth century, as a result of increasing theological skepticism about God's interest in the everyday activities of man,[74] as well as a few prominent scandals in which priests performing these truth-finding rituals had been bribed by the winning side.[75] The ordeal was banned by the Church in 1215.[76] And although trial by battle remained on the books in England until 1819, it fell out of favor in the thirteenth century and all but disappeared by the end of Edward III's reign.[77] Largely by default, trial by jury became the English truth-finding mechanism for serious crimes.

In England, the idea that the state might wrongfully accuse an individual of committing a crime ascended at roughly the same time as the divine perfection of kings descended, and nobles became not the enforcers of the King's law but its principal political targets.[78] The problem was simple: people lacked confidence in the divine truth-finding abilities of kings, yet kings retained the same powers of accusation as they did in the days their powers were thought divine. The criminal law became an important tool in the King's struggle for retaining that power, and prominent anti-royalist

e.g., THEODORE F.T. PLUCKNETT, A CONCISE HISTORY OF THE COMMON LAW 120 (Little, Brown & Co. 5th ed. 1956) (1929).

74. As one English legal historian has put it, "The clergy had never given an unqualified assent to the ordeal; they had been the means of its gradual disuse, as they deemed it an impious reference to Heaven." JOHN PROFFATT, A TREATISE ON TRIAL BY JURY, INCLUDING QUESTIONS OF LAW AND FACT § 28, at 41–42 (Fred B. Rothman & Co. 1986) (1877).

75. One prominent priest admitted that he had felt a moral duty to assist in achieving the "right" result. PLUCKNETT, *supra* note 73, at 114–15.

76. This ban was part of Pope Innocent III's Fourth Lateran Council. *Id.* at 118–19.

77. LLOYD E. MOORE, THE JURY: TOOL OF KINGS, PALLADIUM OF LIBERTY 123 (2d ed. 1988); WHITE, *supra* note 72, at 118; Daniel Klerman, *Settlement and the Decline of Private Prosecution in Thirteenth-Century England*, 19 LAW & HIST. REV. 1 (2001).

78. Many of the most significant English criminal law reforms can be traced to Parliament's own fear of prosecution. These reforms included Parliament's abolition of the Crown's unlimited peremptory challenges in 1305, An Ordinance for Inquests, 1305, 33 Edw., Stat. 4 (Eng.); limitations on the King's right to pardon homicides imposed in 1389, Other Statutes Made at Westminster, 1389, 13 Rich. 2, c. 1 (Eng.); the first right to counsel (in treason cases only) in 1695, An Act for Regulateing of Tryals in Cases of Treason and Misprision of Treason, 1695, 7 & 8 Will. 3, c. 3 (Eng.); and its repeal of the ban of "full defense" (i.e. allowing defense counsel to address the jury) in felony cases in 1836, An Act for Enabling Persons Indicted of Felony to Make Their Defence by Counsel or Attorney, 6 & 7 Will. 4, c. 114 (1836). Some scholars have argued more generally that in both England and America legislators have been willing to implement the most significant protections in criminal law and procedure at times when they believed themselves most at risk of criminal prosecution. *See* Craig S. Lerner, *Legislators as the "American Criminal Class": Why Congress (Sometimes) Protects the Rights of Defendants*, 2004 U. ILL. L. REV. 599.

members of Parliament were occasionally accused on trumped-up charges and executed.[79]

It was this fear—of political repression through unjust criminal prosecution—that caused a kind of neo-classical rediscovery in England of the problem of factual innocence. The idea that the criminal law could be, and was, used as an unjust tool of political repression was a significant and resonating narrative of the Enlightenment—a narrative that had important repercussions in the American colonies. American skepticism, even hatred, of the English criminal justice system was a central part of the pre-revolutionary experience. The new nation's preoccupation with factual guilt coincided exactly with its collective suspicion of our English ancestors' woeful, or at least suspicious, ability to detect the truth in politically charged cases.

Yet even as the jury trial emerged in England and America as the pre-eminent, and humanly flawed, form of truth-detection, it would be a mistake to believe that over the broad swathe of its history it was concerned primarily with factual guilt. It was not. It was much more concerned with the punitive aspects of moral guilt, that is, with the punishment that a just and merciful king or society should impose on the factually guilty. After all, apart from political prosecutions, English life went on, and ordinary criminals needed to be detected and prosecuted. And the overall confidence in the reliability of these tasks remained high.

In fact, throughout the police-less seventeenth and eighteenth centuries, ordinary criminal cases in England were frequently initiated and, in the modern parlance, "put together," by victims or witnesses themselves, with any additional rudimentary investigation done by the magistrates at what we would call the preliminary hearing.[80] Even after the creation of professional police in London in the late 1800s, magistrates retained the power to summarily convict or acquit in misdemeanor cases, and it seems the vast bulk of prosecutions not only terminated at the magistrate level, but frequently enjoyed a legislative exemption from the ordinary presumption of innocence.[81] Parliament might have had serious worries about the

79. Perhaps the most famous examples were the political trials of the 1680s conducted by Judges Jeffreys and Scroggs, and the treason trials of the later Stuarts. *See* JOHN H. LANGBEIN, THE ORIGINS OF ADVERSARY CRIMINAL TRIAL 67–79 (2003).

80. *See* CYNTHIA B. HERRUP, THE COMMON PEACE: PARTICIPATION AND THE CRIMINAL LAW IN SEVENTEENTH-CENTURY ENGLAND 68 (1987); PETER KING, CRIME, JUSTICE AND DISCRETION IN ENGLAND: 1740–1820, at 17 (2000); *see also* John Styles, *Sir John Fielding and the Problem of Criminal Investigation in Eighteenth-Century England*, 33 TRANSACTIONS OF THE ROYAL HIST. SOC'Y 127 (5th series 1983).

81. *See* Bruce P. Smith, *The Presumption of Guilt and the English Law of Theft, 1750–1850*, 23 LAW & HIST. REV. 133 (2005).

truth-finding abilities of political prosecutions against its own members, but the establishment of guilt in ordinary criminal cases was largely a matter of routine, either at the magistrate or judge level, often bolstered by the statutory presumption of guilt.

Indeed, even in ordinary cases that managed to reach the Crown Courts, the most important function of English jurors, as early as the 1300s, was not to assess factual guilt, which was still pretty much a given, but rather to act as a buffer between the guilty and what came to be viewed by ordinary citizens as grossly excessive levels of punishment. Thomas Green describes mid-fourteenth century English jury verdicts as "judgments about who ought to live and who ought to die, not merely determinations regarding who did what to whom and with what intent."[82] Blackstone's famous phrase "pious perjury" describes the not uncommon nullification by seventeenth century juries in cases where they believed death was unwarranted even for a factually guilty defendant.[83] Even as late as the eighteenth century, English jury trials were in fact "sentencing proceedings," whose whole function was to persuade the jury to convict the factually guilty defendant of a lesser non-capital offense.[84]

How could it be that factual guilt was so taken for granted even after trials were no longer a matter of revealed truth? The answer may have something to do with the oath. God-fearing people took the oath seriously. A truth-finding system that gives witnesses, including the accused, the choice between telling the truth and suffering eternal damnation can have a high level of confidence in its accuracy, and needs no myth of factual innocence.[85] As our Anglo-American faith began to wane, so too did our confidence in the oath, and therefore our confidence in the truth-finding abilities

82. GREEN, *supra* note 73, at 98.

83. WILLIAM BLACKSTONE, 4 COMMENTARIES *238–39.

84. John H. Langbein, *Shaping the Eighteenth-Century Criminal Trial: A View from the Ryder Sources*, 50 U. CHI. L. REV. 1, 41 (1983); *see also* J.M. BEATTIE, CRIME AND THE COURTS IN ENGLAND: 1660–1800, at 419–30 (1986).

85. In fact, a high confidence in the oath was reflected in a third kind of medieval trial system—trial by compurgation, sometimes also called "the wager of law." In criminal trials by compurgation, the accused, after taking his oath of innocence, was required to call a designated number of compurgators, or "oath-helpers." The required number and rank of the compurgators varied according to the seriousness of the charge. If the required quantity and quality of compurgators appeared and vouched by their own oaths for the defendant's oath of innocence, the defendant was declared innocent without any further messy inquiry into the actual facts. *See generally* ROBERT VON MOSCHZISKER, TRIAL BY JURY §§ 43–48, at 34–38 (1922). *See also* Albert W. Alschuler, *A Peculiar Privilege in Historical Perspective: The Right to Remain Silent*, 94 MICH. L. REV. 2625 (1996) (analyzing the impact of our modern failure to recognize the importance of the oath on the meaning of the Fifth Amendment's prohibition of "compell[ing]" a witness to testify).

of any of our systems.[86] It is that loss of confidence in the oath that may have become the kernel at the core of the modern myth of factual innocence.

There is almost no data about colonial and early post-colonial American juries, and almost no innocence liturgy from this period. There is no doubt that slavery—the great festering constitutional issue—left in its wake a profound skepticism about southern governments' ability, and indeed even their intent, to treat the newly freed slaves justly in any manner of things, including the criminal justice system. Thus, most of the earliest American innocence literature is associated with abolitionist and post-abolitionist views of racial injustice, slavery itself being a kind of archetypical wrongful conviction.[87] From Reconstruction and Jim Crow forward, there has been a strong and no doubt entirely earned (though largely retrospective) presumption of wrongful conviction whenever all white policemen arrested, and all white juries convicted, black defendants.[88] This only reinforced our already libertarian skepticism from the Revolutionary period.

The result is an American race-based strain of the myth of innocence that is so robust it has been virtually impervious to the winds of changing politics. From Huckleberry Finn to the Ox-Bow Incident, through and beyond World War II, there has been a powerful American narrative about the shabby way the criminal justice system mistreats the disenfranchised and powerless.

This political strain of the myth has somehow metastasized into an overall lack of confidence in the system's truth-detection abilities, quite apart from the race or ethnicity of its targets. Indeed, in the allegedly bucolic and innocent post-WWII period—when confidence in government was arguably at an all time high—Erle Stanley Gardner's Perry Mason was a staple of pop literature, then radio and television.[89] And in the Perry Ma-

86. For example, concerns in the mid-1700s about wrongful convictions at the Old Bailey led to several evidentiary reforms, including rules relating to confessions and corroboration, and allowing a defendant to be represented by a lawyer. Smith, *supra* note 22, at 1198.

87. Not all of the earliest innocence narratives were race-based. For example, there was a notorious case of the wrongful conviction and near-execution (the supposed murder victim showed up at the hanging) of two free, white Vermont men in 1819. *See* STUART BANNER, THE DEATH PENALTY: AN AMERICAN HISTORY 121–22 (2002).

88. Still, I know of no reliable data on the *rates* at which innocent black defendants were railroaded by the criminal law, both North and South, in the last half of the nineteenth century. The appalling image of perfectly innocent black men being lynched without trials is so repugnant that it has drowned out a very different question: what effect did the racism of that period have, and might still be having, on wrongful conviction rates?

89. Gardner published the first of what would be eighty-two Perry Mason novels in 1933. Warner Brothers actually produced six feature Perry Mason films in the mid- to late-1930s, but the stories did not reach mass appeal until a CBS afternoon radio show that ran from 1944 to 1955. Perry Mason had

son stories the police and prosecutors suffered a 100% error rate—the charged person (always white and often well-to-do) was *never* guilty, and was saved not by Henry Fonda or innocence project students but by Raymond Burr.[90]

And then there is O.J. Simpson. In a delicious inversion of the innocence narrative, this time the black defendant is, from all indications, actually guilty,[91] and the system still can't get it right.

What I call in this essay the "myth of factual innocence" is in some sense a distorted version of the presumption of innocence.[92] It is one thing to presume the innocence of an untried defendant, and quite another to presume it of an already convicted one. Of course, the myth of innocence reinforces the presumption of innocence. It is in the trial process itself—where individual jurors are called upon to assess both the factual and moral guilt of an individual defendant—that the myth has its most palliative value. We *want* jurors to believe the arrest and prosecution systems are so completely unreliable that virtually everyone is factually innocent, in order to reinforce the presumption that the particular defendant before them is innocent. We *want* all jurors to be Henry Fondas, and we *want* all jurors to believe there will be a terrible miscarriage of justice if they are not Henry Fondas. But at what cost?

IV. COSTS OF THE MYTH

A. *Loss of Confidence*

The most obvious cost of the myth of factual innocence is the general public's loss of confidence in the criminal justice system, both in policing and in adjudication. More than fifty years of being told by the fourth estate that innocent people are regularly arrested, and only slightly less regularly

three runs on television, all starring Raymond Burr as the world's winningest criminal defense lawyer: once as a weekly series from 1957 to 1966; then in one season as a series in 1973; and finally as intermittent made-for-television movies that ran from 1985 through Burr's death in 1993.

90. Television took back the mantle of innocence in 1963 in *The Fugitive* series, which ran through the 1967 season.

91. Although acquitted in the criminal case, Simpson was found in the civil case to have caused the deaths of Nicole Brown and Ronald Goldman. Rufo v. Simpson, 103 Cal. Rptr. 2d 492, 497 (Ct. App. 2001).

92. The presumption of innocence—at least the obligation of the state to prove a defendant's guilt, if not necessarily beyond a reasonable doubt—seems to be as deeply embedded in the history of civilization as the ideas of truth and falsity, and human fallibility. It traces its roots through Deuteronomy, Sparta, Athens, Trajan's Rome, and the earliest English common law. For a discussion of the history of the presumption of innocence, see Coffin v. United States, 156 U.S. 432, 454–56 (1895). *But see supra* note 81 and accompanying text (discussing the English statutory presumption of misdemeanor guilt frequently operating at the magistrate level).

convicted, has had its effects. The presumption of innocence, at least in the general public's mind, has become almost irrebuttable. With so many innocent folks caught up in the web of such an unreliable system, guilty verdicts themselves are at risk of losing their reliability, and convictions their opprobrium.

This skepticism about the system is palpable in jury selection. In my experience, it is not uncommon for prospective jurors—especially those who have never actually served on a jury—to express the belief that the trial is some kind of battle of lawyers largely unrelated to truth, that the best lawyers usually win, and therefore that poor people who can't afford the best lawyers tend to be wrongfully convicted.[93] This loss of confidence is also quite regularly expressed by prospective jurors in a form some commentators have dubbed "the CSI bias," in which prospective jurors indicate their confidence in the system is so low that they could not convict anyone without irrefutable forensic evidence.[94]

Having said that, I must also say that I do not believe these views are having significant impacts on verdicts, at least in my jurisdiction, both because jurors with the most extreme forms of these views are being excused for cause or peremptorily, and because jurors in large part can put their prejudices aside, actually pay attention to the evidence and follow the instructions, and do the right thing in the case at hand despite grand views about the system as a whole.[95] Nevertheless, the loss in confidence is hurting the system in the following less direct ways.

B. *Undervaluing Public Defenders/Overvaluing Lawyering*

The myth of factual innocence condemns defense lawyers to the same rubbish bin of incompetence as jurors. All these innocent people are in prison because their defense lawyers were not Perry Mason. If you are rich enough to hire Perry Mason, you get off, sometimes even if you are guilty.

93. Just this year I was astonished by a prospective juror in a criminal case who told us in chambers that he could not be fair because he had heard that the lowest ranking law students are the ones that go on to become district attorneys, and that such under-qualified lawyers must surely be prosecuting lots of innocent people, especially ones who can't afford "real lawyers."

94. These views are probably just fallout from the popular television shows that oversell the state of forensic science. Even so, an exaggerated reliance on forensics plays into an exaggerated view of factual innocence. For a thought-provoking criticism of claims that the "CSI effect" is real, see Tom R. Tyler, *Viewing* CSI *and the Threshold of Guilt: Managing Truth and Justice in Reality and Fiction*, 115 YALE L.J. 1050 (2006).

95. *See* John L. Kane, *Reasonable Doubt and Other Shibboleths*, LITIG., Fall 2002, at 22. Moreover, as I've mentioned above, in their everyday lives and for ordinary (that is, non-trial) purposes, people seem to continue to have a high confidence in the reliability of the system. *See supra* text accompanying notes 48–49.

But if you are so poor you must rely on public defenders instead of "real lawyers," your chances of being rightly acquitted are next to zero.

Despite the innocence project anecdotes about sleeping, drunk, and otherwise incompetent defense lawyers, this picture of rampant defense incompetence couldn't be further from the truth, at least in my experience. I have told friends, and even written,[96] that if they get into serious criminal trouble in Denver, the first thing they should do is give away their assets in order to qualify for a public defender. Yes, public defenders are overburdened and underpaid, but on the whole they are also the finest single collection of criminal defense lawyers around, and for good reason—experience. I would stack the best of our public defenders against any private defense lawyer I know.[97]

Somewhat paradoxically, the low esteem into which the myth of innocence casts public defenders simultaneously overvalues lawyering itself, not unlike how it overvalues forensics. Contrary to public perception, the best facts win, not the best lawyers. Trials are contests of facts, not contests of lawyers. Some of the best lawyering I have ever seen has resulted in spectacular losses, some of the worst in spectacular wins. It's the evidence that's important to outcome, not the oratorical or sartorial abilities of the messengers.[98]

The view that the best lawyers win and the worst lawyers lose, that public defenders are bad and highly paid private defense lawyers are good, not only does terrible damage to the public's already waning confidence in the system, it has the pernicious effect of reinforcing all the worst stereotypes of the system as being hopelessly racist and classist. Not only do innocent people get wrongly convicted, so this stereotype goes, it is the poor and disenfranchised—those who cannot afford Perry Mason—who are getting disproportionately wrongfully convicted. Conversely, rich white

96. Morris B. Hoffman, Op-Ed, *Free-Market Justice*, N.Y. TIMES, Jan. 8, 2007, at A19.

97. Here's where I must admit my own popular and scholarly contributions to the myth of public defender incompetence. Along with two economist co-authors, in 2005 I published an econometric study of public defender effectiveness rates as compared to those of private counsel. Morris B. Hoffman et al., *An Empirical Study of Public Defender Effectiveness: Self-Selection by the "Marginally Indigent,"* 3 OHIO ST. J. CRIM. L. 223 (2005). Our data showed that public defenders were less effective than private lawyers, but a closer reading of that data suggested a reason having nothing to do with abilities: public defender clients tend to be self-selected for guilt. I reprised this analysis in an opinion piece published in the New York Times. *See* Hoffman, *supra* note 96.

98. Granted a certain minimum level of competence is necessary. But here again the myth has mixed up incidents with incidence. Sure, there are terrible miscarriages of justice because defense counsel are too incompetent to defend defensible cases (and, of course, miscarriages of justice in the other direction when incompetent prosecutors are too incompetent to prove provable cases). But at what *rates*?

men who are guilty are regularly getting off because of their highly paid lawyers.

People who believe this may watch lots of movies and TV, but they are not spending much time in our courtrooms. As these mistaken beliefs percolate through the culture and through the population of prospective jurors, they make it only more difficult to find jurors who will be able to decide the case on the merits. The myths of innocence, trial gamesmanship, and unequal treatment become self-fulfilling.

C. *Undervaluing Jurors*

While the myth of innocence overvalues lawyering, it undervalues juroring, and for precisely the same reasons. It is because jurors are such dunderheads, in whose midst we can hardly expect a Henry Fonda once a year let alone every day, that they get bamboozled by slick and corrupt prosecutors (when they wrongfully convict) or by slick and greedy big name defense lawyers (when they wrongfully acquit), or so this stereotype goes. This kind of caricature of jurors is as far from the truth as the caricature of lawyers.

In my experience, jurors almost always take their jobs, and oaths, very seriously. It is not at all uncommon for them to express, in our post-verdict debriefings, that their emotions told them one thing but that the facts and law required them to do the other, in either direction. In many cases in which they have returned not guilty verdicts, jurors tell me afterwards that they thought the defendant was probably guilty, but that the prosecution simply did not prove the case beyond a reasonable doubt. Conversely, I have had many jurors, especially in homicide cases, dissolve into tears because they knew the consequences of their guilty verdict but were compelled by the evidence and the instructions to render it anyway.

The myth of innocence contributes to a terribly impoverished view of jurors as either complete idiots or secret racists, incapable in either event of evaluating evidence fairly and honoring their oaths to decide the case based on that evidence and based on laws with which they might not even agree. Again, as with the other aspects of the myth, as this impoverished view becomes accepted truth in the community of prospective jurors, it threatens to self-fulfill.

D. *Increasing the Rate of Wrongful Pleas*

One of the worst effects of the myth of innocence is that its widespread acceptance among the public will itself increase the chances that innocent defendants might plead guilty. After all, if an innocent person is wrongfully accused of a serious crime, and believes the criminal trial system is so unreliable that he has a good chance of being wrongfully convicted of the charged offense despite his innocence, he will be under tremendous pressure to plead guilty to a less serious charge even though he is innocent. And of course because the system is 95% about guilty pleas and only 5% about trials, even a slight increase in the rate of wrongful pleas, unlike a slight increase in the rate of wrongful trial convictions, will have a tremendous impact on the overall numbers of wrongful convictions.

E. Neglecting Moral Guilt

I've saved for last what I believe to be the most profound and damaging cost of the myth of factual innocence: by overemphasizing factual guilt the system neglects moral guilt. This is the central failing of narratives like *12 Angry Men.*

Prospective jurors are unprepared for the arduous task of assessing a defendant's intentionality in part because they so regularly come into our courtrooms assuming trials are only about factual guilt. It is not uncommon in my experience to have jurors let out audible gasps when I move from the instructions dealing with the charges to the ones dealing with the lesser-included offenses based on less culpable mental states. I can imagine what they are thinking: "What? I spent the last week thinking my job was to decide whether the prosecution proved the defendant pulled the trigger. And now, after all the evidence has been presented, and it is clear to everyone (despite the fact that so many innocent people get convicted) that this defendant is not innocent and that he did in fact pull the trigger, it turns out you, judge, have changed everything around and are now asking us to decide what was inside defendant's head at the time he pulled the trigger?"

Granted, in most cases the lawyers will have alerted the jurors to the question of intentionality in their openings, examinations, and closings. This problem can also be blunted by giving some of the elemental and culpability instructions early on. Still, these citizens have spent their adult lives being told that that the system is in shambles, that innocent people are regularly falsely accused and falsely convicted, and therefore that their trial energies will be consumed, as were Henry Fonda's and his colleagues', in the difficult task of ferreting out the innocence lurking behind the insurmountable evidence of guilt.

This perception not only predisposes our jurors to speculate, as did Henry Fonda and his colleagues, about unreasonable alternative factual explanations, and to substitute an any-doubt test for a reasonable doubt test,[99] it also has the potential to prejudice defendants who have defensible cases based on lack of the required mens rea. When the myth is so exclusively focused on factual guilt, and when the myth is overcome by overwhelming evidence, jurors will have little patience with a factually guilty defendant's contention that he is morally and legally innocent because of what was inside his head at the time of the crime. That is, the myth of innocence reinforces what is already, as discussed above, a widespread skepticism about mental defenses.[100]

CONCLUSION

12 Angry Men was a good movie, and everyone interested in the jury system should see it. But it buttresses a long and unfortunate tradition of grossly overestimating the frequency at which factually innocent people are caught up in the criminal justice system.

Yes, we want jurors to force prosecutors to prove both the act and the intention beyond a reasonable doubt. We also should care very much about factually innocent defendants who are wrongfully convicted despite these presumptions and all the other protective mechanisms in place. But by conflating the pre-trial presumption of innocence with a wholly unsupported post-trial presumption that the criminal justice system is highly unreliable, we threaten to turn the myth into reality, especially in our plea-bargain dominated era. And by sending the message to prospective jurors that trials are typically about factually innocent people wrongly accused, we also risk them overlooking the factually guilty but morally innocent, that is, the defendant who committed the act but without the required intention.

So what's a culture to do? To begin with, legal scholars could start a more comprehensive and serious hunt for a meaningful wrongful conviction denominator, instead of continuing to swoon about the numerator.[101] It also wouldn't hurt if they paid some attention to the problem of wrongful acquittals.

Journalists could help by trying to inject some perspective, let alone any critical analysis, into their stories on innocence projects and other con-

99. *See supra* note 4.

100. *See supra* text accompanying notes 55–61.

101. The only serious effort to do so that I am aware of has been by D. Michael Risinger, *Convicting the Innocent: An Empirically Justified Wrongful Conviction Rate*, 97 J. CRIM. L. & CRIMINOLOGY (forthcoming 2007), *available at* http://ssrn.com/abstract=931454. Professor Risinger estimates a lower bound of 3.3% for wrongful *trial* convictions. *Id.* at 15. Given the 95% plea bargaining rate, we must multiply that 3.3% estimate by 5% in order to estimate the overall wrongful conviction rate. That yields 0.165%, a number within the range I propose in this essay (1.95% to 0.0016%), and still a far cry from the histrionics of innocence advocates.

tributions to the mythology of innocence. Having regular crime/court beat writers do these stories, rather than feature or editorial writers, might be one good way to inject perspective.

Trial lawyers and judges can help by making clear early on that a crime consists of both an act and an intention, and by being vigilant in excusing prospective jurors whose focus on the act threatens to blind them to the intention, or whose deeply flawed views about the rate of wrongful convictions threatens to turn them into Henry Fondas hunting for unreasonable doubt.

But I'm not too sanguine. Culture, especially legal-academic culture, is an awfully big battleship to turn. Besides, "Innocent Man Convicted" just sells more movie tickets and newspapers, and gets more attention from student-editors of law reviews, than "Guilty Man Convicted" or even "Guilty Man Acquitted."

[14]

THE ROLE OF THE INNOCENCE ARGUMENT IN CONTEMPORARY DEATH PENALTY DEBATES

*Michael L. Radelet**

I. INTRODUCTION 199
II. DOCUMENTING ERRONEOUS CONVICTIONS 200
III. A MORE ACCURATE CONCEPTION OF INNOCENCE 204
IV. THE DECLINING SUPPORT FOR THE DEATH PENALTY 207
V. EXPLAINING THE DEATH PENALTY'S DECLINING POPULARITY 210
A. Correlation v. Causality 210
B. Factors Contributing to the Death Penalty's Declining Popularity 211
VI. HOW INNOCENCE IS RESURRECTING THE KEY QUESTION: IS DEATH ROW RESERVED FOR THE WORST OF THE WORST? 216
VII. CONCLUSION 219

I. INTRODUCTION

A central component of the death penalty abolitionists' argument from the last 250 years has been the problem of erroneous convictions.[1] Nonetheless, the first systematic data on the prevalence and characteristics of wrongful convictions in capital or potentially capital cases was not published until 1987.[2] Definitive proof of innocence from specimens of DNA left at crime scenes first led to the exoneration of an innocent prisoner in 1989,[3] and then to the

---

* Professor and Chair, Department of Sociology, University of Colorado. This paper was drafted while I was on sabbatical leave from the University of Colorado and a Visiting Scholar at the Irish Centre on Human Rights, National University of Ireland, Galway. I am indebted to William Schabas, Kathleen Cavanaugh, and the faculty and staff of the Centre for providing such a stimulating environment in which to work. I would like to thank Hugo Adam Bedau, Samuel R. Gross, and Eugene Wagner for helpful comments on earlier drafts of this paper.

1. *See* Hugo Adam Bedau & Michael L. Radelet, *Miscarriages of Justice in Potentially Capital Cases*, 40 STAN. L. REV. 21, 22 (1987). This concern can be dated to the wrongful execution of Jean Calas in Toulouse, France, in 1762. *Id.* Calas was burned to death for allegedly murdering his son, supposedly to prevent the son's conversion to the Catholic faith. *Id.* He was exonerated (and his family was paid an indemnity) after a fifty judge panel reviewed the case in 1765. *Id.*; *see, e.g.*, *Jean Calas*, ENCYCLOPEDIA BRITANNICA, http://www.britannica.com/eb/article-9018616/Jean-Calas (last visited Sept. 30, 2008).

2. *See generally* Bedau & Radelet, *supra* note 1, at 27-29 (introducing a strict methodology for examining conviction errors in potentially capital cases).

3. *See* NAT'L INST. OF JUSTICE, U.S. DEP'T OF JUSTICE, CONVICTED BY JURIES, EXONERATED BY SCIENCE: CASE STUDIES IN THE USE OF DNA EVIDENCE TO ESTABLISH INNOCENCE AFTER TRIAL 73-74 (1996), *available at* http://www.ncjrs.gov/pdffiles/dnaevid.pdf. The first inmate exonerated by DNA was David Vasquez in Virginia on January 4, 1989. *Id.*

exoneration of the first death row inmate in 1993.[4] In this Article, I review lessons society learned over the past two decades about erroneous convictions, and I document the falling popularity of the death penalty over the last decade.[5] I then identify major factors that explain the death penalty's declining attractiveness by first focusing on those factors that are not directly related to the innocence question and then zeroing in on the effects of what we are learning about wrongful convictions.[6] I argue that the discovery of the innocence problem has not only directly affected the decline in death penalty support over the past decade but also opened the door for reconsideration of racial bias and arbitrariness, both of which, along with innocence, undermine the notion that death row is reserved for the worst of the worst.[7] I conclude that a combination of these factors and not innocence alone is propelling a reconsideration of the death penalty in American jurisprudence.[8]

II. Documenting Erroneous Convictions

While most leading opponents of the death penalty over the past 250 years have pointed to the possibility of erroneous executions, prior to 1960, those individuals who researched miscarriages of justice did not develop the issue as part of a systematic anti-death penalty critique.[9] By any measure, the foremost pioneer on the subject of wrongful convictions in the United States was Edwin Borchard.[10] In 1932, Borchard described sixty-two American cases and three British cases of innocent defendants convicted of felonies, including twenty-nine defendants convicted of homicide.[11] In his book, Borchard proposed several reforms in criminal procedure that he believed would reduce the risk of error.[12] He devoted only two sentences, however, to the question of capital punishment: "How many wrongfully convicted persons have actually been executed, it is impossible to say. But that these cases offer a convincing argument for the abolition of the death penalty, certainly in cases of convictions on circumstantial evidence, can hardly be gainsaid."[13]

Borchard is one of many scholars to research erroneous convictions yet refrain from developing the issue of erroneous convictions as part of a systematic critique of the death penalty. Other pioneers, such as Erle Stanley

4. *See, e.g.*, TIM JUNKIN, BLOODSWORTH: THE TRUE STORY OF THE FIRST DEATH ROW INMATE EXONERATED BY DNA 258 (2004) (describing Kirk Bloodsworth's story of exoneration).

5. *See* discussion *infra* Parts II, IV.

6. *See* discussion *infra* Part V.

7. *See* discussion *infra* Part IV.

8. *See* discussion *infra* Part VII.

9. *See generally* EDWIN M. BORCHARD, CONVICTING THE INNOCENT: ERRORS OF CRIMINAL JUSTICE (1932) (acknowledging the possibility of erroneous executions yet never developing an anti-death penalty argument as part of his proposed reforms).

10. *Id.*

11. *See id.* at viii.

12. *See id.* at xiii-xxiv.

13. *Id.* at xix.

Gardner and Edward Radin, were silent on the implications of blundered convictions for the future of capital punishment.[14] Still other leading scholars, such as Judge Jerome Frank and his daughter Barbara,[15] and Ronald Huff and his colleagues,[16] called for the abolition of the death penalty after recognizing the possibility of error but did so only in a few paragraphs in their respective books.

The first scholar to do research on erroneous convictions who tied the research to a systematic anti-death penalty critique was Hugo Adam Bedau.[17] He began work on this issue as an assistant to Sara Ehrmann, whose short 1962 critique of the death penalty discussed a dozen or so murder convictions of innocent defendants.[18] Shortly thereafter, Bedau compiled his own summaries of miscarriages of justice in capital or potentially capital cases.[19] Until the mid-1980s, Bedau's modest chapter on the miscarriages of justice in the first two editions of *The Death Penalty in America* was by far the single best source on the subject.[20] As late as 1971, Bedau recognized the paucity of research on this general topic and admonished other opponents of the death penalty not to exaggerate claims of error because it was "false sentimentality to argue that the death penalty ought to be abolished because of the abstract possibility that an innocent person might be executed."[21] Because knowledge about erroneous

14. *See generally* ERLE STANLEY GARDNER, THE COURT OF LAST RESORT (1952) (detailing cases of erroneous convictions but never mentioning their implications on the death penalty); EDWARD D. RADIN, THE INNOCENTS (1964) (providing details of eighty cases).

15. *See* JEROME FRANK & BARBARA FRANK, NOT GUILTY 248 (1957) (providing details of thirty-four cases). In their brief discussion of the death penalty, the authors note that erroneous convictions in capital cases "demonstrate the intolerably monstrous nature of any death sentence: It cannot be undone. It may mean the judicially sanctioned governmental murder of the guiltless." *Id.*

16. *See* C. RONALD HUFF, ARYE RATTNER & EDWARD SAGARIN, CONVICTED BUT INNOCENT: WRONGFUL CONVICTION AND PUBLIC POLICY 161 (1996).

17. *See* Hugo Adam Bedau, *Murder, Errors of Justice, and Capital Punishment*, *in* THE DEATH PENALTY IN AMERICA 434-52 (Hugo Adam Bedau ed., 1st ed. 1964).

18. Sara Ehrmann, *For Whom the Chair Waits*, FED. PROBATION, Mar. 1962, at 14, 14.

19. Bedau, *Murders, Errors, and Capital Punishment*, *supra* note 17. The essay was reprinted, with minor revisions, in 1967. *See* Hugo Adam Bedau, *Murder, Errors of Justice, and Capital Punishment*, *in* THE DEATH PENALTY IN AMERICA 434-52 (Hugo Adam Bedau ed., 2d ed. 1967). In this work, Bedau describes seventy-four cases of defendants wrongly arrested, tried, or convicted for homicide since 1893. *See id.* Bedau reports that seven of the twentieth century cases resulted in a wrongful execution. *See id.* at 438. In contrast to later research on the problem of miscarriages of justice, this essay did not attract any systematic criticism.

20. *See* sources cited *supra* note 19.

21. Hugo Adam Bedau, *The Death Penalty in America: Review and Forecast*, FED. PROBATION, June 1971, at 32, 36. Bedau continues by noting that innocent defendants have been convicted of noncapital crimes: "But one may justifiably reply that the social advantages obtained from capital punishment are too elusive to warrant its preservation, given the unimpeachable record of our failure to convict only the guilty." *Id.* at 36. Defenders of the death penalty frequently misrepresented Bedau's comment as an admission that there is no risk of executing the innocent. *See* HUGO ADAM BEDAU, THE COURTS, THE CONSTITUTION, AND CAPITAL PUNISHMENT, at xvi n.4 (1977).

convictions has grown exponentially in the years since, things have changed considerably.[22]

I met Hugo Bedau in 1981 when he presented a lecture at the University of Florida, where I was a young assistant professor. In 1982, he graciously allowed me to join him in further research on the innocence issue, which we then imagined as basically a summer research project. Now, twenty-seven summers later, we are still researching. While at first our collaboration resembled a post-doctoral fellow working with an eminent professor, over the years, we became close friends and research partners. Our 1987 paper in the *Stanford Law Review* established that, for all but the most hardened skeptics, erroneous convictions are a consistent (albeit infrequent) and inevitable occurrence in modern American courtrooms.[23] And unlike the publications of our predecessors in this field of inquiry, our work quickly became,[24] and remains,[25] a target for impassioned criticism by supporters of the death penalty. Some death penalty supporters, in our opinions, never carefully studied our original work.[26]

Unlike the lack of scholarship on this issue in 1971,[27] today several data sets show the prevalence and characteristics of erroneous convictions. In 1992, Bedau, Constance Putnam, and I expanded our inventory of erroneous convictions to nearly 420 homicide and rape cases.[28] In 2000, Barry Scheck,

22. *See* Ben Coate, Ryan Lewis & Paul Parker, *Miscarriages of Justice: Eye of the Beholder*, 2007 J. INST. JUST. & INT'L STUD. 104, 106.

23. *See* Bedau & Radelet, *supra* note 1; *e.g.*, Stephen J. Markman & Paul G. Cassell, *Protecting the Innocent: A Response to the Bedau-Radelet Study*, 41 STAN. L. REV. 121 (1988) (criticizing our 1987 article and arguing that the risk of convicting an innocent person is too small to be a significant factor in the death penalty debate); *see also* Hugo Adam Bedau & Michael L. Radelet, *The Myth of Infallibility: A Reply to Markman and Cassell*, 41 STAN. L. REV. 161 (1988) (responding to Markman and Cassell).

24. We released the first draft of our paper in 1985. At that time, we included twenty-five examples of inmates executed despite what we called "probable" innocence. We later restricted our analysis to erroneous convictions for homicide and to cases in which courts sentenced innocent defendants to death for rape. This decision led to the exclusion of the cases of Ethel and Julius Rosenberg, which we included in our first draft. In response to our assertion that at least twenty-five executions over the first eighty-five years of the twentieth century were of innocent defendants, Ernest van den Haag, at the time the nation's most prolific pro-death penalty scholar, commented on the number of wrongful executions:

> "[I]f true, a very acceptable number," and added: "All human activities—building houses, driving a car, playing golf or football—cause innocent people to suffer wrongful death, but we don't give them up because on the whole we feel there's a net gain. Here, a net gain in justice is being done."

David Margolick, *25 Wrongfully Executed in U.S., Study Finds*, N.Y. TIMES, Nov. 14, 1985, at A19, *available at* 1985 WLNR 612342.

25. *See, e.g.*, Kansas v. Marsh, 548 U.S. 163, 190 (2006) ("The 1987 article's obsolescence began at the moment of publication."). The fact that a paper cited in a dissenting opinion cited our work aroused Justice Scalia's scorn.

26. For example, we simply do not believe that Justice Scalia read our 1987 work before writing his mean-spirited and off-target analysis of it in 2006. Instead, he (or more likely his clerks) adopted some distorted second- or third-hand account of our work that diehard supporters of the death penalty first penned.

27. *See* Bedau, *Death Penalty: Review and Forecast*, *supra* note 21.

28. *See generally* MICHAEL L. RADELET, HUGO ADAM BEDAU & CONSTANCE PUTNAM, IN SPITE OF INNOCENCE (1992).

Peter Neufeld, and Jim Dwyer added information on nearly 100 cases involving the exoneration of an innocent defendant by DNA evidence.[29] Five years later, Professor Samuel Gross and his colleagues documented 340 felony exonerations (145 exonerations due to DNA evidence) in the fifteen-year period between 1989 and 2003.[30] By October 2008, DNA had vindicated 233 inmates in the United States.[31] According to the Death Penalty Information Center, since 1973, 130 inmates sentenced to death have been exonerated, including 16 whose exonerations were solely or largely due to DNA evidence.[32] Currently, I am involved in a project that documents over 1,200 erroneous convictions in American history.[33]

Estimates of the prevalence of wrongful convictions are, at best, approximate.[34] As Samuel Gross and Barbara O'Brien explain, erroneous convictions are, by their very nature, hidden from view and hidden from analysis.[35] Further, "the ones we know about, exonerations, are clearly a small and unrepresentative sample of all false convictions."[36] Any fair reading of the cases vindicating death row inmates shows a common theme—most owe their freedom to Lady Luck.[37] Despite these problems, Gross and his colleagues estimate that at least 2.3% of those sentenced to death since 1973 have been exonerated, and because only a fraction of the wrongly convicted are exonerated, the proportion of wrongly convicted death row inmates is undoubtedly even higher.[38] Similarly, after examining DNA exonerations in death penalty cases for murder-rapes between 1982 and 1989, Michael Risinger estimated that at least 3.3% of the capital-rape defendants were innocent and that the actual error rate may be closer to 5%.[39] Recent surveys of criminal

29. *See* BARRY SCHECK, PETER NEUFELD & JIM DWYER, ACTUAL INNOCENCE: WHEN JUSTICE GOES WRONG AND HOW TO MAKE IT RIGHT (new ed., New Am. Library 2003) (2000).

30. Samuel R. Gross et al., *Exonerations in the United States 1989 Through 2003*, 95 J. CRIM. L. & CRIMINOLOGY 523 (2005).

31. The Innocence Project Online, http://www.innocenceproject.org/. This figure is current as of October 20, 2008. *Id.* The vast majority of the wrongfully convicted never receive a nickel in compensation, much less any formal apology. *See id.*

32. Death Penalty Info. Ctr., *Innocence and the Death Penalty*, http://www.deathpenaltyinfo.org/innocence-and-death-penalty (last visited Oct. 9, 2008). This list originally started with two dozen cases. *See* Bedau and Radelet, *supra* note 1, at 29 n.40. By 1996, when we transferred the list to the Death Penalty Information Center (DPIC) for regular updates, there were sixty-eight such cases. Michael L. Radelet, William Lofquist & Hugo Adam Bedau, *Prisoners Released from Death Rows Since 1970 Because of Doubts About Their Guilt*, 13 T.M. COOLEY L. REV. 907, 918 (1996). Over the years, the criteria for inclusion changed, so a few of the cases on Bedau and Radelet's original list are no longer included on the DPIC list.

33. ROB WARDEN & MICHAEL L. RADELET, ENCYCLOPEDIA OF WRONGFUL CONVICTIONS (forthcoming 2011). Originally we had hoped to publish this book in 2008.

34. Samuel R. Gross & Barbra O'Brien, *Frequency and Predictors of False Conviction: Why We Know So Little, and New Data on Capital Cases*, 5 J. EMPIRICAL LEGAL STUD. 929 (forthcoming Dec. 2008).

35. *See id.*

36. *Id.*

37. Michael L. Radelet & Hugo Adam Bedau, *The Execution of the Innocent*, 61 LAW & CONTEMP. PROBS. 105, 117-18 (1998).

38. Gross & O'Brien, *supra* note 34, at 15.

39. D. Michael Risinger, *Innocents Convicted: An Empirically Justified Factual Wrongful Conviction Rate*, 97 J. CRIM. L. & CRIMINOLOGY 761, 762 (2007).

justice officials in Ohio and Michigan estimate an error rate of approximately .5% in their own jurisdictions and 1-3% throughout the United States.[40] Defense attorneys have the highest collective estimates of wrongful convictions, followed by judges, police officials, and prosecutors.[41]

Samuel Gross, in one of the most important papers on the miscarriages of justice published in the past two decades, offered a convincing argument that the chances of error in death penalty cases are higher than in other felony prosecutions.[42] Typically, there are more public demands on the police to arrest suspects in homicide cases than in other felony cases, so police might do so even if the evidence of guilt is weak.[43] In extreme cases, the heightened pressure might induce the authorities to mistreat a suspect or to extract a false confession.[44] In a homicide case, more incentive might exist for the actual killer to falsely implicate an innocent person or for a possible witness to perjure himself in return for anticipated favors.[45] Fear of execution might induce some innocent defendants to plead guilty as part of a plea bargain.[46] Jurors who are "death-qualified" to sit in capital trials are more likely to vote guilty than jurors who are dismissed.[47] In short, possible death penalty cases are particularly vulnerable to errors that lead to wrongful convictions.

When DNA tests exonerate a prisoner, they exonerate someone who was totally uninvolved in the homicide. But even some individuals who are involved in the homicide can be classified as innocent.[48] Thus, we now turn our attention to a more accurate, albeit expansive, conceptualization of the problem.

III. A More Accurate Conception of Innocence

There are many additional reasons that lead to the conclusion that the 130 exonerated death row inmates are only the tip of the iceberg of the innocence problem on America's death rows.[49] Most observers would agree that the 130 exonerated death row inmates were behaviorally uninvolved in the homicide for which the court convicted them. Determining criminal responsibility and legal

40. Robert J. Ramsey & James Frank, *Wrongful Conviction: Perspectives of Criminal Justice Professionals Regarding the Frequency of Wrongful Conviction and the Extent of System Errors*, 53 CRIME & DELINQ. 436, 452-54 (2007); Marvin Zalman, Brad Smith & Angie Kiger, *Officials' Estimates of the Incidence of "Actual Innocence" Convictions*, 25 JUST. Q. 72, 80-85 (2008).

41. Ramsey & Frank, *supra* note 40, at 452-53.

42. Samuel R. Gross, *Lost Lives: Miscarriages of Justice in Capital Cases*, 61 LAW & CONTEMP. PROBS. 125, 127 (1998).

43. *Id.* at 133.

44. *Id.* at 135-36.

45. *Id.* at 138.

46. *Id.* at 140.

47. Craig Haney, *On the Selection of Capital Juries: The Biasing Effects of the Death-Qualification Process*, 8 LAW & HUM. BEHAV. 121, 128 (1984).

48. *See infra* Part III (discussing defenses to homicide and varying degrees of crimes).

49. WARDEN & RADELET, *supra* note 33 and accompanying text.

guilt for capital murder involves not only decisions about behavior—who caused the death of another—but also more complicated decisions about cognitive factors—the degree of criminal intent (mens rea) and whether the degree of intent (premeditation) is sufficient to categorize the offender as among the worst of the worst.[50] If a person kills another with diminished mens rea, but nonetheless is convicted of capital murder, he is as innocent as those totally uninvolved in the homicide.[51] Nonetheless, judgments about the defendant's mental state in capital cases are regularly done with imperfection. The following are examples of such imperfect judgments:

- Self-Defense: In Georgia in 1945, an African-American woman named Lena Baker was executed for killing her white employer, Ernest Knight.[52] Baker claimed her employer restrained her and threatened to kill her if she left.[53] During her one day trial, the all-white, all-male jury was unsympathetic.[54] But in 2005, the Georgia Board of Pardons and Paroles granted Baker a formal pardon on the grounds that the evidence proved the homicide was self-defense and that at most Baker merited a charge of voluntary manslaughter.[55]
- Accident: The first inmate sentenced to death in Florida in the modern era was Clifford Hallman, who was condemned on October 12, 1973.[56] When an angry barmaid slapped Hallman and knocked his drink to the floor, he picked up a piece of glass and cut the woman, who eventually died from the wounds.[57] After Hallman arrived on death row, the family of the victim successfully sued Tampa General Hospital, which negligently discharged the victim despite continued internal bleeding.[58] The physician retained to investigate the claim concluded that the wounds were not severe enough to cause the woman's death.[59] In 1979, Florida Governor Bob Graham commuted Hallman's death

50. *See* Hugo Adam Bedau, *Causes and Consequences of Wrongful Convictions: An Essay-Review*, 86 JUDICATURE 115, 115 (2002).
51. *See* Hugo Adam Bedau, *Controversies from Prosecution to Execution, in* THE DEATH PENALTY IN AMERICA 310, 314 (Hugo Adam Bedau ed., 1997). In the preface, Bedau states that the overlapping content between the four books titled THE DEATH PENALTY IN AMERICA is almost nonexistent; therefore, Bedau dropped the edition notation for this publication because it is likely misleading to readers. *See id.* at vii-viii.
52. *Executed U.S. Maid To Be Pardoned*, BBC NEWS, Aug. 16, 2005, http://news.bbc.co.uk/2/hi/americas/4155732.stm.
53. *Id.*
54. *Id.*
55. *Id.*
56. DAVID VON DREHLE, AMONG THE LOWEST OF THE DEAD 188-89 (1995).
57. *Id.*
58. *Id.*
59. *Id.*

sentence to life imprisonment.[60] As of October 2008, thirty-five years after the conviction, Hallman remains in prison.[61]

- Insanity: In 1976, a Nebraska court sentenced Erwin Simants to death for the murders of six people.[62] On appeal, the court overturned Simants's convictions because the sheriff improperly visited the sequestered jurors.[63] At retrial, the court acquitted Simants on the ground of insanity.[64] Similar examples of mentally ill defendants sentenced to death are plentiful.[65]
- Second-Degree Murder: An unknown—and unknowable—number of defendants are sentenced to death because of a wide array of erroneous judgments about their level of criminal intent.[66] In such cases, the defendant undoubtedly caused the death of the victim; but if the defendant had a fairer trial or increased access to proper defenses, a court would likely have convicted the defendant of a non-capital criminal homicide rather than first-degree (or capital) murder. For example, Ernest Dobbert was executed in Florida in 1984 for killing his daughter.[67] As the key witness at trial, Dobbert's thirteen year old son testified that he saw his father kick the victim, but he later recanted this testimony.[68] In a dissent from the Supreme Court's denial of certiorari, written just hours before Dobbert's execution, Justice Thurgood Marshall argued that while Dobbert clearly abused his children, there was substantial doubt concerning the existence of sufficient premeditation to sustain the conviction for first-degree murder: "That may well make Dobbert guilty of second-degree murder in Florida, but it cannot make him guilty of first-degree murder there. Nor can it subject him to the death penalty in that State."[69] If Justice Marshall's assessment was correct, then Dobbert was not guilty of a capital offense, and in this qualified sense Florida executed an innocent man.[70]

---

60. *Id.*; *see also* Michael L. Radelet & Barbara A. Zsembik, *Executive Clemency in Post-*Furman *Capital Cases*, 27 U. RICH. L. REV. 289, 309 (1993).

61. *See* Fla. Dep't of Corr., *Inmate Population Information Detail*, http://www.dc.state.fl.us/activeinmates/detail.asp?Bookmark=1&From=list&SessionID=136906620 (last visited Oct. 15, 2008).

62. Fred W. Friendly, *A Crime and Its Aftershock*, N.Y. TIMES MAG., Mar. 21, 1976, at 16.

63. Simants v. State, 277 N.W.2d 217, 223 (Neb. 1979).

64. State v. Simants, 330 N.W.2d 910, 911 (Neb. 1983).

65. *See generally* Death Penalty Info. Ctr., *Mental Illness and the Death Penalty*, http://www.deathpenaltyinfo.org/article.php?did=782&scid=66 (last visited Aug. 24, 2008) (cataloguing information about mentally ill prisoners on death row).

66. *See* CHARLES L. BLACK, JR., CAPITAL PUNISHMENT: THE INEVITABILITY OF CAPRICE AND MISTAKE 23-29 (2d ed. 1981).

67. Dobbert v. Wainwright, 468 U.S. 1231, 1231 (1984).

68. *Id.*

69. *Id.*

70. *See id.*; BLACK, *supra* note 66, at 23-29.

These four categories indicate that the number of inmates on death row who were factually uninvolved in the homicide constitutes only a small subset of those erroneously convicted of capital murder. There are an unknown number of death row inmates who are arguably guilty of some form of homicide, or innocent by reason of insanity, but who in fact, given fewer flaws in the criminal justice system, should not be guilty of capital murder. They are innocent of capital murder. Only a fraction of death row inmates who were factually uninvolved in the crime are released from death row, and an even smaller fraction of inmates who are legally innocent because of diminished mens rea are released from death row. In short, prosecutors, judges, and jurors make more errors than most Americans realize and many more mistakes than most criminal justice officials would care to admit.

As the public grows more knowledgeable of the inevitability of erroneous convictions, they also become more aware of other faults in the criminal justice system that operate to undermine the belief that death row inmates are the worst of the worst.[71] Indeed, public support for the death penalty declined over the past decade, and other signs indicate that the overall use of the death penalty is declining.[72]

IV. THE DECLINING SUPPORT FOR THE DEATH PENALTY

The use and acceptance of the death penalty in the American criminal justice system has decreased over the last 200 years.[73] We no longer execute robbers and rapists, the range of crimes that carry the death penalty has considerably narrowed, and there is continued concern that the method used to execute is not too painful.[74] Bedau has noted the following specific changes as reasons for the decline of the death penalty: (1) the end of public executions and of mandatory capital sentencing, (2) the introduction of the concept of degrees of murder, (3) the development of appellate review in capital cases, (4) the decline in annual executions, (5) the reduction in the variety of capital statutes, (6) the experimentation with complete abolition of the death penalty, and (7) the search for more humane ways to inflict death as a punishment.[75]

The United States' gradual movement away from the death penalty is part of an international trend that is at least two centuries old and particularly visible over the past thirty years.[76] In 1976, only sixteen countries from around the world abolished the death penalty.[77] By August 2008, the number of

71. *See infra* Parts IV-VI.

72. *See infra* Parts IV-VI.

73. *See generally* THE DEATH PENALTY IN AMERICA 4-16 (Hugo Adam Bedau ed., 1997) (reviewing the history of the death penalty in America).

74. *See id.* at 6-11.

75. *See id.*

76. *See* Amnesty Int'l, *Death Penalty: Abolitionist and Retentionist Countries*, http://www.amnesty international.org/en/death-penalty/abolitionist-and-retentionist-countries (last visited Aug. 21, 2008).

77. *See id.*

abolitionist countries was ninety-one, and forty-six other countries had abolished the death penalty for all ordinary crimes, or in practice had no executions in the past ten years, for a total of 137.[78] Only sixty countries are counted as retentionist.[79] In December 2007, the United Nations General Assembly called for a worldwide moratorium on the death penalty with a view toward abolishing executions.[80] The vote was overwhelming: 104 of the U.N.'s member states supported the resolution, while only 54 opposed the resolution and 29 abstained.[81] The resolution vote represents an extraordinarily rapid and pervasive worldwide move away from the death penalty.[82]

The historical and international rejection of the death penalty parallels the rejection of the death penalty in the United States in the past few decades, although the parallels are more difficult to spot.[83] Over the past dozen years American courtrooms have sentenced fewer and fewer defendants to death:

Number of New Death Row Inmates, 1995-2006[84]

1995 - 326	2001 - 167
1996 - 323	2002 - 169
1997 - 281	2003 - 153
1998 - 306	2004 - 140
1999 - 284	2005 - 138
2000 - 235	2006 - 115

Other signs of the death penalty's decline are apparent.[85] In 2003, former Illinois Governor George Ryan commuted death sentences and pardoned four other inmates after his investigation found massive errors in the sentencing process.[86] In 2007, New Jersey Governor Jon S. Corzine signed a bill repealing

---

78. *See id.*

79. *See id.*

80. *See* Edith M. Lederer, *U.N. Votes Solidly for Death-Penalty Moratorium*, DENV. POST, Dec. 19, 2007, http://www.denverpost.com/ci_7754585?IADID.

81. *See id.* Countries with some of the worst records for respecting human rights joined the United States in opposing the resolution: China, Iran, Syria, North Korea, and Sudan. *See* Warren Hoge, *Assembly Calls for Freeze on Death Penalty*, N.Y. TIMES, Dec. 19, 2007, at A14; Peter Steinfels, *Milestone in Death Penalty Fights, but Still a Way To Go*, N.Y. TIMES, Dec. 22, 2007, at B6.

82. *See* Lederer, *supra* note 80.

83. *See* Hugo Adam Bedau, Michael L. Radelet & Constance E. Putnam, *Convicting the Innocent in Capital Cases: Criteria, Evidence, and Inference*, 52 DRAKE L. REV. 587, 591-96 (2004).

84. BUREAU OF JUSTICE STATISTICS, U.S. DEP'T OF JUSTICE, CAPITAL PUNISHMENT, 2006—STATISTICAL TABLES: TABLE 14. NUMBER OF INMATES RECEIVED UNDER SENTENCE OF DEATH, 1995-2006, http://www.ojp.usdoj.gov/bjs/pub/html/cp/2006/tables/cp06st14.htm (last visited Aug. 21, 2008). We do not know if these figures represent prosecutorial behavior—fewer death sentences are being sought—or jury behavior—fewer death sentences are being recommended or imposed—or both. *See id.* To my knowledge, no data is available regarding how often prosecutors seek death in any states other than those with few death row inmates.

85. *See generally* Bedau, Radelet & Putnam, *supra* note 83; Michael L. Radelet, *The Executioner's Waning Defenses*, *in* THE ROAD TO ABOLITION (Charles Ogletree & Austin Sarat eds., forthcoming 2009).

86. *See* Jodi Wilgoren, *Citing Issue of Fairness, Governor Clears Out Death Row in Illinois*, N.Y. TIMES, Jan. 12, 2003, § 1, at 1. For the text of Governor Ryan's speech in which the commutations were

New Jersey's death penalty, making New Jersey the first state to abolish the death penalty by legislative action and gubernatorial support since Iowa and West Virginia in 1965.[87] In 2007 and 2008, Colorado, Connecticut, Maryland, Montana, Nebraska, and New Mexico seriously discussed eliminating the death penalty completely.[88] Moreover, the annual number of executions has decreased steadily since 1998.[89] Botched executions, which rarely attracted much attention or concern from the American public before the last decade, caused America to stop all executions between September 25, 2007 and April 2008.[90] In 2008, the Supreme Court refused to order any changes in lethal injection methods; however, in a case examining Kentucky's methods, Justice Stevens called for reconsidering whether the death penalty per se violates the Eighth Amendment's prohibition against cruel and unusual punishment.[91]

Public support for the death penalty in the United States has dropped over the past decade.[92] When asking about the death penalty without a specified alternative, Gallup measured Americans' support for the death penalty at 64%

---

announced, see George Ryan, *I Must Act*, *in* DEBATING THE DEATH PENALTY, 218-34 (Hugo Adam Bedau & Paul Cassell eds., 2004). Erroneous convictions, a basic lack of fairness, and racial bias chiefly motivated Governor Ryan's commutations. *See* Michael L. Radelet & Glenn L. Pierce, *The Role of Victim's Race and Geography on Death Sentencing: Some Recent Data from Illinois*, *in* FROM LYNCH MOBS TO THE KILLING STATE: RACE AND THE DEATH PENALTY IN AMERICA 117-49 (Charles Ogletree & Austin Sarat eds., 2006) (describing research on racial bias in death sentencing conducted by Pierce and Radelet at the request of Governor Ryan and his Commission on Capital Punishment).

87. *See* Jeremy W. Peters, *Corzine Signs Bill Ending Executions, Then Commutes Sentences of 8*, N.Y. TIMES, Dec. 18, 2007, at B3. The Nebraska and New Hampshire legislatures also voted to abolish the death penalty, but these two bills were vetoed by governors. *See* John Distaso, *Shaheen Vetoes Death Penalty in NH. Legislators React to Veto*, N.H. UNION LEADER, May 20, 2000, at A1; Robynn Tysver, *Death Penalty Study OK'd*, OMAHA WORLD HERALD, May 28, 1999, News, at 1. In 1979, the Nebraska legislature voted 26-22 to repeal the death penalty, only to see the legislation vetoed by Governor Charlie Thone. *See* Joanne Young, *Life or Death*, LINCOLN J. STAR, Nov. 11, 2007, at A1, *available at* 2007 WLNR 22431357. In 1999, the same legislature passed a bill calling for a moratorium on the death penalty, but this time it was Governor Mike Johanns who vetoed the bill. *See* Tysver, *supra*. In 2000, the New Hampshire legislature voted to end the death penalty, but this bill too suffered a gubernatorial veto. John Kifner, *A State Votes to End Its Death Penalty*, N.Y. TIMES, May 19, 2000, at A16, *available at* 2000 WLNR 3505338; DiStaso *supra*.

88. *See* DEATH PENALTY INFO. CTR., THE DEATH PENALTY IN 2007: YEAR END REPORT 2 (2007), http://www.deathpenaltyinfo.org/2007YearEnd.pdf.

89. *See* DEATH PENALTY INFO. CTR., EXECUTIONS BY YEAR, http://www.deathpenaltyinfo.org/article.php?scid=8&did=146 (last visited Aug. 18, 2008) (giving annual frequencies of executions in the U.S. since 1976). With over 3,000 inmates currently on America's death rows, this pattern could change quickly. *See* DEATH PENALTY INFO. CTR., SIZE OF DEATH ROW BY YEAR, http://www.deathpenaltyinfo.org/article.php?scid=9&did=188#year (last visited Aug. 18, 2008).

90. *See* Baze v. Rees, 128 S. Ct. 1520, 1526 (2008). Executions were stopped pending the Supreme Court's resolution of *Baze v. Rees*, a Kentucky case challenging the drugs used in lethal injections. *See id.* This case was decided in April 2008 and held no constitutional violation in the means by which Kentucky conducts lethal injection. *Id.* For discussion of recent cases of botched executions, see Marian J. Borg & Michael L. Radelet, *On Botched Executions*, *in* CAPITAL PUNISHMENT: STRATEGIES FOR ABOLITION 143-68 (Peter Hodgkinson & William Schabas eds., 2004).

91. *Baze*, 128 S. Ct. at 1542-52; Linda Greenhouse, *After a 32-Year Journey Justice Stevens Renounces Capital Punishment*, N.Y. TIMES, Apr. 18, 2008, at A22.

92. *See* Death Penalty Info. Ctr., *Limiting the Death Penalty*, http://www.deathpenaltyinfo.org/article.php?scid=15&did=411#Religion (last visited Aug. 18, 2008).

in 2005, the lowest level of support in twenty-seven years.[93] Three years later, a Harris Poll found that 63% of respondents supported the death penalty.[94] More importantly, given the alternative of life imprisonment without parole (LWOP), which is available in thirty-five of thirty-six states, recent polls indicate that support for the death penalty and support for LWOP are roughly equivalent.[95] For example, a May 2006 Gallup Poll found that 47% of the American public supports the death penalty while 48% prefer LWOP.[96]

We now turn our attention to possible explanations for this recent decline.

V. EXPLAINING THE DEATH PENALTY'S DECLINING POPULARITY

A. Correlation v. Causality

Are recent declines in the death penalty attributable to a growing recognition of erroneous convictions? Before addressing the question, one must distinguish correlation and causality.[97] For example, while approximately 46.9% of the homicide victims in the United States from 1976 to 2005 were African American, only 13.7% of those executed through the end of 2007 were convicted of killing black victims.[98] Does this correlation prove that the race of the victim is an important factor in explaining who is sentenced to death? No. Homicides that victimize whites might be more aggravated or otherwise more deserving of death for the perpetrator than homicides that victimize blacks.[99] Therefore, researchers attempted to see if numerous other factors can explain the race-of-victim pattern.[100] But ultimately, the race-of-victim effects remain

93. *See* Death Penalty Info. Ctr., *Public Opinion: Gallup Poll Reports Lowest Death Penalty Support*, http://www.deathpenaltyinfo.org/article.php?did=1599&scid=64 (last visited Aug. 18, 2008).

94. *See* Harris Interactive, *Over Three in Five Americans Believe in Death Penalty*, Mar. 18, 2008, http://www.harrisinteractive.com/harris_poll/index.asp?PID=882. This poll did not ask if respondents would still support the death penalty given the option of LWOP. *See id.*

95. *See* DEATH PENALTY INFO. CTR., LIFE WITHOUT PAROLE, http://www.deathpenaltyinfo.org/article.php?did=555&scid=59 (last visited Aug. 18, 2008); Death Penalty Info. Ctr., *Public Opinion About the Death Penalty*, http://www.deathpenaltyinfo.org/article.php?did=209&scid=23 (last visited Aug. 18, 2008); *see also* PollingReport.com, Crime/Law Enforcement, http://www.pollingreport.com/crime.htm (last visited Aug. 18, 2008) (collecting death penalty polls from various polling organizations).

96. Death Penalty Info. Ctr., *National Polls and Studies*, http://www.deathpenaltyinfo.org/article.php?did=2163#gallup606 (last visited Aug. 18, 2008).

97. *See* BUREAU OF JUSTICE STATISTICS, U.S. DEP'T OF JUSTICE, HOMICIDE TRENDS IN THE U.S., http://www.ojp.usdoj.gov/bjs/homicide/race.htm (last visited Aug. 18, 2008) (illustrating the homicide trends by race and whether the trend is a correlation or causality).

98. *See id.* The Death Penalty Information Center reports that 151 of the 1,099 people executed between 1972 and December 31, 2007, were executed for killing African Americans. *See* Death Penalty Info. Ctr., Searchable Database of Executions, http://www.deathpenaltyinfo.org/executions.php (last visited Aug. 18, 2008) (enter black as race of victim and click on "get info").

99. *See* BUREAU OF JUSTICE STATISTICS, *supra* note 97 (illustrating race distribution and type of homicide).

100. *See generally* DAVID C. BALDUS, GEORGE G. WOODWORTH & CHARLES A. PULASKI, JR., EQUAL JUSTICE AND THE DEATH PENALTY: A LEGAL AND EMPIRICAL ANALYSIS (1990) (discussing attempted improvements on the death penalty's arbitrary and discriminatory effects from 1972 to 1987); David C. Baldus & George Woodworth, *Race Discrimination in the Administration of the Death Penalty: An Overview*

even after other possible explanatory factors are considered, giving strong evidence for a race-of-victim effect.[101]

In November 2007, *The Wall Street Journal* published an excellent example of the failure to distinguish correlation from causality in death penalty debates.[102] The article by Roy Adler, Professor of Marketing at Pepperdine University in California, and Michael Summers, Professor of Quantitative Methods at Pepperdine, is astonishing in its simplicity.[103] It examines homicides and executions in the United States from 1979 to 2004 and observes that the former decreased while the latter increased.[104] With that observation, and only that observation, Adler and Summers conclude that each execution prevented seventy-four murders in the following year.[105] No additional "control variables" were used, so the authors failed to determine if the falling homicide rates were due to changing patterns of drug use, ownership of handguns, availability of the alternative punishment of long imprisonment, arrest rates for homicides, or dozens of other possible factors.[106] The authors made no attempt to determine whether more murders are prevented in states that execute prisoners or in states that execute the most or whether the results are stable if other time periods are used.[107] While modest correlation does exist between nationwide homicide frequencies and executions over that time period, to argue that executions are the cause of decreasing homicide rates without considering a plethora of other factors is patently absurd.

B. Factors Contributing to the Death Penalty's Declining Popularity

Some scholars suggest that recent declines in death penalty support are due in large part to, or are solely a consequence of, the publicity given to erroneous convictions.[108] Yet the examples above caution against the premature conclusion that the decline in the death penalty over the past decade has resulted solely from an increasing concern about wrongful convictions. In

---

of the Empirical Research with Special Emphasis on the Post-1990 Research, 39 CRIM. L. BULL. 194 (2003) (discussing empirical evidence regarding the effects of race discrimination on the death penalty).

101. *See* sources cited *supra* note 100.

102. *See* Roy D. Adler & Michael Summers, *Capital Punishment Works*, WALL ST. J., Nov. 2, 2007, at A13.

103. *See id.*

104. *Id.*

105. *Id.*

106. *See id.*

107. *See* Cassandra Stubbs & Ronald J. Allen, Letter to the Editor, *See No Verdict on Death Penalty Deterring Crime*, WALL ST. J., Nov. 8, 2007, at A21.

108. FRANK BAUMGARTNER, SUZANNA L. DEBOEF & AMBER E. BOYDSTUN, THE DECLINE OF THE DEATH PENALTY AND THE DISCOVERY OF INNOCENCE 9 (2008). While these authors have given us an innovative and thought-provoking analysis that details how the innocence card has completely transformed modern death penalty debates, I believe that they miss or fail to appreciate the roles of some important factors, both long-term and short-term, that are contributing to the executioner's demise. *See, e.g.*, James D. Unnever & Francis T. Cullen, *Executing the Innocent and Support for Capital Punishment: Implications for Public Policy*, 4 CRIMINOLOGY & PUB. POL'Y 3, 12-14 (2005).

addition to innocence, what other factors might be contributing to a decline in death sentences and death penalty support? Several factors are no doubt operating.

One obvious factor is the homicide rate. For every 100,000 people, the homicide rate in the U.S. declined from 9.8 in 1991 to 5.7 in 1999.[109] From 1999 to 2005, it stabilized between 5.5 and 5.7.[110] Fewer homicides lead to fewer death row candidates and less outrage about high criminal violence rates, which otherwise lead to more death sentences.[111] This does not mean that falling crime rates directly lead to falling support for the death penalty.[112] As Gross and Ellsworth argued, the drop in crime rates may be an enabling factor; falling crime makes possible a reconsideration of, or debate about, affirmative arguments against the death penalty.[113]

Second, either because of Supreme Court mandates or simple changes in prevailing judicial practices, judges no longer sentence certain categories of offenders to death. In 2002, the Supreme Court prohibited the execution of mentally retarded offenders and decided that judges alone could not pronounce death sentences without input from juries.[114] In 2005, the Court abolished the death penalty for offenders who committed crimes before their eighteenth birthdays.[115] Between 1972 and 1999, Florida courts sentenced 166 offenders to death despite jury recommendations of life imprisonment.[116] While no ban exists on the "override" practice imposed by the Florida Legislature or by the state supreme court, all death sentences handed down since 1999 have had at least seven votes for death.[117]

A third reason for the declining number of death sentences and decreased support for capital punishment is that more and more states are offering LWOP as a sentence for inmates convicted of the most aggravated homicides.[118] More importantly, the public is beginning to realize that LWOP means LWOP— the prisoners will die in prison.[119] On June 17, 2005, Texas became the most recent state to offer LWOP.[120] Today thirty-five of the thirty-six states that use

---

109. *See* BUREAU OF JUSTICE STATISTICS, *supra* note 97.

110. *See id.*

111. *See id.*

112. *See supra* text accompanying notes 95-96.

113. Samuel R. Gross & Phoebe C. Ellsworth, *Second Thoughts: Americans' Views on the Death Penalty at the Turn of the Century*, *in* BEYOND REPAIR? AMERICA'S DEATH PENALTY 7, 12-18 (Stephen P. Garvey ed., 2003).

114. *See* Ring v. Arizona, 536 U.S. 584, 618 (2002); Atkins v. Virginia, 536 U.S. 304, 320 (2002).

115. Roper v. Simmons, 543 U.S. 551, 559-60 (2005).

116. DEATH PENALTY MORATORIUM PROJECT, ABA, EVALUATING FAIRNESS AND ACCURACY IN STATE DEATH PENALTY SYSTEMS: THE FLORIDA DEATH PENALTY ASSESSMENT REPORT, at vii (2006), *available at* http://www.abanet.org/moratorium/assessmentproject/florida/report.pdf.

117. *See id.*

118. Gross & Ellsworth, *supra* note 113, at 33.

119. *See id.*

120. Death Penalty Info. Ctr., *Life Without Parole News and Developments: 2005*, http://www.deathpenaltyinfo.org/article.php?did=2147 (last visited Aug. 26, 2008).

the death penalty also offer LWOP as a sentencing alternative.[121] LWOP dissipates the argument that the death penalty is needed to keep our communities safe from released recidivist murderers. Given the misery of prison life, LWOP also satisfies the jurors' retributive goals.[122] In the vast majority of states, once a jury convicts an offender of one of the most aggravated forms of homicide, jurors and the public know that the offender will die in prison.[123] This knowledge reduces the debate about the death penalty to a debate about how and when death will occur—not where.[124]

The decline in the number of new death sentences may also result from a growing recognition of the death penalty's tremendous fiscal outlays.[125] These costs are incurred not only in cases in which the inmate is eventually executed, but also in cases in which the death penalty is considered but not sought, sought but not obtained, obtained but vacated by appellate courts, or obtained and not carried out for other reasons (e.g., executive clemency or death by other causes while awaiting execution on death row).[126] The staggering costs of the death penalty convinced some death penalty supporters that the high fiscal costs are not worth whatever marginal benefits (in their views) the death penalty provides over LWOP.[127] Twenty years ago, the *Sacramento Bee* estimated that California taxpayers could save some $90 million per year in death penalty costs if the maximum punishment was LWOP.[128] In 2005, the *Los Angeles Times* increased that estimate to $114 million in added annual costs, or $250 million per execution.[129] New Jersey spent over $250 million on the death penalty—without executing anyone—before abandoning the death penalty in 2007.[130] A Maryland study released in 2008 found that the state spent $186 million on the death penalty over the previous two decades, averaging over $37 million per prosecution.[131] Numerous studies by academics, newspapers, state

121. The exception is New Mexico. DEATH PENALTY INFO. CTR., *Life Without Parole*, *supra* note 95.

122. *See* Death Penalty Info. Ctr., *Searchable Database of Executions*, http://www.deathpenaltyinfo.org /executions.php (last visited Aug. 26, 2008). Indeed, 128 of the last 1,099 inmates executed in the United States between 1976 and the end of 2007 (11.6%) dropped their appeals, suggesting that long imprisonment was worse than death. *See id.*

123. *See* Gross & Ellsworth, *supra* note 113, at 47.

124. *See* Richard C. Dieter, *Methods of Execution and Their Effect on the United States*, 35 FORDHAM URB. L.J. 789, 789 (2008).

125. *See* Gross & Ellsworth, *supra* note 113, at 41.

126. *See* Death Penalty Info. Ctr., *Cost of the Death Penalty*, http://www.deathpenaltyinfo.Org/article. php?did=log+scid=7 (last visited Aug. 26, 2008).

127. *Id.*

128. Stephen Magagnini, *Closing Death Row Would Save State $90 Million a Year*, SACRAMENTO BEE, Mar. 28, 1988, at A1, *available at* 1988 WLNR 2113989.

129. *See* Rone Tempest, *Death Row Often Means a Long Life*, L.A. TIMES, Mar. 6, 2005, at B1, *available at* 2005 WLNR 23374489.

130. Robert Schwaneberg, *N.J. Panel Counts Cost of Death Penalty*, STAR-LEDGER (Newark), Sept. 13, 2006, New Jersey at 29, *available at* 2006 WLNR 15895050.

131. Jennifer McMenamin, *Death Penalty Costs Maryland More Than Life Term*, BALT. SUN, Mar. 6, 2008, at B2, *available at* 2008 WLNR 4443762.

legislatures, state supreme courts, and other groups uniformly conclude that seeking a death sentence is far more expensive than seeking LWOP.[132]

Some of the decline in death sentences in the United States in the past decade has likely resulted from a growth in the number of prosecutors and judges who agree with retired California Superior Judge Donald McCartin, who has sentenced nine people to death.[133] McCartin told a reporter in 2008 that his position on the death penalty had changed: "It's a waste of time and taxpayers' money. It costs 10 times more to kill these guys than to keep them alive in prison. It's absurd."[134] People may still like the death penalty, but in the end they concede that whatever benefits it provides are not worth all the cash and all the fuss.[135]

Another reason for a decline in the death penalty in recent years is the erosion of what was once its strongest justification—deterrence.[136] Until fairly recently, general deterrence was the top argument in favor of the death penalty—the idea that murderers need to be executed to send a message to the rest of society not to follow in their footsteps.[137] The general public's support for the idea that the death penalty is a deterrent to murder has dropped precipitously over the past two decades.[138] In a 1985 Gallup Poll, 62% of the respondents answered "yes" to the question, "Do you feel that the death penalty acts as a deterrent to the commitment of murder, that it lowers the murder rate, or not?"[139] Ellsworth and Gross found that belief in the deterrent efficacy of capital punishment consistently hovered around the 60% mark from 1972 to 1991.[140] This fell to 35% in 2004, when the question was last asked.[141] Conversely, the proportion of respondents who stated that the death penalty was

---

132. *See* Death Penalty Info. Ctr., *Costs of the Death Penalty*, *supra* note 126.

133. Gordon Dillow, *Judge McCartin Turns Against Death Penalty*, ORANGE COUNTY REG., Mar. 2, 2008, Local, at 1, *available at* 2008 WLNR 4174545.

134. *Id.* (internal quotations omitted).

135. *See id.*

136. *See* David W. Moore, *Public Divided Between Death Penalty and Life Imprisonment Without Parole*, June 2, 2004, http://www.deathpenaltyinfo.org/article.php?scid=23&did=1029.

137. *See* Robert G. Caldwell, *Why Is the Death Penalty Retained*, 284 ANN. REV. AM. ACAD. POL. & SOC. SCI. 45, 45-53 (1952). As one criminologist wrote in 1952, "The most frequently advanced and widely accepted argument in favor of the death penalty is that the threat of its infliction deters people from committing capital offenses." *Id.*; *see, e.g.*, Ernest van den Haag, *On Deterrence and the Death Penalty*, 60 J. CRIM. L., CRIMINOLOGY & POLICE SCI. 141 (1969). *But see* Hugo Adam Bedau, *Deterrence and the Death Penalty: A Reconsideration*, 61 J. CRIM. L., CRIMINOLOGY & POLICE SCI. 539 (1970) (responding to van den Haag's article).

138. *See* Moore, *supra* note 136.

139. *Id.* This question suffers from unusually poor wording. The death penalty might deter some murders, but it could also stimulate others. *See* William J. Bowers & Glenn L. Pierce, *Deterrence or Brutalization: What Is the Effect of Executions?*, 26 CRIME & DELINQ. 453, 481-82 (1980). Furthermore, the proper question for public policy is the death penalty's marginal deterrent effect—whether it deters homicides over and above the deterrent effect of life imprisonment without parole. *See id.*

140. Phoebe C. Ellsworth & Samuel R. Gross, *Hardening of the Attitudes: Americans' Views on the Death Penalty*, 50 J. SOC. ISSUES 19, 27-28 (1994).

141. Moore, *supra* note 136.

not a deterrent doubled over the last two decades, from 31% to 62%.[142] Similarly, a 2008 Harris Poll found that only 42% of the respondents believed that the death penalty deterred others, down from 63% in 1983.[143] Thus, what was once the leading justification for the death penalty is much less central in contemporary death penalty debates.[144]

Finally, organized religions have slowly but steadily increased their willingness to speak out against the death penalty.[145] Thirty years ago, few organized religions took a stand against the death penalty.[146] Today, the leaders of most major religions—with the important exception of fundamentalist Protestants—publicly oppose capital punishment.[147] The Catholic Church stood against the death penalty for all cases except those with "extreme gravity" until 1997 when even that exception was removed.[148] Not coincidentally, a 2005 poll shows that support for the death penalty among Catholics fell to 48%, down from 68% in 2001.[149] In a 2007 poll, some 47% of Catholics thought they would be disqualified from service on capital juries because of their moral opposition to the death penalty.[150] This change was fueled in part by the most popular death penalty book in American history, *Dead Man Walking*, a memoir by a Catholic nun who worked with death row inmates.[151]

In short, Americans are reevaluating the death penalty for a number of reasons. In this context, we are learning more about wrongful convictions, which raises the following question: how does the innocence factor affect the status and support of the death penalty over the past decade?[152]

142. *Id.*

143. Harris Interactive, *supra* note 96. The Harris Poll asks, "Do you feel that executing people who commit murder deters others from committing murder, or do you think such executions don't have much effect?" *Id.*

144. *See id.*

145. *See* JAMES J. MEGIVERN, THE DEATH PENALTY: AN HISTORICAL AND THEOLOGICAL SURVEY 339 (1997); James J. Megivern, *Religion and the Death Penalty in the United States*, *in* CAPITAL PUNISHMENT: STRATEGIES FOR ABOLITION 116, 141-42 (Peter Hodgkinson & William A. Schabas eds., 2004) [hereinafter Megivern, *Religion and the Death Penalty*].

146. Megivern, *Religion and the Death Penalty*, *supra* note 145, at 121-24.

147. *See* AMERICAN FRIENDS SERVICE COMMITTEE, THE DEATH PENALTY: THE RELIGIOUS COMMUNITY CALLS FOR ABOLITION (1998) (giving statements by thirty of these denominations).

148. *See* U.S. Conference of Catholic Bishops, *Catholic Campaign To End the Use of the Death Penalty*, http://www.usccb.org/sdwp/national/deathpenalty/deathpenaltybrochure.pdf (last visited Aug. 25, 2008); *see also* HELEN PREJEAN, THE DEATH OF INNOCENTS, 129-30 (2005) (recounting the evolution of the Catholic position on the death penalty).

149. Press Release, U.S. Conference of Catholic Bishops, Groundbreaking Zogby Poll Demonstrates Dramatic Rise in Catholic Opposition to Use of the Death Penalty (Mar. 21, 2005), http://www.usccb.org/comm/archives/2005/05-064.shtml.

150. RICHARD C. DIETER, A CRISIS OF CONFIDENCE: AMERICANS' DOUBTS ABOUT THE DEATH PENALTY 1 (2007), http://www.deathpenaltyinfo.org/CoC.pdf.

151. *See* HELEN PREJEAN, DEAD MAN WALKING (1993).

152. *See infra* Part VI.

VI. How Innocence Is Resurrecting the Key Question: Is Death Row Reserved for the Worst of the Worst?

In addition to the above factors, the release of erroneously convicted death row inmates impacts public support for the executioner.[153] As our understanding of the nature and extent of wrongful convictions has increased, stories over the past decade about wrongful conviction cases have made the public more attentive to the problem. A December 2000 poll by the *National Law Journal* found that concerns about wrongful convictions made 31% of the respondents less likely to impose a death sentence.[154] A July 2001 Harris Poll found that 94% of the respondents believed that innocent people are sometimes convicted of murder, a figure that remained steady at 95% in 2008.[155] In 2007, a national poll commissioned by the Death Penalty Information Center found that 87% of the respondents believed that an innocent person was executed in recent years, with over half (55%) saying that this belief affected their views on the death penalty.[156]

Even more important is society's recognition of a broader problem of which innocence is only a part: Is death row reserved for the worst of the worst? If the death penalty operated with precision, only the worst of the worst would be executed, and those who are indeed the worst of the worst would not receive prison sentences. But from a century of research, we now know that the executioner is inexact in exacting his revenge—he shoots targets with a shotgun and not a rifle, and when he scoops up the big fish he inevitably catches schools of little guppies in his net. The release of factually innocent prisoners opens a window through which we can see these larger problems.

One aspect of the problem is the pure arbitrariness that occurs when no factors distinguish individuals sentenced to death from other convicted murderers who are not. Justice Stewart raised this issue in *Furman v. Georgia*, in which he argued that the inability to distinguish individuals sentenced to death from individuals who are not sentenced to death makes the death penalty tantamount to being arbitrarily struck by lightning.[157] Many people who kill one victim are sentenced to death; however, some who kill four or more victims are not executed, and at least one who killed forty-eight victims was not.[158]

153. *See supra* Part V.B.; *infra* notes 173-75 and accompanying text.

154. Death Penalty Info. Ctr., *National Polls and Studies*, http://www.deathpenaltyinfo.org/article.php?did=2163#NLJ/DQ (last visited Aug. 24, 2008); *see also* Unnevar & Cullen, *supra* note 108, at 27 (discussing whether support for the death penalty would potentially lessen with the knowledge that innocent defendants were likely executed on death row).

155. Death Penalty Info. Ctr., *National Polls and Studies*, http://www.deathpenaltyinfo.org/article.php?did=2163#Harris7/01 (last visited Aug. 24, 2008); Harris Interactive, *supra* note 94.

156. DIETER, *supra* note 150, at 5-6.

157. Furman v. Georgia, 408 U.S. 238, 309-10 (1972) (Stewart, J., concurring).

158. *See* Stephanie Hindson, Hillary Potter & Michael L. Radelet, *Race, Gender, Region and Death Sentencing in Colorado, 1980-1999*, 77 U. COLO. L. REV. 549, 566 n.134 (2006). Gary Ridgeway, Washington State's "Green River Killer," was sentenced to life imprisonment in 2003 after confessing and pleading guilty to forty-eight counts of first-degree murder. *See generally* ANN RULE, GREEN RIVER,

Killers who avoid execution often do so only because of pure luck, and killers who end up on death row can often point not only to their crimes but to healthy doses of bad luck as well.[159]

Some arbitrariness in death sentencing is a function of the quality of the defendant's attorney. While even the best attorneys can lose clients to death row, the quality of the defense team, including investigators and experts, especially mental health professionals, makes a huge difference in sentencing outcomes.[160] There are countless examples of defense attorneys who were drunk, using drugs, or sleeping in the courtroom during death penalty trials. Far more common are lazy or unskilled attorneys who are in over their heads or attorneys who are decent and hard-working yet without the resources to match the police or prosecution.

Arbitrariness also results in huge geographic disparities in death sentencing. To explain who is on death row requires considering where the crime occurred, which is often a more powerful explanatory factor than the characteristics of the crime itself. Part of this is due to a national disparity: between 1972 and the end of 2007, 82% of all executions in the United States occurred in the South.[161] Statewide disparities are also common; for example, in Illinois during the 1990s, "the odds of receiving a death sentence for killing a victim(s) in Cook County [were] on average 83.6% lower than for killing a victim(s) in the rural county region of Illinois controlling for the other twenty-six variables in the analysis."[162] In California, counties with the highest rate of death sentencing tend to be rural and to have a higher proportion of white residents.[163]

An additional factor that undermines any contention that the worst of the worst are sentenced to death is the prevalence of racial bias in contemporary death sentencing.[164] Although, this argument fell on deaf ears when presented to the Supreme Court in 1987, in 1990 the U.S. General Accounting Agency reviewed twenty-eight studies that examined the role of race in death

---

RUNNING RED: THE REAL STORY OF THE GREEN RIVER KILLER—AMERICA'S DEADLIEST SERIAL MURDERER (2004).

159. *See infra* notes 160-89 and accompanying text.

160. *See* Stephen B. Bright, *Counsel for the Poor: The Death Sentence Not for the Worst Crime But for the Worst Lawyer*, *in* THE DEATH PENALTY IN AMERICA: CURRENT CONTROVERSIES 275, 276 (Hugo Adam Bedau ed., 1997).

161. *See* DEATH PENALTY INFO. CTR., NUMBER OF EXECUTIONS BY STATE AND REGION SINCE 1976, http://www.deathpenaltyinfo.org/article.php?scid=8&did=186#region (last visited Aug. 23, 2008). Of the 1,099 executions in the U.S. between Jan. 1, 1977, and Dec. 31, 2007, 901 occurred in the South. *See id.* The proportion rises further if only non-consensual executions are counted and if the border state of Missouri is counted as a southern state. *See id.*

162. Glenn L. Pierce & Michael L. Radelet, *Race, Region, and Death Sentencing in Illinois, 1988-1997*, 81 OR. L. REV. 39, 65 (2002).

163. Glenn L. Pierce & Michael L. Radelet, *The Impact of Legally Inappropriate Factors on Death Sentencing for California Homicides, 1990-99*, 46 SANTA CLARA L. REV. 1, 30-31 (2005).

164. David C. Baldus, George Woodworth & Charles A. Pulaski, Jr., *Reflections on the "Inevitability" of Racial Discrimination in Capital Sentencing and the "Impossibility" of Its Prevention, Detection, and Correction*, 51 WASH. & LEE L. REV. 359, 362 (1994).

sentencing.[165] It found a prevalence of racial bias in the post-*Furman* courtroom:

> [A] pattern of evidence indicat[es] racial disparities in the charging, sentencing, and imposition of the death penalty after the *Furman* decision.
>
> In 82 percent of the studies, race-of-victim was found to influence the likelihood of being charged with capital murder or receiving the death penalty . . . . This finding was remarkably consistent across data sets, states, data collection methods, and analytic techniques.[166]

After the GAO study, this pattern appeared repeatedly in later studies.[167] To the degree that individuals who kill whites are several times more likely to be sentenced to death than those who kill blacks in identical crimes, the argument that death row is reserved for the worst of the worst quickly falls apart.[168]

In the past decade, we have also learned that contemporary death sentencing in America is so riddled with error that appellate courts ultimately vacate the majority of death verdicts (and few if any of these appellate courts have reputations for being sympathetic to death-sentenced inmates).[169] James Liebman and his colleagues looked at some 5,800 cases between 1973 and 1995 in which the court imposed a death sentence.[170] They found that "[t]he upshot of this 23-year track record is that, for any given 100 fully reviewed [death] verdicts, an average of 47 were reversed by the state courts, and 68 of the 100 were reversed by either the state or federal courts."[171] In retrials held after reversal, 9% of cases ended in acquittals.[172]

In short, the conviction of the innocent is but one aspect of a larger issue of the basic unfairness of the death penalty.[173] Concerns about executing the innocent have caused some Americans to change their opinion on the death penalty, but a more encompassing factor fueling the change could be an increasing recognition that death sentencing in America is fundamentally unfair.

---

165. *See* McCleskey v. Kemp, 481 U.S. 279 (1987); GEN. GOV'T DIV., U.S. GEN. ACCOUNTING OFFICE, DEATH PENALTY SENTENCING: RESEARCH INDICATES PATTERN OF RACIAL DISPARITIES 2 (1990), *available at* http://archive.gao.gov/t2pbat11/140845.pdf.

166. *Id.* at 5 (footnote omitted).

167. *See* David C. Baldus & George Woodworth, *Race Discrimination in the Administration of the Death Penalty: An Overview of the Empirical Research with Special Emphasis on the Post-1990 Research*, 39 CRIM. L. BULL. 194, 195 (2003); Pierce & Radelet, *supra* note 163, at 31.

168. *See* Baldus & Woodworth, *supra* note 167, at 195.

169. *See* James S. Liebman, *Rates of Reversible Error and the Risk of Wrongful Execution*, 86 JUDICATURE 78, 80 (2002).

170. *Id.*

171. *Id.* at 81; *see also* JAMES LIEBMAN ET AL., A BROKEN SYSTEM, PART II: WHY THERE IS SO MUCH ERROR IN CAPITAL CASES, AND WHAT CAN BE DONE ABOUT IT, at i (2002) (discussing statistics from Liebman's June 2000 report), *available at* http://www2.law.columbia.edu/brokensystem2/report.pdf.

172. Liebman, *supra* note 169, at 82.

173. *See id.* at 80.

VII. CONCLUSION

I now return to the question that inspired this Article: Given that we know we sometimes convict innocent people, what, if anything, does it say about the death penalty? As this Article makes clear, the problem of innocence goes far beyond the 130 innocent defendants exonerated after being sentenced to death.[174] For every inmate released, there are likely many other defendants for whom potentially vindicating DNA evidence is not available and other defendants with plausible innocence arguments that fall short of the standard needed to open the jailhouse doors. Still other inmates on death row did kill someone but did so accidentally, in self-defense, as a consequence of severe mental illness, or without the intent necessary to justify a conviction for capital murder.[175] In short, the 130 inmates who are at the center of the wrongful conviction discussion in death penalty cases are the tip of the iceberg.

Recent discoveries about innocent inmates have changed attitudes about the death penalty. Some previous supporters of the death penalty changed their positions after learning about vindicated death row inmates. Even more importantly, discovery of the innocent exposes many larger flaws of the criminal justice system and capital punishment in particular. Once DNA testing proved that we have put innocent people on death row, a whole range of additional flaws in the criminal justice system (e.g., arbitrariness, racial bias, quality of attorney, and the like) became more plausible.[176] Execution of the innocent is but one aspect of a more encompassing message: the government is fallible.

The discovery of the many miscarriages of justice in capital cases has also, no doubt, caused many pro-death penalty citizens to be more cautious about the death penalty.[177] They are cautious not only because of an elevated consciousness about the plausibility of a defendant's innocence claim, but also because of a growing awareness that those on death row (or candidates for death row) may not be among the worst of the worst.[178] We can imagine that a decade or two ago, the one or two lone holdouts favoring life imprisonment on a death penalty jury would be ostracized, with the majority of the jurors thinking that these holdouts were obstructionist. Those jurors disfavoring the death penalty would be subjected to maximum pressure to change their votes to support death. Today such dissent is more tolerable, and the pressure from pro-death penalty jurors to vote for the death penalty has likely subsided.

Finally, I believe that the innocence argument reopened the fundamental issue of the morality of the death penalty. The question of whether the state may permissibly take the life of one of its citizens under certain circumstances

174. *See supra* note 32 and accompanying text.
175. Bedau & Radelet, *supra* note 1, at 39-40.
176. *See supra* Part VI.
177. One relevant proverb states, "If you can't be good, be careful."
178. *See supra* Part VI.

was pretty much absent from death penalty debates during the 1980s and 1990s. Death penalty abolitionists avoided the question of whether the state should have the right to kill and instead focused on the improprieties and blunders in death penalty decisions.[179] Now the question becomes whether it is moral for the criminal justice system to take lives despite the many imperfections (led by conviction of innocents) and basic unfairness that we now know exists. The question is not about the morality of the death penalty in theory but about the morality of the death penalty as applied by an imperfect criminal justice system. Is it moral to take lives in light of the system's flaws, such as arbitrariness, poor quality attorneys, race discrimination, and the conviction of the innocent? More and more Americans seem to agree with Walter Berns, a supporter of the death penalty, who wrote: "To say that someone deserves to be executed is to make a godlike judgment with no assurance that it can be made with anything resembling godlike perspicacity."[180] The problem of executing the innocent, in the end, seems to shift the relevant question from "Who Deserves to Die?" to the question of "Who Deserves to Kill?"[181]

179. *See* Bedau & Radelet, *supra* note 1, at 24-25.

180. WALTER BERNS, FOR CAPITAL PUNISHMENT: CRIME AND THE MORALITY OF THE DEATH PENALTY 178 (1979).

181. Marvin E. Wolfgang, *We Do Not Deserve To Kill*, 13 T.M. COOLEY L. REV. 977, 990 (1996).

Part III
Race and Religious Discrimination

[15]

South Africa: racism and the death penalty*

Greg Wallance

> The first thing you notice as you come into Central [Prison, Pretoria] is the singing, the sound of the Condemneds. Up behind the huge sign in the Hall saying Stilte/Silence, the Condemneds sing, chant, sing through the day and, before an execution, through the night. At times, the chant is quiet, a distant murmur of quiet humming, softly. Then it swells: you can hear a more strident, urgent note in the swell, sounding through the prison, singing the hymns that will take them through the double doors into the gallows. Fifty, sixty, sometimes seventy at a time up in the Condemneds, singing their fellows through their last nights.
>
> *Bandiet* by Hugh Lewin

On 26 January of this year an extraordinary document was presented to the South African parliament. It is called the 'Report of the Commission of Inquiry into the Penal System of the Republic of South Africa' (hereinafter referred to as the Commission Report), and represents a two-year government study of the cause of, and possible cures for, the alarming rise in crime in that country. Much of the report is concerned with punishment. Some of its recommendations might seem useful, such as 'depenalizing' the pass laws,[1] which regulate travel, residence and work among black and Coloured South Africans. Others are simply frightening, such as the recommendation that the Department of Prisons undertake a study of the use of

*Paper prepared for the Amnesty International Conference on the Abolition of the Death Penalty, Stockholm, 1977.

castration as punishment, not only for the mentally ill, but for the 'sexual criminal'.

But what makes this study so extraordinary is that, in a country that often accounts for half the world's reported executions, the vast majority of which it imposes on blacks,[2] not a single word was devoted to capital punishment. The State President's mandate to the Commission was 'to inquire into the penal system of the Republic of South Africa and to make recommendations for its improvement'. But the Commission members were told in the same paragraph, 'the question whether the death penalty should be retained shall not be inquired into'. This directive was interpreted by the Commission of Inquiry to mean that 'the death sentence has been excluded from the terms of reference of this Commission'.

The South African government is, apparently, satisfied with the presence and application of the death penalty. Nor, significantly, is it inclined to tolerate even mild discussion of race and capital punishment in that country.[3] But the fact remains that in South Africa, race and racism are a fixed, integral and often decisive aspect of the process of capital punishment from the causes of capital crime to the moment, literally, that a condemned person is hanged in Central Prison in Pretoria.

A study of the death penalty in South Africa must consider the statutory and common law criminal offences that carry the death sentence. Of these, the several security laws and the crime of treason involve essentially political offences. The other capital crimes are murder, rape, kidnapping, housebreaking with aggravating circumstances, robbery with aggravating circumstances and child stealing.[4] But more and more, deaths in detention, deaths at the hands of the police who are acting 'in the execution of their duties', and mass killings such as those at Soweto in 1976, are perceived as a form of capital punishment in that they deliberately further a state policy not simply of preserving social or civil order, but of protecting the apartheid system.

Further, two facts must inform this discussion. First, the death penalty is used almost exclusively against blacks. Between 1911 and 1969, for example, approximately 2,000 blacks were sentenced to death for murder. The figure for that period for whites for the same crime was between 75 and 85.[5] The most recent figures from the South African government indicate that from July 1975 to June 1976, 60 persons were executed and, at the end of that period, 86 were awaiting execution. Of the executed, two, at most, were white.[6] Between 1 July 1969 and 30 June 1976, 433 persons were hanged in South Africa. The South Africa government does not provide the racial breakdowns for the executions, but their statistics do indicate that of the 651 offenders under sentence of death, who were admitted to prison in that same period, 33 at most were white.[7]

The second critical point is that the death sentence in South Africa is discretionary. Section 330 of the Criminal Procedure Act provides that in all crimes except murder, the death penalty 'may' be imposed. Although the statute provides a mandatory death sentence for murder, an exception is made 'where the court ... is of the opinion that there are extenuating circumstances'.[8] If a judge finds that such circumstances exist, then he may, although he is not required to, impose a lesser sentence.[9] Thus the practical result is that every sentence of death in South Africa has been imposed at the discretion of a judge with the possible assistance of two assessors.[10]

Common law offences and the death penalty

There are several ways to analyse the racial aspects of capital punishment for common law offences such as murder and rape. One approach is to examine the social process that leads to executions; another is by examining the legal process. Since the legal process is best understood in the context of South Africa's unique social structure, it is appropriate to begin with the social forces that produce a high rate of capital crimes and concomitantly, thousands of death sentences. The great number of executions, an official of the South African embassy explained to this writer, are a necessary response to the high levels of violence which, he remarked, 'in some areas are nothing more (to the residents) than a Sunday afternoon soccer match'. That South Africa is a land of violence is plain. In 1974-5, there were 8,500 murders, 9,000 cases of homicide and 128 cases of infanticide.[11] India, with a population nearly 25 times that of South Africa, only has twice as many murders in a year. The United States, considered a country with a high level of violence, has ten times the population of South Africa, but only two-and-a-half times the number of murders. Crime has increased 50 per cent in South Africa since 1966 while, in the same period, the population has increased only 25 per cent.

Although the great majority of crimes are committed by blacks, whites were reported to have committed 180 murders in 1975-6,[12] a figure that is more than one-third that of the homicides reported in that period in England and Wales,[13] whose combined population is 10 times the size of the white community in South Africa. Moreover, in proportion to the population the overall incidence of violence among whites in South Africa that results in convictions corresponds roughly with the same rate among blacks; however, murder and assault convictions occur among whites in proportion to population at a rate far below that of non-whites.[14]

The high levels of violence among blacks, and the consequent prosecutions for murder in which the death penalty is sought, are no doubt a function of poor economic conditions. In multi-racial societies such as the United States, such conditions often are perceived as a by-product of both contemporary and historic racial discrimination. But in South Africa, apart from the problem of economic inequities, the apartheid policies of the government impact so immediately and harshly on blacks that violent crime can be seen as a direct result of the government's social and political policy. One example is pass laws.

South Africa is possibly the only country in the modern world to use its criminal laws to deter and punish miscegenation (mixed marriages) and social contact between races. The failure of a black to have a passbook in his possession at all times or the failure to obtain approval, recorded in the passbook, for work or living arrangements, is a criminal offence punishable by a fine or imprisonment, which can include forced labour. The result is that South Africa is not so much a police state as it is a 'prison state'. Millions of blacks are detained each year for violation of these laws. Visitors say their most vivid memory of South Africa is the endless lines of blacks outside the police stations or detention centres waiting to explain their failure to have a passbook or the proper authorizations. Each year hundreds of thousands of blacks are jailed for pass law offences.[15] South Africa's prison population, already on a per capita basis the highest in the world,[16] has reached a level where in 1975-6 the number of infants born in prison or jailed with their mothers is greater than the adult prison population of Norway.[17]

The stress placed on blacks by these laws is immense. For example, because of such laws as the Urban Areas Act, a black man who finds a job away from his area of residence must obtain permission to work, to travel to his work, to stay longer than 72 hours, to find a place of accommodation and to remain.[18] His wife and family must obtain permission to visit and to reside with him, the latter being difficult if not impossible to obtain because of the government's desire to limit the number of blacks living outside their designated areas of residence.[19] The result is enforced separation, often, because of difficult and sporadic employment conditions, for years. Moreover, in the 'work' areas no recreational facilities exist for labourers except liquor halls. Blacks are not allowed out of these areas to attend entertainment events. Thus the only outlets for male labourers are prostitutes, homosexuality and alcoholism. It is not a coincidence that the common pattern of murder among blacks in urban areas of South Africa is stabbing that was preceded by heavy drinking.

The pass laws, further, create constant friction between blacks and the authorities. Few blacks consider it morally wrong to violate these laws and, consequently, respect is diminished for all of the government's laws. And little stigma is attached to a prison sentence when so many adults spend time in jail for violating passbook laws. Survival in South Africa for a black depends in large measure on the ability to break laws and get away with it. Indeed, a South African embassy official acknowledged that the pass laws and similar regulations aggravate and stimulate crime among the blacks, but, he added, 'without these [laws], the country couldn't exist'.

Turning to the legal process, there is a connection between racial attitudes and the treatment of offenders convicted of capital crimes. One of the most conspicuous examples is rape.

There is a vigorously asserted belief in South Africa that criminal laws are administered impartially, that, as the Penal Commission Report states,

> ... our judicial system is above reproach. Comparisons are odious and one cannot ... compare the sentences variously meted out by the courts to Blacks and Whites. Their circumstances, their approach to sentences and their general outlook on life differ radically from those of Whites ... Blacks are, on the whole, treated with consummate fairness by both our lower courts as well as the Supreme Court.

Although this statement in itself is revealing, taking the claim of fairness at face value, nowhere is this assertion more at odds with reality than the history of executions in South Africa for the crime of cross-racial rape. The reaction of the government — executive and judicial — to cross-racial rape in South Africa gives the lie to the claim of that country that 'separate development' is not the same as racism.

In a society structured on racial lines, no act, no imaginable form of conduct disregards the artificial racial barriers more than the rape of a white woman by a black man. It is, in the eyes of the white minority, the most unforgivable breach of apartheid. Not only is violence done to the victim, but in a country in which the psychological well-being of the white depends on separation of the races it strikes at the very heart of the white self-image.

Thus, between 1947 and 1969, 288 whites were convicted of the rape of a non-white; 844 blacks were convicted of the rape of white women. Not a single white was executed. Of the convicted blacks, 121 were sentenced to death, of whom 108 were executed.[20] Indeed, there is no record of a white man ever having been executed in South Africa for the rape of a non-white. Moreover, in the area of violent, cross-racial offences, whites, with one-sixth of the population of South Africa, are increasingly responsible for more offences. In 1974-5, for example, 173 cases of rape of a black woman by a white were reported to the police. The figure for non-white rape of whites was 166. In 1975-6 the figures were, respectively, 191 and 166.[21] Yet there is no record of a white receiving the death sentence for cross-racial rape, although since 1969 it has been imposed on blacks in approximately 20 cases.

One way to understand these patterns is that, in imposing

punishment for capital crimes in South Africa, the courts may treat the race of the assailant and that of the victim as an aggravating factor. Indeed, this attitude has been effectively elevated to the status of a legal principle. There is the report of a judge who, in a cross-racial rape case, held that 'the fact that the accused was black and the complainant was white constituted an aggravating feature, since the shock to her would have been all the greater and sentenced the African to death'.[22] One textbook on criminal law, written by a former judge, states that in cases where the accused is a black man and the complainant a white woman, 'difference of race must ... aggravate the seriousness of any *injuria* committed; under certain circumstances there is no doubt that it makes "injurious", what in its absence would not have been so'.[23] In answering a questionnaire on attitudes among lawyers and judges towards the racial factor in the judicial process, one Afrikaner advocate indicated that he thought race played a deliberate and conscious role in capital cases, and added:

> I have in mind rape. I do not regard discrimination as unfair. For a white woman rape, particularly rape by a Non-White, is a terrible experience. For the majority of Bantu women rape, even by a white, is something which can be compensated by the payment of a beast.[24]

The *pro deo* system is another example of the assumption that cross-racial rape by a black is a capital crime, while if committed by a white it is a far less serious offence. *Pro deo* legal assistance, government-appointed counsel for indigent defendants, is provided only where the death penalty is likely in the event of a conviction. Significantly, several lawyers who have practised in South Africa report that in cases charging cross-racial rape by a black, *pro deo* counsel is almost automatically appointed if the defendant is an indigent. The practice is, however, not to appoint *pro deo* counsel for a white indigent defendant where the charge involves cross-racial rape.

As to executions for murder, the figures for cross-racial incidence are not as complete as those for rape. As mentioned, between 1911 and 1968, of approximately 2,000 persons executed for murder, about 75-85 were white. Of these, only six had killed persons who were not white. While figures are not available indicating exactly how many of the executed blacks had killed across the racial line, one estimate is that 'the number runs into hundreds at least'.[25] The same pattern exists in recent years. Between 30 June 1974 and 1 July 1975, 136 death sentences had been imposed for murder. Blacks received 132 of these sentences, whites four. Of the blacks condemned, none had been guilty of killing a black.[26]

The conviction of the non-whites, particularly for the cross-racial crimes, are suspect on racial grounds. The *pro deo* counsel, who represent indigent defendants in capital cases, and thus are the lawyers who appear for blacks accused of capital crimes, are by lawyers and non-lawyers acknowledged to be inexperienced, incompetent and unprepared at trial.[27] More significantly, in a society where it is an aggravating factor in a criminal case if the race of the victim is white and the race of the assailant is black, but not the reverse, the credibility of a black defendant relative to a white complainant is commensurately unequal. One lawyer who practised criminal law in South Africa for 20 years put it this way:

> I knew that if I was defending a white man and the only evidence was that of a black, I had a head start on the prosecution. I didn't have to make the point, it was just there. If it was the reverse, a white man against a colored [defendant], then you had a losing proposition. The word of a black man simply doesn't count against that of a white.

Acceptance of complaints by the police, applications for bail, the use of confessions obtained under duress, the publicity given to a trial — all of these aspects of the criminal justice process in South Africa are influenced significantly by colour. As one former South African lawyer phrased it, 'the fabric of the society' depends on favouring the white over the black.

Further, a racial distinction apparently exists in the willingness of the courts and the executive branch to admit that a mistake may have been made in a capital case. It is the proud assertion of the former Attorney-General of the Transvaal that, 'unlike the United States, unlike England, we have, in capital cases in this country, not had a single miscarriage of justice; not a single case where an innocent person has been executed.[28]

One prominent law professor would agree that is the case with respect to whites: 'I do not know of an instance in South Africa of the execution of a White where there is now a widespread conviction that the court went wrong on the facts or on identity.'[29] But, in discussing this point with respect to non-whites, the same professor refers to the testimony of the Reverend Dr Henry P. Junod, who spent 28 years ministering to prisons, where he spoke with 2,000 blacks in the death cells and witnessed 800 hangings:

> We have had cases where, in front of the gallows we have known that the first Crown witness was the one who should have been where the convicted person was, facing death. We could, naturally, not prove it, but the situation was made perfectly clear by long weeks and months with the accused, and by continuing denials up to the last moment, when nothing more was to be gained by adhering to a false story. We remember one case vividly of a very humble and unobtrusive Karanga, telling the Sheriff:

'Go and tell your Chiefs not to bring men like me to this place anymore ... ' It is indeed terrible to see a man walk his last steps to the gallows under such conditions ... Mistakes have been made to our knowledge: of that we are perfectly sure.[30]

Finally, punishment in South Africa is generally race-conscious and the pattern of executions may be viewed as an extension of the attitude that black offenders deserve harsher treatment for their offences than do whites. Prison diet in South Africa is graded according to race. Whites receive bread twice a day, plus 500 grams of mealie meal (from maize), 200 grams of oats every week and 170 grams of meat five times a week. Blacks (Africans) receive only maize, no oats, bread once a day three times a week, and 125 grams of meat three times per week. Corporal punishment, which exists in few other countries, is used frequently in South Africa, and consists of lashings with a cane. When a black is lashed, he is tied to a wooden frame; his pants are pulled down and he is hit with the cane until his buttocks look, in one observer's words, 'like a freshly-bitten plum'. Whites, however, are always given some protection — after 1973, they were allowed to keep their trousers on — to absorb the blows.[31]

The night before an execution in Central Prison, the white condemned is allowed to hear his favourite music over the prison loudspeaker. The blacks who must face the gallows the next morning are often harassed with petty regulations, such as no smoking rules. And, in a final, savage gesture, symbolic of South African society, when blacks are hanged, 'the same ropes [are] used over and over again, even though many of them [are] full of vomit and saliva from the hangings before'. But, on the rare occasion when a white man is hanged, the executioners provide a new rope.[32]

Political Offences and Deaths in Detention

In addition to treason, the security laws provide for the discretionary use of the death penalty in political cases. The main security laws are the Suppression of Communism Act 1950, as amended by the Internal Security Act of 1976; the Terrorism Act of 1967; the so-called Sabotage Act, and the Unlawful Organizations Act. These laws are broadly drafted to make illegal any act that might change the status quo in South Africa. Under the Terrorism Act, for example, it is a capital offence, *inter alia*, for any resident of South Africa to encourage social or economic change with the assistance of any foreign or international body or institution. One commentator observed that under this law, a

... man who writes lawfully to an agency of the United Nations to

> suggest that a depressed community in South Africa (let us say the Coloured People) be given financial assistance has committed the crime of terrorism! He has committed an act in order to encourage the achievement of social change in co-operation with an international institution.[33]

There is no record of an execution in South Africa under these laws for political offences that do not involve loss of life. One reason is that political trials in South Africa receive a great deal of world attention. Moreover, defendants in these cases do not suffer from inadequate representation and are supported by outside funds. But, in the future, the restraints against execution for political offences may be loosened if black opposition, both violent and non-violent, continues and if the South African government perceives itself as unaffected by world opinion. Indeed, there are signs that this may occur in the near future. In the 'Pretoria 12' trial, where a dozen blacks are charged with terrorist acts, the government took the unprecedented step of announcing its intention, at the start of the trial, to seek the death penalty instead of waiting until the evidence had been brought forth.[34] The South African Minister of Justice, James Kruger, was quoted recently as proposing that the death penalty be mandatory for political offences under the security laws.[35]

Moreover, the death sentence has been imposed — and carried out — for security law offences in the neighbouring countries of Namibia and Zimbabwe. In Namibia, formerly South West Africa, which South Africa has administered since 1966 in violation of a resolution of the United Nations, essentially the same security laws apply as in South Africa. In 1976 two members of the Southwest Africa People's Organization (SWAPO) were convicted under the Terrorism Act of allegedly assisting those responsible for the assassination of a political leader. Both received death sentences which were later overturned when it was revealed that a law partner of the lawyers for the defendants enabled the South African security police to obtain copies of documents relating to the defence's case. An observer for the International Commission of Jurists wrote of the trial: 'It would appear manifest from the opening of the case ... and from the nature and scope of the evidence adduced by the prosecution that the trial was conducted primarily with a view to establishing the guilt of SWAPO rather than that of individual accused persons.'[36] The Rhodesian government, also operating in violation of a United Nation's resolution, has executed at least 60 persons between 1965 and 1975 for political offences. Since April 1975, executions have taken place in secrecy.[37]

Ironically, the race of the accused is less relevant in the application of the internal security laws to political offenders than in the treatment of common law offenders. Although the vast majority of those sentenced under the security laws are black, whites who are convicted of security ofences are dealt with harshly. In 1964, a white man, John Harris, was executed for a bombing that killed one person, an act that was considered a political gesture. Several white men, convicted of political offences and sabotage, are serving life sentences. Breyten Breytenbach, the well-known Afrikaner poet, was convicted in 1975 of Terrorism Act offences for attempting to organize an underground movement against apartheid, and given a nine-year sentence. He has been treated viciously in jail, serving the first two years of his sentence in solitary confinement in a cell adjacent to the death cell at Central Prison.[38] The annual report of the Commissioner of Police for 1975-6, mentions that 'one of the major successes in the sphere of internal security was the arrest and conviction of Breyten Breytenbach'.[39] But, at the same time, because conditions in non-white prisons are far worse than that of the white prison facilities, the harsher treatment of white political prisoners does not compare with the conditions of imprisonment experienced by black political offenders.

Finally, this year world attention focussed on the deaths in detention of black political prisoners. This is a difficult area to examine because of lack of information. But the few facts that are available suggest a pattern.

First, there is an extremely high incidence of deaths among non-political arrestees. In 1976, aside from incidents such as Soweto, 195 people were killed by police 'in the execution of their duties'. All but two of these were black. Of the non-white deaths, 168 were killed while trying to escape arrest. Neither of the whites was killed in the course of an escape. In addition, seven black children were killed by police; all but one were, according to the Minister of Justice, trying at the time to escape arrest. No white juveniles were shot by police.[40]

Secondly, figures for non-political deaths in detention, which may overlap with above figures, reveal that in 1976, 117 persons died in detention. By estimating the numbers of blacks and Coloureds through surname, a rough figure emerges of 80-90 per cent non-white. Of these, approximately 90 per cent died within four days of their arrest. While many of the deaths are attributed to injuries in the course of the crime or in attempting to escape, many are inexplicable. A Johannes Kowane, for example, was arrested for having a 'defective handbrake'. He died in detention two days later of 'natural causes'. An Alfred Mofekung was arrested for not having a passbook in his possession and died five days later of 'natural causes'. Muntulana Luthuli was arrested for 'failing to pay tax'. He died in detention one day later of 'natural causes'. In a country where the great majority of arrested persons are young people under the age of 40, at least 29 blacks died in detention in 1976 of 'natural causes', virtually all of them within a few days of their arrest. The figure for whites is, at most, two.[41]

Thirdly, deaths among political detainees present a similar pattern. In 1976 18 detainees held for violation of the security laws are known to have died in custody.[42] The total since 1963 is at least 45, indicating a surge in such deaths that parallels the increase in the last year and a half of activism among non-whites.[43] Most political prisoners are young men, yet 10 of the deaths in 1976 were reported to have been due to 'natural causes'. Here, explanations are sometimes given, such as 'slipping on soap in shower', which was alleged to be the reason for two of the deaths.[44] In one case of a political detainee's death in detention, the public was informed by the government that an 'unknown' man, detained at an 'unknown' time, had died on an 'unknown' date for 'unknown' reasons.[45] All but a handful of political detainees are black.

These figures suggest a deliberate government policy of brutality towards black common law arrestees and detainees and especially political detainees, particularly when considered with the government's own figures of convictions among its policemen. In 1976 201 policemen were convicted of common assault on, presumably, prisoners, detainees or arrestees, 24 of assault with intent to do grievous bodily harm, seven of culpable homicide and four of murder. This was an increase from 1975 when 170 were convicted of assault and four of culpable homicide. But, of the entire complement of policemen convicted of violent crimes in 1976, the majority of whom were black, only 16 were discharged from the police force.[46] Thus, in 1977, the year of Steve Biko's and others' deaths in detention, assuming the worst of the 1976 offenders were dismissed, the South African police force contained at least 220 men who had committed inexcusable acts of violence on prisoners or detainees, 19 of them having done so with the intent to inflict grievous bodily harm.

GREG WALLANCE

REFERENCES

In addition to the cited references below, this paper has been based on interviews with former members of the South Africa bar, South African journalists and British journalists with experience in that country, emigrés from South Africa, and an official of the South Africa Embassy in London. Especially helpful material was provided by the International Defence and Aid Fund, the African National Congress, the Anti-Apartheid Movement, the South West Africa People's Organization, and the South African Embassy's Information Department.

1 Commission Report. 'Depenalizing' apparently means that violations of the pass laws will still be criminal offences, although jail terms or fines will no longer be imposed.

2 Between 1912, when 24 persons were hanged, and 1969, when 84 were hanged, South Africa climbed to first place in a United Nations survey of the rate of capital punishment throughout the world. In the years 1961 to 1965, 1033 executions were reported to the UN; nearly half of these took place in South Africa. A. Sachs, *Justice in South Africa* (1973).

3 See *Contempt of Court. The Trial of Barend Van Dyk Van Niekerk*, 1970 Acta Juridica 77, 201 (hereinafter cited as Contempt of Court). In 1969, Van Niekerk, a professor of law at the University of the Witwatersrand, published two articles in the *South African Law Journal* that considered the question of capital punishment. In one of these articles he included the result of a survey of advocates on racial attitudes in imposing the death penalty. The survey suggested to Van Niekerk that nearly half of those replying felt that 'justice as regards capital punishment is meted out on a differential basis to the different races, and that 41 per cent who so believe are also of the opinion that such differentiation is "conscious and deliberate" '. Van Niekerk, 'Hanged By The Neck Until You Are Dead', 86 *SALJ* 457, 467 (1969). See 87 *SALJ* 60 (1970). The government of South Africa prosecuted Van Niekerk for contempt of the South African judiciary. The charges were dismissed after the government's presentation of its case.

4 Crim. Proc. Act no. 56 at 1955, 330.

5 *Contempt of Court*, op. cit. The undelivered closing address for Van Niekerk, see above, was published in 1970 Acta Juridica 77. These figures were included in the closing statement and were obtained from statistics provided in the course of the trial by the Under-Secretary of Justice for South Africa. The Van Niekerk figures put the white executions at 75; Albie Sachs, a former South African advocate, places the number at 85. A. Sachs, op. cit.

6 Report of the Commission of Prisons of the Republic of South Africa, for the period 1 July 1975 to 30 June 1976, at 22, 26 (published April 30, 1977) (hereinafter referred to as Prison Report). The data on capital punishment provided by the South Africa government is difficult to interpret for racial significance. For example, we are told in the above report that between 1 July 1975 and 30 June 1976 109 condemned were admitted to prison. Three of these were white. During that period, 60 persons were hanged, but no race breakdown is given. As of 30 June 1976, 86 condemned prisoners were in custody, of whom three were white. The previous year's report (1974-5) informs us that on 30 June 1975 two white condemned were in custody. Thus, it appears that of the five whites present and admitted in 1975-6, three were left in prison under sentence of death by the end of that period. Whether the other two whites were executed is problematic.

7 Prison Reports, op. cit., 1969-76. The execution figures by year are: 1969-70 (80); 1970-71 (80); 1971-72 (56); 1972-73 (55); 1973-74 (43); 1974-75 (59); 1975-76 (60).

8 Crim. Proc. Act no. 56 at 1955, 330.

9 Zeffertt, 'Extenuating Circumstances', 88 SALJ 416, 417 (1971). See *S* v. *Matthee* 1971 (3) SA 769 (AD); *S* v. *Shabalala*, 1966 (2) SA 297 (AD).

10 See Abolition of Juries Act no. 34 of 1969. Although juries, prior to 1969 could make the finding of extenuating circumstances, jury trials in capital cases were rare.

11 Midgely, 'Crime in South Africa', 1 *South Africa Journal of Criminal Law and Criminology* 71, 81 (1977).

12 Annual Report of the Commissioner of the South Africa Police for the year ended June 30, 1976 (hereinafter referred to as Police Report).

13 Criminal Statistics England and Wales 1976.

14 Commission Report. This was for the year 1967-8. Of the total convictions for violent crime in that year, 46, 158 were committed by whites and 398, 106 by non-whites, a ratio of 1 to 8, which corresponded 'roughly' with the ratio of whites to non-whites in the entire population. But for assault the ratio of white

compared with non-white convictions was 1 to 15 (3, 319: 47, 236) and for murder 1:58 (23: 1329).

15 Commission Report.

16 *The Star* (20 January 1973).

17 Prison Report. Between 1 July 1975 and 30 June 1976, 2,870 infants were admitted to, or born in, prison. None were white.

18 Bantu (Urban Areas) Consolidation Act, no. 25 of 1945, *as amended, inter alia*, Bantu Laws Amendment Act, no. 4 of 1976.

19 See ibid., 9 (2); 10; *International Herald Tribune* (4 November 1977). *See also* Commission Report.

20 *Contempt of Court*, op. cit. The figures used by Van Niekerk, see note 5, above, were provided by the government in the course of his trial.

21 Police Report (1975-6).

22 Sachs, op. cit., citing Diemont J. in *S.* v. *Ngubelanga*, 6/10/68, unreported (Cape). *See S.* v. *Germishaya*, van Zijl, J., *quoted in* Maister; R v. D. 1960 (I) SA 151.

23 *Contempt of Court*, op. cit.

24 Ibid.

25 Sachs, op. cit.

26 Prison Reports, op. cit., 1974-75.

27 See Kahn, *The Death Penalty in South Africa*, 18 Tysdskrit Vin Hederdaagse Romeins-Hollandse 108, 136 (1970).

28 Yutar, 'The Office of Attorney-General in South Africa', in *South Africa Journal of Criminal Law and Criminology*, 135.

29 Kahn, op. cit.

30 Ibid. In political cases, there is evidence that witnesses are coerced forcibly into falsifying testimony. Garbus, 'South Africa: The Death of Justice', *New York Review of Books* (4 August 1977). Whether this also occurs in non-political cases is not known.

31 Cook, *South Africa: the imprisoned society* (International Defence and Aid Fund, 1974).

32 Garbus, 'South Africa: the death of justice', *New York Review of Books* (4 August 1977).

33 A.S. Mathews, *Law, Order and Liberty in South Africa* (1971).

34 Garbus, op. cit.

35 *Rand Daily Mail*, (25, 26 August 1977).

36 Press Release, International Commission of Jurists, 11 June 1976.

37 Zimbabwe Briefings no. 1 (Anti-Apartheid Movement, 1977).

38 Garbus, op. cit.

39 Police Report.

40 House of Assembly Debates (Hansaard), 4th Sess, 5th Parliament, 23 March 1977.

41 House of Assembly Debates (Hansaard), 4th Sess., 5th Parliament, 23 February 1977, at 455-66. *See* Commission Report.

42 *Rand Daily Mail* (24 February 1977). The figure of 18 is disputed by the United Nations, which puts reported political detainee deaths in 1976 at 13. 'Violations of Human Rights in South Africa', UN Economic and Social Council, E/CN.4/NGO/198. (10 February 1977). Bernard Levin of *The Times* put the figure at 11 (11 November 1977).

43 *Focus*, No. 12, (September 1977), (News Bulletin of the International Defence and Aid Fund).

44 'Violations of Human Rights in South Africa', op. cit.

45 Rand Daily Mail, (28 June 1969).

46 House of Assembly Debates (Hansaard) 4th Sess., 5th Parliament (23 March 1977). The breakdown by race for convictions in 1976 was: common assault, 81 whites and 120 non-whites; assault with intent to do grievous bodily harm, 5 whites and 19 non-whites; culpable homicide, 3 whites and 4 non-whites; murder, 1 white and 3 non-whites.

[16]

RACISM, WRONGFUL CONVICTIONS, AND THE DEATH PENALTY

HUGO ADAM BEDAU*

INTRODUCTION

Opponents of the death penalty, by virtue of their arguments, tend to divide into two groups. The first and larger group consists of those who oppose this penalty because of the risk of convicting and executing an innocent defendant—or because of the manifest and chronic unfairness that governs the management of our death penalty system, especially when race is at issue. The members of this group oppose the death penalty on what we might call administrative, or practical, grounds. The five Justices constituting the majority in *Furman v. Georgia*[1] advanced arguments of this administrative sort.

The members of this group face a common and familiar objection that is manifest in the following hypothetical question addressed to abolitionists: Suppose our death penalty system were reformed so that there would be no risk of executing the innocent, and so that the racist aspects of the system were completely prevented or remedied. Would you still oppose the death penalty?

There are several possible responses to this challenge. Some abolitionists, no doubt reluctantly, would drop their objections to the death penalty and embrace this risk-free and fairly administered death penalty system. After all, their objections were based entirely on failures in the administration of this punishment, and those objections by hypothesis no longer apply. Other opponents of the death penalty would take the radical line of rejecting the hypothetical question on the ground that it is beyond answering. Why? Because its premise is impossible. This is the line of argument taken by the late Yale law professor Charles Black, Jr., and those he influenced.[2] Black argued that trying to face this hypothetical is as absurd as asking a mathematician to resolve the following conundrum: Suppose π were a rational number, then what?[3] Since we know there is no way to reduce to zero the risk of executing the innocent, and no way to guarantee that the system is wholly without racial bias, there is no need to speculate about what one would say if these conditions were satisfied.

---

* Austin B. Fletcher Professor of Philosophy Emeritus, Tufts University, Medford, MA.
I am much indebted to Dr. C. E. Putnam for counsel and advice in drafting this Essay. Earlier versions were given at the Conference on Race and the Death Penalty at Harvard Law School (May 2006) and at the Annual Meeting of the National Coalition to Abolish the Death Penalty (October 2006).

1. Furman v. Georgia, 408 U.S. 238 (1972).

2. CHARLES L. BLACK, JR., CAPITAL PUNISHMENT: THE INEVITABILITY OF CAPRICE AND MISTAKE 156, 160 (2d ed. 1981).

3. *Id.* at 156.

They never will be satisfied, just as history shows they have never been satisfied to date.[4] Still other opponents of the death penalty would continue their opposition in the face of this hypothetical, but would shift the rationale of their objections either to other administrative shortcomings in the death penalty system—such as its economic costs—or to our inability to find and use a humane and effective method of execution.

Yet other abolitionists would retreat to more abstract and fundamental objections, such as the claim that the death penalty, no matter how it is administered, is a "cruel and unusual punishment" that violates the defendant's right to life. Justice William J. Brennan, Jr.,[5] and Justice Thurgood Marshall[6] advanced arguments of this latter sort in their concurring opinions in *Furman*.

Abolitionists who take this line constitute the second major group of death penalty opponents. They point out that everyone (at least in theory), whether for or against the death penalty, professes to be opposed to convicting, sentencing, and executing the innocent. Surely, they would point out, everyone in favor of the death penalty favors a fair system of punishment. No defender of the death penalty would knowingly choose an unfair system over a fair system, other things being equal. This group of abolitionists argues that what really matters is not whether you are against executing the innocent. What really matters—as the late Henry Schwarzschild was fond of reminding us—is whether you are against executing the *guilty*, or anyway those who have been found guilty by a fair criminal justice system.[7] I am sure that Schwarzschild was right, and I will have no more to say about this second main group of death penalty abolitionists. Let me return, then, to the first group.

I want to focus on questions that have so far not received the attention they merit; they have been neglected, to the best of my knowledge, by all of us, whether we are for or against the death penalty. The questions are these: Are there important similarities, differences, or both, in the merits of the administrative argument from wrongful convictions and of the administrative argument from racial bias? Since most of today's opponents of the death penalty rely on both of these arguments, it is hardly surprising that we do not see these arguments distinguished and evaluated by abolitionists. And since most of today's friends of the death penalty think neither of these arguments is persuasive, it is hardly surprising that the differential merits of the two arguments, if any, are never evaluated from that direction. I propose to remedy this long-standing neglect. My strategy will be to take five topics on the basis of which we can compare and contrast the role of these two arguments, and then to see what the scorecard looks like at the end of my investigation.

4. *Id.* at 17–18, 22, 170.

5. *Furman*, 408 U.S. at 286, 290–91, 305 (Brennan, J., concurring).

6. *Id.* at 358–60 (Marshall, J., concurring).

7. Personal communication with Henry Schwarzschild (1925–1996). Mr. Schwarzschild directed the ACLU's anti-death penalty project beginning in 1976.

I. THE ABOLITION MOVEMENT

The modern abolition movement in the United States began in the early 1960s under the leadership of the NAACP Legal Defense and Educational Fund (LDF).[8] By 1965, the LDF had for several decades undertaken to contest racist practices, whether civil or criminal, lawful or unlawful, all over the nation.[9] The LDF recognized that it could not effectively challenge death penalty cases involving African American defendants—its primary clientele—and at the same time abandon to their fate white defendants in capital cases. The result was a national legal campaign across racial lines to end the death penalty entirely for all crimes and all defendants.[10] What began as the final act of the Civil Rights movement was transformed into a color-blind and race-neutral struggle, and it remains so today.

Playing no role whatever, so far as I know, in the movement at its inception was concern about wrongful death penalty convictions in the strong sense of the term "wrong." No one thought William L. Maxwell in Arkansas was innocent of rape.[11] No one thought William Henry Furman in Georgia was innocent of murder.[12] No one thought Earnest James Aikens in California[13]—with *Furman*, the other leading death penalty case in 1972—was innocent of murder. Unfairly tried, unfairly convicted, and unfairly sentenced: Yes. But wholly innocent of the capital crimes of which they had been charged and convicted: No.

Contrast this with Great Britain, where the wrongful execution of Timothy John Evans in 1953[14] was a vital and continuing source of public anti-death penalty fervor.[15] As for racial aspects of the death penalty in Great Britain, there were none. The contrast in the two narratives, ours in the United States and theirs in Great Britain, could not be sharper. Not until years later, when death penalty cases began to occur in the British West Indies,[16] did race begin to play a role in the struggle against the death penalty in Great Britain.

---

8. HUGO ADAM BEDAU, THE COURTS, THE CONSTITUTION, AND CAPITAL PUNISHMENT 60, 83 (1977); BURTON H. WOLFE, PILEUP ON DEATH ROW 230 (1973). *See generally* MICHAEL MELTSNER, CRUEL AND UNUSUAL: THE SUPREME COURT AND CAPITAL PUNISHMENT 3–19 (1973) (describing the history of the LDF).

9. MELTSNER, *supra* note 8, at 5–7.

10. *See* WOLFE, supra note 8, at 245.

11. *See generally* Maxwell v. Bishop, 398 U.S. 262 (1970).

12. *See generally* Furman v. Georgia, 408 U.S. 238 (1972).

13. *See generally* Aikens v. California, 406 U.S. 813 (1971).

14. LUDOVIC KENNEDY, TEN RILLINGTON PLACE (1961).

15. BRIAN P. BLOCK & JOHN HOSTETTLER, HANGING IN THE BALANCE: A HISTORY OF THE ABOLITION OF CAPITAL PUNISHMENT IN BRITAIN 16 (1997).

16. PENAL REFORM INTERNATIONAL ET AL., COMMONWEALTH CARIBBEAN HUMAN RIGHTS SEMINAR (2000), *available at* http://www.penalreform.org/resources/rep-2000-caribbean-human-rights-en.pdf.

II. JUDICIAL MURDER AND LEGAL LYNCHING

The historic practice of mob lynching in America is important for several reasons, one of which is that it involved both the racial bias and the wrongful conviction objections to the death penalty.[17] Historically, mob lynching has been the paradigm racist mode of quasi- or perhaps pseudo-punishment. Lynchers (at least those in the United States) manifested conspicuous indifference as to whether their victims were truly the guilty murderers or rapists that the lynch mob (usually but not invariably) professed to believe they were.

That brings us to the question: Which of the two objections to lynching was paramount in the minds of its opponents? Was it mainly the objection that an innocent person was likely to be killed if a lynch mob could choose its victims? Or was it mainly the objection that, in the typical mob lynching, an African American man was being treated by whites in a manner that few white men would be treated by other whites? My reading of the lynching narratives and their analysis published in recent years[18] leads me to believe that the two arguments were about equal in their influence on the opponents of mob lynching.

In the past few years, it has become increasingly common for abolitionists to describe our current death penalty system as a system of "legal lynching," defined by historian W. Fitzhugh Brundage as "manipulating the legal system to ensure that blacks accused of rape or murder received the death penalty, the same punishment that would have been meted out by the lynch mob."[19] The point of this description and its use in describing our current death penalty system is obvious. Doing so brings to our attention the ways in which the brutalities of yesterday's practice of mob lynching still cast an ugly shadow over today's new-model death penalty system—the sort of system that then-Governor Mitt Romney in Massachusetts once claimed can and ought to be installed in the criminal law.[20]

As with most analogies, this one sheds light even as it risks distortion through exaggeration. Respect for due process of law and equal protection of the law, conspicuously absent in historic mob lynching, have been for decades firmly established standards by which we can evaluate the performance of the police, prosecutors, judges, juries, and the other officials who manage our death penalty system. These persons know that their official behavior—at least in

---

17. *See* CHARLES J. OGLETREE, JR. & AUSTIN SARAT, FROM LYNCH MOBS TO THE KILLING STATE: RACE AND THE DEATH PENALTY IN AMERICA 1 (2006).

18. *See id.*

19. W. FITZHUGH BRUNDAGE, UNDER SENTENCE OF DEATH: LYNCHING IN THE SOUTH 251 (1997); *see also* JESSE L. JACKSON, SR., JESSE L. JACKSON, JR., & BRUCE SHAPIRO, LEGAL LYNCHING: THE DEATH PENALTY AND AMERICA'S FUTURE (2001); CHRISTOPHER WALDREP, LYNCHING IN AMERICA: A HISTORY IN DOCUMENTS (2006).

20. See ALAN ROGERS, MURDER AND THE DEATH PENALTY IN MASSACHUSETTS 403–06 (2005), for a description of the provisions of the Governor's bill.

principle—is subject to evaluation by such standards; they are not just pro forma norms without practical significance. Seen against the background of mob lynching, our current system of "legal lynching"—if that is what it is (Sacco and Vanzetti used this language in the mid-1920s to describe their case[21])—has to be conceded to be an improvement.

In this regard, it is useful to consider another and older oxymoron of abolitionist rhetoric, "judicial murder"—an epithet found in the anti-death penalty culture of the 1830s at least in Massachusetts.[22] Consider for a moment the similarities and the differences between these two epithets. "Legal lynching" characterizes the death penalty alliteratively as a practice of violence in the streets carried out by a mob acting with self-appointed authority. "Judicial murder" portrays the machinery of death as an authoritative and deliberative enterprise that culminates in a lawful lethal act. The two phrases share the attempt to characterize the death penalty as a system of guilt by association with murder, whether lawless or lawful.

III. THE EMPIRICAL EVIDENCE

The belief that our death penalty system is racially biased is supported by two different kinds of empirical evidence. One kind of support comes from eye-witness accounts, anecdotal testimony, and extensive personal narratives, reporting the myriad ways in which the death penalty system (especially in the South), has had, with grievous unfairness, a particularly significant impact on our African American population.[23] The other kind of evidence is statistical, classically manifest in the outstanding work done in the 1980s by Iowa law professor David Baldus and his associates, culminating in their masterpiece, *Equal Justice and the Death Penalty*.[24] What this research showed, as all students of the subject know, is that there is a significant statistical likelihood that race of victim plays a measurable role in determining who gets sentenced to death and executed.[25] It is virtually impossible to imagine how the conclusions of this research could be impeached or otherwise disregarded as inconclusive. Baldus and his colleagues confirmed the long-standing belief that the best recipe for a death sentence in America involves a cast consisting of a white female murder (or rape) victim and a black male accused of the crime.[26]

By contrast, consider the empirical evidence on the innocence issue. Except for DNA evidence, not available until two decades ago, evidence of innocence is almost always entirely narrative in character. Belief in the wrongful

21. *See* BRUCE WATSON, SACCO AND VANZETTI 75 (2007).

22. *See* ROGERS, *supra* note 20, at 98.

23. AUSTIN SARAT, WHEN THE STATE KILLS: CAPITAL PUNISHMENT AND THE AMERICAN CONDITION 18 (2001).

24. DAVID C. BALDUS, GEORGE G. WOODWORTH & CHARLES A. PULASKI, JR., EQUAL JUSTICE AND THE DEATH PENALTY: A LEGAL AND EMPIRICAL ANALYSIS (1990).

25. *Id.* at 188.

26. *Id.* at 149, 152, 399, 401.

execution of death penalty defendants formerly rested almost entirely on stories that pointed to a defendant's innocence beyond a reasonable doubt. Such evidence is often extremely strong, and while students of the issue might disagree among themselves over the conclusiveness of the evidence in this or that given case, no one seriously disputes the claim that dozens—indeed, hundreds—of persons in the 20th century were wrongly arrested, wrongly indicted, wrongly convicted, wrongly sentenced to death, wrongly denied a new trial, wrongly denied a commutation of their death sentences, or—in some cases (a few? many?)—wrongly executed. Even supporters of the death penalty, such as the late Ernest van den Haag, have conceded that a few of the more than 7,000 legal lynchings in the past century involved the judicial murder of an innocent defendant—although van den Haag and others of his persuasion profess not to know exactly which among these 7,000 cases was one of the wrongful executions.[27]

If I had to choose between arguments that attack the death penalty because of its racial bias and arguments that attack its fallibility, which would I favor and why? History shows that the argument from wrongful conviction is by far the more widely used by American abolitionists. It is as at least as old as the miscarriages of justice that resulted in death by poisoning in the case of Socrates and death by crucifixion in the case of Jesus. Notice, too, that whereas racial bias can lead to wrongful convictions, no one claims that wrongful convictions can lead to racial bias. So far as the magnitude of its impact is concerned, I think that arguments from racial bias—at least in our society—have had the larger impact. But the statistical techniques used by Baldus and others cannot suffice to establish the claim that this or that particular government official acted from racial bias, the criterion on which Justice Lewis F. Powell, Jr., relied in his opinion for the Court in *McCleskey v. Kemp*.[28]

Today, the availability of DNA evidence has dramatically altered the strength of the wrongful conviction argument despite the fact that such evidence is not available in all capital cases. No longer do claims of actual innocence rest solely on narrative evidence. Instead, we now have a powerful statistical tool with which to vindicate claims of actual innocence akin in its strength to the statistical argument from racial bias of twenty years ago. The chief advantage of DNA evidence is that it is highly individuated, since it is focused on the status of a given defendant, one case at a time.[29] This means that both the racial bias argument and the wrongful conviction argument are now driven by narrative, as well as statistical evidence, putting the two arguments more or less on a par with each other.

27. Ernest van den Haag, *The Ultimate Punishment: A Defense*, 99 HARV. L. REV. 1662, 1664 (1986).

28. 481 U.S. 279 (1976).

29. *See* BARRY SCHECK, PETER NEUFELD & JIM DWYER, ACTUAL INNOCENCE: FIVE DAYS TO EXECUTION AND OTHER DISPATCHES FROM THE WRONGLY CONVICTED xv (2000).

IV. DUE PROCESS OF LAW

Which of the two, racism or the risk of executing the innocent, is the greater affront to our purported respect for law and the due process of law? If we could eliminate either racial bias or risk of wrongful conviction, but not both, which of these two defects in our death penalty system ought we to prefer to remedy and why? If we try to argue from the numbers involved in each case, as above, our vote ought to be to remove racial bias. Of course, there are many cases that involve evidence of racial bias as well as evidence that the defendant, although convicted at trial, turns out to be innocent. In the book *In Spite of Innocence* by Michael L. Radelet, Constance E. Putnam, and me on wrongful homicide convictions, the great fraction of the 416 cases we reported for the years 1900 through 1991—about one-third of the total—involved issues of racial bias intertwined with issues of innocence.[30]

If we turn to consider the difference in scope of application presented by the two kinds of arguments, however, we find that the wrongful conviction argument has much the greater application. Potentially *every* capital case is subject to review for the possibility that the trial ended in convicting an innocent defendant. But only a small fraction of all capital cases is subject to review for racial bias.

How much overlap is there in the outcome of the two kinds of arguments we are examining? We can imagine a death penalty system substantially free of racial bias but nonetheless crude and ineffective because it frequently convicts the innocent. It is more difficult to imagine a system that is racially biased but free of errors leading to conviction of the innocent. Thus, to some extent, a remedy for racial bias is likely to reduce the risk of convicting the innocent, but not the converse.

Among the various sorts of remedies to reduce the risk of executing the innocent and avoid the effects of racial bias, which of the two has captured the attention of legal reformers? Consider the Racial Justice Act in this light.[31] This bill was a direct response to the Supreme Court's advice in *McCleskey* to seek the remedy for such racism involved in the death penalty system by persuading the legislatures, state and federal, to construct the appropriate statutory safeguards. Enactment of such a bill would have empowered defense counsel to pursue investigation of prima facie racial bias in the trial courts where race of defendant or of victim (or both) was at issue.[32] This instrument would have constituted a powerful tool in the hands of those who sought to prevent or to attempt to rectify the worst aspects of racism in the death penalty system. The bill died in Congressional Committee in 1994.[33]

---

30. MICHAEL L. RADELET, HUGO ADAM BEDAU, & CONSTANCE E. PUTNAM, IN SPITE OF INNOCENCE: ERRONEOUS CONVICTIONS IN CAPITAL CASES 282–356 (1992).

31. Racial Justice Act of 1988, H.R. 4442, 100th Cong. (1988).

32. *Id.*

33. For further discussion of the Racial Justice Act, see THE DEATH PENALTY IN AMERICA: CURRENT CONTROVERSIES 251 (Hugo Adam Bedau ed., 1997).

Could we imagine parallel legislation, something that might be called the Innocent Defendant Act or the Wrongful Homicide Conviction Act, aimed to address the issue of wrongful convictions in (capital) homicide cases, in the spirit of the Racial Justice Act and its challenge to racism in the system? We do not have to imagine such a law because we already have a model for such legislation. In 2004, Congress enacted the Innocence Protection Act, which can serve as a legislative model for reducing the likelihood of wrongful convictions.[34] How many of the eighty-five remedies proposed to Governor George Ryan in Illinois by his death penalty moratorium commission in 2002 could count as provisions of that Act?[35] This is a topic too large to discuss here, but it is worth noticing that pioneering efforts to remedy procedures in criminal cases, begun by Yale law professor Edwin Borchard, reported in his deservedly famous book *Convicting the Innocent*,[36] did nothing to directly identify and address racist aspects of the criminal justice system. Borchard was concerned exclusively with reporting, preventing, and remedying the error of convicting the innocent,[37] leaving violations of due process, equal protection, and other kinds of procedural errors to be identified and remedied by other investigators at a later date. If racism played a role in the wrongful convictions that Borchard catalogued, it did so only deep in the background. The same can be said of the remedies proposed by Judge Jerome Frank and his daughter Barbara Frank in their book, *Not Guilty*.[38] It is not that racism in the system did not exist in those days. It is rather that it went unnoticed except for a handful of notorious cases, chief of which was that of the Scottsboro Boys in the early 1930s.[39]

V. GOOD FAITH ERROR

Research on wrongful convictions testifies to the presence of what Michael L. Radelet and I called "good faith error."[40] Good faith error occurs when a prosecution witness gives testimony to the effect that the accused is indeed guilty as charged—except that the evidence turns out to be misleading or false even though it was tendered in the sincere belief that it was true.[41] Not only do

34. Innocence Protection Act of 2004, Pub. L. No. 108-405, 118 Stat. 2278 (codified as amended in scattered sections of 18 U.S.C. and 42 U.S.C.).

35. For details on the Illinois commission's proposals, see DEBATING THE DEATH PENALTY: SHOULD AMERICA HAVE CAPITAL PUNISHMENT? 144–47 (Hugo Adam Bedau & Paul G. Cassell eds., 2004), and SCOTT TUROW, ULTIMATE PUNISHMENT: A LAWYER'S REFLECTIONS ON DEALING WITH THE DEATH PENALTY (2003).

36. EDWIN M. BORCHARD, CONVICTING THE INNOCENT: ACTUAL ERRORS OF CRIMINAL JUSTICE (1932).

37. *Id.* at xiii–xxiv.

38. JEROME FRANK & BARBARA FRANK, NOT GUILTY (1957).

39. DAN T. CARTER, SCOTTSBORO: A TRAGEDY OF THE AMERICAN SOUTH (rev. ed. 1979).

40. Hugo Adam Bedau & Michael L. Radelet, *Miscarriages of Justice in Potentially Capital Cases*, 40 STAN. L. REV. 21, 61 (1987); RADELET, BEDAU & PUTNAM, *supra* note 30, at 18.

41. Bedau & Radelet, *supra* note 40, at 61.

such cases exist; research has shown that evidence of this sort was often a paramount cause of the innocent being convicted in homicide cases.[42]

Contrast this with racial bias. It is impossible for someone to act in a racially biased manner, or to accept what he knows is racially biased testimony or other evidence, and to do so in the belief that he is acting in good faith. Racial bias may be unintentional, unwitting, or unknowing. But it is doubtful that it can be tendered in good faith.[43]

This fact about the discrepancy between the arguments and testimony that are racially biased on the one hand, and the arguments and testimony that are tendered in good faith but in error on the other, shows an important difference between the two kinds of evidence. Erroneous but good faith evidence can be excused, and perhaps even in some cases justified. But there is little if any excuse or justification for racial bias, let alone for testimony and arguments based on it.

In addition, since there is no cure for good faith error, there can be no cure for wrongful convictions. Even if we abolish the death penalty, we will continue to convict the innocent. But this is not true where racial bias is concerned. At least in theory, there is a cure for racial bias in the criminal justice system. There was a time when anti-Semitism was widely embraced by American Gentiles.[44] And in the windows of houses on Boston's Beacon Hill, there were once bold signs that read "NINA"—which all concerned knew was code for "No Irish Need Apply."[45] The day when such flagrant ethnic hostility could be openly avowed has passed and has been over for some time. In theory the same could be true of today's racial bias. I see no principled reason why it will not vanish from the scene—even if not as rapidly as we would like.

CONCLUSION

It is not really an oversimplification to insist that racial bias and convicting the innocent are the twin evils paramount in our current death penalty system, as they have been for generations. If we are to believe the friends of the death penalty, the risk of these two evils must be borne patiently in the confidence that the benefits of a death penalty system—even a flawed system such as ours—outweigh the costs. Those of us who have looked with care at our death penalty system may be excused if we are unpersuaded. In our view, the benefits

42. *Id.* at 57 tbl.6.

43. There may be a few counter-examples, however, such as the sincere anti-Semitic Nazi who honestly believed that Jews deserved to die, that the only good Jew was a dead Jew. I must leave to another occasion an examination of claims made by such sincere but deluded fanatics whose morality is repugnant to most of us most of the time. Discussion of this problem originates with the English philosopher R. M. Hare. *See* R. M. HARE, MORAL THINKING: ITS LEVELS, METHOD, AND POINT (1981); R. M. HARE, THE LANGUAGE OF MORALS (1952).

44. Michael N. Dobkowski, *American Anti-Semitism: A Reinterpretation*, 29 AM. Q. 166, 166, 181 (1977).

45. *See* EDWARD M. KENNEDY, AMERICA BACK ON TRACK 3–4 (2006).

are elusive and illusory, the costs palpable and enduring. Let us hope that it will not be too long before those costs lead us to retreat altogether from further use of the death penalty.

Part IV
Gender and Sexuality Issues

[17]

A Nation At War With Itself: The Potential Impact of Uganda's Anti-Homosexuality Bill

Barrie Sander*

Abstract. This paper discusses the Anti-Homosexuality Bill, a private member's Bill tabled before Uganda's Parliament in October 2009. The paper provides a summary of the main provisions of the Bill, a discussion of the motivations behind the Bill and an insight into the different reactions that the Bill has received both within and outside Uganda. The paper then offers a detailed human rights analysis of the proposed offence of "aggravated homosexuality", for which individuals will be liable on conviction to be sentenced to death. The paper concludes that, against the general international trend towards the abolition of the death penalty, recent developments in Uganda are of grave concern to both local Ugandans as well as the international community.

1. Introduction

> The punishment of death is the war of a nation against a citizen whose destruction it judges to be necessary or useful.[116]

Almost 250 years ago, Cesare Beccaria warned of the lethal power of the State to utilise capital punishment as a means to legitimise the arbitrary destruction of any particular group in society whose eradication it deemed "necessary or useful". Most striking about Beccaria's remark is his use of the metaphor of war, in which an entire nation can become embroiled. Such imagery recognises the fundamental importance of the right to life and the fact that undermining this human right can impact on everyone. It recognises the simple but brutal reality that once a State has decided that the right to life is inapplicable in relation to one group of society, there is nothing to stop that same State deciding in the future that the right is inapplicable in relation to other groups.

Beccaria's words of warning now have a renewed relevance in relation to the Anti-Homosexuality Bill, introduced before Uganda's parliament by David Bahati MP on 14 October 2009.[117] The Bill is deeply disturbing not only for its focus on

---

* Barrie Sander is a Trainee Solicitor at Herbert Smith LLP.
Any views expressed herein are the authors' own and do not necessarily reflect the views of Herbert Smith LLP. The paper was written after the author had completed an internship at the African Prisons Project in Kampala, Uganda. During his stay in Uganda, the author worked principally in the condemned (death row) section of Luzira prison assisting the prisoners with their capital mitigation cases. The author would like to thank the Centre for Capital Punishment Studies for coordinating the internship, in particular Ms. Lina Gyllensten and Peter Hodgkinson who were always on hand to offer support and encouragement throughout the experience. The author welcomes any comments on the paper and may be contacted at bjs360@gmail.com.

116 C. Beccaria, On Crimes and Punishments, (1764).

117 BBC News, *Uganda MP urges death for gay sex*, 15 October 2009, available at http://news.bbc.co.uk/1/hi/8308912.stm.

homosexuals, already one the most vulnerable groups in Ugandan society, but also for its potential to incriminate all Ugandans regardless of their sexuality. Arguably, the Bill's most alarming provision is the new offence of "aggravated homosexuality", for which individuals "shall be liable on conviction to suffer death".[118] It is this provision that forms the focus of this paper.

This paper provides a summary of the key provisions of the Anti-Homosexuality Bill, a discussion of what motivated its publication and an insight into the different reactions that the Bill has received both within and outside Uganda. The paper then turns to a detailed human rights analysis of the proposed offence of "aggravated homosexuality", before offering some concluding remarks.

2. Summary of the Anti-Homosexuality Bill

Before delving into a detailed analysis of the specific offence of aggravated homosexuality, it is useful to begin by taking a broader look at the Anti-Homosexuality Bill. At the outset, it is important to note that out of the 18 clauses that make up the Bill, only six introduce new legal provisions.[119] Homosexuality is already an offence under the Penal Code of Uganda,[120] and same-sex marriage is prohibited by the Ugandan Constitution.[121] Despite only a third of the Bill covering new ground, the new provisions are deeply disturbing from a human rights perspective. Indeed, the most controversial aspects of the Bill are those aimed, not directly against homosexuals, but at the wider public.

The Bill sets out an extremely broad, arbitrary and imprecise definition of the offence of homosexuality, expanding beyond the definition that already exists under the Penal Code to include "touching another person with the intention of committing the act of homosexuality".[122] The criminalisation of homosexuality is a clear violation of the freedom from discrimination and right to equal protection of the law guaranteed by the International Covenant on Civil and Political Rights ("ICCPR"),[123] the African Charter on Human and Peoples' Rights ("African Charter"),[124] and the Constitution of Uganda.[125] Arrest and detention on the ground of homosexual activity also violates the freedom from arbitrary arrest or detention guaranteed by the ICCPR,[126] the African Charter,[127] and the Constitution of Uganda.[128] Moreover, the vagueness and potential breadth of the offence of homosexuality could easily unleash a witch hunt

118 Clause 3, Anti-Homosexuality Bill 2009.

119 S. Tamale, *A Human Rights Impact Assessment of the Anti-Homosexuality Bill*, Public Dialogue hosted by the Human Rights & Peace Centre (HURIPEC), Faculty of Law, Makerere University, 18 November 2009, at pp.1-2, available at http://www.huripec.mak.ac.ug/Public_Dialogue_Presentation.pdf.

120 s.145, Ugandan Penal Code.

121 Article 31 (2)(a), Constitution of Uganda.

122 Clause 2, Anti-Homosexuality Bill 2009.

123 International Covenant on Civil and Political Rights ("ICCPR"), G.A. Res. 2200 (XXI), UN GAOR, 21st Sess., Supp. No. 16, at 49, UN Doc. A/6316 (1966), Article 26 (freedom from discrimination and the right to equal protection of the law).

124 African Charter on Human and Peoples' Rights ("African Charter"), OAU Doc. CAB/LEG/67/3 rev. 5, 21 I.L.M. 58 (1982), Articles 2 (freedom from discrimination) and 3 (right to equal protection of the law).

125 Article 21 (freedom from discrimination and the right to equal protection of the law), Constitution of Uganda.

126 ICCPR, *supra* note 8, Article 9.

127 African Charter, *supra* note 9, Article 6.

128 Article 23, Constitution of Uganda.

against homosexuals in local communities as well as enable individuals to bring false accusations against their enemies with the intention of "destroying" their reputations.

The Bill introduces a new offence entitled "Promotion of Homosexuality", which, *inter alia*, provides that any person who produces or disseminates materials to promote homosexuality, funds or sponsors homosexuality, or offers premises for the purposes of promoting homosexuality shall be liable on conviction to up to seven years imprisonment.[129] This provision is particularly dangerous in two respects. First, the provision undermines fundamental freedoms guaranteed by the ICCPR, the African Charter, and the Constitution of Uganda, in particular the freedoms of expression,[130] assembly,[131] and association.[132] Secondly, the provision would criminalise many of the activities of journalists, civil society activists and public health workers. In relation to journalists, the provision would immediately censor any articles that touch on issues of homosexuality. In relation to civil society activists, Amnesty International has warned that the provision would seriously restrict the work of human rights defenders working on sexual orientation or gender identity.[133] Finally, in relation to public health workers, the provision violates the right to health guaranteed by the International Covenant for Economic, Social and Cultural Rights (ICESCR) and the African Charter,[134] and runs directly contrary to the words of the UN Human Rights Committee, which has previously stated that "[c]riminalization of homosexual activity [...] would appear to run counter to the implementation of effective education programmes in respect of the HIV/AIDS prevention".[135] In this regard, Dr. Tamale has pointed out that the provision could lead to the immediate imprisonment of those sponsoring or working for initiatives such as the Most At Risk Populations' Initiative (MARPI) introduced by the Ministry of Health in 2008, which targets specific sections of the population in an effort to curb the spread of HIV/AIDS.[136] As a result, homosexuals will suffer increased stigmatisation within their communities, effectively being driven further underground, while vital outreach and education efforts of public health workers will be stifled.[137]

129 Clause 13, Anti-Homosexuality Bill 2009.

130 ICCPR, *supra* note 8, Article 19 (2); African Charter, *supra* note 9, Article 9; Article 29, Constitution of Uganda.

131 ICCPR, *supra* note 8, Article 21; African Charter, *supra* note 9, Article 11; Article 29, Constitution of Uganda.

132 ICCPR, *supra* note 8, Article 22; African Charter, *supra* note 9, Article 10; Article 29, Constitution of Uganda.

133 Amnesty International, *Uganda: Anti-Homosexuality Bill is inherently discriminatory and threatens broader human rights*, 7 January 2010 ("Amnesty Homosexuality Report"), at p.15. Amnesty International (at p.15, fn. 39) also points to the following reports submitted by the UN Special Representative on human rights defenders, which document past violations against Ugandan human rights activists who work on issues of sexual orientation and gender identity: Report of the Special Representative of the Secretary-General on the situation of human rights defenders, Addendum: Summary of cases transmitted to Governments and replies received, A/HRC/7/28/Add.1, 5 March 2008, paras. 1907-1909; Report of the Special Representative of the Secretary-General on the situation of human rights defenders, A/HRC/4/37/Add.1, March 27, 2007, paras. 559 and 560.

134 International Covenant for Economic, Social and Cultural Rights ("ICESCR"), G.A. Res. 2200A (XXI), UN GAOR, 21st Sess., Supp. No. 16, at 49, UN Doc. A/6316 (1966), Article 12; African Charter, *supra* note 9, Article 16. *See* Amnesty Homosexuality Report, *supra* note 18, at p.10.

135 *Toonen v. Australia*, UN Human Rights Committee, Communication No. 488/1992, U.N. Doc. CCPR/C/50/D/488/1992, 31 March 1994 ("*Toonen* Decision"), at para. 8.5.

136 S. Tamale, *supra* note 4, at pp.8-9.

137 Amnesty Homosexuality Report, *supra* note 18, at p.10. *See also*, S. Lewis, *Lewis says Uganda's anti-*

The Bill also introduces the offence of "Failure to disclose", which provides that any person in authority who fails to report known violations of the Bill within 24 hours will be subject to up to three years imprisonment.[138] By failing to define with sufficient specificity the term "any person in authority", this provision could potentially catch many different types of individuals. For example, it could catch a doctor from whom a homosexual seeks advice:[139] the Bill demands that such a doctor inform the police of the patient's homosexuality within 24 hours, thereby breaching the duty of confidentiality which he owes to his patient, or risk arrest and ultimately imprisonment. Priests, teachers, landlords, employers, politicians and lawyers could all be subjected to a similar fate. Most harrowing of all is the vivid image provided by Dr. Tamale of "a mother who is trying to come to terms with her child's sexual orientation [...] [being] dragged to police cells for not turning in her child to the authorities".[140] While one of the stated objectives in the Bill is "to protect the traditional family",[141] this provision clearly does more to promote its destruction. By laying the foundations for a culture of spying amongst the Ugandan population, this provision also directly violates the right to privacy guaranteed by the ICCPR and the Constitution of Uganda.[142]

Beyond introducing new offences, the Bill also contains an extra-territorial provision which states that a citizen or permanent resident of Uganda can be prosecuted for any of the offences under the Bill even if they are committed outside the borders of Uganda.[143] This provision elevates the offences under the Bill to a similar status as crimes such as terrorism, treason and the promotion of war on chiefs, which currently benefit from extra-territoriality under the Ugandan Penal Code.[144] Not only is such elevation unjustifiable, but also the provision is unenforceable in practice.[145]

Finally, the Bill purports to nullify any international treaties ratified by Uganda whose provisions contradict the spirit and provisions enshrined in the Bill.[146] This provision represents a flagrant violation of public international law. First, the provision disregards the principle of *pacta sunt servanda* enshrined in Article 26 of the Vienna Convention on the Law of Treaties (VCLT), which affirms that "[e]very treaty in force is binding upon the parties to it and must be performed by them in good faith".[147] Secondly, by giving primacy to Ugandan domestic legislation over Uganda's international treaty obligations, the provision breaches Article 27 of the VCLT, which

gay Bill must go, Stephen Lewis Foundation, 24 November 2009, who claims that the Bill "put[s] at risk [...] the entire apparatus of AIDS treatment, prevention and care" (available at: http://www.stephenlewisfoundation.org/news_item.cfm?news=3208).

138 Clause 14, Anti-Homosexuality Bill 2009.

139 S. Tamale, *supra* note 4, at pp.6-7.

140 S. Tamale, *supra* note 4, at p.7.

141 Preamble 1.1, Anti-Homosexuality Bill 2009.

142 ICCPR, *supra* note 8, Article 17; Article 27, Constitution of Uganda. *See also* the *Toonen* Decision, *supra* note 20, at para. 8.2, where the Human Rights Committee noted that "it is undisputed that adult consensual activity in private is covered by the concept of 'privacy'."

143 Article 16, Anti-Homosexuality Bill 2009.

144 *See* s.4 (2), Ugandan Penal Code.

145 *See* S. Tamale, *supra* note 4, at p.9, asking whether the government is "going to storm the bedrooms of consenting adults, or deploy spies to follow them when they travel abroad in order to establish who they have slept with and how they did it".

146 Article 18, Anti-Homosexuality Bill 2009.

147 Vienna Convention on the Law of Treaties ("VCLT"), 1155 UNTS 331, 23 May 1969, Article 26.

prohibits the invocation of a State's internal law as justification for its failure to perform an international treaty.[148] Finally, the provision is not in conformity with the grounds for terminating, denouncing or withdrawing from a treaty under Part V of the VCLT, which exclusively governs such actions and must be complied with for this purpose.[149]

From this brief summary of the most important provisions that are introduced by the Anti-Homosexuality Bill, two points are clear. First, both the spirit and substance of the Bill mark a significant departure from Uganda's human rights obligations enshrined both in international human rights treaties and the Constitution of Uganda. Secondly, far from focusing its aim exclusively at Uganda's homosexual population, the Bill targets all Ugandans regardless of their sexuality. As Dr. Tamale has forcefully argued:[150] "Those sitting back and thinking, 'Get them Bahati!' may be shocked one day when it is them that this law throws in jail".

3. The Motivation Behind the Tabling of the Anti-Homosexuality Bill

Having summarised the main provisions of the Anti-Homosexuality Bill, it is useful at this stage to consider what motivated the creation and tabling of such a Bill in Uganda at this time.

The preamble to the Anti-Homosexuality Bill sets out the official motivations behind the Bill, including a need to strengthen the family unit, defend the culture of Uganda, and protect Uganda's children from sexual abuse and exploitation.[151] These laudable aims are in stark contrast to the method adopted by the Bill to achieve them. The juxtaposition between the aims and methods adopted by the Bill leads one to suspect that other motivations lie behind the Bill. In this regard, at least three other unofficial rationales of the Bill are possible.

First, it must be remembered that the Anti-Homosexuality Bill is a private member's Bill, introduced by David Bahati MP. One rationale behind the Bill's introduction may be little more than opportunism by David Bahati MP, who has now become a household name both at home and internationally. By releasing the Bill, David Bahati MP, a previously unknown politician, has achieved widespread notoriety.

Secondly, there is increasing evidence that the Bill is at least partly the result of US conservative evangelists, who have been encouraging homophobic attitudes in Uganda by alleging that homosexuals are trying to "recruit" children and that homosexuality is a habit that can be "cured".[152] In particular, several journalists have claimed that the impetus for harsher legislation against homosexuals in Uganda is

148 VCLT, *supra* note 32, Article 27: "A party may not invoke the provisions of its internal law as justification for its failure to perform a treaty. This rule is without prejudice to article 46."

149 *See* VCLT, *supra* note 32, Article 42: "The termination of a treaty, its denunciation or the withdrawal of a party, may take place only as a result of the application of the provisions of the treaty or of the present Convention. The same rule applies to suspension of the operation of a treaty."

150 S. Tamale, *Why Anti-Gay Bill Should Worry Us*, The Monitor, 3 November 2009, available at http://www.faruganda.org/index.php?option=com_content&view=article&id=10%3Aopnion&catid=1%3Anews&Itemid=3.

151 Preamble 1.1, Anti-Homosexuality Bill 2009.

152 *See* X. Rice, *Uganda considers death sentence for gay sex in bill before parliament*, The Guardian, 29 November 2009, available at: http://www.guardian.co.uk/world/2009/nov/29/uganda-death-sentence-gay-sex.

rooted in a seminar given in Kampala in March 2009 by three US evangelists (Scott Lively, Don Schmierer and Caleb Lee Brundidge) to "expose the truth behind homosexuality and the homosexual agenda".[153] For three days, the US visitors discussed how "the gay movement is an evil institution" whose goal is "to defeat the marriage-based society and replace it with a culture of sexual promiscuity".[154] After the conference, Stephen Langa, the Ugandan organiser of the event, arranged for a petition signed by thousands of Ugandans to be delivered to Parliament in April 2009.[155] Against this background, it is unsurprising that the Anti-Homosexuality Bill arrived only months later, explicitly citing "the attempts of sexual rights activists seeking to impose their values of sexual promiscuity on the people of Uganda" as one of its rationales.[156]

Finally, the timing of the Bill so soon after the September 2009 riots in Kampala, which left over 20 Ugandans dead and 40 injured,[157] has led some commentators to conclude that another potential rationale for the Bill is "the sinister way it could be used to stifle political debate and quell dissent to the ruling NRM party" in the run up to the 2011 elections.[158] A recent report issued by Human Rights Watch has emphasised the fragility of Uganda's democracy and recalled how previous national elections in 2001 and 2006 were "marred by politically motivated violence, intimidation, and bribery of voters, virtually none of which were either investigated or prosecuted".[159] Dr. Tamale recently warned that "when people at the locus of power are feeling vulnerable and their power is being threatened, they will turn against the weaker groups in society".[160] In exactly this fashion, the Anti-Homosexuality Bill may eventually become little more than a tool to be exploited for political gain.

While it may be impossible to identify the overriding rationale behind the Anti-Homosexuality Bill, it is clear from the above discussion that the existence of the Bill has served to shine a light on the increasingly dangerous external homophobic

---

See X. Rice, *supra* note 37. *See also* S. Nakaweesi-Kimbuge and F. Mugisha, *Bahati's bill: A convenient distraction for Uganda's government*, Pambazuka News, 16 October 2009, available at: http://www.pambazuka.org/en/category/features/59556, noting in particular that "it costs a considerable amount of money, time and processes to table a private-member's bill, which begs the question of how the MP from Kabale District is financing this process?"; T. McVeigh, P. Harris, and B. Among, *Anti-gay bigots plunge Africa into new era of hate crimes*, The Observer, 13 December 2009; J. Gettleman, *Americans' Role Seen in Uganda Anti-Gay Push*, New York Times, 3 January 2010, available at: http://www.nytimes.com/2010/01/04/world/africa/04uganda.html; and S. Monjeza and T. Chimbalanga, *West turns Africa into gay battlefield*, The Sunday Times, 17 January 2010, available at: http://www.timesonline.co.uk/tol/news/world/africa/article6991023.ece.

154 *See* J. Gettleman, *supra* note 38.

155 *See* X. Rice, *supra* note 37.

156 Preamble 1.1, Anti-Homosexuality Bill 2009.

157 P. Greste, *Royal riots expose Uganda tensions*, BBC News, 17 September 2009, available at: http://news.bbc.co.uk/1/hi/world/americas/8260130.stm.

158 A. Rubin, *Uganda's Anti-Homosexuality Bill: Satan's Agents and the Real Reason Behind It*, Huffington Post, 18 December 2009, available at: http://www.huffingtonpost.com/ariel-rubin/ugandas-anti-homosexualit_b_397090.html. *See also*, A. Rubin, *Anti-gay bill diversionary – Latigo*, The Independent, 16 December 2009, where opposition leader, Morris Latigo, claims that "[i]t is a very good bill terms of opening up possibilities for mischief in Ugandan politics" (available at: http://www.independent.co.ug/index.php/column/interview/69-interview/2282-anti-gay-bill-diversionary-latigo).

Human Rights Watch, *Preparing for the Polls: Improving Accountability for Electoral Violence in Uganda*, 4 December 2009, at p.1.

160 S. Tamale, *supra* note 4, at p.4.

influences on Uganda as well as the ongoing political tensions that are building as the 2011 elections approach.

4. REACTION TO THE ANTI-HOMOSEXUALITY BILL

Ever since its publication, the Anti-Homosexuality Bill has divided opinion, a point exemplified by the compilation of key statements and opinions on the Bill put together by the Civil Society Coalition on Human Rights and Constitutional Law, which has asked the question "Should Uganda be killing its gays or killing the Anti-Homosexuality Bill?".[161]

Supporters of the Bill have tended to advance several homophobic arguments to justify their position. Some have argued that human rights are inapplicable to homosexuals. For instance, the Church of Uganda has emphasised the need to "[e]nsure that homosexual practice or the promotion of homosexual relations is not adopted as a human right".[162] In addition, Ugandan Ethics Minister James Nsaba Buturo has previously stated that "homosexuals can forget about human rights",[163] arguing that "[i]f we accept that homosexuals are a minority group then robbers are going to come to us to say that 'we too are a minority group'".[164] Such an argument is deeply flawed, the obvious distinction between robbers and homosexuals being that robbers choose to cause a specific harm to others, whereas homosexuals do not cause harm to anyone and should not be criminalised for being who they are.[165] As emphasised most forcefully by Article 1 of the Universal Declaration on Human Rights, "[a]ll human beings are born free and equal in dignity and rights".[166]

Others have argued that the fate of the Bill should be left to the Ugandan people to decide.[167] Yet, as Andrew Mwenda has noted, "the biggest threat to homosexuals is actually society since over 90% of [Uganda's] population is hostile to them".[168] This

---

161 Civil Society Coalition on Human Rights and Constitutional Law, *Uganda's Anti-Homosexuality Bill – The Great Divide*, December 2009 ("Civil Society Coalition Report"), at p.1.

162 *See* Church of Uganda, *Church of Uganda's Position on the Anti Homosexuality Bill 2009*, 9 February 2009, at p.3, available at: http://churchofuganda.org/wp-content/uploads/2010/02/COU-official-position-on-the-Anti-Homosexuality-Bill-2009..pdf. *See also* S. Naturinda, *Cultural Leaders Request Legislators to Pass Gays Bill*, The Monitor, 30 April 2010, reporting on the statement of the Forum for Kings and Cultural Leaders in Uganda, in which they "note[d] with alarm how western governments and their agencies are aggressively pushing for the legitimisation of homosexuality which to us is not a human right, but a human vice", available at: http://allafrica.com/stories/201004300042.html.

163 *See* AFP News Service, *Minister breaks ranks in Uganda's Anti-gay bill debacle*, 8 January 2010, available at: http://www.theequatorian.com/index.php?option=com_content&task=view&id=739&Itemid=293. *See also,* David Bahati MP who argues that in Uganda "we don't recognise homosexuality as a right" (J. Mmali, *Uganda fear over gay death-penalty plans*, BBC News, 22 December 2009, available at: http://news.bbc.co.uk/1/hi/8412962.stm).

164 *See* AFP News Service, *UN "Spreading Homosexuality"*, 3 April 2009, available at: http://www.news24.com/Content/Africa/News/965/944efddd78c84ecea8b8283eff969f0a/03-04-2009-10-08/UN_spreading_homosexuality.

165 One of the misconceptions behind the Bill is the erroneous belief expressed by David Bahati MP that "people are [not] born gays. It is foreign influence at work" (*see* T. McVeigh, P. Harris, and B. Among, *supra* note 38).

166 Universal Declaration of Human Rights, G.A. Res. 217A (III), U.N. Doc A/810 at 71 (1948), 10 December 1948, Article 1.

167 Civil Society Coalition Report, *supra* note 46, at p.3.

168 A. Mwenga, *Bahati: Don't usurp God's power*, The Independent, 10 November 2009, available at: http://www.independent.co.ug/index.php/the-last-word/the-last-word/3-the-last-word/2083-bahati-dont-usurp-gods-power.

hostility was vividly highlighted in January 2010 when thousands of children demonstrated in Kampala in favour of the Bill, with one fifteen year-old claiming that he was "happy to be part of those demonstrating to show the world that gays have no place in Uganda".[169] I have also personally witnessed Ugandan hostility towards homosexuality whenever I discussed the Bill with locals during my stay in Uganda.[170] For example, during a discussion on the subject during a lecture I gave at Makerere University in Kampala,[171] I was struck when one student declared that "homosexuality is the same as mass murder". When probed, he argued that "homosexuality undermines procreation" (another common argument put forward by supporters of the Bill); "since homosexuals are not able to have children, they are slowly destroying the human race".[172] Such an argument is unsound: to equate not having children with murder equally catches within its scope many heterosexual couples who consensually choose not to have children as well as many impotent men and women who are unable to have children.

Such debates with local students or local communities always end up highly charged. Any mention of the human rights of homosexuals is dismissed as an affront to Ugandan culture, "an immoral Western import",[173] an attempt to impose colonial views on Africa.[174] There are two problems with this argument. First, it must be remembered that homosexuality existed prior to Europeans entering Uganda.[175] According to President Museveni, "[t]hey were not persecuted but were not encouraged either".[176] It was in fact a British colonial law which first criminalised homosexuality in Uganda: if anything, it is homophobia which is the colonial intrusion,

---

169 G. Magga, *Thousands of children demonstrate in favour of anti-gay bill*, 22 January 2010, available at: http://en.afrik.com/article16829.html.

170 On this point, *see* B. Sander, *Uganda's Anti-Homosexuality Bill: A Disturbing Affront to Human Rights*, 5 December 2009, available at: http://www.internationallawbureau.com/blog/?p=1032.

171 B. Sander & K. Akers, *Guest Lecture: Capital Punishment*, Makerere University, Faculty of Law, 13 November 2009.

172 *See also* AFP News Service, *supra* note 49, where it is noted that Ugandan Ethics Minister James Nsaba Buturo has previously argued that "homosexuality threatens the future of civilisation because homosexual sex does not produce children"; and Church of Uganda, *supra* note 47, at p.2, claiming that "[f]rom a plain reading of Scripture [...] homosexual practice has no place in God's design of creation, the continuation of the human race through procreation, or His plan of redemption".

173 *See* J. Gettleman, *supra* note 38.

174 *See* AFP News Service, *supra* note 48, where Ugandan Ethics Minister James Nsaba Buturo is quoted as claiming that "[n]obody, nobody, nobody has the right to think for Ugandans. Nobody has the right to impose their values on a sovereign state"; *See also* AFP News Service, *supra* note 49, where Minister Buturo is quoted as claiming that "[a]t the United Nations there are attempts by some nations to impose homosexuality on the rest of us [...] We have learned that they want to smuggle in provisions on homosexuality"; E. Gyezaho, *Museveni Warns Against Homosexuality*, The Daily Monitor, 16 November 2009, quoting President Museveni as claiming that "European homosexuals are recruiting in Africa" (available at: http://allafrica.com/stories/200911161991.html); and T. McVeigh, P. Harris, and B. Among, *supra* note 38, quoting David Bahati MP as stating that the Bill aims to "protect the cherished culture of the people of Uganda against the attempts of sexual rights activists seeking to impose their values of sex promiscuity on the people of Uganda".
See also, S. Nakaweesi-Kimbugwe and F. Mugisha, *Bahati's bill: A convenient distraction for Uganda's government*, Pambazuka News, 16 October 2009, who emphasise that "African cultures, in all their diversity, have always embraced people who are different" and ultimately "reject the use of [...] African identity to support and legislate the persecution of [homosexual] Ugandans, their allies and anyone willing to consider the right to equality for all" (available at: http://www.pambazuka.org/en/category/features/59556).

176 *See* E. Gyezaho, *supra* note 59.

not the affirmation of human rights.[177] Secondly, although there exists a right to culture,[178] this right is limited at the point at which it impinges upon another human right.[179] Ugandans cannot invoke cultural rights to justify the Anti-Homosexuality Bill's numerous derogations from other human rights and fundamental freedoms. As Diana Ayton-Shenker has emphasised:[180]

> [C]laiming cultural relativism as an excuse to violate or deny human rights is an abuse of the right to culture. [...] Rather than limit human rights to suit a given culture, [...] traditional cultural values [should be invoked] to reinforce the application and relevance of universal human rights [...] This approach not only encourages greater tolerance, mutual respect and understanding, but also fosters more effective international cooperation for human rights.

In this regard, the African value of tolerance and respect for others should be invoked in response to those who argue that homosexuality is an affront to African culture. To this end, Article 28 of the African Charter calls on all individuals "to respect and consider his fellow beings without discrimination, and to maintain relations aimed at promoting, safeguarding and reinforcing mutual respect and tolerance".[181]

At the other end of the spectrum, individuals and groups who condemn the Anti-Homosexuality Bill can broadly be divided into three categories. First and foremost, upon its publication, the Bill immediately attracted the protest of several human rights and civil society organisations. In particular, a coalition of 17 local and international human rights organisations criticised the Bill in the strongest terms for fundamentally undermining the rights of one of Uganda's most marginalised groups.[182] Secondly, some religious organisations as well as prominent religious leaders have voiced their opposition to the Bill. Dr. Rowan Williams, the Archbishop of Canterbury, condemned the Bill for its "shocking severity" as well as its potential "to turn pastors into informers".[183] Rick Warren, the most powerful evangelical in the US, has condemned the Bill as "unjust, extreme and un-Christian toward homosexuals".[184] Even a group of Ugandan clergymen have opposed the death penalty provisions of the Bill.[185] The final group consists of various governments from within the international community. Thus far, the Swedish Minister of International Development has threatened to cut

177 *See also* S. Tamale, *supra* note 4, at p.5, noting that "Europe imported legalized homophobia to Africa".

178 *See,* for example, ICESCR, *supra* note 19, Article 15; and African Charter, *supra* note 9, Article 22.

179 *See* D. Ayton-Shenker, *The Challenge of Human Rights and Cultural Diversity*, United Nations Background Note, available at: http://www.un.org/rights/dpi1627e.htm.

180 D. Ayton-Shenker, *supra* note 64.

181 African Charter, *supra* note 9, Article 28.

182 Civil Society Coalition on Human Rights and Constitutional Law, *Uganda: Anti-gay bill threatens basic rights and freedom*, 16 October 2009, available at: http://www.amnesty.org.uk/news_details.asp?NewsID=18454.

183 G. Pitcher, *Dr. Rowan Williams: taking a break from Canterbury travails*, The Daily Telegraph, 12 December 2009, available at: http://www.telegraph.co.uk/news/newstopics/religion/6792671/Dr-Rowan-Williams-taking-a-break-from-Canterbury-travails.html.

184 *See* H. Chua-Eoan, *Rick Warren Denounces Uganda's Anti-Gay Bill*, Time Magazine, 10 December 2009, available at: http://www.time.com/time/world/article/0,8599,1946921,00.html.

185 *See* S. Naturinda, *Clergy – Jail Gays, Don't Hang Them,* The Daily Monitor, 29 October 2009, available at: http://allafrica.com/stories/200910290674.html.

aid to Uganda,[186] while the Bill has attracted diplomatic protests from Canadian Prime Minister Stephen Harper,[187] British Prime Minister Gordon Brown,[188] and US Secretary of State Hilary Clinton.[189]

It seems that the international pressure from foreign governments in particular has begun to have some impact in Uganda, with President Museveni recently distancing himself from the Bill and warning that "[i]t's a foreign policy issue, and we must handle it in a way in which it does not compromise our principles but also takes into account our foreign policy interests".[190] In addition, Ugandan Ethics Minister James Nsaba Buturo has conceded that the death penalty provisions may be dropped as a result of the international uproar.[191] Even David Bahati MP has conceded that he is open to amending the proposed law albeit "without putting the values of the country at risk".[192] While these statements are broadly to be welcomed, it remains the case that the Bill even in a watered-down form would still breach numerous rights and fundamental freedoms guaranteed by international human rights treaties and the Constitution of Uganda. As Frank Mugisha has noted:[193]

> He [Museveni] seems to be saying that the law should be watered down due to foreign interests. But he should rather be talking about the interests of minorities in Uganda. He should come out and say that the entire bill is just wasting time.

---

186 *See* R. Muhmuza, *Sweden to cut aid over anti-gay law,* The Daily Monitor, 3 December 2009, available at: http://www.monitor.co.ug/News/National/-/688334/816884/-/wfj05e/-/index.html.

187 *See* S. Rennie, *Harper tells Ugandan president Canada 'deplores' African country's law targeting gays*, The Canadian Press, 29 November 2009, available at: http://www.thefreepress.ca/article/GB/20091129/CP02/311299974/-1/fernie/harper-tells-ugandan-president-canada-deplores-african-countrys&template=cpArt.

188 *See* J. Chapman, *Gordon Brown caught up in gay rights storm as Uganda debates death penalty for homosexuals*, The Daily Mail, 30 November 2009, available at: http://www.dailymail.co.uk/news/worldnews/article-1232081/Gordon-Brown-caught-gay-rights-storm-Uganda-debates-death-penalty-homosexuals.html. *See also*, R. Muhumuza, *Bahati Faces UK Travel Ban*, The Monitor, 21 April 2010, reporting that British authorities have started a process that could see David Bahati banned from visiting the UK if the Anti-Homosexuality Bill were passed, available at: http://allafrica.com/stories/201004201124.html.

189 *See* H. Clinton, *Remarks on the Human Rights Agenda for the 21st Century*, Speech at Georgetown University, Washington DC, 14 December 2009, available at: http://www.state.gov/secretary/rm/2009a/12/133544.htm. *See also*, Naturinda, *supra* note 47, recalling that US President Obama had also referred to the Bill as "odious".

190 *See* X. Rice, *Uganda president hints at softer anti-gay bill*, The Guardian, 13 January 2010, available at: http://www.guardian.co.uk/world/2010/jan/13/uganda-anti-gay-bill-president.

See X. Rice, *Uganda rows back on draconian anti-gay law after western outrage*, The Guardian, 14 January 2010, available at: http://www.guardian.co.uk/world/2010/jan/14/uganda-backpedals-on-gay-law.

192 *See* J. Tugume, *Bahati says he's willing to amend gays Bill*, The Daily Monitor, 21 January 2010, available at http://www.monitor.co.ug/News/National/-/688334/846608/-/whdk2g/-/index.html.

193 *See* X. Rice, *supra* note 76.

5. THE OFFENCE OF AGGRAVATED HOMOSEXUALITY: A HUMAN RIGHTS ANALYSIS

Although Uganda remains a retentionist state,[194] in the past decade the death penalty has scarcely been used in practice. No civilians have been executed in Uganda since May 1999, when 28 death row inmates were hanged at Luzira Prison.[195] In terms of military personnel, two soldiers were executed by firing squad in 2002, and three soldiers were executed in March 2003.[196] The clear lack of action taken by the executive to implement death sentences has led the Supreme Court of Uganda, in the landmark January 2009 case of *Attorney General v. Susan Kigula & 417 others* ("*Kigula* Judgement"), to call for a fresh debate on the desirability of the death penalty in the Ugandan Constitution:[197]

> [W]e wish to urge that the Legislature should reopen debate on the desirability of the death penalty in our Constitution, particularly in light of findings that for many years no death sentences have been executed yet the individuals concerned continue to be incarcerated on death row without knowing whether they were pardoned, had their sentences remitted, or are to be executed. The failure, refusal or neglect by the Executive to decide on those death sentences would seem to indicate a desire to do away with the death penalty.

The encouraging words of the Supreme Court need to be placed in context. It is conceded that internationally the abolitionist movement can point to significant progress: the African Commission of Human and Peoples Rights (ACHPR) has issued a succession of resolutions calling on African states to observe a moratorium on the death penalty;[198] 50 participants representing different African Union member states and national human rights commissions appealed for a moratorium on the death penalty at a recent conference organised by ACHPR in September 2009;[199] and over one hundred countries voted in favour of resolutions on the "Moratorium on the use of the death penalty" at the UN General Assembly in December 2007 and 2008.[200] However, it must also be remembered that Uganda voted against both UN General Assembly resolutions in 2007 and 2008, and while no executions have been carried out in the past decade, Uganda's civilian and military courts have continued to impose the death sentence.[201] In addition, public opinion towards the death

194 Amnesty International Report 2009, *The State of the World's Human Rights* ("Amnesty Annual Report 2009"), at p.337.

195 International Federation of Human Rights (FIDH), *International Fact-Finding Mission – Uganda: Challenging the Death Penalty*, Report No. 425/2, October 2005 ("FIDH Report"), at p.16.

196 FIDH Report, *supra* note 80, at p.16.

197 *Attorney General v. Susan Kigula & 417 others*, Supreme Court of Uganda, Constitutional Appeal No. 03 of 2006, 21 January 2009 ("*Kigula* Judgement"), at p.63.

198 *See*, most recently, the final communiqué of the 44th session of the African Commission on Human and Peoples' Rights, held at Abuja from 10 to 24 November 2008. *See also* Amnesty International, *African Commission calls for a moratorium on the death penalty*, 5 December 2008, available at: http://www.unhcr.org/refworld/docid/493e3ae22c.html.

199 *See*, N. Bishumba, *AU Urges Members to Emulate Rwanda on Death Penalty*, The New Times, 28 September 2009, available at http://allafrica.com/stories/200909280004.html.

200 UN General Assembly, Third Committee, Resolution 62/149, 18 December 2007 (104 votes in favour, 54 against and 29 abstentions). Resolution 62/149 was reaffirmed in December 2008 with a slightly stronger majority (105 votes in favour, 48 against and 31 abstentions).

201 Amnesty Annual Report 2009, *supra* note 79, at p.337.

penalty remains largely in favour of its retention.[202] Most damaging of all, the Supreme Court in the *Kigula* Judgement, while finding that the mandatory imposition of the death penalty was a violation of the Constitution of Uganda,[203] upheld the constitutionality of the death penalty *per se* as well as hanging as a legitimate method of execution.[204]

Against this background, when the *Kigula* Judgement was first rendered by the Supreme Court, it was uncertain what kind of impact it would have on the future of the death penalty in Uganda: would the executive heed the calls of the Supreme Court to reopen the debate on the desirability of the death penalty or would the Supreme Court's finding that the death penalty *per se* does not violate the Constitution be used to justify the continued retention of the death penalty as a legitimate form of punishment in Uganda?

While the Anti-Homosexuality Bill does not provide a comprehensive answer to this question, it nonetheless represents the first indication since the *Kigula* Judgement as to whether the death penalty has a future role within the Ugandan criminal justice system.[205] As noted at the very beginning of this paper, the Bill introduces the new offence of aggravated homosexuality punishable by death.[206] It is useful at this point to quote the provision in full:

> '3. Aggravated Homosexuality
>
> (1) A person commits the offence of aggravated homosexuality where the –
>
> (a) Person against whom the offence is committed is below the age of 18 years;
> (b) Offender is a person living with HIV;
> (c)Offender is a parent or guardian of the person against whom the offence is committed;
> (d) Victim of the offence is a person with disability;
> (e) Offender is a serial offender; or
> (f) Offender applies, administers or causes to be used by any man or woman any drug, matter or thing with intent to stupefy or overpower him or her so as to there by enable any person to have unlawful carnal connection with any person of the same sex.

202 In 2001, President Museveni set up a Constitutional Review Commission (CRC) to conduct a review of the Constitution of Uganda. One of the themes of the review focused on public opinions towards the death penalty. It emerged that 42.5% of those consulted were in favour of abolition while 57.5% were against (*see* F. Gorchs-Chacou & C. Sculier, *The Death Penalty in the Great Lakes Region of Africa: Protagonists, Arguments and Strategies*, World Coalition Against the Death Penalty, May 2008, at p.12). It should also be noted that, in its submissions to the CRC, the Ugandan Human Rights Commission did not recommend the full abolition of the death penalty, but instead argued that the CRC should merely amend the Constitution to remove political offences from the list of crimes subject to the death penalty (*see* FIDH Report, *supra* note 80, at p.12).

203 *Kigula* Judgement, *supra* note 82, at p.45.

204 *Kigula* Judgement, *supra* note 82, at p.34.

205 *See* B. Sander, *Uganda: Anti-Homosexuality Bill – Time to Denounce Death Penalty*, The Monitor, available at http://deathpenaltynews.blogspot.com/2009/10/uganda-anti-homosexuality-bill-time-to.html, where I argue that "the tabling of the Bill will provide the necessary impetus for a constructive debate in the legislature on the desirability of the death penalty in Uganda".

206 Clause 3, Anti-Homosexuality Bill 2009.

(2) A person who commits the offence of aggravated homosexuality shall be liable on conviction to suffer death.

(3) Where a person is charged with the offence under this section, that person shall undergo a medical examination to ascertain his or her HIV status.'

By introducing this provision, the Anti-Homosexuality Bill indicates a continued willingness by at least some Ugandan members of Parliament to use the death penalty in draft legislation; it seems that, at least for those members of Parliament who support the Bill, the death penalty is still regarded as a legitimate form of punishment within Uganda. Such support still exists in Uganda despite the extremity of the death penalty as a form of punishment, a point forcefully emphasised by the Constitutional Court of South Africa:[207]

> Death is the most extreme form of punishment to which a convicted criminal can be subjected. Its execution is final and irrevocable. It puts an end not only to the right to life itself, but to all other personal rights which had vested in the deceased [...] It leaves nothing except the memory in others of what has been and the property that passes to the deceased's heirs.

Against this background, this final section of the paper sets out a detailed human rights analysis of the offence of aggravated homosexuality in an effort to illustrate the various ways in which the provision violates Uganda's obligations under public international law.

5.1 Extending the Application of the Death Penalty

First and foremost, the offence of aggravated homosexuality is problematic for the very fact that it extends the application of the death penalty beyond existing crimes.

Subjecting a new offence to the death penalty goes directly against the spirit of the UN General Assembly, which has stated that "the main objective to be pursued in the field of capital punishment is that of progressively restricting the number of offences for which the death penalty may be imposed".[208] In addition, the new offence shows particular disregard for resolutions 2004/67 and 2005/59, in which the UN Commission on Human Rights called upon all States that still retained the death penalty "to progressively restrict the number of offences for which it could be imposed and, at least, not to extend its application to crimes to which it did not at present apply".[209] In a similar vein, the Human Rights Committee has emphasised

207 *State v. T Makwanyane and M Mchunu*, Case No. CCT/3/94, 6 June 1995 ("Makwanyane Judgement"), at para. 26. *See also*, *Edwards and Others v. The Bahamas*, Inter-American Commission on Human Rights, Report No. 48/01, 4 April 2001, para. 132: "It is also generally recognized that the death penalty is a form of punishment that differs in substance as well as in degree in comparison to other forms of punishment. It is the absolute form of punishment that results in the forfeiture of the most valuable of rights, the right to life, and once implemented, is irrevocable and irreparable".

208 UN General Assembly Resolution 32/61, *Capital Punishment*, adopted on 8 December 1977, Resolutions and Decisions adopted by the General Assembly during its 32nd Session, at p.136, Clause 1.

209 The UN Commission on Human Rights adopted Resolution 2004/67 on the question of death penalty

that the "[e]xtension of the scope of application of the death penalty raises questions as to the compatibility with article 6 of the [ICCPR]".[210] In fact, the Human Rights Committee has previously criticised Lebanon for extending the death penalty to new crimes, even going so far as to confirm that this was "not compatible with Article 6 of the ICCPR".[211] Finally, the UN Special Rapporteur on extrajudicial, summary or arbitrary executions has stated his belief that "the reintroduction of the death penalty and the extension of its scope [...] contravene the spirit and purpose of article 6 of the ICCPR, as well as the international trend towards the progressive restriction of the number of offences for which the death penalty may be imposed".[212]

In this way, the offence of aggravated homosexuality breaches public international law by the mere fact that it introduces a new capital punishment offence, thereby expanding the scope of application of the death penalty in Uganda.

5.2 The Most Serious Crimes Threshold

Article 6 (1) of the ICCPR sets out a qualified right to life,[213] pursuant to which an individual may lawfully be deprived of his life, provided it is not carried out "arbitrarily" and provided the carefully crafted set of conditions in Article 6 (2), (4) and (5) are adhered to. One such condition is that the death penalty may be imposed "only for the most serious crimes".[214] Although the African Charter is silent on this issue, the condition has found the support of the African Commission on Human and Peoples' Rights, which has requested States to "limit the imposition of the death penalty only to the most serious crimes".[215] This limitation on the scope *ratione materiae* of the death penalty is firmly supported by the general principle of criminal law that penalties must be proportionate to the crime.[216] Against this background, Professor Schabas has submitted that this limitation "is an international norm applicable to states whether or not they have ratified one or other of the applicable treaties".[217]

---

on 21 April 2004, and resolution 2005/59 on 20 April 2005. It was the 8th time such a resolution was adopted by the Commission on Human Rights since 1997.

210 UN Human Rights Committee, *Concluding Observations on the Third Periodic Report of Peru*, UN Doc. CCPR/C/79/Add.67, at para. 15, referred to by W.A. Schabas, The Abolition of the Death Penalty in International Law, at p.104 (Cambridge University Press, 2002).

211 UN Human Rights Committee, *Concluding Observations, Lebanon*, UN Doc. CCPR/C/79/Add.78, at para. 20, referred to by W.A. Schabas, *supra* note 95, at p.104.

212 The Special Rapporteur on extrajudicial, summary or arbitrary executions, Report on Mission to the USA, UN Doc. E/CN.4/1998/68/Add.3, 22 January 1998, at para. 145.

213 ICCPR, *supra* note 8, Article 6 (1) ("Every human being has the inherent right to life. This right shall be protected by law. No one shall be arbitrarily deprived of his life"); W.A. Schabas, *International Law and the Death Penalty: reflecting or promoting change?*, in P. Hodgkinson and W.A. Schabas (eds), Capital Punishment: Strategies for Abolition, at p.41 (Cambridge University Press, 2004). *See also* the American Convention on Human Rights, (1978) 1144 UNTS 123, Article 4 (2) and the European Convention on Human Rights, (1955) 213 UNTS 221, Article 2. *See also* African Charter, *supra* note 9, Article 4: "Human beings are inviolable. Every human being shall be entitled to respect for his life and the integrity of his person. No one may be *arbitrarily* deprived of this right" (emphasis added). It is notable that, unlike other international human rights treaties, the African Charter is silent on the subject of the death penalty itself.

214 ICCPR, *supra* note 8, Article 6 (2).

215 African Commission on Human and Peoples' Rights, *Resolution Urging States to Envisage a Moratorium on the Death Penalty*, 13th Activity Report of the African Commission on Human and Peoples' Rights, OAU Doc. AHG/Dec/153(XXXVI), Annex IV.

216 W.A. Schabas, *supra* note 98, at p.45.

217 W.A. Schabas, *supra* note 98, at p.50.

The "most serious crimes" concept is imprecise. In this regard, Professors Hood and Hoyle have remarked that the concept "was, in reality, a 'marker' for the policy of moving towards abolition through restriction, nothing more specific than that".[218] As the international community has begun to witness a trend towards the abolition of the death penalty, the "most serious crimes" concept has been dynamically interpreted in an increasingly restrictive manner.[219] The Human Rights Committee has even demanded that the expression "be read restrictively" since the death penalty is "a quite exceptional measure".[220] In this light, the concept is now generally understood to refer to offences that are life-threatening or lead to the loss of life. In 1984, the Economic and Social Council of the UN adopted a resolution proclaiming that the scope of the concept "should not go beyond intentional crimes with lethal or other extremely grave consequences".[221] In a similar vein, the UN Secretary General has commented that "offences should be life-threatening, in the sense that this is a very likely consequence of the action",[222] while the Human Rights Committee has concluded that the imposition of the death penalty for "crimes that do not result in loss of life" is contrary to Article 6 of the ICCPR.[223] Finally, this position is also supported by the UN Special Rapporteur on extrajudicial, summary or arbitrary executions, who has stated that the death penalty should only be imposed "where it can be shown that there was an intention to kill which resulted in the loss of life".[224]

Whilst the above statements in themselves are sufficient evidence that the offence of aggravated homosexuality does not fall within the scope of the "most serious crimes" concept, it is also worth pointing out that various statements have been made specifically in relation to the criminalisation of homosexuality in this context. In this regard, the Human Rights Committee has stated that "committing a third homosexual act" cannot be characterised as the most serious crime and is therefore incompatible with Article 6 of the ICCPR.[225] In addition, the former UN Special Rapporteur on extrajudicial, summary or arbitrary executions has concluded that it is "unacceptable that in some States homosexual relationships are still punishable by death", arguing that the "most serious crimes" concept is "a stipulation which clearly excludes matters of sexual orientation".[226]

---

218 R. Hood and C. Hoyle, The Death Penalty: A Worldwide Perspective, at p.130 (Oxford University Press, 4th ed., 2008).

219 R. Hood and C. Hoyle, *supra* note 103, at p.131.

220 UN Human Rights Committee, *General Comment No. 6: The Right to Life (Art. 6)*, 16th Session, 30 April 1982 ("General Comment No. 6"), at para. 7.

221 Resolution 1984/50, *Safeguards Guaranteeing Protection of Those Facing the Death Penalty*, Economic and Social Council, approved on 25 May 1984, Article 1.

222 UN Secretary General, *Crime Prevention and Criminal Justice: Capital punishment and implementation of the safeguards guaranteeing protection of the rights of those facing the death penalty*, UN Doc. E/2000/3, 31 March 2000, at para. 79.

223 UN Human Rights Committee, *Concluding observations of the Human Rights Committee: Iran (Islamic Republic of)*, UN Doc. CCPR/C/79/Add.25, at para. 8.

224 Special Rapporteur on extrajudicial, summary or arbitrary executions, *Civil and Political Rights, Including the Questions of Disappearances and Summary Executions*, A/HRC/4/26, 29 January 2007, at para. 65.

225 UN Human Rights Committee, *Concluding observations of the Human Rights Committee: Sudan*, UN Doc. CCPR/C/79/Add.85, 19 November 1997, at para. 8.

226 Special Rapporteur on extrajudicial, summary or arbitrary executions, *Civil and Political Rights, Including the Questions of Disappearances and Summary Executions*, E/CN.4/2001/9, 11 January 2001, at para. 50.

The conclusion that the offence of aggravated homosexuality fails to meet the "most serious crimes" threshold demanded by public international law for the imposition of the death penalty is further supported by international criminal law. The jurisdiction of the International Criminal Court (ICC) is "limited to the most serious crimes of concern to the international community as a whole".[227] The Rome Statute specifically defines the crimes that meet this threshold as the following:[228] the crime of genocide; crimes against humanity; war crimes; and the crime of aggression. Crucially, the death penalty was "deliberately excluded" from the Rome Statute,[229] although Article 80 ensures that States can retain the death penalty as a punishment when implementing the Statute into domestic legislation.[230] Nonetheless, the exclusion of the death penalty as form of punishment that can be rendered by the ICC represents "an important benchmark in an unquestionable trend towards universal abolition of capital punishment".[231] Moreover, the exclusion of the death penalty from the Rome Statute also leads to an "ICC paradox":[232] if one accepts the premise that to ratify the Rome Statute is to accept its definition of "the most serious crimes", the paradox arises that while the ICC cannot impose the death penalty even for crimes within its jurisdiction, there remain individual States that retain the death penalty not only for these crimes but also for other far less serious offences. In this way, by creating a new offence of aggravated homosexuality, Uganda is equating consensual sexual relations between same-sex partners with genocide, crimes against humanity, war crimes and the crime of aggression. If passed, the Anti-Homosexuality Bill would lead to the incongruous position that a Ugandan who is convicted of the offence of aggravated homosexuality could be sentenced to death whereas a Ugandan who is convicted of the offence of genocide by the ICC in The Hague could receive a maximum sentence of life imprisonment.[233]

In light of the preceding discussion, it is clear that the offence of aggravated homosexuality fails to meet "the most serious crimes" threshold demanded by public international law for the imposition of the death penalty. Consequently, as presently drafted, the offence is in clear violation of Article 6 (2) of the ICCPR.

5.3 Other Breaches of the ICCPR

Beyond "the most serious crimes" threshold, Article 6 (2) of the ICCPR also requires that offences made subject to the death penalty must "not [be] contrary to the

227 Rome Statute of the International Criminal Court, adopted on 17 July 1998 ("Rome Statute"), Article 5.

228 *Report of the Special Rapporteur on torture and other cruel, inhuman or degrading treatment of punishment*, A/HRC/10/44, Human Rights Council 7th Session ("Report of the Special Rapporteur on Torture"), 14 January 2009, at para. 32.

229 Rome Statute, *supra* note 112, Article 5.

230 Rome Statute, *supra* note 112, Article 80: "Nothing in this Part affects the application by States of penalties prescribed by their national law, nor the law of States which do not provide for penalties prescribed in this Part".

231 W.A. Schabas, An Introduction to the International Criminal Court, at p.316 (Cambridge University Press, 3rd ed., 2007).

232 *See* K. Akers, *Retention and Ratification: The ICC Paradox*, Centre for Capital Punishment Studies Report 2007, at p.91*ff.*, available at: http://home.wmin.ac.uk/docs/CCPS/CCPSReport2007.pdf.

233 Rome Statute, *supra* note 112, Article 77 (1) (b).

provisions of the present Covenant".[234] In this regard, the offence of aggravated homosexuality is problematic in at least four respects.

First, as has been noted earlier in this paper,[235] the offence of homosexuality,[236] upon which the offence of aggravated homosexuality is based, violates the freedom from discrimination, the right to equal protection of the law, and the freedom from arbitrary arrest or detention guaranteed by the ICCPR.[237]

Second, the offence of aggravated homosexuality also violates the freedom from discrimination and the right to equal protection of the law by subjecting individuals living with HIV as well as those who have a disability to the more severe penalty of death.[238]

Third, the provision prohibiting same-sex relations with a person below the age of 18 years,[239] appears to apply even if the accused is also under the age of 18.[240] This is in clear violation of Article 6 (5) of the ICCPR which provides that "[s]entence of death shall not be imposed for crimes committed by persons below eighteen years of age".[241]

Finally, the offence of aggravated homosexuality provides that a person charged pursuant to this provision "shall undergo a medical examination to ascertain his or her HIV status".[242] Mandatory HIV tests represent a clear violation of an individual's freedom from arbitrary or unlawful interference with his privacy as well as their right to liberty and security of the person guaranteed by the ICCPR.[243]

5.4 The Mandatory Death Penalty

A final point to note is that the offence of aggravated homosexuality appears to impose a mandatory death penalty. In particular, the Bill provides that a person who commits the offence of aggravated homosexuality "*shall* be liable on conviction to suffer death".[244] Should this language be deemed to be mandatory in nature, it would contravene both public international law as well Ugandan constitutional law.

In terms of Ugandan constitutional law, the Supreme Court in the *Kigula* Judgement recently ruled that "all those laws on the statute book in Uganda which provide for a mandatory death sentence are inconsistent with the Constitution and therefore are void to the extent of that inconsistency".[245]

---

234 ICCPR, *supra* note 8, Article 6 (2).
235 *See supra* note 8 and accompanying text.
236 Clause 2, Anti-Homosexuality Bill 2009.
237 ICCPR, *supra* note 8, Articles 9 (freedom from arbitrary arrest or detention), and 26 (freedom from discrimination and the right to equal protection of the law).
238 ICCPR, *supra* note 8, Article 26.
239 Clause 3 (1) (a), Anti-Homosexuality Bill 2009.
240 Clause 3 (1) (a), Anti-Homosexuality Bill 2009.
241 ICCPR, *supra* note 8, Article 6 (5).
242 Concern that this may be the case was first indicated by Amnesty International: *see* Amnesty Homosexuality Report, *supra* note 18, at p.13.
243 ICCPR, *supra* note 8, Articles 9 (right to liberty and security of person) and 17 (right to privacy).
244 Clause 3, Anti-Homosexuality Bill 2009 (emphasis added).
245 *Kigula* Judgement, *supra* note 82, at p.45.

Under public international law, the mandatory death sentence has been held to violate Article 6 (1) and (2) of the ICCPR. In *Thompson v. St. Vincent and the Grenadines*, the Human Rights Committee considered that "a system of mandatory capital punishment" was an arbitrary deprivation of the right to life contrary to Article 6 (1) of the ICCPR since it would "deprive the author of the most fundamental of rights, the right to life, without considering whether this exceptional form of punishment is appropriate to the circumstances of his or her case".[246] In addition, in *Lubuto v. Zambia*, the Human Rights Committee held that the mandatory imposition of the death sentence violates Article 6 (2) of the ICCPR since such a system prevents a court from considering any mitigating circumstances, which is essential in making an accurate determination of whether the offence in question meets "the most serious crimes" threshold.[247] Finally, it has even been suggested by Professor Schabas that since Article 6 (4) of the ICCPR requires that all death sentences be subject to commutation or reprieve, "it appears that the spirit of the Covenant opposes mandatory death sentences".[248]

Such flagrant disregard for both public international law and the recent ruling of the Supreme Court of Uganda is deeply disturbing. Although the Anti-Homosexuality Bill is yet to be passed into law, the mere tabling of the Bill in its current form indicates a clear affirmation of the use of capital punishment and a deeply dismissive attitude to the rule of law in Uganda.

6. Conclusion

This paper has set out a focused discussion on the potential impact of the Anti-Homosexuality Bill. It has been demonstrated that, if passed, the Bill would undermine countless provisions of public international law as well as the Constitution of Uganda. Particularly alarming is the new capital punishment offence of aggravated homosexuality, which runs against the general international trend towards the abolition of the death penalty within the international community.

At present it is unclear whether the increasing scrutiny of the Anti-Homosexuality Bill by the international community will lead to the Bill's demise. Encouraging indications that the Bill may be dismissed can be taken from the recommendations recently released by a committee of Cabinet, set up specifically to advise the government on the Bill. The committee's report noted that the Bill had "technical defects in form and content" and concluded that only the provision regarding the promotion of homosexuality had any merit.[249]

Regardless of the Bill's survival, most distressing of all is the fact that anti-homosexual sentiment in Uganda appears to have blinded the local population to the

246 *Thompson v. St. Vincent and the Grenadines*, UN Human Rights Committee, Communication No. 806/1998, 5 December 2000, at para. 8.2.

247 *Lubuto v. Zambia*, UN Human Rights Committee, Communication No. 390/1990, 31 October 1995, at para. 7.2.

248 W.A. Schabas, *supra* note 95, at p.111.

249 *See* R. Muhumuza, *Cabinet Committee Rejects Bahati Bill*, The Monitor, 8 May 2010, available at: http://allafrica.com/stories/201005070948.html.

wider implications of such legislation, which, unbeknown to most, is of grave concern to everyone. As Dr. Tamale recently concluded:[250]

> The lesson [to be] drawn from [...] chapters in our recent history is that today it is homosexuals under attack; tomorrow it will be another exaggerated minority.

250 S. Tamale, *supra* note 4, at p.5.

[18]

Chivalry Is Not Dead:

*Murder, Gender, and the Death Penalty**

Steven F. Shatz† and Naomi R. Shatz††

ABSTRACT

Chivalry—that set of values and code of conduct for the medieval knightly class—has long influenced American law, from Supreme Court decisions to substantive criminal law doctrines and the administration of criminal justice. The chivalrous knight was enjoined to seek honor and defend it through violence and, in a society that enforced strict gender roles, to show gallantry toward "ladies" of the same class, except for the women of the knight's own household, over whom he exercised complete authority. This article explores, for the first time, whether these chivalric values might explain sentencing outcomes in capital cases. The data for the article comes from our original study of 1299 first degree murder cases in California, whose death penalty scheme accords prosecutors and juries virtually unlimited discretion in making the death-selection decision. We examined sentencing outcomes for three particular types of murder where a "chivalry effect" might be expected—gang murders, rape-murders, and domestic violence murders. In cases involving single victims, the results were striking. In gang murders, the death-sentence rate was less than one-tenth the overall death-sentence rate. By contrast, in rape-murder cases, the death-sentence rate was nine times the overall death-sentence rate. The death-sentence rate for single-victim domestic violence murders was roughly 25% lower than the overall death-sentence rate. We also examined, through this study and earlier California studies, more general data on gender disparities in death sentencing and found substantial gender-of-defendant and gender-of-victim disparities. Women guilty

---

† Phillip and Muriel Barnett Professor, University of San Francisco School of Law. A.B., 1966, University of California, Berkeley, J.D., 1969, Harvard Law School. Professor Shatz gratefully acknowledges the invaluable assistance of former U.S.F. students Tiffany Danao, Natalie Davis, Jaime Herren, Mary Johnson, and Jessica Simmons, who did the initial reading and coding of the data for the empirical study discussed in the article.

†† Clerk, Hon. Ralph D. Gants, Massachusetts Supreme Judicial Court. B.A., 2004, Barnard College, J.D., 2008, Yale Law School. The authors thank the participants at the U.S.F. faculty scholarship workshop for their comments and suggestions, which helped shape our thinking at an early stage of this project, and Susan Freiwald, Maya Manian, Nina Rivkind, and Julia Simon-Kerr for their thoughtful and careful reading of previous drafts of this article.

of capital murder were far less likely than men to be sentenced to death, and defendants who killed women were far more likely to be sentenced to death than defendants who killed men. We argue that all of these findings are consistent with chivalric norms, and we conclude that, in prosecutors' decisions to seek death and juries' decisions to impose it, chivalry appears to be alive and well.

INTRODUCTION 65
I. CHIVALRY IN THE LAW 70
  A. Chivalry and the Supreme Court 70
  B. Chivalry and Criminal Justice 74
    1. Self-defense 75
    2. Heat of Passion 76
    3. Rape 78
    4. Domestic Violence 79
  C. Chivalry and the Death Penalty 81
    1. Rape and the Death Penalty 81
    2. Gender and the Death Penalty 83
II. THE CALIFORNIA DEATH PENALTY SCHEME: VIRTUALLY UNFETTERED DISCRETION 87
  A. The California Death Penalty Scheme 88
  B. The Current Study 92
III. THE DEATH PENALTY AND PARTICULAR KINDS OF MURDERS 95
  A. Gang Murders 96
  B. Rape-Murders 99
  C. Domestic Violence Murders 103
IV. THE DEATH PENALTY AND GENDER 105
  A. Gender of the Defendant 105
  B. Gender of the Victim 107
CONCLUSION 110

INTRODUCTION

In his 1962 memoir, Clinton Duffy, the former warden of San Quentin State Prison,[1] tells a story about Eithel Spinelli, the first woman to be executed in California.[2] In 1941 when Spinelli was on California's death row, thirty male inmates at San Quentin prison sent a petition to Duffy:

> A lengthy document, it said, among other things: that Mrs. Spinelli's execution would be repulsive to the people of California; that no woman in her right mind could commit the crime charged to her; that the execution of a woman

1. San Quentin is the prison where executions in California are held. CAL. PENAL CODE § 3603 (West 2010).
2. CLINTON DUFFY, 88 MEN AND 2 WOMEN 134–41 (1962).

would hurt California in the eyes of the world; that both law and the will of the people were against the execution; that Mrs. Spinelli, as the mother of three children, should have special consideration; that California's proud record of never having executed a woman should not be spoiled.

The signers offered to draw straws to take her place in the gas chamber.[3] For Duffy, the petition by these hardened criminals, some of them slated for execution themselves, confirmed the chivalrous reaction evoked by the prospect of executing a woman.[4] Duffy himself "was sure that, for no other reason than her sex, her sentence would be commuted to life imprisonment."[5] The inmates' reaction cannot be explained on the basis that Spinelli was a particularly attractive or sympathetic person. According to Duffy, Spinelli was the head of a criminal gang and apparently had directed the killing of a gang associate to prevent him from "talking" about another gang murder.[6] She was the "coldest, hardest character, male or female" Duffy had ever known and was also utterly unattractive: "a hag, evil as a witch, horrible to look at."[7]

At the time of Spinelli's execution, chivalric values regularly found expression in the law as a whole, in the administration of criminal justice, and in the application of the death penalty.[8] In more recent years, chivalry in the law has come under attack. For some scholars, the story of the San Quentin inmates' gallantry—their reluctance to see a female murderer executed—is reflective of archaic paternalism[9] and of gender stereotyping of women as the weaker, more passive sex.[10] Do chivalric norms affect the administration of the present-day death penalty, as they apparently did in Spinelli's time? While scholars have written about the significant gender-of-defendant disparities in death sentencing,[11] this broader question has yet to be addressed. Using empirical data

---

3. *Id.* at 136.
4. *Id.* at 135–37; *see* Andrea Shapiro, *Unequal Before the Law: Men, Women and the Death Penalty*, 8 AM. U. J. GENDER SOC. POL'Y & L. 427, 457 (2000) (citing the Spinelli story as an example of chivalry); Elizabeth Rapaport, *Equality of the Damned: the Execution of Women on the Cusp of the 21st Century*, 26 OHIO N.U. L. REV. 581, 588–89 (2000) (same).
5. DUFFY, *supra* note 2, at 134.
6. *Id.*
7. *Id.* at 136. That Spinelli was executed despite the chivalric response may be explained by the fact that chivalry does not protect all women equally and that Spinelli's crime, her behavior, and even her appearance were altogether unfeminine. *See* Victor L. Streib, *Death Penalty for Female Offenders*, 58 U. CIN. L. REV. 845, 879 (1990) [hereinafter Streib, *Death Penalty (Article)*]; Joan W. Howarth, *Executing White Masculinities: Learning From Karla Faye Tucker*, 81 OR. L. REV. 183, 211 (2002) ("Most of the women charged with capital murder are not sufficiently feminine—because of poverty, mental illness, race, or the violent agency of the crime of which they are accused, to earn the full protection of womanhood through informal immunity from being charged as capital defendants.").
8. See *infra* Part I.
9. Shapiro, *supra* note 4, at 456–57.
10. Jenny E. Carroll, Note, *Images of Women and Capital Sentencing Among Female Offenders: Exploring the Outer Limits of the Eighth Amendment and Articulated Theories of Justice*, 75 TEX. L. REV. 1413, 1418 (1997).
11. *See infra* Part I.C.2.

drawn from a recent study of death sentencing in California, we explore whether chivalric norms might explain sentencing outcomes in death penalty cases—that is, whether there is a discernible "chivalry effect."[12]

Chivalry incorporated a broad set of cultural norms[13] when it emerged as a comprehensive code of conduct among knights in the High Middle Ages.[14] However, three central norms of medieval chivalry define the present inquiry: the elevation of honor above all virtues, the strict sex roles subordinating women to male protectors, and the class limits to chivalry.

Honor was the core value of chivalry and the most important of the three virtues of the chivalric knight.[15] For the chivalrous knight, honor had an intimate relationship with violence, and the essence of chivalry was its regulation of honor violence.[16] As Richard Kaeuper has emphasized, "The vast and complex literature of chivalry celebrates knightly violence even as it attempts to reform or deflect it into channels where it would produce less social damage."[17] Chivalry placed the highest value on winning honor with knightly prowess.[18] Most honorable was the display of prowess during war, but honor could also be won through the use of violence in tournaments or private disputes.[19] As Kaeuper explains,

> Only after reading scores of works of chivalric literature can we fully appreciate the utterly tireless, almost obsessional emphasis placed on personal prowess as the key chivalric trait. Not simply one quality among others in a list of virtues, prowess often stands as a one-word definition of chivalry in these texts.[20]

Consequently, violence was an accepted means for settling any dispute between knights, especially any perceived affront to honor. Violence might be

---

12. The California death penalty scheme provides an ideal vehicle to examine the role of chivalry in death sentencing because of the sweeping discretion afforded prosecutors and juries in the death selection process and because of the availability of substantial empirical evidence on the operation of the scheme. *See infra* Part II.
13. Although there is no doubt that chivalry as an ideal took hold at some point in the High Middle Ages, its temporal and geographical scope is unclear and the extent to which knights adhered to the code is unknown. JOHN FRASER, AMERICA AND THE PATTERNS OF CHIVALRY 38–39 (1982).
14. The term "chivalry" was used in other senses by medieval writers, *see* RICHARD KAEUPER, CHIVALRY AND VIOLENCE IN MEDIEVAL EUROPE 4 (1997), but our concern is with chivalry as a code of conduct.
15. F. J. C. Hearnshaw, *Chivalry and its Place in History*, *in* CHIVALRY: A SERIES OF STUDIES TO ILLUSTRATE ITS HISTORICAL SIGNIFICANCE AND CIVILIZING INFLUENCE 1, 27–33 (Edgar Prestage ed., 1928). The other two important virtues were gallantry (or courtesy)—the quality displayed by the San Quentin inmates—and Christian piety. *See generally id.* at 1–33.
16. KAEUPER, *supra* note 14, at 7–9.
17. *Id.* at 160.
18. *Id.* at 129–30.
19. *See generally id.* at 129–160.
20. *Id.* at 135 (citations omitted).

precipitated by even an apparently trivial affront, for example, an assertion of better lineage, a dispute over whose lady was fairer, a request for a knight's name, or even the question, "Why are you so sad?"[21] Violence was also honorable when used to win a lady from another knight or to protect ladies.[22]

Chivalry enforced strict gender roles because it was a code of conduct only for men; women could not earn honor through physical or martial prowess.[23] While knights were enjoined to be gallant toward ladies, chivalric literature was of two minds concerning women, sometimes idealizing them as inspiring knights to great achievement and sometimes denouncing them as a distraction and impediment to real male concerns,[24] but always judging them in terms of whether they brought honor to men. Insofar as chivalry addressed relations between men and women, "women seem to have been considered property in much chivalric literature, prizes to be won by knightly prowess or to be defended against the prowess of others."[25]

Because women could not achieve honor and would in fact be in danger in the often-violent world, their place was in the home.[26] However, notwithstanding the gallantry generally demanded of knights, chivalry had no solicitude for a knight's wife. The honorable knight, as ruler of his home, was permitted and even expected to physically punish his wife if she "misbehaved."[27] In the words of C. Quince Hopkins, "[T]he 'Age of Chivalry' was a hard time for victims of domestic violence, when physically 'chastising' one's wife was considered an honorable knight's duty."[28]

Medieval society was divided into rigid classes, and chivalry was a code of conduct only for the knightly class. According to F.J.C. Hearnshaw, this was one of the principal vices of chivalry: "[Chivalry] was an exclusive class-institution; it placed a gulf between the knightly order and the commonalty, and restricted its code of honour and courtesy peculiarly to members of its own caste; it generated a contempt for social inferiors and a disregard for their feelings. . . ."[29] As a consequence of adherence to a code of conduct that only governed relations within the knightly class and a "brutal indifference to human suffering,"[30] chivalric knights engaged in public and private warfare felt no inhibitions against attacking common people and laying waste to their property.[31]

21. *Id.* at 159.
22. *Id.* at 226–27.
23. *Id.* at 213.
24. *Id.* at 211–12.
25. *Id.* at 226.
26. RICHARD W. KAEUPER & ELSPETH KENNEDY, THE BOOK OF CHIVALRY OF GEOFFROI DE CHARNY: TEXT, CONTEXT AND TRANSLATION 191–93 (1996).
27. MARGI LAIRD MCCUE, DOMESTIC VIOLENCE: A REFERENCE HANDBOOK 26 (1995).
28. C. Quince Hopkins, *Rescripting Relationships: Towards a Nuanced Theory of Intimate Violence as Sex Discrimination*, 9 VA. J. SOC. POL'Y & L. 411, 421 (2001).
29. Hearnshaw, *supra* note 15, at 31.
30. *Id.* at 30 (quoting JOHN RICHARD GREEN, A SHORT HISTORY OF THE ENGLISH PEOPLE 182 (1874)).
31. *See* KAEUPER, *supra* note 14, at 176–85.

The interplay among these three norms is best illustrated by the chivalric knights' particular and peculiar view of the crime of rape. The rules of chivalry were quite clear that raping or otherwise harming a "lady" was unacceptable unless the knight had "won" her in combat with her male protector:

> The custom and policy at the time were as follows: any knight meeting a damsel who is alone should slit his own throat rather than fail to treat her honourably, if he cares about his reputation. For if he takes her by force, he will be shamed forever in all the courts of all lands. But if she is led by another, and if some knight desires her, is willing to take up his weapons and fight for her in battle, and conquers her, he can without shame or blame do with her as he will.[32]

Thus the harm caused by the rape of an unaccompanied lady was the dishonor brought on her male protector and the offending knight. Further, because chivalry imposed duties on the knight only in regard to ladies of his class, no dishonor attached to the rape of peasant women.[33] Nor would the chivalrous knight, who was entitled to employ physical violence against his wife, suffer dishonor if he used force to obtain sex from her.[34]

These three norms of medieval chivalry become our standards for evaluating whether there is a chivalry effect in the modern administration of the death penalty. In Part I, by way of background, we explore the role of chivalry in the law and the recent attacks on chivalry. In particular, we review the existing evidence that chivalry has played a role in decisions of the Supreme Court, in the general operation of the criminal justice system, and in the administration of the death penalty. In Part II, we describe the operation of California's death penalty scheme and the empirical research that is the subject of this article. This research examined cases where an adult defendant was found guilty of first degree murder and was statutorily death-eligible (such murders being referred to as "capital murders") to determine the existence of patterns in death sentencing. In Part III, we analyze disparities in the application of the death penalty in the case of three "gendered" forms of capital murder: gang murders, rape-murders, and domestic

---

32. *Id.* at 227 (citing a translation of Chrétien de Troyes's medieval poem *Lancelot, the Knight of the Cart*).

33. SUSAN BROWNMILLER, AGAINST OUR WILL: MEN, WOMEN AND RAPE 290 (1975) (citing the writings of Andrew the Chaplain).

34. *See generally* James A. Brundage, *Implied Consent to Intercourse*, *in* CONSENT AND COERCION TO SEX AND MARRIAGE IN ANCIENT AND MEDIEVAL SOCIETIES 245, 245–56 (Angeliki Laiou ed., 1993) (explaining the medieval concept of conjugal debt and its implications for the use of force to obtain sex within a marriage). In fact until very recently, in this country, a man using force against his wife to obtain sex was not guilty of rape. WAYNE R. LAFAVE, CRIMINAL LAW § 17.4(d) (5th ed. 2010). Although no state any longer retains an absolute version of the common law "marital immunity" rule, "[t]he law in more than half the states today makes it harder to convict men of sexual offenses committed against their wives." Michelle J. Anderson, *Marital Immunity, Intimate Relationships, and Improper Inferences: A New Law on Sexual Offenses by Intimates*, 54 HASTINGS L.J. 1465, 1468–73 (2003).

violence murders. In Part IV, we examine disparities in sentencing outcomes by gender of defendant and gender of victim. We conclude that chivalric norms may explain the disparities we identify and that when prosecutors and jurors are given unguided discretion to make life and death decisions, those enduring norms may play a significant role in determining who lives and who dies.

I. CHIVALRY IN THE LAW

Chivalry has exerted a powerful influence on American culture throughout the nation's history,[35] particularly in the South, where the pursuit and defense of honor has often justified violence[36] and where the modern death penalty has flourished.[37] As a persistent element of American culture, chivalry was, until recently, an accepted feature of the law and legal institutions. In recent years, feminist scholars and lawyers have challenged the role of chivalric norms in constitutional interpretation, in criminal justice, and in the use of the death penalty.

A. Chivalry and the Supreme Court

For most of the United States' history, the Supreme Court endorsed a chivalric view of women and women's place in society, emphasizing the distinct roles that women and men were meant to occupy, in cases such as *Bradwell v. State* (1872),[38] *Muller v. Oregon* (1908),[39] and *Hoyt v. Florida* (1961).[40] In *Bradwell*, the Court upheld Illinois's refusal to allow women to practice law, explaining:

> The civil law, as well as nature herself, has always recognized a wide difference in the respective spheres and destinies of man and woman. Man is, or should be, woman's protector and defender. . . . The paramount destiny and mission of woman are to fulfil [sic] the noble and benign offices of wife and mother.[41]

In *Muller*, the Court upheld a state law limiting the hours a woman could

35. *See* FRASER, *supra* note 13; *see also* Andrew Taslitz, *Willfully Blinded: On Date Rape and Self-Deception*, 28 HARV. J.L. & GENDER 381, 407 (2005) ("[T]hough the term is rarely used, there is ample empirical evidence of a powerful 'chivalry' norm continuing in modern American culture.").
36. *See* Donald Dripps, *The Fourteenth Amendment, the Bill of Rights, and the (First) Criminal Procedure Revolution*, 18 J. CONTEMP. LEGAL ISSUES 469, 498–99 (2009). The Ku Klux Klan and related racist and xenophobic organizations justified their use of violence in chivalric terms. *See generally* NANCY MACLEAN, BEHIND THE MASK OF CHIVALRY (1994).
37. The eleven states of the former Confederacy have conducted 73% of the post-*Furman* executions. *See* DEATH PENALTY INFO. CTR., FACTS ABOUT THE DEATH PENALTY (2010) *available at* http://www.deathpenaltyinfo.org/FactSheet.pdf.
38. 83 U.S. 130 (1872).
39. 208 U.S. 412 (1908).
40. 368 U.S. 57 (1961).
41. 83 U.S. at 141.

work, citing women's "physical structure and performance of maternal functions" as justifying protective legislation.[42] In *Hoyt*, the Court upheld a state law excusing women from jury service because, as the "center of home and family life," women had "special responsibilities" justifying relief from civic duties.[43] In these cases and others, the Court both expressed and relied on the chivalric view that a woman's place was in the home, while a man's role was to engage in civic life and to protect women.

In the 1970s, in response to critiques by second-wave feminists, the Court's views changed. In a string of cases addressing women's participation in the public sphere, the Court held that discrimination—even "positive" discrimination—with regard to women was invidious and denied them an equal role in society. The Supreme Court first articulated this principle in *Reed v. Reed*,[44] holding that a law that gave preference to men in the administration of estates violated the Equal Protection Clause.[45] The Court found that while there was a legitimate goal of reducing the workload of the probate courts, choosing administrators solely on the basis of their sex was not a rational way to accomplish that goal.[46] Two years later, the Court emphasized that even laws intended to benefit women are unconstitutional if they differentiate on the basis of sex. In *Frontiero v. Richardson*, Justice Brennan, writing for the Court, explicitly rejected the reasoning of *Bradwell*, writing, "There can be no doubt that our Nation has had a long and unfortunate history of sex discrimination. Traditionally, such discrimination was rationalized by an attitude of 'romantic paternalism' which, in practical effect, put women, not on a pedestal, but in a cage."[47] The Court reiterated this understanding in *Mississippi University for Women v. Hogan*, holding that "if the statutory objective is to exclude or 'protect' members of one gender because they are presumed to suffer from an inherent handicap or to be innately inferior, the objective itself is illegitimate."[48]

J.E.B. v. Alabama ex rel. T.B.[49] may be the high water mark of the Supreme Court's refusal to allow government actions to be based on gender stereotypes. *J.E.B.* was a paternity action prosecuted by the state of Alabama on behalf of the mother against J.E.B., the putative father.[50] During jury selection, the state, not irrationally, used its peremptory strikes to remove all the male jurors, assuming that they would identify with the putative father.[51] Conversely, J.E.B. used his strikes to remove female jurors.[52] Because the jury *venire* was

42. 208 U.S. at 421.
43. 368 U.S. at 62.
44. 404 U.S. 71 (1971).
45. *Id.* at 76.
46. *Id.*
47. Frontiero v. Richardson, 411 U.S. 677, 684 (1973).
48. 458 U.S. 718, 725 (1982).
49. 511 U.S. 127 (1994).
50. *Id.* at 129.
51. *Id.*
52. *Id.*

two-thirds women, the state succeeded in empanelling an all-female jury that found against J.E.B.[53] The Court found the state's actions unconstitutional.[54] The Court pointed out the history of excluding women from juries and noted that such exclusion was based on stereotypes of women as too fragile for the duties of civic life.[55] The Court forcefully rejected reliance even on stereotypes that might be based on a "shred of truth."[56] The Court held that distinguishing between men and women based on sex-based stereotypes violates the Constitution, stating: "Today we reaffirm what, by now, should be axiomatic: Intentional discrimination on the basis of gender by state actors violates the Equal Protection Clause, particularly where, as here, the discrimination serves to ratify and perpetuate invidious, archaic, and overbroad stereotypes about the relative abilities of men and women."[57] Thus, even though the reliance on gender stereotypes in this case worked to the mother's advantage, the Court understood that such reliance would, in the end, disadvantage women.[58]

Despite this apparent progress, chivalry continues to play a role in cases involving access to and control over women's bodies. For example, in *Michael M. v. Superior Court*, the Court upheld California's gender-specific statutory rape law (which criminalized sex with underage girls, but not sex with underage boys) by finding that it served the government interest of preventing teenage pregnancy because "males alone can 'physiologically cause the result which the law properly seeks to avoid.'"[59] In upholding the gendered law, the Court reinforced stereotypes about women, men, and sex: that, when it comes to sex, the male is the aggressor and the female the passive victim, and, consequently, that females need the protection of the state. Feminist critics of California's law

---

53. *Id.*
54. *Id.*
55. *Id.* at 131–32.
56. *Id.* at 140.
57. *Id.* at 130–31.
58. The Court's progress toward eliminating chivalry in its legal reasoning in cases involving women's entrance into, and acceptance in, various aspects of the public sphere has not been a smooth road, nor one tread by all members of the Court. For example, in *United States v. Virginia*, 518 U.S. 515 (1996), although the majority held that the Virginia Military Institute's (VMI) policy of excluding women from admission violated the constitutional guarantee of equal protection, Justice Scalia's dissent was, in part, a eulogy for the vanishing role of chivalry in our culture. In arguing that VMI should have been allowed to exclude women from admission, Scalia extolled the value of the "manly 'honor'" for which he believed VMI stood. *Id.* at 601 (Scalia, J., dissenting). He quoted from VMI's "Code of a Gentleman," the chivalric rules by which the students at VMI were to conduct their lives:

    > Without a strict observance of the fundamental Code of Honor, no man, no matter how "polished," can be considered a gentleman. The honor of a gentleman demands the inviolability of his word, and the incorruptibility of his principles. He is the descendant of the knight, the crusader; he is the defender of the defense-less and the champion of justice . . . or he is not a Gentleman.

    Id. at 602. After reciting the Code of a Gentleman, Justice Scalia lamented, "I do not think any of us, women included, will be better off for its destruction." *Id.* at 603.
59. 450 U.S. 464, 457 (1981) (quoting Michael M. v. Superior Court, 601 P.2d 572, 575 (Cal. 1979)). This statement is baffling; it is axiomatic that males *alone* cannot cause pregnancy.

and the Court's holding have argued that "[t]he state restricts the young woman's sexual behavior for reasons related to sexist notions of what makes females valuable. The state does not merely restrict the young woman's freedom; it also treats her sexuality as a thing that has a value of its own and must be guarded."[60]

Michael M. can be viewed as just one link in a chain of cases in which the Court has reinforced chivalric sex stereotypes by failing to acknowledge how the state's regulation of matters involving women's physical bodies reifies gender stereotypes. The chain runs from *Roe v. Wade*[61] (which treated abortion as a "purely physiological phenomenon" rather than examining the potential sex discrimination inherent in abortion regulation[62]), through *Geduldig v. Aiello*[63] and *General Electric Co. v. Gilbert*[64] (which held that pregnancy discrimination is not sex discrimination), to the Court's recent and troubling decision in *Gonzales v. Carhart*[65] (which upheld federal regulation of late-term abortions as serving the government's interest in protecting women).[66]

In *Carhart*, as justification for banning an abortion procedure thought by many physicians to be safer for their patients than alternative procedures, the government argued that abortion causes serious mental health problems for women and thus is harmful to women who choose it.[67] Thus, the Partial Birth Abortion Ban Act was to some extent positioned as a public health measure to protect women from psychological harm.[68] Justice Kennedy, writing for the Court, endorsed this view, relying on affidavits from women "who claimed to have been coerced into and harmed by abortion."[69] Justice Kennedy echoed the theme used by the proponents of the Act, questioning a woman's capacity to make rational decisions with the observation that "it seems unexceptionable to conclude some women come to regret their choice to abort the infant life they once created and sustained."[70] In addition to endorsing the view that women

---

60. Frances Olsen, *Statutory Rape: A Feminist Critique of Rights Analysis*, 63 TEX. L. REV. 387, 406 (1984).
61. 410 U.S. 113 (1973).
62. Cary Franklin, *The Anti-Stereotyping Principle in Constitutional Sex Discrimination Law*, 85 N.Y.U. L. REV. 83, 128 (2010).
63. 417 U.S. 484 (1974).
64. 429 U.S. 125 (1976).
65. 550 U.S. 124 (2007).
66. According to Reva Siegel, the Court's apparent reliance on gender stereotypes in this area occurs because "[t]he Court typically reasons about reproductive regulation in physiological paradigms, as a form of state action that concerns physical facts of sex rather than social questions of gender." Reva Siegel, *Reasoning from the Body: A Historical Perspective on Abortion Regulation and Questions of Equal Protection*, 44 STAN. L. REV. 261, 264–65 (1992); *see also* Franklin, *supra* note 62, at 128.
67. Reva B. Siegel, *The Right's Reasons: Constitutional Conflict and the Spread of Women-Protective Antiabortion Argument*, 57 DUKE L. J. 1641, 1642 (2008) [hereinafter *The Right's Reasons*].
68. Maya Manian, *The Irrational Woman: Informed Consent and Abortion Decision-Making*, 16 DUKE J. GENDER L. & POL'Y 223, 224 (2009).
69. Siegel, *The Right's Reasons*, *supra* note 67, at 1642.
70. 550 U.S. at 159.

cannot make rational health care decisions for themselves, the Court also implied that women's true or most important identity role was that of a mother, with Justice Kennedy explaining that "[r]espect for human life finds an ultimate expression in the bond of love the mother has for her child."[71]

Thus, the *Carhart* majority relied upon two chivalric themes—that women lack the capacity to make decisions and therefore need the protection of men (in the guise of the state) and that a woman's true calling is motherhood—resurrecting a reliance on chivalry that the Court had seemed to reject in other contexts. As Justice Ginsburg charged in dissent:

> "This way of thinking reflects notions about women's place in the family and under the Constitution—ideas that have long since been discredited . . . . This Court has repeatedly confirmed that '[t]he destiny of the woman must be shaped . . . on her own conception of her spiritual imperatives and her place in society . . . .'"[72]

B. Chivalry and Criminal Justice

In the modern state, the criminal law replaced the chivalric code as the regulator of violent behavior. Yet, for a time in this country, honor-based killings were excused in law or in fact. For example, dueling was illegal at the common law, but it was an acceptable custom in the early nineteenth century and persisted up to the Civil War, especially in the South.[73] Well into the twentieth century, a number of states treated a different kind of "honor" killing as a justifiable homicide—a husband's killing of a man caught in the act of adultery with his wife.[74] All such laws have since been repealed.[75] Nonetheless, in its regulation of violent crime, the criminal law has continued to recognize and apply chivalric norms, in particular in regard to defenses to homicide—self-defense and heat of

71. *Id.* Reinforcing the idea that a woman's one true calling is motherhood, Justice Kennedy ignored the fact that the women he was referring to were precisely women who did not want to become mothers and who did not consider the fetus they carried to be a child. *See* Manian, *supra* note 68, at 225 ("*Carhart*'s portrayal of women evokes a century-old societal view of femininity . . . [and] reflects a gender-stereotyped view of women's nature.").

72. 550 U.S. at 185 (quoting in part Planned Parenthood of Se. Pa. v. Casey, 505 U.S. 833, 852 (1992)). At least one author, however, has argued that the majority's woman-protective argument is in fact merely an extension of feminist arguments, raised in the context of abortion, rape, and domestic violence, regarding women's psychological trauma. Jeannie Suk points out that *Roe* also relied on the notion of psychological harm to women—in that case from carrying to term an unwanted pregnancy—as a justification for making abortion legal. Jeannie Suk, *The Trajectory of Trauma: Bodies and Minds of Abortion Discourse*, 110 COLUM. L. REV. 1193 (2010).

73. C.A. Harwell Wells, Note, *The End of the Affair? Anti-Dueling Laws and Social Norms in Antebellum America*, 54 VAND. L. REV. 1805, 1818 (2001).

74. Lois J. Frankel, *Sex Discrimination in the Criminal Law: The Effects of the Equal Rights Amendment*, 11 AM. CRIM. L. REV. 469, 500–01 & n.244 (1973).

75. The four states that had such laws into the 1970s were Georgia, New Mexico, Texas, and Utah. Jeremy D. Weinstein, *Adultery, Law, and the State: A History*, 38 HASTINGS L.J. 195, 230–36 (1986).

passion—and in regard to crimes committed primarily against women: rape and domestic abuse.[76]

1. Self-defense

The law of self-defense (and defense of another) makes justifiable a homicide where the defendant kills under the reasonable belief that the defendant (or another) will suffer an imminent deadly attack by an aggressor.[77] Although the defense might be explained on utilitarian grounds—if a life is to be lost, better that it be the life of the aggressor than the life of the innocent defendant—at least two aspects of the defense echo chivalric values.

First, the general rule, and the rule in California, is that the defense applies even when the defendant could safely have retreated from the encounter and thereby avoided the loss of life.[78] The "no-retreat" rule serves no utilitarian purpose, so it can only be justified on the basis of the so-called "true man" doctrine.[79] That doctrine holds that the true man cannot be expected to suffer the loss of dignity and honor that would result from fleeing his assailant because the virtue of the true man is worth more than the life of an aggressor.[80] This doctrine is a product of chivalric values:

> The judicial proponents of the "true man" doctrine—which constituted a sharp break with English common law—were located in the South and West. By virtue of the slave culture in the former and the frontier culture in the latter, both of these regions had inherited rich systems of honor that put a premium on physical displays of courage and on violent reactions to slights.[81]

To critics of this "true man" doctrine, it was those very chivalric values that did not belong in the criminal law:

> The feeling at the bottom of the [rule] is one beyond all law; it is the feeling which is responsible for the duel, for war, for lynching; the feeling which leads a jury to acquit the slayer of his wife's paramour; the feeling which would compel a true man to kill the ravisher of his daughter.[82]

Second, although the defense is in theory gender-neutral, feminists have argued that, as applied, it is a man's defense and of little use to women. This is

76. The following discussion focuses on California law because the study referred to in Parts II and III was done in California, but California law is not unrepresentative of the law generally.
77. LAFAVE, *supra* note 34, at § 10.4; *see, e.g.*, People v. Randle, 111 P.3d 987 (Cal. 2005).
78. LAFAVE, *supra* note 34, at § 10.4(f); *see, e.g.*, People v. Holt, 153 P.2d 21, 24 (Cal. 1944).
79. Dan M. Kahan, *The Secret Ambition of Deterrence*, 113 HARV. L. REV. 413, 429–35 (1999).
80. *Id.* at 431.
81. *Id.* at 432–33.
82. Joseph H. Beale, Jr., *Retreat from a Murderous Assault*, 16 HARV. L. REV. 567, 577, 581 (1903).

most clear with regard to the "imminence" element of the defense. Men, because of their generally greater size and strength or because of their acculturation and experience with violence, or both,[83] are far more likely than women to be able to respond successfully to the threat of immediate deadly force.[84] Thus, when women kill in response to a threatened or actual attack (or a series of threatened or actual attacks)—most often in the context of domestic abuse—the killing may occur during a period of relative calm when the woman can gain the upper hand, for example, when the attacker is asleep.[85] Men, on the other hand, often can—and are often raised to believe they should—respond to threats immediately with physical violence.[86]

2. Heat of Passion

The heat of passion defense mitigates murder to voluntary manslaughter when the defendant has killed in the heat of passion upon adequate provocation.[87] At the common law, there were a limited number of categories of adequate provocation: adultery by a spouse, mutual combat, assault to oneself, assault to a family member, or unlawful arrest.[88] Under modern codes, and in California, provocation is no longer limited to specific categories but extends to any conduct that would provoke the reasonable person.[89] Even more clearly than self-defense, the heat of passion defense is based on chivalric norms.

From its origins in English common law, the theory of the heat of passion defense was that the defendant's intentional killing was mitigated by the victim's affront to the defendant's honor. The case of *Regina v. Mawgridge*[90] is usually cited as the leading common law case on the defense. There, Chief Justice Holt explained why each of the categories of provocation recognized by the law constituted an affront to the defendant's honor that partially justified the killing,

83. *See* State v. Wanrow, 559 P.2d 548, 558 (Wash. 1977) ("In our society women suffer from a conspicuous lack of access to training in and the means of developing those skills necessary to effectively repel a male assailant without resorting to the use of deadly weapons.").

84. Relying on research in the natural and social sciences disclosing gender-based differences in the processing of emotions by the brain—in particular, that in a stressful situation, men reach emotional clarity quickly, while women wrestle with emotional complexity—Katharine K. Baker has argued that self-defense and heat of passion are gendered defenses. Katharine K. Baker, *Gender and Emotion in Criminal Law*, 28 HARV. J.L. & GENDER 447, 460 (2005) ("As long as men react immediately, thoughtlessly, and without emotional struggle, their violent acts are minimized or excused.").

85. For that reason, some activists and scholars have sought to expand the doctrine of self-defense to cover such situations by seeking to admit evidence regarding "battered women's syndrome." *See infra* notes 119–121 and accompanying text.

86. *See* Joshua Dressler, *When "Heterosexual" Men Kill "Homosexual" Men: Reflections On Provocation Law, Sexual Advances, And The "Reasonable Man" Standard*, 85 J. CRIM. L. & CRIMINOLOGY 726, 735–36 (1995) (comparing the responses of men and women to provocation).

87. LAFAVE, *supra* note 34, at § 15.2.

88. *Id.* at § 15.2(b).

89. *See id.*

90. (1707) 84 Eng. Rep. 1107 (K.B.).

and he acknowledged that the law "may seem hard" for making such killings a crime at all.[91] In sum, the provocation-based defenses "partially excused men for behaving in accord with outdated notions of masculinity and honor."[92] A defense based on affronts to honor is a gendered defense because "honor violence" historically has been sanctioned for men, not women.[93] Consequently, men invoke the heat of passion defense far more often than do women.[94]

More recently, many American courts have tended to recast the defense as an excuse defense, along the lines of the Model Penal Code's reduction to manslaughter of killings resulting from "the influence of extreme mental or emotional disturbance for which there is a reasonable explanation or excuse."[95] The result in these courts has been to focus less on the nature of the provoking incident and whether the incident would affront the honor of a reasonable man and to focus more on the intensity of the defendant's emotion and its psychological effects.[96] Consistent with that approach, the California Supreme Court has expanded the defense by holding that the provocation may be sufficient to invoke the defense even if not falling within the four categories of provocation recognized at the common law, so long as the defendant's reason was "disturbed or obscured by some passion . . . to such an extent as would render ordinary men of average disposition liable to act rashly or without due deliberation and reflection . . . ."[97]

Even this expanded defense, divorced of its roots in "honor violence," remains deeply gendered. Men are the predominant beneficiaries of the doctrine because here the criminal law follows "boys' rules."[98] As Joshua Dressler explains,

> What is important here . . . is not simply that the average male is more susceptible to violent loss of self-control than is the average woman. It is also necessary to consider how men and women respond to affronts, *i.e.*, to provocations. Women usually submit stoically to their victimization or deny their status as victims by blaming themselves ("I deserve this treatment"); men are more likely to characterize themselves as victims of injustice, or to think

---

91. *Id.* at 1115.
92. Henry F. Fradella, *From the Legal Literature*, 42 CRIM. L. BULL. 775, 775 (2006).
93. Caroline Forell, *Gender Equality, Social Values and Provocation Law in the United States, Canada and Australia*, 14 AMER. U. J. GENDER SOC. POL'Y & L. 27, 31 (2006).
94. "The origins of the provocation defense are deeply gendered; it was created for and has always been used far more often by men than women." *Id.* at 31; *see also*, SAMUEL PILLSBURY, JUDGING EVIL: RETHINKING THE LAW OF MURDER AND MANSLAUGHTER 147–55 (1998) (arguing that provocation-based defenses permit outdated, sexist views about gender roles to control the legal system in a manner that systematically discriminates against women).
95. MODEL PENAL CODE § 210.3 (1962).
96. PILLSBURY, *supra* note 94, at 131.
97. *People v. Berry*, 556 P.2d 777, 780 (Cal. 1976) (quoting *People v. Valentine*, 169 P.2d 1, 12 (Cal. 1946)).
98. Dressler, *supra* note 86 at 735 (citing SUSAN ESTRICH, REAL RAPE 60 (1987)).

that their self-worth has been attacked, and to act offensively as a result. One glance at the common law categories of "adequate provocation" shows that the defense has served a male interest, by mitigating the predominantly male reaction of retaliating for affronts and other "injustices."[99]

3. Rape

Rape has always been acknowledged as among the worst of the violent crimes.[100] However, consistent with chivalric norms, only certain cases of rape have historically been punished by our legal system. The law of rape has always been characterized on the one hand by severe condemnation of the crime[101] and the imposition of extreme penalties[102] and on the other hand by the exclusion of spouses from those protected by the rape laws,[103] a tolerance of "acquaintance" rape,[104] and trial rules (e.g., requiring corroboration of the victim's testimony, permitting evidence of the woman's prior sexual conduct or reputation for chastity, and authorizing cautionary jury instructions which impugn the victim's credibility)[105] that make even the conviction of "stranger" rapists difficult.

This treatment of rape reflects chivalric attitudes regarding sexual violence. As noted above, the rules of chivalry were very clear that raping or otherwise harming a "lady" was unacceptable. Yet no such disapproval applied to the rape of peasant women, or to a knight's sexual abuse of his wife.[106] In the modern history of rape law, the race, social class, and sexual behavior of the victim have all influenced the degree of outrage over her rape.[107] Particularly in the South, fear of black men raping white women was a driving force behind capital rape laws.[108] Rape of a black woman, on the other hand, was not a crime for much of our nation's history.[109] Thus, although rape has long been seen as a particularly awful crime, it is only a certain kind of rape—namely the rape of a chaste, white woman by a stranger—that has been punished harshly by the criminal law.[110]

---

99. *Id.* at 736 (citations omitted).

100. *See* Coker v. Georgia, 433 U.S. 584, 597 (1977) ("Short of homicide, [rape] is the 'ultimate violation of self.'").

101. *See id.* ("[Rape] is highly reprehensible, both in a moral sense and in its almost total contempt for the personal integrity and autonomy of the female victim . . . .").

102. *See infra* notes 128–144 (discussing the application of the death penalty in rape cases).

103. BROWNMILLER, *supra* note 33, at 380–82.

104. *Id.* at 351–52.

105. *Id.* at 368–74.

106. *Id.* at 290, 380–82 (citing a treatise by twelfth-century writer Andrew the Chaplain and later discussing the marital rape exemption).

107. *See generally* Dorothy E. Roberts, *Rape, Violence, and Women's Autonomy*, 69 Chi.-Kent L. Rev. 359 (1993).

108. Corey Rayburn, *Better Dead than Raped?: The Patriarchal Rhetoric Driving Capital Rape Statutes*, 78 ST. JOHN'S L. REV. 1119, 1128 n.58. (2004).

109. Jeffrey J. Pokorak, *Rape as a Badge of Slavery: The Legal History of, and Remedies for, Prosecutorial Race-of-Victim Charging Disparities*, 7 NEV. L.J. 1, 6 (2006).

110. *See* Phyllis L. Crocker, *Crossing the Line: Rape-Murder and the Death Penalty*, 26 OHIO N.U. L. REV. 689, 706–08 (2000) (explaining the stereotype of a white woman forcibly raped by a stranger and the reluctance of a jury to convict beyond those circumstances) [hereinafter

In recent years, the feminist movement has succeeded in bringing many changes to rape laws. In California, for example, the legislature enacted a spousal rape statute[111] and rape shield laws protecting the victim from questioning about her prior sexual conduct,[112] and the California Supreme Court held that the prosecution need not prove the victim's physical resistance in order to sustain a rape charge.[113] Nevertheless, in practice, prosecutors in rape cases still face evidentiary hurdles not faced in non-gendered crimes. As one scholar explains, "The problem . . . is that when a man rapes a woman in circumstances that do not fit the stereotype of a rape, which is most of the time, the woman's credibility will be suspect."[114]

4. Domestic Violence

In the 1970s and 1980s, at the height of the women's rights movement, feminists, along with their efforts to reform rape laws, raised the issue of domestic violence and criticized the state, the police, and the courts for their gender bias and reluctance to intervene in "domestic matters."[115] Again, advocates were successful in changing laws and practices. California, for example, enacted legislation that increased the penalties for domestic violence,[116] required a certain police response in domestic violence cases,[117] and mandated domestic violence training for court employees.[118] The legislature also sought to protect women victims of domestic violence by making expert testimony regarding "battered women's syndrome" admissible in a criminal case,[119] and the California Supreme Court has recognized "battered women's

Crocker, *Crossing the Line*].

111. CAL. PENAL CODE § 262 (West 2010).

112. CAL. EVID. CODE §§ 782, 1103(c) (West 2010).

113. People v. Barnes, 721 P.2d 110 (Cal. 1986).

114. Crocker, *Crossing the Line*, *supra* note 110, at 708.

115. Jeannie Suk, *Criminal Law Comes Home*, 116 YALE L.J. 2, 11–12 (2006); Deborah M. Weissman, *The Personal is Political*, 2007 B.Y.U. L. REV. 387, 396 (2007).

116. *See, e.g.*, CAL. PENAL CODE §§ 273.5, 243(e)(1) (West 2010).

117. *See id.* § 836(c).

118. *See* CAL. GOV. CODE § 68555 (West 2010).

119. The 1991 legislation added Evidence Code § 1107(a) which provided, *inter alia*, that "expert testimony is admissible . . . regarding battered women's syndrome, including the physical, emotional, or mental effects upon the beliefs, perceptions, or behavior of victims of domestic violence." 1991 CAL. STAT. 3612–13. The section was subsequently amended to be gender-neutral and to eliminate reference to a "syndrome," and it now provides that expert testimony is admissible regarding "intimate partner battering and its effects." CAL. EVID. CODE § 1107(a) (West 2010). Since expert testimony on battered women's syndrome was originally admitted on the basis of research purporting to show that *women* victims of battering relationships exhibited a common pattern of responses to that experience (*see generally* LENORE WALKER, BATTERED WOMAN (1979) and THE BATTERED WOMAN SYNDROME (1984)), the amendment has the effect of undercutting the justification for such expert testimony. Scholars challenging the validity of the research on battered women's syndrome have called into question whether expert testimony should ever have been allowed on the subject. *See, e.g.*, David L. Faigman & Amy J. Wright, *The Battered Woman Syndrome in the Age of Science*, 39 ARIZ. L. REV. 67 (1997).

syndrome" as a mitigating or even excusing factor for a domestic violence survivor's killing of her abuser.[120] Throughout the country, states have adopted civil and criminal protection orders that could exclude the abuser from the family home.[121]

Nevertheless, the responses to domestic violence have not been wholly emancipatory for women. For example, police mandatory arrest policies, prosecutorial "no-drop" policies,[122] and court- or probation department-imposed criminal protection orders[123]—adopted to prevent coercion of the domestic violence victim by the abuser—have created obstacles to victims of domestic violence being treated as fully autonomous under the law. Such policies deny agency to victims of domestic violence under the chivalric and paternalistic assumption that women cannot make the "right" decisions for themselves about whether they need state intervention in their violent relationships.[124] Rather than recognizing the many reasons that survivors of domestic violence may choose to stay in their relationships despite such violence or the reasons they may want to end those relationships privately without police or court involvement, these policies assume a childlike naïveté on the part of women and transfer control over women's private lives to the state, allowing the state to take steps to end women's intimate relationships.

A defendant's use of battered women's syndrome evidence in a murder case is similarly problematic because it seems to rely on the assumption that a woman lacks autonomy in a domestic relationship.[125] While such evidence can help the factfinder understand the psychological effects of being in a battering relationship and thereby explain the defendant's conduct, such syndrome evidence has pathological implications that can compromise a defendant's claim

---

120. People v. Humphrey, 921 P.2d 1 (Cal. 1996).

121. Suk, *supra* note 115, at 15–16 ("The protection order was to be a legal tool that would transform the home from a wife's prison into her fortress. It would ban the husband from the space in which his power over her found expression.").

122. Mandatory arrest policies require police to arrest one or both individuals when they respond to domestic violence calls. "No-drop" policies require prosecutors who handle domestic violence cases to prosecute them despite requests by the victim to drop the charges.

123. Recently, criminal courts have begun to routinely issue orders of protection in cases involving domestic violence, whether or not the victim wants such an order in place, and regardless of the relationship between the parties. *See* Suk, *supra* note 115, at 42–50. State departments of probation and parole have also developed policies making such orders conditions of supervised release. *See e.g.*, Moller v. Dennison, 849 N.Y.S.2d 645 (N.Y. App. Div. 2008); Dawson v. State, 894 P.2d 672, 680 (Alaska Ct. App. 1995); People v. Jungers, 25 Cal. Rptr. 3d 873 (Cal. Ct. App. 2005). These provisions impose a "de facto" divorce on couples who have experienced domestic violence, even over the explicit objections of the "victim" that the policies purport to protect. Suk, *supra* note 115, at 42; *In re* Williams v. N.Y. State Div. of Parole, 899 N.Y.S.2d 146, 148 (N.Y. App. Div. 2010), *lv. denied* 15 N.Y.3d 710 (2010).

124. "Perpetrators no longer are able to manipulate the system by coercing the victim into dropping the charges; control has been shifted from the perpetrator to the government." Deborah Epstein, *Effective Intervention in Domestic Violence Cases: Rethinking the Roles of Prosecutors, Judges, and the Court System*, 11 YALE J.L. & FEMINISM 3, 16 (1999).

125. *See* Suk, *supra* note 72, for a discussion of how battered women's syndrome developed and became accepted into the law within a feminist discourse on trauma.

that she acted as a reasonable person and the killing was a justified response to finding herself held hostage by an individual with physical, financial, or social power over her.

As has been true in other areas of the criminal law, the attacks on the chivalric norm granting the husband authority over his wife and the right to use physical force against her have brought about significant changes. Aya Gruber describes the success of feminist efforts in this area: "Society moved from viewing domestic violence as legitimate or private to regarding batterers as among the lowest forms of criminals."[126] Nevertheless, as in the other areas of criminal law discussed, chivalry continues to affect the administration of the law. The law of self-defense continues to embody the "true man" doctrine, heat of passion continues to be a gendered defense, and rape prosecutions—particularly in the case of "date rape" or spousal rape—encounter unique obstacles. So too the law continues to take a more lenient view toward domestic violence crimes, even murder,[127] and to demean female victims by treating them as less than fully autonomous beings.

C. Chivalry and the Death Penalty

Chivalric norms may affect the choice of crimes to which the death penalty is applied or the treatment of the sexes as defendants or victims in murder cases. In the past, the issue of chivalry and the death penalty has been examined in the context of rape defendants and female murder defendants.

1. Rape and the Death Penalty

Chivalry, rape, and the death penalty have a linked history in the United States. The feminist critique of the death penalty as a punishment for rape begins with the epidemic of lynchings—primarily in the South and primarily of African American men[128]—in the late nineteenth and early twentieth centuries. It is estimated that there were 4,743 deaths by lynching between 1882 and 1968, with the overwhelming majority occurring between 1889 and 1918.[129] According to Stuart Banner,

> Lynching was a form of unofficial capital punishment, adjudication of guilt and execution by groups lacking the formal authority for either. The victims were usually black, the executioners usually white. The line between a lynching and an official execution could be thin. The participants in lynchings often included the very same people who, in their official capacities, administered the criminal justice system. Official trials and executions in the South could take place astonishingly fast, so fast as to closely resemble

126. Aya Gruber, *Rape, Feminism, and the War on Crime*, 84 WASH. L. REV. 581, 584 (2009).
127. *See infra* Part III.
128. FRANK ZIMRING, THE CONTRADICTIONS OF AMERICAN CAPITAL PUNISHMENT 90 (2003).
129. *Id.*

lynchings, when a case carried racial implications.[130]

At its height, lynching was much more common than official capital punishment,[131] enjoyed substantial public support among whites,[132] and virtually never resulted in prosecution of any of the responsible parties.[133] Thus, lynching was a substitute for judicial process and execution and a precursor of the modern death penalty.[134]

Although lynchings were first and foremost a vehicle for racial oppression, the justifications given for the practice were seen by feminists to oppress women as well. The myth that supported the lynchings was that the lynching victims were guilty of rape or other sexual behavior toward a (white) woman, and the lynchings were justified in chivalric terms as necessary to redeem the woman's honor.[135] In her biography of Jessie Daniel Ames, the leader of the Association of Southern Women for the Prevention of Lynching (ASWPL) in the 1930s, Jacquelyn Dowd Hall explained the dilemma that lynching posed for women:

> The lynch mob in pursuit of the black rapist thus represented the trade-off implicit in the code of chivalry, for the right of the southern lady to protection presupposed her obligation to obey. The connotations of wealth and family background attached to the position of the lady in the antebellum South faded in the twentieth century, but the power of "ladyhood" as a value construct remained. The term denoted chastity, frailty, graciousness . . . . Internalized by the individual, this ideal regulated behavior and restricted interaction with the world. If a woman passed the tests of ladyhood, she could tap into the reservoir of protectiveness and shelter known as southern chivalry . . . . Together the practice of ladyhood and the etiquette of chivalry functioned as highly effective strategies of control over women's behavior as well as powerful safeguards of caste restrictions.[136]

Ames's response on behalf of the ASWPL was to rebel against "the crown of chivalry which has been pressed like a crown of thorns on our heads."[137] While Ames and her supporters did not reject the norms of ladyhood outright, they sought to "strike down the apologetics of lynching by disassociating the

---

130. STUART BANNER, THE DEATH PENALTY—AN AMERICAN HISTORY 229 (2002).

131. *Id.*

132. *See* HORTENSE POWDERMAKER, AFTER FREEDOM 389 (1939) (citing a 1930s study showing that 64% of whites thought that lynching for rape was justifiable).

133. Dripps, *supra* note 36, at 499 n.132 (2009) ("less than 1% of lynchings in period 1900–1930 resulted in conviction of any responsible individual").

134. As lynchings declined in the mid-twentieth century, the number of legal executions increased, and the "high-lynching" states (including all the states of the former Confederacy) became the "high-execution" states in the post-*Furman* era. *See* ZIMRING, *supra* note 128 at 89–114.

135. JACQUELYN DOWD HALL, REVOLT AGAINST CHIVALRY 145–46 (1979).

136. *Id.* at 151–52.

137. *Id.* at 167.

image of the lady from its connotations of female vulnerability and retaliatory violence."[138] They attacked the paternalism inherent in the justification for lynching, arguing that "the presumptive tie between lynching and rape cast white women in the position of sexual objects—ever threatened by black lust, ever in need of rescue by their white protectors."[139]

When lynching died out after 1930, use of the death penalty for rapists grew.[140] From 1930 until the *Furman* decision in 1972, 455 men were executed for rape in the United States, almost 90% of them African Americans.[141] Many feminists continued to oppose capital punishment for rapists. In *Coker v. Georgia*,[142] Ruth Bader Ginsburg (now Justice Ginsburg of the U.S. Supreme Court) was the lead attorney on an amicus brief for the American Civil Liberties Union and others, including five women's rights organizations.[143] The brief argued that the death penalty for rape was a product of chivalry:

> The death penalty for rape should be rejected as a vestige of an ancient, patriarchal system in which women were viewed both as the property of men and as entitled to a crippling "chivalric protection." It is part of the fabric of laws and enforcement practices surrounding rape which in fact hamper prosecution and convictions for that crime, thus leaving women with little real protection against rape.[144]

Although the Court in *Coker* held that the death penalty was a disproportionate punishment for rape of an adult woman and therefore was unconstitutional under the Eighth Amendment, the Court did not address the "chivalry" argument.

2. Gender and the Death Penalty

The chivalry hypothesis suggests that female defendants would be favored by the criminal justice system and that they would be convicted of lesser crimes or receive lesser sentences than similarly situated men. Recent studies have

---

138. *Id.* at 194.

139. *Id.* Lillian Smith, a post-World War II civil rights leader, described the ASWPL campaign against lynching in these terms: "The lady insurrectionists . . . said calmly that they were not afraid of being raped; as for their sacredness, they could take care of it themselves; they did not need the chivalry of lynching to protect them and they did not want it." *Id.* at 196.

140. As the lynchings diminished, the "high-lynching" states (including all the states of the former Confederacy) became the "high-execution" states in the post-*Furman* era. *See* ZIMRING, *supra* note 128 at 89–114.

141. *See* Furman v. Georgia, 408 U.S. 238, 364 (1972).

142. 433 U.S. 584 (1977).

143. The women's rights organizations were the National Organization for Women Legal Defense and Education Fund, the Women's Law Project, the Center for Women Policy Studies, the Women's Legal Defense Fund, and Equal Rights Advocates, Inc. Brief for American Civil Liberties Union et al. as Amici Curiae Supporting Petitioner, Coker v. Georgia, 433 U.S. 584 (1977) (No. 75-5444), 1976 WL 18142.

144. *Id.* at 6; *see also* Rayburn, *supra* note 108, at 1126 ("the only way to guarantee exclusive control of [women] by husbands was to threaten the ultimate punishment: death.").

shown that at all stages of the criminal judicial process female defendants are treated more leniently than males[145] and that in homicide cases male offenders generally receive longer sentences than female offenders.[146] An earlier study concluded: "A review of the post-1975 literature suggests that the chivalry hypothesis is now wholly accepted."[147]

Studies of gender and the death penalty have, for the most part, focused on the gender of the defendant and have consistently found that women are sentenced to death and executed at significantly lower rates than men.[148] A study of the death penalty applied to women from 1973-2005 found that at every stage of the process female defendants appear to be diverted away from the death penalty at a greater rate than men. While 10% of people arrested for murder are women, only 2% of death sentences imposed at trial are imposed upon women,[149] and women account for only 1.1% of persons actually executed.[150] Men arrested for murder are six times more likely to be sentenced to death than are women arrested for murder.[151] Many scholars have posited that the reason for this discrepancy is chivalric beliefs.[152] The theory, affirmed by studies of attitudes toward female offenders,[153] argues that women "are stereotyped as weak and passive, creating and continuing men's protective attitude toward women."[154] That any women at all are executed is explained by the fact that those women did not fit the stereotypical feminine role because they were women of color or lesbians or had in some way rejected the prescribed wife-and-mother role.[155]

Dissenting from the conclusion that chivalry explains the scarcity of

---

145. Sergio Herzog & Shaul Oreg, *Chivalry and the Moderating Effect of Ambivalent Sexism*, 42 LAW & SOC'Y REV. 45, 47 (2008); Shapiro, *supra* note 4, at 452.

146. Edward L. Glaeser & Bruce Sacerdote, *Sentencing in Homicide Cases and the Role of Vengeance*, 32 J. LEGAL STUD. 363, 371 (2003).

147. Ilene H. Nagel & John Hagan, *Gender and Crime: Offense Patterns and Criminal Court Sanctions*, *in* 4 CRIME AND JUSTICE, AN ANNUAL REVIEW OF RESEARCH 113 (M. Tonry & N. Morris eds. 1983).

148. Victor L. Streib, *Rare and Inconsistent: The Death Penalty for Women*, 33 FORDHAM URB. L.J. 609, 621–22 (2006) [hereinafter Streib, *Rare and Inconsistent*]. The conclusion is based on the number of women arrested for murder by jurisdiction, rather than the number of arrests, prosecutions or convictions for capital murder. *Id.* at 620.

149. VICTOR L. STREIB, DEATH PENALTY FOR FEMALE OFFENDERS 3 (2006), *available at* http://www.deathpenaltyinfo.org/FemDeathDec2005.pdf [hereinafter STREIB, DEATH PENALTY (REPORT)].

150. *Id.*

151. Victor L. Streib, *Gendering the Death Penalty: Countering Sex Bias in a Masculine Sanctuary*, 63 OHIO ST. L.J. 433, 442 (2002).

152. *See* Herzog & Oreg, *supra* note 145, at 47. *But see* Streib, *Rare and Inconsistent*, *supra* note 148, at 627 (finding no pattern or rational explanation of the gender discrepancies in the application of the death penalty).

153. *See* Herzog & Oreg, *supra* note 145, at 66.

154. Shapiro, *supra* note 4, at 456.

155. Carroll, *supra* note 10, at 1421; Joan W. Howarth, Review Essay, *Feminism, Lawyering, and Death Row*, 2 S. CAL. REV. L. & WOMEN'S STUD. 401, 417 n.86 (1992); Streib, *Death Penalty (Article)*, *supra* note 7, at 879.

women sentenced to death, Elizabeth Rapaport is one of the few researchers to argue in favor of other explanatory factors.[156] While acknowledging that "[t]here are deep cultural inhibitions against the deliberate killing of women"[157] and that male murderers are substantially more likely to receive a death sentence than female murderers,[158] she has argued that "[t]he fundamental reason why so few women murderers are death sentenced is that women rarely commit the kinds of murders that are subject to capital punishment," particularly felony-murders.[159] Rather, she argues that when women murder, they overwhelmingly murder family members, and domestic murder is rarely treated as seriously by the criminal justice system as stranger murder.[160] As discussed in Part IV, the empirical data from California calls into question these broad assertions.[161]

The chivalry hypothesis suggests that crimes against women would be more harshly punished than similar crimes against men. At least in the case of homicide, there is a general consensus that, regardless of the gender of the offender, killing a woman results in a longer sentence than killing a man.[162] This disparity exists even in forms of homicide where intent of the offender plays no

---

156. Elizabeth Rapaport, *Some Questions About Gender and the Death Penalty*, 20 GOLDEN GATE U. L. REV. 501 (1990).

157. *Id.* at 503.

158. *Id.* at 505. Rapaport asserted that male murderers are "twenty times" more likely to be sentenced to death, but that figure, based on death sentences from a single year (1986) when only three women were sentenced to death, is clearly exaggerated. *See* STREIB, DEATH PENALTY (REPORT) *supra* note 151, at 444 tbl. 2.

159. Rapaport, *supra* note 156, at 509–10. This argument contains a significant ambiguity: it is not clear whether Rapaport is arguing that women do not commit the kinds of murders that are, by statute, capital murders or do not commit the kinds of capital murders that usually result in a death sentence.

160. Of course, what Rapaport may be noticing is simply that chivalric values influence voters and legislatures as well as judges and juries—leading them to discount domestic violence and exclude domestic murders from the list of capital murders. *See infra* notes 170–73 and accompanying text.

161. For example, while Rapaport presumes that felony-murderers are more likely candidates for the death penalty than other murderers, in this study, at least, that depends entirely on the underlying felony. Murderers who killed during theft-related felonies (the most common capital felony-murders) were rarely sentenced to death, even more rarely than domestic violence murderers. And, although Rapaport is correct that domestic violence murders constitute a higher percentage of capital murders for women than for men and that the death penalty is underused for domestic violence murders, in this study, most capital murders by women (75%) were not domestic violence murders, while the only woman to receive a death sentence did commit a domestic violence murder. Rapaport also contends that male murderers are more likely to have prior convictions for violent crimes, making them better candidates for a death sentence. Rapaport, supra note 156, at 510. She offers no evidence for this assertion other than the fact that men commit more than 95% of violent crimes. However, if women commit approximately 5% of violent crimes and approximately 5% of capital murders (*see infra* Part IV.A), then, as a statistical matter, the female murderer is no less likely than the male murderer to have committed prior violent crimes.

162. Glaeser & Sacerdote, *supra* note 146, at 375–76. Of course, as has been noted with sentencing discrepancies based on the gender of the offender, the *type* of woman in question plays a role. Offenders who kill women who do not conform to traditional ideas of appropriate femininity and womanhood, such as prostitutes, do not receive sentences that are as long as those who kill "stereotypical" women victims. *See id.* at 373.

role, such as vehicular homicide.[163] Three empirical studies primarily focused on race of victim disparities in death sentencing have noted that the odds of a death charge or death sentence are significantly higher if the victim is a woman rather than a man.[164] However, scholarship discussing the issue of women as victims in capital cases has focused almost exclusively on rape-murder and has documented that it is punished more severely than other forms of murders.[165]

Despite the apparent solicitude for women reflected in the heavy use of the death penalty in rape-murder cases, Phyllis Crocker argues that making rape-murderers death-eligible manages to de-emphasize women and incorporate chivalric stereotypes rather than emphasize the abhorrent nature of the crime of rape.[166] Crocker's studies of the application of the death penalty to rape-murder have found that whether a homicide preceded by sexual assault is punished by the death penalty depends both on whether the defendant and victim were strangers and on the races of the defendant and victim.[167] As Crocker points out, if the death penalty were being used to punish the experience of rape—the violence and harm the victim suffers—it would not matter whether the defendant was a stranger or an acquaintance, black or white. Instead, the death penalty is deployed to strongly condemn rapes that fit the stereotypical definition of "real" rape, which focuses on the identities of the participants rather than the nature of the crime. Further, Crocker argues that once a rape becomes a rape-murder, the stereotypes and evidentiary hurdles attendant to simple rape trials evaporate, and juries require less evidence of rape in rape-murder cases than in rape cases.[168] While at first blush this might appear to be a victory for feminists, it again illustrates the ways in which the criminal justice system discounts the agency of women. As Crocker puts it, "When a woman is alive to testify about the rape, her credibility is questioned. In a rape-murder case, when the woman is dead, her inability to speak speaks for her; her silence, when dead, is more powerful than her voice when alive."[169]

---

163. *Id.* at 376–78.

164. *See* Stephanie Hindson, Hillary Potter & Michael L. Radelet, *Race, Gender, Region and Death Sentencing in Colorado, 1980–1999*, 77 U. COLO. L. REV. 549, 564–65 (2006); Michael L. Radelet & Glenn L. Pierce, *Choosing Those Who Will Die: Race and the Death Penalty in Florida*, 43 FLA. L. REV. 1, 25–26 (1991); Michael J. Songer & Isaac Unah, *The Effect of Race, Gender, and Location on Prosecutorial Decisions to Seek the Death Penalty in South Carolina*, 58 S.C. L. REV. 161, 190 (2006).

165. *See, e.g.*, Phyllis L. Crocker, *Is the Death Penalty Good for Women?*, 4 BUFF. CRIM. L. REV. 917 (2001).

166. *Crocker*, Crossing the Line, *supra* note 110, at 693.

167. *Id.* at 702–03.

168. *Id.* at 710–15. Crocker discusses cases from Ohio where defendants were given the death penalty for rape-murders in which the rapes fell outside the stereotyped "real" rape of a stranger on an unsuspecting female victim. For example, she discusses a case in which the victim was drunk and/or high and voluntarily walked with the defendant into the woods; and another case where the only evidence supporting the rape charge was a witness who had said the defendant intended to kill the victim because "she would tell" (though what she would tell was never established). *Id.*

169. *Id.* at 704.

In stark contrast to rape-murder, domestic violence murders rarely are prosecuted as capital crimes in most states.[170] Because domestic violence murders often are seen as heat of passion murders or (if the survivor of the domestic violence is the killer) the product of "battered women's syndrome," the killer may not be prosecuted for murder at all. Even when a domestic violence murderer is convicted of first degree murder and is death-eligible, a death sentence is rarely imposed.[171] This leniency toward domestic violence murderers is particularly troubling in light of the fact that women are much more likely to be murdered by intimate partners than under other circumstances.[172] As was noted earlier, this is consistent with the culture of chivalry, wherein spousal violence was traditionally either condoned or ignored by the law because it was a private matter between the partners.[173]

* * *

Over the last forty years, struggles against chivalry in the formal law and in the administration of the law have frequently succeeded. Nevertheless, the victories have not been complete, and, despite much progress, chivalric norms appear to remain deeply embedded in American culture, continuing to influence decision-making at all levels of the legal system. It should come as no surprise, therefore, that chivalry affects the most profound decisions that prosecutors and jurors make: the decisions to seek and to impose the death penalty.

II. THE CALIFORNIA DEATH PENALTY SCHEME: VIRTUALLY UNFETTERED DISCRETION

In the 1972 landmark decision of *Furman v. Georgia*,[174] the Supreme Court held that the death penalty, as then administered in the United States, violated the Eighth Amendment. Although there was no majority opinion in *Furman*, all five justices in the majority focused on the infrequency with which the death penalty was imposed.[175] Justices Stewart and White, in particular,

---

170. Elizabeth Rapaport, *Capital Murder and the Domestic Discount: A Study of Capital Domestic Murder in the Post-*Furman *Era*, 49 S.M.U. L. Rev. 1507 (1996). *But see* Carolyn B. Ramsey, *Intimate Homicide: Gender and Crime Control, 1880–1920*, 77 U. COLO. L. REV. 101 (2006) (challenging the historical accuracy of this assertion by looking at cases from the turn of the twentieth century that demonstrate that prosecutors and courts treated intimate homicides by men very seriously).

171. *See infra* Part III.C.

172. Dana M. Britton, *Feminism in Criminology: Engendering the Outlaw*, 571 ANNALS AM. ACAD. POL. & SOC. SCI. 57, 64 (2000).

173. *See* JONATHAN SIMON, GOVERNING THROUGH CRIME 181 (2007) (discussing how courts have "sheltered" spousal violence under a privacy doctrine).

174. 408 U.S. 238 (1972).

175. 408 U.S. at 248 n.11 (Douglas, J., concurring); *id.* at 291–95 (Brennan, J., concurring); *id.* at 309–10 (Stewart, J., concurring); *id.* at 313 (White, J., concurring); *id.* at 354 n.124, 362–63 (Marshall, J., concurring). It was the Justices' understanding that only 15–20% of death-eligible murderers were being sentenced to death. This was the figure cited by Chief Justice Burger, writing for the four dissenters. *Id.* at 386 n.11 (Burger, C.J., dissenting). Justice Powell, also writing for the four dissenters, cited similar statistics. *See id.* at 435 n.19 (Powell, J., dissenting). Justice Stewart, in turn, cited to the Chief Justice's statement as

emphasized that the relative infrequency of its application created the risk that it would be arbitrarily applied.[176] In subsequent cases, the Court cited the opinions of Justices Stewart and White as embodying the *Furman* holding.[177] In *Zant v. Stephens*,[178] the Court held that, to meet the *Furman* concern about the risk of arbitrary enforcement, the states, by statute, were required to "genuinely narrow," by rational and objective criteria, the death-eligible class.[179] The Court later explained the point of the *Furman/Zant* rule as follows:

> As the types of murders for which the death penalty may be imposed become more narrowly defined and are limited to those which are particularly serious or for which the death penalty is particularly appropriate . . . [juries] will impose the death penalty in a substantial portion of the cases so defined. If they do, it can no longer be said that the penalty is being imposed wantonly and freakishly or so infrequently that it loses its significance as a sentencing device.[180]

Thus, the Court seemed to say that the measure of a constitutional death penalty scheme was whether death was imposed on a "substantial portion" of those who were death-eligible, that is, whether the scheme produced a higher death-sentence rate than the pre-*Furman* rate.[181] While the Supreme Court was insisting that death penalty schemes be narrowly drafted so that the death penalty is in fact imposed on a substantial portion of the death-eligible class, California was proceeding in the opposite direction.

A. The California Death Penalty Scheme

The present California death penalty scheme was enacted through the 1978 Briggs Death Penalty Initiative six years after *Furman*.[182] According to its author, State Senator John V. Briggs, the initiative was intended to "give

---

support for his conclusion that the imposition of death was "unusual." *Id.* at 309 & n.10 (Stewart, J., concurring). Subsequently, in *Gregg v. Georgia*, the plurality reiterated this understanding: "It has been estimated that before *Furman* less than 20% of those convicted of murder were sentenced to death in those States that authorized capital punishment." 428 U.S. 153, 182 n.26 (1976) (plurality opinion).

176. Justice Stewart found that the death sentences at issue in *Furman* were "cruel and unusual" because, of the many persons convicted of capital crimes, only "a capriciously selected random handful" were sentenced to death. 408 U.S. at 309–10 (Stewart, J., concurring). Justice White concluded that, "the death penalty is exacted with great infrequency even for the most atrocious crimes and . . . there is no meaningful basis for distinguishing the few cases in which it is imposed from the many cases in which it is not." *Id.* at 313 (White, J., concurring).

177. *See* Gregg v. Georgia, 428 U.S. 153, 188–89 (1976) (plurality opinion); Maynard v. Cartwright, 486 U.S. 356, 362 (1988).

178. 462 U.S. 862 (1983).

179. *Id.* at 877.

180. Penry v. Lynaugh, 492 U.S. 302, 327 (1989) (quoting *Gregg*, 428 U.S. at 222 (White, J., concurring)).

181. *See id.* at 327.

182. Death Penalty Act, Initiative Measure Proposition 7 (Nov. 7, 1978).

Californians the toughest death-penalty law in the country."[183] By "the toughest death penalty law," the proponents meant the law "which threatens to inflict that penalty on the maximum number of defendants."[184] That "toughest death penalty law" has since been expanded by the voters on three occasions since 1978[185] and is the broadest death penalty scheme in the country.[186]

The California Penal Code starts with an expansive definition of first degree murder[187] and then enumerates thirty-three special circumstances that make a first degree murderer death-eligible (i.e., that make the murder "capital murder").[188] This extensive list of special circumstances covers almost all forms of first degree murder, because virtually all first degree murders are either

---

183. *Ballot Propositions and Key Races*, 9 CAL. J. (SPECIAL SECTION) 5 (Oct. 1978).

184. Carlos v. Superior Court, 672 P.2d 862, 871 n.13 (Cal. 1983).

185. *See* Crime Victims Justice Reform Act, Initiative Measure Proposition 115 § 9 (June 5, 1990); 1995 CAL. STAT. 478, *enacted by* Proposition 196 § 2 (Mar. 26, 1996); 1998 CAL. STAT. 629, *enacted by* Proposition 18 (Mar. 7, 2000); Gang Violence and Juvenile Crime Prevention Act, Initiative Measure Proposition 21 § 11 (Mar. 7, 2000).

186. Amended Declaration of David C. Baldus at ¶ 69 Ashmus v. Wong, Civ. No. C93-00594-TEH (N.D. Cal.). ("[T]he rate of death eligibility among California homicide cases is the highest in the nation by every measure. This result is a product of the number and breadth of special circumstances under California law."). In fact, the California scheme is so broad that the death sentencing rate among death-eligible cases is "over two-thirds lower than the death sentencing rate in pre-*Furman* Georgia." *Id.* at ¶ 71. *See also* Tuilaepa v. California, 512 U.S. 967, 994 (Blackmun, J., dissenting) (noting that California's special circumstances create "an extraordinarily large death pool"); Symposium, *Report of Governor's Council on Capital Punishment*, 80 IND. L.J. 1, 9 (2005) (citing California and Illinois as having exceptionally broad definitions of death-eligibility).

187. There are twenty-one categories of first degree murder in California. CAL. PENAL CODE § 189 (West 2010).

188. *Id.* § 190.2(a). The thirty-three special circumstances may be grouped as follows:
Two "other murder" circumstances: the defendant was convicted of more than one murder ((a)(3)) or was previously convicted of murder ((a)(2));
Eight "victim" circumstances: the defendant intentionally killed a peace officer ((a)(7)), federal law enforcement officer or agent ((a)(8)), firefighter ((a)(9)), witness ((a)(10)), prosecutor or former prosecutor ((a)(11)), judge or former judge ((a)(12)), elected official or former elected official ((a)(13)), or juror ((a)(20));
Six "manner" circumstances: the murder was committed by a destructive device, bomb, or explosive planted ((a)(4)) or mailed ((a)(6)) or was intentionally committed by lying in wait ((a)(15)), by the infliction of torture ((a)(18)), by poison ((a)(19)), or by shooting from a motor vehicle ((a)(21));
Four "motive" circumstances: the defendant committed the murder for financial gain ((a)(1)); to escape arrest ((a)(5)); because of the victim's race, color, religion, national origin, or country of origin ((a)(16)); or to further the activities of a criminal street gang ((a)(22);
Twelve "commission of a felony" circumstances: the murder was committed while the defendant was engaged in, or an accomplice to, robbery ((a)(17)(A)), kidnapping ((a)(17)(B)), rape ((a)(17)(C)), forcible sodomy ((a)(17)(D)), child molestation ((a)(17)(E)), forcible oral copulation ((a)(17)(F)), burglary ((a)(17)(G)), arson ((a)(17)(H)), train wrecking ((a)(17)(I)), mayhem ((a)(17)(J)), rape by instrument ((a)(17)(K)), or carjacking ((a)(17)(L)); and
One "catchall" circumstance: the murder was especially heinous, atrocious, or cruel ((a)(14)). This last circumstance was held unconstitutional on vagueness grounds. *See* People v. Superior Court (Engert), 647 P.2d 76, 77–78 (Cal. 1982); *accord* People v. Wade, 750 P.2d 794, 804 (Cal. 1988)). Consequently, the "heinous, atrocious, or cruel" circumstance was ignored for purposes of the studies discussed in this article.

premeditated killings or felony-murders.[189] Most premeditated murders are capital murders under California's unique "lying in wait" special circumstance[190] that makes death-eligible a murderer who intentionally kills his victim by surprise and from a position of advantage.[191] As for felony-murder, currently all but one (torture) of the thirteen felonies that may be the basis for a first degree felony-murder conviction are also special circumstances,[192] and California is one of only a handful of states where a defendant would be death-eligible for an unintentional, even wholly accidental, killing during a felony.[193]

The most significant category of commonly occurring first degree murders not expressly covered by the special circumstances are domestic violence murders.[194] Many domestic violence killings do not result in a murder conviction at all. Men, in particular, have been able to make use of the heat of passion defense to negate malice and reduce such killings to voluntary manslaughter.[195] Similarly, victims of domestic violence who kill their abusers have been able to use battered women's syndrome to prove self-defense or imperfect (unreasonable) self-defense, reducing the crime to voluntary manslaughter.[196] Still, some domestic violence killings do result in first degree murder convictions. Even in the absence of a special circumstance explicitly covering domestic violence murders,[197] many such murders are made capital murders by

---

189. *See* Loving v. United States, 517 U.S. 748, 755–56 (1996) (holding that a death penalty scheme that made death-eligible all those who committed premeditated murders or felony-murders would encompass so many murders it would "not narrow the death-eligible class in any way consistent with our cases.")

190. *See* CAL. PENAL CODE § 190.2(a)(15) (West 2010).

191. People v. Morales, 770 P.2d 244, 260–61 (Cal. 1989).

192. *Compare* CAL. PENAL CODE § 189 *with* § 190.2(a)(17) (West 2010). Torture, although not one of the felony-murder special circumstances, is a special circumstance when occurring in conjunction with an intentional killing. CAL. PENAL CODE § 190.2(a)(18) (West 2010).

193. The other states are Florida, Georgia, Idaho, Maryland, and Mississippi. Steven F. Shatz, *The Eighth Amendment, the Death Penalty, and Ordinary Robbery-Burglary Murderers: A California Case Study*, 59 FLA. L. REV. 719, 761 (2007).

194. For purposes of this article, we employ the definition of domestic violence used by the California legislature:

> "Domestic violence" means abuse committed against an adult or a minor who is a spouse, former spouse, cohabitant, former cohabitant, or person with whom the suspect has had a child or is having or has had a dating or engagement relationship. For purposes of this subdivision, "cohabitant" means two unrelated adult persons living together for a substantial period of time, resulting in some permanency of relationship. Factors that may determine whether persons are cohabiting include, but are not limited to, (1) sexual relations between the parties while sharing the same living quarters, (2) sharing of income or expenses, (3) joint use or ownership of property, (4) whether the parties hold themselves out as husband and wife, (5) the continuity of the relationship, and (6) the length of the relationship.

CAL. PENAL CODE § 13700(b) (West 2010).

195. *See* People v. Berry, 556 P.2d 777, 778 (Cal. 1976).

196. *See supra* notes 119–120 and accompanying text.

197. Significantly, although rape is a special circumstance making a murderer death-eligible, rape of a spouse is not. *Compare* CAL. PENAL CODE §§ 261–262 (West 2010) *with* CAL. PENAL CODE § 190.2(a)(17)(C) (West 2010).

one or more existing special circumstances—for example, multiple murder,[198] financial gain,[199] torture,[200] or lying in wait.[201]

The breadth of capital murder in California gives prosecutors and juries extraordinary discretion to select defendants for death, and in practice, that discretion is not otherwise limited. Prosecutors have unfettered discretion in their decisions to seek the death penalty in capital murder cases.[202] After a defendant has been convicted of first degree murder and a special circumstance has been found true at the guilt phase of a capital trial, the sentencing jury is accorded virtually unlimited discretion in its decision. The jurors are instructed to consider a list of eleven factors and told to weigh the aggravating factors against the mitigating factors in reaching their decision (although they are not told which factors are aggravating or mitigating).[203] The jurors are not required to agree on aggravating and mitigating factors, and they do not have to make findings in support of, or otherwise explain, their penalty decision.[204] And, although the California Supreme Court ostensibly will engage in individual proportionality review[205]—potentially a *post hoc* limitation on prosecutors' and juries' exercise of discretion— the court has never found a death sentence to be disproportionate in its more than thirty years of reviewing death sentences under the current law.

The California death penalty scheme is unique, not only for its breadth, but also because it is a product of direct democracy, unmediated by the legislature or the courts. The legislature has had no role in the enactment or repeated expansions of the 1978 death penalty law, and with the exception of its 1982 decision holding unconstitutional the "heinous, atrocious, or cruel" special circumstance,[206] the California Supreme Court has taken no role in limiting death-eligibility.[207]

The California death penalty scheme is also dysfunctional. Former Chief Justice Ron George testified to its dysfunction before the California Commission

198. *See, e.g.*, People v. Bunyard, 200 P.3d 879 (Cal. 2009) (defendant kills his wife and the fetus she is carrying).

199. *See, e.g.*, People v. Crew, 74 P.3d 820 (Cal. 2003) (defendant kills his wife to get possession of her bank accounts and other property).

200. *See, e.g.*, People v. Cole, 95 P.3d 811 (Cal. 2004) (defendant kills his sleeping girlfriend by setting her on fire).

201. *See, e.g.*, People v. Ceja, 847 P.2d 55 (Cal. 1993) (defendant kills the mother of his child by luring her out of her house).

202. *See, e.g.*, People v. Ramirez, 139 P.3d 64, 117 (Cal. 2006) (holding that prosecutorial discretion to seek the death penalty does not violate the federal Constitution); People v. Gray, 118 P.3d 496, 543 (Cal. 2005) (same).

203. *See* CAL. PENAL CODE § 190.3 (West 2010).

204. *See* People v. Solomon, 234 P.3d 501, 539 (Cal. 2010).

205. *See, e.g.*, People v. Lenart, 88 P.3d 498, 512–13 (Cal. 2004); People v. Lawley, 38 P.3d 461, 508–509 (Cal. 2002).

206. People v. Superior Court, 647 P.2d 76, 77–78 (Cal. 1982).

207. In *Carlos v. Superior Court*, 672 P.2d 862 (Cal. 1983) (en banc), the court interpreted section 190.2 to require proof of intent to kill for a special circumstances finding. Less than four years later, the court held that interpretation to be erroneous and overruled *Carlos* in *People v. Anderson*, 742 P.2d 1306, 1325–31 (Cal. 1987).

on the Fair Administration of Justice,[208] and the Commission agreed with his testimony.[209] In the thirty-three years between the reinstatement of the death penalty in 1977 and the end of 2010, over 900 defendants were sentenced to death.[210] However, only thirteen were executed.[211] More than six times as many inmates died of natural causes or suicides during that time.[212] As of the end of 2010, there were 713 prisoners on death row,[213] the largest death row in the country. Executions in California are so infrequent that they cannot serve a penological purpose. Even those scholars who contend that the death penalty has a deterrent effect concede that it cannot deter when executions are as infrequent as they are in California.[214] Nor can the death penalty serve a retributive purpose when most of those selected as the "worst of the worst" are never executed.[215]

Prosecutors, and even some jurors, are doubtless aware of these facts. For those who are, their decisions to seek or impose the death penalty may not be based on an expectation that an execution will actually result. Instead, they might intend "to 'send a message' of extreme disapproval for the defendant's acts."[216] Still, the prosecutors' and jurors' choices regarding who should receive this message would seem to be just as valid an expression of their values as a sentence they believe will be carried out. Given the virtually unfettered discretion accorded to prosecutors and jurors in making those choices, California offers an ideal laboratory for exploring the expression of contemporary cultural values in the administration of the death penalty.

B. The Current Study

To test how prosecutors and juries[217] use their virtually unfettered

---

208. CAL. COMM'N ON THE FAIR ADMIN. OF JUSTICE, FINAL REPORT 114 (Gerald Uelman ed., 2008), *available at* http://www.ccfaj.org/documents/CCFAJFinalReport.pdf.

209. *Id.* at 116–17.

210. CAL. DEP'T OF CORR. & REHAB., CONDEMNED INMATE SUMMARY (2011), *available at* http://www.cdcr.ca.gov/Capital_Punishment/docs/CondemnedInmateSummary.pdf.

211. *Inmates Executed 1978–Present*, CAL. DEP'T OF CORR. AND REHAB., http://www.cdcr.ca.gov/Capital_Punishment/Inmates_Executed.html (last visited Nov. 5, 2011). One other prisoner sentenced to death was executed in another state. *Id.*

212. CAL. DEP'T OF CORR. & REHAB., CONDEMNED INMATES WHO HAVE DIED SINCE 1978 (2011), *available at* http://www.cdcr.ca.gov/Capital_Punishment/docs/CONDEMNEDINMATESWHOHAVEDIEDSINCE1978.pdf.

213. CAL. DEP'T OF CORR. & REHAB., *supra* note 210.

214. See Joanna M. Shepherd, *Deterrence Versus Brutalization: Capital Punishment's Differing Impacts Among States*, 104 MICH. L. REV. 203, 233–42 (2005).

215. *See* Furman v. Georgia, 408 U.S. 238, 311-12 (1972) (White, J., concurring) ("[W]hen imposition of the penalty reaches a certain degree of infrequency, it would be very doubtful that any existing general need for retribution would be measurably satisfied. Nor could it be said with confidence that society's need for specific deterrence justifies death for so few when for so many in like circumstances life imprisonment or shorter prison terms are judged sufficient, or that community values are measurably reinforced by authorizing a penalty so rarely invoked.").

216. Caldwell v. Mississippi, 472 U.S. 320, 331 (1985) (quoting Maggio v. Williams, 464 U.S. 46, 54–55 (1983) (Stevens, J., concurring)).

217. We refer to "juries" as the sentencers because, although in theory a defendant could waive a

discretion, we examined 1299 cases of defendants convicted of first degree murder during the three-year period from 2003 through 2005. The cases were identified and the data gathered by means of a defense subpoena in a capital case. The defendant in that case challenged the constitutionality of the California death penalty law under the Eighth Amendment because of its overbreadth and subpoenaed pre-sentence reports ("PSRs") for all defendants convicted of first degree murder during the period in order to present empirical evidence in support of his challenge.[218] Because the quality of the information contained in the PSRs varied from county to county and many of the PSRs were produced with substantial redactions, the information was supplemented with appellate decisions where available.[219] In 117 of the 1299 cases, the defendant committed the murder while a juvenile, and therefore was not death-eligible.[220] In the remaining cases, we categorized the case as "capital murder" where a special circumstance was admitted or found true or where a special circumstance could have been found beyond a reasonable doubt by the factfinder.[221] In 182 cases, we found that the murder was not a capital murder. That is, based on the facts contained in the PSR and any related appellate opinion, if available, there was not substantial evidence to permit an appellate court to uphold a special circumstances finding. Of the remaining 1000 cases we classified as capital murder cases, a special circumstance was found in 509 cases and could have been found based on the facts set forth in the other 491 cases. Thus, 84.6% of the adult first degree murder cases were factually capital cases. In 55 of the 1000 capital cases (5.5%), the defendant was sentenced to death.

---

jury at the penalty phase of a capital case, this is almost never done and was not done in any case that went to a penalty phase in the current study. The study is based on sentencing outcomes, so no distinction is made between prosecutors and juries—that is, we do not attempt to separately analyze prosecutors' charging decisions. In fact, there is reason to assume that the decisions of prosecutors and juries are closely aligned since the main factor driving some prosecutors' decisions whether to seek the death penalty is their assessment of the likelihood of obtaining a death verdict. *See* Dashka Slater, *The Death Squad* (1992), *reprinted in* NINA RIVKIND & STEVEN F. SHATZ, CASES AND MATERIALS ON THE DEATH PENALTY 316, 317 (3d ed. 2009) (quoting a leading death penalty prosecutor in California). In any case, the actions of both prosecutors and juries are expressions of prevailing cultural norms.

218. The PSRs were produced under a court protective order prohibiting the disclosure of confidential information. We do not cite to any individual cases in this article with the exception of the cases resulting in a death sentence (which were identified independently of the PSRs).

219. There were some defendants for whom no PSR was produced and some PSRs that did not provide sufficient usable information, but we estimate that the 1299 cases represent 98–99% of the first degree murder cases (and all of the death cases) during the period.

220. *See* CAL. PENAL CODE §190.5(A) (West 2010).

221. In making this latter determination, we applied two principles: (1) we treated as controlling a factfinder's determination that no special circumstance was proved, unless that determination was made by a jury and there was overwhelming evidence of jury nullification; and (2) where no finding was made, we determined, by reference to appellate decisions on similar facts, whether an appellate court would have upheld such a special circumstances finding had such a finding been made.

The following graph sets forth this distribution of cases.

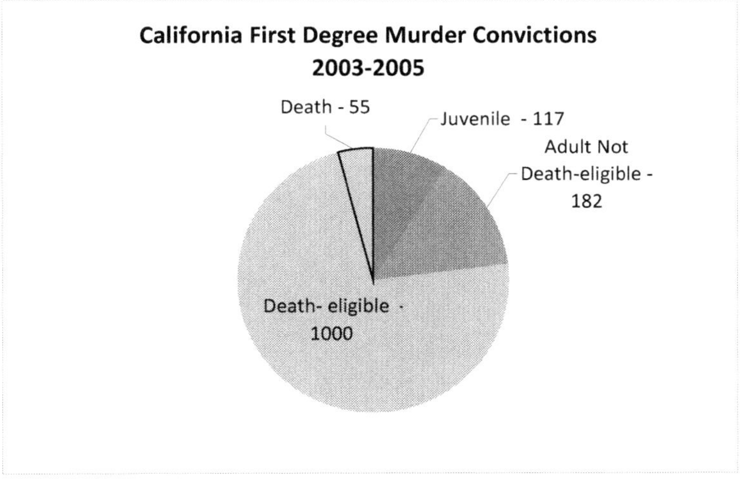

We examined the data to determine if there were disparities in death sentencing outcomes correlated with certain types of capital murder or with the gender of the defendants and victims. The present study is, in certain respects, both more comprehensive and more precise than prior studies addressing gender disparities in other jurisdictions.[222] It is more comprehensive in that we examined the different ways in which chivalric norms might affect death sentencing. It is more precise in that (as was true of the two earlier California studies described below) our data is derived from cases in which the defendant was death-eligible rather than more general arrest or homicide data. Some of our findings have to be viewed with caution for two reasons. First, the number of death sentences in the study is relatively small, creating a significant margin of error as to some findings. Second, the sentence in any given case may be determined by factors other than the nature of the crime or the gender of the parties—for example, legitimate factors such as the quality of the witnesses and other evidence or the past record of the defendant, or illegitimate factors such as the race of the victim or the location of the killing. At the same time, to the extent that our findings in the current study suggest the existence of a "chivalry effect,"[223] such findings tend to be corroborated by the general evidence of the role of chivalric norms in American society, by the findings of other researchers, and, in particular, by data drawn from two earlier studies of California's death penalty—a study based on a sample of 404 first degree murder appeals decided in the period 1988–1992 ("Appellate Study") and a study of 473 first degree

---

222. *See supra* Part I.C.2.

223. Our hope is that our findings will spur further empirical research exploring a possible chivalry effect in the death penalty.

murder cases for murders committed in Alameda County during the period 1978–2001 ("Alameda Study").[224]

III. The Death Penalty and Particular Kinds of Murders

Although the sweep of the special circumstances in California makes the overwhelming majority of adult first degree murderers death-eligible, death-sentence rates demonstrate that prosecutors and jurors consider certain kinds of murders to be more aggravated (i.e., more "death-worthy") than others. Previous California studies have established that two classes of capital murders are considered more highly aggravated (i.e., they produce a significantly higher death-sentence rate) than other commonly occurring types of capital murder.[225] First are the cases in which the defendant has murdered more than one person: prior murder[226] or multiple murder cases[227] (hereafter "multiple murder"). Second are the cases where the defendant intentionally inflicted or attempted to inflict additional serious physical or psychological harm beyond the killing itself: torture,[228] rape or other sexual assault,[229] mayhem,[230] or kidnapping[231] (hereafter "additional-injury murder").[232] By contrast, most cases not falling within these two categories of highly aggravated murders fell into one of two other large categories: the theft-related felony-murders (robbery,[233] burglary,[234] and carjacking[235]) and what might be termed "ordinary premeditated murders" (lying in wait[236] and drive-by shooting[237]).[238] The current study confirms that multiple

224. These two earlier studies were conducted by Professor Shatz, who gathered and analyzed the data for the current study. The Appellate Study was based on all published murder appeals and all unpublished murder appeals decided by the First Appellate District of the Court of Appeal during the study period. The Alameda Study was based on all first degree murder convictions for murders committed during the study period. Consequently, the Appellate Study primarily covered murders committed in the 1980s while the Alameda Study primarily covered murders committed in the 1980s and 1990s. Only portions of the data from the earlier studies have been published. *See* Steven F. Shatz & Nina Rivkind, *The California Death Penalty: Requiem for* Furman?, 72 N.Y.U. L. REV. 1283, 1326–38 (1997) (using data from the Appellate Study); Shatz, *supra* note 193, at 736–45 (using data from both studies).

225. *See* Shatz, *supra* note 193, at 739–44. A substantial majority of the murders in the current study were committed post-1999.

226. CAL. PENAL CODE § 190.2(a)(2) (West 2010).

227. *Id.* § 190.2(a)(3).

228. *Id.* § 190.2(a)(18).

229. *Id.* §§ 190.2(a)(17)(C)-(F), (17)(K).

230. *Id.* § 190.2(a)(17)(J).

231. *Id.* § 190.2(a)(17)(B).

232. Certain other kinds of murders identified by the special circumstances may be considered equally aggravating, but they occur so infrequently in the cases (e.g., murder for financial gain or murder of a peace officer) that their effect cannot be measured. *See id.* §§ 190.2(a)(1), (7).

233. *Id.* § 190.2(a)(17)(A).

234. *Id.* § 190.2(a)(17)(G).

235. *Id.* § 190.2(a)(17)(L).

236. *Id.* § 190.2(a)(15).

237. *Id.* § 190.2(a)(21).

murders and additional-injury murders continue to be viewed as the most death-worthy. In capital cases falling within one or both of these categories, the death-sentence rate was 14.4%. By contrast, the death-sentence rate for all other cases was 1.6%.

Against this background, we examine three kinds of murders—gang murders, rape-murders, and domestic violence murders—all of which have a significant gender component and thus may shed light on the chivalry question. In order to avoid the distortion created by the aggravating effect of multiple murder, we limit our consideration to cases with a single victim and no prior murder conviction for the defendant. In such cases, the overall death-sentence rate was 3.4%. In the case of each of these "gendered" murders, we compare the death-sentence rate for that kind of murder with the death-sentence rate for all other single-victim capital cases in the study.

A. Gang Murders

The rise in gang violence in recent decades prompted the addition of the "gang motive" special circumstance in 2000.[239] That circumstance makes death-eligible a defendant convicted of first degree murder who "intentionally killed the victim while the defendant was an active participant in a criminal street gang . . . and the murder was carried out to further the activities of the criminal street gang."[240] In the current study, gang murder was the most commonly occurring special circumstance, appearing in 31.5% of all cases and in 33.9% of the capital cases.[241] Gang murder is a gendered crime. In the study, while women constituted about 6.8% of the non-gang murderers, they constituted only 3.3% of the gang murderers. The gender disparity is even greater with regard to the victims of gang murders—they are disproportionately men. In single-victim non-gang capital murders in the study, women were the victims in 30.5% of the cases; in gang murder cases, women were the victims in only 6.7% of the cases. In short, gang murder cases usually involve men killing men.

The facts of the hundreds of gang murders are depressingly repetitive, tending to follow one of three patterns. In one version, in the manner of the Jets and the Sharks in *West Side Story*, gang members in one gang agree with members of a rival gang to confront each other. *People v. Sanchez*[242] is a case in that mode. There, the two defendants, Sanchez and Gonzalez, were members of rival gangs and were convicted of first degree murder under the following circumstances. Sanchez and a fellow gang member drove to a house where Gonzalez and his fellow gang member were standing outside. The Sanchez car

---

238. The gang murder special circumstance, the most commonly occurring special circumstance in the current study, was not added to section 190.2(a) until 2000 and so was not considered in the earlier studies.

239. *See id.* § 190.2(a)(22).

240. *Id.* We refer to such murders coming within this special circumstance as "gang murders."

241. Adults committing a gang murder before 2000 and juveniles were not death-eligible.

242. 29 P.3d 209 (Cal. 2001).

made several passes in front of house, with the defendants engaging in provocative conduct. On the third pass, the defendants opened fire on each other, killing an innocent bystander. In the second version, the members of one gang plan and carry out an attack on members of a rival gang (or persons they believe to be members of a rival gang) in retaliation for an offense that they believe the other gang committed. For example, in *People v. Shabazz*,[243] the defendant learned the location of a car believed to have been used in a drive-by shooting by a rival gang, went to the location, and, on finding a rival gang member in the car, opened fire, killing the rival's companion. The third version is typified by *People v. Medina*,[244] where an unplanned encounter between gang members at a party escalated from a verbal confrontation to a fistfight to a shooting.[245]

The California Supreme Court, relying on the testimony of police gang experts, has referred to gang violence as being the product of gangs' "code of honor,"[246] and the Court has described the genesis of the violence as follows:

> [G]ang members view behavior that disrespects their gang as a challenge and a "slap in the face" which must be avenged. Gang members perceive that, if no retaliatory action is taken in the face of disrespectful behavior, the challenger and others will view the gang member and the gang itself as weak. . . . [V]iolence is used as a response to disrespectful behavior and disagreements and as a means to gain respect.[247]

Scholars who have studied street gangs confirm the views of the court: if a gang member suffers an insult, his honor and status are at stake, and the only way to save face is to retaliate with violence.[248] Violence, then, is meant to "defend the 'honor of males; to secure and defend the reputation of their local area and the honor of their women.'"[249] As such, violence is deeply tied to notions of masculinity.[250]

Gang rules of conduct thus can be seen as a modern incarnation of chivalry.[251] Mirroring knightly violence, gang violence is deployed to define and defend territorial boundaries, to achieve power by vanquishing rival gangs and

---

243. 130 P.3d 519, 521–22 (Cal. 2006).
244. 209 P.3d 105, 108 (Cal. 2009).
245. For first-hand accounts of life in California gangs, see CUPCAKE BROWN, A PIECE OF CAKE 105–37 (2006); STANLEY TOOKIE WILLIAMS, BLUE RAGE, BLACK REDEMPTION 79–210 (2004).
246. People v. Cervantes, 29 P.3d 225, 235 (Cal. 2001).
247. 209 P.3d at 109.
248. LARRY J. SIEGEL & BRANDON C. WELSH, JUVENILE DELINQUENCY: THEORY, PRACTICE, AND LAW 311 (2009).
249. John M. Hagedorn, *Gang Violence in the Postindustrial Era*, 24 CRIME & JUST. 365, 373 (1998) (quoting in part Walter Miller, *Violent Crime in City Gangs*, *in* DELINQUENCY, CRIME, AND SOCIAL PROCESS 707 (Donald R. Cressey & David Ward eds. 1969)).
250. *Id.* at 398. Our focus here is on the *conduct* of the gang members. The complex psychological, economic, and social factors that cause persons to join gangs and that create the honor culture described here are beyond the scope of this article.
251. *Id.* at 371–72 (gang violence between neighborhood peer groups mimics feudal rivalries).

taking their territories, and above all to defend and protect the honor of the gang and gang members. Like knightly violence, gang violence also is a means to address even trivial personal affronts. Just as the chivalric knight might have responded with violence to a request for his name,[252] so a gang member might respond violently to the question, "Where are you from?"[253] Indeed, in the world of gangs, as was true in the world of knights, death in service to the gang may even be a path to honor and glory.[254]

Despite the sheer number of gang murders in California and the grip that gang violence has on many communities, the gang murders studied almost never resulted in a death sentence. Of the fifty-five death-sentenced defendants in the study, only six had committed a proved or provable gang murder, and five of those six had committed multiple murders. Thus, out of 296 single-victim gang murder cases, only one defendant (0.3%) was sentenced to death, and that case was atypical because the defendant was convicted of intentionally killing a police officer to effect an escape from custody.[255] It would seem that, consistent with chivalric norms, Californians (as represented by prosecutors and jurors) were more tolerant of killings among men in the context of defending the honor of groups or individuals than of almost any other form of capital murder. To suggest that prosecutors' and jurors' refusal to impose the death penalty for gang murders is an expression of chivalric norms is not to assert that prosecutors and jurors mistake gang members for knights of the Round Table. Rather, it is to argue that their outrage at the murderer is tempered by the same "boys will be boys" attitude that accepted the often "heedless violence"[256] of the medieval knights.

While the extraordinarily low death-sentence rate for gang murders strongly suggests a societal tolerance for "honor violence" and is consistent with such tolerance expressed in other aspects of the criminal law,[257] other factors may be at work. The low death-sentence rate may be due in part to the fact that the victims in gang murders are overwhelmingly men and, as we discuss

252. See *supra* note 21 and accompanying text.

253. People v. Medina, 209 P.3d 105, 111 (Cal. 2009).

254. In the words of rapper The Notorious B.I.G.—perhaps one of the most famous casualties of gang violence—"you're nobody til somebody kills you." THE NOTORIOUS B.I.G., *You're Nobody*, *on* LIFE AFTER DEATH (Bad Boy Records 1997). The idea that dying to defend one's honor or to defend or protect others is admirable has also been a recurring theme in the popular imagination of knighthood. *See, e.g.*, JOE DARION & MITCH LEIGH, *The Impossible Dream*, MAN OF LA MANCHA (1964) (describing the requirements of a knight as "to be willing to march into hell for a heavenly cause").

255. *See* Wendy Thomas Russel, *Cop Killer Gets Death; Daryle Black's Murderer to be Executed*, LONG BEACH PRESS-TELEGRAM, May 10, 2003, at A1. The extraordinarily low death-sentence rate for single-victim gang murders cannot be explained on the hypothesis that a higher percentage of gang murder cases involve multiple victims. In fact, the percentage of gang murder cases that are multiple murder cases is 11.2%, significantly lower than the percentage for non-gang murder cases, 16.0%.

256. *See* KAEUPER, *supra* note 14, at 29.

257. *See supra* notes 73–99 and accompanying text.

below,[258] the death penalty is far more likely to be imposed for murder of a woman than murder of a man. Other characteristics of the victims may also contribute to the low death-sentence rate. Victims of gang violence are more likely to be racial minorities and to be living in the more marginal communities where gangs operate, and the victims may be, or may be perceived as being, themselves participants in the gang culture.[259] Consequently, prosecutors and juries may deem such victims less worthy of the "protection" of the death penalty.

Though these factors suggest that a societal tolerance for honor violence may not be the only explanation for the treatment of gang murders, they do not refute the chivalry hypothesis. To the extent that the death penalty is imposed according to the gender of the victim, it is an expression of chivalric values. Similarly, disparities in the use of the death penalty based on the race and class of the victims recall the rigidly class-based distinctions in medieval times defining to whom the knight owed a duty of protection. In sum, whether the observed failure to employ the death penalty in gang murder cases is due entirely to a tolerance for honor violence or, instead, to certain characteristics of the victims, that failure strongly suggests a chivalric effect.

B. Rape-Murders

The data in the current study demonstrates that rape-murder is the crime most likely to result in a death sentence. In single-victim rape-murder cases, the death-sentence rate was 31.7%, almost sixteen times the rate for all other single-victim capital cases (2.0%). This strikingly disproportionate use of the death penalty in rape-murder cases, marking rape-murderers as the worst of the worst, appears even more noteworthy in light of the fact that murderers in this category may or may not have actually committed a rape—an attempt is enough—and may or may not have intended, or even foreseen, the death.[260] Rape is the quintessential "gendered" crime.[261] In California, while rape-murder could in

---

258. *See infra* notes 312–319 and accompanying text.

259. Interestingly, this pattern holds true even when the victim is an innocent bystander and has not assumed the risks of gang life. *See, e.g.*, People v. Shabazz, 130 P.3d 519, 522 (Cal. 2006), People v. Sanchez, 29 P.3d 209, 215 (Cal. 2001).

260. The felony-murder special circumstances apply if the murder was committed while the defendant was engaged in the commission or attempted commission of certain felonies, CAL. PENAL CODE § 190.2(a)(17), and the California Supreme Court has held that, in the case of the felony-murder special circumstances, the prosecution need not prove that the defendant had any *mens rea* as to the killing. *See, e.g.*, People v. Mitcham, 824 P.2d 1277, 1295 (Cal. 1992); People v. Earp, 978 P.2d 15, 66 (Cal. 1999).

261. Rape is defined as an act of sexual intercourse accomplished by "force, violence, duress, menace, or fear of immediate and unlawful bodily injury" or under various other circumstances inconsistent with the victim's consent. CAL. PENAL CODE § 261 (West 2010). Sexual intercourse is defined as any penetration of the victim's vagina or external genital organs. *Id.* § 263; People v. Karsai, 182 Cal. Rptr. 406, 411 (Ct. App. 1982). The California Judicial Counsel's pattern jury instructions read as follows:

To prove that the defendant is guilty of this crime, the People must prove that:

theory be committed in other ways,[262] in virtually all cases, the crime is committed (and, in every case in the study, was committed) by a man against a woman.[263]

Setting aside momentarily the critique of rape and rape-murder prosecutions as determined by class and race bias[264]—likely a product of chivalric norms that defined only certain "ladies" as deserving of the knight's protection—the question remains whether the disproportionate use of the death penalty can be explained as a chivalry effect. The extraordinary 31.7% death-sentence rate may best be appreciated by comparing death sentences for single-victim rape-murders and for multiple murders. There is consensus among those who have studied the death penalty that, if there is to be a death penalty, defendants who kill more than one victim should be death-eligible[265]—that they are clearly among the worst of the worst.[266] Three recent proposals to reform and narrow the death penalty at the state level all would retain multiple murder as a death-eligibility factor. For example, the Governor's Commission in Illinois recommended the reduction of death-eligibility factors in Illinois from twenty to five, retaining multiple murder.[267] The Massachusetts Governor's Council on Capital Punishment, called upon to draft a "model" death penalty law, would have created a death penalty scheme with only six death-eligibility factors, including multiple murder.[268] Finally, the non-governmental Constitution Project would have retained multiple murder as one of only five death-eligibility factors.[269] No similar consensus exists regarding rape-murder. In fact, none of

---

> 1. The defendant had sexual intercourse with a woman;
>
> . . .
>
> 3. The woman did not consent to the intercourse; AND
>
> 4. The defendant accomplished the intercourse by [any of the means listed in § 261].
>
> *Sexual intercourse* means any penetration, no matter how slight, of the vagina or genitalia by the penis.

JUDICIAL COUNCIL OF CAL., CRIMINAL JURY INSTRUCTIONS, No. 1000 (2011).

262. Rape-murder could be committed in the following ways: by a woman against a man if she were to kill him in course of trying to have sexual intercourse with him without his consent; by a woman against a woman, if she aided a man's attempt to rape the victim; or by a man against a man, if the defendant killed another man to facilitate the rape of a woman.

263. In one case in the study, *People v. Morales*, the defendant in a rape-murder case killed four victims, including a man. *See Murderer of 4 Family Members Gets Death*, L.A. TIMES, Aug. 24, 2005.

264. *See supra* notes 107–110 and accompanying text.

265. *See, e.g.*, David Baldus, *When Symbols Clash: Reflections on the Future of the Comparative Proportionality Review of Death Sentences*, 26 SETON HALL L. REV. 1582, 1605 (1996); Alex Kozinski & Sean Gallagher, *Death: The Ultimate Run-On Sentence*, 46 CASE W. RES. L. REV. 1, 30 (1995).

266. *See* Kansas v. Marsh, 548 U.S. 163, 206 (2006) (Souter, J., dissenting) ("[T]he death penalty must be reserved for 'the worst of the worst.'").

267. GOVERNOR'S COMM'N ON CAPITAL PUNISHMENT, REPORT 65, 67 (2002), *available at* http://www.idoc.state.il.us/ccp/ccp/reports/commission_report/complete_report.pdf.

268. Joseph L. Hoffman et al., *Report of the Governor's Council on Capital Punishment*, 80 IND. L.J. 1, 7, 8 (2005).

269. THE CONSTITUTION PROJECT, MANDATORY JUSTICE: THE DEATH PENALTY REVISITED

the three above reform proposals would have included rape-murder as a capital crime. However, California's prosecutors and jurors disagree.[270] In California, the death-sentence rate for rape-murders is almost twice that for defendants guilty of multiple murder and more than three times the death-sentence rate for defendants who kill "only" two victims.[271] That California prosecutors and jurors would see killing one person in the course of a rape or attempted rape as so much more heinous than killing two people is on its face remarkable[272] and requires an explanation.

Feminist scholars have long argued that rape should not be viewed as a sexual act but as an especially aggravated form of violence and dominance perpetrated primarily by men against women in an assertion of power.[273] As such, rape has been analogized to torture,[274] and both U.S.[275] and international courts have held rape to be torture under international law.[276] Torture, like rape, is a special circumstance under California law.[277] The circumstance requires proof that the defendant intentionally acted to inflict extreme physical pain on the victim while alive and intentionally killed the victim.[278]It would seem that,

xxiv-xxv (2006), *available at* http://www.constitutionproject.org/manage/file/30.pdf. The Constitution Project, housed at Georgetown University, seeks to develop bipartisan solutions to contemporary issues. Its Death Penalty Initiative was co-chaired by the Honorable Charles F. Baird, former judge of the Texas Court of Criminal Appeals; the Honorable Gerald Kogan, former Chief Justice of the Florida Supreme Court; and Beth A. Wilkinson, the prosecutor in the Oklahoma City bombing case. *Id.* at xxxvii.

270. The views of California prosecutors and jurors are likely more representative of American cultural norms than those of the various commissions, which were dominated by legal or criminal justice professionals and which were obliged to issue reports defending their recommendations in rational terms.

271. Only when defendants have killed three or more victims does their death-sentence rate exceed the death-sentence rate for single-victim rape-murder defendants. The death-sentence rate for rape-murders is also substantially higher than for other forms of capital murder which some might think are particularly heinous, such as murder of a child or murder for financial gain (contract murders or murders to collect life insurance).

272. To the extent that this hierarchy of values is based on comparative harms inflicted on victims, prosecutors and jurors seem to think that rape plus death is worse than death plus death or that rape is a fate worse than death, a position that has been strongly disputed by some feminist scholars. In praising the feminist movement for changing societal ideas about rape, Susan Jacoby has written, "But the most important change brought about by the women's movement is abandonment of the antediluvian notion that rape is 'a fate worse than death.' Nothing is worse than death . . . ." Susan Jacoby, *Thank Feminists for Rape Reforms*, BALT. SUN, Aug. 13, 2002, at 11A.

273. *See generally* BROWNMILLER, *supra* note 33, at 377; Martha Chamallas, *Lucky: The Sequel*, 80 IND. L.J. 441, 461–67 (2005) (discussing the sex/violence dichotomy).

274. *See* NANCY VENABLE RAINE, AFTER SILENCE 258 (1998).

275. Zubeda v. Ashcroft, 333 F.3d 463, 472–73 (3d Cir. 2003); Doe I v. Unocal Corp., 395 F.3d 932, 945 (9th Cir. 2002). Congress has also defined torture to include rape. *See, e.g.*, Torture Victims Relief Act of 1998, Pub. L. No. 105-320, § 3, 112 Stat. 3016 (codified at 22 U.S.C. § 2152(3) (2006)).

276. *See* Bonita C. Meyersfield, *Reconceptualizing Domestic Violence in International Law*, 67 ALB. L. REV. 371, 394–95 (2003) (discussing decisions of international tribunals recognizing rape as a form of torture).

277. CAL. PENAL CODE § 190.2(a)(18) (West 2010).

278. People v. Jennings, 237 P.3d 474, 498 (Cal. 2010).

measured by either the depravity of the defendant or the harm to the victim, the torture-murderer—who has killed intentionally after inflicting extreme physical pain—is at least as deserving of the death penalty as the rape-murderer—who may not have killed intentionally and may have done no more than attempt the rape. However, that is not the outcome California prosecutors and jurors reach. The death-sentence rate for single-victim torture-murder cases in the study was 9.0%, less than one-third the death-sentence rate for single-victim rape-murder cases. The disproportionate use of the death penalty in rape-murder cases, particularly in comparison with its use in multiple murder and torture murder cases, confirms that rape continues to be viewed as a singular crime requiring the harshest of punishments.

Since chivalric times, rape (and therefore rape-murder) has never been viewed as simply a crime against the female victim; rather, it has been viewed, perhaps even primarily, as a crime against the honor of the man who was her protector (her husband or her father)[279] because it was a crime against the man's property:

> The historical origin of the death penalty for rape lies in the long standing view of rape as a crime of property where the aggrieved was not the woman but her husband or father. In the Southern states this view coalesced with a tradition which valued white women according to their purity and chastity . . . .[280]

The excessive use of the death penalty to punish rape-murders reflects a societal view that "elevates [women's] chastity to the very essence of their identity."[281] These views concerning the special harms caused by rape, and thus by rape-murder, found voice in Chief Justice Burger's dissent in *Coker v. Georgia*,[282] where he wrote: "Rape . . . is destructive of the human personality. The remainder of the victim's life may be gravely affected, and this in turn may have a serious detrimental effect upon her husband."[283] While explaining the harms caused by rape, the Chief Justice conflated the experiences of the victims with the effect rape has on the men to whom rape victims "belong."

The extraordinary disparity in the employment of the death penalty in single-victim rape-murder cases—almost sixteen times the rate for other single-victim cases and almost twice the rate for multiple murder cases—may have less to do with the heinousness of rape-murder compared to other forms of capital murder and more to do with outdated notions about honor, violence, and sex.

---

279. BROWNMILLER, *supra* note 33, at 376; *See also* KAEUPER, *supra* note 14, at 225–26.

280. Brief for American Civil Liberties Union et al. as Amici Curiae Supporting Petitioner, *supra* note 143 at 6. *See also* Rayburn, *supra* note 108, at 1126 ("the only way to guarantee exclusive control of [women] by husbands was to threaten the ultimate punishment: death.").

281. Rayburn, *supra* note 108, at 1154.

282. Coker v. Georgia, 433 U.S. 584 (1977).

283. *Id.* at 612 (Burger, C.J., dissenting).

C. Domestic Violence Murders

In contrast to rape-murderers, domestic violence murderers seldom are sentenced to death. The data from the current study confirms that domestic violence murders are disproportionately excluded at all levels, first by the voters' definition of death-eligibility and then by the prosecutors' and juries' charging and sentencing decisions. Single-victim domestic violence murders constituted 12.8% of all first degree murders in the current study, 9.3% of the capital murders, and 6.9% of the death sentences. When domestic violence murderers are death-eligible under one of the existing special circumstances, they are sentenced to death at a lower-than-average rate. In the current study, the death-sentence rate in single-victim domestic violence capital murders was 2.6%, below the 3.7% death-sentence rate for all other single-victim capital murders. So stated, the disparity may not appear substantial, but, in light of the fact that more than 66% of the victims in single-victim domestic violence capital murders were women[284] and that the death penalty is otherwise disproportionately applied in woman-victim cases,[285] the result is striking. In single-victim domestic violence cases in the study, women were the victims in fifty-three cases. The fifty-three cases resulted in one death sentence, a death-sentence rate (1.9%) less than one-seventh the death-sentence rate for women victims in other single-victim cases (14.5%). While the numbers are small, the data from the Appellate Study is similar: a death-sentence rate of 2.7% where women were the victims in single-victim domestic violence murders in contrast to a death-sentence rate of 18.5% for non-domestic violence murders involving a single woman victim.

This relative tolerance for domestic violence murderers—consistent with the chivalric norm that the knight was the unquestioned master of his household—is troubling in light of the fact that women are much more likely to be murdered by intimate partners than under other circumstances.[286] Until recently, the law either condoned or ignored spousal violence as a private matter between the partners.[287] Cases from around the country demonstrate the patriarchal views that judges (mostly male) have regarding domestic violence and domestic violence murder.[288] One aspect of this patriarchal belief can be a sense of identification with the defendant on the part of the judge. For example, in one 1995 case that may not be typical but reflects the persistence of chivalric norms, a man had been arrested four times for domestic violence against his ex-wife, and the judge had sentenced him to one eight-hour domestic violence

---

284. This contrasts with an overall rate for female victims in single-victim capital murder cases of 21.6%. *See infra* Part IV.B.

285. *See infra* Part IV.B.

286. Britton, *supra* note 172, at 64.

287. *See* SIMON, *supra* note 173, at 181 (discussing how spousal violence has been "sheltered" by the courts under a privacy doctrine).

288. *See* Lynn Hecht Schafran, *There's No Accounting for Judges*, 58 ALB. L. REV. 1063, 1063–67 (1995) (describing cases where judges espoused such views).

program.[289] After the man killed his wife (the day after completing the program) the judge stated that he had given him such a light sentence because, having gone through a divorce himself, he had identified with the defendant and why he was angry.[290] The fact that the death penalty is seldom implemented in cases of domestic violence murder highlights that, whether the discounting is done by the voters, the prosecutor, or the jury, society does not condemn the murder of a present or past intimate partner to the same degree that it rejects the murder of any other victim.

Another reason for the tolerance shown toward domestic violence murderers may be a misguided belief on the part of voters, prosecutors, and juries that the victim of a domestic violence murder is somehow partly responsible for her own death. This view holds that women provoke or instigate domestic violence against themselves or unreasonably fail to take steps to end the abuse.[291] For example, one judge expressed this belief in a case where a man tracked down his wife who was trying to flee their abusive marriage and shot her five times in the face.[292] The judge imposed a minimal sentence, which the defendant served on the weekends.[293] The judge reasoned that the victim "provoked" her husband by not telling him she was leaving.[294] Further, even if the victim did nothing that a prosecutor or jury may believe "provoked" the murder in that moment, these decision-makers may believe that simply by being involved with an abusive man a woman has some responsibility for her own murder. As we discuss below, the decision-making process for capital jurors is often deeply personal, and jurors are more likely to impose a death sentence when they feel personally threatened by the defendant.[295] In cases of domestic violence, jurors may feel that they would never get themselves into a situation where they were being abused or that if they were in an abusive relationship they would have the sense to leave before it turned deadly. Thus, they may have trouble identifying with the victim. Such an attitude represents a deep misunderstanding of the dynamics of domestic violence: the manipulation by the abuser, the time taken to break down the victim's feelings of self worth[296] and

289. *Day One: Soft on Domestic Violence?* (ABC television broadcast, Feb. 2, 1995) (LEXIS).

290. *Id.*

291. *See, e.g.*, Kathleen Waits, *Battered Women and Family Lawyers: The Need for an Identification Protocol*, 58 Alb. L. Rev. 1027, 1051–52 (1995).

292. *Court Backs Judge Who Found Slayer Had Been Provoked,* N.Y. TIMES, July 17, 1984, at A22; *Life Insurance Changes Judge's Mind on Sentence*, N.Y. TIMES, June 30, 1983, at A14 [hereinafter *Life Insurance*]; Schafran, *supra* note 288, at 1065–66.

293. *Life Insurance*, *supra* note 292; Schafran, *supra* note 288, at 1066.

294. *Life Insurance*, *supra* note 292; Schafran, *supra* note 288, at 1066; *see also* Sarah M. Buel, *Access to Meaningful Remedy: Overcoming Doctrinal Obstacles in Tort Litigation Against Domestic Violence Offenders*, 83 Or. L. Rev. 945, 969 (discussing a judge who granted summary judgment in a civil case for assault based on the husband's argument that the wife had not sought medical attention or contacted the police when he punched her).

295. *See infra* Part IV.A.

296. *See, e.g.*, *Domestic Violence*, NAT'L CTR. FOR VICTIMS OF CRIME http://www.ncvc.org/ncvc/main.aspx?dbName=DocumentViewer&DocumentID=32347#3 (last visited Nov. 5, 2011); *Domestic Violence*, U.S. DEP'T OF JUSTICE: OFFICE ON

avenues of escape, and the power and control that the abuser wields over the victim. This misunderstanding may explain why prosecutors and juries have less sympathy for domestic violence murder victims and less inclination to impose the death penalty on their murderers.

* * *

The sentencing results for these three "gendered" types of murder—gang murder, rape-murder, and domestic violence murder—highlight the ways in which the California death penalty is applied in accordance with chivalric ideas. The dichotomy now-Justice Ginsburg once noted, whereby "women [are] viewed both as the property of men and as entitled to a crippling 'chivalric protection,'"[297] led to a strikingly different application of the death penalty in the case of the gender-based crimes of rape-murder and domestic violence murder. The death-sentence rate for single-victim rape-murders that were not domestic violence murders was 33.3%, while the death-sentence rate for single-victim domestic violence murders that were not rape-murders was 2.7%. When murders occurred in the context of a culture in which honor violence is endemic—gang murders—or in the context of an intimate relationship where violence has long been tolerated—domestic violence murders—the severity of those murders tended to be discounted and the death penalty rarely employed. The treatment of these three particular kinds of murder in the cases in this study sheds light on the parallels between chivalric culture and our current society, indicating that in contexts where gender plays a salient role in crime, we may still adhere to medieval views on the interplay between gender and violence.

IV. The Death Penalty and Gender

The disparities in death sentencing for "gendered" murders form the background for a discussion of the broader issue of gender and the death penalty. This section examines whether there are gender-of-defendant or gender-of-victim disparities in the administration of the death penalty and, if so, whether those disparities are consistent with a chivalry effect.

A. Gender of the Defendant

The data in the current study confirms the most well-known aspect of the relationship of gender to the death penalty—that women murderers are sentenced to death at a significantly lower rate than men. In the cases examined, fifty-one women were convicted of capital murder (5.1% of the 1000 defendants convicted of capital murder), and only one, Angelina Rodriguez, was sentenced to death.[298] She was convicted of killing her husband by poisoning him, plainly

---

VIOLENCE AGAINST WOMEN, http://www.ovw.usdoj.gov/domviolence.htm (last visited Nov. 5, 2011).

297. Brief for American Civil Liberties Union et al. as Amici Curiae Supporting Petitioner, *supra* note 143, at 11.

298. *See* Anna Gorman, *Jury Calls for Poisoner's Death*, L.A. TIMES, Nov. 13, 2003, at B3.

violating chivalric norms by her choice of victim (a lady should not be killing her "lord and master"[299]) and her choice of means (killing by stealth is dishonorable because it denies the victim the opportunity to defend himself[300]), thus making her a likely candidate for a death sentence. While the numbers in the current study are, independently, too small to prove the existence of a gender-of-defendant disparity, when combined with the data from the earlier studies, these numbers confirm the findings of previous researchers.[301] Combining the data from all three California studies, women constituted 5.3% of the death-eligible defendants convicted of first degree murder and not sentenced to death, but only 1.2% of the defendants sentenced to death.

Two explanations, both consistent with chivalric norms, suggest why death-eligible women convicted of first degree murder are so infrequently sentenced to death. The simple explanation is that women are sentenced to death at a lower rate than men because of chivalric attitudes on the part of prosecutors and juries. Because women are stereotyped as weak, passive, and in need of male protection, prosecutors and juries may be reluctant to impose the death penalty upon them.[302] In this sense the criminal justice system treats women almost like children—considered less rational and less able to make appropriate decisions, they are held to a lower moral standard when they transgress societal rules. Some authors argue that "the relative dependence of women on men translates into a diminished culpability and an increased possibility of rehabilitation" in the eyes of prosecutors and juries.[303] Of course, some women *are* sentenced to death. That too can be explained in chivalric terms; women who receive the death penalty tend to be women who do not fit traditional, idealized notions of femininity (e.g., prostitutes, lesbians, and women of color) and thus do not benefit from this attitude of chivalry.[304]

The second reason relates to the role that "future dangerousness" plays in death penalty decisions. Studies of decision-making by capital juries indicate that a major factor in their sentence choice is whether they believe the defendant, if allowed to live, will pose a danger to others.[305] Some states, including the two

---

299. At the common law, the wife who killed her husband was regarded as having committed a crime worse than murder: "[S]he not only breaks through the restraints of humanity and conjugal affection, but throws off all subjection to the authority of her husband. And therefore the law denominates her crime, a species of treason . . . ." Edward Christian, *Notes on the Thirteenth Edition* of WILLIAM BLACKSTONE, COMMENTARIES ON THE LAW OF ENGLAND, 445 (13th ed. 1800).

300. *See* JOHN BELLAMY, CRIME AND PUBLIC ORDER IN ENGLAND IN THE LATER MIDDLE AGES 54 (1973) ("[Homicide by stealth] was heinous, not because of any evil preparations, but because it caught a man off his guard.").

301. *See supra* notes 145–173 and accompanying text.

302. Shapiro, *supra* note 4, at 456. This theory has been suggested as the reason for the low rates of women tried, convicted, and sentenced for crimes in general. *See* Herzog & Oreg, *supra* note 145, at 47.

303. Carroll, *supra* note 10, at 1418.

304. Herzog & Oreg, *supra* note 145, at 48–49.

305. John H. Blume et al., *Future Dangerousness in Capital Cases: Always "At Issue,"* 86 CORNELL L. REV. 397, 398 (2001).

with the highest execution rates—Texas and Virginia—expressly make future dangerousness an aggravating factor. However, the Supreme Court has assumed that juries consider the issue even in states, like California, that do not identify it as an issue for the jury.[306] Studies of capital juries by the Capital Jury Project have confirmed that assumption. Even in cases where the state does not place the future dangerousness of the defendant at issue, jurors still consider future dangerousness in making their sentencing decisions.[307] Jurors not only consider the issue, but place unwarranted weight on it, because they "grossly underestimate how long capital murderers not sentenced to death stay in prison."[308]

In considering future dangerousness, jurors seem primarily to consider whether the defendant could be a danger to them personally, rather than the likelihood that the defendant would pose harm to someone else.[309] One consequence is that jurors tend to identify with victims who were killed by strangers, rather than by acquaintances,[310] and with victims who were themselves "innocent," rather than those engaged in risky or illegal behavior.[311] Women defendants are likely to be physically smaller and weaker than most men, and their appearance, coupled with cultural assumptions about women's capacity for violence, means that even women who have committed capital murder will be perceived as less dangerous to the jurors personally than male defendants committing similar crimes.

B. Gender of the Victim

While past studies have examined gender-of-defendant disparities, gender-of-victim disparities have only been noted in passing in studies focused on other issues.[312] However, the gender-of-victim disparities found in the present study are striking. Women were the victims in 21.9% of the single-victim capital cases. In those cases, the death-sentence rate was 10.9%, more than seven times the rate when men were the victims (1.5%). The earlier California studies also reflect significant gender-of-victim disparities, although not of the same order as the present study. In the Appellate Study, the comparable figures were 14.0% for female victim cases and 5.7% for male victim cases. In the Alameda Study, the figures were 18.4% for female victim cases and 5.7% for male victim cases.[313]

---

306. *See* California v. Ramos, 463 U.S. 992, 1008 (1983); *see generally* Blume, et al., *supra* note 305.
307. *See generally* Blume, et al., *supra* note 305.
308. William J. Bowers & Benjamin D. Steiner, *Death by Default: An Empirical Demonstration of False and Forced Choices in Capital Sentencing*, 77 TEX. L. REV. 605, 648 (1999).
309. Scott E. Sundby, *The Capital Jury and Empathy: The Problem of Worthy and Unworthy Victims*, 88 CORNELL L. REV. 343, 364–65 (2003).
310. *Id.* at 359.
311. *Id.* at 364.
312. *See supra* note 164, and accompanying text.
313. As to what might explain the apparent increase in the gender-of-victim disparity over time, two factors should be noted: (1) the percentage of first degree murder convictions based on

This gender-of-victim disparity is produced in part, but only in part, by the high death-sentence rate for rape-murders (where all the victims were women) and the low death-sentence rate for gang murders (where the victims were disproportionately men). When rape-murders are excluded from consideration, the death-sentence rate in the current study for female victim cases is 4.9% compared to 1.5% in male victim cases. The disparity also persists in the earlier California studies when rape-murders are excluded. In the Appellate Study, the death-sentence rate for female victim cases was 10.3%, as against the 5.7% for male victim cases. In the Alameda Study, the comparable figures were 17.5% and 5.7%, respectively. Excluding the gang murder cases along with the rape-murder cases further reduces the gender-of-victim disparity in the current study, but the disparity remains substantial. Excluding both rape-murder and gang murder cases, a death sentence was imposed in 5.6% of the female victim cases and only 2.1% of the male victim cases.[314] If all three gendered crimes identified earlier are excluded, the respective death-sentence rates are: 7.9% in female victim cases and 2.0% in male victim cases. These figures are set out in the following chart:

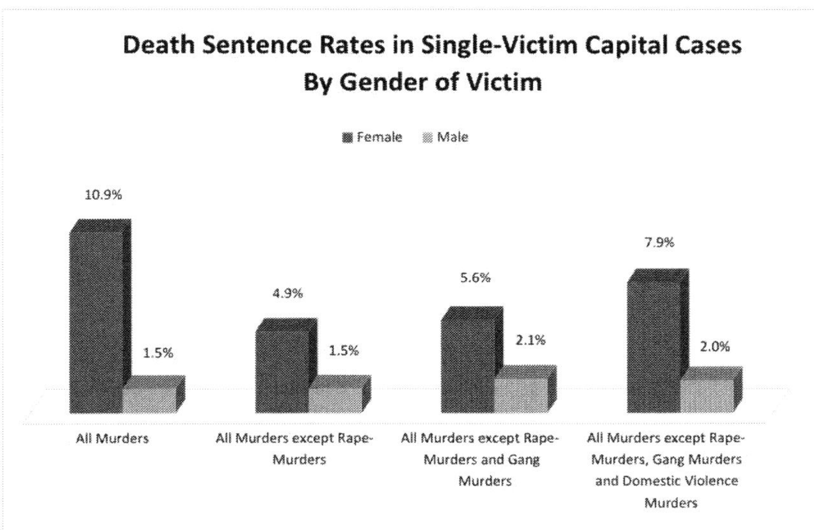

That prosecutors and jurors found the murder of a woman by someone other than an intimate partner so much more aggravated than the murder of a

---

gang killings has increased significantly and men are disproportionately the victims in gang killings, where the death penalty is rarely imposed; and (2) there has been a substantial decline in the absolute number, and the percentage, of capital case defendants sentenced to death, which may exaggerate disparities as use of the death penalty becomes more narrowly focused on particular kinds of murders, such as rape-murder.

314. There is no comparable data from the earlier California studies on gang murders.

man or a woman in the course of domestic violence is consistent with chivalric norms, which allowed knights to kill other men and gave them plenary power over women in their household but held that killing any other woman was dishonorable because she was defenseless. In an age when killings were committed by armored knights engaged in hand-to-hand combat, women were especially vulnerable and in need of protection. Whether they remain relatively more vulnerable today, when a substantial majority of murders are committed with firearms,[315] is unclear. Nonetheless, studies of capital juries' decision-making confirm that jurors are still influenced by such views. Although the jurors interviewed by the Capital Jury Project claimed that the victim's gender was irrelevant to their decisions,[316] in actual cases, jurors were more likely to return a sentence of death if the victim was female.[317] The researchers found that the degree to which the victim was perceived to be innocent (not engaged in "risky behavior")[318] or helpless played a significant role in the jurors' decisions.[319] Presumably the jurors concluded that female victims—except victims of domestic violence—were more innocent or more vulnerable than male victims. These factors help explain why California, consistent with chivalric norms, punishes male-on-male violence or male-on-female violence within the home (which may be seen as the male's prerogative or for which the female victim may be seen as partly to blame) less severely than stranger (usually male) violence toward a supposedly innocent and helpless female.

* * *

The data reveals disparities in death sentencing by both the gender of the defendant and the gender of the victim, with the gender of the victim having an even greater impact on penalty outcomes than the gender of the defendant.[320] As

---

315. See U.S. DEPT. OF JUSTICE, MURDER VICTIMS BY WEAPON, 2005–2009 (2010), *available at* http://www2.fbi.gov/ucr/cius2009/offenses/expanded_information/data/shrtable_08.html.

316. Stephen P. Garvey, *Aggravation and Mitigation in Capital Cases: What Do Jurors Think?*, 98 COLUM. L. REV. 1538, 1556 (1998); Sundby, *supra* note 309, at 347 (finding that only 5% of jurors said they would be much more likely to vote for death if the victim were female). At least some jurors, however, recognized that they found the murder of women to be more troubling than the murder of men. One female juror described her process in deciding how bad the case she sat on was this way: "I thought about a scale—the cliche of thinking about Manson, but that kind of crime, that kind of mass murder, serial murder involving children or women as the worst. I don't know why that seems to me—children in particular and, unfairly, women before men." Sundby, *supra* note 309, at 368.

317. Sundby, *supra* note 309, at 357–58.

318. *Id.* at 364.

319. *Id.* at 352.

320. This pattern replicates the pattern consistently found in studies of race and the death penalty, from the seminal study of the Georgia death penalty by Professor Baldus and others (the basis for the constitutional challenge in *McCleskey v. Kemp*, 481 U.S. 279 (1987)) to the recent eight-state study by the American Bar Association which found that "Every state studied appears to have significant racial disparities in its capital system, particularly those associated with the race of the victim." AM. BAR ASS'N, STATE DEATH PENALTY ASSESSMENTS: KEY FINDINGS 5 (2007), *available at* http://www.abanet.org/moratorium/assessmentproject/keyfindings.doc. That both the race of the victim and the gender of the victim seem to have a substantial effect on death sentencing raises the troubling possibility that the victim's identity may matter as much or more to

noted, these disparities cannot be explained away by the nature of the murders. Treating women as less culpable and less to be feared when they murder and weaker and more in need of society's protection when they are victims is a clear expression of chivalric values.

CONCLUSION

Forty years ago, in his concurring opinion in *Furman*, Justice Marshall warned that giving juries "untrammeled discretion" in capital cases was "an invitation to open discrimination."[321] His concern was not only about racial discrimination but also about gender discrimination: "There is . . . overwhelming evidence that the death penalty is employed against men and not women. . . . It is difficult to understand why women have received such favored treatment since the purposes allegedly served by capital punishment seemingly are equally applicable to both sexes."[322] Justice Marshall's concern about gender discrimination has not found voice in later cases. In fact, in *McCleskey v. Kemp*, Justice Powell, writing for the majority, rejected defendant McCleskey's claim that a complex statistical study proved a substantial risk of racial bias in capital sentencing.[323] The Justice wrote that "the claim that his sentence rests on the irrelevant factor of race easily could be extended to apply to claims based on unexplained discrepancies that correlate to membership in other minority groups, and even to gender."[324] Justice Powell thus made clear his view that considering gender disparities in death penalty sentencing was an extreme to which the Court would not go. The Court has never since mentioned the issue. The lower courts have been similarly dismissive of claims of gender disparities in death sentencing, finding that such claims are foreclosed by *McCleskey*.[325]

Recently, and apparently for the first time, the California Supreme Court addressed a "chivalry" challenge to a defendant's death sentence. In *People v. Carasi*, the male defendant, Carasi, and his girlfriend, Lee, were charged with the double murder of Carasi's mother and his former girlfriend.[326] The prosecution sought the death penalty against both defendants.[327] The prosecution's evidence was that the defendants had plotted the murders, lured the women victims to a parking garage, and then stabbed the victims to death.[328] Both defendants moved for severance on several occasions, and one of Carasi's arguments was that a joint trial with a female co-defendant would inevitably put him at a disadvantage at the penalty phase because of "misplaced chivalry" by

---

prosecutors and juries than the nature of the crime or the character of the defendant.

321. Furman v. Georgia, 408 U.S. 238, 365 (1972) (Marshall, J., concurring).

322. *Id.*

323. 481 U.S. 279.

324. *Id.* at 315–17.

325. *See, e.g.*, Harris v. Pulley, 885 F.2d 1354 (9th Cir. 1988).

326. 190 P.3d 616, 622 (Cal. 2008).

327. *Id.*

328. *Id.* at 622–23.

the jury.[329] As the United States Supreme Court has recognized, the issue of relative culpability can be a "critical issue" in the penalty phase of a death penalty case.[330] Nevertheless, the motions were denied, both defendants were convicted of first degree murder, and the special circumstances were found true.[331] At the joint penalty phase, Carasi was sentenced to death.[332] The jury was unable to agree on Lee's sentence, and she subsequently received life without possibility of parole.[333] On appeal, the California Supreme Court dismissed Carasi's "chivalry" challenge out of hand.[334] The court found no reason to believe that chivalry might have affected the result because Carasi had offered "only generalized assumptions about cultural stereotypes and gender biases in criminal cases" to justify his claim.[335] The Court held that there was evidence in the record that could have justified the different outcomes and noted that the jury was instructed to consider each defendant individually, "based solely on the evidence applicable to that defendant."[336]

Two theories, both reminiscent of Justice Powell's opinion for the majority in *McCleskey*, may explain the courts' indifference to the possible influence of chivalric norms, in general, and gender, in particular, on death sentencing. First, the courts may view the documented disparities—such as treating the murder of a woman as especially heinous (except when she is the victim of domestic violence)—as natural or, in Justice Powell's words, "inevitable."[337] Certainly, the Justice's dismissive reference to possible claims based on gender suggests as much. Second, the courts' concern may be that an attack on chivalry in the death penalty may be, in effect, an attack on the death penalty itself.[338] From its roots in the lynching culture[339]—the "peculiar chivalry"[340]—to the present emphasis on retribution and "honoring the victim" as the justifications for its use,[341] the

329. *Id.* at 639, 649.

330. Green v. Georgia, 442 U.S. 95, 97 (1978).

331. 190 P.3d at 639, 622.

332. *Id.* at 622.

333. *Id.* at 622 n.2.

334. *Id.* at 649.

335. *Id.*

336. *Id.* at 649–50 (quoting CAL. JURY INSTRUCTIONS 8.84 (2005)). It is not clear whether the court rejected the defendant's claim because it found that the mere fact of gender-of-defendant disparities in the application of the death penalty failed to establish that there was a risk of gender bias in sentencing or because proving a *risk* of gender bias was insufficient if the defendant could not prove gender bias in his case.

337. McCleskey v. Kemp, 481 U.S. 279, 312 (1987).

338. Justice Powell voiced this concern about McCleskey's challenge: "Given . . . safeguards already inherent in the imposition and review of capital sentences, the dissent's call for greater rationality is no less than a claim that a capital punishment system cannot be administered in accord with the Constitution." *Id.* at 313 n.37.

339. *See supra*, notes 128–139 and accompanying text.

340. JAMES W. MARQUART, SHELDON EKLAND-OLSON & JONATHAN R. SORENSEN, THE ROPE, THE CHAIR, AND THE NEEDLE: CAPITAL PUNISHMENT IN TEXAS, 1923–1990, at 38–65 (1994) (chapter discussing the history of rape, race, and "peculiar chivalry" in the United States).

341. *See* Sister Helen Prejean, *Our Need to Journey With Clergy and Laity who are Ambivalent*

death penalty itself seems to have an intimate relationship with chivalric norms.

In the forty years since *Furman*, the attacks on chivalry in the areas of constitutional law and the general administration of criminal justice[342] have been successful in bringing about significant changes in the law. However, the empirical evidence demonstrating a tolerance for honor killings (as reflected in the negligible use of the death penalty in gang murders), a grossly disproportionate use of the death penalty for rape-murderers coupled with its scant use for domestic violence murderers, and the substantial disparities in death sentencing based on the genders of defendants and victims strongly suggests that little has changed with regard to the administration of the death penalty. The promise of *Furman* and succeeding cases was that the modern death penalty would be administered in a rational, non-arbitrary manner[343]—that capital punishment would "be imposed fairly, and with reasonable consistency, or not at all."[344] The promise of *J.E.B.* was that the law would not be administered on the basis of "invidious, archaic, and overbroad" gender stereotypes.[345] Despite these promises, when prosecutors and jurors are called upon to make a life or death decision unconstrained by legal standards, chivalry appears to be alive and well.

About Capital Punishment, and Then to Act Together for its Abolition, 4 RUTGERS J. OF LAW & RELIGION 31, 35 (2002) (noting that victims' families seek and judges impose the death penalty to honor victims). Recently, California Supreme Court Justice Moreno asserted in a concurring opinion that the purpose of a penalty phase "is not to honor the victim but to decide whether the defendant should receive a death sentence," but no other justice joined him in that position. People v. Verdugo, 236 P.3d 1035, 1073–74 (Cal. 2010) (Moreno, J., concurring); *see also* People v. Kelly, 171 P.3d 548, 576 (Cal. 2007) (Moreno, J., concurring and dissenting) (criticizing the victim impact evidence on the ground that "the punishment phase of a criminal trial is not a memorial service for the victim") (quoting Salazar v. State, 90 S.W.3d 330, 335–36 (Tex. Crim. App. 2002)).

342. *See supra* Parts I.A, I.B.

343. *See* Jurek v. Texas, 428 U.S. 262, 276 (1976); Kansas v. Marsh, 548 U.S. 163, 203 (Souter, J., dissenting).

344. Eddings v. Oklahoma, 455 U.S. 104, 112 (1982).

345. J.E.B. v. Alabama *ex rel.* T.B., 511 U.S. 127, 130 (1994). To say that a death penalty scheme administered on the basis of gender stereotypes violates the promise of *J.E.B.* is not to say that a defendant would succeed with an Equal Protection challenge to the scheme. The defendant making such a challenge would have the same problem Warren McCleskey had in *McCleskey v. Kemp*, 481 U.S. 279 (1987)—the difficulty of proving that either the prosecutor or the jurors in his or her case was acting with discriminatory intent.

[19]

Zina (Adultery) Under Islamic Law in Nigeria: The Gender Issues in Amina Lawal's Case

Aminu Adamu Bello*

Introduction

Several Women non-governmental organizations were involved in the defence of Amina Lawal in her *Zina* (adultery) trial. After her acquittal, it appeared that there was unanimity in the conclusion that women and women organizations have acquired significant knowledge of Islam and, supposedly, Islamic law, to marshal appreciable arsenal in the defence of women living under *Shari'a* or Islamic law. This is interesting, not just for the fact that there is a supposition that hitherto knowledge of *Shari'a* or Islamic law was the privileged domain of men alone, but that there existed the perception that aspects of *Shari'a* or Islamic law were biased and prejudiced against women. It would seem several women organizations believe that *Shari's* is anti women because the laws were made by men.

The amount of literature now available advancing this position is staggering, with most of them coming from established local and international NGOs. As civil society organizations, the NGOs have added their weight to the discussion on the perceived *Shari'a* gender-bias against women and are championing a crusade to ensure that women are given adequate protection under the new *Shari'a* criminal justice system.

The involvement of the NGOs in highlighting the gender sensitive elements in the *Shari'a* (subsequently, Islamic law)[1] in Nigeria only serve to confirm their role as a part of society that has a life of its own, which is distinct from the state and fairly autonomous from it,[2] thus enabling them to influence and affect public attitudes towards an issue. It is because of this that any observation emanating from civil society organizations is being taken seriously. On the issue of the adultery cases decided by *Shari'a* courts in Nigeria, civil society organizations have acquired front seats and are generating critical material, including advocating strongly that the legislature should hasten the process of repealing all laws, including religiously-inspired laws that discriminate against women.

---

* Faculty of Law, University of Abuja

[1] In this paper, the term Islamic law will be used to refer to the Katsina State *Shari'a* Penal Code in spite of what it calls itself. This is because this writer believes that the contents of the Code do not represent the totality of *Shari'a* principles but aspects of the Maliki jurisprudence especially since 'the outcome of the enactment and enforcement of [*sharia*] principles by state institutions is always a matter of secular law and not of *Shari'a* as the religious normative system of Islam.' See generally Abdullahi Ahmed An-Na'im, '*Shari'a* in the Secular State: A Paradox of Separation and Conflation' in Peri Bearman, Wolfhart Heinrichs and Bernard G. Weiss eds., *The Law Applied: Contextualizing the Islamic Shari'a*, I.B. Tauris & Co Ltd., London, 2008, p.322

[2] Ibrahim, Jibrin, 'Democracy and Minority Rights in Nigeria: Religion, Shari'a and the 1999 Constitution', Paper for the Conference on "Globalisation, State Capacity and Self-Determination in Muslim Context', organized by the Centre for Global International and Regional Studies, University of California-Santa Cruz, Santa Cruz, 7th to 10th March 2002

Hauwa Ibrahim, a counsel in the defence team of Amina Lawal is one such source of material. It is not only from her defence pleadings (?) that it is apparent that one could conclude that she considered her work as a gender specific assignment,[3] her published reflections after Amina's acquittal also show how much pressure she said she was under while challenging what she has come to see as gender bias in the adjudication of sexual offences under Islamic law.[4]

In line probably with the thinking within some Non-Governmental Organisations, (NGO), Hauwa had come to see her presence in the Amina Lawal case as championing a course other than that of a counsel defending a client. In the material chronicling her supposed travails as a female counsel before an Islamic *Shari'a* court, Hauwa said she had to continuously think of the client as a peasant woman and accordingly psych herself up to defend the woman from a gender-biased criminal justice system[5]. While this may be an inference from some material on the issue,[6] and may not be sufficient grounds to justify any form of generalization, it nonetheless provides sufficient grounds to warrant some reflections on the amount of gender-centric material which the Amina Lawal case generated.

Perhaps it is instructive that one of the references with direct bearing on perceived gender bias in the Amina Lawal's case is the discharge of Amina's accomplice in the alleged crime with nothing other than a chance for him to accuse Amina of impugning his integrity. Given the evidential rules required for conviction in the crime of adultery adopted by Katsina State and encoded in the State *Shari'a* Penal Code, four people must give evidence supporting the prosecution's case or, according to Maliki jurisprudence, the pregnancy of a woman will *prima facie*, and subject to some exceptions, provide the ground for proof and possible conviction. That Amina's accomplice maintained that he never made a confession meant that Amina could have been charged for defaming him (*qadhf*). This position irks women rights activists and has remained a sour point that continues to provide reasons for complaints about the treatment of women by Islamic law. While feminist issues have been alive and active within civil society organizations in Nigeria for quite sometime, the new *Shari'a* Penal Codes have, evidently, produced such heightened public involvement that the

---

[3] Ibrahim, Hauwa and Lyman, Princeton N., 'Reflections on the New Shari'a Law in Nigeria' Africa Policy Studies Program at the Council on Foreign Relations, American University Washington College of Law, 2004

[4] Ibid

[5] Ibid: This position has since been refuted by the lead Counsel in the two celebrated adultery cases in Nigeria to date. See, Yawuri, A.M., 'On Defending Safiyatu Hussaini and Amina Lawal' in Philip Ostien et al, (eds.), *Sharia Implementation in Northern Nigeria: A Sourcebook*, Vol. IV, pp.129-139

[6] Ibid, Also, translation(s) of *Safiya Hussaini v. The State*, in Philip Ostien et al, (eds.), *Shari'a Implementation in Northern Nigeria: A Sourcebook*, Vol. V, pp.32-51: also *Amina Lawal v. The State*, in Philip Ostien et al, (eds.), *Shari'a Implementation in Northern Nigeria: A Sourcebook*, Vol. V, pp.52-107

Nigerian Civil Society organizations are now significantly influencing the direction of the discourse in pursuance of women emancipation.[7]

It may bear clarifying that the provisions of some Nigerian statutes providing for criminal liability in the jurisdiction have not been perceived as biased against women, probably because none has so far been challenged as discriminating.[8] Even so, existing customary laws have been giving women and women organizations concern such that they have continuously fought for changes in the ones perceived as bad laws.

The statues establishing criminal liabilities in Nigeria, the Criminal Code and the Penal Code, did not include the application of customary law in criminal cases. The Nigerian Criminal Code provides that 'no person shall be tried or punished in any court in Nigeria for an offence except under express provisions of the code *or of some Act or Law which is in force in, or forms part of law of Nigeria*[9] (emphasis added). The Penal Code[10] also provides at s.3 (2) that 'after the commencement of this law no person shall be liable to punishment under native law and custom'[11] for which purpose Islamic law had been treated as customary law. Until recently therefore, the Nigerian legal system was not concerned with determination of criminal cases in native or area courts. In the case of *Alkamawa v Bello*,[12] the Supreme Court, per Wali, JSC, held, obiter, that Islamic law is 'a complete system of universal law more certain and permanent and more universal than the English Common Law.'[13] It would seem, probably, that along with the allowances made in the 1999 Constitution, the *Alkamawa* case set the stage for serious consideration of enactment of criminal law statutes that would check perceived vices and immorality. This has enabled some states in Nigeria, including Katsina State where Amina's *zina* ordeal transpired, to 'expanded the application of the *Shari'a* legal system'[14] to include criminal law provisions, thus clearly justifying 'the intimate authority in the people ... to decide

---

[7] Cf. BOABAB, WOCOL etc

[8] This paper will not engage in any arguments relating to some provisions of the Nigerian Criminal Code (s.353 Indecent Assault) and the Penal Code (s.55 allowing wife beating) on whether they are discriminatory against women or not.

[9] Section 4, Criminal Code Act

[10] Applicable in the Northern Nigeria states with predominant muslim populations

[11] The Penal Code Law is the source from which most of the eleven states which have established Sharia legal system deviated and availed themselves of the provisions of s.6(2) and s.6(5)(k) of the 1999 Constitution. Section 6(2) states: 'The Judicial powers of a state shall be vested in the courts to which this section relates, being courts established, subject as provided by this Constitution, for a State' while the courts to which this section apply include at section 6(5) (k) 'such other courts as may be authorized by law to exercise jurisdiction at first instance or on appeal on matters with respect to which a House of Assembly may make laws. Somehow, Ruud Peters takes exception to a situation in Nigeria where, in exercise of constitutional powers, states create courts and rules of evidence. He observes that Evidence is a federal matter and since Sharia has implicit laws as to evidence, there is a conflict with the constitution, see *Islamic Criminal Law in Nigeria,*

[12] (1998) 8 NWLR (Pt. 56.561)

[13] Ibid, 173

[14] Ladan, M.T. *Introduction to Jurisprudence, Classical and Islamic*, Malthouse Press Limited, 2006, p.285

whether a particular mode of punishment is acceptable within their respective borders.'[15]

In our present discussion, we will not be seeking justification for the penalty of *zina* outside the particular statute, (the Katsina State *Shari'a* Penal Code Law) because, whatever is said for or against the codification of the *hudood* in Katsina State, it is today the law that governs criminal adjudication in the state in respect of all those who profess the Islamic faith and every other person who may willingly submit to the jurisdiction of the *Shari'a* Courts in the state. It is only within the *Shari'a* Penal Code that prosecution and defence must marshal ammunition for their respective positions. It will therefore serve no purpose to venture into seeking justification for the enforcement of *hudood* as positive law in Katsina State. What this paper intends to do is look at the law and respond to the claim that the *hudood* provisions in the Katsina State *Shari'a* Penal Code have singled out women for oppression. This is therefore a response to suggestions that Islamic law oppresses women.

This paper will look at the gender issues which commentaries on the trial of the Amina Lawal's adultery case have highlighted. It will discuss facts that were disclosed in the charge against Amina Lawal before the *Shari'a* Court. This will include what the Katsina *Shari'a* Penal Code Law describes constitutes the offence of adultery and if this is capable of interpretation as discriminatory. It will also review the process of litigation and level of access to justice that manifested throughout the trial of Amina Lawal while also trying to isolate areas that could lend themselves to interpretation as gender biased against women. It will also argue that the perceived discrimination of women by Islamic law does not exist within the parameters of Islamic criminal law but essentially, and for arguably good reasons, resides within the province of Islamic personal (civil) law, especially the Islamic law of inheritance. To import personal law argument into criminal law would appear to be a non-issue in as much as Islamic criminal law has made categorical and specific provisions to deal with identified crimes, criminal activity and criminals.

A. The Case against Amina Lawal[16]

Amina Lawal was arrested, along with an accomplice, one Yahayya Mohammed, in Kurami, a village in Katsina State in Northern Nigeria.[17] They were both arraigned before the *Shari'a* Court Bakori, for the crime of adultery. The case was first heard on the 15th of January 2002. Police Prosecutor, Corporal Idris Adamu of the Nigeria Police Command, on behalf of the Katsina State Commissioner of Police, prosecuted.

---

[15] Zydney Mannheimer, Michael J., *When the Federal Death Penalty is "Cruel and Unusual"*, University of Cincinnati Law Review, Vol. 74, (2006) 821

[16] *Amina Lawal v. The State,* KTS/SCA/FT/86/2002, supra note 6

[17] Ojeih, Francis E. 'AMINA LAWAL – Nigerian Constitution and Sharia legal system: A battle for Supremacy?', in M.M. Gidado, C.U. Anyanwu and A.O. Adekunle (eds.), *CONSTITUTIONAL ESSAYS* [Nigeria Beyond 1999: Stabilizing the Polity through Constitutional Re-engineering] *In Honour of Bola Ige*, 2004, Chenglo Limited, Enugu, pp.305-314

Amina Lawal and Yahayya Mohammed were charged jointly, it would seem, with continuously committing the offence of *zina* from the time their courtship began, that is about eleven months ago, and continuing up until quite recently[18] as a result of which the 1st accused, Amina Lawal, became pregnant and eventually gave birth to a baby girl.

Prosecution had led evidence to prove that Amina Lawal was a Muslim woman who was previously married but now divorced. That at the time of arrest, she had confessed to having had illegal sexual intercourse with a man, identified as one Yahayya, *which could have resulted in her pregnancy*. On the evidence of the birth of her baby, Amina Lawal was charged with the offence of adultery, contrary to the provision of the Katsina State *Shari'a* Penal Code Law[19] which defined the crime of adultery (*zina)*, as follows:

> Whoever, being a man or a woman fully responsible, has sexual intercourse through the genital of a person over whom he has no sexual rights and in circumstances in which no doubt exists as to the illegality of the act, is guilty of the offence of zina.[20]

During the trial, Amina reportedly confessed to committing adultery with her accomplice, Yahayya. The accomplice said he did not commit adultery with her. The court discharged and acquitted Yahayya and proceeded to convict Amina upon the circumstantial evidence of her pregnancy and the birth of a child outside legal marriage.

There is a prevailing misunderstanding that an unmarried woman, including divorced women should not be charged with adultery in the first place.[21] This presumption appears to be predicated on the feeling that since sexual activity is a perfectly healthy and normal human activity, there is no rational basis for criminalising the act, especially where the alleged criminal has already acquired a taste for the act. This taste, the argument would continue, having been imbibed as it were, within legal marital relationship and that just because the marriage has broken down, the estranged spouse(s) should not be burdened by any feeling of guilt. This argument is inconsistent with Islamic law.

All schools of Islamic jurisprudence qualify extra-marital sexual relations resulting in intercourse as either fornication or *zina*. Though both are implied in the *Qur'anic* proscription,[22] hadith law establishes a distinction between illegal sexual activities of a married person from that of an unmarried person. It is in the evidential rules for

---

[18] The exact wordings in the translation of the Record of Proceedings in Ostien, et al, (eds.), Op. Cit., note 6

[19] Katsina State Sharia Penal Code Law No. 2 of 2001

[20] Ibid, Section 124

[21] Ojeih, F. E. Op. Cit., note 17, p.313

[22] *Qur'an* 17:32

proof of the offence and whether the penalty upon conviction are appropriate, just and fair that scholars of the various Schools of Islamic law and even scholars within the same School of Islamic law have continued to engage. For this paper, all references to Islamic law will maintain the position of the Maliki Islamic law jurisprudence.

Three issues are pertinent for our discussion of gender bias in the Amina Lawal case. One, the insistence and predication of prosecution on the evidence of pregnancy as proof of *zina*; two, the absence of an accomplice in a charge of *zina* due to an initial discharge of the co-accused, and three, the presumption that women are denied access to justice under Islamic law.

B. Proof of adultery and the inadmissibility of consensual sex as a defence

The three general means of proof of *zina* are confession, evidence of four unimpeachable (male) eye witnesses and manifestation of pregnancy in the unmarried woman. For proof by confession to lead to conviction and the application of the *hadd* punishment, the person confessing must be an adult and in full and complete mental health. In this situation, one confession (*Iqrar*) is often sufficient to convict[23] but the confessor may be persuaded to retract such confession in any way whatsoever (*mutlaqan*) or even run away during implementation of the *hadd* punishment.[24] Retraction of the confession is acceptable on its own and will lead to acquittal, but some Maliki scholars and jurists have maintained that for the retraction to avail a defendant, it must be accompanied with some defensive plea of what amounts to some doubt, justification or defence (*shubhah).*[25] Malik is reported to have said:

> As for him who confesses committing fornication and then says, I didn't do so, and said it was for so and so reasons, that it'll be accepted from him and he won't be punished because this punishment is for Allah, it can't be done without either clear proof on whosoever does so or by his confession. If he confesses, he'd be punished.[26]

Four unimpeachable male witnesses that saw the *res–in–res* are required for proof of *zina* by evidence.[27] Evidence may be taken jointly or severally on condition that the time spent in between the testimonies is short.[28] This four witness rule is claimed to

[23] Sanusi, S. L., 'The Hudood Punishment in Northern Nigeria: A Muslim Criticism', available at www.uga.edu/islam/sanusi.htm p.6, citing Ibn Qudamah, *Al-Mughmi*, Vol. 10, esp. pp.191 ff; Al-Jazairi, *Kitabul fiqh ala 'l-Madhahib al-Arba'*, Vol 5 75, 94 and passim; M. Abu Hassaan, *Ahkam al-Jareemah wa 'l-Uqoobah fi 'l-Shariah al-Islamiyyah* 255-257; Ibn Hazm, *Al-Muhalla*, Vol II, 155-157

[24] Ibid

[25] Uthman, M.B., 'Protecting the Rights of Accused Persons through the Proper Implementation of the Shari'a Procedural Guarantees in Northern Nigeria', in Joy Ngozi Ezeilo, Muhammed Tawfiq Ladan, Abiola Afolabi-Akiyode (eds.) *Shari'a Implementation in Nigeria Issues & Challenges on Women's Rights And Access to Justice,* Women's Aid Collective (WACOL), 2003, p.186

[26] *Al-Muwatta' (The Approved)*, supra note 100, hadith no. (1563) 14

[27] Uthman, M.B., Op. Cit., note 25, p.186

[28] Ibid

have been imposed through divine revelation to require the strongest possible direct evidence before any allegations might be made against a woman's chastity.[29]

The manifestation of pregnancy in an unmarried woman resident in the jurisdiction constitutes sufficient ground to accuse a woman of *zina.* Her silence about her state of pregnancy until it is discovered supports the establishment of a *prima-facie* case against her.[30] In the case of a woman who is divorced or whose husband has died and is found to be pregnant or has a child without first remarrying, Maliki law holds that such pregnancy or child belongs to the former or dead husband. The former husband may however repudiate the pregnancy or child through *Li'an.*[31] This Maliki position is espoused as follows:

> And if she [the widow or divorced woman] gives birth to a child after (the waiting period) before expiry of the maximum gestation for pregnancy it is attached to the (former/dead) husband unless the husband (if alive) rejects it with the oath of *Li'an.*[32]

From the above, it is obvious that where a divorcee or a widow has a child within the maximum gestation the child belongs automatically to the previous husband unless he is willing to go through the process of *Li'an.*[33] The woman will avert the *hadd* of *zina* if she makes a counter oath of *Li'an.*[34]

It will be a defence to a charge of *zina* however if the woman is able to prove that the pregnancy was not due to consensual sex outside marriage. One way to do this is to claim that she was raped. According to Imam Malik:

> The established practice with us concerning the woman that is found to be pregnant and without husband, who claims that 'I was raped' or 'I got married' is that these defences will not be admissible and the *hadd* penalty will be applied upon her except she can advance evidence to support her claim of marriage or rape such as her turning up bleeding if she is a virgin, or screaming until she is found defiled, or similar corroborative evidence that establishes her claim of her defilement.[35]

---

[29] Shah, Nik Noriani Nik Badli, 'Man Made Codifications of Hudud Law', Sisters in Islam, Kaula Lumpur, 2002, online at http://www.sistersinislam

[30] Ibid, citing al-Tasuliy, (n.d.) *al-Bahjah Fi Sharh al Tuhufah*, A.A al-sa'ud & Uthman al-Tayyib, Kano, Vol. II, p.357

[31] Sanusi, L.S., Op. Cit., note 23

[32] Ibid, citing Muhammad Ulaysh, *Minah al-Jaleel, Sharh 'ala Mukhtasar Sayid Khaleel*, 4:307

[33] *Li'an* is a process in which a husband takes an oath before a court four (4) times, each time swearing by Allah that his wife is guilty of *zina.* He completes the oath by saying: "Allah's curse be upon me if I am a liar in my accusation of *zina* against my wife" (he is expected to name her).

[34] The woman also swears four times with her own conclusion like this: "Allah's wrath be upon me if he is truthful in his accusation of *zina* against me."

[35] Uthman, M. B., Op. Cit., note 25, p. 187, citing Abdul-Baqi, M.F. (n.d.) *al-Muwatta li Imamil A'immati Malik bin Anas (R.A)*, Maktabah Anas bin Malik p. 647

Thus, Malik has acknowledged the possibility that pregnancy can result from an unwilling sexual act and has established a number of safeguards that aim to assure that no innocent party is convicted unjustly, the principal safeguard of which is physical evidence as undeniable proof of rape.[36] Other safeguards are the timeframe within which the matter is reported.[37] Also, the character of the alleged rapist,[38] and that of the woman making the allegation become points at issue.[39] In the event, for instance, that the man alleged to have committed the rape is seen by witnesses making away with the woman until she is found defiled, this is a different case altogether[40] and a presumption is established to support the woman's plea of rape.

The issue of extra-marital consensual sex is completely non-existent in Islam so that any argument that extra-marital sex could be consensual will not be a defence in a charge of *zina*. The *Qur'anic* injunction which says: 'Nor come nigh to adultery: For it is a shameful (deed) And an evil, opening the road (To other evils)'[41] makes a simple and categorical prohibition

Under the Nigerian Criminal Code, adultery is not seen as a crime[42] but can be pleaded in support of a petition for divorce[43] where the court is compelled to take notice if there is any form of condonation of adultery by the spouse pleading it as a ground,[44] which condonation may vitiate and defeat the petition, according to the discretion of the court.[45] It would appear that this attitude to adultery has been formed based on the concept of consensual sex. This concept maintains that the legitimacy of sex flows from mutual consent, not from any formal status. It rejects the traditional definition of lawful sex, which presupposes a marital bond.[46] The principle dismantles the moral boundary between marital and premarital sex, between marriage and cohabitation.[47] Under Islamic law, it is only the genital sex within a marital relationship that is legitimate and not subject to any form of sanction.

---

[36] Al-Zurqaani, Hashiyat *Al-Zurqani Ala Muwatta' Al Imam Malik*, Beirut, Dar Al-Ma'rifah, 1989, Vol. 4, p.150.

[37] Uthman, M. B., Op. Cit., note 25, p.187, citing Ibn Rushd, *Bidayatul Mujtahid wa Nihayatul Muqatsid*, Vol I, pp.353-354

[38] Ibid, p.188, citing Ibn Juzay, *al-Qawanin al-Fiqhiyya*; Tasuliy, *Bahjah*, Vol II, p.356

[39] Ibid, citing Al-Tasuliy, *Bahjah*, Vol II, p.356

[40] Ibid, p.189

[41] *Qur'an* 17:32, Abdullah Yusuf Ali (trans.), Amana Corp., 1983

[42] *Aoko v Fagbemi & other*, (1961) 1 N.L.R. p400, (the accused was charged, tried and convicted for adultery. On appeal, his conviction was quashed because the offence of adultery is not defined and penalized under the Nigeria Criminal Code Act).

[43] S. 28(a), Matrimonial Causes Act 1970

[44] *Tinubu v Tinubu* [1959] WNLR 316; *Craig v Craig* (1962) 16 NLR 103

[45] *Onwudiwe v Onwudiwe* [1957] WRNLR 98, where the court refused to exercise its discretion because of failure to file discretionary statements

[46] Khan, Ali, 'Hermeneutics of Sexual Order', *Santa Clara Law Review*, Vol.31, 1990, p.84 also available online at http://ssrn.com/abstract=979394 (Khan advances the argument that 'marriage dwells upon an historically ingrained precept that genital sex is legitimate within a socially contracted relationship. Through the ritual of marriage, genital sex acquires a new meaning: it becomes marital sex: a new reality, a new symbol, which represents a bond, a commitment, a family'.)

[47] Ibid

C. Penalty for Adultery under Maliki Law/Katsina Shari'a Penal Code Law

It has already been observed that to assume simply that because of the nomenclature or title *Shari'a* or *Shari'a* Penal Law, the content of such enactment represents *Shari'a* is actually deceptive. This is because codification realistically obviates the principles of *Shari'a* as the religious normative system of Islam. For this same reason, this paper has maintained all references to the law as Islamic law and not *Shari'a*. So, it is safe, for the present purpose, to continue on the understanding that the provisions in the Katsina State *Shari'a* Penal Code Law represent only an aspect of *Shari'a* as espoused by a particular jurisprudential school, in this case, the Maliki Islamic Law Jurisprudence. This singular distinction would validly put paid to and indeed negate any claim to the validity of making different choices within the diversity of the variously accepted interpretations of the *shari'a*, unless indeed the varying interpretations are those obtainable within the Maliki *madhab*.

In Nigeria, it is only the interpretation of Islamic law per Maliki jurisprudence that is tenable at law which would seem to agree with the assertion that 'what is assumed to be Muslim in one community may be unknown or even be considered un-Islamic, in other Muslim communities,'[48] a position that will also effectively remove the discussion of the judicial processes employed in the Nigerian *Shari'a* Courts from any kind of comparison with any other outside the Katsina/Nigerian jurisdiction, except where the Maliki Law also exists and forms the basis of that other jurisdiction's legal framework.

The penalty for *zina* under Maliki Islamic law is not gender biased. The penalty of death by stoning falls on all persons who are either married or divorced, once they are convicted of the crime, irrespective of gender. Unmarried convicts would ordinarily have been charged with the crime of fornication and not adultery.[49] It may help to define the boundaries of adultery and fornication as sexual offences under Maliki Islamic law with the following two authentic Hadith.

The first reports an incident of alleged adultery/fornication during the lifetime of the Prophet (SAW) involving a young unmarried man and a married woman, which incident resulted in the young man being punished with one hundred lashes and exile for one year and the married woman, who confessed to adultery with the unmarried

[48] Umar, M.S., 'Gender Issues in Application of Islamic Law in Nigeria', *Aljami'ah*, Vol 45, No.1, 2007 M/1428 H, p.43, citing Ayesha M. Imam, Mufuliat Fijabi, and Hurera Akilu-Atta, '*Women's Rights in Muslim Laws: A Resources Document*', BOABAB for Women's Human Rights, Lagos, 2005, p. 14

[49] It is not presumed that a clear distinction exists between 'fornication' and 'adultery' in Islamic law. However, it is significant that the point is made that unmarried persons, who have not been previously married , are not given the same punishment for indulging in consensual sexual relations as those who were once married but were found to have committed the offence after the dissolution of their marriage. It is therefore the punishment that differ and apparently, the effect of extra-marital sexual relation on marriage and the protection of progeny that elicits the direct and unequivocal punishment stipulated for persons who are either married, widowed or divorced, convicted of engaging in 'consensual' sexual relations.

young man, being stoned to death.[50] The second ahadith and perhaps the most frequently cited is attributed to Umar Ibn al-Khattab, RAA, who is reported to have said 'stoning is a duty laid down in God's Book for married men and women who commit adultery when proof is established, or if there is pregnancy, or a confession.'[51]

One of Professor Asifa Quraishi's papers asks the questions: 'Who demands the stoning of women for adultery?' In it, she advances the argument that *Shari'a* per se, as the Law of God does not demand the stoning of women for adultery. She distinguishes the sources of Islamic law and concludes that it is indeed the work of the jurisprudents that eventually created the penalty of stoning for the crime of zina under Islamic law.

According to Professor Quraishi, the *Qur'anic* evidentiary rules make it impossible to secure a conviction for the crime of adultery because it was unlikely that 'sex will take place in front of four people who are willing to testify to it, with the risk that maybe one of the other witnesses might chicken out, and then the rest end up being lashed for making an unsubstantiated accusation.'[52] She also points out that 'in the time of the Prophet, they [the people] didn't drag people in and prosecute them for *zina*'[53] especially because there was no feeling and a desire that the 'people's private lives—especially women's—should be closely monitored, and any sexual indiscretion should result in a criminal prosecution for consensual extramarital sex.'[54] It would appear that women activists are concerned that the enactment of Islamic law creates such a monitoring permission that curtails the freedoms enjoyed by women. The suggestion however that the sentences for adultery discriminate against women, because they are more severe than the penalties for men convicted of adultery[55] does not draw from any source of Islamic law since married men and married women convicted of the offence are liable to stoning according to Maliki law.

D. Grounds of Amina's acquittal

The grounds upon which Amina Lawal succeeded at appeal were both substantive and procedural. Islamic law prohibits adultery and includes it in the list of *hadd* offences for which there are specified penalties in the Qur'an.

When the Katsina State *Shari'a* Court of Appeal heard Amina's appeal, it considered several issues including (1) statutory composition of the court that tried Amina at first

[50] SM: 3210, reproduced in Souaiaia, Ahmed E., *Human Rights & Islam: The Divine and the Mundane in Human Rights Law,* iUniverse Inc, (2003) p.61

[51] SM 3201, reproduced in Souaiaia, Ahmed E. note 53 supra, p.60

[52] Quraishi, Asifa, 'Who Demands the Stoning of Women?: A Description of Islamic Law and Constitutionalism' *Berkeley Journal of Middle Eastern & Islamic Law*, Vol. 1, pp.163-177, 2008, also available online at http://www.ssrn.com/abstract=1140204

[53] Ibid

[54] Ibid

[55] Zuhur, Sherifa, 'Gender, Sexuality and the Criminal Laws in the Middle East and North Africa: A Comparative Study', *Women for Women's Human Rights* (WWHR)-New Ways, Inonu Cad. Saadet Apt. No: 37/6 Gumussuyu 4437, Istanbul, Turkey, 2005, p. 22

instance, (2) gestation period for fertilized embryos, (3) circumstances and method of apprehension of alleged offender(s). Eventually, the Katsina State *Shari'a* Court of Appeal discharged and acquitted Amina Lawal on the following grounds:

> (1) That one judge was present during Lawal's initial conviction instead of the three required under Islamic Law. Therefore the court was not properly constituted;
> (2) That under proper interpretation of *Shari'a* law, babies can remain in gestation in a mother's womb for over five years, thereby creating the possibility that her ex-husband could have fathered the child;
> (3) That the policeman who first arrested Amina in 2002 should have been flogged because he did so in violation of Islamic law which requires four witnesses to the crime.

From the foregoing, it would appear that the second reason touched on substantive law. It states that embryos could be in gestation for periods of up to five years with the consequence that a previous husband is liable to accept paternity of a child born as a result of this pregnancy, unless he refutes by swearing the oath of l*i' an*. This was sufficient to acquit Amina Lawal and substantive Maliki Islamic law would have been satisfactorily applied and implemented.[56]

E. The Claim of Gender Discrimination

Islamic law has the means to safeguard justice based on its own principles, procedures,[57] but this has been challenged, it would seem, by the assertion that the *Shari'a* Penal Codes have been heavily stacked against women and poor Muslims while allowing influential Muslim elites to escape prosecution of corruption and the stern punishment of *hudood*.[58] What this would seem to imply is that the various *hudood* cases that have been decided were resolved in consideration of reasons that do not include adherence to the law and due process. It is probably to emphasis this feeling that it has been claimed that:

> The success of the [Amina Lawal] appeal was partly the result of campaigns by activist constituencies of human rights, women's rights, democracy promotion, local and international non-governmental organisations, the European Union, embassies of Western countries in Nigeria and local and international media commentators.[59]

It is further claimed that the Amina Lawal appeal succeeded because there was pressure on the *Qadis* of the Katsina State *Shari'a* Court of Appeal to find all possible ways to discharge and acquit thereby de-escalating the tension that has been building

[56] Sanusi, L. S., Op. Cit., note 23
[57] Von Struensee, Vanessa M.G., *The Punishment of Death by Stoning for Offence of Zina (Adultery); Sharia in Nigeria and its Impact on Muslim Women*, abstract at http://papers.ssrn.com/so13/papers.cfm?abstract_id=570148, accessed 13th January, 2008
[58] Umar, M. S., Op. Cit., note 48, p. 51
[59] Ibid, pp.39-40

both locally and internationally and at the same time averting the unwanted scrutiny from hostile quarters.[60] While activists would feel comfortable with these assertions, the same groups would have defeated their claims to improved knowledge of Islamic law and how they collectively pursued the defence of hapless women (including Amina Lawal) charged with the offence of adultery under the *Shari'a* Penal Codes.

Mohammed S. Umar's analysis of gender issues in the application of Islamic law in Nigeria[61] includes an extensive review of the effort of several civil society organisations in the defence of women charged with adultery under Islamic law in Nigeria. However, his conclusion that the involvement of strategic non-governmental organizations like BAOBAB helped to improve 'religious literacy [which] can be [an] effective response to the hegemonic politics of religious revival, which seems to demand subordination of women as a necessary tenet of Islam[62] only inflates claims that indeed Islamic law oppresses women. No where in his paper did he avert his mind to the existence of female Islamic Scholars of repute during and after the time of the Prophet Mohammad (SAW). This line of reasoning does not help at all in furthering the course of education for the uneducated, especially religious education, so that the application of Islamic law can be treated in all its ramifications from the point of knowledge.

In the Amina Lawal case, the issues that could be distilled as likely to have constituted bias against her as a woman may be listed under the following headings:

1. Pregnancy of the alleged offender

It is obvious that pregnancy can only manifest in a woman and Amina Lawal is a woman whose pregnancy was indeed the reason for her arraignment for trial before a *Shari'a* court in Bakori, Katsina State in Nigeria. Ordinarily, the manifestation of pregnancy in a woman today will raise no eyebrows. Indeed, until the enactment of the *Shari'a* Penal Codes in Nigeria, pregnancy out of wedlock was simply a moral issue that was left to the families concerned to tackle. While Islamic law equates morality with the normative religious law, the *Shari'a*, it also established prohibitions against unlawful sex such as fornication, adultery and instituted the conventional institutions of marriage and family as aspects of a moral framework designed to bring order and stability to human sexuality.[63]

During the period in Nigerian history when the Penal Code provision ousted criminal jurisdiction from customary courts,[64] the Islamic law had been treated as customary law. Issues termed as criminal under Islamic law were therefore not taken to court and were left in the realm of morality which the state was unwilling or unable to enforce.

[60] Ibid, p. 51
[61] Ibid
[62] Ibid
[63] Khan, A., Op. Cit., note 46, p.50
[64] Section 3(2), Penal Code Law 1960

In the event that a Muslim man accused his wife of adultery, there was nothing in the laws of Nigeria that could have assisted him other than resorting to divorcing the woman, after swearing to the oath of *li 'an*. The marriage would have been dissolved after the accused woman also swears to the oath of *li 'an*. No prosecution would have ensured for any offence. However, it is presumed that the child born as a result of any pregnancy that might have resulted will not be ascribed to the former husband. This is also the situation when the paternity of the pregnancy of a woman is being challenged by her husband. A pregnancy is therefore *prima facie* evidence that could support a charge of *zina* against a woman, and a woman only. A man cannot get pregnant. He cannot be charged for *zina* on the evidence of a pregnancy, even where the woman claims the man is responsible. Such claim would introduce the issue of consent, showing that the woman knew what she was doing with the man and also that she knew that one of the consequences of the activity was pregnancy. Where the man she accuses denies her claim, she may be charged for *qadhf* even where the accusation is of rape, i.e. absence of consent on the part of the woman.

2. Absence of an Accomplice/Collaborator in the Offence

Amina Lawal's purported accomplice, one Yahayya, was not charged and prosecuted beyond the court of first instance because he said he did not have illegal sexual intercourse with Amina.[65] The way and manner in which Yahayya was discharge and acquittal was frowned at by the Katsina State *Shari'a* Court of Appeal. The Bakori *Shari'a* Court had only asked Yahayya to swear to an oath, supposedly, an oath of suspicion. In its reaction to the oath taking, the Katsina State Court of Appeal said that:

> There is no authority that says that a person accused of *zina* should take an oath in the absence of evidence. The *Shari'a* Court Bakori erred when it administered the oath on Yahayya Mohammed. It is wrong to administer the oath of suspicion in this type of case.[66]

The court also emphasized that cases like the one under consideration are proved by the evidence of four witnesses, confession or pregnancy and that in the absence of any of these, the charge is not proved and the informants or complainants shall receive punishment for qadhf. 'Therefore it was wrong to administer an oath in this case.'[67] The Katsina State *Shari'a* Court of Appeal did not however say it was wrong to have discharged and acquittal Yahayya of the charge of adultery due to lack of evidence to support a charge against him.

The main argument of those who claim that there is gender bias in the treatment of women for the offence of adultery under the applicable Islamic law in Nigeria is that, where pregnancy is used as a basis for the prosecution of the offence, there must in

[65] *Amina Lawal v. Katsina State*, Supra note 6
[66] Ibid p.103
[67] Ibid

fact be the presence of two persons, a male and a female, since the female who eventually becomes pregnant cannot be said to be the single architect of her own pregnancy. This same argument turns on its head when it is further claimed that pregnancy alone cannot be proof of adultery because pregnancy could result from non-consensual sex. Introducing and insisting that an accomplice/collaborator must be charged confirms sexual activity, either consensual or non-consensual. In the event that it is non-consensual, the applicable Islamic law in Nigeria provides for several methods of proof including victim's allegation that she was raped,[68] or that she was deceived into having sex by one claiming to be her husband.[69] Consensual non-marital sex constitutes adultery if sexual partners are married, but not to each other or they were once married, but are now divorced; the same constitutes fornication where sexual partners have never been married.

The absence of an accomplice/collaborator in the offence of *zina* is therefore not an expression or indication of gender bias. To insist that a person who has availed himself of a defence under the law should have been charged in order to sustain the *zina* charge against the accused defeats the purpose of legal presumption of innocence. The accused has several defences, as the outcome of the appeal which discharged her has shown, to prove that her pregnancy was not as a result of consensual sex, out of legal wedlock.[70] That she did not plead non-consensual sex, but was still discharged and acquitted speaks volumes for a legal system that sets out to ensure the delivery of substantive and procedural justice.

3. The question of access to justice

Various claims that women and the poor are at the receiving end of the Islamic justice system because they lack the wherewithal to access justice and that 'the *zina* laws are far more difficult for uneducated and poor women to counter'[71] only reflects the inherent contradictions within all modern legal systems. No modern legal system has perceptible ready-made inbuilt mechanisms that ensure all persons have equal and unfettered access to justice. To claim that such a system really exists will be further from the truth.

In all legal systems, there are established courts and the procedures to be followed to institute and maintain causes. Almost all judicial systems provide for an education process that ensures that practitioners receive some legal training to participate in the system. Today, legal representation is *sine-quo-non* to access to justice. It is presumed that only those who are knowledgeable in the workings of the judiciary and the

---

[68] Al-Zurqaani, Hashiyat *Al-Zurqani Ala Muwatta' Al Imam Malik,* Beirut, Dar Al-Ma'rifah, 1989, Vol. 4, p.150

[69] See especially Uthman, M. B., Op. Cit., note 25, p180

[70] There is a worrisome issue that may arise however, where artificial insemination may indeed make for a successful pregnancy in a woman. It may be sometime yet before it is known how the hadd law would handle such a situation.

[71] Ibid

judicial system can 'speak' the language of the law.[72] The Islamic legal system admits of legal representation and indeed places a burden on the judge to guide litigants where they have no legal advisers.

F. Observations

The prosecution/respondent in the Amina Lawal *zina* case built its case on the *Qur'anic* proscription of illegal extra-marital consensual sex and the codification of the offence in the Katsina State *Shari'a* Penal Code Law. The Qur'an, says: 'Nor come nigh to adultery: For it is a shameful (deed) And an evil, opening the road (To other evils).'[73]

In his commentary on this verse, Abdullah Yusuf Ali maintains that:

> Adultery is not only shameful and inconsistent with any self-respect or respect for others, but it opens the road to many evils. It destroys the basis of the family; it works against the interests of children born or to be born; it may cause murders and feuds and loss of reputation and property, and also loosen permanently the bonds of society. Not only should it be avoided as a sin, but any approach or temptation to it should be avoided.[74]

Abdullah Yusuf Ali sees the act of *zina* as capable of causing:

1. Shame: this may not be readily acceptable in communities where the definition of shame does not include repercussions for acts that are morally wrong essentially because such societies dwell on claims and counter claims as to the validity of morality as a regulator of human behaviour and interactions. In societies where morality is a non-issue, the concept of criminalizing consensual sex is unheard of and frequently vehemently challenged;[75]
2. *Zina* brings about disrespect for self and others because of the intimacy involved in the act of sexual penetration. Many relationships are destroyed where expectations are established that give the impression that a lasting intimate relationship may ensure, and such expectations are dashed once parties have experienced sexual penetration. Unfortunately, prostitution thrives where the urge is simply to satisfy a craving or, for some female participants, to make money from male patrons;[76]
3. *Zina* may lead to other evil vices (moral misdeeds), including acts calculated at hiding the fact that parties are involved in sexual relationship. In this respect, any activity that may appear to shield

[72] See Oba, A., Legal Education
[73] *Qur'an* 17:32, Abdullah Yusuf Ali (trans.), Amana Corp., 1983
[74] Ibid, Footnote 2215, at p.703
[75] Khan, Ali, Op. Cit., note 46
[76] Some anti-*hadd* advocates have even expressed the view that poverty is responsible for some women going into prostitution in order to raise money to look after themselves and in some cases, also look after their children either from a previous marriage or born out of wedlock (as a result of zina or rape).

sexual partners from prying eyes (within a society with clear moral values that emphasize marital sex only), may readily be accepted as legitimate way to hide the zina act;

4. *Zina* destroys the basis of the family: The concept of family is another issue which creates conflicts when consensual sex is discussed. This is because most concepts of the family presume that procreation is the only justifiable reason for engaging in sexual penetration.[77] However, this is contested, including the expressed position that sexual penetration may and could indeed be indulged in for pleasure and nothing more. Those who express this view would insist that the pleasure derived by participants does not have to lead to conception. Also, it is possible to have a family without an intention to procreate, hence sexual penetration within marriage losses its value. Indeed marriage itself is often discountenanced;
5. *Zina* works against the interest of the children especially when consideration of paternity and progeny are introduced. Several countries, including Nigeria have made it illegal to discriminate against a citizen solely on the basis of the circumstances of his birth.[78] This constitutional provision has been interpreted to mean that it is illegal to consider a person illegitimate where such a person was born outside of legal marriage.[79]
6. *Zina* may cause severe disruptions to societal values including loss of reputation and property.[80]

Ibn Kathir's commentary on the same verse is also illuminating. According to the exegete, Allah says, forbidding His servants to commit *zina* or to approach it or to do anything that may lead to it: '(And come not near to unlawful sex. Verily, it is a Fahishah (immoral sin) meaning a major sin, (and an evil way.) meaning, a terrible way to behave.'[81]

He then proceeds to state:

> Imam Ahmad recorded Abu Umamah saying that a young man came to the Prophet and said, "O Messenger of Allah! Give me permission to commit *Zina* (unlawful sex)." The people surrounded him and rebuked him, saying, "Stop! Stop!" But the Prophet said, (Come close).The young man came to him, and he said, (Sit down) so he sat down. The Prophet said, (Would you like it (unlawful sex) for your mother) He said, "No, by Allah, may I be ransomed for you." The Prophet said, (Neither do the people like it for their mothers.) The Prophet said, (Would you like it for your daughter) He said, "No, by Allah, may I be

[77] Khan, Ali, Op. Cit., note 46

[78] Section 42 (2), Constitution of the Federal Republic of Nigeria, 1999

[79] It is probably only in the situation where a husband divorces his wife through *li'an* that the child born of the pregnancy will be deprived of a father's name and would also not inherit from him.

[80] Societies which do not consider consensual sex wrong between unmarried couples, often frown at the same act if it is done by a married couple or even where only one of the consenting partners is married. See for instance *Aoko v Fagbemi & other,* (1961) 1 N.L.R.; *Tinubu v Tinubu* [1959] WNLR 316; *Craig v Craig* (1962) 16 NLR 103

[81] *Qur'an* 17:32, *Tafsir Ibn Kathir*, (Abridged) Volume 1, Parts 1 & 2, Darussalam Publishers, available online at http://www.tafsir.com

> ransomed for you." The Prophet said, (Neither do the people like it for their daughters.) The Prophet said, (Would you like it for your sister) He said, "No, by Allah, may I be ransomed for you." The Prophet said, (Neither do the people like it for their sisters.) The Prophet said, (Would you like it for your paternal aunt) He said, "No, by Allah, O Allah's Messenger! May I be ransomed for you." The Prophet said, (Neither do the people like it for their paternal aunts.) The Prophet said, (Would you like it for your maternal aunt) He said, "No, by Allah, O Allah's Messenger! May I be ransomed for you." The Prophet said, (Neither do the people like it for their maternal aunts).[82]

The *Qur'anic* exegeses on the subject of *zina* (adultery) are quite extensive. Their conclusion is that the prescribed punishment for the offence is a deterrent. Yet, the crime is still being committed and interaction and living in community with non-muslims who do not criminalize adultery has opened up avenues of criticism of the Islamic legal system in this respect. More so when the Universal Declaration of Human Rights has pitched a system of purportedly non-religious human rights schemes against Islamic Human Rights Schemes throughout the world.[83]

Several non-governmental organisations mounted their campaigns against the *hadd* for *zina* upon a challenge of the offence and its punishment as being in contravention of human right schemes and also allude to Arab cultural treatment of women. In several of her works, the Moroccan writer, Fatima Mernissi[84] has referred to the institution of polygamy in Islam as allowing male sexuality to remain promiscuous while keeping women in check to be used simply as agents of man's sexual gratification,[85] to be discarded as men pleased. According to her:

> Whereas polygamy deals with the intensity of the male's sexual drive, repudiation deals with its instability. Repudiation prevents the man from losing his sexual appetite through boredom. It aims at supplying a new set of sexual objects within the framework of marriage, to protect him against the temptation of *zina*.[86]

It would appear that even though Mernissi has argued that for a Muslim man, the only person he is allowed to love is his mother,[87] her conclusions almost always is that

---

[82] Ibid

[83] See for instance An-Na'im, A.A., Op. Cit., note 1

[84] *Behind the Veil: Male female Dynamics in a Muslim Society*, Al Saqi Books, London, 1985; *The Harem Within: Tales of a Moroccan Girlhood*, Bantam, London, 1997; *Women's Rebellion and Islamic Memory*, Zed Books, London, 1996; *Women and Islam: An Historical and Theological Enquiry*, Basil Blackwell, Oxford, 1991

[85] *Women's Rebellion*, p.49. In 'A Feminist Interpretation of Women's Right in Islam', Kurzman, Charles (ed.), *Liberal Islam: A Sourcebook*, OUP, Oxford, 1996, pp.122-126, Mernissi claims the ease with which women are manipulated is in part due to the tradition of misogyny within Islamic history, implying that this tradition has persisted and has influenced many an Islamic scholar and leader who do not want their powers diminished in the allocation of resources.

[86] Ibid: Mernissi has implored that 'until we arrive at the conception of woman as an equal and responsible citizen...as a resource to be managed and as a talent to be developed, every development project in the Arab world will be doomed to failure.' See *Women's Rebellion*, p.55. It is compelling to note that as much as Islam was revealed from the Arabian Peninsula, there is a difference between Arabism and Islam such that Arab culture and tradition is not necessarily Islamic culture and tradition.

[87] Ibid, p.121

women should not be asking for equality with men, but seek instead for a re-examination of attitudes to sexual relations that will take each gender as capable of creative ingenuity and contribution to the development of the community.[88] However, some international non-governmental organisations engaged in human rights advocacy deftly refused to acknowledge Mernissi's conclusions and instead concentrated on the wrongly perceived 'barbaric and savage' nature of Islam and indeed the African continent as the pivot of their campaigns. This attitude must have advised the reasoning of BOABAB for Women's Human Rights, the Nigerian non-governmental organisation that was in the forefront of campaigns and defence of Amina Lawal, to request and advice caution in NGO strategy of engagement of the Nigerian government on the issue of the *hadd* of *zina*.

In BOABAB's publicised advisory,[89] the NGO said:

> Dominant colonialist discourses and the mainstream international media have presented Islam (and Africa) as the barbaric and savage Other. Please do not buy into this. Accepting stereotypes that present Islam as incompatible with human rights not only perpetuates racism but also confirms the claims of right-wing politico-religious extremists in all our contexts.[90]

BOABAB also enjoined NGOs to always remember that the point for human right activists is 'to question who is invoking Islam (or whatever belief/discourse) for what purposes, and also to acknowledge and support internal dissent within the community involved'[91] and not allow themselves to be 'engaged in wholesome condemnation of peoples' belief and cultures, which is seldom accurate or effective in changing views within the affected community.'[92]

Conclusion

It is arguable whether previous rulings in respect of the *hadd* of *zina* may be among those *Shari'a* rulings that could be contextualized, amended, adapted, extended or abrogated,[93] but what is certain is that the Prophet of Islam and the *Qur'anic* revelation did not come up with exact and specific guidelines for women in terms of conduct, dressing and the regulation of cross-sexual interaction.[94] Illegal sexual relations are however explicitly prohibited. The *Qur'anic* prohibitions are unequivocal. No Muslim man or woman would readily confess to engaging in illegal consensual sex. It is instructive that even Amina Lawal, though illiterate, sought legitimacy in the legal system that the world had assumed was bent on condemning her. According to her counsel, Aliyu Musa Yawuri,

---

[88] *Beyond the Veil*, p.176

[89] Iman, Aisha, Medar-Gould, Sindi, 'How Not to Help Amina Lawal' in Cockburn, Alexander & St. Clair, Jeffry, (eds.), *Counterpunch*, available online at http://www.counterpunch.org/imam05152003.html

[90] Ibid

[91] Ibid

[92] Ibid

[93] Sanusi, L.S., 'Shariah and the Woman Question', *Weekly Trust Newspaper*, Kaduna, 18th September, 2000

[94] Ibid

> Amina Lawal is a Muslim; she lives in a Muslim community. She believed that the *Sharia*, under which she was convicted and sentenced to death, should contain some mechanism that could allow her appeal and set her free. In other words, she yearned for legitimacy.[95]

The trial and conviction; appeal, discharge and acquittal of Amina Lawal in the charge of *zina* under the Katsina State *Shari'a* Penal Code Law was not gender biased.

[95] Yawuri, A.M., Op. Cit., note 5, p. 133

Part V
Juveniles

[20]

END NATURAL LIFE SENTENCES FOR JUVENILES*

JEFFREY FAGAN
Columbia University

In 2005, the U.S. Supreme Court in *Roper v. Simmons* (125 S. Ct. 1183) banned executions of persons who commit capital murder before they reach age 18. *Roper* overturned death sentences for 72 people in 18 states (Streib, 2005). Most (but not all) were resentenced to natural life or life in prison without the possibility of parole (or JLWOP).[1] Juvenile justice advocates now want to extend *Roper's* maturity heuristic, proportionality analysis, aversion to errors, and deference to international laws and norms to argue for a constitutional ban on natural life sentences for adolescent offenders. This move could have a far greater reach than did *Roper*, potentially affecting more than 2,250 inmates in 42 states.[2] But extending *Roper* raises difficult normative, constitutional and policy questions. Does the *Roper* logic fit when the crime is other than murder? When the sentence is less than death? A retreat from natural life sentences requires a confrontation in state legislatures with three decades of increasingly harsh punishment legislation aimed at juvenile offenders, and with its underlying fear-driven instinct to remove serious youthful offenders categorically and permanently from our midst. The policy options and mobilization strategies to counter this trend emerge not only from *Roper's* jurisprudence but also from the coupling and alignment of natural life sentences with a broader discourse on the principles of juvenile justice and youth policies.

DIVERSITY AMONG STATES IN JLWOP ELIGIBILITY

Currently, 42 states permit juvenile life without parole (JLWOP) sentences (Human Rights Watch-Amnesty International, 2005, hereafter HRW-AI). Colorado banned JLWOP sentences in 2006, and five other

---

* Dustin Crawford, Arie Rubinstein, Mark Favors, Erin Wallace, Jennifer DiCastro and Jason Stramaglia provided excellent research assistance.

1. Information regarding individuals resentenced after *Roper v. Simmons* was compiled by searching respective states' department of corrections websites for offenders listed by Streib (2005). In some states, the department of corrections websites did not provide inmate search capabilities or did not have information on a particular offender.

2. A complete list of states and their JLWOP sentencing statutes appears in a detailed report by Human Rights Watch and Amnesty International, The Rest of Their Lives: Life Without Parole for Child Offenders in the United States (2005). Available online: http://hrw.org/reports/2005/us1005/5.htm#_Toc114638402. The list of statutes also is available from the author.

states have abolition legislation pending.[3] Among the nine states that prohibit JLWOP sentences, four prohibit LWOP sentences at any age.

No consensus exists among the states for the minimum age of a natural life sentence: Fourteen states allow a minor to be tried as an adult at any age and sentenced to JLWOP. In seven states, all life sentences deny the possibility of parole, regardless of age. Some states, such as California, limit JLWOP sentences to persons convicted of capital crimes or "special circumstances" crimes that include felony murder, capital murder, or terrorism. Most JLWOP sentences require a conviction for capital homicide and felony murder. But many states have much broader statutory horizons that extend to crimes other than homicide, including lesser degrees of homicide or manslaughter, robbery, aggravated assault, rape, and nonviolent felonies such as burglary and drug selling (Massey, 2006). Other states (e.g., Louisiana, South Carolina) permit or mandate natural life sentences for minors as a second or third *strike*.

Although they are widely authorized across the states, the use of JLWOP sentences has varied over time. JLWOP sentences were extremely rare before 1980 (HRW-AI, 2005). The number rose steadily throughout the 1980s, reaching 50 in 1989, and peaking at 152 in 1996; since then, JLWOP sentences have declined sharply to 54 in 2003 (HRW-AI, 2005). This downward trend mirrors the sharp decline in juvenile death sentences over the same period, a decline that exceeded the decline in the rate of juvenile homicide arrests and the overall decline in the homicide and violent crime rates (Fagan and West, 2005).[4]

---

3. Michigan, Florida, California, Mississippi, and Illinois. For example, four bills in the Michigan Senate would eliminate LWOP for minors sentenced before their 18th birthday. SB 0006 would change the "Code of Criminal Procedures" to prohibit the court from sentencing youth 17 years and under with imprisonment for life without parole eligibility. SB 0009 would change "Corrections Code of 1953" to require that individuals 17 years or younger when they committed a crime be eligible for parole after having served a minimum of 10 years. SB 0028 would change the "Probate Code of 1939" to allow the court to impose any sentence on a juvenile that could be imposed on an adult convicted of the offense for which the juvenile was convicted, except imprisonment for life without parole eligibility. SB 0040 would amend Michigan Penal Code 1931 PA 328 to include a statement prohibiting individuals 17 years and younger from being sentenced to life imprisonment without parole eligibility. In California, SB 999 would eliminate JLWOP sentences for first-degree murder and replace them with indeterminate sentences of 25 years to life.

4. However, JLWOP sentencing practices for all degrees of murder seemed to harden during this time (HRW-AI, 2005). The increase in the rate of JLWOP sentences per juvenile homicide arrest indicates that the decline is certainly not a sign of evolving norms or a dissolving of the national consensus. According to the thorough HRW-AI study, the proportion of homicide defendants below age 18 years who received LWOP sentences rose sharply: The share of adolescents convicted of murder who received sentences of natural life rose from 2.86% in 1990 to 9.05% in 2000.

Not only is there heterogeneity in the statutory architecture of JLWOP sentences, but there also is wide variability in the willingness of states to use it. The HRW-AI report (2005) shows enormous variation across states in their use of JLWOP sentences. JLWOP rates in Delaware, Illinois, and Maryland are low despite high juvenile arrest rates for violent crimes, but Pennsylvania and Michigan have high JLWOP rates but low youth violence arrest rates. Juvenile arrests for violence are comparable in Michigan and New Jersey; yet Michigan has sentenced 306 youth to LWOP compared with none in New Jersey. Missouri has high juvenile arrest rates and high rates of youths serving natural life sentences.

The architecture of JLWOP statutes seems to shape this variation. The eight states where natural life sentences are mandatory for specific crimes have the highest JLWOP rates (per youth population). The lowest rates are in five states where the sentence is discretionary—that is, statutes that assign sentencing judges discretion based on individualized assessments. In this statutory design, JLWOP has the deepest and widest reach when legislatures in effect delegate sentencing authority to prosecutors whose charging decisions have the power to foreclose any latitude in sentencing once the case reaches the criminal court.

INTERNATIONAL NORMS AND COVENANTS

The *Roper* Court nodded to international norms, noting ". . .the stark reality that the United States is the only country in the world that continues to give official sanction to the juvenile death penalty." Here, abolitionists are on firm ground: international norms strongly oppose natural life sentences for minors (HRW-AI, 2005). The norms and practices of other nations reveal the jurisprudential isolation and outlier status of American law and policy on this question. Only three countries authorize and use natural life sentences for minors: the United States, South Africa, and Israel (HRW-AI, 2005). None use it as often or as broadly as U.S. courts. HRW-AI (2005) reports that only four juvenile offenders were serving natural life sentences in South Africa in 1999 and four in Israel as of 2002. Several countries explicitly ban JLWOP sentences: Austria, Ireland, Japan, Switzerland, Sweden, and the United Kingdom. In Canada, a sentence of LWOP is prohibited for juvenile offenders, and the harshest penalty a juvenile can receive is life with the possibility of parole in five to 10 years.

JLWOP sentences violate several international covenants (Goliath, 2003; HRW-AI, 2005), including Articles VII (right to special protection), XXV (right to due process), and XXVI (right to protection against cruel, infamous, or unusual punishment) of the American Declaration of the Rights and Duties of Man. Article 37 of the Convention of Rights of the Child, which has been signed and ratified by every country but the United

States and Somalia, explicitly prohibits LWOP sentences for juvenile offenders under the age of 18 years. In the United Nations, JLWOP sentences also violate the U.N. *Standard Minimum Rules for the Administration of Juvenile Justice* (i.e., the *Beijing Rules*), which hold that detention of children should only occur as a last resort and for the shortest length of time possible.

THE PROPORTIONALITY OF NATURAL LIFE SENTENCES FOR CHILDREN AND ADOLESCENTS

The jurisprudential bar is both different and higher for those hoping to extend *Roper's* calculus to the case of natural life sentences for adolescents. The problem is not the design of blanket rules that instantiate the rationality of an age-based classification as a proxy for human development and various aspects of behavior (Emens, 2005). Law is good at that when it comes to adolescence (Scott and Steinberg, 2003). The *Roper* Court's proportionality analysis, and its resulting bright line on age, was simplified by its longstanding "death is different" jurisprudence that treats execution as a separate category with its own precedents and rules [e.g., *Woodson v. North Carolina* U.S. 280 (1976)], and whose culpability bar is highest. Because of the low culpability bar and weak track record of proportionality analyses in LWOP case law, JLWOP sentences — whether authorized or mandated legislatively — can run afoul of the jurisprudence of the juvenile death penalty. Accordingly, the constitutionality of JLWOP sentences may turn on how legislatures form their views of the severity of natural life sentences for adolescents.

DEATH IS DIFFERENT, BUT IS JLWOP DIFFERENT?

The U.S. Supreme Court, as well as federal and state appellate courts, has generally adopted narrow Eighth Amendment proportionality principles in noncapital cases, thereby affirming natural life sentences for nonviolent crimes such as drug selling or "Three-Strikes" violations.[5] In juvenile LWOP cases, differing views of the proportionality of JLWOP sentences have led some courts to invalidate these sentences and others to affirm

5. Decisions such as *Ewing v. California* (2003) (upholding a life sentence under California's Three Strikes Law for the theft of three golf clubs worth $399 each), *Rummel v. Estelle* (1980) (affirming a LWOP sentence for the theft of $120.75 worth of goods via credit card fraud), and *Harmelin v. Michigan* (1991) (upholding a LWOP sentence in a drug distribution case for a first-time offender) are typical, standing in contrast to *Solem v. Helm* (1983), where the Court reversed a LWOP sentence for a chronic property offender.

them.[6] This admixture of proportionality standards for juveniles in these cases is hardly surprising. Courts are conflicted over whether age is a fiction in proportionality analyses, and the conflict is heightened when sentencing goals move from retributive to instrumental. If the legislatures are inchoate on proportionality principles, it is not surprising that appellate judges also disagree on exactly what proportionality means, how it might

6. In *Harris v. Wright* (1995), the Ninth Circuit rejected the notion that a sentence of natural life for an adolescent is fungible with execution: "Youth has no obvious bearing on this problem. . ..Accordingly, while capital punishment is unique and must be treated specially, mandatory life imprisonment without parole is, for young and old alike, only an outlying point on the continuum of prison sentences. Like any other prison sentence, it raises no inference of disproportionality when imposed on a murderer." But in *People v. Miller* (2002), the court overturned an LWOP sentence for a first-time, 15-year-old Illinois offender, after finding the LWOP sentence so disproportionate to the defendant's role as a passive lookout that it "shocks the moral sense of the community." The Court was critical of the Illinois felony murder law whose wide net and diluted notions of culpability would offend *Roper's* logic.

State courts are inconsistent in their views of age as a factor in assessing the proportionality of natural life sentences. In *State* v. *Massey* (1990), the Washington State Court of Appeals rejected age as a factor in the proportionality analysis of a life sentence for a 13-year-old convicted of murder, narrowly defining proportionality as "only a balance between the crime and the sentence imposed." But in *Workman v. Kentucky* (1968), the Kentucky Supreme Court held that JLWOP sentences for two 15-year-old males convicted of rape "under all circumstances shocks the general conscience of society today and is intolerable to fundamental fairness." And in *Naovarath v. State* (1989), the Nevada Supreme Court overturned a natural life sentence of a 13-year-old convicted of first-degree murder for shooting a man who had been sexually molesting him. The Court, pointing to the "undeniably lesser culpability of children for their bad actions, their capacity for growth, and society's special obligation to [them]," held that JLWOP sentence constituted severe cruel and unusual punishment: "To adjudicate a thirteen year old to be forever irredeemable and to subject a child of this age to hopeless, lifelong punishment. . .is not a usual or acceptable response to childhood criminality."

Even when courts consider age, structured sentencing may preclude its relevance in sentencing. In *State v. Mitchell* (1998), a Minnesota court rejected a proportionality challenge brought by a 15-year-old who had been sentenced to natural life (albeit with parole review after 30 years). Although age was obviously a mitigating factor, the trial judge could not impose a lesser sentence since JLWOP was mandatory once the case was transferred to the criminal court, where any sentencing discount for diminished culpability was forfeited. In *State v. Standard* (2003), the South Carolina Supreme Court discounted age altogether and invoked an instrumentalist definition of proportionality in affirming a natural life sentence under the state's "Two-Strikes Law" for a 15-year-old with a prior armed robbery conviction who was later convicted of first-degree burglary and grand larceny and sentenced to LWOP. The Court ruled that *Standard*'s sentence was within the bounds of society's current and evolving standards, citing the minority of states that authorize the sentence on very young juvenile offenders (see, also, *State v. Mitchell,* 1998).

be defined operationally in law and policy, what its limits are when punishment serves nonretributive purposes, and whether states can have different proportionality standards and principles that operate simultaneously (Frase, 2005).

THE THINNEST OF LINES BETWEEN NATURAL LIFE AND DEATH

The *Roper* Court casually entered this debate, perhaps unintentionally. Justice Kennedy's opinion toyed with the notion that for adolescents, a natural life sentence is on the same proportionality plane as a death sentence. First, he noted in passing that ". . .the punishment of life imprisonment without the possibility of parole is itself a severe sanction, in particular for a young person." Then, he invoked the incomplete development of adolescents as a discount on proportionality, stating that ". . .[w]hen a juvenile offender commits a heinous crime, the State can exact forfeiture of some of the most basic liberties, but the State cannot extinguish his life *and his potential to attain a mature understanding of his own humanity*" (emphasis added) (*Roper v. Simmons*, 2005, at 1197). The Court seemed to reject *any* punishment that would permanently mortgage or foreclose the possibility of the realization of full human development. Finally, the majority opinion concluded that minors might well imagine life without parole to be the same, if not worse, than death because most of their lives lie ahead. "To the extent the juvenile death penalty might have residual deterrent effect, it is worth noting that the punishment of life imprisonment without the possibility of parole is itself a severe sanction, in particular for a young person" (*Roper v. Simmons*, 2005, at 1196). By these proportionality standards, both the juvenile death penalty and the JLWOP sentence fail a constitutional or commonsense test of the retributive and deterrence goals of punishment. It is only when the sentencing goals drift toward the instrumental that the *Roper* logic and its extension to JLWOP become moot.

The idea that LWOP is the equivalent of death for an adolescent is not only enduring, but it is also a challenge to the *Harris* Court's dismissal of proportionality analyses in non-capital cases. John Stuart Mill (1868) characterized a natural life sentence as a "living tomb." Logan (1998) cites both historical and contemporary evidence that modern courts have characterized JLWOP as a "slow death sentence" that is "equally severe" to a death sentence. Anticipating *Roper*, the Nevada Supreme Court in *Naovarath v. Nevada* (1989) characterized JLWOP as "virtually hopeless lifetime incarceration" that is ". . .a denial of hope" that renders "good behavior and character improvement" immaterial and, worse, is cancerous to human development: "To adjudicate a thirteen-year-old to be forever irredeemable and to subject a child of this age to hopelessness or near hopelessness is the hallmark of [this] punishment" ([*Naovarath v. Nevada,* (1989, at 948)]. The *Naovarath* Court also raised doubts about the deterrent effects of JLWOP for younger offenders: "It is questionable as to whether a 13-year-old can even imagine or comprehend what it means to be imprisoned for 60 years or more."

The severity of punishment of a natural life sentence is also an empirical question, but the available facts let us estimate its boundaries. Most of this evidence, such as the recent newspaper series by Liptak (2005) and Florio et al. (2005), is descriptive. One of the very few systematic empirical studies on prisoners serving LWOP sentences confirms the protracted deterioration of humanity that occurs when one is imprisoned for life. In the 1920s, Sir Alexander Patterson studied the effects of long-term imprisonment on both young and older offenders as part of a parliamentary review of capital punishment in the United Kingdom (Patterson, 1951 [1930]). As part of his report for the British Parliament's *Select Committee on Capital Punishment*, he visited men serving life sentences in English prisons at 6-week intervals for nearly a year. He recorded a deterioration that "will permanently impair something more precious that the life of the physical body," and he equated life sentences with "a death sentence where the inevitable end is reached by the imperceptible stages of institutional decay instead of by one full stroke" (p. 485). The Select Committee recommended that life sentences include review and the possibility of release after 20 years. Patterson also recommended that "inasmuch as 21 is the age when full civil responsibility is assumed, it should also be the age below which no one should be sentenced to death" (p. 487).[7]

Patterson's description of the emotional and spiritual decay of long prison terms comports with Streib's (1995) characterization of early incarceration as a lifetime sentence to psychological and physical (often sexual) abuse in prison. The facts side with this view. For example, Forst et al. (1989) show the elevated risks of physical and sexual abuse when minors are transferred to the criminal court and sentenced as adults to prison, which is a consequence of transfer and waiver laws that are essential moving parts of the JLWOP process (Logan, 1998). Thus, natural life sentences for juveniles are in yet another way a disfiguring punishment, certainly a dimension of "cruel" but, again, not all that unusual. The link between violent subjugation of youths in prison and their long-term spiritual and emotional decay suggests that ". . .life in prison is as severe, if not more severe . . ..for a juvenile than is the death penalty" (Streib, 1995:776).

7. The recommendations of the Select Committee were hardly unanimous. Six Conservative members withdrew from the committee in an effort to discredit the report. See Calvert (1931:v–xii).

MISTAKES

The recent newspaper series (Florio et al., 2005; Liptak, 2005) and television documentaries (Frontline, 2007) illustrate how the spacious net of JLWOP statutes can permanently incarcerate young offenders whose culpability—whether convicted of felony murder or a second drug offense—may be attenuated. These cases illustrate one of *Roper's* central concerns: the inability of judges and juries to accurately render individualized assessments about whether a teenager's immaturity and developmental deficits attenuates his or her culpability. It also shows how mandatory JLWOP sentences can result when culpability is low. The number of mistakes—whether errors in determining guilt or in divining culpability—is a difficult empirical question. Errors are all too common in death penalty cases (Forst, 2003; Liebman et al., 2000), including juvenile death penalty cases (Gross et al., 2005), but we discover many of these errors because of strong due process footprints (Garrett, 2008) and the close attention of skilled death penalty lawyers. No such footprints exist in most JLWOP cases, and certainly, fewer legal resources are available when death is not at stake. Accordingly, the same risks of error that cautioned the courts in *Roper* and 4 years earlier in *Atkins v. Virginia* (2002) (banning the execution of mentally retarded persons)—inflated culpability assessments, false confessions, ineffective assistance to counsel, all leading to wrongful conviction—are present equally for JLWOP but with significantly less appellate recourse.

Errors in capital cases, as Justice Kennedy reminds us in *Roper*, are not correctable. Unless natural life sentences become reviewable as to the matter of (im)maturity or guilt, and until defense resources routinely provide lawyers who are sufficiently skilled and trained specifically for the punishment at hand, similar mistakes are likely given the wide statutory net and the absence of (super) due process to protect against mistakes such as those that occur in capital cases even after remedies are exhausted (Garrett, 2008). Indeed, the *Roper* opinion reflects the fear that mistakes will happen, at least in part, because of the irrationality of judgments among prosecutors, judges, and juries about the culpability and danger of youths (Emens, 2005). In *State v. Mitchell* (1998), the appellate opinion notes how this fear of youth crime has metastasized in state legislatures into two-strike and three-strike laws aimed at youths and that promote mandatory JLWOP sentences. The *Mitchell* court notes that whether or not natural life sentences for minors are cruel, they certainly are no longer unusual.

STRATEGY AND TACTICS

Opponents of natural life sentences for minors have three avenues to proceed within states; local contexts guide the choice of strategies. First, many of the waiver and transfer statutes that make possible JLWOP sentences delegate—de facto—transfer decisions to prosecutors and legislators through the coupling of unreviewable charging decisions with mandatory JWLOP provisions. These expansive waiver laws deregulate punishment and remove judges from any role other than procedural traffic cop and evidentiary gatekeeper. Narrowing or reversing these laws can reduce the reach of JLWOP statutes. Some states have reduced the scope of these laws, whereas others—such as Connecticut—have simply reversed the statutory trends of the past 30 years to criminalize delinquency by raising the age of majority to 18 years and by restricting waiver eligibility. Robust empirical evidence shows that these laws offer no crime-control benefits and instead expose high numbers of minors to the iatrogenic effects of criminal court sentences (McGowan, 2006). The same may also be true of the felony murder rule, where little evidence exists of marginal deterrence, and where there may be unanticipated and perverse effects resulting in victim substitution (Klick and Garoupa, 2006). These facts can offset the demand for retribution that seems to fuel spacious JLWOP and transfer laws.

Second, narrowing JLWOP eligibility to capital crimes would reduce the reach of these statutes drastically and mitigate some of their errors. Evidence of fractured proportionality could be persuasive to state legislators when the actual human faces of excessive punishment are visible so that parents and legislators can forge a sense of linked fate to animate advocacy for legislative change. These laws are used wantonly and promiscuously, and personalized proportionality analyses can reveal the moral hazard in the expansion of natural life sentences for persons of compromised culpability.

Third, of course, is the pursuit of abolition within states. The success of the efforts in Colorado, and the story of state efforts that aggregated to the *Atkins* decision (Ellis, 2003), charts a path and a strategy for building a persuasive consensus of states. The *Atkins* decision was the result of time-consuming work by local coalitions of mental health advocates, voluntary organizations in the disability community, and mental health professionals, who worked with death penalty opponents within both the legal and the advocacy communities (Ellis, 2003). Their work uniquely juxtaposed legislative action with constitutional analysis. The legitimacy of their constitutional argument with both legislatures and the Court was enhanced by the intersection of advocacy interests with the professional judgments of clinicians and scientists. The same work was done in the interval between *Stanford v. Kentucky* (1989) and *Roper*, although with more limited success, to produce abolition of juvenile death sentences in five states. Here, the argument and the penal calculus are simpler: What extra benefits to crime control or to retributive justice do we gain from a sentence of life without parole for an immature juvenile than we now gain from sentences of 40 or 50 years? The answer, given the reality and severity of prison, is nothing at all.

REFERENCES

ACLU of Michigan
2004 Second Chances: Juveniles Serving Life Without Parole in Michigan Prisons. Lansing: ACLU of Michigan.

Calvert, E. Roy
1931 The Death Penalty Enquiry: The Evidence Reviewed. London: Gollancz Publishers.

Ellis, James W.
2003 Disability advocacy and the death penalty: The road from *Penry* to *Atkins*. New Mexico Law Review 33:173–201.

Emens, Elizabeth
2005 Aggravating youth: *Roper v. Simmons* and age discrimination. Supreme Court Review 2005:51–102.

Fagan, Jeffrey
2003 *Atkins*, adolescence and the maturity heuristic: Rationales for a categorical exemption for juveniles from capital punishment. New Mexico Law Review 33:207–292.

Fagan, Jeffrey and Valerie West
2005 The decline of the juvenile death penalty: Scientific evidence of evolving norms. Journal of Criminal Law and Criminology 95:427–500.

Feld, Barry C.
2004 Competence, culpability, and punishment: Implications of *Atkins* for executing and sentencing adolescents. Hofstra Law Review 32:463.

Florio, Gwen, Sue Lindsay, and Sarah Langbein
2005 Locked Up Forever. Rocky Mountain News (September 16). Available online: http://www.rockymountainnews.com/drmn/local/article/0,1299, DRMN_15_4083343,00.html.

Forst, Brian A.
2003 Errors of Justice: Nature, Sources and Remedies. New York: Cambridge University Press.

Forst, Martin A., Jeffrey A. Fagan, and T. Scott Vivona
1989 Youth in prisons and training schools: Perceptions and the consequences of the treatment custody dichotomy. Juvenile and Family Court Journal 40:1–15.

Frase, Richard S.
2005 Excessive prison sentences, punishment goals, and the Eighth Amendment: "Proportionality" relative to what? Minnesota Law Review 89:571–655.

Frontline
2007 When Kids Get Life. Frontline (May 8). Available online: http://www.pbs.org/wgbh/pages/frontline/whenkidsgetlife/.

Garrett, Brandon
2008 Judging innocence. Columbia Law Review. In press.

Goliath, Patricia
2003 Juveniles and life imprisonment. De Rebus (May):22–27.

Gross, Samuel R., Kristen Jacoby, Daniel J. Matheson, Nicholas Montgomery, and Sujata Patil
2005 Exonerations in the United States 1989 through 2003. Journal of Criminal Law & Criminology 95:523–602.

Human Rights Watch and Amnesty International
2005 The Rest of Their Lives: Life Without Parole for Child Offenders in the United States. New York: Human Rights Watch.

Klick, Jonathan and Nuno M. Garoupa
2006 Differential victimization: Efficiency and fairness justifications for the felony murder rule. Florida State University College of Law, Public Law Research Paper No. 244. Available online: http://ssrn.com/abstract=951795.

Liebman, James, Jeffrey Fagan, Valerie West, and Jonathan Lloyd
2000 Capital attrition: Error rates in capital cases, 1973-1995. Texas Law Review 78:1839–1865.

Liptak, Adam
2005 Locked away forever after crimes as teenagers. New York Times (October 3).

Logan, Wayne A.
1998 Proportionality and punishment: Imposing life without parole on juveniles. Wake Forest Law Review 33:681–725.

Massey, Hillary J.
2006 Disposing Of Children: The Eighth Amendment and Juvenile Life Without Parole After Roper. Boston College Law Review, 47: 1083 – 1118.

McGowan, Andrea, Robert Hahn, Akiva Liberman, Alex Crosby, Mindy Fullilove, Robert Johnson, et al.
2006 Effects on violence of laws and policies facilitating the transfer of juveniles from the juvenile justice system to the adult justice system: A systematic review. American Journal of Preventive Medicine 32:7–28.

Mill, John Stuart
1868 Collected Works, XXVIII. London, U.K.: Routledge.

Patterson, Alexander
1951 Minutes of Evidence, The Select Committee on Capital Punishment. Originally printed in Sir Alexander Paterson (1930), Paterson on Prisons: The Collected Papers of Sir Alexander Paterson. London, U.K.: F. Muller.

Scott, Elizabeth and Laurence D. Steinberg
2003 Blaming youth. Texas Law Review 81:799–840.

Streib, Victor L.
1995 Sentencing juvenile murderers: Punish the last offender or save the next victim? University of Toledo Law Review 26:765–786.
2005 The juvenile death penalty today: Death sentences and executions for juvenile crimes, January 1, 1973–February 28, 2005. Available online: http://www.law.onu.edu/faculty_staff/faculty_profiles/coursematerials/streib/juvdeath.pdf.

CASES CITED

Atkins v. Virginia, 536 U.S. 304 at 218 (2002).
Ewing v California, 538 U.S. 11 (2003).
Harmelin v. Michigan, 501 U.S. 957 (1991).
Harris v. Wright, 93 F.3d 581, 585 (9th Cir. 1996).
Lockyer v. Andrade, 538 U.S. 63, 79-83 (2003).
Naovarath v. Nevada, 105 Nev. 525 (1989).
People v. Miller, 202 Ill. 2d. 328 (2002).
Roper v. Simmons, 125 S. Ct. 1183 (2005).
Rummel v. Estelle, 445 U.S. 263 (1980).
Solem v. Helm, 463 U.S. 277 (1983).
Stanford v. Kentucky, 492 U.S. 361 (1989).
State v. Massey, 803 P.2d 340, 348 (Wash. Ct. App. 1990).
State v. Mitchell, 577 N.W.2d 481 (Minn. 1998).
State v. Standard, 569 S.E.2d 325, 329 (2002), cert. denied, 537 U.S. 1195 (2003).
Workman v. Kentucky, 429 S.W.2d 374, 378 (Ky. 1968).
Woodson v. North Carolina, 428 U.S. 280 (1976).

Jeffrey Fagan is a Professor of Law and Public Health at Columbia University. He is a fellow of the American Society of Criminology, a member of the MacArthur Research Network on Adolescent Development and Juvenile Justice and the National Consortium on Violence Research. He is former vice-chair of the Committee on Law and Justice of the National Research Council.

[21]

Juvenile Parricide Offenders Sentenced to Death

Kathleen M. Heide

Department of Criminology, University of South Florida, Tampa, Florida, USA

Jessica McCurdy

Georgetown University Law Center, Georgetown University, Washington DC, USA

Abstract: Most accounts of youths who kill parents describe the plight of the severely abused child who kills to end long-standing abuse. Although there is recognition among scholars and practitioners that youths who kill parents to get money, to gain freedom, or to express hatred do exist, the literature has not focused on them. This research looks closely at cases of juveniles sentenced to death from 1973 to 2005, a period when juvenile murderers were eligible for capital punishment in many states, to determine if there were any cases of youths killing parents represented among this population. Of the 205 juveniles sentenced to death during this period, four killed one or more parents. This manuscript presents an in-depth analysis of one of these cases and then provides summaries of the others. These cases contain startling similarities in regard to offender motives and backgrounds and differ markedly from cases presented in the professional literature.

Keywords: parricide, matricide, patricide, murder, juvenile murderers, death penalty, capital punishment, adolescent development, juvenile justice

The killing of parents, often referred to as parricide, has evoked horror since antiquity, as evidenced in Greek and Roman mythology dating back hundreds of years (Heide, 1992). In the United States, analyses of homicides from the mid-1970s through 2002 in which the victim-offender relationship was known have consistently indicated that approximately 2% involved biological parents as victims (Boots & Heide, 2006; Heide, 1989). The public tends to be particularly concerned when parents are slain by minors. Analyses of parricide incidents from 1976 through 1999 have shown that the involvement of juveniles

---

Paper presented in part at the Academy of Criminal Justice Sciences in March 2007, Seattle, WA.

Address correspondence to Kathleen M. Heide, University of South Florida, Department of Criminology, 4202 East Fowler Avenue, Social Sciences Room 107, Tampa, FL 33620. E-mail: kheide@cas.usf.edu

in killing their parents has been substantial. Approximately one of four fathers (25%) and one of six mothers (17%) killed over the 24-year period were slain by children under 18 (Heide & Petee, 2007).

Juveniles who killed their parents have frequently been portrayed sympathetically by the media as mistreated youths who killed those who brutalized them and other family members (Blais, 1985; Boots & Heide, 2006; Kleiman, 1988; Prendergast, 1983, 1986; Tofexis, 1992; Walker, 1989). The murder of Richard Jahnke, Sr., in Wyoming by his teenage son and daughter in the early 1980s, for example, brought national attention in the United States to the predicament of abused children who kill parents out of terror or desperation. The compassionate portrayal given by the media eventually led the governor of Wyoming to commute the sentences of these two adolescents and forever imprinted in the public mind the prototypical case of "the severely abused child" (Heide, 1992).

The dilemma of the "battered child" has resulted in legislative changes in several states (Heide, Boots, Alldredge, Donerly, & White, 2005). Evidence also exists that lay people's decisions to transfer juvenile parricide offenders to adult court (Stalans & Henry, 1994) and jury decisions to hold these youths accountable are likely to be affected by claims of abuse (Haegerich & Bottoms, 2000). Indications of a change in attitude and practice are also evident in sentencing and even sometimes in actions taken by grand juries and judges (Heide, 1992).

Based on her clinical experiences and review of the literature, Heide (1992) identified three types of children who kill parents: the severely abused child, the severely mentally ill child, and the dangerously antisocial child. The severely abused child kills a parent because she or he is terrified or desperate to end the abuse and sees no other way out. Abuse is long-standing and typically is easily documented in these cases. The severely mentally ill child kills a parent because of a serious underlying mental illness. The pathology typically has been ongoing for years and has been clinically diagnosed. The dangerously antisocial child kills a parent in furtherance of selfish aims, such as freedom or money.

Most accounts of youths who kill parents in the professional literature describe the severely abused child (Corder, Ball, Haizlip, Rollins, & Beaumont, 1976; Duncan & Duncan, 1971; Ewing, 1997; Heide, 1992, 2003; Lennings, 2002; Mack, Scherl, & Macht, 1973; Marleau, Auclair, & Millaud, 2006; Post, 1982; Russell, 1984; Sadoff, 1971; Sargent, 1962; Scherl & Mack, 1966; Schlesinger, 1999; Tanay, 1973, 1976; Wertham, 1941). Although there is recognition among scholars and practitioners that youths who kill parents to get money, to gain freedom, or to express hatred do exist (Heide, 1997; Hillbrand, Alexandre, Young, & Spitz, 1999), the literature has not focused on them. There are only a few cases of adolescent parricide offenders in the scholarly literature who were diagnosed as psychotic prior to the killings (Benedek &

Cornell, 1989; Foucault, 1975; McCully, 1978; Medlicott, 1955; Mouridsen & Tolstrup, 1988; Tucker & Cornwall, 1977).

Among children and adolescents, severe mental illness, which is commonly found among adult parricide offenders, is typically ruled out (Ewing, 1997; Heide, 1992). The question frequently becomes, as Heide pointed out in *Why Kids Kill Parents*, "Was the juvenile really a battered child or was she or he simply 'a psychopath'?" (1992, p. 12–13). The two categories are not mutually exclusive. Abuse and neglect are commonly noted in the backgrounds of young parricide offenders who appear dangerously antisocial, sometimes making classification difficult (Ewing, 1997; Heide, 1992). Indeed, some abused youths who kill parents have conduct disorders and, if not treated effectively, may be diagnosed in adulthood as having antisocial personality disorders (Heide, 1992).

Heide (1997) has cautioned lawyers and mental health professionals to look beyond the abuse in cases of adolescents who kill mothers (matricide) or fathers (patricide) to determine the driving force behind the murder. Some youths who have been severely abused do not bond with others. They are filled with rage and hatred, do not have a prosocial value system, do not feel guilt when they hurt others, do not experience remorse for their misdeeds, and are incapable of empathy. Their ability to exercise sound judgment and make good decisions, which is already limited to some extent by their adolescent brains, may also be further compromised by the neurobiological effects of trauma (Heide & Solomon, 2006). The likelihood of these youths behaving impulsively is further compounded when they ingest large quantities of alcohol and drugs (Heide & Solomon, 2006). Thus, in these cases, abuse is a contributing factor to violent behavior and is partly responsible for these youths becoming dangerously antisocial.

This research looked closely at cases of juveniles prosecuted as adults and sentenced to death from 1973 to 2005, a period when juvenile murderers were eligible for capital punishment in many states, to determine if there were any cases of youths killing parents represented among this population. In 1973, the death penalty was restored in many states to conform to the U.S. Supreme Court's guidelines in *Furman v. Georgia* (1972). A few years later, in *Gregg v. Georgia* (1976), the court held that the death penalty was not cruel and unusual punishment under the Eighth Amendment if the jury was provided with standards to guide their decision making, such as aggravating and mitigating factors, and their recommendation was subject to meaningful appellate review. Up until 1988, a murderer of any age could be sentenced to death. The case of *Thompson v. Oklahoma* (1988) was interpreted to prohibit the execution of a youth under age 16 years of age only in states where the minimum age of execution was not legislated. One year later, the court limited the application of the death penalty to juveniles 16 and older. The court held in *Stanford v. Kentucky* (1989) and its companion case *Wilkins v. Missouri* (1989) that sentencing individuals for murders that they committed at ages 16 or 17 did not violate the Eighth Amendment. For many years the United States stood alone among Western industrialized nations in allowing the execution of individuals for murders that they committed as juveniles (Heide, 1999). In 2005, the U.S. Supreme Court held in *Roper v. Simmons* (2005) that sentencing convicted murderers to death for killings they committed while under the age of 18 was unconstitutional under the Eighth Amendment.

Examining youths under 18 sentenced to death from 1973 to 2005 provided a unique opportunity to look closely at juvenile parricide cases judged to be among the most egregious and to see what the case materials revealed about these young killers in light of the currently available literature on juvenile parricide offenders. One could hypothesize that, if such cases existed on death row, these youths would appear very differently from parricide cases often profiled in the news. Clearly juries must have found that aggravating factors outweighed mitigating factors and judges must have agreed with their findings. What would be the underlying dynamics behind these murders? Would the record provide convincing data that these youths fit the profile of the dangerously antisocial child as opposed to the other two types of parricide offenders? Would available information indicate that these individuals had histories of severe mental illness or extensive childhood maltreatment that might have contributed to their homicidal behavior?

METHODOLOGY

There is currently no national database that records the system processing of individuals arrested for murder. The Supplementary Homicide Report database maintained by the Federal Bureau of Investigation (FBI) provides national data on homicides reported and the characteristics of arrestees. It does not contain information on charges filed against arrestees, convictions obtained, and dispositions given (FBI, 2006). Thus, while it is possible to know how many juveniles were arrested for killing parents, it is not possible to discern from any existing database what percentage of these individuals were charged with first-degree murder, convicted as charged, and sentenced to death when it was constitutionally permissible. Available studies indicate that imposition of death sentences is exceedingly rare; less than 2% of arrests for intentional criminal homicide result in a sentence of death (Pastore & Maguire, 2001; Snell & Maruschak, 2002).

Victor Streib, professor of law at Ohio Northern University, is the leading authority on juveniles sentenced to death in the United States. One of the databases he created and has maintained consists of juveniles who were sentenced to death in the United States from 1973 until 2005. Streib identified 205 juveniles who had been placed on death row during this 32-year period (2005). His listing contained the name, age, state of residence, race, and the current legal status of the offender. From this list, Streib's publications and papers were consulted for additional case-related information (Streib, 1987, 1998, 2003a, 2003b, 2004, 2005, 2007; Streib & Sametz, 1989). It was possible to determine the relationship of the victim and the offender in 152 of the 205 cases. In four of these cases, juveniles had killed individuals identified as parents of some type. In three of the incidents, a biological parent and stepparent were among the victims killed. In the remaining case, a female cousin who raised the boy from the time he was two and was considered his foster mother was slain. No cases involved adoptive parents.

A list of the remaining 53 cases for which information was not available was sent to Streib. Most of these cases involved juveniles who were sentenced to death in earlier years and had their cases overturned. Streib reviewed his original files on these 53 cases and confirmed that none involved juveniles who had killed biological, step-, adoptive, or foster parents.

Accordingly, of 205 juveniles who were sentenced to death over the 32-year period, only four (2%) had been sentenced to death for murdering one or more parents. Those four juveniles were Sean Sellers, Frederick Lashley, Stephen McGilberry, and Mark Anthony Duke. Sellers and Lashley were executed. In contrast, Duke's and McGilberry's sentences were commuted to life in prison after the U.S. Supreme Court handed down its decision in *Roper v. Simmons* (2005).

This article examines these four cases using available writings from the Sean Sellers case and case-related materials with respect to all four cases. The analysis of the Sellers case is more in-depth than the other three cases because it was highly publicized and extensive case-related materials are available. Some of these materials include his personal writings about his life and reflections on his criminal behavior, which provide insight into the factors that contributed to his killing his parents. Thereafter a brief overview of the cases of the other three boys is provided, followed by discussion of the motivational dynamics behind these crimes. The article concludes by examining these cases in light of the court's decision in *Roper v. Simmons*, addresses the study's limitations, and makes suggestions for future research.

SEAN SELLERS: AN IN-DEPTH CASE ANALYSIS

Sean Sellers was born on May 18, 1969, in California. His father was reportedly an alcoholic. When Sellers was three or four years old, his parents divorced. Shortly thereafter his mother, Vonda, married Paul Bellofatto, a truck driver. From that point on, Sellers stayed with friends and relatives while his mother and stepfather traveled extensively. By the time he was 16, Sellers had moved over 30 times (Amnesty International, 1998).

During the times Sellers stayed with his relatives he was abused both physically and emotionally. There were signs that Sellers was troubled as an adolescent; he reportedly wet the bed when he was 12 and 13 years of age. When he wet the bed, his uncle would make him wear a diaper. If Sellers wet the bed two nights in a row, he was forced to wear a soiled diaper on his head (Amnesty International, 1998). In addition, he reported being beaten frequently by both his mother and grandfather, and molested by an older relative (Sellers, "Confession," n.d.). Despite this treatment, Sellers apparently had a close relationship with his relatives. He continually tried to please them and to fit in with their ideals. For example, he frequently went with his uncles to hunt and was encouraged to take part by pulling off the animals' legs. When he did not perform adequately, he was called a "wimp" by his uncles and stepfather and was admonished to do better (Amnesty International, 1998).

It was during his early childhood that Sellers reportedly began experiencing the first signs of his later mental illness. By the time he was six or seven years old, he had begun to hear voices in his head. Sellers indicated that he did not say anything to his parents because he thought it was normal. He had also become increasingly paranoid. At times he would brush the carpet of his room a certain way so he would know if anyone had entered his room. Frequent mood swings also characterized his adolescence, going from a state of euphoria to suicidal depression (Amnesty International, 1998).

In his personal writings Sellers stated that when he looked back on his life, he saw his turning point being at the age of 13. At that point in his life he did four things: "played football, practiced Ninjutsu, collected comic books, and played Dungeons & Dragons (D&D)" (Sellers, "Exposing," n.d.). He and his family had moved to Colorado where he was "really, really happy." He was in the Civil Air Patrol and had become the cadet commander of his squadron. When he was 15, however, his parents decided to move again to Oklahoma against his strong protests. After the move, Sellers's involvement in D&D and the occult increased exponentially, and he felt extremely angry toward his parents for making him move. He also experienced heartbreak in the form of rejection by his girlfriend. It was then that he decided that he hated God, as "God had failed [him]" (Sellers, "Exposing," n.d.).

Sellers combined this new belief in Satanism with his prior love of Ninjutsu and D&D to form a group called the Elimination. By the age of 15 Sellers was practicing Satanic rites on a daily basis and had become increasingly obsessed with the theories behind good and evil. He performed acts of self-mutilation, drank blood, and took drugs. However, he felt that there was a "barrier" between him and the power he craved. He believed that barrier was that he had not yet committed murder (Sellers, "Exposing," n.d.).

Motivational Dynamics Behind the Killing of Robert Bower

Sellers's first homicide, that of Robert Bower, took place after several discussions with his friends in the Elimination. This group performed rituals in order to invoke the power of Satan. Sellers wrote that there was a "barrier put up between us and the power they needed to invoke." As a result the teens began to break biblical commandments, until only one remained: "Thou shall not murder" (Sellers, "Exposing," n.d.).

The group started talking about ways they could break this commandment until "after a lust ritual with [Sellers's] second priest, Satan took over [their] actions" (Sellers, "Exposing," n.d.). On the night of September 8, 1985, Sellers and a friend drove to a convenience store whose owner had previously insulted Sellers's friend's girlfriend and had refused to sell them beer. It was there that they killed Robert Paul Bower. Sellers recalled that

> after much conversation with the man who thought that we were friends, my friend distracted him and I raised the gun from beneath the counter, pointed it at his head, and squeezed the trigger. It missed. I fired again. My friend cut him off from getting away. The second shot had only injured him. I caught him. His terror stricken eyes searched mine for mercy behind the smoking barrel. I squeezed the trigger and he collapsed, knocked back from the impact—dead. (Sellers, "Exposing," n.d.)

After the killing, Sellers reported that they walked out of the store and back to their car where they "laughed as the evil delight of our action gripped us" (Sellers, "Confession," n.d.). In the weeks following Bower's murder, Sellers became more involved in Satanic rituals and began consuming drugs frequently. Eventually the Elimination disbanded, but Sellers continued practicing rituals on his own. He wrote that his thoughts of that time in his life were that he was not happy and that the "blood, drugs, sex, hate, all of it had become boring" (Sellers, "Exposing," n.d.).

Sellers also recalled the effect that the killing had on his psyche:

> After that, I had killed someone. Sometimes I wanted to tell Dad so he'd be proud of my strength. He'd see me as strong, not weak. And sometimes I didn't even remember doing it. I didn't live under a constant awareness that I'd killed someone. Most of the time I didn't even know what I'd done. It was that blinking in my mind. The person who couldn't do it didn't know he did, then blink, the person who did do it, remembered. That's the best I can explain that. When I was that person, that murderer, I felt superior. I looked down on people with the secret knowledge that I had killed and was capable of killing them too. When I was not that person I was just a confused teenager, going to school, working, learning to drive, still full of anger, and counting the days when I'd be 18 so I could move OUT of that house. (Sellers, "Confession," n.d.)

Motivational Dynamics Behind the Killings of Sellers's Parents

Sellers recalled that he was very angry with his parents and life in general in the weeks preceding the double parricide. He described fights with his mother over a girl, Angel, he loved and his mother "hated." It all came to a head one afternoon when his mother told him, "You want to leave? Go. Pack your shit and get the fuck out!" (Sellers, "Confession," n.d.). Sellers did leave that day, but that night his stepfather came and forced him to return to the house. Sellers stated that things grew increasingly worse from there:

> Mom ranted about Angel, we even got into a physical fight over her. It wasn't much of a fight. Mom wailed on me like she always did, but now I was bigger than her, and I just pushed her. All the while that blinking was getting worse in my mind. I couldn't get away. I couldn't move out. I decided to kill my mother. I bought some rat poison and put it in her coffee, but it didn't work, even when I served her 3 cups of it. But after that, blink! and everything was different. We argued, but I just wanted to leave, I didn't want to kill her. Then blink! and I'd be planning her death. (Sellers, "Confession," n.d.)

Sellers killed both of his parents on March 5, 1986. He recalled that on that night, he

> continually thought about suicide. I just wanted to get out. I sat there in my pickup wishing I had either the guts to blow my brains out, or for a way to find a new world and leave everything behind. I had been up for three days. I was out of speed. Tonight I would get some sleep. I drove home, did some homework, performed a ritual and slept. (Sellers, "Exposing," n.d.)

Sellers reported that he fell asleep, woke up, and proceeded to take a gun and shoot his parents (Sellers, "Exposing," n.d.). Sellers maintained that he could not remember what happened after that point and that his next clear memory was "of a jail cell two days later" (Sellers, "Exposing," n.d.). Years after the crime, Sellers related that he started to regain some of his lost memories and revealed some of what had happened that night:

> One night that blink happened and when I came home from work I was the cold murderer who had killed Robert Bower. I went to their room before they went to bed and took Dad's .44 revolver from the drawer beside the bed. I put it in my room and waited for them to go to bed. Dad talked to me about rebuilding the engine of my pickup together. When they were in bed I went to my room, did a ritual, dressed only in my black underwear, and then crept quietly into their room. There was nothing but cold hatred in me. There was some sense of, "Sean needs to be free and this will free him. This is the only way." That was not a conscious thought, just a sensation. It's like that was the motivation behind it. I wasn't committing murder, I was removing an obstacle from my way. I was knocking down a door to a prison cage. All I felt, however, was coldness. I put the gun close to Dad's head and fired, then immediately fired again at Mom's head. Her head raised up, neck craning backward, and I fired again. Then I laid the gun down in the hallway and went back to the room. (Sellers, "Confession," n.d.)

Sellers then went to his friend Richard's house where they planned what they would tell the police.

Sellers's Arrest, Conviction, and Subsequent Case Processing

Sellers was arrested shortly thereafter and brought to the jail where he woke up with no memory of the event, except for an "overwhelming sense of guilt" (Sellers, "Exposing," n.d.). From there he was given a public defender who was provided with $750 to spend on any expert witness fees and their travel costs. The public defender's main defense in Sellers's case was that he had been brainwashed by Satanism and D&D (Sean Richard Sellers, n.d.). A defense psychologist testified that Sellers was not capable of forming the intent to commit first-degree murder for one of two reasons: (1) he did not know right from wrong and was therefore insane or (2) he suffered from automatism and was "legally unconscious," meaning that he was unaware of what he was doing when he killed all three people (Amnesty International, 1998).

The jury was *not* given the option to find Sellers guilty of first-degree manslaughter if they had doubts that he was able to form the intent necessary for murder. The judge limited the jury's options to two possible verdicts—to find Sellers guilty of first-degree murder or to acquit him. The jury found Sellers guilty of first-degree murder. Following the verdict, the judge did not instruct the jury to consider Sellers's age at the time of the crime, 16, to be a mitigating circumstance in deciding whether to recommend a life or death sentence. Rather, the judge left it up to the jury to decide if age should be considered a factor. On October 2, 1986, the jury, believing that Sellers represented a continuing danger to society, recommended that Sellers be executed (Amnesty International, 1998).

Dorothy Otnow Lewis, a psychiatrist renowned for her research with violent juveniles, including those on death row, examined Sellers several months after he was sentenced to death. She diagnosed him as being chronically psychotic, noting that he exhibited symptoms of paranoid schizophrenia and major mood disorder. Six years after the trial, Sellers was diagnosed as having Multiple Personality Disorder (MPD), now known as Dissociative Identity Disorder (DID), by three mental health professionals who performed several sophisticated tests and recognized that the voices and blackouts that Sellers reported experiencing as a child and as an adolescent were consistent with a DID diagnosis (Amnesty International, 1998). The experts concluded that one of the alter personalities likely did not know the difference between right and wrong. This alter likely had executive control of Sellers's body at the time of the murders (Amnesty International, 1998).

During the course of investigating Sellers's DID, it was discovered that Sellers had brain damage, which he sustained from head injuries as a child. Based on this new information, Sellers petitioned the Oklahoma Court of Criminal Appeals (OCCA) for post-trial consideration of newly discovered evidence. The OCCA refused to consider the evidence and denied Sellers's appeal for a new trial. Sellers next sought habeas corpus relief from the federal courts. Although the federal district court noted that there was "significant neurological and psychological evidence" that Sellers suffered from brain damage and DID, it denied him relief. The court maintained that the evidence did not amount "to a truly persuasive demonstration of actual innocence nor meet the extraordinarily high threshold of showing that a constitutional violation will occur" if Sellers was executed. The Tenth Circuit Court of Appeals noted that the introduction of this new evidence could cause a jury to find Sean Sellers innocent of the crime if it believed that an alter personality had committed the crime. The Tenth Circuit Court, however, felt compelled to restrict its ruling to whether the sentence violated the Constitution and not to correcting errors of fact made at trial. The court indicated that application for executive clemency was a possible venue for Sellers (Amnesty International, 1998).

On January 27, 1999, the parole board denied clemency to Sellers despite the fact that one of the jurors who originally recommended the death penalty spoke on his behalf. She said that the jury sentenced Sellers to death to make sure that he would be confined for life, but that jurors did not expect that Sellers would ever be executed. She also stated that, if the jury had been aware of his mental disorder, it would have changed his sentence (Sean Richard Sellers, n.d.). All five board members denied clemency. Sean's death sentence was carried out on February 5, 1999; he was the first person in 40 years to be executed for crimes committed under the age of 17 (Amnesty International, 1998).

Formal Diagnosis

Evidence from available sources suggests that Sellers could have suffered from five different disorders: a psychotic disorder, DID, mood disorder, substance abuse, and conduct disorder. Sellers was diagnosed as psychotic within months of his conviction by a psychiatrist with extensive expertise in youth violence. Prior to this diagnosis, Sellers had reported hearing voices in his head and experiencing periods of paranoia. These symptoms, which are symptoms frequently seen in individuals diagnosed as psychotic, are also encountered in those who suffer from DID.

In 1992, three mental health professionals diagnosed Sellers as having DID. EEG tests and other tests administered years after the trial provided strong evidence that this diagnosis might have been the more appropriate of the two. In 1992, there was more awareness of DID than at the time of Sellers's trial and more sophisticated tests were available to confirm the diagnosis (Amnesty International, 1998).

Sellers clearly experienced depression as a teenager. He described in his own writings a near suicide attempt. After a girl he had been dating broke up with him, he decided to kill himself. As he was pointing the gun at his head, he decided not to pull the trigger and instead called a friend. Sellers also described thoughts of suicide in the weeks before he killed his parents (Sellers, "Exposing," n.d.).

Available evidence clearly indicates that Sellers abused drugs and possibly alcohol. In the nights before his parents' deaths, he had been using amphetamines and marijuana frequently and had experimented with other types of recreational drugs (Sellers, "Exposing," n.d.). It is not clear whether Sellers was dependent on drugs. Sellers did not mention withdrawal of any type occurring during those first few days in jail. However, it is possible that he was dissociated from his experiences and might not have been aware of physiological discomfort. His involvement in drugs prior to his arrest likely affected his mental state by intensifying his impulsivity and anger, and easily could have affected his judgment and ability to control his behavior (Fendrich, Mackesy-Amiti, Goldstein, Spunt, & Brownstein, 1995).

Available data suggested Sellers met the criteria to support a diagnosis of conduct disorder. He had run away from home in the past, was involved in illegal activities (such as the murder of Robert Bower), and was heavily involved in drugs (Sellers, "Confession," n.d.). Because he committed the murders and was arrested prior to age 18, a diagnosis of antisocial personality disorder is not warranted (American Psychiatric Association, 1994).

Heide's Typology of Parricide Offenders

Sellers is not easily classified into one of Heide's three types of parricide offenders (1992). The difficulty of classifying him is foremost due to the inability of the authors to conduct an in-depth evaluation of him and to have access to the reports of mental health professionals who evaluated him previously. Available data indicate that Sellers has some characteristics of the mentally ill child and the severely abused child. However, as will be discussed below, he seems to be most representative of the dangerously antisocial child. Sellers's history of severe abuse, his diagnosis of DID, and his expressed antisocial ideals must be weighed when considering which specific type of parricide offender Sellers best exemplifies. In addition, *the driving force behind the actual crime must be determined before deciding upon a specific type*.

The strongest evidence that Sellers was physically abused comes from his own writings. He stated that he was spanked and hit frequently by his mother hard enough to cause his lips to swell, as well as beaten by his grandfather (Sellers, "Confession," n.d.). His mother would reportedly "wail" on him when they got into fights when Sellers was a teenager. She would also belittle his friends, especially his girlfriend Angel (Sellers, "Confession," n.d.), which falls into the category of emotional or psychological abuse (Heide, 1992). His uncle, who would frequently humiliate him if he wet the bed or failed to act "manly" enough, also emotionally abused him (Amnesty International, 1998).

Sellers was exposed to several violent acts against animals and was encouraged to take part in them himself. When he refused, as mentioned earlier, his uncle and stepfather berated him, which suggests that he was verbally abused by family members. After Sellers murdered Robert Bower, he stated that he "wanted to tell Dad so he'd be proud of my strength. He'd see me as strong, not weak" (Sellers, "Confession," n.d.). In addition to evidence of physical, psychological, and verbal abuse, Sellers reportedly also was sexually abused. When he was about eight years old, an older relative who lived in the same apartment complex reportedly molested Sellers (Sellers, "Confession," n.d.).

These experiences, if true, suggest that Sellers was exposed to several types of ongoing abuse. Extreme and pervasive abuse is often found in the histories of individuals diagnosed with DID (American Psychiatric Association, 1994; van der Hart, Nijenhuis, & Steele, 2006). Sellers might have come to a breaking point in late adolescence after his attempts to remove himself from the situation failed. There is some evidence that Sellers was mentally fragile from the time he was a child. He reportedly experienced blackouts, heard voices in his head from the time he was six or seven years old, and exhibited signs of paranoia (Amnesty International, 1998).

After Bower's death, Sellers reported that he experienced "blinks" in which he was a completely different person. Apparently he would "blink" and be a coldhearted killer, then "blink" again and be a normal, confused adolescent. Sellers stated that it was during the times when he was the "killer" persona that the murders of Bower and his parents occurred (Sellers, "Confession," n.d.). From this evidence, and the fact that he was formally diagnosed with DID six years after the crimes, it can be assumed that Sellers suffered from mental illness, which quite likely was caused or exacerbated by the abusive environment in which he was raised.

The evidence that Sellers also fit the typology for a dangerously antisocial child comes mostly from essays that he wrote several years after the homicides. To be diagnosed with conduct disorder, which is a main factor in identifying a dangerously antisocial child, there must be a demonstration of having participated in three or more forms of disruptive behavior (American Psychiatric Association, 1994; Durand & Barlow, 2006). As noted above, Sellers appeared to meet these criteria. Also statements such as "I was removing an obstacle from my way" and "There was nothing but cold hatred in me" (Sellers, "Confession," n.d.) point toward Sellers being a dangerously antisocial child. In addition, two former wardens and a former death row unit manager at the institution where Sellers was being held described Sellers as a manipulator who behaved best when visitors from the Christian community were in close proximity (Sean Richard Sellers, n.d.).

There are data in Sellers's case that are components of all three types of parricide offenders. Critical in understanding Sellers is determining the motivating factor behind the crime. Assuming that Sellers had been abused in his past, evidence shows that the abuse was not severe and extensive enough at the time of the double parricide to make Sellers believe that his life was in significant danger from his parents. In the altercation with his mother over his girlfriend, there was no indication of any immediate threat to his life at the time of the killings or in the time frame immediately preceding. In fact, in the days prior to the killings, it is likely that Sellers had little or no contact with his parents, as he was "up for three days" and was out of amphetamines, indicating that he had been under the influence of drugs for the past three days (Sellers, "Exposing," n.d.). As such, Sellers would not fit the typology of a severely abused child at the time of the crime because he clearly did not kill to end the abuse or because he was terrified.

The evidence for classifying Sellers as the "mentally ill child" type of parricide offender is mixed. Sellers claimed that when he murdered Richard Bower he was suffering from "blinks" where he would continually switch back and forth between two identities, the "killer" and himself. He also referenced "the blinks" prior to murdering his parents. Perhaps, the killings of Bower and his parents could be interpreted as evidence of his DID, with the "killer" persona taking over for that period of time. However, there is not enough evidence to support severe mental illness as being the definitive force behind the murders. In other words, Sellers did not kill Bower and his parents simply because he was mentally ill, delusional, or in an altered state of consciousness. Although he likely was suffering from mental illness at the time of both homicidal incidents, mental illness *alone* did not propel him to kill.

The final type, the dangerously antisocial child, is the one with the most supporting evidence. Sellers's self-reported feelings at the time of the crime provide the most evidence. He stated that he was "removing an obstacle from [his] way" and reported that he felt nothing but "cold hatred" (Sellers, "Confession," n.d.). Both of these statements, which reportedly reflect what happened during and immediately preceding the crime, point towards the primary motivation in the commission of the crime and are consistent with the "dangerously antisocial child."

It is possible that Sellers might best be classified as a mixed type—mentally ill and dangerously antisocial. It is hard to evaluate the extent to which mental illness played a primary role in the killing of Sellers's parents. It is not clear whether the blackout Sellers experienced was due to DID. The heavy use of drugs prior to the murders likely influenced Sellers's judgment and perceptions and makes it difficult to assess the role that mental illness played in the double killings.

COMPARATIVE CASES

Less information is available for the three other boys who were sentenced to death for the killing of parents and, in two of these three cases, other family members. Lashley acted alone to kill his foster mother. McGilberry conspired with a friend to kill his mother, stepfather, stepsister, and stepsister's son. Duke planned with his friends to murder his father, his father's girlfriend, and her two children. Not surprisingly, available data indicate that these cases were particularly egregious. The limited materials available on the backgrounds of these boys and the dynamics behind these murders make classifying these offenders into one of Heide's three types difficult. Once again, an in-depth assessment of the youth is necessary to make a definitive determination of the adolescent parricide offender type. The data that are on the record, however, provide some evidence that these three juvenile parricide offenders might very well have fit into the dangerously antisocial parricide offender type.

Frederick Lashley

Little is known about Frederick Lashley's childhood before he was removed from the care of his father at the age of two. Apparently, his mother had left him with his father, who severely abused him, until Janie Tracy (Lashley's cousin) took him in. Tracy essentially became Lashley's mother and provided for him in St. Louis, Missouri. She was physically disabled because of a neuromuscular problem and had had brain surgery which left a soft spot on her head (*State of Missouri v. Frederick Lashley*, 1984). This physical disability might have impaired her ability to supervise Lashley, as he was reported to have begun consuming alcohol at the age of ten. He also said that during his teens he was suicidally depressed (*Application for Grant of Reprieve or Commutation of Sentence*, 1993).

Tracy had gone to visit her sister hours before her murder on April 9, 1981. While she was gone, Lashley, 17, removed the bulb from the light socket on his cousin's front porch. He then entered the home, grabbed a cast-iron skillet from the kitchen, and waited inside for Tracy to return in order to rob her. Tracy returned home later that night. After discovering that the light was out, Tracy entered the darkened house where Lashley proceeded to hit her on the head with the skillet so hard that it broke in two. Medical evidence also revealed that a knife was thrust through the soft spot on her head to pierce her brain. Following the killing, Lashley took his foster mother's car keys and $15 from her purse, locked the door, and drove off in her car. Slightly after midnight he was picked up by the police while still driving the stolen car (*State of Missouri v. Frederick Lashley*, 1984).

Lashley was high on phencyclidine (PCP), one of the dissociative drugs, at the time of the killing. These types of drugs "distort perceptions of sight and sound and produce feelings of detachment—dissociation—from the environment and self" (NIDA Report Series, n.d.). PCP has always been associated with paranoid delusions and violent behavior (American Council for Drug Education, n.d.). The defense attorney who represented him had no prior death penalty training; Lashley was his first capital case. After his conviction, Lashley tried to appeal his sentence based on the fact he was a juvenile at the time of the crime, but the sentence was upheld. Twelve years later on July 28, 1993, he was executed (*Application for Grant of Reprieve or Commutation of Sentence*, 1993).

Stephen McGilberry

Stephen McGilberry, 16, was living in Jackson County, Mississippi, with his mother, stepfather, stepsister, and her three-year-old son when he brutally bludgeoned them to death with a bat on October 23, 1994 (Streib, 2005). Shortly before the murders, McGilberry's driving privileges were revoked due to his receiving bad grades in school and losing his job. This punishment reportedly embarrassed McGilberry because he did not want his friends to see his mother driving him to school (*McGilberry v. State*, 1999). The plan to kill his family grew out of this sense of humiliation.

McGilberry's original plan was to steal his stepsister's car and drive it to New Orleans in order to sell it for cash or drugs. A week before the murders, McGilberry approached his friend Meyer Ashley with the idea of killing his family. They worked out a plan, but the Friday before, Ashley decided not to go through with it. So McGilberry approached his other friend, Chris Johnson 14, with the plan on Saturday. That night, McGilberry had a dream of killing his family. When he woke, he went to Johnson's house where they worked out the details of the plan (*McGilberry v. State*, 1999).

The two boys returned to McGilberry's house later that day. They decided to use utility knifes to slit open the occupants' throats. However, the sleeping position of McGilberry's stepfather made this impossible. They then went to the garage where they proceeded to smoke a cigarette and revise the plan. Johnson noticed a baseball bat in the garage and suggested that they use that to knock the family unconscious, and then drop them over the pier. Because McGilberry's mother was awake, they decided to stash a few bats outside of McGilberry's bedroom window until everyone was asleep (*McGilberry v. State*, 1999).

Once everyone was asleep, the boys took the bats and split up. McGilberry was to kill his stepfather and stepsister, while Johnson was to kill McGilberry's mother and stepsister's son. However, Johnson did not hit McGilberry's mother hard enough to kill her, so McGilberry went back and hit her again "because she was suffering." The boys then took some money and credit cards from the stepsister's purse and drove off in her car to a friend's house (*McGilberry v. State*, 1999).

Later that night, the stepsister's fiancé found the bodies and called the police. When they arrived they realized that there was a missing member of the family and contacted McGilberry's friend to tell him to come home. When

McGilberry arrived on the scene, he was read his Miranda rights. He then waived his rights and proceeded to confess to all four murders. The jury convicted him of four capital murder charges and sentenced him to death (*McGilberry v. State*, 1999). Following the Supreme Court ruling in *Roper v. Simmons* (2005), McGilberry was released into the general prison population to serve a life sentence.

Mark Anthony Duke

Mark Anthony Duke was 16 when he cold-bloodedly murdered his father, his father's girlfriend, and her two daughters (aged six and seven) in their home in Shelby County, Alabama, on March 22, 1997 (Streib, 2005). Duke reportedly wanted to kill his father because his father refused to let Duke borrow the family's truck. After his father denied him access to the truck, Duke went to a friend's house to plan his father's murder with his friends. Duke decided that he also needed to kill his father's girlfriend and her two children to eliminate any witnesses.

Duke enlisted the help of his friends in planning how to carry out the killings and how to hide the evidence afterward (*Roper v. Simmons* Amicus Brief, 2004). Duke instructed the three boys how to clean the prints off of two weapons, a .45 caliber gun and a .32 caliber gun. Duke and his friends returned to Duke's house where he instructed his friends, Michael Ellison and David Collums, to meet Brandon Samra and him in the neighborhood behind the house (*Roper v. Simmons* Amicus Brief, 2004).

Then Duke and Samra entered the house where the girlfriend, Dedra Hunt, was sitting on the couch with her two children. Duke had instructed Samra to kill Hunt while he killed his father and the two children. Because his father was nowhere in sight, the two boys went up to the master bedroom to look for him. When they did not find him, they returned to the kitchen, where they saw him sitting on the fireplace in the living room (*Roper v. Simmons* Amicus Brief, 2004)

As they planned, Duke went after his father and Samra after Hunt. Duke shot his father at close range, but did not kill him. When his father started pleading for his life, Duke tried to fire another shot, but the gun was jammed. So Duke proceeded to stab and hit his father several times, then cleaned the gun out and shot him between the eyes. He reportedly told his father as he shot him that he would see him in hell (*Roper v. Simmons* Amicus Brief, 2004).

Meanwhile, Samra had shot Hunt in the head, but the bullet only knocked out some of her teeth. Hunt grabbed her children and ran upstairs in order to escape Samra. Samra followed, but Hunt was able to lock herself and one of her children in the bathroom of the master bedroom. Samra was unable to pry the door open, so he waited until Duke was finished killing his father. When he arrived, Duke kicked a hole in the door and was able to unlock it. As they entered the bathroom, Duke immediately shot Hunt, killing her instantly. He found the child hiding in the shower and proceeded to slice open her throat (*Roper v. Simmons* Amicus Brief, 2004).

The other child was found hiding under a bed in one of the upstairs bedrooms. When Duke tried to cut her throat as he had done to her sister, she struggled so hard that he was unable to accomplish the task. So he asked Samra to help him, but Samra refused until Duke yelled at him. Then Duke held her down while Samra killed her. After the murders, Duke grabbed his father's wallet and left the house to dispose of the knives in a storm drain. Samra and Duke met up with the other two boys who were waiting for them as they had planned. Duke warned the other boys that if any of them told, he would kill them as well (*Roper v. Simmons* Amicus Brief, 2004).

The boys washed up and threw the dirty clothes in a dumpster. In order to establish an alibi, they then went to go see a movie, but did not stay for long. Instead they went out to eat and play pool. The next morning Duke had the other boys come with him to ransack the house so it would look like a robbery. After rehearsing their alibi, they called the police. At their trial both Samra and Duke were convicted of four charges of capital murder and sentenced to death. Duke's sentence was recently reversed to life in prison, however, due to the Supreme Court's ruling (*Roper v. Simmons* Amicus Brief, 2004).

CONCLUSIONS AND IMPLICATIONS

This article examined four cases of juveniles sentenced to death for killing their parents between 1973 and 2005, a period when sentencing individuals under 18 in the United States was constitutionally permissible. These parricide cases were identified by reviewing case summaries of juveniles sentenced to death during this period and consulting with Victor Streib, the leading expert on U.S. juveniles sentenced to death.

Conclusions in this article are based on the information cited and are made with caution. Had the authors been able to review the actual case materials and to interview the boys soon after they committed the murders, conclusions and interpretations might have been different. In the Sellers case, more information was available for review and analysis, including Sellers's personal writings, than for the three remaining cases. Even in the Sellers' case, however, psychiatric evaluations, psychological testing, and medical reports that were completed years after Sellers's killings were not available for perusal. This limitation is not easily overcome, as two of the four individuals—Sellers and Lashley—have been executed. The other two individuals whose sentences were commuted to life—McGilberry and Duke—are more than ten years older than they were at the time of their crimes. Their reflections today as men in their late 20s of their thoughts and behavior more than a decade ago might be very different from their experiences at 16 years of age when each was involved in killing four people.

The similarities between the cases of McGilberry and Duke are startling, beginning with the reason the two murdered their families (loss of driving privileges) to their cold-blooded planning before and after the multiple murders. If the facts reported are accurate, both of these boys killed to further selfish instrumental reasons. The driving force behind these murders is consistent with the profile of the dangerously antisocial child.

Lashley would also seem to fit into this group of severely antisocial children. His removing the lightbulb from the front porch prior to the robbery-homicide provides evidence of premeditation. He too was motivated for instrumental gain and had intended from the onset to rob his foster mother. Although Lashley, unlike the other three boys, did not murder a biological parent, the victim in his case was indeed related to him and had been the central person in his life for 14 years. This woman had raised him from the time that he was 2 years old to age 16, when he ambushed and killed her.

The murders committed by the comparison cases all seem especially heinous and cruel. McGilberry bludgeoned his family to death with a baseball bat. Duke used a knife and a gun to murder his whole family, which included two young children, even after they pleaded for mercy. Lashley thrust a knife into the soft spot of his foster mother's head after he had knocked her unconscious.

Sellers's case differs from the other three in four ways. First, he was the only youth known to have murdered prior to the parricide. Second, Sellers claimed to have had experienced memory loss during the crime, whereas available information on the other three boys' accounts suggest that they knew exactly what they were doing and that they were aware that their conduct was wrong. Third, Sellers was reportedly the only one to have been diagnosed by mental health professionals as suffering from a major mental disorder (psychosis or DID), although these diagnoses were made after his conviction. Fourth, Sellers was the only individual to have had a reported history of physical, sexual, and emotional abuse *throughout* his childhood.

It is important to note that Lashley did experience abandonment and abuse during the first few years of his life. Early profound abuse and bonding breaks can lead to an attachment disorder, setting the foundation for hatred and anger and interfering with the development of empathy (Heide & Solomon, 2006). In her studies of juveniles condemned to death in the United States, Lewis and her colleagues (Lewis et al., 1988; Lewis, Yeager, Blake, Bard, & Strenziok, 2004) documented abuse in nearly every case. In a study of 18 men on death row in Texas for murders they committed as juveniles, Lewis et al. (2004) reported that 17 came from extremely violent or abusive families.

It is indeed possible that McGilberry and Duke suffered some child maltreatment, although no substantiated reports of abuse were uncovered during our review. Extreme abuse and neglect are often found in the histories of individuals who commit acts of human cruelty (Magid & McKelvey, 1987). The viciousness with which McGilberry and Duke hunted down their parents and the people their parents loved suggests that something happened to these boys that affected their ability to empathize with human beings. Their detachment from others must have been extreme to have allowed them to plot and carry out the killing of three small children, in addition to their parents.

The Supreme Court's decision in *Roper v. Simmons* (2005) set aside the death penalty for juveniles in recognition that youths, on the average, are not as developmentally mature as adults. Recent scientific findings have indicated that the prefrontal cortex is not fully developed until individuals are between 20 and 25 years old. This part of the brain is responsible for higher functions such as deliberation, judgment, and decision making. Research has also established that brain development is negatively affected by early and profound abuse and neglect. If adolescents who are abused or neglected abuse alcohol and drugs, it is likely that the negative effects will be amplified. Put another way, healthy adolescents raised in functional households can be expected to act impulsively on occasion simply because the higher centers of the brain are not as fully developed as those of adults. If these adolescents have been severely abused and neglected, their ability to stop and think about their actions and to regulate strong emotion is further compromised. If these youths abuse drugs and alcohol, the effects are likely to be additive, meaning that they are less likely to be able to access higher cortical functions to evaluate their decisions and are more likely to behave impulsively (Heide & Solomon, 2006).

These advances in science and the groundbreaking work done by Lewis and her colleagues provide convincing data that all adolescents who act violently, particularly those who murder another human being, should be given psychiatric, neurological, neuropsychological, and educational assessments to determine what factors are influencing their behavior. All of the juveniles on death row in Texas examined by Lewis and her colleagues had signs of prefrontal cortex dysfunction, which can be caused or exacerbated by abuse (Lewis, Yeager, Blake, Bard, & Strenziok, 2004). Available evidence, including the review of the four cases above, suggests that all too often young murderers are often not provided with comprehensive assessments (Heide & Solomon, 2003; Myers, 1992). Accordingly, the extent to which mental illness, neurological deficits, intelligence, environment, and family background have contributed to their behavior is not known.

In the four cases of parricide offenders sentenced to death, the driving force appeared to be the desire to achieve an instrumental, selfish gain and to remove an obstacle. The extent to which early abuse and mental illness contributed to the development of these antisocial youth remains unknown. Knowing the etiology of the antisocial character can be fundamental in preventing this psychopathology in the future. In addition, knowing the pathways that led individuals to plan and execute the cold-blooded killings of those who gave them life would seem essential in developing effective interventions and determining if these individuals can be safely returned to society.

Although juveniles can no longer be sentenced to death for murders they committed prior to age 18, they can be sentenced to life without the possibility of parole in more than 40 states (ACLU of Michigan, 2004). Life imprisonment gives no opportunity for those juveniles who committed their crimes because of immaturity, desperate home situations, or childhood trauma to rehabilitate themselves and reenter society. Instead, they will spend their entire adulthood in prison for a crime committed before the courts judged them to be mature enough to see R-rated movies, to have an alcoholic beverage, or to enter into a legal contract.

Interestingly, the juvenile court was founded more than 100 years ago in recognition of the fact that it was inappropriate to hold juveniles as accountable as adults (Roberts, 2004). In the last 20 years, the United States has moved increasingly to holding juveniles more accountable. Each of the states has mechanisms to move juveniles into adult court where they face longer sentences, including life sentences, and have far fewer treatment and educational resources (Benekos & Merlo, 2008; Heide, 1999).

Research findings leading us to a better understanding of the brain and the endocrine system (Heide & Solomon, 2006) are posing a serious challenge to the current "get tough" public policy with juveniles in the United States. There is evidence that judges, legislators, and even the public are beginning to grapple with the issue of how to deal with today's young violent lawbreakers (Benekos & Merlo, 2008). As science reveals more about the brain and documents individual or group differences in the capacity to control feelings, thoughts, and behavior, the criminal justice system will increasingly face the dilemma: How does society hold young people morally culpable; ensure that the law is fair, just, and humane to those who are constitutionally more at risk of responding and behaving maladaptively through no fault of their own; and, at the same time, protect society?

REFERENCES

ACLU of Michigan. (2004). *Second chances: Juveniles serving life without parole in Michigan prison*. Detroit, MI: Author.

American Council for Drug Education. (n.d.). *Basic facts about drugs: PCP and LSD*. Retrieved August 28, 2007, from http://www.acde.org/common/LSD-PCP.pdf

American Psychiatric Association. (1994). *Diagnostic and statistical manual of mental disorders* (4th ed.). Washington, D.C.: Author.

Amnesty International. (1998). *USA: Killing Hope—The imminent execution of Sean Sellers*. Retrieved August 28, 2007, from http://web.amnesty.org/library/Index/ENGAMR511081998

Application for grant of reprieve or commutation of sentence. (1993, July 23). Retrieved March 20, 2006, from http://www.umsl.edu/~phillips/dp/Lashley.html

Benedek, E., & Cornell, D. (1989). Clinical presentations of homicidal adolescents. In E. Benedek & D. Cornell (Eds.), *Juvenile homicide* (pp. 37–57). Washington, D.C.: American Psychiatric Press.

Benekos, P. J., & Merlo, A. V. (2008). Juvenile justice: The legacy of punitive policy. *Youth Violence and Juvenile Justice*, *6*(1), 28–46.

Blais, M. (1985, March 10). The twisting of Kenny White. *Tropic (The Miami Herald)*, p. 10–17.

Boots, D. P., & Heide, K. M. (2006). Parricides in the media: A content analysis of available reports across cultures. *International Journal of Offender Therapy and Comparative Criminology*, *50*, 418–445.

Corder, B. F., Ball, B. C., Haizlip, T. M., Rollins, R., & Beaumont, R. (1976). Adolescent parricide: A comparison with other adolescent murder. *American Journal of Psychiatry*, *133*(8), 957–961.

Duncan, J. W., & Duncan, G. M. (1971). Murder in the family. *American Journal of Psychiatry*, *127*(11), 74–78.

Durand, V. M., & Barlow, D. H. (2006). *Essentials of abnormal psychology*. Belmont, CA: Thomson/Wadsworth.

Ewing, C. P. (1997). *Fatal families: The dynamics of intrafamilial homicide*. Thousand Oaks, CA: Sage.

Federal Bureau of Investigation. (2006). *Murder and homicide*. Retrieved August 28, 2007, from http://www.fbi.gov/ucr/05cius/offenses/expanded_information/murder_homicide.html

Fendrich, M., Mackesy-Amiti, M. E., Goldstein, P., Spunt, B., & Brownstein, H. (1995). Substance involvement among juvenile murderers: Comparisons with older offenders based on interviews with prison inmates. *International of Journal of Mental Health and Addiction*, *30*, 1363–1382.

Foucault, M. (Ed). (1975). *I, Pierre Riviere, having slaughtered my mother, my sister, and my brother: A case of parricide in the nineteenth century*. New York: Pantheon Books.

Furman v. Georgia, 408 U.S. 238 (1972).

Gregg v. Georgia, 428 U.S.153 (1976).

Haegerich, T. M., & Bottoms, B. L. (2000). Empathy and jurors' decisions in patricide trials involving child sexual abuse allegations. *Law and Human Behavior*, *24*, 421–448.

Heide, K. M. (1989). Parricide: Incidence and issues. *The Justice Professional*, *4*(1), 19–41.

Heide, K. M. (1992). *Why kids kill parents*. Columbus: Ohio State University Press.

Heide, K. M. (1997). Dangerously antisocial kids who kill their parents: Understanding the phenomenon better. In P. Latimore (Ed.), *Proceedings of the fifth annual meeting of the Homicide Research Working Group, 1996 June 9–12, Santa Monica, CA* (pp. 228–233). Washington, D.C.: National Institute of Justice.

Heide, K. M. (1999). *Young killers: The challenge of juvenile homicide*. Thousand Oaks, CA: Sage.

Heide, K. M. (2003). Youth homicide: A review of the literature and a blueprint for action. *International Journal of Offender Therapy and Comparative Criminology*, *47*(1), 6–36.

Heide, K. M., Boots, D., Alldredge, C., Donerly, B., & White, J. R. (2005). Battered child syndrome: An overview of case law and legislation. *Criminal Law Bulletin, 41*(3), 219–239.

Heide, K. M., & Petee, T. (2007). Parricide: An empirical analysis of 24 years of data. *Journal of Interpersonal Violence, 22*(11), 1382–1399.

Heide, K. M., & Solomon, E. P. (2003). Treating today's juvenile homicide offenders. *Youth Violence Juvenile Justice, 1*(1), 5–31.

Heide, K. M., & Solomon, E. P. (2006). Biology, childhood trauma, and homicide: Rethinking justice. *International Journal of Law and Psychiatry, 29*, 220–233.

Hillbrand, M., Alexandre, J. W., Young, J. L., & Spitz, R. T. (1999). Parricide: Characteristics of offenders and victims, legal factors, and treatment issues. *Aggression and Violent Behavior, 4*(2), 179–190.

Kleiman, D. (1988). *A deadly silence*. New York: Atlantic Monthly Press.

Lennings, C. J. (2002). Children who kill family members: Three case studies from Australia. *Journal of Threat Assessment, 20*(2), 57–72.

Lewis, D. O., Pincus, J. H., Bard, B., Richardson, E., Prichep, L. S., Feldman, M., & Yeager, C. (1988). Neuropsychiatric, psychoeducational, and family characteristics of 14 juveniles condemned to death in the United States. *American Journal of Psychiatry, 145*(5), 584–589.

Lewis, D. O., Yeager, C. A., Blake, P., Bard, B., & Strenziok, M. (2004). Ethics questions raised by the neuropsychiatric, neuropsychological, educational, developmental, and family characteristics of 18 juveniles awaiting execution in Texas. *Journal of American Academy of Psychiatry and Law, 32*(4), 408–429.

Mach, J. E., Scherl, D. J., & Macht, L. B. (1973). Children who kill their mothers. In E. J. Anthony & C. Koupernik (Eds.), *The child in his family* (pp. 319–332). New York: Wiley.

Magid, K., & McKelvey, C. A. (1987). *High risk: Children without a conscience*. New York: Bantam Books.

Marleau, J. D., Auclair, N., & Millaud, F. (2006). Comparison of factors associated with parricide in adults and adolescents. *Journal of Family Violence, 21*, 321–325.

McCully, R. S. (1978). The laugh of Satan: A study of a familial murderer. *Journal of Personality Assessment, 42*(1), 81–91.

McGilberry v. State, 741 So. 2d 894 (1999).

Medlicott, R. W. (1955). Paranoia of the exalted type in a setting of *folie a deus*: A study of two adolescent homicides. *British Journal of Medical Psychology, 28*, 205–223.

Mouridsen, S. E., & Tolstrup, K. (1988). Children who kill: A case study of matricide. *Journal of Child Psychology and Psychiatry, 29*, 511–515.

Myers, W. C. (1992). What treatments do we have for children and adolescents who have killed? *Bulletin of American Academy of Psychiatry and Law, 20*(1), 47–58.

NIDA report series: Hallucinogens and dissociative drugs. (n.d.). Retrieved August 28, 2007, from http://www.nida.nih.gov/ResearchReports/Hallucinogens/halluc2.html

Pastore, A. L., & Maguire, K. (2001). *Bureau of Justice statistics: Sourcebook of criminal justice statistics*. Washington, D.C.: Department of Justice.

Post, S. (1982). Adolescent parricide in abusive families. *Child Welfare, 61*(7), 445–455.

Prendergast, A. (1983, May 26). It's you or me, Dad. *Rolling Stone*, 41–44, 66–67.

Prendergast, A. (1986). *The poison tree*. New York: Avon Books.

Roberts, A. R. (2004). The emergence of the juvenile courts and probation services. In A. R. Roberts (Ed.), *Juvenile justice sourcebook* (pp. 163–181). New York: Oxford University Press.

Roper v. Simmons. (2005). Retrieved March 20, 2006, from http://supct.law.cornell.edu/supct/html/03-633.ZS.html

Roper v. Simmons amicus brief. (2004). Retrieved March 20, 2006, from http://websolutions.learfield.com/deathrow/gestalt/go.cfm?objectid=6FBB22D2-6D7F-473A-AF77EF2803092AB3

Russell, D. H. (1984). A study of juvenile murderers of family members. *International Journal of Offender Therapy and Comparative Criminology*, *28*(3), 177–192.

Sadoff, R. L. (1971). Clinical observations on parricide. *Psychiatry Quarterly*, *45*(1), 65–69.

Sargent, D. (1962). Children who kill: A family conspiracy? *Journal of Social Work*, *7*, 35–42.

Scherl, D. J., & Mack, J. E. (1966). A study of adolescent matricide. *Journal of American Academy of Child Psychiatry*, *5*(2), 569–593.

Schlesinger, L. B. (1999). Adolescent sexual matricide following repetitive mother-son incest. *Journal of Forensic Sciences*, *44*(4), 746–749.

Sean Richard Sellers. (n.d.). Retrieved October 1, 2005, from http://www.clarkprosecutor.org/html/death/US/sellers512.htm

Sellers, S. (n.d.). *Exposing Satanism*. Retrieved October 1, 2005, from http://www.exposingsatanism.org/seansellers.htm

Sellers, S. (n.d.). *The confession of my crimes*. Retrieved August 28, 2007, from http://www.clarkprosecutor.org/html/death/US/sellers512.htm

Snell, T., & Maruschak, L. M. (2002). *Bureau of Justice statistics bulletin: Capital punishment 2001*. Washington, D.C.: Department of Justice.

Stalans, L. J., & Henry, G. T. (1994). Societal views of justice for adolescents accused of murder: Inconsistency between community sentiment and automatic legislative transfers. *Law and Human Behavior*, *18*, 675–696.

Stanford v. Kentucky, 492 U.S. 361 (1989).

State of Missouri v. Frederick Lashley. (1984). Retrieved March 20, 2006, from http://websolutions.learfield.com/deathrow/gestalt/go.cfm?objectid=6FBB22D2-6D7F-473A-AF77EF2803092AB3

Streib, V. L. (1987). *Death penalty for juveniles*. Bloomington, IN: Indiana University Press.

Streib, V. L. (1998). Moratorium on the death penalty for juveniles. *Transnational Law and Contemporary Problems*, *61*(4), 55–87.

Streib V. L. (2003a). *The juvenile death penalty today: Death sentences and executions for juvenile crimes—January 1, 1973 to December 31, 2002* [report dated January 9, 2003]. Ohio Northern University, Claude W. Pettit College of Law. Retrieved August 28, 2007, from http://64.233.179.104/scholar?hl=en& lr=&q=cache:Pez_m82uYXkJ:www.internationaljusticeproject.org/pdfs/JuvdeathDec2002-streib.pdf

Streib V. L. (2003b). *The juvenile death penalty today: Death sentences and executions for juvenile crimes—January 1, 1973 to June 30, 2003* [report dated July 1, 2003]. Ohio Northern University, Claude W. Pettit College of Law. Retrieved August 28,

2007, from http://64.233.179.104/scholar?hl=en&lr=&q= cache:koQEZOVfamwJ: www.law.onu.edu/faculty/streib/juvdeath.pdf+author:%22 Victor+Streib%22

Streib V. L. (2004). *The juvenile death penalty today: Death sentences and executions for juvenile crimes—January 1, 1973 to April 30, 2004* [report dated May 4, 2004]. Ohio Northern University, Claude W. Pettit College of Law. Retrieved August 28, 2007, from http://209.85.165.104/search?q=cache:1KPw8g_c08AJ:www.international justiceproject.org/pdfs/JuvDeathApril2004.pdf+The+juvenile+death+penalty+ today:+ death+sentences+and+executions+for+juvenile+crimes,+January+1,+1973+to+April+ 30,+2004.&hl=en&ct=clnk&cd=1&gl=us

Streib, V. L. (2005). *The juvenile death penalty today: Death sentences and executions for juvenile crimes—January 1, 1973 to December 31, 2004* [report dated January 31, 2005]. Ohio Northern University, Claude W. Pettit College of Law. Retrieved August 28, 2007, from http://www.thejusticeproject. org/national/juveniles/ resource-kit/facts-and-figures/17100.pdf

Streib, V. L. (2007). *Juvenile death*. Ohio Northern University, Claude W. Pettit College of Law. Retrieved August 28, 2007, from http://www. law.onu.edu/faculty/ streib/documents/JuvDeath.pdf

Streib, V. L., & Sametz, L. (1989). Executing female juveniles. *Connecticut Law Review, 22*(1), 3–59.

Tanay, E. (1973). Adolescents who kill parents: Reactive parricide. *Australia and New Zealand Journal of Psychiatry, 7*, 263–277.

Tanay, E. (1976). Reactive parricide. *Journal of Forensic Sciences, 21*(1), 76–82.

Thompson v. Oklahoma, 487 U.S. 815 (1988).

Tofexis, A. (1992, November 23). When kids kill abusive parents. *Time*, 60–61.

Tucker, L. S., & Cornwall, T. P. (1977). Mother-son “folie `a deux”: A case of attempted patricide. *American Journal of Psychiatry, 134*(10), 1146–1147.

van der Hart, O., Nijenhuis, E. R. S., & Steele, K. (2006). *The haunted self*. New York: W. W. Norton.

Walker, L. (1989). *Sudden fury*. New York: St. Martin’s Press.

Wertham, F. (1941). *Dark legend*. New York: Duell, Sloan, and Pearce. Witkins v. Missouri, 492 U.S. 361 (1989).

Part VI
Victim Issues

[22]

Trauma Therapy for Death Row Families

WALTER C. LONG, JD
Private Law Practice, Austin, Texas, USA

The family members of death row inmates undergo unique suffering that includes disenfranchised grief and intense psychological trauma. In Texas, where executions occur at a rate of 1 every 2 weeks, this class of trauma victims presumably is large, a fact that should generate public mental health concern. Yet the class remains virtually unknown to the therapeutic community. Very little has been done to address the trauma healing needs of death row families. This theoretical paper proposes that structural therapy designed to reengage attachment relationships and reempower family members' innate resources to emotionally regulate one another may provide one of the most effective means of helping this population survive trauma.

KEYWORDS *death penalty, capital punishment, torture, human rights, trauma, disenfranchised grief, ambiguous loss, PTSD, structural family therapy*

INTRODUCTION

From 1982 until August 2011, the state of Texas executed 473 people, for many years at a pace of about one person every 2 weeks (Texas Department of Criminal Justice, 2009). Currently, more than 300 await execution. Each of those sentenced to death and executed came from a family. Recent studies have documented the psychological distress experienced by the family members of death row inmates (Adcock, 2010; Beck, Blackwell, Leonard, & Mears, 2003; Beck & Britto, 2006; Beck, Britto, & Andrews, 2007; Beck &

Received 14 December 2009; accepted 14 September 2010.
Address correspondence to Walter C. Long, JD, P.O. Box 41557, Austin, TX 78704. E-mail: waltlong@aol.com

Jones, 2007; Byrd, 2000; Jones & Beck, 2006; King, 2003, 2006, 2007; Sharp, 2005; Vandiver, 1998; see also Radelet, Vandiver, & Berardo, 1983). These studies suggest that death sentences cause serious emotional and psychological damage in these families, identifying symptoms consistent with dysthymic disorder, posttraumatic stress disorder (PTSD), complex PTSD, complicated and disenfranchised grief, guilt, and shame (Beck et al., 2007; Jones & Beck, 2006; Sharp, 2005). Concern has even been raised about the intergenerational consequences of death sentencing (Beck & Jones, 2007). However, so far the literature contains no therapies designed to address death row families' unique struggle with trauma.

This article proposes a theoretical structural family therapy to ameliorate the pain of death row families. A basic assumption of family therapy is that families have within themselves unused possibilities (Minuchin & Fishman, 1981) for emotional regulation that may be their best source of healing. The death penalty is a relational assault, threatening and then totally severing family ties (King, 2007). Therefore, family therapies that enhance intrafamilial attachment relationships through restructuring of the family and provision of tools for emotional regulation may provide the most hope for ameliorating the death row families' distress. The therapist's skilled shaping of the attachment relationships within and between the family's subsystems, combined with his or her experiential training in dyadic emotional regulation (e.g., Fosha, 2001) and assistance with meaning making, may best promote lasting relief in families suffering the trauma of a death sentence (Armour, 2003; Van Ecke, Chope, & Emmelkamp, 2006).

OVERVIEW OF THE LITERATURE

The literature on death row families has been primarily descriptive and diagnostic. Depression is so frequently reported as to be a common denominator. For example, Jones and Beck (2006) found that out of 24 death row family members, 16 experienced depression for more than 2 years. Ten out of the 11 who were primary support persons for death-sentenced inmates were depressed. Among these, "depression led to loss of jobs, home, and even life" (p. 283). Most studies have also reported social isolation, stigma, guilt, and prolonged and distorted grieving (inter alia; Jones & Beck, 2006; Sharp, 2005; King & Norgard, 1999; Smykla, 1987).

Most recently, Elizabeth Beck and colleagues have focused on death row families' experiences of disenfranchised grief and nonfinite loss to capture "the nature and intensity of the families' bereavement" (Beck & Jones, 2007; Beck et al., 2007; Jones & Beck, 2006, p. 284). *Disenfranchised grief*, a concept developed by Kenneth Doka, "occurs when a loss cannot be openly acknowledged, publicly mourned, or socially supported" (Doka, 1989; Jones & Beck, 2006, p. 285). Community approval of an inmate's execution denies social support to the family members, causing them to feel isolated and ashamed (Beck et al., 2007). Their resulting disenfranchised grief manifests "high levels of distress and disorganization" and resists healing (Jones & Beck, 2006, p. 285). *Nonfinite loss*, in turn, refers to losses "slowly manifested over time" (Jones & Beck, 2006, p. 284). Much like experiencing the slow demise of a terminally ill family member, the relatives of death row inmates find themselves entrapped between a present marred by frequent losses of hoped-for milestones and the dreaded future appointed time of execution. Sharp (2005) described death row family members as locked into what she called a BADD cycle of disenfranchised grieving (bargaining, activity, disillusionment, and desperation).

The vocabulary of disenfranchised grieving accurately captures the experience of these families, and the interminable quality of nonfinite loss is an important addition to understanding. However, the experience of loss is not only suspended in time but radically ambiguous, as death row families often navigate repeated appellate events that alternately bestow and dash hopes before execution finally occurs (Radelet et al., 1983). Furthermore, grief categories are insufficient to capture the nature of the external stressor causing pathology and distress: homicide. Miller (2009) found that the survivor distress of family members of murder victims is proportional to the perceived intentionality of the killing. Death row families are forced to deal with not only intentionality but elaborate, public premeditation and planning. Trauma is a category that must be carefully considered when examining their experience and looking for solutions to their pain.

The death sentence, culminating in execution, exposes death row family members to at least two interacting kinds of trauma of great intensity and long duration: (a) PTSD and (b) ambiguous loss. Beck and her colleagues (2007) found symptoms of PTSD in 16 of the 24 family members in their study. They concluded that death row family members' trauma stems from their experience of social isolation coupled with the "overwhelming sense of powerlessness that is inherent in the experience of death row" (p. 129).

Pauline Boss (2006) coined the term *ambiguous loss* to describe a kind of *ongoing* trauma caused by a continuing external relational stressor. Ambiguous loss more accurately than nonfinite loss captures the seemingly interminable survival/extinction emotional stress of death row family members. According to Boss, ambiguous loss occurs when a family member is physically absent but psychologically present, or physically present but psychologically absent. Before and after execution, the inmate, imagined as terrified and isolated, takes on an imposing role in the psychological life of the family. Every prison visit with the actual inmate similarly is a struggle against the frightening future for psychological presence. The death sentence creates a limbo of chronic uncertainty, upsets the family's systemic processes, rearranges normal family relationships, prevents passage through the normal stages of grief, and undermines resilience. Violent death has been held to have four grief stages: (a) initial shock and alertness; (b) survivor search for the lost loved one; (c) disorganization and difficulty in functioning; and, finally, (d) *mitigation*, defined as "healthy adaptation to the reality of the death of the loved attachment object and an ability to reinvest in another" (Parkes, 1970; Stevens-Guille, 1999, p. 55). Ambiguous loss stands in the way of mitigation for death row family members.

Family members of death row inmates intensely identify with their missing death-sentenced member. Frequently they report that "they feel like they are on death row with their loved one" (Jones & Beck, 2006, p. 296). They often become enmeshed with the prisoner and his own fear, losing awareness of their own psychological boundaries. In their experience of ambiguous loss, the physically absent prisoner becomes very present as the controlling member of their psychological family, bearing an imagined highly aroused affective state and often remaining thus present for many years after the execution takes place. He is a "family ghost" that must be addressed in the course of therapy for a death row family (Minuchin & Fishman, 1981, p. 57).

METHOD

I am not a therapist but a graduate student in counseling psychology and a Texas criminal defense attorney with years of experience representing death row inmates in their habeas corpus appeals and working with their families. Unless otherwise explicitly sourced, my opinions are formed from experiences in my law practice and the public accounts of family members given to the Texas After Violence Project (TAVP), a nonprofit oral history organization that I founded. One purpose of TAVP is to provide materials that can be used in social science study of community violence and capital punishment. The organization itself takes no policy position on the death penalty; rather, it is designed to listen without judgment, promote dialogue, and make a record for history. Upon receiving final consent from narrators with adherence to institutional review board guidelines, TAVP releases the stories for archiving and public access in the University of Texas library system. The judgments expressed herein are my own.

DEATH SENTENCE TRAUMA AND THE NATURAL SUPPORT SYSTEM

The death penalty is indistinguishable from torture in legal description and similar in affective consequences (Cerna, 1997; Vogelman & Lewis, 1994). The United Nations Convention Against Torture defines *torture* as including any "act by which severe pain or suffering, whether physical or mental, is intentionally inflicted on a person . . . punishing him for an act he . . . has committed" (United Nations Convention Against Torture, 1988, Article 1). *Death sentencing* unquestionably causes severe "mental" suffering "which cannot be relieved by developing more 'humane' methods of killing" (Vogelman & Lewis, 1994). "From the moment the sentence is pronounced, the prisoner is forced to contemplate the prospect of being taken away to be put to death at an appointed time" (Vogelman & Lewis, 1994, quoting Amnesty International, 1989, p. 61). The prisoner's family members likewise are forced to contemplate this while, in a number of states (including Texas), from sentencing to execution physical contact between prisoner and family also is prohibited (Byrd, 2000). The "intense fear, helplessness, [and] horror" observed in clinical assessment of PTSD is "common" in death row families (Beck et al., 2007, p. 125).

"The core experiences of psychological trauma are disempowerment and disconnection from others" (Herman, 1997, p. 133). Traumatic events demonstrate contempt for people's dignity and autonomy, sending them the message that they are nothing, destroying their belief that they can be themselves in relation to others (Herman, 1997). An execution is such an event, "not only depriv[ing] the prisoner of all vestiges of human dignity, [but] . . . ultimate[ly] desecrat[ing] the individual as a human being. It is the annihilation of the very essence of human dignity" (*Kindler v. Canada*, 1992, p. 241). It causes trauma in those with ties to the person under such assault, whether they are advocates, friends, or family members. For those attached to the defendant, executions can smash beliefs they may have had in a meaningful, safe, and fair world.

Posttraumatic stress is a process in which dysregulation caused by traumatic exposure becomes hardwired into the brain's responses to stimuli (Van der Kolk, 2006). Healing trauma involves seeking methods that can assist sufferers to find the capacity to cognitively evaluate their emotions again. "It is critical that they gain enough distance from their sensory imprints and trauma-related emotions so that they can observe and analyze these sensations and emotions without becoming hyperaroused or engaging in avoidance maneuvers" (Van der Kolk, 2003, p. 187). Once they are able to achieve such distance, they can viscerally (not just intellectually) discover that remembrance of traumatic events does not necessarily lead them to have overwhelming emotions and that they can achieve competent self-regulation and self-soothing (Van der Kolk, 2006).

Van der Kolk (2003) has laid out three "critical steps" for treating PTSD: (a) *safety:* "After having been traumatized, [it] is critical that the victim re-establish contact with his or her natural support system"; (b) *anxiety management:* practical skills taught in therapy may include "deep muscle relaxation, breathing control, role playing, covert modeling, thought stopping, and guided self-dialogue"; and (c) *emotional processing:* this involves the victim learning to remember the traumatic event without feeling helpless, that is, learning to remember *without reexperiencing* the event and learning that the event had "a beginning, a middle, and an end" and "now belongs to . . . personal history" (pp. 188–189).

The theoretical structural therapy model that I propose attempts to apply Van der Kolk's critical steps of treatment to death row families. The model should enhance the potential of the natural support system of the family to nurture its own subsystems. It does that, first, by having the therapist attend to the nature and strength of the attachment relationships in each family subsystem, calculating which to support in which configurations (in order to avoid excluding any members and to enhance the chances of the entire family's reempowerment) and, second, by having the therapist strategically meet with subsystems and experientially show those subsystems how to emotionally regulate themselves and to emotionally process their trauma so that they can begin doing that on a self-sustaining basis within the family, creating a cycle of healing to replace the cycle of trauma.

AMBIGUOUS LOSS AND THE FAMILY GHOST

It is my perception that death row families have a very potent ghost member. Minuchin and Fishman (1981) described "families with a ghost" as follows:

> A family which has experienced death or desertion may have problems reassigning the tasks of the missing member. . . . Problems in these families may be experienced by family members as issues of incomplete mourning. But if the therapist operates on this assumption, she may crystallize the family instead of helping them move toward a new organization. From the therapeutic point of view, this is a family in transition. Previous shapes are handicapping the development of new structures. (p. 57)

The family ghost is common terminology in family therapy. Harry Stack Sullivan (1972) defined *family ghosts* as presences who are "exterior to sensual contact—effective by virtue only of the individual's faith in their past or present existence elsewhere" (p. 47). Carl Whitaker made ghosts real by bringing absent family members into therapy sessions (Haley & Hoffman, 1967).

Experiencing ambiguous loss, death row family members inevitably find themselves in an ongoing traumatic transition with a family ghost that can last many years. Their ghost is the *imagined* to-be-executed or executed inmate, specifically visualized or contemplated as being traumatized, or having been traumatized or killed. A subsystem between a death row family member and the ghost can become a kind of *pas de deux* family within a family, dangerously enmeshed within itself and disengaged from the rest. Mothers frequently respond to the death penalty's destruction of their attachment relationship with their child by dissolving their boundaries. A Texas mother told TAVP how, when her son was given an execution date, she "successfully committed suicide, but the paramedics brought her back." Her son survived that date but was executed shortly thereafter. I observed another Texas mother in an apparent state of catatonia days before her son's execution. She was in my law office, with her head on a desk, completely unresponsive to any kind of stimulus from other family members who were trying to reach her. She could have been dissociating or manifesting *tonic immobility*, a state in animals and humans elicited by extreme fear coupled with overwhelming physical restraint that prevents fight or flight. Tonic immobility is induced in lab animals by inverting them on their backs and restraining them until they stop struggling (Marx, Forsyth, Gallup, Fuse, & Lexington, 2008). This is not far removed, of course, from the mental picture of an execution. Reporters witnessing actual executions have described a characteristic wail let out by the inmates' mothers (Willett, 2000). Recently, a reporter described a mother weeping inconsolably, stamping her feet, and pressing her head against the unyielding viewing chamber glass while her son, strapped on his back to the table, was killed (Turner, 2009).

Enmeshment with the ghost can be subtle yet potent. In a story given to TAVP, the brother of a young man executed many years previously recounted numbness and memory loss that he had experienced since the execution, which was carried out on the eve of his own high school graduation. When it happened, everything became a "blur." At the funeral, he sat next to his grandfather without recognizing him. God, he said, stripped him of memories, "wipe[d] out everything for [him] like a disk clean-up on a laptop or something." Years later, he continued to feel somewhat distant from his family, which had always been a loving, functional family, even during the years of his brother's imprisonment.

Starting when he was about 10 years old, his parents traveled to death row weekly to see his brother. He had gone on many of those trips and loved his brother deeply. But not infrequently, his father would walk into the house and mistakenly greet him by his brother's name. Because his parents were "always scared of getting another phone call," they treated him as though he were his brother, only kept under tighter rein. He understood that his parents' obsession with saving his brother robbed him of some of the attention and care they otherwise would have bestowed upon him. Nevertheless, at one point, he accused his father of not loving him.

Years after the execution, the young man still wore a custom-made t-shirt bearing a color photo of his brother and his parents on the front. The shirt represented the tight emotional bond he had with his brother. But he could recall virtually nothing of what his brother had told him during the many prison visits. Instead, he was possessed by his sensations of his brother in danger. He clearly remembered empathizing with his brother's emotional turmoil when an unlikely stay of execution had occurred:

> If I was to tell you that at 1:45 we was going to take you to this place and strap you down and kill you, you think you'd be able to deal with that? You see what I'm saying? . . . And then they gave him a steak? So it was like, they took him down there, strapped him in, and was going to do everything to him, and then be like, "Nah, we're not going to kill you today. Come back another day."

As the reprieve proved temporary and the family's initial euphoria turned to dread, he became angry at ongoing efforts to save his brother, whom he perceived to be subjected to many indignities on death row. What would his brother be saved for? More of the same maltreatment? Now he felt ashamed for a thought that had passed his mind then: *"Go ahead and kill him."*

The young man continued to feel as though there was no one who could share his experience. "How can you address someone who just lost their brother to lethal injection? . . . You can't even, you don't even know what to say to that person." He recognized that his own family or other families that similarly had gone through executions might understand him, but he observed, "They have a hard time dealing with it themselves, so how are you going to ask advice of them?" He described himself as being basically "inside the box," which is remarkable, because this is exactly how he had seen his brother during visits. The visitation room on Texas's death row contains a long row of slender, sterile, white metal cubicles ("boxes") with steel mesh doors at the back for introduction and extraction of the inmate and a wall of thick glass on the front separating the inmate and his family members.

The young man evokes therapeutic concern because of the effect that the family ghost has had on his maturation and individuation process and on his continuing experiences of isolation and numbness. The traumatizing image of his brother in danger appears to have effected a block between him and his otherwise loving parents, enhancing ongoing trauma for all and inhibiting their capacity to be fully present and to emotionally regulate one another.

A PROPOSED THERAPY FOR DEATH SENTENCE TRAUMA

The daunting nature of the therapeutic work of restoration cannot be overstated. Death row families often already are victimized by economic poverty, racial discrimination, and some degree of dysfunction long before the crime leading them to experience death row occurs. The death sentence further disrupts the very attachment bonds that otherwise are the most critical resource for their trauma healing (Allen & Bloom, 1994). With otherwise intact families, I believe a therapist taking a family structural approach should try to accomplish several things: (a) strategically form secure relationships with family members to help them experientially understand dyadic emotional regulation; (b) continuously map the family's subsystems; (c) move subsystems together, helping them discover and use their innate potential for mutual emotional regulation; (d) reassign or redefine the role of the family ghost in relation to all subsystems, including the family as a whole; and (e) help the family in its process of meaning making and the pursuit of what matters.

Strategic Formation of Secure Relationships

Van der Kolk's first critical step to trauma recovery is reestablishing contact with the natural support system, because secure attachment bonds are the best defense against "trauma induced pathology" (Johnson, 2002, p. 25). Humans are communal creatures who receive through the subconscious communication of their physiologies the key to their mutual thriving. Attachment is "the interactive regulation of synchrony between psychobiologically attuned organisms" (Schore, 2003, p. 64). Secure contact with an attachment figure—a parent, child, sibling, spouse, lover, friend, teammate, fellow soldier, or colleague—is an innate survival mechanism. A secure attachment provides a safe base from which to explore the world as well as a haven where feelings of distress can be expressed in ways that elicit support. "The building blocks of secure bonds are emotional accessibility and responsiveness" (Johnson, 2002, p. 39). A secure bond is the single most important treatment for trauma, because it literally "tranquilizes the nervous system" (Johnson, 2002, p. 44, quoting Schore, 1994).

The therapist needs to nurture his or her own secure attachment relationship with each participating individual family member in order to help each experience dyadic emotional regulation. Diana Fosha (2001) defined *dyadic regulation* as mutual coordination between family members of their emotion-handling strategies:

> Optimal dyadic regulation of emotion [means that] each partner is open and communicates to the other, who responds openly in turn. The partners remain engaged and oriented toward one another even when things get difficult. Mutual coordination does not mean perfect empathy and flawless mutual attunement. It means being motivated to maintain connection and communication even in the face of discord and difficulty without withdrawing into oneself and closing up or putting up a wall. (p. 228)

The therapist joins the family as an extraordinary source of empathy and as an expert in sharing emotional insight. In each dyadic relationship the therapist forms a subsystem model that he or she hopes will be good for replication between and within the family's other subsystems. The end goal is "eventually enabling each member to use each other and the family as a secure base" (Stevenson-Hinde, 2007, p. 340).

Continuous Mapping of Family Subsystems

The therapist continuously maps the family's kaleidoscopically relating subsystems because his or her process of joining each subsystem as an expert member of the family has to be dynamic, adjusting to developments within and between enmeshed or disengaged subsystems (Minuchin & Fishman, 1981). Traumatic events, and especially death sentences and executions, disengage family subsystems because they dramatically increase each subsystem's sense of isolation and powerlessness. The relationship style of almost any particular subsystem likely will be one that is enmeshed with the family ghost. Until the ghost is reassigned and the family has reached a point of emotional stability, the map is going to show lines (broken or whole, but dominant) between every subsystem and the ghost (the missing family member perceived through the state's traumatizing actions).

Moving Subsystems to Find Optimal Emotional Regulation

While facilitating the family subsystems' general and specific understandings of the trauma and its effects, the therapist mindfully needs to move the subsystems toward one another so as to help them uncover their own unused potential to optimally assist one another with emotional regulation. The therapist strategizes with regard to which subsystems are ready, which ones could have the greatest influence on balancing and releasing the potentialities of the whole family subsystem or significant other parts, and so forth.

Reassigning the Ghost

The therapist helps the subsystems to become securely emotionally reattached vertically and horizontally with one another according to appropriate family roles instead of dysfunctionally bonded to the traumatic image of the missing family member and, in some cases, the event that disappeared him. The therapist must simultaneously assist the family to reintegrate the missing member in stable ways that, for example, may honor his memory (especially if injustice in addition to the execution is perceived), may involve attempted reconciliatory acts with the aggrieved family on the other side of the crime or the community, or may simply involve concerted effort to recall and recount the dignity of that individual and his benign roles in the family before the crime occurred. Emotionally reattached subsystems have to be liberated from the linkage with the traumatizing image of the executed family member that causes intrafamilial walls.

Assisting Meaning Making and the Pursuit of That Which Matters

In addition to relocating the subsystems, the therapist needs to help the family reconstitute its previously nurturing and grounding schemas—its meaningful stories about its secure place in the world—by "incorporating new and adaptive cognitions" and by undertaking empowering actions (Allen & Bloom, 1994, p. 426). Armour (2003) noted that "studies have shown that finding meaning occurs less often for persons dealing with violent death" (p. 523). She proposed placing meaning creation within the context of "the intense pursuit of what matters," a program of intense meaning generating ventures that enable survivors of homicide to "relearn the self" and "relearn the world" (p. 525). The program has a couple of elements that may meet the needs of execution survivors: (a) fighting for what's right and (b) living in ways that give a purpose to the executed family member's death. The incorporation of *doing* into meaning making engages the body as well as mind in the reconstitution of the self following the traumatic event. The essential meaning making must reconstitute the individual's and family's senses that they have achieved a position within the community that is beyond shame. Maercker and Muller (2004) found that an individual's "self-perceived rejection by extended social environments (e.g., acquaintances, colleagues, local authorities)" could have a stronger association with PTSD symptoms than self-perceived rejection by family members (p. 350). In a recent case on which I worked, survivors of the executed inmate posted his obituary in the local newspaper, recounting his many achievements and good deeds during his decades on death row. This possibly unprecedented act was a good first step toward their healing.

REFERENCES

Adcock, C. (2010). The collateral anti-therapeutic effects of the death penalty. *Florida Coastal Law Review, 11*, 289–320.

Allen, S., & Bloom, S. (1994). Group and family treatment of post-traumatic stress disorder. *Psychiatric Clinics of North America, 17*, 425–437.

Amnesty International. (1989). *When the state kills: The death penalty: A human rights issue*. London, England: Amnesty International.

Armour, M. (2003). Meaning making in the aftermath of homicide. *Death Studies, 27*, 519–540.

Beck, E., Blackwell, B., Leonard, P., & Mears, M. (2003). Seeking sanctuary: Interviews with family members of capital defendants. *Cornell Law Review, 88*, 382–418.

Beck, E., & Britto, S. (2006). Using feminist methods and restorative justice to interview capital offenders' family members. *Affilia, 21*(1), 59–70.

Beck, E., Britto, S., & Andrews, A. (2007). *In the shadow of death: Restorative justice and death row families*. New York, NY: Oxford University Press.

Beck, E., & Jones, S. (2007). Children of the condemned: Grieving the loss of a father to death row. *Omega, 56*(2), 191–215.

Boss, P. (2006). *Loss, trauma, and resilience: Therapeutic work with ambiguous loss*. New York, NY: Norton.

Byrd, R. (2000). A "last hug" before execution: The case in favor of contact visitation for death row inmates in Texas. *Scholar: St. Mary's Law Review on Minority Issues, 2*, 249–288.

Cerna, C. (1997). Universality of human rights: The case of the death penalty. *ILSA Journal of International and Comparative Law, 3*, 465–475.

Doka, K. (1989). *Disenfranchised grief: Recognizing hidden sorrows*. Lexington, MA: Lexington Books.

Fosha, D. (2001). The dyadic regulation of affect. *JCLP/In Session: Psychotherapy in Practice, 57*(2), 227–242.

Haley, J., & Hoffman, L. (1967). The growing edge: An interview with Carl Whitaker. In J. Haley & L. Hoffman (Eds.), *Techniques of family therapy* (pp. 265–360). New York, NY: Basic Books.

Herman, J. (1997). *Trauma and recovery: The aftermath of violence—From domestic abuse to political terror*. New York, NY: Basic Books.

Johnson, S. (2002). *Emotionally focused couple therapy with trauma survivors: Strengthening attachment bonds*. New York, NY: Guilford.

Jones, S., & Beck, E. (2006). Disenfranchised grief and nonfinite loss as experienced by the families of death row inmates. *Omega, 54*, 281–299.

Kindler v. Canada, 6 CRR (2d) 193 (SCC) at 241 (Cory, J.) (1992). Retrieved from http://www.canlii.org/en/ca/scc/doc/1991/1991canlii78/1991canlii78.html

King, R. (2003). *Capital consequences: Families of the condemned tell their stories*. New Brunswick, NJ: Rutgers University Press.

King, R. (2006). The impact of capital punishment on families of defendants and murder victims' family members. *Judicature, 89*, 292–296.

King, R. (2007). No due process: How the death penalty violates the constitutional rights of the family members of death row prisoners. *Boston University Public Interest Law Journal, 16*, 195–253.

King, R., & Norgard, K. (1999). What about our families? Using impact on death row defendants' family members as a mitigating factor in death penalty sentencing hearings. *Florida State University Law Review, 26*, 1119–1174.

Maercker, A., & Muller, J. (2004). Social acknowledgment as a victim or survivor: A scale to measure a recovery factor of PTSD. *Journal of Traumatic Stress, 17*, 345–351.

Marx, B., Forsyth, J., Gallup, G., Fuse, T., & Lexington, J. (2008). Tonic immobility as an evolved predator defense: Implications for sexual assault survivors. *Clinical Psychology: Science and Practice, 15*(1), 74–90.

Miller, L. (2009). Family survivors of homicide: I. Symptoms, syndromes, and reaction patterns. *American Journal of Family Therapy, 37*, 67–79.

Minuchin, S., & Fishman, C. (1981). *Family therapy techniques*. Cambridge, MA: Harvard University Press.

Parkes, C. (1970). The first year of bereavement: A longitudinal study of the reaction of London widows to the death of their husbands. *Psychiatry, 4*, 444–467.

Radelet, M., Vandiver, M., & Berardo, F. (1983). Families, prisons, and men with death sentences: The human impact of structured uncertainty. *Journal of Family Issues, 4*, 593–612.

Schore, A. (1994). *Affect regulation and organization of the self*. Hillsdale, NJ: Erlbaum.

Schore, A. (2003). *Affect dysregulation and disorders of the self*. New York, NY: Norton.

Sharp, S. (2005). *Hidden victims: The effects of the death penalty on families of the accused*. New Brunswick, NJ: Rutgers.

Smykla, J. (1987). The human impact of capital punishment: Interviews with families of persons on death row. *Journal of Criminal Justice, 15*, 331–347.

Stevens-Guille, M. (1999). Intersections of grief and trauma: Family members' reactions to homicide. In C. Figley (Ed.), *Traumatology of grieving: Conceptual, theoretical, and treatment foundations* (pp. 53–69). Philadelphia, PA: Brunner/Mazel.

Stevenson-Hinde, J. (2007). Attachment theory and John Bowlby: Some reflections. *Attachment & Human Development, 9*, 337–342.

Sullivan, H. (1972). *Personal psychopathology: Early formulations*. New York, NY: Norton.

Texas Department of Criminal Justice. (2011). *Executed offenders*. Retrieved from http://www.tdcj.state.tx.us/stat/executedoffenders.htm

Turner, A. (2009, November 20). Board's plea fails to stop execution. Retrieved from *Houston Chronicle* website: http://www.chron.com/CDA/archives/archive.mpl?id=2009_4814871

United Nations Convention Against Torture and Other Cruel, Inhuman or Degrading Treatment or Punishment, art. 1, Dec. 10, 1984, S. Treaty Doc. No. 100-20 (1988), 1465 U.N.T.S. 113.

Van der Kolk, B. (2003). Posttraumatic stress disorder and the nature of trauma. In M. Solomon & D. Siegel (Eds.), *Healing trauma: Attachment, mind, body, and brain* (pp. 168–195). New York, NY: Norton.

Van der Kolk, B. (2006). Clinical implications of neuroscience research in PTSD. *Annals of the New York Academy of Sciences, 40*, 1–17.

Van Ecke, Y., Chope, R., & Emmelkamp, P. (2006). Bowlby and Bowen: Attachment theory and family therapy. *Counseling and Clinical Psychology Journal, 3*(2), 81–108.

Vandiver, M. (1998). The impact of the death penalty on families of homicide victims and of condemned prisoners. In J. Acker, R. Bohn, & C. Lanier (Eds.), *America's experiment with capital punishment: Reflections on the past, present and future of the ultimate penal sanction* (pp. 477–505). Durham, NC: Carolina Academic Press.

Vogelman, L., & Lewis, S. (1994). Life after death row: Posttraumatic stress and the story of Philip Takedi. *South African Journal of Psychology, 24*(2). Retrieved from http://www.csvr.org.za/wits/papers/paplsl.htm

Willett, J. (2000, October 12). *Witness to an execution*. Retrieved from the National Public Radio website: http://www.npr.org/programs/atc/witness/

[23]

CONTESTING THE VICTIM CARD: Closure Discourse and Emotion in Death Penalty Rhetoric

Nancy Berns*

Drake University

Closure for crime victims' families has become an important cultural narrative in the past two decades. This paper furthers our understanding of motivational framing and emotional resonance by illustrating how death penalty advocates use emotion-domain expansion to tap into the popular concept of "closure." By arguing that the death penalty can bring closure and healing to crime victims' families, advocates expand their emotional appeal. Abolitionists have also embraced closure and argue that other options are preferable for victims' families. Implications of this process include shifts in death penalty rhetoric, new feeling rules, emotive dissonance, and the institutionalization of closure.

The promise of "closure" for crime victims and their families has become a prominent cultural narrative for defining not only victims' needs but also the broader concept of justice. Used to tell stories about an array of issues, including grief, victimization, the criminal justice system, and capital punishment, *closure discourse* has emerged as a powerful new framework for talking about social problems and a contemporary example of what scholars have identified as cultural resources (Best 1999), cultural narrations (Snow and Benford 1988), moral vocabularies (Ibarra and Kitsuse 1993), emotional discourses (Loseke 2000), or cultural themes (Hilgartner and Bosk 1988; Gamson 1992). In particular, closure has become a popular rhetorical resource in the cultural toolkit (Swidler 1986) of both death penalty advocates and abolitionists and has proved useful for doing social problems emotion work (Hochschild 1979; Loseke 2000).

There is no agreement about what closure is, how it should be defined, or even whether or not it exists. And for those who do believe in its existence, there is no consensus about how it can be achieved. Some argue that killing the murderer will bring closure to the families of homicide victims. Others argue that only forgiveness will bring closure. And, significantly, many families of murder victims argue that there is no such thing as closure and therefore disdain the word.

Tapping into the cultural narrative of closure has been particularly useful for death penalty advocates because it allows them to broaden their emotion claims for why the death penalty is necessary. No longer are death penalty supporters simply advocating killing offenders; rather they are offering healing and closure for victims' families. Although critics argue that the pro-death penalty closure argument is still really about vengeance, the rhetoric surrounding closure has opened up public support and opportunities for the institutionalization of closure in the criminal justice system. Death

*Direct all correspondence to Nancy Berns, Department for the Study of Culture and Society, Drake University, 105D Howard Hall, Des Moines, IA 50311; e-mail: nancy.berns@drake.edu

penalty advocates made use of closure first, but abolitionists have countered with their own therapeutic claims about what victims' families need. Abolitionists challenge the new emotion claims pushed by death penalty advocates, but they also embrace the concept of closure to frame their own claims such as advocating restorative justice, forgiveness, and life without parole as routes to closure.

In this article I address how death penalty claimsmakers use closure discourse to expand the emotion domain of their claims and the implications of this process, including feeling rules, emotive dissonance, counterclaims, and the institutionalization of closure.

LITERATURE REVIEW

For this study, I draw from several fields of literature, including studies on death penalty rhetoric, the social construction of social problems, and the sociology of emotion.

Death Penalty Rhetoric

There have been many studies on death penalty rhetoric (e.g., Bedau 1987, 2004; Haines 1996, 1992; Galliher et al. 2002; Kirchmeier 2002; Lynch 2002; Haney and Greene 2004; Sarat 2005). However, only a few have included the role of closure in the debate; most notable are Zimring (2003), Kanwar (2001), and Bandes (2000). All three of these scholars criticize the use of closure as a justification for the death penalty. Zimring (2003) shows that prior to 1989 closure did not appear in death penalty stories in the United States, but by 2001 there were more than 500 stories per year mentioning closure and capital punishment. Kanwar (2001:216) argues that "the cultural production of a feeling of closure" for victims has become an independent justification for the death penalty. Kanwar and Bandes both discuss how victims seek closure in different ways: some through mercy and others through vengeance.

The claim that emotions play a key role in the death penalty debate is not new. Advocates on both sides have been working hard for decades to produce arguments that resonate not only with the public's intellect, but also its emotions. The abolitionist movement struggled to find an argument that appealed to a mainstream majority because so many of its reasons for opposing the death penalty put them on the side of murderers. For example, the sanctity of life argument holds that human life has infinite value and must be protected at all costs (Bedau 1987; Sarat 2005). Related arguments include the violation of the Eighth Amendment, which forbids cruel and unusual punishment and the immorality of the state killing people (Bedau 1987; Sarat 2005). It is difficult to gather widespread public support for a movement when critics can easily charge movement supporters of siding with "evil offenders" over "innocent victims." In what Sarat (2005) calls the "new abolitionism," the post-Furman era of death penalty debate saw a new rhetoric emerge that allowed abolitionists to oppose capital punishment in a way that had mass appeal: Innocent people may be executed. The larger scope of this argument includes fairness, constitutional issues of practice, and racial/class discrimination, but perhaps the most effective part has been the fear of convicting and executing innocent people. This allows abolitionists to "be on the side" of innocent people rather than just murderers—a strategy that appeals to a larger section of society (Radelet and Bedau 1998). The growing evidence that innocent people are being convicted and placed on death row has been the lynchpin in the new abolitionism (Radelet and Bedau 1998; Sarat 2005; Unnever and Cullen 2005). Research indicates that it is an argument that may be having significant impact on reshaping public opinion (Fan, Keltner, and Wyatt 2002; Sarat 2005; Unnever and Cullen 2005).

Historically, two key rationales in favor of the death penalty have been deterrence and retribution. Expressive values associated with the death penalty center around the idea of retribution—allowing societal expressions of moral outrage, giving the offender his or her just deserts, and reinforcing a shared sense of community norms (Banner 2002). With the success of new abolitionism, presumed benefits of capital punishment in terms of deterrence had to compete with concerns about the byproducts of implementing the death penalty, including lack of due process, executing the innocent, high costs, and racial discrimination (Acker 2003). Furthermore, with an expanding body of literature questioning deterrence effects and the public's growing awareness of the death penalty's economic costs, the argument for the death penalty started to face stiff challenges (Acker 2003; Bohm 2003).

Pro-death penalty advocates have countered the innocence argument by denying that any innocent person has been executed and arguing that safeguards are in place to prevent wrongful conviction. However, a more effective counter argument to the new abolitionism is the pro-death penalty advocates' rhetorical shift to focusing on closure for victims' families. The closure argument not only expands their emotion domain, but also shifts death penalty rhetoric away from offenders and onto victims' families. Zimring, Kanwar, and Bandes provide a good beginning for thinking about closure as a rhetorical argument in the death penalty debate. However, their discussions only begin our inquiry and stop short of examining how abolitionists have responded to the new rhetoric. I examine the use of closure by death penalty advocates and the results of that use, and then show how abolitionists have countered with their own claims about victims and closure, which has not been investigated in any previous study. Analyzing abolitionists' responses to the new closure claims also contributes to the research Benford and Hunt (2003) argue is needed to better understand the interactional dynamics of counterframing and reframing.

Social Problems and Emotions

Grounded in social constructionism, this article furthers our understanding of motivational framing and emotional resonance by illustrating how death penalty advocates use what I call *emotion-domain expansion* to tap into the increasingly popular concept of closure. I will first briefly highlight previous scholarship that lays the foundation for my analysis, and then define emotion-domain expansion and outline the stages that emerge in this process.

A large body of research on social problems uses social constructionism to study the claimsmaking activities of advocates, officials, media, and others who shape social problems (e.g., Best 1987, 1990; Spector and Kitsuse 1977; Holstein and Miller 1993;

Loseke 2003). In particular, I build on Joel Best's concept of "domain expansion." Best argues that claimsmakers frequently reconstruct a problem in order to expand its scope or to renew interest. "Claimsmakers are likely to offer a new definition, extending the problem's domain or boundaries, and find new examples to typify just what is at issue" (Best 1990:66).

Frame analysis is compatible with the concept of domain expansion. Snow et al. (1986) identified four types of frame alignment processes that are used to increase movement participation: amplification, extension, bridging, and transformation. Furthermore, Snow and Benford (1988) specified three types of framing as necessary for successful rhetoric: diagnostic, prognostic, and motivational. Although motivational framing involves convincing people why they should care (Loseke 2003) and includes emotions, it is the least researched and understood part of the framing process (Benford 1997; Berbrier 1998; Schrock, Holden, and Reid 2004). Berbrier (1998:440) expanded on the frame alignment perspective in his use of "cultural affectations" to explain how "emotionally laden values and culturally resonant claims" are aligned. Schrock et al. (2004) furthered our understanding of motivation framing and the use of emotions in their discussion of "emotional resonance." Constructionist scholars have also linked successful claims-making and frame alignment to the ability of advocates and social movement leaders to connect to available cultural resources (Best 1991, 1999). Having a strong connection between a social problem frame and the larger culture is important for cultural resonance (Snow and Benford 1988; Gamson and Modigliani 1989; Benford and Snow 2000).

Cultural resources are important because they provide language already familiar to people, which strengthens cultural resonance. There were multiple social and cultural events that shaped language and narratives relating to victims and closure. Death penalty advocates did not invent the concept of closure. Like other social problems claimsmakers, they drew from existing cultural resources. During the 1960s and 1970s, numerous social movements developed that changed how we think about victims and victimization (Best 1999). Closure talk emerged in this cultural and political context. Diverse movements such as feminism, civil rights, crime victims' rights, restorative justice, and law-and-order conservatism helped set the stage for closure discourse. Hundreds of organizations grew out of the larger crime victims' rights movement. Groups such as Mothers Against Drunk Driving (MADD), Murder Victims' Families for Reconciliation (MVFR), and Parents of Murdered Children significantly changed how we think about crime victims and their role in the criminal justice system. Furthermore, popular culture, including talk shows, movies, television shows, and self-help books, has introduced formats and rhetoric that contribute to a melodramatic focus on crime victims, revenge, and a need for therapeutic closure. New forms of victimization and melodrama appeared on television talk shows, which became increasingly popular in the 1980s (Lowney 1999). In this format, talk shows produce a compassionate emotional climate involving outrage over suffering and calls for punishment and shame for the villains. Today most talk shows, movies, and news coverage about crime and other social problems include the victim as a central character and use emotions to drive the story.

This study also draws on Arlie Hochschild's approach to emotion culture in explaining the role of emotion in social problems work. Hochschild (1983:18) defines feeling rules as "standards used in emotional conversation to determine what is rightly owed and owing in the currency of feeling." People engage in emotion management in order to make feelings or their presentation of feelings conform to cultural feeling rules. When they fail to do this, they may experience emotive dissonance, a disconnect between what they feel and what they think they are supposed to feel. Social problems scholar Donileen Loseke (2000) argues that claimsmakers can draw upon moral and emotional discourses as cultural resources to persuade audiences to feel outrage or sympathy. Loseke extends emotion work to include "the work of constructing claims that can be evaluated through widely circulating feeling rules" (Loseke 2000:44).

Building on these bodies of scholarship, I use the term "emotion-domain expansion" to describe the identification of new aspects of an established social problem that produce strong emotional responses. Emotion-domain expansion is the macro analogue of emotion mining, which refers to "the search for and development of potential emotional capital in workers' experiences that had not been previously recognized by the workers as related to their job" (Schweingruber and Berns 2005:681). Likewise, advocates and social-movement leaders search for emotions that relate to their social problem but which had not previously been connected.

The analysis in this article emphasizes the use of emotion to construct social problems and mobilize social movement support as a dynamic process involving the interplay of rhetoric and social context. I highlight several possible stages of this dynamic: (1) Activists engage in emotion-domain expansion to expand the emotions connected to a social problem and potentially increase support for their claims. Emotion-domain expansion involves using preexisting culturally significant emotional concepts, for example, closure, as cultural resources. (2) Emotion-domain expansion involves creating feeling rules, that is, making claims about how people involved in the social problem are supposed to feel. (3) As with other feeling rules, those created and institutionalized through emotion-domain expansion result in emotive dissonance for those unwilling or unable to follow them. (4) The resulting emotive dissonance may become a cultural resource for additional claimsmaking or counterclaimsmaking. (5) Successful emotion-domain expansion claims and related feeling rules may become institutionalized.

METHODS

This article is based on a qualitative analysis of a wide range of documents related to the death penalty debate, including newspaper and popular magazine articles, Web sites, social science and law journal articles, court cases, and books. I located these sources using periodical indexes, Web searches, and concentrated reading on pro- and anti-death penalty rhetoric. A broad range of academic and popular sources were used in order to capture the diversity of the claims made about the death penalty. The data collection was guided by theoretical sampling (Strauss and Corbin 1998), that is, the sample is not intended to be representative of the entire population of death penalty rhetoric. Instead, sampling was organized on the basis of the concepts and connections developed during the analysis. For instance, as it became clear that emotions were an important part of death penalty rhetoric, I began to note the emotion claims made by claimsmakers on each side, the feeling rules they put forward, and claims about emotive dissonance. I also connected claims to institutionalized practices of the criminal justice system, including victim impact statements and right-to-view statutes. Finally, I attempted to situate both rhetoric and institutional practices within the historical development of death penalty law and practice, closure rhetoric within the larger culture, and other cultural and legal contexts. For this article, which is part of a larger project on closure, selective coding was used to connect the concepts of feeling rules, emotion-domain expansion, and emotive dissonance to other relevant concepts and to validate these relationships. The analysis involved constant comparison between the developing theory and the data. While conducting the analysis I continued theoretical sampling until I reached theoretical saturation (Strauss and Corbin 1998).

A NEW RETRIBUTION: CLOSURE AND THERAPEUTIC VENGEANCE

In this article, I outline five stages involved in emotion-domain expansion and the implications that follow. First, using death penalty rhetoric, I show how activists engage in emotion-domain expansion to expand the emotions connected to a social problem and potentially increase support for their claims. Even though retribution has always been an argument for pro-death penalty advocates, the potential mass appeal of the retribution argument magnifies when the emotion-domain is expanded beyond vengeance and expressions of morality and norms to include closure and healing for victims' families. Death penalty rhetoric now has a *new retribution* that helps to counter new abolitionism.

Death penalty claimsmakers use closure discourse to expand the emotion-domain of their claims and construct feeling rules, especially for families of homicide victims. There are three main threads in the overarching argument in the pro-death penalty closure rhetoric. First, the death of the killer will provide closure for victims' families who cannot move on until the offender is dead. Second, it is right and therapeutic for families of victims to want the killer to suffer and, in some versions of the argument, only watching the offender's execution can provide closure. And finally, one cannot advocate for both the offenders and the families of victims; thus any advocacy on behalf of murderers disrespects the victims and their families. These three arguments intertwine in various ways, and embedded in them are feeling rules that affect not only victims' families but also the larger public.

Pro-Death Penalty Closure Claims

The most central claim in pro-death penalty closure discourse is that the death of the killer is needed for victims' families to move on, find closure, and heal. In a more extreme version of the claim, victims will only find closure and healing by watching the offender get executed. One method of framing the "death as closure" argument is through testimonies. On the Pro-Death Penalty site, there are summaries of pending executions (and archives of past executions) that include victims' families' testimonies regarding an execution. Many of those testimonies refer to "closure" and "justice" in regards to the execution, although the uses of these terms vary. For example:

> Bill Spurrier said the execution will bring him a sense of closure. "I know he'll never be able to commit another murder," he said. Dolores Spurrier said she went to every one of Braun's trials and got to know relatives of the other victims. "I think everybody is just glad that it's going to happen," she said. "It will be some closure. But I don't think you would ever really get over it." Other representatives of the victims' families are planning to be at the execution. Salais, who spoke through her tears, said she is not excited at the coming execution but resolved that it will bring closure and bring peace to her brother. "It is something I have to do. Once he is executed, I will know it is over. My brother can be at peace, and I can get on with my life." ("October 1999 Executions" 1999)

Another common claim is that offenders, even while imprisoned, continue to "haunt" victims' families. For example, the following quote appeared on the Balanced Politics Web site:

> The death penalty gives closure to the victim's families who have suffered so much. Some family members of crime victims may take years or decades to recover from the shock and loss of a loved one. Some may never recover. One of the things that helps hasten this recovery is to achieve some kind of closure. Life in prison just means the criminal is still around to haunt the victim. A death sentence brings finality to a horrible chapter in the lives of these family members. (Balanced Politics.org 2007)

A second main theme in the pro-death penalty closure rhetoric is that it is therapeutic for families of victims to want the killer to suffer and therefore they are right to have and express this desire. This claim links vengeance with compassion and healing. The next two examples show how vengeance and retribution are constructed as entitlements for victims' families. In a 2002 column for *The Times-Herald*, James Wallace argues that Michigan needs to use capital punishment to support victims' families. He describes an execution as a "privilege" for the victims' families.

> But what right do we have, as a society of non-victims, to deny the loved ones of a murdered victim the privilege of seeing their predator suffer the supreme sacrifice he bestowed upon his victim? We need to line up behind the victims and not the side of the predators. We need to rally our forces and get this death penalty on the ballot again and this time let us succeed in the successful changing of the law. (Wallace 2002:1)

Similarly, in a letter to the editor in *The New York Times*, Stephen Sultan argues that the victim's family is entitled to retribution and closure.

> The Old Testament philosophy of "an eye for an eye" has always been a valid argument for the death penalty, particularly in the case of police officers. The victim's family is entitled to retribution and closure. Some may call it vindictiveness, but it is really vindication. This is the only rational argument, since the death penalty has never been a deterrent to murder. (Sultan 1997)

A third main theme in the pro-death penalty closure rhetoric is that one cannot advocate for both the offenders and the families of victims; thus any advocacy on behalf of murderers disrespects the victims' families. This claim frames those in favor of the death penalty as the only true advocates for victims' families. The Pro-Death Penalty Web site focuses on homicide victims' families as a primary framework. On the home page of this site, there is a prominent section labeled "Who speaks for the victims of those we execute?" Pro-death penalty closure discourse emphasizes that it advocates for the victims' families as opposed to the offender, which they argue is what the abolitionists do. This type of claim is an example of what Benford and Hunt (2003) call an attack on the collective character of a counter movement group. Retribution arguments have always claimed to be for victims' families and simultaneously attacked abolitionists for favoring the enemy. However, in the new retribution claims, the emphasis is on healing and closure and not just vengeance.

Many claims focus on more than one of the main themes described above. All three of these main arguments are found in an article by Jim Blair on a political Web site.

> First, the old argument: closure for the families of the victims. As long as the killer of their children/spouse/"significant other" lives, most people can't get on with their lives. . . . The opponents of capital punishment like to see themselves as "kinder and gentler," but that depends on whether you look at it from the perspective of the criminal or the family/friends of the victims. "Dead Man Walking" (book more so than movie) makes it clear that Sister Helen Prejean has much more love for the killer, than for the parents of his victims. Now in most states, . . . there is little or nothing done for the relatives/friends of the victim, even if the state does have capital punishment. But in some states, Florida, for example, there IS some consideration. There the relatives are invited to watch the execution. When will some state let them "throw the switch"? Can compassion reach that far? (Blair 1998)

The three main threads discussed just now provide a foundation for the pro-death penalty closure rhetoric. Along with constructing feeling rules, which are discussed later, the closure rhetoric has shifted our focus from offenders to victims' families. The argument that the death penalty is needed to provide closure for victims' families takes the focus away from the offender—and thus away from issues of due process and fairness—and places it on victims' families. Focusing on closure shifts the focus away from the public's growing concern about executing innocent people and embraces even more fully a desire for retribution—only this time retribution is cast in the context of sympathy for victims' families, which broadens the emotion-domain without disrupting traditional death penalty rhetoric. Advocates reconstructed their claims about capital punishment to include a new type of retribution, which focuses on closure for victims' families.

The closure argument expands the emotion-domain of pro-death penalty discourse from just killing an offender to closure, healing, and justice for victims' families. The expansion of emotion claims to include closure and healing for victims' families further broadens the number of people who may be persuaded to support capital punishment. Although there will remain a significant number of people who support retribution, for others, advocating someone's death may lead to emotive dissonance. The closure argument expands the emotion-domain of pro-death penalty rhetoric by including those who can identify more with helping grieving family members move on with their lives. And, yet, it does not alienate those supporters who continue to respond more to explicit retribution and vengeance—a traditional claim in pro-death penalty rhetoric. In short, closure for victims' families is a "nicer" way to support capital punishment. Furthermore, death penalty advocates can use the more uplifting rhetoric of closure and therapy for victims in order to mask particularly difficult problems of capital punishment, such as race/class discrimination, questions of innocence, and incompetent legal counsel. This strategy of masking particularly difficult issues has been used in the framing of other problems, including domestic violence (Berns 2004).

FEELING RULES AND EMOTIVE DISSONANCE

Emotion-domain expansion by advocates of a particular issue also shapes feeling rules, which may result in emotive dissonance. The second stage explains the construction of feeling rules, which are claims about how people involved in the social problem are supposed to feel. The third stage in the process describes emotive dissonance that results from the inability or unwillingness to follow the created feeling rules.

Death penalty advocates have used closure discourse to expand the emotion-domain of death penalty claims and helped shape feeling rules for families and friends of homicide victims. Hochschild (1979, 1983:18) defines feeling rules as "standards used in emotional conversation to determine what is rightly owed and owing in the currency of feeling." When the feeling rules fail, or do not produce the emotions promised, individuals may experience dissonance or a disconnect between what they feel and what they think they should feel (Hochschild 1983).

Arguing that victims' families will not find closure until the offender is dead constructs feeling rules about grief management. Three of these feeling rules are: (1) After an execution, victims' families will be relieved and have a sense of closure; (2) the pain felt when a loved one is murdered is so great that only the same suffering on the part of the offender can bring healing; and (3) supporting the death penalty is a proper way to show support and sympathy for victims of crime and their families.

Like all formula stories, the stories of the typified family members who follow these rules may apply to some people but most may experience some level of disconnect. For some victims' families, the death penalty and/or witnessing executions leaves them with emotive dissonance—they do not feel the closure promised. A common response from families of homicide victims after viewing an execution is that it still hurts; or there was not the closure I was expecting; or I'm even angrier. The formula story prepares family members to expect peace or a sense of relief, but some instead feel worse. In an article for the *Christian Science Monitor*, staff writers Dante Chinni and Peter Grier describe how executions are not the end of grief for families. Their article gives many examples people expressing emotive dissonance, as in this quote:

> As she watched Ricky McGinn lying in front of her in the death chamber, Mozelle Hamm could not find it in herself to forgive him. He had murdered her granddaughter, Christi Jo, and now the state of Texas was going to give him his own back. Finally, after the waiting, the trial, the appeals, she would at least know—for certain this time—that McGinn would never hurt anyone again. But then, as the execution spooled out in front of her last Sept. 27, something happened. Or rather, it didn't happen. Ms. Hamm felt . . . less than one might suppose. There was no flood of relief. There was no lifting of weight, no sense of turning a personal page. And today, months later, that is the message Mozelle Hamm has for the Oklahoma City bombing survivors and victim relatives who were to watch Timothy McVeigh's execution: Remember, closure is for doors. (Chinni and Grier 2001)

Methods of execution have evolved in an effort to make them more humane, which, interestingly, has complicated the rhetoric of retribution. An increasing objection to capital punishment is that is "too easy," "too quick," and without enough pain. These objections are usually tied to executions by lethal injection. Tapping into the victims' families' claim that the execution of the offender did not provide enough satisfaction, some death penalty opponents argue that executions fail to provide the closure victims hope for (and death penalty advocates promise) because the executions themselves are too serene to provide justice. Judy Busch of Oklahoma City witnessed the execution of Floyd Medlock, who had killed her seven-year-old granddaughter. After the execution, Busch said that she did not leave fully satisfied. "It was so quick and so sterile and so serene," she says. "It left me feeling angry, I guess" (Lauerman 2001:1).

Research has found little evidence that people "find closure" through executions or victim impact statements (Domino and Boccaccini 2000; Armour 2002; Mosteller 2003). Defense attorney Michael Goodwin (1997) argues that the right-to-view statutes intended to help families may actually make things worse. He claims that after viewing executions, some families have felt disappointment and a desire for more vengeance rather than closure. This may be in part because they think the offender died too easily or they wish they could watch him be tortured and in more pain. These research claims and witness testimonies support the argument that many experience emotive dissonance in relation to pro-death penalty feeling rules.

ABOLITIONISTS AND CLOSURE DISCOURSE

In death penalty rhetoric, the emotive dissonance discussed in the previous section serves as a cultural resource for abolitionists to counter and reframe the closure-by-execution claims and to construct new feeling rules that reject the need for capital punishment. This fourth stage extends the emotion-domain expansion process outlined in this article.

The abolitionists' counterclaims to the new retribution discourse both challenge death penalty advocates' arguments and embrace closure as a way to frame their own arguments. First, abolitionists have constructed their own discourse to claim that closure can only come through means other than capital punishment, such as life without parole, forgiveness, or meeting the offender. Second, abolitionists point to this emotive dissonance as proof that pro-death penalty arguments are faulty. They construct the dissonance itself as a new social problem, and use it to recruit alienated family members to their cause. A major new claim for abolitionists is that the death penalty is a problem because it is a barrier for victims' families to actually find closure; executions do *not* provide closure for victims' families and can only make things worse. In this section, I discuss several specific closure arguments used by death penalty opponents and show how emotive dissonance has become a cultural resource for abolitionist claimsmaking.

Challenging Closure-by-Execution while Embracing Other Closure Claims

Death penalty opponents' closure discourse includes five specific claims, not all of which are made by the same advocates and some of which contradict each other. These are: (1) executions do not bring closure for victims' families; (2) life in prison is a better option than the death penalty because the capital punishment appeals process prolongs the false hope of closure; (3) life in prison is a better option than the death penalty because it is more retributive and thus will provide closure for those wanting revenge; (4) closure can be found in forgiveness and letting go of anger; and (5) executions hinder the possibility of closure by preventing any reconciliation between the offender and the families of his victim.

The first claim, that executions do not bring closure for victim's families, directly counters the claim that watching an execution brings closure and that this "therapeutic vengeance" can result in any lasting satisfaction. The most common examples used as evidence that viewing executions does not bring closure are quotes from family members who found little to no satisfaction after watching an offender die. Death penalty opponents argue that a focus on vengeance and hate will only result in more anger, not in healing. Furthermore, they claim that prosecutors create false hopes that the execution will help victims and bring them some satisfaction. In the *Pastoral Statement on Capital Punishment* signed by 21 pastors and posted on the Web site run by the Connecticut Network to Abolish the Death Penalty, the authors explain why the death penalty hurts more than it helps.

> Rarely does the death penalty bring "closure" to victims. Usually, it serves only as one more attempt by society to enact vengeance when it feels violated. Many believe the death penalty is needed in order to bring closure to the families of victims. In time, many family members learn to deal with the devastation of homicide through a process of healing. Some advocates of capital punishment impede this process as they promise the family that they will "feel better" after the execution of the perpetrator. So, for years a family member remains a "victim," waiting for the event that will make her/him feel better. Sometimes the "event" never occurs. When it does, however, there is no evidence of "closure." Many family members, following an execution, say something akin to: "Why don't I feel better?" Indeed, the day following the execution of Timothy McVeigh, The Hartford Courant's front page was plastered with quotes from family members of those killed in the Oklahoma City bombing. The banner headline read: "IT STILL HURTS." (Bennett 2005:1)

Countering the claim that the death penalty can provide closure is important for abolitionists. However, when abolitionists embrace the concept of closure in their own claims, they are able to advocate for victims' families while supporting their larger interest of challenging capital punishment.

The second claim, that life in prison is a better option than the death penalty because the capital punishment appeals process prolongs the false hope of closure, counters the claim that the death penalty gives finality to the justice process—an ending—that helps provide the families with closure. This claim argues that the death penalty prolongs families suffering because they are forced to wait for years while offenders appeal their sentences. In an article for *The Salon*, one of the oldest and most popular online magazines, Michelle Goldberg explains that research does not support the perception that executions bring closure. Goldberg interviewed many family members whose loved one's killers had been executed and yet they did not find the relief they had anticipated. As part of this article, she quotes Richard Moran, sociologist and author of *Executioner's Current*.

> If anything prevents closure, it's the death penalty. If you have a trial in which the person is sentenced to life imprisonment, it's over, that's it. If the person is sentenced to death, you will be contacted by authorities and will relive that murder every two years for the next 15 years. Then, if they finally do execute the person, then you can start beginning your closure. What it does is, it puts off any healing. Wounds are being reopened and whole process is being prolonged. (Goldberg 2003:4)

Posted on the Death Penalty Information Center's (2006) Web site, an op-ed article in the *Baltimore Sun* described a judge's decision to sentence a man to life without parole rather than the death sentence so that the victims' families would not have to go through years of appeal (Judge Imposes Life 2003). On the same Web site, in another op-ed article from *Newsday*, Kathy Dillon argues that capital punishment may do the opposite of bringing closure for families:

> Far from bringing closure, a capital prosecution may do the opposite. After a death sentence is handed down, the legal proceedings drag on for years with the outcome left uncertain at best. The emotional wounds of victims' family members are opened again and again. (Dillon 2004:1)

The third claim, that life in prison is a better option than the death penalty because it is more retributive, draws upon the rhetoric of revenge to challenge capital punishment and makes use of families' reported lack of satisfaction while witnessing executions. This allows them to challenge the death penalty argument without dismissing the idea that victims' families can find satisfaction in the suffering of the killer. In other words, people can believe that revenge will bring closure, but support life without parole rather than the death penalty. As in the following example, life in prison without parole can be framed as "the ultimate revenge" and better than capital punishment. Mr. O'Hair, the Detroit prosecutor said, "If you're after retribution, vengeance, life in prison without parole is about as punitive as you can get." Mr. Davis said a desire "to extract a pound of flesh" was behind many of the arguments for capital punishment. "But that pound of flesh comes at a higher price than a lifetime of incarceration" (Bonner and Fessenden 2000:1).

The fourth claim, that closure can be found in forgiveness and letting go of anger, offers a different route to closure, one not focused on vengeance. This claim draws upon restorative justice movement rhetoric and institutionalized victim–offender reconciliations programs. One of the "frequently asked questions" on the New Mexico Coalition to Repeal the Death Penalty's Web site is "What about victims' families? Don't they need 'closure?' " The answer both denies that executions bring closure and explains that closure only comes from healing and forgiveness:

> Many victims' family members oppose the death penalty. We know executions won't bring back our loved ones and they won't provide "closure." We have learned through very painful personal experience that closure only comes with healing and forgiveness. Healing comes through letting go of the anger. Keeping alive the hate and rage we have felt in the aftermath of a murder simply gives the murderer continuing control over our lives. (New Mexico Coalition 2006)

Related to this claim is the fifth, that executions may hinder the possibility of closure by preventing any reconciliation between the offender and the families of his victim. If forgiving the offender is a route to closure, life in prison makes this a continuing possibility. This claim is found in an article from the Death Penalty Information Center.

> Representative Cushing emphasized the need of victims for healing and forgiveness, asking his colleagues to abolish the death penalty "because if the state kills them, that forever forecloses the possibility that those of us who are victims might be able to figure out how to forgive." ("Victims and the Death Penalty" 2006)

These last two arguments attempt to expand the emotion-domain for opposing capital punishment by introducing hope for forgiveness and reconciliation as valid emotional responses. By arguing that killing an offender takes away any meaningful change of closure, abolitionists try to convince people to oppose the death penalty for the sake of the victims' families. This allows them to directly counter the emotion claims of death penalty advocates, but still be viewed as advocating for victims.

Don't Kill in My Name

Another way that emotive dissonance plays a role in the death penalty debate is by motivating family members to participate in abolitionist advocacy. Some family members, angry that they were given false hope of closure by execution, now passionately oppose the death penalty. Lifton and Mitchell use victims' families' testimonies to argue that at best closure is elusive and more likely nonexistent. Examples they give include the father of a murder victim shouting at a reporter who asked about closure: " 'Don't use that word with me,' he said. 'I hate that word. I don't know who made that word up. There is no closure. So many people don't seem to understand that. There is no closure' " (Lifton and Mitchell 2000:204).

In a testimony to a U.S. Senate subcommittee, Vicki Schieber explained that there is no closure and that linking closure to the death penalty is problematic.

> The word *closure* is invoked so frequently in discussions of victims and the death penalty that victims' family members jokingly refer to it as "the c word." But I can tell you with all seriousness that there is no such thing as closure when a violent crime

> rips away the life of someone dear to you. As my husband and I wander through the normal things that we all do in our daily lives, we see constant reminders of Shannon and what we have lost. Killing Shannon's murderer would not stop the unfolding of the world around us with its constant reminders of unfulfilled hopes and dreams. . . . Indeed, linking closure for victims' families with the execution of the offender is problematic for two additional reasons: first, the death penalty is currently applied to only about one percent of convicted murderers in this country. If imposition of that penalty is really necessary for victims' families, then what of the 99% who are not offered it? Second, and even more critical from a policy perspective, a vague focus on executions as the potential source of closure for families too often shifts the focus away from other steps that could be taken to honor victims and to help victims' families in the aftermath of murder. (Schieber 2006)

A particularly valuable testimony for abolitionists comes from converts: those who used to favor the death penalty but changed their view after a loved one was killed. Tom Mauser's son, Daniel, was a 15-year-old sophomore when he was among the murdered at Columbine High School in Littleton, Colorado, in 1999. On a memorial Web site honoring his son, Mauser answers the question: "Now that you've had a child murdered, has your opinion on the death penalty changed in any way?"

> Yes. Prior to Columbine, I considered myself a mild supporter of the death penalty—not liking it, but seeing it as somewhat as a deterrent. My reservations about the death penalty were mostly practical ones—for example, the fact that death sentence appeals cost taxpayers so much. Since Columbine, I have come to strongly oppose the death penalty. I have come to learn, based on talking with a few other parents of murdered children, that there is little closure in seeing a murderer put to death. I believe that a victim's parent gains revenge with an execution, but not closure. I recognize that some parents say they do reach closure, but I question that, wondering if they merely feel societal pressure to acknowledge they have found closure. I say that because I have observed some in this community who want very much to hear no more about Columbine and to hear us say we're finding closure. I believe that closure comes with reconciliation, with honoring one's child in a positive way, and with making a closer spiritual connection with God. (Daniel Mauser 2007)

Embracing the concept of closure for victims' families has been important for abolitionists in the capital punishment claimsmaking competition. A focus on due process for offenders allows critics to claim they do not care about victims and families. By expanding the emotion-domain to include closure and healing for victims' families, abolitionists are better able to compete with the new pro-death penalty rhetoric and to recruit families of murder victims to their cause.

INSTITUTIONALIZATION OF CLOSURE CLAIMS IN CAPITAL CASES

The final stage describes the institutionalization of successful claims and feeling rules constructed through emotion-domain expansion. Although I am discussing feeling rules and institutionalization in separate sections, the interaction between these stages should not be read as a linear process, but rather as a dynamic and ongoing interaction. The institutionalization of closure refers to the establishment of opportunities for victims to achieve closure within the legal system. I will focus specifically on two practices related to capital cases: victim impact statements and right-to-view statutes. These practices embed closure within the criminal justice system as well as normalize and establish closure as part of "justice." The institutionalization of closure furthers its impact beyond a mere rhetorical tool as closure becomes something that people try to achieve within the legal system. Cultural narratives are made more "real" through institutional practices (Foucault 1978; Swidler 1995).

Victim Impact Statements (*Payne v. Tennessee* 1991)

Victim impact statements, which are not limited to death penalty cases, acknowledge the importance of feelings of victims' families and have legitimated punishment for therapeutic reasons. Though not all victims support the death penalty or call for vengeance, victim impact statements opened the door for the institutionalization of closure. The U.S. Supreme Court's *Payne* decision in particular gives legal support for legitimizing this new type of retribution. Closure discourse has allowed victims' rights advocates more success in the justice system whereas expressions of intense emotions such as grief, shame, and vengeance are usually not allowed in legal discourse (Kanwar 2001). However, closure discourse is being allowed within the legal system and specific "performances" for and by victims—such as victim testimony—have been institutionalized to allow for the emotional satisfaction (Kanwar 2001:239). How victim impact statements are used and what types of statements are allowed continue to be negotiated within each state.

In *Booth v. Maryland* (1987), the Supreme Court considered for the first time whether the Eighth Amendment prohibits a capital sentencing jury from considering victim impact evidence. In the *Booth* decision, the Supreme Court ruled that evidence from victim impact statements was prejudicial. Two years later, in *South Carolina v. Gathers* (1989), the Court ruled that characteristics about the victim that the defendant did not know ahead of time had no bearing on the crime and should not be allowed for sentencing consideration (Culbert 2001; Blume 2003). Only two years after *Gathers*, the Supreme Court reversed its position on victim impact statements for capital cases. In *Payne v. Tennessee* (1991), the court ruled that the Eighth Amendment does not prohibit a capital sentencing jury from considering victim impact evidence. It is likely that the change in personnel on the court between 1989 and 1991, along with growing public pressure from the victims' rights movement, led to the court's reversal. In its decision, the court offered several reasons for why it reversed its position, including three that mesh nicely with the victims' rights movement: (1) victim impact statements help describe the magnitude of the crime; (2) the justice system is weighted unfairly in favor of the defendant and the victim should be allowed to argue for the appropriateness of the death penalty; and (3) allowing victims to give their testimonies will help redress some of the harm caused by the crime (Culbert 2001). The use of victim impact evidence is shifting from "providing information to the sentencing court to seeking catharsis or closure. Society, in a pop-psychology-way, appears to have embraced the propriety of statements directed at defendants for the purpose of helping to heal the victim" (Mosteller 2003:554).

Right-to-View Statutes

Another result of the victims' rights movement was right-to-view legislation, which allows victims' families to witness the execution of their family member's killer. Right-to-view legislation is important for pro-death penalty claims about closure because this provides the means (execution) to the end (closure for victims' families). This connection institutionalizes the claim that the death penalty is needed for victims' families. No longer is closure for victims' families "just rhetoric," but is now an institutional practice. Closure has become "real" and victim-impact statements and executions have been successfully framed as a means to achieving closure. Although the rhetoric of closure is related to victim impact discourse, it is absolutely central in the right-to-view argument.

One pivotal case used in pro-death penalty rhetoric involves Brooks Douglass, a legislator from Oklahoma who pushed through right-to-view legislation in Oklahoma in 1996 in time for his sister and him to view the execution of one of the men who killed their parents. In 1979, when Douglass was 16, two men entered his family's home in Okarche, Oklahoma, raping his sister and killing their parents. Douglass said that he saw the viewing of an execution as an opportunity for closure (Goodwin 1997).

In spring 2001, Timothy McVeigh's case became a rallying cry for death penalty advocates and a high-profile forum for the discussion of whether families should be allowed to view an execution. McVeigh murdered 168 men, women and children and seemed to show no remorse for his actions. Vice President Dick Cheney said, "I think if there ever was a man who deserved to be executed, it's probably Timothy McVeigh" (Bedau 2004:212). Closure became a central theme in media coverage of the case and a powerful rhetorical tool for politicians, prosecutors, and advocates pushing for the death penalty (Shapiro 1997; Bedau 2004). Entertainment Network, Inc., an Internet company in Florida, unsuccessfully claimed that McVeigh's execution needed to be broadcast on the Web in order to give the country closure (Pearl 2003). Attorney General John Ashcroft used the closure argument in his decision to allow closed circuit TV to publicize McVeigh's execution for the victims and their families. Ashcroft said that he "hopes his closed-circuit TV show can help Oklahoma City's bereaved meet their need to close this chapter in their lives" (Rich 2001:23). In the end, more than 1,000 people were given the opportunity to view McVeigh's execution in June 2001, but fewer than 300 did (Pearl 2003).

Pro-Death Narratives in Institutionalization of Closure

The two practices I have discussed, victim impact statements and right-to-view legislation, support pro-death penalty claims more than abolitionist rhetoric. Those victims' families who oppose the death penalty are not given the same space and time in court as those who favor the death penalty (Shapiro 1997; Bandes 1999; Kanwar 2001; Burr 2003). Critics of victim impact statements voice concern over the state's discrimination regarding which victims get to talk. Courts have barred victims from giving their testimony because they oppose the death penalty (Shapiro 1997; Bandes 1999). In a 2002 report, Renny Cushing, the executive director of MVFR, argues, "family members who oppose the death penalty are silenced, marginalized, and abandoned, even by the people who are theoretically charged with helping them" (Cushing and Shaffer 2002:6). Cushing said that they published the Dignity Denied report to push for policies in victim services agencies "to develop a protocol that recognizes opposition to the death penalty as a valid response to the trauma of murder" (Cushing and Shaffer 2002:7).

This concern broadens when prosecutors are also given the discretion to deny opportunity to victims who do not fit the ideal image of a victim and thus would not be convincing enough (Bandes 1999; Kanwar 2001; Nadler and Rose 2003; Sundby 2003). Prosecutors use this discretion to allow testimony only from victims who support the state's case for the death penalty (Henderson 1998; Bandes 1999; Blume 2003).

There could be institutional practices that favor abolitionist claims about closure. For example, we could have a "right to keep offender alive" so that victims' families can find answers about the murder and possibly forgive the offenders. Or a "right to avoid the appeals process" because it drags out the legal trials. Or the "right to not have my name used in killing someone else." There are a few prosecutors who listen to victims' families who oppose the death penalty and instead seek a plea bargain for life in prison (Karamanian 1998), and there are advocates who are trying to use victim impact statements as a way to voice compassion for defendants and opposition to the death penalty. But these exceptions do not carry the weight of institutionalized practices like the right-to-view legislation.

DISCUSSION

The emotion-domain expansion efforts of death penalty advocates and opponents alike have implications for social problems scholars and also for participants in the criminal justice system. The death penalty is not the only social problem that has been shaped by emotion-domain expansion. In fact, closure discourse is just one instance of what Frank Furedi (2004) called "therapeutic claims-making." Other examples of emotion-domain expansion abound but full investigations of them, including their propagation of feeling rules, are rare. For instance, pro-life groups, such as The Silent No More Awareness Campaign, have engaged in emotion-domain expansion by arguing that abortion "is harmful emotionally, physically and spiritually to women and others" (Silent No More 2007). These emotions have been medicalized as "post-abortion syndrome" and have been institutionalized via Justice Anthony Kennedy's majority decision in *Gonzales v. Carhart* (2007:29), which held that "[s]evere depression and loss of esteem can follow" for "women [who] come to regret their choice to abort the infant life they once created and sustained." Meanwhile, Planned Parenthood has attempted to counter this type of emotion claim by selling T-shirts and other products with the slogan "I had an abortion," suggesting that having abortion is not as "fraught with emotional consequence" as Justice Kennedy claimed.

Cases of emotion-domain expansion such as these raise a number of avenues of investigation for social problems scholars. First, what emotions are involved in emotion-domain expansion and how do they vary by type of movement and historical era? Certainly fear is an important emotion for all manner of social problems claims and has been for some time. However, other emotions may rise and fall in popularity. Since "[r]ules for managing feeling are implicit in any ideological stance" (Hochschild 1979:566), new ideological positions toward social problems may result in changed feeling rules. However, this area remains understudied.

Second, how do people implicated in feeling rules constructed by social problems negotiate them? Although there is a large emotion management literature, most of it focuses on on-the-job emotion management. This article has examined the results of emotive dissonance for social problems claimsmakers. But how are new feeling rules experienced by individuals implicated in the social problems? How do families of murder victims negotiate competing claims about how they should feel? How do families set their own feeling rules and what are the implications for family members when they disagree about these rules? How do women who have had abortions or are contemplating having one deal with reports that abortion is supposed to be followed by "post-abortion syndrome" or that other women are advertising their abortions on T-shirts? Research into these questions is needed to understand the complete effects of emotion claimsmaking.

Third, what are the ways that emotion claims can be institutionalized? In the case of the death penalty, institutionalization of closure claims has involved changes in the criminal justice system, such as victim impact statements and right-to-view execution policies. Death penalty opponents have been less successful in institutionalizing their claims within the criminal justice system, but victim-offender reconciliation programs provide an institutional base for some of their closure claims. Abortion opponents have been successful getting some of their emotion claims institutionalized into case law, but most medical institutions have thus far not embraced "post-abortion syndrome." These two examples suggest that potential routes of institutionalization for emotion-domain expansion claims include legal (via legislation or case law), medical, or nonprofit institutions. However, emotion claims may be institutionalized elsewhere, such as policies and practices of businesses, media organizations, and educational institutions.

Fourth, how do social problems claimsmakers select and publicize potentially problematic incidents to increase the resonance of the emotion claims? Death penalty advocates highlight heinous crimes like Timothy McVeigh while death penalty opponents look for people who have benefited from victim–offender reconciliation. Similarly, abortion proponents and foes search for women and others affected by abortion who can testify to their strong emotions, or lack thereof. However, there have been few studies that have examined how claimsmakers construct these cases and claims. One notable exception is Arnold Arluke's (2006) study of how anti-animal cruelty advocates select cases of animal abuse to highlight in advertising campaigns. More of this detailed examination of social problems work is needed.

For participants in the criminal justice system, the closure formula story poses the same troubles that other institutionalized formula stories do: many people are unwilling or unable to fit their experience to the story. The connection between vengeance and closure creates new problems based on its institutionalization. As studies of the legal system have shown, participants may be forced to adopt their selves to institutional expectations, to develop a "legal self" (Hopper 2001). Just as for stalking victims seeking legal protection (Dunn 2001) and divorce clients seeking to demonstrate their morality (Hopper 2001), participants in death penalty cases need to follow feeling rules to gain the assistance of other actors in the legal process. These feeling rules prescribe that after an execution, victims' families will be relieved and have a sense of closure; the pain felt when a loved one is murdered is so great that only the same suffering on the part of the offender can bring healing; and supporting the death penalty shows your support for the murdered victims. For the families of murder victims, though, the stakes are even higher since the closure formula story promises not just success in the legal system but relief from the terrible pain of having a loved one murdered. However, the organization of our death penalty system makes this result unlikely for the vast majority of these family members. The majority of homicide cases do not involve capital punishment. Not only is closure through execution unavailable to these families, they may be left blaming the criminal justice system for denying them this relief. This type of closure is also unavailable for families of victims whose killers were not caught and therefore have no target for their anger. Also denied this type of closure are those family members who do not support the death penalty. Not only do they oppose the mechanism that is supposed to give them relief, but also the justice system may deny them the opportunity to tell their story and whatever satisfaction that may bring. In addition, others may believe that their lack of desire for closure by execution suggests a lack of real grief for the murder victim (Kay 2006:231). Even for those few family members who embrace these feeling rules and see a loved one's murderer executed, many report not experiencing the closure predicted.

Death penalty abolitionists draw on this pool of emotive dissonance to make their own claims, some of which are also about grief management. Among the feeling rules embedded in abolitionist closure rhetoric are that closure only comes through forgiveness and/or letting go of the anger; life without parole will help you heal quicker; and meeting with the offender will provide relief. Just as with the closure-through-vengeance story, though, the claim that closure will result from meeting with and forgiving a murderer imprisoned for life is not going to fit the experience of many family members.

Closure, embedded in both pro- and anti-death penalty rhetoric, is a goal that many people are seeking. However, whatever the particular ritual or practice that is said to achieve it, it is inevitable that many will fail to find this promised, but elusive, relief for their grief.

CONCLUSION

Capital punishment will continue to be fiercely debated. This article illustrates how claimsmakers, both for and against the death penalty, have expanded the emotion-domain of their rhetoric by focusing on the possibility of families of murder victims achieving closure. The pro-death penalty closure argument has shifted the death penalty debate and has significant implications for victims, offenders, and the criminal justice system. Abolitionists have challenged pro-death penalty claims and embraced closure as a way to frame their own issues. The overarching message in the anti-death penalty rhetoric on closure is that the death penalty does *not* provide closure for victims' families and can make things worse.

Emotions have long been an important part of storytelling. It is not surprising, then, that particularly powerful cultural narrations are often those that resonate emotionally with an audience. Playing the victim card, as death penalty advocates and opponents do, can involve the exploitation of sensitive, intimate and volatile topics, not unlike the emotional manipulation used on talk shows. Victims' families have become a new resource for both sides of the capital punishment debate looking to expand the emotion-domain of their claims. Influenced by other social movements and a popular cultural climate that has increasingly focused on victims, melodrama, and emotion, the crime victims' rights movement constructed a need for closure. Other advocates followed this construction with "answer-claims" arguing in effect, "we know how you can find closure." "Executions," says one side. Yet others say "Life without parole" or even "forgiveness." These answers are for people who are grieving, but they originate from long-standing interests of advocates who have reframed the debate to tap into the hunt for closure. Not only has closure discourse dramatically shifted death penalty rhetoric from the offender to the victims' families, but closure has also become something people may be desperate to find through a variety of feeling rules when it is not at all clear that one can "close" the unbearable pain of having a loved one murdered.

ACKNOWLEDGMENTS

The author thanks Joel Best, Renee Cramer, Kathe Lowney, Mike Radelet, and David Schweingruber for reading earlier versions of this paper. Thank you also for the helpful suggestions from the anonymous reviewers at *The Sociological Quarterly*.

REFERENCES

Acker, James R. 2003. "The Death Penalty: An American History." *Contemporary Justice Review* 6(2):169–86.

Arluke, Arnold. 2006. *Just a Dog: Understanding Animal Cruelty and Ourselves*. Philadelphia, PA: Temple University Press.

Armour, Marilyn Peterson. 2002. "Journey of Family Members of Homicide Victims." *American Journal of Orthopsychiatry* 72(3):372–82.

Balanced Politics.org 2007. "Should the Death Penalty Be Banned as a Form of Punishment?" Retrieved August 17, 2007 (http://www.balancedpolitics.org/death_penalty.htm).

Bandes, Susan. 1999. "Victim Standing." *Utah Law Review* 2:331–47.

——. 2000. "When Victims Seek Closure: Forgiveness, Vengeance and the Role of Government." *Fordham Urban Law Journal* 27(5):1599–606.

Banner, Stuart. 2002. *The Death Penalty: An American History*. Cambridge, MA: Harvard University Press.

Bedau, Hugo. 1987. *Death Is Different: Studies in the Morality, Law, and Politics of Capital Punishment*. Boston, MA: Northeastern University Press.

——. 2004. "The Present Situation of the Death Penalty in the United States." Pp. 205–14 in *Death Penalty: Beyond Abolition*, edited by Roger G. Hood and Robert Badinter. Strasbourg, France: Council of Europe Publishing.

Benford, Robert D. 1997. "An Insider's Critique of the Social Movement Framing Perspective." *Sociological Inquiry* 67:409–30.

Benford, Robert D. and Scott A. Hunt. 2003. "Interactional Dynamics in Public Problems Marketplaces: Movements and the Counterframing and Reframing of Public Problems." Pp. 153–18 in *Challenges and Choices: Constructionist Perspectives on Social Problems*, edited by James A. Holstein and Gale Miller. New York: Aldine de Gruyter.

Benford, Robert D. and David A. Snow. 2000. "Framing Processes and Social Movements: An Overview and Assessment." *Annual Review of Sociology* 26:611–39.

Bennett, James H. 2005. "Pastoral Statement on Capital Punishment." Jan. 12 post. Retrieved June 7, 2005 (http://www.ctchurches.org/pscapitalpunishment.htm).

Berns, Nancy. 2004. *Framing the Victim: Domestic Violence, Media and Social Problems*. Hawthorne, NY: Aldine de Gruyter.

Best, Joel. 1987. "Rhetoric in Claims-Making." *Social Problems* 34:101–21.

——. 1990. *Threatened Children: Rhetoric and Concern about Child-Victims*. Chicago, IL: University of Chicago Press.

——. 1991. "Road Warriors' on 'Hair-Trigger Highways': Cultural Resources and the Media's Construction of the 1987 Freeway Shootings Problem." *Sociological Inquiry* 61:327–45.

——. 1999. *Random Violence: How We Talk about New Crimes and New Victims*. Berkeley: University of California Press.

Berbrier, Mitch. 1998. "Half the Battle': Cultural Resonance, Framing Processes, and Ethnic Affectations in Contemporary White Separatist Rhetoric." *Social Problems* 45(4):431–50.

Blair, Jim. 1998. "For a Pro-Life Death Penalty." From Blair's personal Web site. Retrieved March 18, 2006 (http://www.philosofiles.com/big/philosophy/blair-forprolifedeath.shtml).

Blume, John H. 2003. "Ten Years of Payne: Victim Impact Evidence in Capital Cases." *Cornell Law Review* 88:257, 268.

Bohm, Robert M. 2003. *Deathquest II*. 2d ed. Cincinnati: Anderson.

Bonner, Raymond and Ford Fessenden. 2000. "States with No Death Penalty Share Lower Homicide Rates." *New York Times*, September 22, p. 1.

Booth v. Maryland. 1987. 482 U.S. 299.

Burr, Richard. 2003. "Litigating with Victim Impact Testimony: The Serendipity that Has Come from Payne v. Tennessee." *Cornell Law Review* 88:517–29.

Chinni, Dante and Peter Grier. 2001. "For Survivors, Execution Isn't the End." *The Christian Science Monitor*, June 11, p. 1.

Culbert, Jennifer L. 2001. "The Sacred Name of Pain: The Role of Victim Impact Evidence in Death Penalty Sentencing Decisions," Pp. 103–35 in *Pain, Death, and the Law*, edited by Austin Sarat. Ann Arbor: University of Michigan Press.

Cushing, R. R. and S. Shaffer. 2002. *Dignity Denied: The Experience of Murder Victims' Family Members Who Oppose the Death Penalty*. Cambridge, MA: Murder Victims' Families for Reconciliation.

Daniel Mauser memorial Web page. 2007. "Frequently Asked Questions." Retrieved August 15, 2007 (http://www.danielmauser.com/FAQs.html).

Death Penalty Information Center. 2006. "Victims and the Death Penalty." Retrieved June 10, 2006 (http://www.deathpenaltyinfo.org/node/732).

Dillon, Kathy. 2004. "Avoid Death Sentences: Give Cop Killers Life without Parole." Op Ed, *Newsday*, September 21. Retrieved March 16, 2006 (http://www.deathpenaltyinfo.org/node/1258).

Domino, Marla L. and Marcus T. Boccaccini. 2000. "Doubting Thomas: Should Family Members of Victims Watch Executions?" *Law and Psychology Review* 24:59–75.

Dunn, Jennifer L. 2001. "Innocence Lost: Accomplishing Victimization in Intimate Stalking Cases." *Symbolic Interaction* 24(3):285–313.

Fan, David P., Kathy A. Keltner, and Robert O. Wyatt. 2002. "A Matter of Guilt or Innocence: How News Reports Affect Support for the Death Penalty in the United States." *International Journal of Public Opinion Research* 14:439–52.

Foucault, Michel. 1978. *The History of Sexuality*. vol. 1, London: Penguin.

Furedi, Frank. 2004. *Therapy Culture*. London: Routledge.

Galliher, John F., Larry W. Koch, David Patrick Keys, and Teresa J. Guess. 2002. *America without the Death Penalty: States Leading the Way*. Boston, MA: Northeastern University Press.

Gamson, William A. 1992. *Talking Politics*. Cambridge, England: Cambridge University Press.

Gamson, William A. and Andre Modigliani. 1989. "Media Discourse and Public Opinion on Nuclear Power." *American Journal of Sociology* 95:1–37.

Goldberg, Michelle. 2003. "The 'Closure' Myth." *The Salon*. Retrieved June 7, 2005 (http://archive.salon.com/news/feature/2003/01/21/closure/index_np.html).

Gonzales v. Carhart. 2007. 550 U.S.

Goodwin, Michael L. 1997. "An Eyeful for an Eye—An Argument against allowing the Families of Murder Victims to View Executions." *Brandeis Journal Family Law* 36:585.

Haines, Herbert. 1992. "Flawed Executions, the Anti-Death Penalty Movement, and the Politics of Capital Punishment." *Social Problems* 39:301–14.

——. 1996. *Against Capital Punishment: The Anti-Death Penalty Movement in America, 1972–1994*. New York: Oxford University Press.

Haney, Craig and Susan Greene. 2004. "Capital Constructions: Newspaper Reporting in Death Penalty Cases." *Analyses of Social Issues & Public Policy* 4(1):129–51.

Henderson, Lynne. 1998. "Co-opting Compassion: The Federal Victims' Rights Amendment. (Criminal Law Symposium)." *St. Thomas Law Review* 10(3):579–606.

Hilgartner, Stephen and Charles L. Bosk. 1988. "The Rise and Fall of Social Problems." *American Journal of Sociology* 94:53–78.

Hochschild, Arlene. 1979. "Emotion Work, Feeling Rules, and Social Structure." *American Journal of Sociology* 85:551–75.

——. 1983. *The Managed Heart: The Commercialization of Human Feeling*. Berkeley: University of California Press.

Holstein, James A. and Gale Miller. 1993. "Social Constructionism and Social Problems Work." Pp. 151–72 in *Reconsidering Social Constructionism*, edited by J. Holstein, and G. Miller. Hawthorne, NY: Aldine de Gruyter.

Hopper, Joseph. 2001. "Contested Selves in Divorce Proceedings." Pp. 127–41 in *Institutional Selves: Troubled Selves in a Postmodern World*, edited by Jaber F. Gubrium, and James A. Holstein. New York: Oxford University Press.

Ibarra, Peter R. and John I. Kitsuse. 1993. "Vernacular Constituents of Moral Discourse." Pp. 25–58 in *Reconsidering Social Constructionism*, edited by James A. Holstein, and Gale Miller. Hawthorne, NY: Aldine de Gruyter.

"Judge Imposes Life Sentence for Victims' Sake. 2003". *Baltimore Sun*, July 26. Retrieved May 5, 2006 (http://www.deathpenaltyinfo.org/node/732).

Kanwar, Vik. 2001. "Capital Punishment as 'Closure': The Limits of a Victim-Centered Jurisprudence." *New York University Review of Law & Social Change* 27(2–3):215–55.

Karamanian, Susan. 1998. "Victims' Rights and the Death-Sentenced Inmate: Some Observations and Thoughts." *St. Mary's Law Journal* 29(4):1025–35.

Kay, Judith W. 2006. "Murder Victims' Families for Reconciliation." Pp. 230–45 in *Handbook of Restorative Justice*, edited by Dennis Sullivan and Larry Tifft. London: Routledge.

Kirchmeier, Jeffrey L. 2002. "Another Place beyond Here: The Death Penalty Moratorium Movement in the United States." *University of Colorado Law Review* 73:1.

Lauerman, Kerry. 2001. "Killing as 'Closure.'" *The Salon*. Retrieved June 7, 2005 (http://archive.salon.com/news/feature/2001/04/14/mcveigh/index.html).

Lifton, Robert Jay and Greg Mitchell. 2000. *Who Owns Death?: Capital Punishment, The American Conscience, and the End of Executions*. New York: William Morrow.

Loseke, Donileen R. 2000. "Ethos, Pathos, and Social Problems: Reflections on Formula Narratives." Pp. 41–54 in *Perspectives on Social Problems*. Vol. 12, edited by James A. Holstein and Gale Miller. Greenwich, CT: JAI.

——. 2003. *Thinking about Social Problems*. 2d ed. Hawthorne, NY: Aldine de Gruyter.

Lowney, Kathleen S. 1999. *Baring Our Souls: TV Talk Shows and the Religion of Recovery*. Hawthorne, NY: Aldine de Gruyter.

Lynch, Mona. 2002. "Capital Punishment as Moral Imperative: Pro-Death-Penalty Discourse on the Internet." *Punishment & Society* 4(2):213–36.

Mosteller, Robert P. 2003. "Victim Impact Evidence: Hard to Find the Real Rules." *Cornell Law Review* 88(2):543–54.

Nadler, Janice and Mary R. Rose. 2003. "Victim Impact Testimony and the Psychology of Punishment." *Cornell Law Review* 88:419–56.

New Mexico Coalition to Repeal the Death Penalty. 2006. "Frequently Asked Questions." Retrieved May 3, 2006 (http://nmrepeal.org/FAQ2.htm#b).

Payne v. Tennessee. 1990. 501 U.S. 808.

Pearl, Matthew. 2003. "Dante and the Death Penalty: How Capital Punishment Fails Its Audience." *Legal Affairs*, January/February. Retrieved May 28, 2009 (http://www.legalaffairs.org/issues/January-February-2003/review_pearl_janfeb2003.msp).

Pro-Death Penalty.com. 1999. "October 1999 Executions." Retrieved July 17, 2007 (http://www.prodeathpenalty.com/Pending/99/oct99.htm).

Radelet, Micahel L. and Hugo Adam Bedau. 1998. "The Execution of the Innocent." *Law and Contemporary Problems* 61:105–24.

Rich, Frank. 2001. "It's Closure Mongering Time." *New York Times*, April 28, p. A-23.

Sarat, Austin. 2005. "Innocence, Error, and the 'New Abolitionism': A Commentary." *Criminology & Public Policy* 4(1):45–54.

Schieber, Vicki. 2006. "Testimony to the Subcommittee on the Constitution, Civil Rights and Property Rights Committee on the Judiciary US Senate." Retrieved July 17, 2007 (http://www.constitutionproject.org/pdf/SchieberTestimonySenate02_01_06.pdf).

Schrock, Douglas, Daphne Holden, and Lori Reid. 2004. "Creating Emotional Resonance: Interpersonal Emotion Work and Motivational Framing in a Transgender Community." *Social Problems* 51(1):61–81.

Schweingruber, David and Nancy Berns. 2005. "Shaping the Selves of Young Salespeople through Emotion Management." *Journal of Contemporary Ethnography* 34(6):679–706.

Shapiro, Bruce. 1997. "Victims' Rights—and Wrongs." *Salon.com.* Retrieved June 5, 2005 (http://www.salon.com/june97/news/news970613.html).

"Silent No More Awareness". 2007. Retrieved October 28, 2007 (http://www.silentnomoreawareness.org).

Snow, David A. and Robert D. Benford. 1988. "Ideology, Frame Resonance, and Participant Mobilization." Pp. 197–217 in *From Structure to Action: Social Movement Participation across Cultures*, edited by Bert Klandermans, Hanspeter Kriesi, and Sidney Tarrow. Greenwich, CT: JAI.

Snow, David A., E. Burke Rochford, Jr, Steven K. Worden, and Robert D. Benford. 1986. "Frame Alignment Processes, Micromobilization, and Movement Participation." *American Sociological Review* 51:464–81.

South Carolina v. Gathers. 1989. 490 U.S. 805.

Spector, Malcolm and John I. Kitsuse. 1977. *Constructing Social Problems*. Hawthorne, NY: Aldine de Gruyter.

Strauss, Anselm and Juliet Corbin. 1998. *Basics of Qualitative Research*. 2d ed. Thousand Oaks, CA: Sage.

Sultan, Stephen. 1997. "Case for Death Penalty." A letter to the editor in *New York Times*, August 18. Retrieved August 17, 2007 (http://www.nytimes.com/1997/03/29/opinion/l-case-for-death-penalty-356140.html).

Sundby, Scott E. 2003. "The Capital Jury and Empathy: The Problem of Worthy and Unworthy Victims." *Cornell Law Review* 88:343–81.

Swidler, Ann. 1986. "Culture in Action." *American Sociological Review* 51:273–86.

——. 1995. "Cultural Power and Social Movements." Pp. 25–40 in *Social Movements and Culture*, edited by Hank Johnston and Bert Klandermans. New York: Routledge.

Unnever, James D. and Francis T. Cullen. 2005. "Executing the Innocent and Support for Capital Punishment: Implications for Public Policy." *Criminology Public Policy* 4(1):3–32.

Wallace, James. 2002. "Death Penalty Offers Closure to Murder Victims' Loved Ones." *The Times-Herald*, August 20.

Zimring, Franklin. 2003. *The Contradictions of American Capital Punishment*. New York: Oxford University Press.

[24]

PROLOGUE: CAPITAL PUNISHMENT

Capital punishment as a form of killing is more controversial than many. Most Western societies have abolished it, with the notable exception of the United States. Even after abolition, however, many people in these societies continue to support the death penalty, and elsewhere it remains standard practice. Peter Hodgkinson, Seema Kandelia and Rupa Reddy take this debate forward through a discussion of the politics of capital punishment, religious perspectives, and the rights and responses of primary and secondary victims.

The focus on secondary victimisation in this chapter is a particularly interesting one. Most discussions of capital punishment weigh the rights of the victim against the human rights of the perpetrator and the morality of killing in the name of the state. However, few of these discussions acknowledge that capital punishment creates new victims in the form of the partners and families of the perpetrator. This group attracts less sympathy than the families of the victims of crime (see for example Condry 2007), but they too are innocent and lose a loved one at the hands of someone else – in this case, state authority. What new perspective does this put on our definitions of killing?

References

Condry, R. (2007) *Families Shamed: The consequences of crime for relatives of serious offenders.* Cullompton: Willan Publishing.

Capital Punishment: Creating More Victims?

Peter Hodgkinson, Seema Kandelia and Rupa Reddy

Introduction

This chapter examines the issue of why we kill in the context of capital punishment. In particular, it will look at justifications for the death penalty that revolve around addressing the needs of victims in homicide cases. Our major contention is that the death penalty, whilst purporting to help victims' families to achieve 'justice' on behalf of the deceased, and 'closure' for themselves after the trauma of homicide, in fact creates a form of 'secondary victimisation'[4] (Goodey 2005: 157) and further victims, including the families of the condemned. Far from usefully addressing the aftermath of homicide for victims' families, this chapter argues that the death penalty and its processes, from the initial prosecution to the end of the lengthy appeals process, reproduce and widen the scope of victimisation.

Key to this is the question of who constitutes a 'victim'. In homicide cases the 'primary victim' is the deceased, and therefore for the purposes of our argument when referring to the category of 'secondary victim' we mean the families of the deceased, sometimes known as 'co-victims' or 'survivors' (Hodgkinson 2004: 335). However, we also argue that the families of the offender in capital cases should be considered to fall within the category of secondary victims. Both sets of families are affected by the original crime and have to endure the capital process. However, whilst the needs of survivors are to some extent being acknowledged and addressed, the needs of the families of offenders are not (Sharp 2005).

The first section of this chapter examines the theoretical and practical role of victims in the criminal justice system, specifically in capital cases. We will show that although in Anglo–American jurisdictions the right to punish has theoretically been all but completely passed into the power of the state, the

---

4 A term often used by rape victims when they refer to the 'aggressive and embarrassing cross-examination' to which they are subjected by police and at trial.

participation of victims has been gradually increasing. Whilst this has largely been in the area of 'service rights' dealing with their material and psychological needs, they have also had increasing input into the procedural aspects of capital cases. The second section argues that, although seemingly helpful to victims, problems relating to procedural participation have contributed greatly to further secondary victimisation of victims' families. Furthermore, we argue that as well as aggravating the experiences of the families of homicide victims, the death penalty also creates new victims in the form of the families of offenders, who therefore should be included in the category of secondary victims. We conclude by examining restorative justice as one possible means for overcoming some of these problems.

The experience of the family of the homicide victim in capital punishment

The criminal justice system attempts to fulfil a number of aims in relation to prevention of crime and protection of the public. Sentencing is only one aspect of this system. Broadly speaking, in Anglo–American legal systems the right to punish an offender has been removed from the individual victim to the state. The reasoning for this is based on social contract theory and posits that citizens in a sovereign state give up their personal right to punish those that have harmed them; in return the state acts as a 'proxy retaliator' and protects law and order on behalf of the citizen (Ashworth 2005: 71; Garland 2001: 109–10). A major reason for enforcing this social contract revolves around the protection of the rule of law, and the need to ensure that decisions which may affect individual rights, such as punishment, are taken impartially and independently rather than by individuals with an emotional involvement in the decision (Ashworth 2005).

As well as ensuring fair treatment of suspects and offenders, the removal of punishment from the private sphere also prevents social disorder in the form of vigilantism or reprisal killings (Ashworth 2002; Kanwar, 2001). An extreme example of the potential results of the breakdown of the rule of law in this respect are the long running 'blood feuds' found in certain regions of Albania. In the latter jurisdiction, the Kanun legal code enshrined customary practices dating back to the fifteenth century, including principles relating to personal honour. According to this code, violations of honour such as the killing of an individual often result in reprisal killings of male members of the killer's family, triggering a blood feud, which can continue for many years.[5]

However, it does not follow from this reasoning that the victim, or in the

5 Ismail Kadare, one of Albania"s most eminent authors, provides an authoritative analysis of the Kanun system through the vehicle of fiction in *Broken April* (1991). See also Albanian Human Rights Group (2000–2001).

case of homicide, secondary victims, should have no role in the criminal justice system. At its most basic, in capital cases the right to some level of involvement arises from the fact that they are forced into the involuntary role of victim as a result of the homicide. Secondary victims may also have a vested interest in ensuring that the oft-stated aims of punishment are fulfilled, namely deterrence, incapacitation and retribution. The death penalty incapacitates offenders, thus protecting potential future victims. Perhaps more relevant is the issue of whether the death penalty acts as a general deterrent to murder. Although the harm they have already suffered cannot be reversed, many victims' family members may still have an interest in ensuring that others do not suffer a similar trauma. The ongoing debate as to the deterrent value of the death penalty has been fraught with methodological disagreements; yet despite a lack of conclusive evidence as to its effectiveness, deterrence continues to be cited as a primary justification for the death penalty (Hodgkinson 2004). As Hood (1996) argues, in utilitarian terms:

> The issue is not whether the [death penalty] deters some people, but whether, when all the circumstances surrounding the use of capital punishment are taken into account, it is a more effective deterrent than the alternative sanction: most usually imprisonment for life or very long indeterminate periods of confinement. (p.1)

There are also principled arguments against the deterrence justification based on Kantian desert theory, which argues that the offender's sentence should be determined only in relation to the crime committed, rather than for other reasons such as the potential future deterrent effect.[6] Desert theory is highly relevant to secondary victims since it incorporates legitimate desire for revenge for the harm inflicted into a more impartial assessment of the punishment based on proportionality. It is also important because its analysis of crime creates an imbalance between the law-abiding citizen and the offender, thus giving an unfair advantage to the offender which can only be redressed through punishment (Clarkson et al. 2007).

In relation to victims of serious crimes such as homicide, critics of desert theory have questioned whether any punishment can adequately redress the harm caused by the offence and whether the theory differs significantly from the more emotional impetus of revenge (Lacey 1988). In the context of the death penalty, victims' groups have also used the desert justification to lobby for harsher punishment, as opposed to a more impartial assessment of sentence based on proportionality. Thus, one reason why the right to punish has been

6 See Von Hirsch (1976) for further discussion of the basis of the debate around desert theories of punishment.

removed from victims in the state model described above is to ensure that the desire for private revenge is tempered by an impartial and independent assessment of the resultant punishment. In this sense desert theory acts as a limitation upon the victim's participation in the punishment process.

Addressing victim needs: participation in capital punishment

Although the justifications for limiting the formal role of victims and their families is important, nonetheless the victim, and in the case of homicide the victim's family, has always taken some part in the prosecution of such cases, largely through their evidence as witnesses during the trial. The question becomes not *whether* the victim or secondary victim should participate in the prosecution of the offence, but exactly *what level* of involvement they can or should have. The latter has changed significantly in recent years in all criminal cases, including homicide cases. This has taken the form of two levels of participation. The first, and probably most significant, is an increase in 'service rights', including the right to be kept informed of the progress of the case, the status of the offender, and the right to receive appropriate support throughout the legal process (Sanders and Young 2007: 657). The second is an increase in procedural rights, namely the ability to give a statement on the impact or harm which the offence has caused. The question of what influence such statements have on sentencing is discussed in greater detail below.

Worldwide research on secondary victims of homicide shows an overall deficiency of support services (Hodgkinson 2004). The organisation Victim Support in the UK offers a range of material and psychological support services to secondary victims,[7] and this issue has been a prominent aspect of political lobbying on behalf of victims in the USA. However, most countries appear to have very little in the way of service provision for crime victims in general and none for the families of homicide victims and the condemned. The Jamaican government, despite problems of infrastructure and funding, provides a victim support unit, which also provides a service for the families of homicide victims and a recently drafted victims' charter which provides rights to information and service provision in relation to victims' involvement with the criminal justice system.[8] In Trinidad and Tobago, an independent victim support service has been set up by the non-governmental Caribbean Centre for Human Rights.[9]

7 See http://www.victimsupport.org.uk/vs_england_wales/index.php for further information on this government- funded but independent organisation.

8 Available at http://www.jis.gov.jm/victims_charter.pdf

9 The CCHR Victim Support Project started in November 2006 and has already shown tremendous progress with counsellors identified, volunteers recruited and trained, and a sample of homicide victims' families contacted and surveyed. As of June 2007, the VSP has made over 60 calls to families affected by homicide, identifying them from newspapers or from word of mouth. Nine families have been referred for counselling despite the stigma attached to counselling in Trinidad & Tobago.

Increases in victim participation in the criminal justice system are often presented in the form of a balance between the rights of offenders and victims, whereby 'the rights of victims and offenders are posited as being diametrically opposed' (Edwards 2004: 970), and any extension of victims' rights must come at the cost of a concurrent incursion into the rights of the defendant. This is not necessarily accurate in the case of service rights, since unless the conflict lies in an allocation of scarce resources, services to assist victims do not detract from the due process rights afforded to defendants. However, the increasing procedural role of victims may have a more significant effect on the treatment of offenders.

In England and Wales, the Crown Prosecution Service's Code of Practice states that the consequences for the victim and the views of the victim or their family must be taken into account when making the decision to prosecute.[10] Sentencing reports already take account of the harm caused to victims and wider society in determining the retributive severity of the sentence and the level of incapacitation required to protect victims (including potential future victims; Ashworth 2005). The Victim Personal Statement scheme allows victims to convey information to the court on how the crime has affected them (*ibid.*). However, the statement does not necessarily have to be taken into account in determining the sentence, and a lack of consistency is evident in relation to the circumstances in which this occurs (*ibid.*). In a more recent pilot scheme launched in five courts in England, the families of homicide victims have been given the opportunity to present the court with a statement on the effect of the crime on them, between conviction and sentence, which may possibly have more influence on sentencing outcomes.[11]

In the USA, advocacy by individual victims and groups of victims (including secondary victims) has had some success in increasing the participation of victims at a number of stages of the legal process. The level of formal participation has largely taken the form of the use of Victim Impact Statements at the sentencing stage of capital trials, an issue first raised in the Supreme Court in *Booth v. Maryland*,[12] where such evidence was declared inadmissible. Since then, the Supreme Court in the case of *Payne v. Tennessee* has deemed the introduction of certain types of victim impact evidence as

Assistance is provided in a number of ways, for example, by providing emotional support, referrals to counsellors and supermarket hampers. The VSP has recruited the support of one psychiatrist and 17 psychologists and has a number of doctors they can call upon to advise them when necessary. Projects at the planning stage include working with the families of the condemned, the prison system, victims in jail, and the development of restorative justice initiatives.

10 See http://www.cps.gov.uk/victims_witnesses/codetest.html

11 See the government consultation which launched this pilot scheme, available at http://www.dca.gov.uk/consult/manslaughter/manslaughter.htm. See Sweeting et al. 2008 for the findings of the evaluation of that pilot scheme http://www.justice.gov.uk/docs/research-victims-advocates.pdf

12 *Booth v. Maryland* 482 US 496 (1987)

admissible.[13] This comprises information on, firstly, the victim's character and contribution to society and, secondly, the impact of the murder on their family (Hoffmann 2002–3). A third type of evidence concerning the opinion of the secondary victims about the sentence was not ruled on in the case and thus remains inadmissible (*ibid.*).

Conflict continues in the academic and political debate on this issue, with some arguing that the benefit of victim impact evidence is that it helps the victim's family in homicide cases to gain 'closure' from the trauma caused by the crime.[14] In the context of analogous evidence in the UK, Erez (1999) argues that such participation empowers victims by making them more visible within the criminal justice system, which has two effects: it is both cathartic, even if it does not necessarily have the desired level of impact, and it has a beneficial influence on assessing proportionality of sentence by fully informing the court of the effects of the crime. Hoffmann acknowledges that whilst there may be some negative effects to admitting such evidence, such as influencing the impartiality of the sentence or further victimisation of the secondary victims, the benefits outweigh these. Specifically, he argues that the jury in US capital cases are currently left to assume (in the absence of further information) that 'the survivors would prefer to see the defendant sentenced to death' (Hoffmann 2002–3: 540) and that if survivor opinion evidence were allowed in very strictly constrained circumstances, at least the intellectual dishonesty this situation caused would be alleviated (*ibid.*: 542). Indeed, secondary victims who advocate less harsh punishment would be incorporated into the system, which is currently not the case.[15] Therefore it could be argued that a demonstrably positive effect exists in allowing the family to inform the court of the harm caused by the crime and its ongoing effect.

The participation of victims in sentencing decisions is not a recent development in other legal jurisdictions, and the other end of the spectrum is demonstrated by the example of *Shari'ã* systems.[16] In these, although the state still takes on the overall role of regulating crimes, as in Anglo-American systems, the role of the victim is very different. Of the three categories of crime contained in the *Shari'ã*, the *Qesas* principles provide a number of options for dealing with crimes such as homicide. One is the talionic 'eye for an eye' punishment which gives the victim 'the right to inflict or have inflicted upon the perpetrator the same harm as the victim suffered', including death (Bassiouni 2004: 182). The second option is victim compensation (*diyya*),

13 *Payne v. Tennessee* 501 US 808 (1991)

14 See Mosteller (2002–3) for a discussion as to the use of concepts of 'closure' and 'catharsis' to justify the use of victim impact evidence in the USA.

15 See Hodgkinson (2004) for a more detailed analysis of this issue.

16 See Bassiouni (2004) for a detailed discussion on all aspects of the death penalty in relation to the *Shari'ã*.

which is encouraged in part to avoid reprisal killings leading to longstanding 'blood feuds' that could result from the first option (Bassiouni 2004). The third option is set out as the most preferable: forgiveness by the victim and their heirs instead of the infliction of further harm or compensation (*ibid.*). In practice, a number of Islamic jurisdictions[17] have enacted criminal law provisions which have the effect of restricting the availability of the death penalty to specific types of premeditated murder circumstances, thus diminishing the facility of the victim's family to dictate the sentence of the offender (*ibid.*). The state in these jurisdictions thus takes a more prominent 'sovereign state' role in dealing with the offender, albeit not to the same degree as Anglo–American systems.[18]

The issue of what level of participation victims should take in sentencing relates to the issue of the rule of law, and the desire for an independent and impartial assessment of the sentence an offender should receive. One major point which arises from the discussion of both the American and *Shari'ã* systems is that in capital cases this level of procedural participation by secondary victims inevitably leads to inconsistency and arbitrariness. The type and severity of sentence is determined by how merciful or retributive the secondary victims are in each individual case rather than by a set of predetermined sentencing rationales (Hoffmann 2002–3; Hodgkinson 2004; Ashworth 2005). This may be exacerbated by the finding that the fate of the defendant is determined not necessarily on the facts but on just how articulate and persuasive the secondary victims are (Hoffmann 2002–3). The sentence is assessed using other factors besides the aims of sentencing, such as 'just deserts' or deterrence.[19]

Unintended consequences of capital punishment: the phenomenon of secondary victimisation

Beyond the issue of the treatment of offenders and the rule of law, a major problem with increasing the rights of victims to participate in the legal process is that they may misinterpret the importance of their role. For example, if their participation proves to be less influential than they were led to expect, they

17 Bassiouni (2004) cites Algeria, Egypt, Iraq, Jordan, Lebanon, Morocco, Syria and Tunisia as examples.

18 An interesting consequence of this level of influence by the family of homicide victims in certain *Shari'ã* systems has been noted in relation to so-called 'honour killings', where the murder of a female family member is often carried out by members of her own family (see Chapter 1). This leads to a situation where the offender is simultaneously a secondary victim. If the offender not only belongs to, but was indeed sanctioned by the victim's family to commit the offence, then the latter may be more concerned with representing the interests of the offender than seeking 'justice' on behalf of the deceased victim. For a detailed exposition of this issue in relation to the law in Pakistan see Warraich (2005).

19 Nadler and Rose (2002–3) examine in detail the effects of victim impact testimony on juror assessment of punishment in capital trials in the USA.

could experience a type of 'secondary victimisation' (Edwards 2005). In the case of the victim's family, the powerlessness they experience at the involuntary and violent loss of their loved one may to some extent be compounded if the court then ignores their opinion on whether the death penalty should be used (Hoffmann 2002–3). In this way, victim personal statement schemes can raise and then dash the hopes of the victim's family and exclude them whilst ostensibly seeming to empower them (Sanders and Young 2007; Ashworth 2005).

Hoffmann suggests that in capital cases this could be alleviated if victims' families are clearly informed of the role of their evidence from the outset, and that it will only be one of numerous considerations in determining sentence (Hoffmann 2002–3; Ashworth 2005). This would also reduce the potential for further arbitrariness and inconsistency in sentencing, since all parties would be clearly aware of the role of victim impact evidence from the outset. Compounding the potential for inconsistency and further victimisation of family members is discrimination between victims, with courts at times giving precedence to the views of those whom they see as more 'worthy' than others. Often, the exercise of this discretion is based on how retributive the victims' family are and thus can further victimise those not deemed to satisfy this standard (Hodgkinson 2004).

One of the primary reasons governments give for retaining the death penalty is that it is necessary to address the needs of crime victims in attaining 'closure' after the trauma of homicide (Hodgkinson & Schabas 2004). Yet Kanwar (2001: 215) argues in the context of the USA that although 'nothing expresses the impossibility of closure more dramatically than the death penalty', nonetheless 'a feeling of closure for the secondary victims has become, at least implicitly, an independent justification for the retention and enforcement of the death penalty' (*ibid.*: 216). The case of Timothy McVeigh, the Oklahoma City bomber who drove a truck loaded with explosives into a federal office building in April 1995, killing 168 people, demonstrates that this is a complex issue for those affected by murder. After witnessing McVeigh's execution, Kathleen Treanor, whose daughter died in the bombing, stated 'It's a demarcation point...it's a period at the end of a sentence. It's the completion of justice and that's what I'll remember about today' (CNN.com 2001b). A survey carried out by ABC News/Washington Post in April 2001 reported that 60 per cent of the US population surveyed think that the death penalty is fair because it gives satisfaction and 'closure' to the families of the victims (Langer 2001).

However, not all victims' families find that retribution, in the form of execution of the criminal, gives them 'closure'. In contrast to Kathleen Treanor's view, Bud Welch stated that he would not find closure 'by taking Timothy McVeigh out of his cage to kill him. It will not bring my little girl back' (CNN.com 2001a). The relief secondary victims feel when the offender is executed at the end of the lengthy appeals process is often short-lived. Kanwar (2001) gives the example of Linda Kelley, the first secondary victim to view the execution of an offender in Texas in 1996, and describes how her responses developed from the belief that viewing the execution of the murderer of her two children would help give her 'closure'; happiness after the execution mixed with anger at the offender's last words; ambivalence that he had escaped further suffering; then an eventual questioning of whether witnessing the execution had in fact given her 'closure' in any real sense, since it had not changed the fact that her children were still gone. This shows that the belief that the process of capital punishment can achieve 'closure' is largely illusory.[20]

Creating more victims: families of the offenders

The death penalty not only impacts on the family of the victim, but also the family of the offender, yet the latter is almost always overlooked in any discussion on the death penalty. Both families experience suffering as a result of the homicide, one through loss of a loved one, the other through the loss by execution, and neither through any 'fault' of their own. Both sets of families have similar needs and concerns and therefore, we argue, should be recognised as 'victims'. Even though both sets of families experience significant trauma following the murder, the response from the community, from the media, most victim groups, the state and the criminal justice system differs significantly, with most sympathy reserved for the families of the victim.

While justifications of deterrence and retribution underpin continued strong support for capital punishment, it is very important to be aware of the 'incidental' or 'collateral' affects of the death penalty in its application. One aspect of this concerns the offenders' families who, due to their marginalisation and the hostility directed to them as well as to their family member, the suspect, express a deep level of hurt and anger that the state wants to kill their loved one. It is difficult for the families of the condemned to understand how the state, which is meant to be protecting all of its citizens from harm, can be responsible for the death of their loved one – there is no one 'on their side' (Sheffer and Cushing 2006: 15).

A number of studies have examined the impact that the death penalty has had on offenders' families. Many of these focus on the individual stories outlining the experiences of the family. They document the shock and distress that families of offenders experience upon learning of the crimes committed

20 See Lithwick (2006) and Domino and Boccaccini (2000) for a further discussion on whether killing brings 'closure' to victims' families.

by their loved ones. They highlight feelings of pain, loss and depression, similar to those experienced by family members of the victims. Offenders' families also suffer psychiatric and physical problems such as Post-Traumatic Stress Disorder, weight gain/loss, and addiction to alcohol or drugs, as well as having to bear the financial burden of having a loved one facing a capital trial. Further to this are feelings of profound guilt and anxiety about a capital trial and the possibility of execution (King 2005; Sharp 2005; King 2004; Beck et al, 2002; Vandiver 1989; Smykla 1987).

While members of the victims' family are critical of the criminal justice system, this seems to be much more prominent for family members of the offender. In many cases, the lack of compassion from police, prosecutors, defence attorneys, judges and society as a whole can compound the distress of the offender's family (Beck et al. 2002; Eschholz et al. 2003). However, anecdotal evidence suggests that differences in the criminal justice system's treatment of families are not only a question of degree; there also is a qualitative difference. Beck highlights a case in which the mothers of two offenders were 'instructed to refrain from crying or showing emotion. They compared this to the treatment of the victim's family members, who were given tissues and breaks when they were overcome with emotion' (Beck et al. 2002: 401). In another example of differential treatment, the victim's family was placed prominently in sight of the jury, whereas the offender's relative was deliberately placed out of their sight (*ibid.*: 401). In addition, the offender's family's history of violence and abuse can be brought into the public sphere ostensibly as part of the mitigating process though actually further stigmatising the offender's family in the eyes of the jury.

In some jurisdictions, family members are not afforded a basic right to know when their loved one will be executed or in some cases where the body is buried after the execution. In Japan and Taiwan, for example, the administration of the death penalty is clouded in secrecy. In particular, the execution date is not made known to the condemned or to his or her family; the condemned is only informed an hour or so before the execution, which leaves the inmates in a constant state of anxiety, not knowing if each day is their last, while family members are only informed of the execution after it has taken place (Johnson 2006; FIDH 2003; Ryden 2001).

Similarly, in Uzbekistan, the implementation of the death penalty prior to abolition[21] was widely condemned by the international community. Family members of those on death row were not informed of the date or place of execution nor where the body had been buried. Then UN Special Rapporteur on Torture, Theo van Boven, stated that:

21 Uzbekistan abolished the death penalty in January 2008.

> The complete secrecy surrounding the date of execution, the absence of any formal notification prior to and after the execution and the refusal to hand over the body for burial are believed to be intentional acts, fully mindful of causing family members turmoil, fear and anguish over the fate of their loved one(s). The practice of maintaining families in a state of uncertainty with a view to punishing or intimidating them and others must be considered malicious and amounting to cruel and inhuman treatment. (2003: para. 65)

These kinds of criminal justice practices can only add to the suffering of offenders' families, not least by taking away the possibility of saying goodbye. The counter argument offered by the family members of a murder victim is that they do not get an opportunity to say goodbye either; however, this poses the question of whether the family members of the offender, who are also not party to the crime, should be subjected to the same suffering. The intention in these jurisdictions seems to be to add to the retributive element of the offender's punishment by the means described above. The problem, however, is that this applies the 'rebalancing' aim of desert theory to secondary victims, rather than the primary victim and offender.

Furthermore, the stigma of capital offences more often than not filters through to the treatment of offenders' families in the wider community. In many cases, they are attributed blame for the offenders' family environment or upbringing and are therefore also perceived as guilty by association. In the press, for example, the effect the crime has had on the offenders' family members is frequently overlooked. In one study, Beck and colleagues (2002: 400) reported that, of nineteen families of capital defendants interviewed, all felt that the media was 'problematic and hostile' towards them. They note that the manner of reporting, for example the media's portrayal of the offender as some kind of 'monster', can further exacerbate the suffering of offenders' families.

Within any discussion of the effects of the death penalty on offenders' families, it should not be forgotten that family members include not only parents, partners and siblings, but in some cases, young children. The effect of having a parent placed on death row and executed can have a tremendous impact on a child's life, though little formal research has been conducted on the issue.[22] King (2006: 296), noting a case in which a son became extremely distressed after the execution of his father who then within a year was also facing a capital charge, argues that:

---

22 There have, however, been some studies on the criminality of children of incarcerated parents. See Beck et al (2007) for a more detailed discussion on this issue.

> ... society failed Little Hameen. He was a victim, just as much as the young man who Abdullah killed, yet society did not acknowledge him as such. We offered him no support or understanding, no counseling or services, not even any condolences. We killed his father and left him to figure out how to live with his rage and pain.

A key point in this case is that Little Hameen's father, Abdullah, had undergone an extraordinary rehabilitation, and was expected to receive clemency. Little Hameen testified on his father's behalf; however testimony from another secondary victim advocating the execution resulted in the Delaware Board of Pardons refusing him clemency. This case illustrates the problems of allowing victim evidence to influence capital procedures, and in particular, the ways in which the capital punishment system constructs victims' families' concerns as more 'worthy' of attention than those of offenders' families, despite the similarities of their victimisation.

There are few resources for families of the condemned. The majority of victims' groups tend to focus on the needs and concerns of the primary victim or in the case of homicide, their family members. For the families of the offender, what little support and attention there is comes mainly from religious groups, researchers or sympathetic members of the community who may also have lost someone to murder. In the USA, a few organisations recognise the suffering of the condemned's family. These include Murder Victims' Families for Reconciliation (MVFR), Murder Victims' Families for Human Rights (MVFHR), and the Journey of Hope. These organisations share similar beliefs, include members of both sets of families, and are firmly opposed to the death penalty. MVFR's opposition is that:

> ... endless trials re-open emotional wounds and put off the time when real healing can begin, the vast resources and attention spent on the death penalty is better spent supporting victims and preventing crime in the first place...executions create more families who have lost a loved one to killing, and many of us think it is just plain wrong for the state to kill. (MVFR, n. d.)

Similarly, MVFHR (n. d.) recognise that 'Family members of the executed have been made orphans, widows, and childless. Family members of the victims have been re-victimized over and over by mandatory appeals and overwhelming media attention on the offender.' This highlights once more the unintended consequences of capital punishment and its further victimisation of the families of both victims and offenders.

Restorative justice initiatives

The majority of discussions on the value of the death penalty have focused extensively on its retributive and deterrent elements. As discussed throughout this chapter, however, the application of the death penalty causes unintended harm, certainly to the family members of the condemned, and possibly to the family members of the victim. This further victimisation of the families of those involved in capital trials has not yet been fully recognised by the criminal justice system, and where it has is accepted as an unavoidable casualty of the process. However, partly in recognition of this, a practice that is gaining more popularity, particularly in the USA, is victim–offender mediation based on restorative justice principles, where the offender is viewed as an integral part of the healing process for victims. Restorative justice recognises the harm caused to individuals, their families and the community, rather than a more abstract conception of harm to society. Restorative justice thus attempts to engage all stakeholders, including the offender, in dealing with the aftermath of a crime in a way that encompasses accountability and healing (Umbreit et al. 2002).

Although restorative justice measures are widely used for non-violent crimes, little research has been conducted into the value of restorative justice measures for victims of serious violent crimes, particularly families of homicide victims. Whilst its value comparatively may be limited in capital cases there is, we argue, significant scope for its application to both sets of secondary victims. Some studies have found significant benefits to adopting restorative justice measures as a supplementary approach to the criminal justice process in capital cases (Eschholz et al. 2003; Umbreit and Vos 2000).

In the context of homicide, victim–offender mediation (also referred to as victim–offender conferencing, victim–offender dialogue, victim–offender reconciliation) brings together the family members of the homicide victim and the offender (and the offender's family where appropriate) in the presence of a trained mediator. The process gives victims and/or their families a chance to tell the offender of their pain, fear and the extent to which the crime has impacted upon them. It also gives them the chance to ask questions that only the offender can answer, for example, what happened in the final moments, what were the victim's final words and so forth. For the offender, taking part in the mediation allows him or her to understand the effects of their crime, to take responsibility and to express remorse. The process also enables offenders' families to reach out to the victims' families and apologise or share their grief (Eschholz et al. 2003; Umbreit et al. 2002).

Although victim–offender mediation may not be appropriate in all cases, it seems that in some, it has more a positive and longer-lasting impact on victims' (and offenders') families than the traditional criminal justice responses of execution or witnessing the execution. One study assessing the impact of victim–offender dialogue programmes involving crimes of severe violence found that of the 78 participants (victims, family members and offenders) that took part in victim–offender mediation, all but one was satisfied with the outcome, with 71 participants expressing that they were 'very satisfied' (Umbreit et al. 2002: 15). With this in mind, restorative justice arguably produces better results for victims and secondary victims in terms of their recovery from trauma from the homicide and constitutes a more constructive approach to dealing with the aftermath of homicide for all those affected. It fully acknowledges the needs of both sets of families and views them both as an equal and integral part of the healing process, rather than constructing a hostile opposition between them, as the capital punishment process invariably does.

Conclusion

The experience that the families of homicide victims have of the capital punishment system is in a state of continuous appraisal. In this chapter, we have argued for the importance of developing protocols through which the experiences of all other actors could be examined. However, by widening the participation of those whom we would describe generically as secondary victims, we must acknowledge that inadvertently and paradoxically in the case of the families of homicide victims, this has brought with it a number of negative unintended consequences, which could have been avoided and should now be corrected to avoid them in future. This includes, in particular, the much-lauded policy to permit the families of the victim to witness the execution as the defining vehicle through which 'closure' could be most effectively achieved. The strong anecdotal evidence from the narrative of such families is that, far from achieving 'closure', the experience of watching someone being put to death adds another dimension of distress, thus compounding the suffering. Typically, at this point the state absolves itself of any further responsibility to these particular constituents.

Increased participation of the victim's family in the trial and all subsequent appeals and clemency hearings causes further arbitrariness and inconsistency in a system which already suffers from these deficiencies of the rule of law.[23] Although increased participation in the death penalty process may benefit those victims' families supportive of capital punishment, it prejudices those who oppose it. This chapter has attempted to bring to the forefront of the phenomenon of secondary victimisation, the circumstances of offenders' families, which whilst analogous in many ways to those of the victims' families, are more often than not neglected in the discussion about capital punishment. Our contention is that this group should be distinguished alongside the victims' family as two groups equally deserving of improved service rights.

23 See Hoffmann (2002–3) for more detailed discussion of this point.

We believe too that more effort should be made to apply the principles of restorative justice so as to provide some solutions to the problems faced by both sets of families.

The death penalty not only affects the families of the victims and the condemned but many others too. Studies have shown that individuals involved in the operation and administration of the death penalty such as lawyers, judges, jurors, law enforcement and prison staff, wardens, chaplains, medical professionals and execution teams are affected to various degrees by their involvement in death sentences (Owens and Owens 2003). Capital jurors, for example, experience secondary victimisation as illustrated in numerous studies of their roles and experiences. These attest to the trauma experienced by sizeable percentages of respondents, especially those referred to as 'holdouts' who persist, in the face of immense pressure from the rest of the jury, against voting in favour of death (Fleury-Steiner 2004; Bowers et al. 1998; Eisenberg et al. 1996; Sundby 2005). Surprisingly, very few empirical clinical studies have been conducted to evaluate whether any pathological changes have been experienced by those who witness executions (Freinkel et al. 1994). However, one can draw conclusions from the narrative descriptions of media witnesses to executions, and the chaplains and prison wardens who are required to attend executions, whose accounts are replete with examples of a continuum of adverse affects experienced by those who are present at the execution (Pickett 2002; Willett & Rozelle 2004; Reid & Gurwell 2001).

These accounts demonstrate further the ways in which capital punishment re-creates and creates further victimisation in its purported quest to address the needs of those victimised by homicide. The use of capital punishment as a response to homicide creates ripples of suffering extending far beyond the primary victim and offender, or indeed, the current class of secondary victims. Thus the issues explored in this chapter, if taken together with other analyses of the negative effects of the death penalty, fuel the argument that capital punishment creates more problems than it solves.

References

Albanian Human Rights Group (2000—2001) 'The Kanun Bastardised, Dossier: The Blood Feud', *Albanian Human Rights Group Periodical Magazine for Human Rights* 2.

Ashworth, A. (2005) *Sentencing and Criminal Justice*, 4th Ed. Cambridge: Cambridge University Press.

Ashworth, A. (2002) 'Responsibilities, Rights and Restorative Justice.' *British Journal of Criminology* 42, 578–95.

Bassiouni, C. (2004) 'Death as a Penalty in the Shari'ã' in P. Hodgkinson and W.A. Schabas, eds., *Capital Punishment: Strategies for Abolition*. Cambridge: Cambridge University Press.

BBC News (2005) 'Families "to Have Voice in Court".' 1 September 2005, at http://news.bbc.co.uk/1/hi/uk/4202618.stm.

Beck, E., Britto, S. and Andrews, A. (2007) *In the Shadow of Death. Restorative Justice and Death Row Families.* New York: Oxford University Press.

Beck, E., Blackwell, B. S., Leonard, P. B. and Mears, M. (2002) 'Seeking Sanctuary: Interviews with Family Members of Capital Defendants.' *Cornell Law Review* 88, 382–418.

Booth v. Maryland 482 US 496 (1987).

Bowers, W.J., Sandys, M. and Steiner, B.D. (1998) 'Foreclosed Impartiality in Capital Sentencing: Jurors' Predispositions, Guilt-Trial Experience, and Premature Decision Making.' *Cornell Law Review* 83(6) 1476–1556.

Clarkson, C.V., Keating, H.M. and Cunningham, S.R. (2007) *Criminal Law: Texts and Materials*, 6th Ed. London: Sweet and Maxwell.

CNN.com (2001a) 'Some Oklahoma City bombing families fight for McVeigh's life.' 4 May 2001, http://edition.cnn.com/2001/US/05/04/mcveigh.families/index.html.

CNN.com (2001b) 'McVeigh execution: A 'completion of justice'.' 11 June 2001. http://edition.cnn.com/2001/LAW/06/11/mcveigh.02/index.html.

Crown Prosecution Service, Code for Prosecutors, http://www.cps.gov.uk/victims_witnesses/codetest.html.

Department for Constitutional Affairs, 'Hearing the relatives of murder and manslaughter victims: The Government's plans to give the bereaved relatives of murder and manslaughter victims a say in criminal proceedings, available at http://www.dca.gov.uk/consult/manslaughter/manslaughter.htm.

Domino, M. L. and Boccaccini, M. T. (2000) 'Doubting Thomas: Should Family Members of Victims Watch Executions?' *Law and Psychology Review* 24, 59.

Edwards, I., (2004) 'An Ambiguous Participant: The Crime Victim and Criminal Justice Decision-Making.' *British Journal of Criminology* 44, 967–82.

Eisenberg, T., Garvey, S.P. and Wells, M.T., (1996) 'Jury Responsibility in Capital Sentencing: An Empirical Study.' *Buffalo Law Review* 44, 339–380.

Erez, E. (1999) 'Who's Afraid of the Big Bad Victim? Victim Impact Statements as Victim Empowerment and Enhancement of Justice' *Criminal Law Review* 545–56.

Eschholz, S., Reed, M. D., Beck, E., and Leonard, P. B. (2003) 'Offenders' Family Members' Responses to Capital Crimes. The Need for Restorative Justice Initiatives.' *Homicide Studies* 7(2), 154–181.

Fleury-Steiner, B., (2004) *Jurors' Stories of Death – How America's Death Penalty Invests in Inequality.* Ann Arbor: University of Michigan Press.

Frienkel, A., Koopman, C., and Spiegel, D. (1994) *Dissociative symptoms in media eyewitnesses of an execution.* American Journal of Psychiatry 151: 9.

Garland, D. (2001) *The Culture of Control: Crime and Social Order in Contemporary Society.* Oxford: Oxford University Press.

Goodey, J. (2005) *Victims and Victimology – Research, Policy and Practice.* Longman Criminology Series. London: Pearson Education Ltd.

Hodgkinson, P. and Schabas, W.A. (2004) *Capital Punishment: Strategies for Abolition.* Cambridge: Cambridge University Press).

Hoffmann, J. (2002–3) 'Revenge of Mercy? Some Thoughts About Survivor Opinion Evidence in Death Penalty Cases.' *Cornell Law Review* 88, 530–42.

Hood, R. (1996) *Capital Punishment, Deterrence and Crime Rates*, Seminar on the Abolition of the Death Penalty, Kiev, 28–9 September 1996, Council of Europe Parliamentary Assembly, Doc. AS/Jur (1996) 70.

International Federation for Human Rights (FIDH) (2003) *The Death Penalty in Japan: A Practice Unworthy of a Democracy International Federation for Human Rights*, International Mission of investigation. Report No. 359/2, May 2003.

Jamaica Government Victim Charter http://www.jis.gov.jm/victims_charter.pdf.

Johnson, D. T. (2006) 'Japan's Secretive Death Penalty Policy: Contours, Origins, Justifications, and

Meanings.' *Asian-Pacific Law & Policy Journal* 7(2), 62–124.

Kadare, I. (1991) *Broken April*. London: The Harvill Press.

Kanwar, V. (2001) 'Capital Punishment as 'Closure': The Limits of Victim-Centred Jurisprudence.' *Review of Law and Social Change* 27, 215–55.

King, R. (2006) 'The Impact of Capital Punishment on Families of Defendants and Murder Victims Family Members.' *Judicature* 89(5), 292–6.

King, R. (2005) *Capital Consequences: Families of the Condemned Tell Their Stories*. New Brunswick, New Jersey and London: Rutgers University Press.

King, K. (2004) 'It Hurts So Bad: Comparing Grieving Patterns of the Families of Murder Victims With Those of Families of Death Row Inmates.' *Criminal Justice Policy Review* 15(2), 193–211.

Lacey, N. (1988) *State Punishment: Political Principles and Community Values*. London: Routledge.

Langer, G. (2001) 'Death Penalty Ambivalence', 10 May 2001, ABC News, available at http://abcnews.go.com/sections/us/DailyNews/poll010504_deathpenalty.html.

Lithwick, D. (2006) 'Does Killing Really Give Closure?' *Washington Post* 26 March 2006, available at http://www.washingtonpost.com/wp-dyn/content/article/2006/03/24/AR2006032402340.html.

Mosteller, R. P. (2002-3) 'Victim Impact Evidence: Hard to Find the Real Rules' *Cornell Law Review* 88, 543–54.

Murder Victims' Families for Reconciliation. http://www.mvfr.org/ (accessed 27 March 2008).

Murder Victims' Families for Human Rights. http://www.murdervictimsfamilies.org/ (accessed 27 March 2008).

Nadler, J. and Rose, M. R. (2002–3) 'Victim Impact Testimony and the Psychology of Punishment.' *Cornell Law Review* 88, 419–56.

Owens, V.S. and Owens, D.C. (2003) *Living Next Door to the Death House*. Cambridge: William B. Eerdmans Publishing Company.

Payne v. Tennessee 501 US 808 (1991).

Pickett, C. with Carlton S. (2002) *Within these Walls: Memoirs of a Death House Chaplain*. New York: St. Martins Press.

Reid, D. with Gurwell, J. (2001) *Have a seat, please*. Huntsville, Texas: Texas Review Press.

Ryden, E., ed. (2001) *Taiwan Opposes the Death Penalty: Proceedings of the Fujen University International Conference on the Abolition of the Death Penalty*, 24-16 June 2001, Department of Law & John Paul II Peace Institute, Fujen Catholic University.

Sanders, A. and Young, R. (2007) *Criminal Justice*, 3rd Ed. Oxford: Oxford University Press.

Sharp, S. F. (2005) *Hidden Victims: The Effects of the Death Penalty on Families of the Accused*. New Brunswick, New Jersey and London: Rutgers University Press.

Sheffer, S and Cushing, R. (2006) *Creating More Victims: How Executions Hurt the Families Left Behind*. Cambridge, Massachusetts: Murder Victims' Families for Human Rights.

Smykla, J. O. (1987) 'The Human Impact of Capital Punishment: Interviews with Families of Persons on Death Row.' *Journal of Criminal Justice*, 15, 331–47.

Sundby, S. (2005) 'A life and death decision: a jury weighs the death penalty.' Basingstoke: Palgrave Macmillan.

Sweeting, A., Owen, R.,Turley, C., Rock, P., Garcia-Sanche, M.,Wilson L. and Khan, U. (2008) *Evaluation of the Victims' Advocate Scheme Pilots*. Ministry of Justice Research Series 17/08, October 2008.

Umbreit, M. S., Coates, R. B., Vos, B. and Brown, K. (2002) *Executive Summary: Victim Offender Dialogue in Crimes of Severe Violence. A Multi-Site Study of Programs in Texas and Ohio*, Centre for Restorative Justice & Peacemaking in collaboration with National Organization for Victim Assistance, 1 December 2002.

Umbreit, M. S. and Vos, B. (2000) 'Homicide survivors meet the offender prior to execution: Restorative justice through dialogue.' *Homicide Studies* 4(1), 63–87.

Van Boven, T. (2003) *Mission to Uzbekistan.* Report of the Special Rapporteur on the question of torture, Theo Van Boven, submitted in accordance with Commission resolution 2002/38, Economic and Social Council/Commission on Human Rights, Fifty-ninth session, E/CN.4/2003/68/Add.2, 3 February 2003.

Vandiver, M. (1989) 'Coping with Death. Families of the Terminally Ill, Homicide Victims, and Condemned Prisoners' in Radelet, M. L. (ed) *Facing the Death Penalty. Essays on a Cruel and Unusual Punishment* (Philadelphia, Temple University Press).

Victim Support http://www.victimsupport.org.uk/vs_england_wales/index.php.

Von Hirsch, A. (1976) *Doing Justice – The Choice of Punishments.* New York: Hill and Lang.

Warraich, S. A. (2005) "Honour killings' and the law in Pakistan.' In L. Welchman and S. Hossain, eds., *'Honour': Crimes, Paradigms and Violence Against Women.* London: Zed Books.

Willett, J. and Rozelle, R. (2004) Warden. Albany, Texas: Bright Sky Press.

Name Index

Abel, R. 199
Abu-Jamal, Mumia 137
Acker, James R. 475
Adamu, Idris 402
Adcock, C. 459
Adler, Roy 291
Ahmed, Imam 414
Aikens, Earnest James 319
Akers, Kerry Ann xvii, xxvii, 235–48
Alexandre, J.W. 434
Alldredge, C. 434
Allen, S. 466, 469
Ambler, Leah xx, 107–29
Ames, Jessie Daniel 367
Ancel, Marc 83, 156–7
Andrews, A.B. 226, 230, 459
Arluke, Arnold 490
Armour, M. 460, 469, 482
Ashcroft, John 488
Ashley, Meyer 447
Ashworth, A. 500, 503, 505–6
Auclair, N. 434
Ayton-Shenker, Diana 337

Babcock, Sandra xv, 21–35
Bahati, David 329, 333, 338
Baker, Lena 285
Baldus, David 321
Ball, B.C. 434
Bandes, Susan 474–5, 488–9
Banner, Stuart 366, 475
Bard, B. 450–51
Barker, R. 222
Barlow, D.H. 444
Bassiouni, C. 504–5
Beaumont, R. 434
Beccaria, Cesare 329
Beck, Elizabeth 459–63, 508–9
Bedau, Adam 287, 488
Bedau, Hugo Adam 257, 281–2, 317–26, 474–5
Bello, Aminu Adamu xxv, 399–417
Bellofatto, Paul 437
Benedek, E. 434
Benekos, P.J. 452
Benford, Robert D. 473, 475–6, 480
Bennett, C. 227
Bennett, James H. 483
Berardo, F. 460
Berbrier, Mitch 476
Bergegren, Astrid 83–4
Berns, Nancy xxvi, 473–96
Berns, Walter 300
Best, Joel 473, 475–6, 492
Biko, Steve 312
Bingham, Thomas 7, 9
Black, Charles Jr 317
Blackstone, William 270
Blackwell, B. 459
Blair, Jim 480
Blais, M. 434
Blake, P. 450–51
Bloom, S. 466, 469
Blume, John H. 224–5, 487, 489
Boccaccini, Marcus T. 482
Bogo, M. 227, 230
Bohm, Robert M. 475
Bonner, Richard 484
Boon, Andy xx, 185–201
Boots, D. 433
Borchard, Edwin 280, 324
Bosk, Charles L. 473
Boss, Pauline 461
Bossuyt, Marc 165–6
Bottoms, B.L. 434
Bower, Robert Paul 439–41, 444–5
Bowers, W.J. 513
Bradford, Caycie xvii, 131–50
Branson, D. 222
Bread, Angel 25
Brennan, William J. Jr 318, 356
Breyer, Stephen 32, 135
Breytenbach, Breyten 312
Britto, S. 459
Broda, Christian 84
Broom, Romell 145
Brown, Gordon 338

Brownstein, H. 443
Brundidge, Caleb Lee 334
Bunzo, Akama 114
Burr, Raymond 272
Burr, Richard 488
Bush, George W. xv, 30
Byrd, R. 460, 463

Cabral Barreto, Ireneu 104
Camargo, Rafael 30, 34
Camus, Albert 104
Carroll, Jenny xxv
Cassin, René 153
Cerna, C. 462
Chaskalson, Arthur 79
Cheney, Dick 488
Chenwi, Lilian xix, 55–79
Chinni, Dante 480, 482
Chong Jin, Wee 8
Chope, R. 460
Christi Jo 482
Chuan, Ong Ah 4
Cicero, M. Tullius 265
Clapham, Andrew 105
Clarke, R.S. 167
Clarkson, C.V. 501
Clemens, Aaron xxv
Clinton, Hilary 32, 338
Cohen, M.B. 227, 230
Coke, C.J. 43
Collums, David 448
Condry,R. 497
Corbin, Juliet 477–8
Corder, B.F. 434
Core, J. 223, 225
Cornell, D. 435
Cornwall, T.P. 435
Corzine, Jon S. 288
Cramer, Renee 492
Crawshaw, Nancy 96
Crocker, Phyllis 371
Crutcher, Sarah xxv
Culbert, Jennifer L. 487
Cullen, Francis T. 475
Cushing, R.R. 489, 507

Dando, Shigemitshu 117
De Icaza, Carlos 28
De Meyer, Arnoud 98
Demetriou, Andreas 96
Dennis, M.J. 173
Dike 266
Dillon, Kathy 484
Diplock, William 7, 19, 43
Dobbert, Ernest 286
Doka, Kenneth 460
Domino, Marla L. 482
Donerly, B. 434
Dowd Hall, Jacquelyn 367
Dowrick, Frank 83
Dressler, Joshua 362
Duffy, Clinton 350–51
Duke, Mark Anthony 437, 448–50
Duncan, G.M. 434
Duncan, J.W. 434
Dunn, Jennifer L. 491
Durand, V.M. 444
Dwyer, Jim 283

Edmondson, Drew 27
Edward III, King of England 268
Edwards, I. 502, 506
Ehrmann, Sara 281
Eisenberg, T. 513
Ellis, James W. 429
Ellison, Michael 448
Ellsworth, Phoebe 292, 294
Emens, Elizabeth 424
Emmelkamp, P. 460
Erez, E. 504
Eschholz, S. 508, 511
Evans, Timothy John 319
Ewalt, P. 227, 229, 231
Ewing, C.P. 434–5

Fagan, Jeffrey xiii, xxv, 16, 421–32
Fan, David P. 475
Faulder, Joseph Stanley 24
Fay, Michael 18
Fendrich, M. 443
Fessenden, Ford 484
Fierro Reyna, Cesar Roberto 26–7
Fishman, C. 462, 464, 468
Fitzhugh Brundage, W. 320
Fleury-Steiner, B. 513
Florio, Gwen 428
Fogel, Jeremy 144
Fonda, Henry 251–3, 272, 275–6
Forst, Brian A. 428
Forsyth, J. 465

Fosha, Diana 460, 467
Foucault, Michel 435, 487
Franck, Hans Göran 89
Frank, Barbara 281, 324
Frank, Jerome 281, 324
Frase, Richard S. 426
Freinkel, A. 513
Furedi, Frank 489
Furman, William Henry 319
Fuse, T. 465

Galić, Stanislav 211–12
Galliher, John F. 474
Gallup, G. 465
Gamson, William A. 473, 476
Gardner, Erle Stanley 271, 280
Garland, D. 500
Garlicki, Lech 102
Garoupa, Nuno M. 429
Garrett, Brandon 428
Gawande, Atul 136
George, Ron 376
Ginsburg, Ruth Bader 32, 359, 368, 390
Glassman, U. 222, 227
Globerman, J. 227, 231
Goldberg, Michelle 484
Goldstein, P. 443
Goodey, J. 499
Goodwin, Michael 482, 488
Gothard, S. 226
Gotoda, Masaharu 113
Graham, Bob 285
Grassian, Stuart 136
Green, Thomas 270
Greene, Susan 474
Grier, Peter 480, 482
Griffin, James 82
Gross, Samuel 283–4, 292, 294
Grossman, B. 222, 227, 230
Gruber, Aya 366
Gumboh, Ester xiii, 203–20
Gurwell, J. 513

Haegerich, T.M. 434
Haines, Herbert 474
Haizlip, T.M. 434
Haley, J. 464
Hallman, Clifford 285–6
Hamm, Mozelle 482
Haney, Craig 474
Hanks, Tom 254
Harper, Stephen 338
Hasegawa, Sukehiro 114
Hauwa, Ibrahim 400
Hearnshaw, F.J.C. 353
Heide, Kathleen M. xxv, 433–56
Henderson, Lynne 489
Henry, Brad 28–9
Henry, G.T. 434
Herman, J. 463
Hilgartner, Stephen 473
Hillbrand, M. 434
Hochschild, Arlie 473, 477, 481, 490
Hodgkinson, Peter xx, xxvi, 103, 185–201, 499–516
Hoffman, J. 504–6
Hoffman, L. xxi, 464
Hoffman, Morris B. 251–81
Holden, Daphne 476
Holder, Eric 32
Holmes, Oliver Wendell Jr 263
Holstein, James A. 475
Holt, John 361
Hood, Roger 52, 89, 163, 343, 501
Hopkins, C. Quince 353
Hopper, Joseph 491
Hoyle, C. 343
Hudson, J. 223, 225
Huff, Richard 281
Humphrey, John P. 152–3
Hunt, Dedra 448
Hunt, Scott A. 475, 480
Hussein, Saddam 180–81

Ibarra, Peter R. 473

Jahnke, Richard Sr 434
Jarman-Rhode, L. 227
Johnson, D.T. 508
Johnson, S. 467
Jones, S. 460–62
Justicia 266

Kagan, Elena 32
Kajiyama, Hiroshi 114
Kalu, Ogbu xxv
Kambanda, Jean 214
Kandelia, Seema xxvi, 499–516
Kanwar, Vik 474–5, 487–9, 500, 506–7
Karamanian, Susan 489

Kathir, Ibn 414
Kay, Judith 491
Kelley, Linda 507
Keltner, Kathy A. 475
Kennedy, Anthony 358, 428, 489
Ki Moon, Ban 180
King, R. 460, 508–9
Kirchmeier, Jeffrey L. 474
Kitsuse, John I. 473, 475
Kleck, G. 225
Kleiman, D. 434
Klick, Jonathan 429
Knight, Ernest 285
Kolar, P. 227
Kong, Yong Vui 3, 7, 15–16, 18–20
Kowane, Johannes 312
Kruger, James 311

Lacey, N. 501
Lager, P. 227
LaGrand, Karl 25
LaGrand, Walter 25
Lashley, Frederick 437, 446, 44, 449–50
Lauerman, Kerry 482
Lawal, Amina 399–400, 402–3, 408–11, 416–17
Lay, Kenneth 262
Leahy, Patrick 32
Leal García, Humberto 32, 34
Lebron, Tiffany xxv
Lennings, C.J. 434
Leonard, P. 459
Leone, U. 158
Letsas, George 98
Levine-Jorano, N. 230
Levy, J. 204, 206
Lewin, Hugh 303–15
Lewis, D.O. 450–51
Lewis, Dorothy Otnow 441
Lewis, S. 462–3
Lexington, J. 465
Lidbom, Carl 85–7, 98, 102
Lidgard, Bertil 84
Liebman, James 298, 438
Lifton, Robert Jay 485
Liptak, Adam 427–8
Liu J. 10
Lively, Scott 334
Logan, D. 223
Logan, Wayne A. 426–7
Long, Walter C. xxvi, 459–71
Loseke, Donileen 476–7
Loving, Susan 28
Lowney, Kathe 492
Lowney, Kathleen S. 476
Lumet, Sidney 253, 255
Luthuli, Muntulana 312
Lynch, Mona 474

Mach, J.E. 434
Macht, L.B. 434
Mackesy-Amiti, M.E. 443
Maddox, K. 227
Maercker, A. 469
Magid, K. 451
Maguire, K. 436
Malachy, Nelson 19
Malik, Imam 404–6
Mann, C. 225
Marleau, J.D. 434
Marshack, E. 227
Marshall, Thurgood 135, 286, 318, 395
Maruschak, L.M. 436
Marx, B. 465
Mason, Perry 273–4
Massey, Hilary J. 422
Massie, Robert 144
Mauser, Daniel 486
Maxwell, William L. 319
McCartin, Donald 294
McCully, R.S. 435
McCurdy, Jessica xxv, 433–56
McDermott, Yvonne xvii, 3–20
McFall, J. 227
McGilberry, Stephen 437, 446–50
McGinn, Ricky 482
McGowan, Andrea 429
McKelvey, C.A. 451
McVeigh, Timothy 483, 488, 490, 506
Mears, M. 459
Medellín, José 31, 33
Medlicott, R.W. 435
Medlock, Floyd 482
Mendes, Douglas L. xviii, 37–53
Merlo, A.V. 452
Mernissi, Fatima 415–16
Meron J. 211
Mill, John Stuart 426
Millaud, F. 434
Miller, Gale 475
Miller, L. 461

Miller, P. 222, 224, 227
Minuchin, S. 462, 464, 468
Mitchell, Greg 485
Modigliani, Andre 476
Mofekung, Alfred 312
Mohammed, Abdulrahaman Zakaria 246
Mohammed, Yahayya 402–3
Mokuau, N. 227, 229, 231
Monguya Mbenge, D. 72
Montgomery, Amelia xxvii
Moran, Richard 484
Moreno Ramos, Roberto 26–7
Morgan, Ivan 42, 236
Morris, Norval 157
Mosteller, Robert P. 482, 488
Mouridsen, S.E. 435
Mowbray, A. 98, 100
Mugisha, Frank 338
Muller, J. 469
Musa Yawuri, Aliyu 416
Museveni, Yoweri 336, 338
Mwenda, Andrew 335
Myers, W.C. 451

Nadler, Janice 489
Neufeld, Peter 283
Nguyen Tuong Van 19
Nicol, Danny 90
Nijenhuis, E.R.S. 444
Norgard, K. 460
Nsaba Buturo, James 335, 338

O'Brien, Barbara 283
Oehlers, Alfred 18
Opsahl, Torkel 82
Owens, D.C. 513
Owens, V.S. 513

Pallikarides, Evagoras 96
Parkes, C. 462
Pastore, A.L. 436
Patten, Chris 173
Patterson, Alexander 427
Pearl, Matthew 488
Petee, T. 434
Pickett, C. 513
Pocar J. 211
Post, S. 434
Powell, Lewis F. 322, 395–6
Pratt, Earl 42, 236
Preamble E. 88
Prejean, Helen 480
Prendergast, A. 434
Prinze, Freddie Jr 254
Putnam, Constance 282, 323

Quraishi, Asifa 408

Radelet, Michael L. xxi, 257, 279–300, 323–4, 460–61, 474, 492
Radin, Edward 281
Rapport, Elizabeth 370
Reddy, Rupa xxvi, 499–516
Reed, Joyce G. xx, 221–33
Reid, D. 513
Reid, Lori 476
Reiman, J. 225
Reza, Elizabeth xxv
Rich, Frank 488
Risinger, Michael 283
Roberts, A.R. 452
Robertson, A.H. 81
Robinson, Mary 176
Rodriguez, Angelina 390
Rogge, M. 224, 227
Rohrer, Glenn E. xx, 221–33
Rollins, R. 434
Romney, Mitt 320
Roosevelt, Eleanor 153
Rose, Mary R. 489
Ross, Michael 137
Rozelle, R. 513
Rubio, Ruperez 85
Ruffolo, M. 222, 224, 227
Rüth, Alexandra 103
Ryan, George 288, 323
Ryden, E. 508

Sacco, Ferdinando Nicola 257, 321
Sametz, L. 437
Samra, Brandon 448
Sander, Barrie xxiii, 329–47
Sanders, M. 502, 506
Sarat, Austin 192, 196, 474–5
Saunders, J.A. 41
Sax, H. 154
Schabas, William xv, 87, 99, 151–83, 342, 506
Schaefer, R. 225
Scheck, Barry 282
Scheingold, S. 192, 196

Scherl, D.J. 434
Schieber, Vicki 485–6
Schlesinger, L.B. 434
Schmierer, Don 324
Schneck, D. 222, 224, 227
Schore, A. 467
Schorr, S. 223, 225
Schrock, Douglas 476
Schwarzschild, Henry 318
Schweingruber, David 477, 492
Scott, Elizabeth 424
Seemungal, Florence 52
Sellers, Sean Richard 437–45, 449–50
Shae, Bobby 192–3
Shaffer, S. 489
Shamash 266
Shanmugam, K. 17
Shapiro, Bruce 488–9
Sharp, S.F. 460–61, 499, 508
Shatz, Naomi R. xxv, 349–97
Shatz, Steven F. xxv, 349–97
Shearer, P. 230
Sheffer, S. 507
Shinomiya, Satoru 128
Shortnacy, Michael xxv
Simants, Erwin 286
Simpson, O.J. 272
Smykla, J.O. 460, 508
Snell, T. 436
Snow, David A. 473
Soering, Hans 97, 135
Solomon, E.P. 435, 450–52
Sotomayor, Sonia 32
Spector, Malcolm 475
Spinelli, Eithel 350–51
Spitz, R.T. 434
Spunt, B. 443
Spurrier, Dolores 479
Stalans, L.J. 434
Stanley Williams, Mark 144
Stanley, C. 199
Stebbins, D. 223–4, 226
Steele, K. 444
Steib, Victor L. 427
Steinberg, Laurence D. 424
Stevens, John Paul 31, 135
Stevens-Guille, M. 462
Stevenson-Hinde, J. 468
Stewart, Potter 296
Stewart, Potter 372–3
Strafer, M. 162
Strauss, Anselm 477–8
Streib, Victor xxv, 436–7, 447–9
Strenziok, M. 450–51
Strom, G. 227
Sugiura, Seiken 113
Sullivan, Harry Stack 464
Sultan, Stephen 479
Summers, Michael 291
Sundby, Scott E. 489, 513
Swidler, Anne 473, 487

Tamale, S. 331–2, 334, 347
Tanay, E. 434
Tarulevicz, Nicole 18
Terzieff, Juliette xxv
Thanh Le, Hung 28
Thatcher, Margaret 167
Tochi, Iwuchukwu Amara 19
Tofexis, A. 434
Tolstrup, K. 435
Torres Aguilera, Osbaldo 26–9, 34
Towle, C. 230
Tracy, Janie 446
Treanor, Kathleen 506
Trilsh, Mirja 103
Tucker, Carla Fay 176
Tucker, L.S. 435
Türmen, Riza 100–101
Turner, A. 465

Umamah, Abu 414
Umar, Mohammed S. 410
Umbreit, M.S. 511–12
Unnever, James D. 475
Urofsky, M.L. 162

Van Boven, Theo 508
Van den Haag, Ernest 322
Van der Hart, O. 444
Van der Kolk, B. 463–4, 467
Van der Linden, René 104
Van Ecke, Y. 460
Vandiver, M. 460, 508
Vanzetti, Bartolomeo 257, 321
Vito, G. 225, 228
Vogelman, L. 462–3
Vos, B. 511

Walker, L. 434
Wallace, James 479

Wallance, Greg 312
Warren, Rick 337
Welch, Bud 506
Wertham, F. 434
West, Valerie 422
Whitaker, Carl 464
White, Byron 372–3
White, J.R. 434
White, W.S. 162
Willet, J. 465, 513
Williams, Rowan 337
Wohlwend, Karen 93, 104
Wolf, Amanda xxv
Wyatt, Robert O. 475

Yeager, C.A. 450–51
Yorke, Jon xvi, 81–105
Young, J.L. 434
Young, R. 502, 506
Yusuf Ali, Abdullah 413

Zimring, Franklin 474